Marketing Communications
Third Edition

PEARSON

We work with leading authors to develop the strongest learning experiences, bringing cutting-edge thinking and best learning practice to a global market. We craft our print and digital resources to do more to help learners not only understand their content, but to see it in action and apply what they learn, whether studying or at work.

Pearson is the world's leading learning company. Our portfolio includes Penguin, Dorling Kindersley, the Financial Times and our educational business, Pearson International. We are also a leading provider of electronic learning programmes and of test development, processing and scoring services to educational institutions, corporations and professional bodies around the world.

Pearson Custom Publishing enables our customers to access a wide and expanding range of market-leading content from world-renowned authors and develop their own tailor-made book. You choose the content that meets your needs and Pearson Custom Publishing produces a high-quality printed book.

Every day our work helps learning flourish, and wherever learning flourishes, so do people.

To learn more please visit us at: www.pearsoncustom.co.uk

PEARSON CUSTOM PUBLISHING

Marketing Communications
Third Edition

Compiled from:

Essentials of Marketing Communications
by Chris Fill

Marketing Communications:
Interactivity, Communities and Content
Fifth Edition
by Chris Fill

PEARSON

Harlow, England • London • New York • Boston • San Francisco • Toronto • Sydney • Auckland • Singapore • Hong Kong
Tokyo • Seoul • Taipei • New Delhi • Cape Town • Sao Paulo • Mexico City • Madrid • Amsterdam • Munich • Paris • Milan

Pearson Education Limited
Edinburgh Gate
Harlow
Essex CM20 2JE

And associated companies throughout the world

Visit us on the World Wide Web at:
www.pearsoned.co.uk

First published 2009
This Custom Book Edition © Pearson Education Limited 2012

Compiled from:

Essentials of Marketing Communications
by Chris Fill
ISBN 978 0 273 73844 2
Copyright © Pearson Education Limited 2011

Marketing Communications:
Interactivity, Communities and Content
Fifth Edition
by Chris Fill
ISBN 978 0 273 71722 5
Copyright © Prentice Hall Europe 1994, 1999
Copyright © Pearson Education Limited 2006, 2009

All rights reserved. No part of this publication may be reproduced, stored in a retrieval system, or transmitted in any form or by any means, electronic, mechanical, photocopying, recording or otherwise, without either the prior written permission of the publisher or a licence permitting restricted copying in the United Kingdom issued by the Licensing Agency Ltd, Saffron House, 6–10 Kirby Street, London EC1N 8TS.

ISBN 978 1 78134 239 8

Printed and bound in Great Britain by 4edge, Hockley.
www.4edge.co.uk. FSC Certified

Contents

Chapter 1	The scope of marketing communications Chapter 1 in Essentials of Marketing Communications by Chris Fill	2
Chapter 2	Communication: interactivity and conversations Chapter 2 in Essentials of Marketing Communications by Chris Fill	30
Chapter 3	Audiences: attitudes, behaviour and decision-making Chapter 3 in Essentials of Marketing Communications by Chris Fill	55
Chapter 4	Integrated marketing communications Chapter 9 in Marketing Communications: Interactivity, Communities and Content Fifth Edition by Chris Fill	86
Chapter 5	Marketing communications: strategies, tactics and planning Chapter 10 in Marketing Communications: Interactivity, Communities and Content Fifth Edition by Chris Fill	117
Chapter 6	Agencies: practice, regulation and international communications Chapter 7 in Essentials of Marketing Communications by Chris Fill	153
Chapter 7	Shaping relationships with marketing communications Chapter 8 in Essentials of Marketing Communications by Chris Fill	177
Chapter 8	Advertising and strategy Chapter 16 in Marketing Communications: Interactivity, Communities and Content Fifth Edition by Chris Fill	210
Chapter 9	Media planning and behaviour: delivering the message Chapter 27 in Marketing Communications: Interactivity, Communities and Content Fifth Edition by Chris Fill	234

Chapter 10	**Traditional media** Chapter 24 in Marketing Communications: Interactivity, Communities and Content Fifth Edition by Chris Fill	264
Chapter 11	**Interactive marketing communications** Chapter 14 in Essentials of Marketing Communications by Chris Fill	290
Chapter 12	**Digital media** Chapter 25 in Marketing Communications: Interactivity, Communities and Content Fifth Edition by Chris Fill	315
Chapter 13	**Public relations and sponsorship** Chapter 10 in Essentials of Marketing Communications by Chris Fill	351
Chapter 14	**Direct marketing and personal selling** Chapter 11 in Essentials of Marketing Communications by Chris Fill	379
Chapter 15	**Sales promotion, exhibitions and product placement** Chapter 12 in Essentials of Marketing Communications by Chris Fill	403

Marketing Communications
Third Edition

Chapter 1
The scope of marketing communications

Marketing communications is concerned with the methods, processes, meanings, perceptions and actions associated with the ways in which products, services and brands are presented to, are considered by, and through which interaction can occur with audiences.

Aims and learning objectives

The primary aim of this introductory chapter is to explore some of the key concepts associated with marketing communications. In addition readers are encouraged to consider the scope and purpose of marketing communications and to develop an appreciation of the key characteristics of the main tools of the communications mix and the way in which the mix is changing.

The learning objectives of this chapter are to enable readers to:

1. explain the scope, role and tasks of marketing communications;
2. describe how marketing communications can be used to engage audiences;
3. explore ways in which the environment can influence the use of marketing communications;
4. write brief notes about the key characteristics of the marketing communications mix;
5. identify and explain the key differences between marketing communications used in consumer and business markets.

Introduction

Organisations such as Apple, O$_2$, Tesco, Santander, Haier, Nokia, BBC, Gillette, Microsoft, Chanel, Boeing, Oxfam and Petrobras all operate across a number of sectors, markets and countries and all use a variety of marketing communications tools, media and messages to communicate with their various audiences. These audiences consist not only of people who buy their products and services but also of people and organisations who might be able to influence them, who might help and support them by providing, for example, labour, finance, manufacturing facilities, distribution outlets and legal advice, or who are interested because of their impact on parts of society or the business sector in particular.

There is no universally agreed definition of marketing communications and there are many interpretations of the subject. The origin of many definitions rests with a promotional outlook where the purpose was to use communications to persuade people to buy products and services. The focus was on products, one-way communications, and the perspective was short term. The expression 'marketing communications' emerged as a wider range of tools and media evolved and as the scope of the tasks these communications activities were expected to accomplish expanded.

In addition to awareness and persuasion, new goals such as developing understanding and preference, and reminding and reassuring customers, became recognised as important aspects of the communications effort. Direct marketing activities heralded a new approach as one-to-one and two-way communications began to shift the focus from mass to personal communications. Now a number of definitions refer to an integrated perspective. This view has gathered momentum since the mid-1990s and has become an essential part of the marketing communications vocabulary. With the integrative perspective a stronger strategic and long-term orientation has developed, although the basis for many marketing communication strategies appears to still rest with a promotional mix orientation.

The key issue is that marketing communications has the potential to provide added value, and it achieves this through the development of appropriate customer relationships. Marketing communications can enable organisations to share understanding, and some would argue that it creates opportunities for value creation (Vargo and Lusch, 2004). Above all else, marketing communications should be an audience-centred activity.

> Marketing communications is an audience centred activity which attempts to encourage engagement between participants and provoke conversations.

This definition has two key points. The first concerns the notion that marketing communications is audience-centred. Traditionally marketing communications has been used to convey product-related information to customer audiences. Today, marketing communications needs to connect with a range of stakeholders who have links and relationships with the organisation, each of varying dimensions. In a customer centric world, marketing communications should seek to provide value for the target audience, based on their needs. Marketing communications should be an audience-centred activity. In that sense, it is important that messages be based on an understanding of both the needs and environment of the audience. To be successful, marketing communications should be grounded in the behaviour and information-processing needs and style of the target audience; an outside-in approach.

Viewpoint 1.1 — O₂ audience orientation

As if to emphasise the need to be audience-oriented, O₂ developed a campaign called 'A world that revolves around you'. The campaign was based on the insight that pre-pay customers felt neglected. This helped establish the campaign objectives, namely to improve retention and loyalty, and in doing so demonstrate that O₂ regarded pre-pay customers as important. Customers were offered the opportunity of a 10 per cent refund of their top-ups every three months.

By understanding the media used by this customer segment it became possible to develop a media mix that was oriented around the target audience. The first phase of the campaign was based around creating awareness and for this traditional media, such as broadcast, outdoor and print media were sufficient. However, this alone would not encourage retention, interaction with the audience was necessary and this required an understanding of which media they use and when they use it. This was achieved by first plotting the path a typical customer took each day and then second, selecting media that fitted with this pattern. Information was gathered by talking to customers online, when on their mobiles, during top-ups, or in O₂ stores. The result of this was a media plan that involved email, postcards, SMS, MMS, a WAP site, a seeded message in online chatrooms and brand street events. Approximately 50 per cent of O₂'s customers took part in the campaign.

Source: Based on Bashford (2007); Anon (2009)

Question
How does this O₂ example demonstrate an audience orientation?

Task
Track the route you follow each day (to work, college, university), work out your media behaviour at home and then work out the media opportunities that a brand of your choice has to reach you.

Exhibit 1.1 The O₂ Arena
Image courtesy of Alamy Images/Ace Stock Ltd.

The second key point concerns the word *engagement*, or the nature of the communication that can occur between people and between people and machines. Engagement refers to audience captivation, a moment achieved through the use of communication tools, media and people to deliver messages that are relevant, meaningful, of interest and which arouse curiosity. Such captivation may last seconds, such as at the impact of a stunning ad, the sight of a beautiful person or the emotion a piece of music might bring to an individual. Alternatively, engagement may be protracted and last hours, days, weeks, months or years, depending on the context and the level of enjoyment or loyalty felt towards the event, object or person. Whatever the duration engagement enables the communication of messages that are understood, are rich in information or emotional content and which have meaning for the participants. In turn these messages provoke people to talk about their experiences. These conversations may be conducted through face-to-face, ear-to-ear or various electronic formats.

Marketing communications is a complex activity and is used by organisations with varying degrees of sophistication and success. The issue of engagement is examined in greater depth later in this chapter.

The scope of marketing communications

At a basic level, marketing communications, or promotion as it was originally known, is used to communicate elements of an organisation's offering to a target audience. Marketing communications can carry a brand's promise to customers. This promise might refer to the attributes and features of a product/service, its performance characteristics. It might however, focus on the benefits, the functional and emotional feelings and experiences that customers can enjoy through purchase and consumption. Sometimes marketing communications are used to promise on both elements.

Duncan and Moriarty (1997) and Grönroos (2004) suggest that the scope of marketing communications should incorporate four main dimensions. The first of these is that organisations develop a set of **planned** communication events, which are developed through research, resourced, timed and delivered to targeted audiences. These are largely controlled communications unlike those arising from **unplanned** or unintended customer experiences. These might occur through empty stock shelves, accidents or word-of-mouth communications. In addition to these there are marketing communications experienced by audiences relating to both their experience from **using products** (how tasty is this smoothie?) or **the consumption of services** (just how good was the service in that hotel, restaurant or at the airport?). These dimensions of marketing communications are represented at Figure 1.1 (Hughes and Fill, 2007).

Figure 1.1 helps demonstrate the breadth of the subject and the inherent complexity associated with managing communication with audiences and the way they engage with a brand. Although useful in terms of providing an overview, this framework requires elaboration in order to appreciate the detail associated with each of the elements, especially planned marketing communications. This book builds on this framework and in particular considers issues associated with both planned and unplanned aspects of marketing communications.

Planned or formalised marketing communications incorporates three key elements: tools, media and messages, known collectively as the marketing communications mix. The main communication tools are advertising, sales promotion, public relations, direct marketing, personal selling and added-value approaches such as sponsorship, a subpart of public relations. Messages can be primarily informative or emotional but are usually a subtle blend of both dimensions reflecting the preferences and needs of the target audience. To help get these messages through to their audiences, organisations use two main types of media. One type refers to traditional media such as print and broadcast, cinema and outdoor. The other refers to the increasing use of digital media, and the Internet in particular, in order to listen to, interact and converse with audiences.

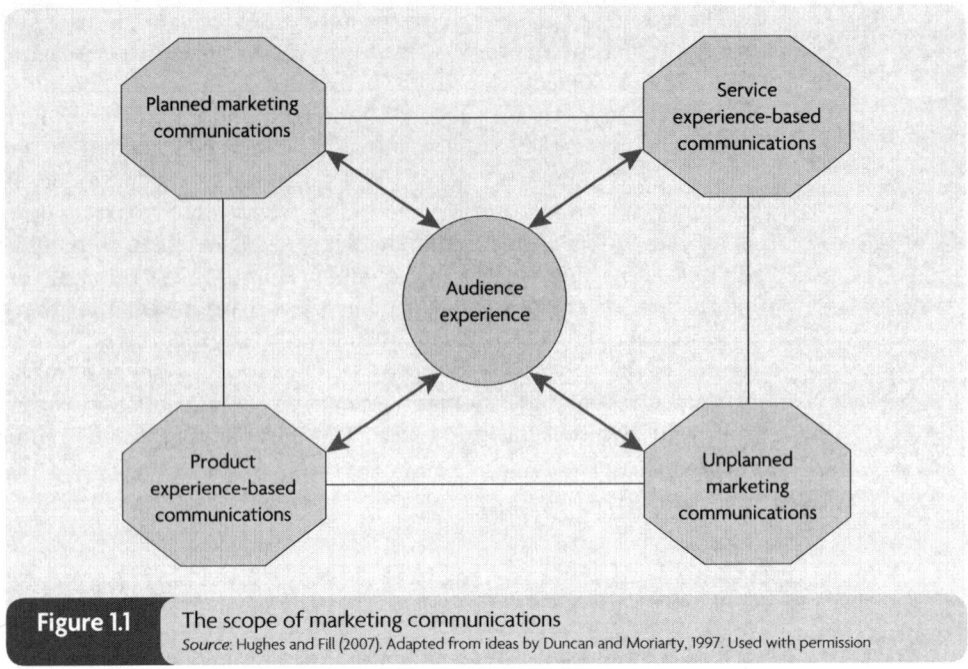

Figure 1.1 The scope of marketing communications
Source: Hughes and Fill (2007). Adapted from ideas by Duncan and Moriarty, 1997. Used with permission

Unplanned marketing communications involve communications that have not been anticipated and hence are relatively uncontrollable. These may be both positive and negative but here the emphasis is more on how the organisation reacts to and manages the meanings attributed by audiences to these messages. For example, unsolicited comments by third-party experts, changes in legislation or regulations by a government, the actions of competitors, failures in the production or distribution processes or perhaps the most potent of all communications, word-of-mouth comments between customers, all impact on the way in which organisations and brands are perceived and the images and reputations that are developed. Many reports, for example JMW (2010), have reported the relative effectiveness of these approaches and that the vast majority find that people use word of mouth recommendation when making purchasing decisions, rather than advertising, preferring to see others using the product. Not surprisingly, many leading organisations recognise the power and influence of word-of-mouth communication and actively seek to shape the nature, timing and speed with which it occurs. In other words, they attempt to control the uncontrollable and the planned and the unplanned begin to merge.

When considering the scope of marketing communications it is important to consider the broad industry context in which marketing communication events occur. Figure 1.2 illustrates the industry context, setting it out within an audience perspective. Planned marketing communications are developed and delivered through the five principal tools mentioned earlier. The media play an increasingly influential role in marketing communications activities and provide an important contextual dimension. What is communicated, the content of the message, is also important. Organisations invest heavily in trying to understand their audiences and to develop messages that resonate with them. These three elements are examined later in this chapter and again in Part 3. The final contextual element concerns people, processes and systems. Most marketing communications require people to establish, maintain and intervene in communication processes and often these are enabled through the use of technology. Indeed, digital technology has been pivotal in shaping the current marketing communications environment, whether it be through mobile phones, webpages, or call centres they are used extensively by organisations to provide customer support.

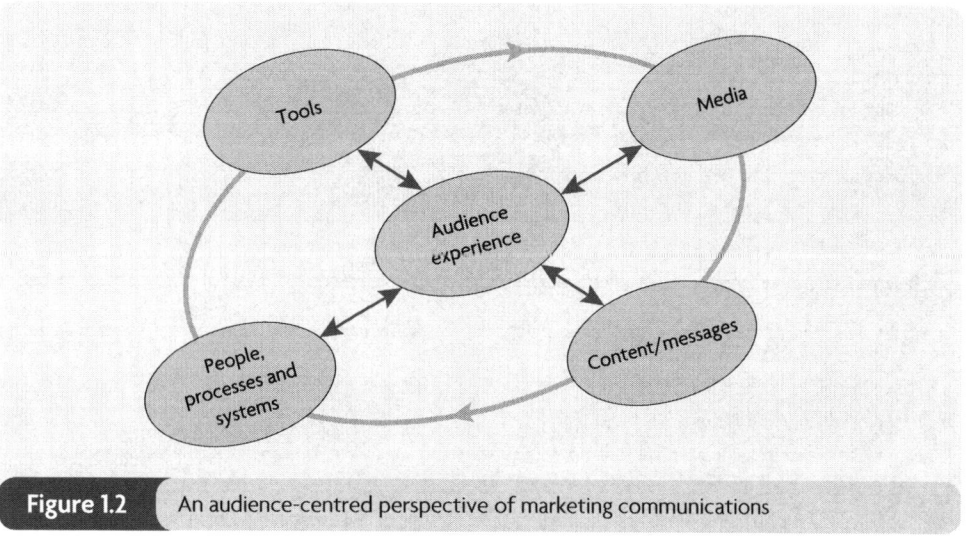

Figure 1.2 An audience-centred perspective of marketing communications

The role of marketing communications

Organisations communicate with a variety of audiences in order to pursue their marketing and business objectives. Marketing communications can be used to engage with a variety of audiences and in such a way that meet the needs of the audience. Messages should encourage individual members of target audiences to respond to the focus organisation (or product/brand). This response can be immediate through, for example, purchase behaviour or use of customer care lines, or it can be deferred as information is assimilated and considered for future use. Even if the information is discarded at a later date, the communication will have attracted attention and consideration of the message.

Viewpoint 1.2 Iced apples or will it be pears?

The campaign used by Magners during the summer of 2006 to roll out their brand of cider across the UK was based primarily on observational consumer research. The basis for the campaign was to position the drink as 'naturally refreshing' by showing it poured over ice, in an apple orchard and in a pint bottle.

One of the first tasks undertaken on the Bulmer's brand in the early 1990s was to elevate cider out of the 'embarrassed-to-be-seen-drinking' category and to do this C&C, the owner, repositioned Bulmer's closer to beer by adding long-neck bottles and cans to its on tap offering. C&C then observed 40- and 50-something golfers choosing Bulmer's to quench their thirst. This led to campaigns that helped to encourage drinkers to consider cider as a refreshing drink. Magners contains a high level of natural apple juice content and a lower alcohol content than other ciders, so it is much easier to make refreshment the key point of differentiation. These elements were critical when repositioning Magners as a quality, refreshing drink rather than a cheap intoxicant, which was how cider was largely viewed in the UK.

In 1997 C&C noticed consumers were adding ice to Bulmer's draught to cool it down. This use of ice was then adopted in Magners' campaigns. By showing consumers how to serve and drink the product it helped to create a clear point of difference for the brand. It was the first cider brand to do this and its success has led to competitive responses such as Sirrus from Scottish & Newcastle, especially formulated to be poured over ice.

The Magners' cider brand struggled to sustain its initial success, partly due to poor summer weather and competitor reactions. The 'over-ice' positioning was copied easily by competitors, and those that had big marketing budgets, squashed Magners' attempt to establish a strong market position. In 2009 the C&C Group launched Magners Pear in an attempt to broaden its portfolio. The launch campaign featured the use of television, outdoor and digital media. The campaign also used sales promotion in the form of sampling activity to encourage trial tasting and familiarity plus a competition based around a Magners 'pub finder' mobile application.

Source: Based on Baker (2006); Simm (2008); Alarcon (2009)

Question

To what extent was the depiction of cider poured over ice a temporary form of engagement?

Task

Observe the way five different drinks brands are presented to audiences. What point of differentiation do they use and how similar are they?

The reason for using marketing communications will vary according to the prevailing situation or context but the essential goal is to provoke an audience response. This response might be geared to developing brand values and the positive thoughts an individual might have about a brand. This is grounded in a 'thinking and feeling orientation', a combination of both cognitive thoughts and emotional feelings about a brand. Another type of response might be one that stimulates the audience to act in particular ways. Referred to as a behavioural or sometimes brand response, the goal is to 'encourage particular behaviours'. For example, these might include sampling a piece of cheese in a supermarket, encouraging visits to a website, placing orders and paying for goods and services, sharing information with a friend, registering on a network, opening letters, signing a petition or telephoning a number. See Figure 1.3 for a list of the factors that can drive engagement opportunities.

Apart from generating cash flows, the underlying purpose of these responses can be considered to be a strategic function of developing relationships with particular audiences and or from (re)positioning brands. For example, LV=, an insurance brand, moved from a behavioural strategy based on daytime direct response tv advertising, to one based on developing brand values. The goal was to boost awareness of its mutual status (rather than a plc) and so reposition the brand as a premium insurer (Brownsell, 2010a).

Engagement therefore can be considered to be a function of two forms of response. The quality of engagement cannot be determined but it can be argued that marketing communications

Figure 1.3 Factors that drive engagement opportunities

should be based on driving a particular type of response that captivates an individual. For example, Sarah Copley, Sales and Marketing Director for Virgin Trains explained that for several years the company spent time developing and building the brand values particularly at a time when the product was not complete. However, now Virgin Trains have a focus on growing passenger numbers (Brownsell, 2010b), a behavioural strategy that requires a complementary communications approach.

From this it can be concluded that the primary role of marketing communication is to engage audiences. Where engagement occurs an individual might be said to have been positively captivated, and as a result opportunities for activity should increase. Engagement acts as a bridge, the mechanism through which brands and organisations link with target audiences and through which the goals of both parties can be achieved: mutual value.

Engagement suggests that understanding and meaning has been conveyed effectively. At one level, engagement through one way communication enables target audiences to understand product and service offers, to the extent that the audience is sufficiently engaged to want to enter into further communication activity. At another level, engagement through two-way or interactive communication enables information that is relationship specific (Ballantyne, 2004) to be exchanged. The greater the frequency of information exchange the more likely collaborative relationships will develop. So, the role of marketing communications is to engage audiences.

The tasks of marketing communications

Bowersox and Morash (1989) demonstrated that communication plays an important part in the process through which information flows as it can help accomplish one or more key tasks:

First, marketing communications can act as a differentiator, particularly in markets where there is little to separate competing products and brands. Mineral water products, such as Perrier and Highland Spring, are largely similar: it is the communications surrounding the products that have created various brand images, enabling consumers to make purchasing decisions. In these cases it is the images created by marketing communications that enable people to differentiate one brand from another and position them so that consumers' purchasing confidence and positive attitudes are developed.

Second, communications can also be used to reinforce experiences and beliefs. This may take the form of reminding people of a need they might have or reminding them of the benefits of past transactions with a view to convincing them that they should enter into a similar exchange. In addition, it is possible to provide reassurance or comfort either immediately prior to an exchange or, more commonly, post-purchase. This is important as it helps to retain current customers and improve profitability, an approach to business that is much more cost-effective than constantly striving to lure new customers. Brands are often refreshed, in order that they maintain currency among the target audience and remain competitive.

The third task identified was that communication can inform and make potential customers aware of an organisation's offering. No purchase can be made without prior awareness. Sometimes audiences need to be educated, shown how to use a product or service or advised about why a product might be helpful. The fourth and final task is to use communication to persuade current and potential customers of the desirability of either trialling a product, buying a product or to enter into a relationship.

Therefore, communication can build images about a brand; that is differentiate it, reinforce memories and understanding, inform and make audiences aware of a brand's presence and finally persuade an individual to buy and consume a product or service. To put it another way: DRIP (Fill, 2002). See Table 1.1 for an example.

Table 1.1 DRIP elements of marketing communications

DRIP element	Examples
Differentiate	Cravendale milk is better for us than ordinary milk because it is finely filtered, making it purer for a fresher taste.
Reinforce	McCain used communications to reassure consumers about the nutritional content of its products.
Inform/make aware	The Environment Agency and Flood Action Week inform various organisations, such as the Met Office, local media and the general public of the new flood warning codes.
Persuade	Cillit Bang... bang and the dirt is gone

At a higher level, the communication process not only supports the transaction, by informing, persuading, reinforcing or differentiating, but it also offers a means of exchange itself. Communications involve intangible benefits, such as the psychological satisfactions associated with, for example, the entertainment value of television advertisements or the experiences within a sponsored part of a social network.

Communications can also be seen as a means of perpetuating and transferring values and culture to different parts of society or networks. For example, it is argued that the way women are portrayed in the media and stereotypical images of very thin or 'size zero' women are dysfunctional in that they set up inappropriate role models. The form and characteristics of the communication process adopted by some organisations (both the deliberate and the unintentional use of signs and symbols used to convey meaning) help to provide stability and continuity.

Other examples of intangible satisfactions can be seen in the social and psychological transactions involved increasingly with the work of the National Health Service (NHS), charities, educational institutions and other not-for-profit organisations, such as housing associations. Not only do these organisations recognise the need to communicate with various audiences,

Viewpoint 1.3 Chocolate DRIPs

Green & Black's is a very successful premium organic brand of chocolate. Their use of marketing communications might be to:

- differentiate it from other chocolate brands;
- remind/reassure customers of the taste and experience of the brand;
- inform and educate the market about the ethics and economics of Fairtrade and the nutritional benefits of chocolate;
- persuade potential consumers and retailers to purchase and distribute Green & Black's respectively.

Question
Which of these tasks are the most important? Justify your view.

Task
Think of a campaign for a brand of your choice and consider how the DRIP model can be applied.

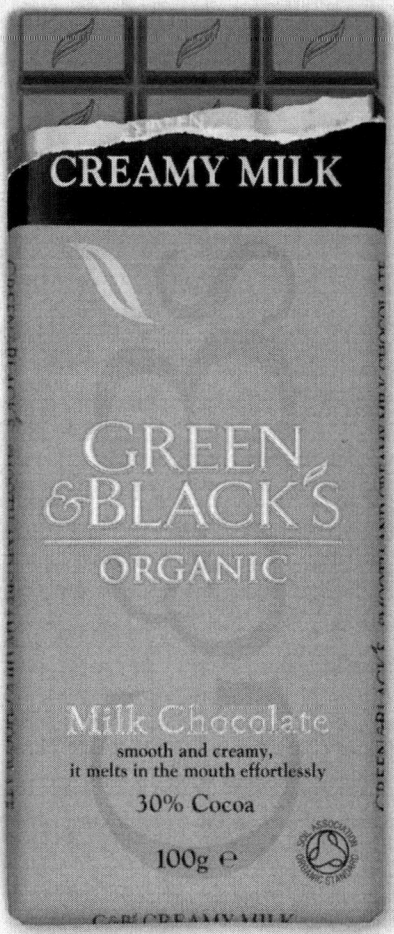

Exhibit 1.2 Green and Black's 'Creamy Milk' chocolate
Image courtesy of Brave

but also they perceive value in being seen to be 'of value' to their customers. There is also evidence that some brands are trying to meet the emerging needs of some consumers who want to know the track record of manufacturers with respect to their environmental policies and actions. For example, the growth in 'Fairtrade' products, designed to provide fairer and more balanced trading arrangements with producers and growers in emerging parts of the world, has influenced Kraft that they should engage with this form of commercial activity. Sainsbury's claim that all of their bananas are Fairtrade, while Typhoo have claimed for some time on their packaging, 'care for tea and our tea pickers'.

The notion of value can be addressed in a different way. All organisations have the opportunity to develop their communications to a point where the value of their messages represents a competitive advantage. This value can be seen in the consistency, timing, volume or expression of the message. Heinonen and Strandvik (2005) argue that there are four elements that constitute communication value. These are the message content, how the information is presented, where the communication occurs and its timing. In other words, the all-important context within which a communication event occurs. These elements are embedded within marketing communications and are referred to throughout this book.

Environmental influences

The management of marketing communications is a complex and highly uncertain activity. This is due in part to the nature of the marketing communication variables, including the influence of the environment. The environment can be considered in many different ways, but for the purposes of this opening chapter, three categories are considered; the internal, external and market environments. The constituents of each of these are set out in Figure 1.4.

Internal influences

The internal environment refers primarily to the organisation and the way it works, what its values are and how it wants to develop. Here various forces seek to influence an organisation's marketing communications. The overall strategy that an organisation adopts should have a huge impact. For example, how the organisation wishes to differentiate itself within its target markets will influence the messages and media used and, of course, the overarching positioning and reputation of the company. Brand strategies will influence such things as the way in which brands are named, the extent to which sales promotions are an integral part of the

Figure 1.4 The environmental influences that shape marketing communications

communication mix and how they are positioned. The prevailing organisational culture can also be extremely influential. For a long time the hierarchical management structure and power culture at Procter and Gamble led to the establishment of a pattern of behaviour whereby the marketing communication messages were largely product benefit oriented rather than emotionally driven, as at their arch rivals Unilever.

The amount of money available to the marketing communication budget will influence the media mix or the size of the sales force used to deliver messages. Apart from the quality and motivation of the people employed, the level of preferences and marketing skills deployed can impact on the form of the messages, the choice of media, and the use of agencies and support services. Finally, the socio-political climate of the firm shapes not only who climbs the career ladder fastest, but how and to which brands scarce marketing resources are distributed.

Marketing communications is regarded as one of the elements of the marketing mix and is primarily responsible for the communication of the marketing offer and the brand promise, sometimes referred to as the brand proposition. Although recognising that there is implicit and important communication through the other elements of the marketing mix (through a high price, for example, symbolic of high quality), it is the task of a planned and integrated set of communication activities to communicate effectively with each of an organisation's stakeholder groups.

Marketing communications is sometimes perceived as only dealing with communications that are external to the organisation. It should be recognised that good communications with internal stakeholders, such as employees, are also vital if, in the long term, successful favourable images, perceptions and attitudes are to be established. Influences through the work force and the marketing plan can be both positive and effective. For example, staff used in B&Q and Halifax advertising are intended to project internal values that should reflect positively upon the respective brands.

Market influences

Market influences are characterised by partial levels of control and typified by the impact of competitors. Competitors occupy particular positions in the market and this shapes what others claim about their own products, the media they use, the geographic coverage of the sales force and their own positioning. Intermediaries influence the nature of business-to-business marketing communications. The frequency, intensity, quality and overall willingness to share information with one another are significant forces. Of course, the various agencies an organisation uses can also be very influential. Marketing research agencies (inform about market perception, attitudes, and behaviour), communication agencies (determine what is said and then design how it is said, what is communicated) and media houses (recommend media mixes and when it is said) all have considerable potential to influence marketing communications.

However, perhaps the biggest single market group consists of the organisation's customers and network of stakeholders. Their attitudes, perceptions and buying preferences and behaviours, although not directly controllable, (should) have a far reaching influence on the marketing communications used by an organisation.

External influences

As mentioned earlier, the external group of influencers are characterised by the organisations' near lack of control. The well known PEST framework is a useful way of considering these forces. Political forces, which can encompass both legal and ethical issues, shape their use of marketing communication through legislation, voluntary controls and individual company attitudes towards issues of right and wrong, consequences and duties and the formal and informal communications an organisation uses. Indeed, increasing attention has been placed upon ethics and corporate responsibility to the extent that in some cases a name and shame culture might be identified.

Economic forces, which include demographics, geographics and geodemographics, can determine the positioning of brands in terms of perceived value. For example, if the government raise interest rates then consumers are more inclined not to spend money, especially on non-staple products and services. This may mean that marketing communications needs to convey stronger messages about value and to send out strident calls-to-action.

Social forces are concerned with the values, beliefs and norms that a society enshrines. Issues to do with core values within a society are often difficult to change. For example, the American gun culture or the once prevalent me-orientation with respect to self-fulfilment, set up a string of values that marketing communications can use to harness, magnify and align brands. The current social pressures with regard to obesity and healthier eating habits have forced fast-food companies such as McDonald's to introduce new menus and healthier food options. As a result, marketing communications not only has to inform and make audiences aware of the new menus but also convey messages about differentiation and positioning plus provide a reason to visit the restaurant.

Technological forces have had an immense impact on marketing communications. New technology has revolutionised traditional forms of marketing communications and led to more personalised, targeted, customised and responsive forms of communication. What was once predominantly one-way communications based upon a model of information provision and persuasion, has given way to a two-way model in which integration with audiences and where sharing and reasoning behaviours are enabled by digital technology, is now used frequently with appropriate target audiences.

New forms of marketing communications have been developed in response to changing environmental conditions. For example, public relations are now seen by some to have both a marketing and corporate dimension. Direct marketing is now recognised as an important way of developing relationships with buyers, both consumer and organisational, while new and innovative forms of communication through sponsorship, floor advertising, video screens on supermarket trolleys and checkout coupon dispensers, plus Internet and associated technologies, mean that effective communication requires the selection and integration of an increasing variety of communication tools and media.

The marketing communications mix

Successful marketing communications involves integrating three elements into combinations that have the potential to engage target audiences. The elements that need to be mixed are the tools, media and messages and, collectively these are referred to as the marketing communications mix.

As stated earlier, there are five principal marketing communications tools: advertising, sales promotion, public relations, direct marketing and personal selling. In addition to these tools or methods of communication, there are the media, or the means by which advertising and other marketing communications messages are conveyed. Tools and media should not be confused as they have different characteristics and seek to achieve different goals. Also, just in case you were thinking something is missing, the Internet is a medium not a tool.

To complete the trilogy, messages need to be conveyed to the target audience. Whereas organisations were primarily responsible for the content of messages, today an increasing number of messages are developed by consumers, and shared with other consumers. This last point is referred to as word-of-mouth communication.

In the past decade there have been some major changes in the communications environment and in the way organisations communicate with their target audiences. Digital technology has given rise to a raft of different media at the same time that people have developed a variety of ways to spend their leisure time. This is referred to as media and audience fragmentation respectively, and organisations have developed fresh combinations of the communications mix in order to reach their audiences effectively. For example, there has been a dramatic rise in the use of direct-response media as direct marketing has become a key part of many campaigns. The Internet and digital technologies have enabled new interactive forms of communication, where the receiver has greater responsibility for their part in the communication process. An increasing number of organisations are using public relations to communicate messages about the organisation (corporate public relations) and also messages about their brands (marketing public relations).

The traditional mix has evolved dramatically. Originally brands were developed through the use of advertising to generate 'above-the-line' mass communication campaigns. The strategy was based around buying space in newspapers and magazines, or advertising time (called spots) in major television programmes that were watched by huge audiences (20+ million people in the UK). This strategy required media owners to create programmes (content) that would attract brand owners because of the huge, relatively passive audiences. By interrupting the audience's entertainment, brand owners could talk to (or at) their markets in order to sell their brands.

However, since the days of just two commercial television stations there has been a proliferation of media. Audiences no longer use the television as their main form of information or entertainment and newspaper readership has fallen steadily in recent years. It has been suggested that consumers now use media to satisfy four additional needs:

- to discover;
- to participate;
- to share;
- to express themselves.

Rather than passive media involvement, these motivations, as they are referred to, require active engagement with media. Consumers now have a choice of media and leisure activities, they decide how and when to consume information and entertainment. Consumers are now motivated and able to develop their own content, be it through text, music or video and consider topics that they can share with friends on virtual networks. Thus, media and messages are the key to reaching consumers today, not the tools. More direct and highly targeted, personalised communication activities using direct marketing and the other tools of the mix now predominate. (See Figure 1.5.)

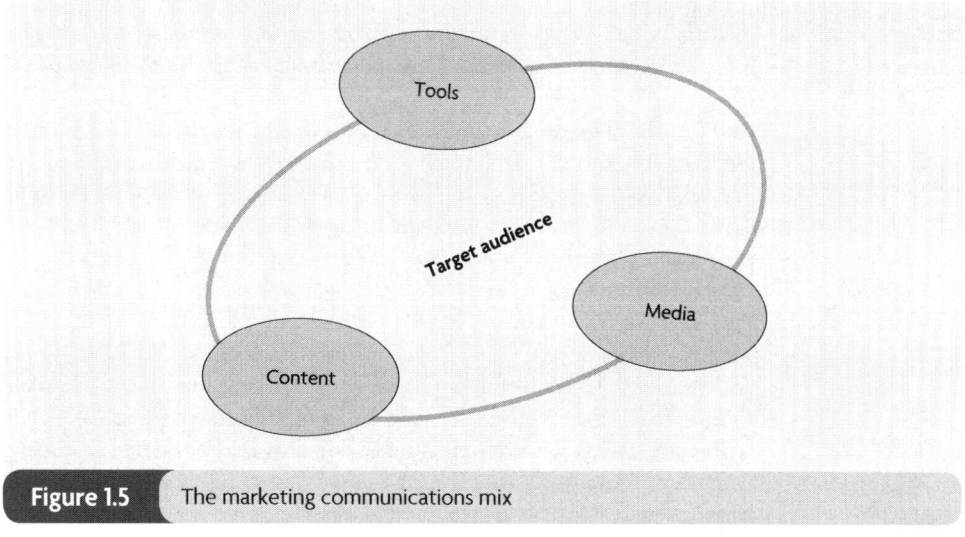

Figure 1.5 The marketing communications mix

Philips and Cooper (2008) refer to the digital reworking in 2008, of the iconic 1990s 'Hello Boys' ad for Wonderbra. The original ad was delivered through posters and PR which required audiences to 'spectate'. The contemporary version involves video content developed online and conversations stimulated through a variety of digital seedings. See www.edelman.co.uk/case-studies/wonderbra-dita-von-teese for more detail about this case and the extraordinary campaign results. These included an immediate product sell-out and, at the time, the most watched YouTube video on launch day. Here content, conversation and engagement are demonstrated wonderfully.

The new mix represents a shift in approach. The conventional format represents an *intervention*-based approach to marketing communications, one based on seeking the attention of a customer who might not necessarily be interested. The shift is towards *conversation*-based marketing communications, where the focus is on communications with and between members of an audience who may have contributed content to the campaign. This has a particular impact on direct marketing, interactive communications and, to some extent, personal selling.

The tools of the MCs mix

Advertising

Advertising is a non-personal form of mass communication that offers a high degree of control for those responsible for the design and delivery of advertising messages. However, the ability of advertising to persuade the target audience to behave in a particular way is suspect. Furthermore, the effect on sales is extremely hard to measure. Advertising also suffers from low credibility in that audiences are less likely to believe messages delivered through advertising than they are messages received through some other tools and word-of-mouth communication.

The flexibility of this tool is good because it can be used to communicate with a national audience or a particular specialised segment. Although the costs can be extremely high, a vast number of people can be reached with a message, so the cost per contact can be the lowest of all the tools in the mix. Advertising is explored in Chapter 9.

Sales promotion

Sales promotion comprises various marketing techniques, which are often used tactically to provide added value to an offering. The aim is to accelerate sales and gather marketing information. Like advertising, sales promotion is a non-personal form of communication but has a greater capacity to target smaller audiences. It is controllable and, although it has to be paid for, the associated costs can be much lower than those of advertising. As a generalisation, credibility is not very high, as the sponsor's goals are easily identifiable. However, the ability to add value and to bring forward future sales is strong and complements a macroeconomic need, which focuses on short-term financial performance. Sales promotion techniques and approaches are the subject of Chapter 12.

Personal selling

Personal selling is traditionally perceived as an interpersonal communication tool that involves face-to-face activities undertaken by individuals, often representing an organisation, in order to inform, persuade or remind an individual or group to take appropriate action, as required by the sponsor's representative. A salesperson engages in communication on a one-to-one basis where instantaneous feedback is possible. The costs associated with interpersonal communication are normally very high.

This tool, considered in Chapter 11, differs from the previous two in that, while still lacking in relative credibility and control, the degree of control is potentially lower, because the salesperson is free at the point of contact to deliver a message other than that intended (Lloyd, 1997). Indeed, many different messages can be delivered by a single salesperson. Some of these messages may enhance the prospect of the salesperson's objectives being reached (making the sale), or they may retard the process and so incur more time and hence costs. Whichever way it is viewed, control is lower than with advertising.

Public relations

Public relations is concerned with establishing and maintaining relationships with various stakeholders and with enhancing the reputation of the organisation. This indicates that public relations should be a part of the wider perspective of corporate strategy. The increasing use of public relations, and in particular publicity, is a reflection of the high credibility attached to messages conveyed through this form of communication.

Publicity involves the dissemination of messages through third-party media, such as magazines, newspapers or news programmes. There is no charge for the media space or time but there are costs incurred in the production of the material. There is a wide range of other tools used by public relations, such as event management, public affairs, sponsorship and lobbying. It is difficult to control a message once it is placed in the media channels, but the endorsement offered by a third party can be very influential and have a far greater impact on the target audience than any of the other tools in the marketing communications mix.

Viewpoint 1.4 Associating with extreme Red Bulls

The energy drink Red Bull was first launched in the mid 1980s but its development in Britain continues to be strong, with sales steadily increasing year on year and maintaining a near 30 per cent market share. There are several factors contributing to this performance, not least of them being the quality of the product and the perceived value consumers derive from drinking the brand.

The brand makes use of a wide range of marketing communications tools and media, with a message that is based around the distinctive, slim silver can, that it is cool to drink Red Bull. The brand uses television, print and cinema as key media channels to reach their 14–19-year-old target audience, and to build brand awareness. However, this is not enough to sustain contemporary brands and so they use other activities to build a brand experience for users, based around excitement, adrenalin, danger and youth culture. To achieve this Red Bull associate themselves with extreme sports (e.g. Formula 1, the Red Bull Air Race World Series, street culture and music events). This builds credibility that in turn fosters word-of-mouth communication.

Source: Based on Turner (2008), www.redbull.com

Question
To what extent is the brand experience a more important driver of sales than the quality of the product and its various attributes?

Task
Make a list of five events with which Red Bull might associate themselves.

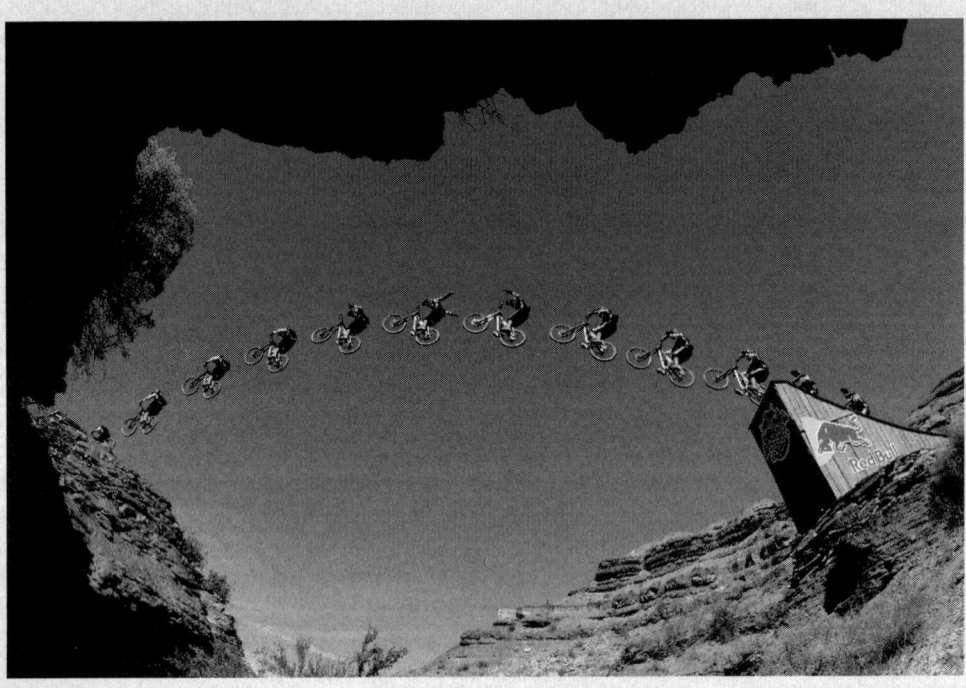

Exhibit 1.3 A Red Bull event: Red Bull Rampage, Virgin, Utah 2010
Image © John Gibson/Red Bull Photofiles

This non-personal form of communication offers organisations a different way to communicate, not only with consumers but also with many other stakeholders.

Direct marketing

The four elements of the communications mix discussed so far have a number of strengths and weaknesses. As a response to some of the weaknesses that revolve around costs and effectiveness, direct marketing emerged in the 1990s as a new and effective way of building relationships with customers over the long term.

Direct marketing represents a shift in focus from mass to personalised communications. In particular, the use of direct mail, telemarketing and the fast-developing area of interactive marketing communications, represents 'through-the-line' communications. By removing the face-to-face aspect of personal selling and replacing it with an email communication, a telephone conversation or a direct mail letter, many facets of the traditional salespersons' tasks can be removed, freeing them to concentrate on their key skill areas.

Direct marketing seeks to target individual customers with the intention of delivering personalised messages and building a relationship with them based on their responses to the direct communications. In contrast to conventional approaches, direct marketing attempts to build a one-to-one relationship, a partnership with each customer, by communicating with the customers on a direct and personal basis. If an organisation chooses to use direct marketing then it has to incorporate the approach within a marketing plan. This is because distribution is different and changes in the competitive environment may mean that prices need to change. For example, charges for packing and delivery need to be incorporated. The product may also need to be altered or adapted to the market. For example, some electrical products are marketed through different countries on home shopping channels and websites. The electrical requirements of each country or region need to be incorporated within the product specification of each country's offering. In addition to these changes, the promotion component is also different, simply because communication is required directly with each targeted individual. To do this, direct-response media must be used.

In many cases, direct-response media are a derivative of advertising, such as direct mail, magazine inserts and television and print advertisements that use telephone numbers and web addresses to encourage a direct response. However, direct response can also be incorporated within personal selling through telemarketing and sales promotions with competitions to build market knowledge and develop the database, which is the key to the direct marketing approach.

This text regards direct marketing as a management process associated with building mutually satisfying customer relationships through personal and intermediary-free interaction and dialogue. Direct-response media are the primary forms of communication when direct marketing is an integral part of the marketing plan.

The Internet is both a distribution channel and communication medium, one that enables consumers and organisations to communicate in radically different ways. It allows for interactivity and is possibly the best medium to enable dialogue. Communication is two-way, often interactive, and very fast, allowing businesses and individuals to find information and enter exchange transactions in such a way that some traditional communication practices and shopping patterns are being reconfigured.

The key characteristics of the communication tools

Each of the tools of the communication mix performs a different role and can accomplish different tasks. This reflects their different capabilities, their various attributes and key characteristics. These are the extent to which each of the tools is controllable, whether it is paid for by the sponsor and whether communication is through mass media or undertaken personally. One additional characteristic concerns the receiver's perception of the credibility of the source of the message. If the credibility factor is high then there is a greater likelihood that a message from that source will be accepted by receivers.

The 4Cs framework set out at Table 1.2, depicts the key characteristics and shows the relative effectiveness of the communication tools across a number of different characteristics. These are the ability of each to communicate, the credibility they bestow on messages, the costs involved and the control that each tool can maintain.

Media and the MCs mix

There is a huge and expanding variety of media used to convey messages to target audiences. For ease of understanding it is helpful to categorise these into six main classes. These consist of broadcast, print, outdoor, digital, in-store and other media classes. Of these the digital class is growing the most and is the most influential. These classes can be broken down into types and vehicles, all of which are explored in greater detail in Chapter 13.

There is a trend to move resources from traditional media to digital media. Each of these classes have particular characteristics that makes the decision to use particular combinations of media, referred to as the media mix, a complex and challenging marketing decision.

Key differences between traditional and digital media

A comparison of traditional and digital media provides an interesting insight into the capabilities of the two main forms of media. These are set out in Table 1.3. Space (or time) within

Table 1.2 The 4Cs framework – a summary of the key characteristics of the tools of marketing communications

	Advertising	Sales promotion	Public relations	Personal selling	Direct marketing
Communications					
Ability to deliver a personal message	Low	Low	Low	High	High
Ability to reach a large audience	High	Medium	Medium	Low	Medium
Level of interaction	Low	Medium	Low	High	High
Credibility					
Given by the target audience	Low	Medium	High	Medium	Medium
Costs					
Absolute costs	High	Medium	Low	High	Medium
Cost per contact	Low	Medium	Low	High	High
Wastage	High	Medium	High	Low	Low
Size of investment	High	Medium	Low	High	Medium
Control					
Ability to target particular audiences	Medium	High	Low	Medium	High
Management's ability to adjust the deployment of the tool as circumstances change	Medium	High	Low	Medium	High

Table 1.3 Comparison of traditional and digital media

Traditional media	Digital media
One-to-many	One-to-one and many-to-many
Greater monologue	Greater dialogue
Active provision	Passive provision
Mass marketing	Individualised marketing
General need	Personalised
Branding	Information
Segmentation	Communities

traditional media is limited and costs rise as demand for the limited space/time increases. Internet space is unlimited so absolute costs remain very low and static, while relative costs plummet as more visitors are recorded as having been to a site. Another aspect concerns the focus of the advertising message. Traditionally, advertisers tend to emphasise the emotional rather than information aspect, particularly within low-involvement categories. Digital media allow focus on the provision of information and so the emotional aspect of advertising messages tends to have a lower significance. As branding becomes a more important aspect of Internet activity, it is probable that there will be a greater use of emotions, especially when the goal is to keep people at a website, rather than driving them to it.

Digital media allow focus on the provision of information and so the emotional aspect of online advertising messages tends to have a lower significance. Apart from the obvious factor that digital media, and the Internet in particular, provide interactive opportunities that traditional media cannot provide, it is important to remember that opportunities-to-see are generally driven by customers rather than by the advertiser that interrupts viewing or reading activities. People drive the interaction at a speed that is convenient to them; they are not driven by others.

Management control over some Internet-based marketing communications is relatively high, as not only are there greater opportunities to control the position and placement of advertisements, promotions and press releases, but it is also possible to change the content of these activities much more quickly than is possible with traditional media. The goals outlined above indicate the framework within which advertising needs to be managed.

Messages and the MCs mix

Brand related messages have two main sources. One is the organisation itself in terms of how it chooses to present their organisation or brand, a planned aspect of marketing communications. What organisations say and how they say it needs careful consideration. The other source involves audiences and the brand messages that customers create and communicate, both positive and negative. These messages may be directed to the brand or shared with one another. In an age of interaction, individual consumers can create and share content with others, and these are largely unstructured and unplanned communications.

What is common to both the planned and unplanned messages is that they both contain two elements, information and emotion. Ensuring that the right balance of information and emotions is achieved and that the presentation of the message is appropriate for the target audience represents a critical part of the planned communication process for agencies, clients and individuals.

Messages should reflect a balance between the need for information and the need for pleasure or enjoyment in consuming the message. Messages can be product oriented and rational or customer-oriented and based on feelings and emotions. All messages contain information and emotional content, it is the balance between the two that needs to be managed according to the task and context.

Messages where there is high-involvement require an emphasis on the information content, in particular the key attributes and the associated benefits. This style is often factual and product oriented. Where there is low-involvement the message should contain a high proportion of emotional content and seek to develop brand values through imagery and associations. These issues are discussed in Chapter 15.

Messages should be developed that enable recipients to not only respond to the source but to also encourage them to talk to others through conversation, offline or online. For example, when Toyota launched the up-rated Prius, social media was an important element of the campaign. Woods (2009) reports that use was made of organic search in order to increase visibility of information about the Prius, but in addition model previews, news stories, videos and other influential content was seeded across relevant websites, all in an attempt to provoke conversation about the brand.

In addition to considering the attributes of both traditional and digital media, it is also worth considering the content of the information that each is capable of delivering. These are set out in Table 1.4.

Table 1.4 Comparison of content

Websites/Internet	Traditional media
Good at providing rational, product-based information	Better at conveying emotional brand values
More efficient as costs do not increase in proportion to the size of the target audience	Costs are related to usage
Better at prompting customer action	Less effective for calling to action except point-of-purchase and telemarketing
Effective for short-term, product-oriented brand action goals and long-term corporate identity objectives	Normally associated with building long-term values
Average at generating awareness and attention	Strong builders of awareness
Measures of effectiveness weak and/or in the process of development	Established methodologies, some misleading or superficial (mass media); direct marketing techniques are superior
Dominant orientation – cognition	Dominant orientation – emotion

As mentioned earlier, digital media are superior at providing rational, product-based information whereas traditional media are much better at conveying emotional brand values. The former have a dominant cognition orientation and the latter an emotional one. There are other differences, but the predominant message is that these types of media are, to a large extent, complementary, suggesting that they should be used together, not one independently of the other.

Criteria when selecting the mix

Using the key characteristics it is possible to determine the significant criteria organisations should consider when selecting communication tools (see Table 1.5 on p. 26). These are as follows:

- the degree of control required over the delivery of the message;
- the financial resources available to pay a third party to transmit messages;
- the level of credibility that each tool bestows on the organisation;
- the size and geographic dispersion of the target audiences;
- the communication tasks each tool is best at satisfying.

Control

Control over the message, particularly in traditional mass media communication, is necessary to ensure that the intended message is transmitted to and received by the target audience. Furthermore, this message must be capable of being understood in order that the receiver can act appropriately. Message control is complicated by interference or negative 'noise' that can corrupt and distort messages. For example, the media spotlight shone brightly on Eurostar when a number of trains broke down in the channel tunnel during the 2009 Christmas period. The disruption for thousands of passengers, many stranded for hours in the tunnel, generated negative media comments about the company. All advertising and campaign work was stopped immediately by Eurostar and only resumed six months later (Clark, 2010).

Advertising and sales promotions can allow for a high level of control over the message, from design to transmission. Interestingly, they afford only partial control or influence over the feedback associated with the original message.

Control can also be an important factor when considering online and digital-based communications. For example, the ability to place banner ads, to bid for sponsored links and determine keyword rankings in search engines requires control and deliberation. However, it should be noted that message control is an ambiguous term. Brand owners desire control over message placement and seeding but they also want people to talk about their brands. In this context owners sacrifice control over what is said about a brand, who says it and in which context. Engagement is about provoking conversations and that implies that there is virtually no control over this aspect. Planned marketing communications carries a high level of control, whilst unplanned word-of-mouth conversations carry little control.

Financial resources

Control is also a function of financial power. In other words, if an organisation is prepared to pay a third party to transmit the message, then long-term control will rest with the sponsor for as long as the financial leverage continues. However, short-term message corruption can exist if management control over the process is less than vigilant. For example, if the design of the message differs from that originally agreed, then partial control has already been lost. This can happen when the working relationship between an advertising agency and the client is less than efficient and the process for signing off work in progress fails to prevent the design and release of inappropriate creative work.

Advertising and sales promotion are tools that allow for a high level of control by the sponsor, whereas public relations, and publicity in particular, is weak in this aspect because the voluntary services of a third party are normally required for the message to be transmitted.

There is a great variety of media available to advertisers. Each media type (for example television, radio, newspapers, magazines, posters and the Internet) carries a particular cost, and the financial resources of the organisation may not be available to use particular types of media, even if such use would be appropriate on other grounds.

Credibility

Public relations is highly credible because receivers perceive the third party as unbiased and endorsing the offering. They view the third party's comments as objective and trustworthy in the context of the media in which the comments appear.

At a broad level, advertising, sales promotion and, to a slightly lesser extent, personal selling are tools that can lack credibility, as perceived by a target audience. Because of this, organisations often use celebrities and 'experts' to endorse their offerings. The credibility of the spokesperson is intended to distract the receiver from the sponsor's prime objective, which is to sell the offering. Credibility, as we see shall later, is an important aspect of the communication process and of marketing communications.

Dispersion – size and geography

The size and geographic dispersion of the target audience can be a significant influence on the choice of tools. A national consumer audience can only be reached effectively if tools of mass communication are used, such as advertising and sales promotion. Similarly, various specialist businesses require personal attention to explain, design, demonstrate, install and service complex equipment. In these circumstances personal selling – one-to-one contact – is of greater significance. The tools of marketing communications can enable an organisation to speak to vast national and international audiences through advertising and satellite technology, or to single persons or small groups through personal selling and the assistance of word-of-mouth recommendation.

Table 1.5 Key selection criteria for the tools of the marketing communications mix

	Advertising	Sales promotion	Public relations	Direct marketing	Personal selling
Level of control	Medium	High	Low	High	Medium
Level of cost	High	Medium	Low	Medium	High
Level of credibility	Low	Medium	High	Medium	Medium
Level of dispersion High	Low	Medium	High	High	Medium
Low	Medium	High	High	Medium	High
Primary tasks	Differentiating Informing	Persuading	Differentiating Informing	Persuading Reinforcing	Persuading

Source: Baines *et al.* (2011)

Communication tasks

Each communication tool has particular strengths therefore the selected mix of tools should be based on a combination of tools designed to accomplish particular DRIP tasks. One of the reasons direct marketing has become so successful is that it delivers a call-to-action and is therefore a very good persuasive tool as well as being good at reinforcing messages. Advertising on the other hand is much better at differentiating offerings and informing audiences about key features and benefits.

At this point it is worth consolidating our understanding about the role, the tasks and the marketing communications mix. The role is to engage audiences, the tasks are to DRIP and through the selection and deployment of the elements of the mix, organisations seek to engage audiences and achieve their goals (DRIP). The marketing communications universe portrays this visually (see Figure 1.6).

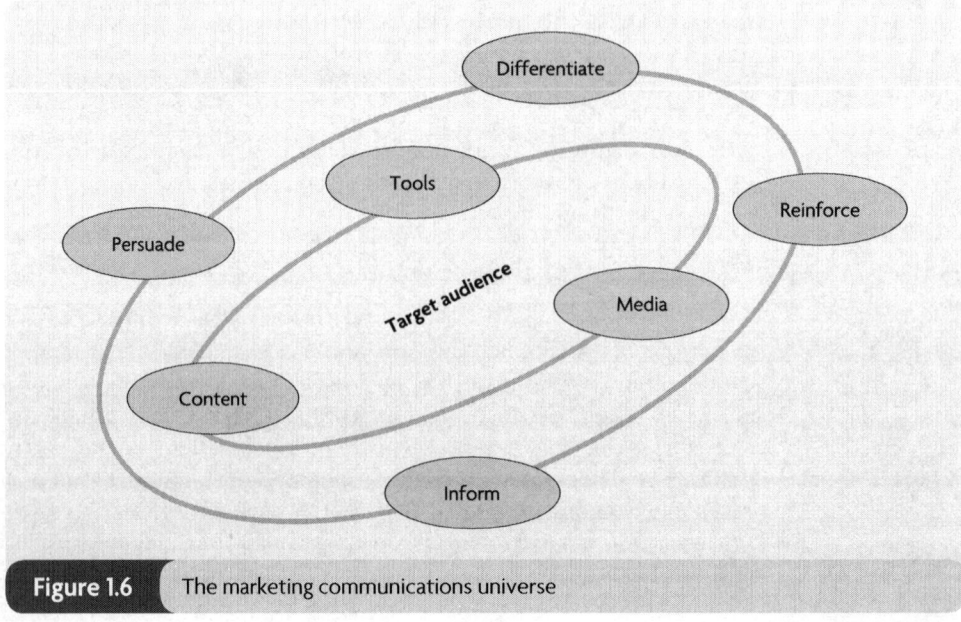

Figure 1.6 The marketing communications universe

Communication differences

Having identified the need to communicate with a number of different audiences, it seems appropriate to conclude this opening chapter by examining the differences between communications used by and targeted at two very different and specific audiences. These are organisations (commonly referred to as business-to-business) and those aimed at consumer markets. Some writers (Brougaletta, 1985; Gilliland and Johnston, 1997) have documented a variety of differences between consumer and business-to-business markets. The following is intended to set out some of the more salient differences (see also Table 1.6).

Message reception

The contextual conditions in which messages are received and ascribed meanings are very different. In the organisational setting the context is much more formal, and as the funding for the purchase is to be derived from company sources (as opposed to personal sources for consumer market purchases) there may be a lower orientation to the price as a significant variable in the purchase decision. The item is intended for company usage, whereas products bought in a consumer context are normally intended for personal consumption.

Table 1.6 Differences between consumer and business-to-business marketing communications

	Consumer-oriented markets	Business-to-business markets
Message reception	Informal	Formal
Number of decision-makers	Single or few	Many
Balance of the promotional mix	Advertising and sales promotions dominate	Personal selling dominates
Specificity and integration	Broad use of communications mix with a move towards integrated mixes	Specificity use of below-the-line tools but with a high level of integration
Message content	Greater use of emotions and imagery	Greater use of rational, logic and information-based messages although there is evidence of a move towards the use of imagery
Message origin	Increasing use of user-generated content	Limited use of user-generated materials
Length of decision time	Normally short	Longer and more involved
Negative communications	Limited to people close to the purchaser/user	Potentially an array of people in the organisation and beyond
Target marketing and research	Great use of sophisticated targeting and communication approaches	Limited but increasing use of targeting and segmentation approaches
Budget allocation	Majority of budget allocated to brand management	Majority of budget allocated to sales management
Evaluation and measurement	Great variety of techniques and approaches used	Limited number of techniques and approaches used

Number of decision-makers

In consumer markets a single person very often makes the decision. In organisational markets decisions are made by many people within a buying centre. This means that the interactions of the participants should be considered. In addition, a variety of different individuals need to be reached and influenced and this may involve the use of different media and message strategies.

The balance of the communications mix

The role of advertising and sales promotions in business-to-business communications is primarily to support the personal selling effort. This contrasts with the mix that predominates in consumer markets. Personal selling plays a relatively minor role and is only significant at the point of purchase in some product categories where involvement is high (cars, white goods and financial services), reflecting high levels of perceived risk. However, the increasing use of direct marketing in consumer markets suggests that personal communications are becoming more prevalent and in some ways increasingly similar to the overall direction of business-to-business communications.

The constituent tools of the marketing communications mix

Business-to-business markets have traditionally been quite specific in terms of the tools and media used to target audiences. While the use of advertising literature is very important, there has been a tendency to use a greater proportion of 'below-the-line' activities. This compares with consumer markets, where a greater proportion of funds have been allocated to 'above-the-line' activities. It is interesting that the communications in the consumer market are moving towards a more integrated format, more similar in form to the business-to-business model than was previously considered appropriate.

Message content

Generally, there is high involvement in many business-to-business purchase decisions, so communications tend to be much more rational and information-based than in consumer markets. However, there are signs that businesses are making increased use of imagery and emotions in the messages.

Message origin

Increasingly, consumers are taking a more active role in the creation of content. Blogging for example, is important in both consumer and business markets, but the development of user-generated-content and word-of-mouth communication is becoming a significant part of consumer-based marketing communications activities.

Length of purchase decision time

The length of time taken to reach a decision is much greater in the organisation market. This means that the intensity of any media plan can be dissipated more easily in the organisational market.

Negative communications

The number of people affected by a dissatisfied consumer, and hence negative marketing communication messages, is limited. The implications of a poor purchase decision in an organisational environment may be far-reaching, including those associated with the use of the product, the career of participants close to the locus of the decision and, depending on the size and spread, perhaps the whole organisation.

Target marketing and research

The use of target marketing processes in the consumer market is more advanced and sophisticated than in the organisational market. This impacts on the quality of the marketing communications used to reach the target audience. However, there is much evidence that the business-to-business markets organisations are becoming increasingly aware and sophisticated in their approach to segmentation techniques and processes.

Budget allocation

The sales department receives the bulk of the marketing budget in the organisation market and little is spent on research in comparison with the consumer market.

Measurement and evaluation

The consumer market employs a variety of techniques to evaluate the effectiveness of communications. In the organisation market, sales volume, value, number of enquiries and market share are the predominant measures of effectiveness.

There can be no doubt that there are a number of major differences between consumer and organisational communications. These reflect the nature of the environments, the tasks involved and the overall need of the recipients for particular types of information. Information need, therefore, can be seen as a primary reason for the differences in the way communication mixes are configured. Advertising in organisational markets has to provide a greater level of information and is geared to generating leads that can be followed up with personal selling, which is traditionally the primary tool in the promotional mix. In consumer markets, advertising used to play the primary role with support from the other tools of the promotional mix. This is not always true today as organisations use other tools such as public relations, combined with digital media, to reach particular audiences. Interestingly, digital media are helping to reconfigure the marketing communications mix and perhaps reduce the gulf and distinction between the mix used in business-to-business and consumer markets. Throughout this book, reference will be made to the characteristics, concepts and processes associated with marketing communications in each of these two main sectors.

Summary

In order to help consolidate your understanding about this introduction to marketing communications, here are the key points summarised against each of the learning objectives:

1 Explain the scope, role and tasks of marketing communications

The scope of marketing communications embraces an audience-centred perspective of planned, unplanned, product and service experiences. The role of marketing communications is to engage audiences with a view to provoking relevant conversations. The tasks of marketing communications are based within a need to differentiate, reinforce, inform and persuade audiences to think and behave in particular ways.

2 Describe how marketing communications can be used to engage audiences

Engagement is a function of two elements. The first is the degree to which a message encourages thinking and feeling about a brand, the development of brand values. The second is about the degree to which a message stimulates behaviour or action. Engagement may last a second, a minute, an hour, a day or even longer.

3 Explore ways in which the environment can influence the use of marketing communications

The internal, market and external environments all influence the use of marketing communications. The internal environment refers to employees, the culture, the financial resources and the marketing skills available to organisations. The market environment refers principally to the actions of competitors and the perceptions and attitudes held by customers towards an organisation or its brands.

The external environment can be considered in terms of the PEST framework. The influence of anyone of these elements on marketing communications can be significant, although the impact is usually generic and affects all organisations rather than any single band or organisation.

4 Write brief notes about the key characteristics of the marketing communications mix

The marketing communication mix consists of the tools, media and messages used to reach, engage and provoke audience-centred conversations. The five tools, six classes of media and two broad types of message can be configured in different ways to meet the needs of the target audience.

5 Identify and explain the key differences between marketing communications used in consumer and business markets

The way in which the marketing communication mix is configured for consumer markets is very different from the mix used for business markets. The tools, media and messages used are all different as the general contexts in which they operate require different approaches. Business markets favour personal selling, consumer markets, advertising. Both make increasing use of digital media whilst rational messages are predominant in business markets, and emotional based messages tend to prevail in consumer markets.

Review questions

1. Prepare brief notes about the scope of marketing communications, including a definition.
2. What is the role of marketing communications and identify the key tasks that it is required to undertake?
3. Name the three main elements that make up the marketing communications mix. Which one is critical?
4. How do each of the tools compare across the following criteria: control, communication effectiveness and cost?
5. How does direct marketing differ from the other tools of the mix?
6. How does the external environment influence an organisation's marketing communications?
7. Identify five different advertisements that you think use direct-response media. How effective do you think they might be?
8. How does the content delivered through traditional media differ from that delivered through digital media?
9. What criteria should be used when configuring a marketing communications mix?
10. Explain how marketing communications tools and media might be used differently to reach business rather than consumer markets.

References

Alarcon, C. (2009) Magners pushes Pear variant in marketing drive, *Marketing Week*, Thursday 30 April, retrieved 18 August 2009 from www.marketingweek.co.uk/news/magners-pushes-pear-variant-in-marketing-drive/2065279.article

Anon (2009) Marketing Society – Ledge Edge Award Winner – O_2, *Marketing*, 10 June, 7.

Baines, P., Fill, C. and Page, K. (2011) *Marketing*, 2nd edn, Oxford: Oxford University Press.

Baker, A. (2006), 'Cider brand rules', *Brand Republic*, 9 August, retrieved 5 December 2007 from www.brandrepublic.com/news/search/article/576158/cider-brand-rules/

Ballantyne, D. (2004) Dialogue and its role in the development of relationship specific Knowledge, *Journal of Business and Industrial Marketing*, 19(2), 114–123.

Bashford, S. (2007) Collaboration is imperative, *Marketing*, 13 December, 4–5.

Bowersox, D. and Morash, E. (1989) The integration of marketing flows in channels of distribution, *European Journal of Marketing*, 23(2), 58–67.

Brougaletta, Y. (1985) What business-to-business advertisers can learn from consumer advertisers. *Journal of Advertising Research*, 25(3), 8–9.

Brownsell, A. (2010a) LV = flags mutual status with primetime activity, *Marketing*, 31 March, 9.

Brownsell, A. (2010b) Keeping Virgin firmly on track, *Marketing*, 10 February, 22–23.

Clark, N. (2010) Eurostar plots mag to boost customer loyalty, *Marketing*, 17 February, 4.

Duncan, T.R. and Moriarty, S. (1997) *Driving Brand Value*, New York: McGraw Hill.

Fill, C. (2002) *Marketing Communications*, 3rd edn. Harrow: Financial Times Prentice-Hall.

Gilliland, D.I. and Johnston, W.J. (1997) Toward a model of business-to-business marketing communications effects. *Industrial Marketing Management*, 26, 15–29.

Grönroos, C. (2004) The relationship marketing process: communication, interaction, dialogue, value. *Journal of Business and Industrial Marketing*, 19(2), 99–113.

Heinonen, K. and Strandvik, T. (2005) Communication as a element of service value. *International Journal of Service Industry Management*, 16(2), 186–98.

Hughes, G. and Fill, C. (2007), Redefining the nature and format of the marketing communications mix. *The Marketing Review*, 7(1), 45–57.

JMW (2010) Jack Morgan Worldwide, Experience brands and the new engagement model, retrieved 13 June 2010 from http://www.jackmorton.com/takeaway/downloads/files/New_Engagement_Model_Exp_Brands.pdf

Lloyd, J. (1997) Cut your rep free, *Pharmaceutical Marketing* (September), 30–32.

Philips, R. and Cooper, J. (2008) PR Essays: Conversation with content, *Marketing*, 26 November, 15.

Simms, J. (2008) Here today, gone tomorrow? *Marketing*, 13 March, 17.

Turner, C. (2008) How Red Bull invented the 'cool' factor, *UTALK Marketing*. Retrieved 12 February 2008 from www.utalkmarketing.com/pages/article

Vargo, S.L. and Lusch, R.F. (2004) Evolving to a new dominant logic for marketing, *Journal of Marketing*, 68 (January), 1–17.

Woods, A. (2009) Searching in social circles, *Marketing*, 2 December, 39–41.

Chapter 2
Communication: interactivity and conversations

Communication is concerned with interpreting messages and sharing meaning. Only by using messages that reduce levels of ambiguity and which share meaning with audiences, can it be hoped to stimulate meaningful interaction and dialogue. To create and sustain valued conversations the support of significant others is often required. These may be people who are experts, those who share common interests, those who have relevant knowledge or have access to appropriate media channels.

Aims and learning objectives

The aims of this chapter are to introduce communication theory and to set it in the context of marketing communications.

The learning objectives of this chapter are to:

1. understand the linear model of communication and appreciate how the various elements link together and contribute to successful communication;
2. examine the impact of the media and personal and influences on the communication process;
3. demonstrate the characteristics of the influencer and interactional forms of communication;
4. explain the characteristics associated with opinion leaders, formers and followers;
5. examine the nature and characteristics associated with word-of-mouth communication;
6. describe the processes of adoption and diffusion as related to marketing communications.

Introduction

It was established in the previous chapter that marketing communications is partly an attempt by an organisation/brand to create and sustain a dialogue with its various audiences. It is also important to encourage members of these audiences to talk amongst themselves about a brand. As communication is the process by which individuals share meaning, each participant in the communication process needs to be able to interpret the meaning embedded in the messages, and be able to respond in an appropriate way.

For this overall process to work, information needs to be transmitted to, from and among participants. It is important, therefore, that those involved with marketing communications understand the complexity of the process. Through knowledge and understanding of the communications process, participants are more likely to achieve their objective of sharing meaning with each member of their target audiences and so have an opportunity to enter into a dialogue.

This chapter examines several models of the communication process. It considers the characteristics associated with word-of-mouth communications and looks at the way products and ideas are adopted by individuals and markets.

A linear model of communication

Wilbur Schramm (1955) developed what is now accepted as the basic model of mass communications (Figure 2.1). The components of the linear model of communication are:

Source: the individual or organisation sending the message.
Encoding: transferring the intended message into a symbolic style that can be transmitted.
Signal: the transmission of the message using particular media.
Decoding: understanding the symbolic style of the message in order to understand the message.

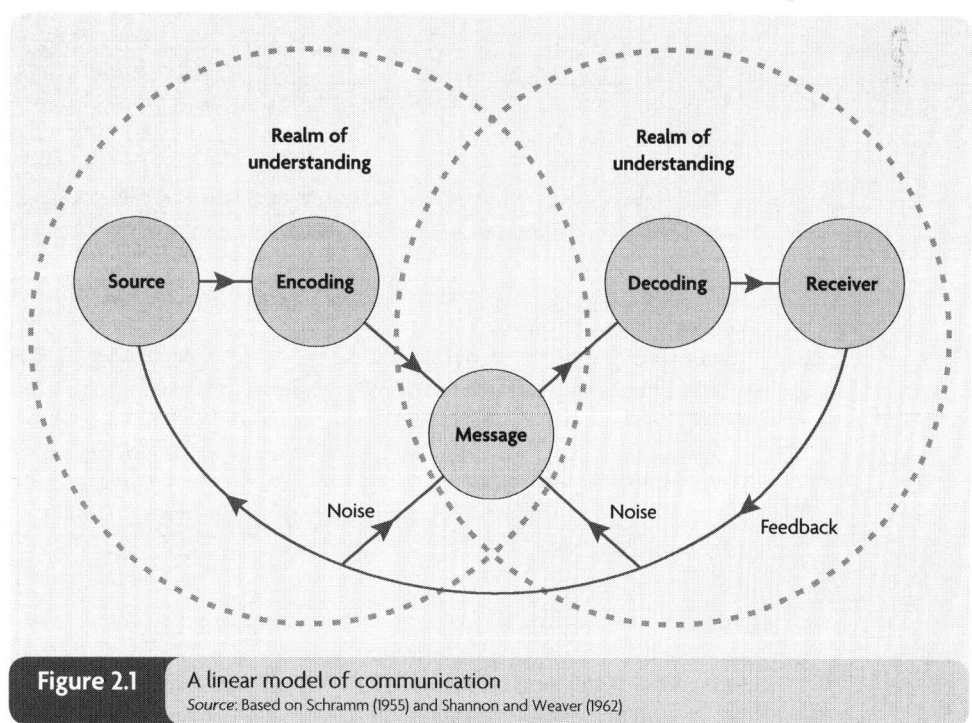

Figure 2.1 A linear model of communication
Source: Based on Schramm (1955) and Shannon and Weaver (1962)

Receiver: the individual or organisation receiving the message.
Feedback: the receiver's communication back to the source on receipt of the message.
Noise: distortion of the communication process, making it difficult for the receiver to interpret the message as intended by the source.

This is a linear model that emphasises the 'transmission of information, ideas, attitudes, or emotion from one person or group to another (or others), primarily through symbols' (Theodorson and Theodorson, 1969). The model and its components are straightforward, but it is the quality of the linkages between the various elements in the process that determine whether a communication event will be successful.

Source/encoding

The source, an individual or organisation, identifies a need to transmit a message and then selects a combination of appropriate words, pictures, symbols and music to represent the message to be transmitted. This is called encoding. The purpose is to create a message that is capable of being understood by the receiver.

There are a number of reasons why the source/encoding link might break down. For example, the source may fail to diagnose a particular situation accurately. By not fully understanding a stakeholder's problem or level of knowledge, inappropriate information may be included in the message, which, when transmitted, may lead to misunderstanding and misinterpretation by the receiver. By failing to appreciate the level of education of the target receiver, a message might be encoded in words and symbols that are beyond the comprehension of the receiver.

Some organisations spend a great deal of time and expense on marketing research, trying to develop their understanding of their target audience. The source of a message is an important factor in the communication process. A receiver who perceives a source lacking conviction, authority, trust or expertise is likely to discount any message received from that source, until such time as credibility is established.

Most organisations spend a great deal of time and expense recruiting sales representatives. The risk involved in selecting the wrong people can be extremely large. Many high-tech organisations require their new sales staff to spend over a year receiving both product and sales training before allowing them to meet customers. From a customer's perspective, salespersons who display strong product knowledge skills and who are also able to empathise with the individual members of the decision-making unit are more likely to be perceived as credible. Therefore, an organisation that prepares its sales staff and presents them as knowledgeable and trustworthy is more likely to be successful in the communication process than one that does not take the same level of care.

The source is a part of the communication process, not just the generator of detached messages. Patzer (1983) determined that the physical attractiveness of the communicator, particularly if it is the source, contributes significantly to the effectiveness of persuasive communications.

This observation can be related to the use, by organisations, of spokespersons and celebrities to endorse products. Spokespersons can be better facilitators of the communication process if they are able to convey conviction, if they are easily associated with the object of the message, if they have credible expertise and if they are attractive to the receiver, in the wider sense of the word.

This legitimate authority is developed in many television advertisements by the use of the 'white coat', or product-specific clothing, as a symbol of expertise. By dressing the spokesperson in a white coat, they are immediately perceived as a credible source of information ('they know what they are talking about'), and so are much more likely to be believed.

Signal

Once encoded, the message must be put into a form that is capable of transmission. It may be oral or written, verbal or non-verbal, in a symbolic form or in a sign. Whatever the format chosen, the source must be sure that what is being put into the message is what is required to be decoded by the receiver.

The channel is the means by which the message is transmitted from the source to the receiver. These channels may be personal or non-personal. The former involves face-to-face contact and word-of-mouth communications, which can be extremely influential. Non-personal channels are characterised by mass media advertising, which can reach large audiences.

Information received directly from personal influence channels is generally more persuasive than information received through mass media. This may be a statement of the obvious, but the reasons for this need to be understood. First, the individual approach permits greater flexibility in the delivery of the message. The timing and power with which a message is delivered can be adjusted to suit the immediate 'selling' environment. Second, a message can be adapted to meet the needs of the customer as the sales call progresses. This flexibility is not possible with mass media messages, as these have to be designed and produced well in advance of transmission and often without direct customer input.

Viewpoint 2.1   Is this what you really meant?

When developing names or taglines for global brands it is important to choose a name that translates appropriately into all the languages. The encoding process, the name of the car, cleaner, biscuit or fashion accessory should be well researched and capable of being decoded by the target audience in such a way that there is meaning, sense and value. The following are examples where the encoding process had not been properly considered:

- When the European hardware store chain 'Götzen' opened in Istanbul they had to change the name as 'Göt' means 'ass' in Turkish.
- 'Traficante' is an Italian brand of mineral water. In Spanish, it means drug dealer.
- Clairol's 'Mist Stick', curling iron had problems when launched in Germany because 'Mist' is slang for manure.
- A mainstream UK bank informed audiences in a recent advertising campaign that to show the soles of your feet in Thailand is a very rude gesture and, to give the thumbs up sign in Turkey, has quite the opposite meaning to its symbolism of cool acceptance here in Britain.
- Finally, workers in an African port saw a consignment with the international symbol for 'fragile' (a wine glass with snapped stem) on the side. They assumed it meant that they had been sent a cargo of broken glass and immediately pitched all the cases overboard into the harbour.

Sources: Based on: www.i18nguy.com/translations and www.sourceuk.net/indexf.html?03590

Question
To what extent should the encoding process be researched?

Task
Search the web and find your own examples of communications where different meanings have emerged.

Decoding/receiver

Decoding is the process of transforming and interpreting a message into thought. This process is influenced by the receiver's realm of understanding, which encompasses the experiences, perceptions, attitudes and values of both the source and the receiver. The more the receiver understands about the source and the greater their experience in decoding the source's messages, the more able the receiver will be to decode the message successfully.

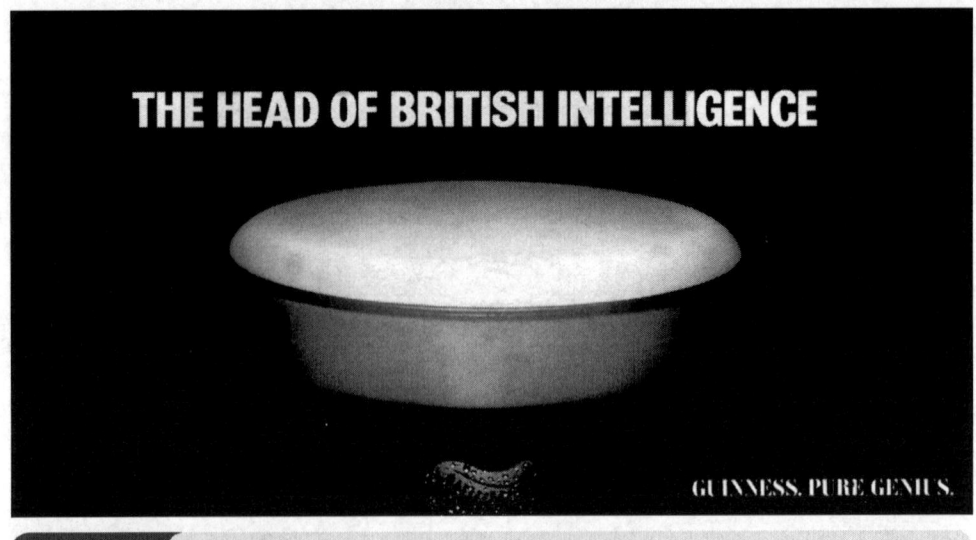

Exhibit 2.1 Decoding Guinness
Here decoding requires an understanding of two different interpretations of the word 'head'. The 'head' of the beer and the 'head' of a spy organisation. Humour is generated through the suggestion that the beer (Guinness) is intelligent.
Image courtesy of The Advertising Archives

Feedback/response

The set of reactions a receiver has after seeing, hearing or reading the message is known as the response. These reactions may vary from the extreme of calling an enquiry telephone number, returning or downloading a coupon or even buying the product, to storing information in long-term memory for future use. Feedback is that part of the response that is sent back to the sender, and it is essential for successful communication. The need to understand not just whether the message has been received but also which message has been received is vital. For example, the receiver may have decoded the message incorrectly and a completely different set of responses may have been elicited. If a suitable feedback system is not in place then the source will be unaware that the communication has been unsuccessful and is liable to continue wasting resources. This represents inefficient and ineffective marketing communications.

The evaluation of feedback is vital if effective communications are to be developed. Only through evaluation can the success of any communication be judged. Feedback through personal selling can be instantaneous, through overt means such as questioning, raising objections or signing an order form. Other means, such as the use of gestures and body language, are less overt, and the decoding of the feedback needs to be accurate if an appropriate response is to be given. For the advertiser, the process is much more vague and prone to misinterpretation and error.

Feedback through mass media channels is generally much more difficult to obtain, mainly because of the inherent time delay involved in the feedback process. There are some exceptions, namely the overnight ratings provided by the Broadcasters' Audience Research Board to the television contractors, but as a rule feedback is normally delayed and not as fast. Some commentators argue that the only meaningful indicator of communication success is sales. However, there are many other influences that affect the level of sales, such as price, the effect of previous communications, the recommendations of opinion leaders or friends, poor competitor actions or any number of government or regulatory developments. Except in circumstances such as direct marketing, where immediate and direct feedback can be determined, organisations should use other methods to gauge the success of their communication activities, for example, the level and quality of customer enquiries, the number and frequency of store visits, the degree of attitude change and the ability to recognise or recall an advertisement. All of these represent feedback, but, as a rough distinction, the evaluation of feedback for mass communications is much more difficult to judge than the evaluation of interpersonal communications.

Noise

A complicating factor, which may influence the quality of the reception and the feedback, is noise. Noise, according to Mallen (1977), is 'the omission and distortion of information', and there will always be some noise present in all communications. Management's role is to ensure that levels of noise are kept to a minimum, wherever it is able to exert influence.

Noise occurs when a receiver is prevented from receiving all or part of a message in full. This may be because of either cognitive or physical factors. For example, a cognitive factor may be that the encoding of the message was inappropriate, thereby making it difficult for the receiver to decode the message. In this circumstance it is said that the realms of understanding of the source and the receiver were not matched. Another reason noise may enter the system is that the receiver may have been physically prevented from decoding the message accurately because the receiver was distracted. Examples of distraction are that the telephone rang, or someone in the room asked a question or coughed. A further reason could be that competing messages screened out the targeted message.

Some sales promotion practitioners are using the word 'noise' to refer to the ambience and publicity surrounding a particular sales promotion event. In other words, the word is being used as a positive, advantageous element in the communication process. This approach is not adopted in this text.

Realms of understanding

The concept of the 'realm of understanding' was introduced earlier. It is an important element in the communication process because it is a recognition that successful communications are more likely to be achieved if the source and the receiver understand each other. This understanding concerns attitudes, perceptions, behaviour and experience: the values of both parties to the communication process. Therefore, effective communication is more likely when there is some common ground – a realm of understanding between the source and receiver.

Some organisations, especially those in the private sector, spend a huge amount of money researching their target markets and testing their advertisements to ensure that their messages can be decoded and understood. The more organisations understand their receivers, the more confident they become in constructing and transmitting messages to them. Repetition and learning are important elements in marketing communications. Learning is a function of knowledge and the more we know, the more likely we are to understand.

Factors that influence the communication process

The linear, sequential interpretation of the communication process fails to accurately represent all forms of communication. It was developed at a time when broadcast media dominated commercial communication and can be argued to no longer provide an accurate representation of contemporary communication processes. Issues concerning media and audience fragmentation, the need to consider social and relational dimensions of communication and the impact of interactive communication have reduced the overall applicability of the linear model.

However, there are two particular influences on the communication process that need to be considered. First, the media used to convey information, and second, the influence of people on the communication process. These are considered in turn.

The influence of the media

The dialogue that marketing communications seeks to generate with audiences is partially constrained by an inherent time delay based on the speed at which responses are generated by the participants in the communication process. Technological advances now allow participants to conduct marketing communication-based 'conversations' at electronic speeds. The essence of this speed attribute is that it allows for real-time interactively based communications, where enquiries are responded to more or less instantly.

New, digital-based technologies and the Internet in particular, provide an opportunity for interaction and dialogue with customers. With traditional media the tendency is for monologue or at best delayed and inferred dialogue. One of the first points to be made about these new, media-based communications is that the context within which marketing communications occurs is redefined. Traditionally, dialogue occurs in a (relatively) familiar context, which is driven by providers who deliberately present their messages through a variety of communication devices into the environments that they expect their audiences may well pass or recognise. Providers implant their messages into the various environments of their targets. Yuan *et al.* (1998) refer to advertising messages being 'unbundled', such as direct marketing, which has no other content, or 'bundled' and embedded with other news content such as television, radio and webpages with banner ads. Perhaps more pertinently, they refer to direct and indirect online advertising. Direct advertising is concerned with advertising messages delivered to the customer (email) while indirect advertising is concerned with messages that are made available for a customer to access at their leisure (websites).

Digital media-based communications tend to make providers relatively passive. Their messages are presented in an environment that requires targets to use specific equipment to actively search them out. The roles are reversed, so that the drivers in the new context are active information seekers, represented by a target audience (members of the public and other information providers such as organisations), not just the information providing organisations.

The influence of people

The traditional view of communication holds that the process consists essentially of one step. Information is directed and shot at prospective audiences, rather like a bullet is propelled from a gun. The decision of each member of the audience to act on the message or not is the result of a passive role or participation in the process. Organisations can communicate with different target audiences simply by varying the message and the type and frequency of channels used.

The linear model has been criticised for its oversimplification, and it certainly ignores the effect of personal influences on the communication process and potential for information deviance. To accommodate these influences two further models are introduced, the influencer model and the interactional model of communication.

The influencer model of communication

The influencer model depicts information flowing via media channels to particular types of people (opinion leaders and opinion formers; see pp. 45–46) to whom other members of the audience refer for information and guidance. Through interpersonal networks, opinion leaders not only reach members of the target audience who may not have been exposed to the message, but may reinforce the impact of the message for those members who did receive the message

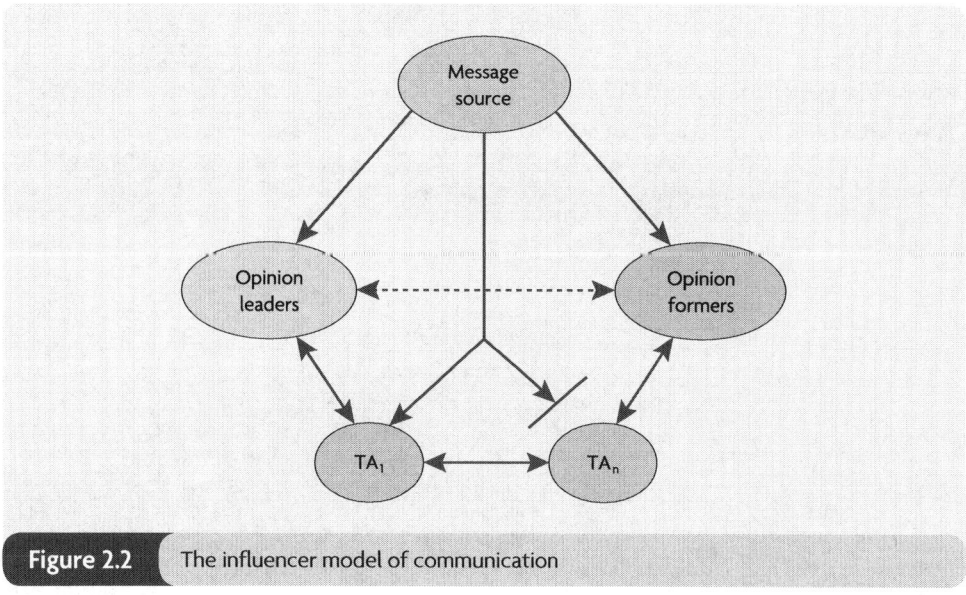

Figure 2.2 The influencer model of communication

(Figure 2.2). For example, feedback and comments from travellers on Tripadvisor.com assist others when making travel plans, and constitutes opinion leadership. However, editors of travel sections in the Sunday press and television presenters of travel programmes fulfil the role of opinion former and can influence the decision of prospective travellers through their formalised knowledge.

Sometimes referred to as the two-step model, this approach indicates that the mass media do not have a direct and all-powerful effect over their audiences. If the primary function of the mass media is to provide information, then personal influences are necessary to be persuasive and to exert direct influence on members of the target audience.

The influencer approach can be developed into a multi-step model. This proposes that communication involves interaction among all parties to the communication process (see Figure 2.3). This interpretation closely resembles the network of participants who are often involved in the communication process.

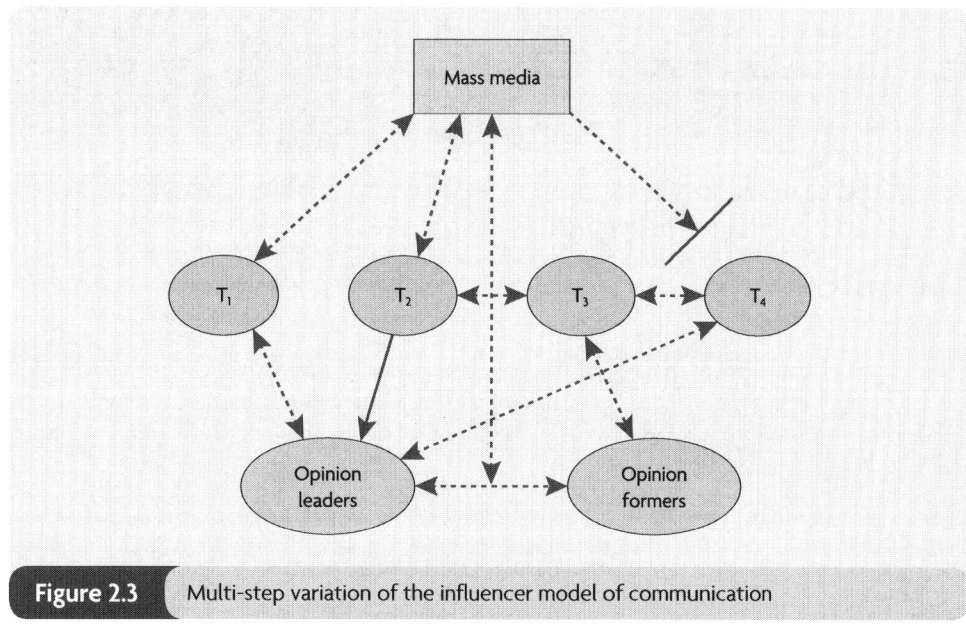

Figure 2.3 Multi-step variation of the influencer model of communication

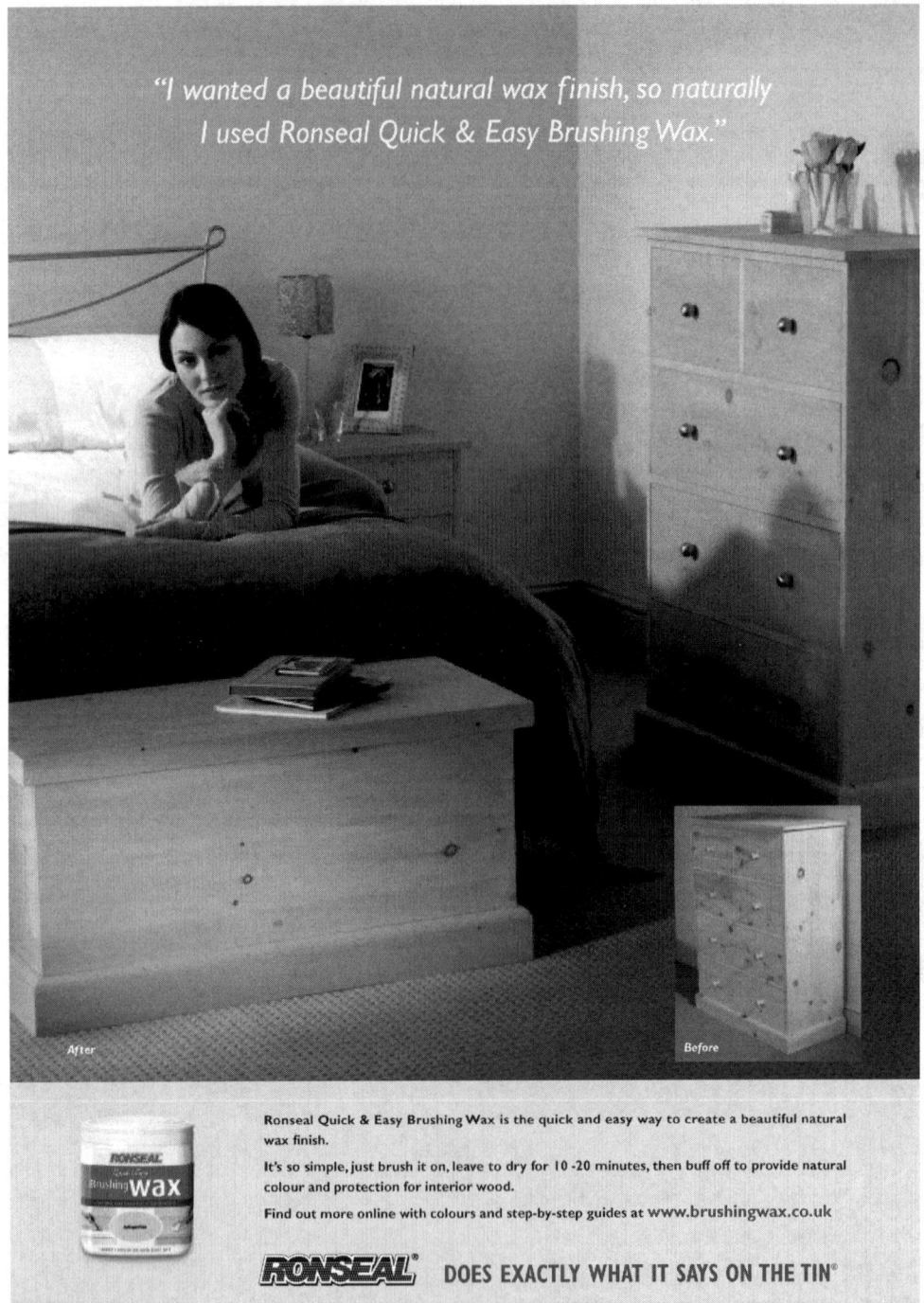

Exhibit 2.2 Brushing Wax print ad
This ad uses the principles of opinion leadership (a representative of the target audience) to convey the product benefits
Image courtesy of Ronseal Ltd.

Interactional model of communication

The models and frameworks used to explain the communication process so far should be considered as a simplification of reality and not a true reflection of communication in practice. The linear model is unidirectional, and it suggests that the receiver plays a passive role in the process. The influencer model attempts to account for an individual's participation in the communication process. These models emphasise individual behaviour but exclude any social behaviour implicit in the process.

The interactional model of communication attempts to assimilate the variety of influences acting upon the communication process. This includes the responses people give to communications received from people and machines. Increasingly communication is characterised by attributing meaning to messages that are shared, updated and a response to other messages. These 'conversations' can be termed interactional and are an integral part of society. Figure 2.4 depicts the complexity associated with this form of communication.

Interaction is about actions that lead to a response. The development of direct marketing helped make significant inroads in the transition from what is essentially one-way to two-way and then interactive-based communication. Digital technology has further enabled this interaction process. However, interaction alone is not a sufficient goal simply because the content of the interaction could be about a radical disagreement of views, an exchange of opinion or a social encounter.

Ballantyne refers to two-way communication with audiences in two ways. First, as a 'with' experience, as manifest in face-to-face encounters and contact centres. He also distinguishes a higher order of two-way communication based on communication 'between' parties. It is this latter stage that embodies true dialogue where trust, listening and adaptive behaviour are typical. These are represented diagrammatically in Table 2.1.

A key question emerges, what is interaction and what are its key characteristics? If we can understand the dynamics and dimensions of interactivity then it should be possible to develop more effective marketing communications. In the context of marketing communications,

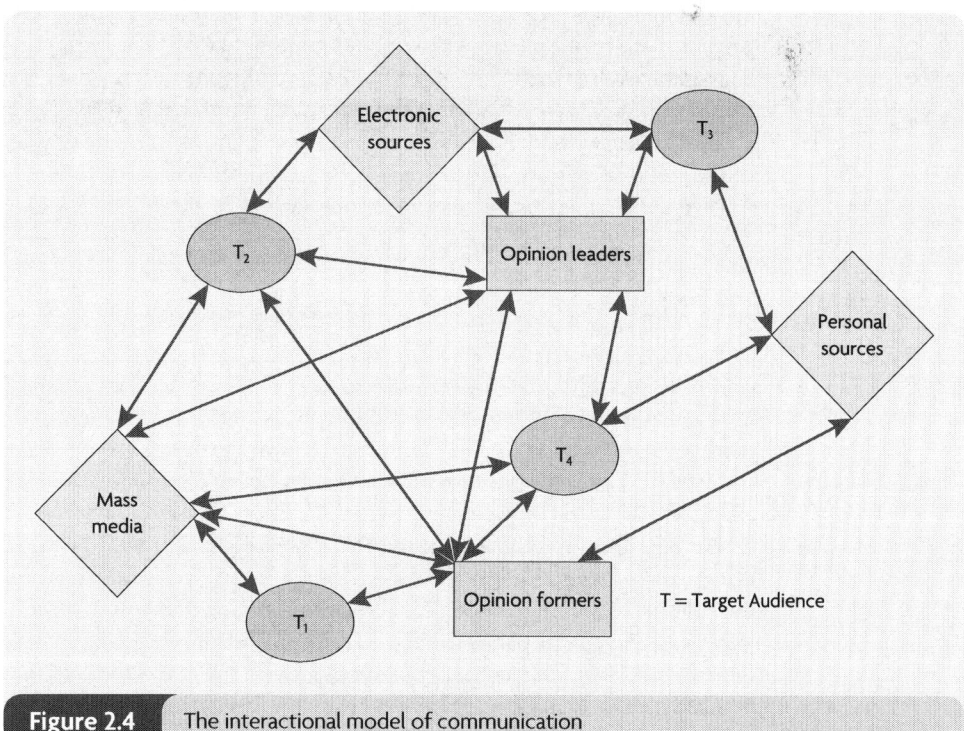

Figure 2.4 The interactional model of communication

Table 2.1 Communication matrix

Direction	Mass markets	Portfolio/mass-customised	Networks
One-way Planned communications designed to inform and persuade Medium to high wastage	Communication 'to' Planned persuasive messages aimed at securing brand awareness and loyalty; e.g. communication of USPs and ESPs	Communication 'for' Planned persuasive messages with augmented offerings for target markets; e.g. communicating targeted lifecycle products, guarantees, loyalty programmes	
Two-way Formal and informal with a view to listening and learning Minimal wastage		Communication 'with' Integrated mix of planned and interactively shared knowledge; e.g. face to face, direct (database), contact centres, interactive b2b Internet portals	Communication 'between' Dialogue between participants based on trust, learning and adaptation with co-created outcomes; e.g. key account liaison, expansion of communities, staff teamwork

Source: Ballantyne (2004), Emerald Group Publishing Ltd. Used with permission

interactivity can be considered from one of two perspectives. One is the technology, tools and features (e.g. multimedia, www, online gaming) that provide for interaction. The second, according to Johnson *et al.* (2006) is the added value that interactivity is perceived to bring to the communication process.

Arising out of interaction is dialogue. This occurs through mutual understanding and a reasoning approach to interactions, one based on listening and adaptive behaviour. Dialogue is concerned with the development of knowledge that is specific to the relationship of the parties involved. Ballantyne refers to this as 'learning together' (Ballantyne, 2004: 119).

The adoption of dialogue as the basis for communication changes an organisation's perspective of its audiences. Being willing and able to enter into a dialogue indicates that there is a new emphasis on the relationships organisations hold with their stakeholders. Dialogue requires interaction as a precursor. In other words, for dialogue to occur there must first be interaction and it is the development and depth of the interaction that leads to meaningful dialogue.

The influencer model is important because it demonstrates the importance of people in the communication process. However, successful communication is often determined by the level of interactivity the communication encourages.

Word-of-mouth communications

Consumer-to-consumer conversations about products, services and brand related marketing messages and meanings are naturally occurring events. Buyers, potential buyers and non-buyers exchange information without influence or being prompted by the brand owner. However, many organisations use word-of-mouth as an integral part of their marketing communications and deliberately encourage people to have positive conversations about their particular brand.

Word-of-mouth (WoM) communications are characterised as informal, unplanned and unsolicited conversations. These recommendations provide information and purchasing support and serve to reinforce an individual's purchasing decisions. At the heart of this approach is the source credibility that is assigned to people whose opinions are sought after and used in the purchase decision process. Those who provide information in WoM communications can be characterised as informal experts who are unbiased, trustworthy and who can be considered to be objective. Personal influence is important and can enrich the communication process.

Unlike advertising, where messages are primarily linear and unidirectional, WoM communication is interactive and bidirectional.

Definition and motives

Arndt (1967: 66) sets out word-of-mouth as 'an oral, person-to-person communication between a receiver and a communicator whom the receiver perceives as non-commercial, regarding a brand, product, or service'. Put in more simple terms, word of mouth concerns the sharing of an opinion among people independent from the company or its agents (Santo, 2006: 29).

Stokes and Lomax (2002) define word-of-mouth communication as 'interpersonal communication regarding products or services where the receiver regards the communicator as impartial'. This simple definition was developed from some of the more established interpretations that failed to accommodate contemporary media and the restrictions concerning the perceived independence of the communicator.

People like to talk about their product (service) experiences for a variety of reasons that are explored in the next section. However, by talking with a neighbour or colleague about the good experiences associated with a holiday, for example, the first-hand 'this has actually happened to someone I know' effect will be instrumental in the same views being passed on to other colleagues, irrespective of their validity or overall representation of similar vacations. Mazzarol *et al.* (2007) identify the 'richness of the message' and the 'strength of the implied or explicit advocacy' as important triggers for WoM. Palmer (2009) brings these together and refers to WoM as information people can trust as it comes from people just like them and it helps them make better decisions.

Helm and Schlei (1998: 42) refer to WoM as 'verbal communications (either positive or negative) between groups such as the product provider, independent experts, family, friends and the actual or personal consumer'. However, as discussed later, organisations now use electronic WoM techniques in a commercial context in order to generate brand based conversations based around a point of differentiation. Indeed, an important point is that WoM is transmitted person-to-person through a variety of media (Lam, *et al.*, 2009).

One important question that arises is, why do people want to discuss products or advertising messages? Bone (1995) cited by Stokes and Lomax (2002) refers to three elements of WoM (see Table 2.2).

Dichter (1966) determined that there were four main categories of output WoM.

1 Product involvement

People, he found, have a high propensity to discuss matters that are either distinctly pleasurable or unpleasurable. Such discussion serves to provide an opportunity for the experience to be relived, whether it be the 'looking for' or the 'use' experience, or both. This reflects the product and service experience elements of marketing communications, identified as part of the scope of the topic, in Chapter 1.

Table 2.2 Elements of word-of-mouth communication

Element of WoM		Explanation
Direction	Input WoM	Customers seeking recommendation prior to purchase
	Output WoM	Expression of feelings as a result of the purchase experience
Valence		The positive or negative feelings resulting from the experience
Volume		The number of people to which the message is conveyed

Source: After Bone (1995)

2 Self-involvement

Discussion offers a means for ownership to be established and signals aspects of prestige and levels of status to the receiver. More importantly, perhaps, dissonance can be reduced as the purchaser seeks reassurance about the decision.

3 Other involvement

Products can assist motivations to help others and to express feelings of love, friendship and caring. These feelings can be released through a sense of sharing the variety of benefits that products can bestow.

4 Message involvement

The final motivation to discuss products is derived, according to Dichter, from the messages that surround the product itself, in particular the advertising messages and, in the business-to-business market, seminars, exhibitions and the trade press, which provide the means to provoke conversation and so stimulate word-of-mouth recommendation.

Marketing communications can be used to stimulate conversations, by using these motivations as the anchor for the messages.

People who identify very closely with a brand and who might be termed brand advocates often engage in word-of-mouth communications. Advocacy can be demonstrated not only through word-of-mouth communications but also through behaviour, for example, by wearing branded clothing or using tools and equipment. The issue of advocacy is explored further in Chapter 8 in the section on loyalty and retention schemes.

Viewpoint 2.2 Spreading the word about Hovis

Founded in 1888, Hovis has become an established household name in the UK bread market. Hovis uses WoM in its attempt to regain the market leadership, both deliberately, and perhaps as a secondary aspect of its branded communications. The planned approach seeks to drive awareness by recruiting 800 advocates to help support the launch of their Hearty Oats brand. Referred to as a 'marketing advocacy campaign', women over 35 were identified as the best opinion leaders (advocates), partly because of their interest in health issues, social networking and a tendency to be early adopters of emerging trends. Selected advocates, as Hovis refers to them, were sent samples and they were encouraged to feedback comments and exchange recipes. The expectation is that they will talk amongst their friends and acquaintances, both off and online, about their positive feelings towards the Hearty Oats (and Hovis) brand.

The secondary approach borrows on Dichter's ideas about why people talk about products and services. When Hovis recognised the difficulties their brand was facing (declining quality, poor packaging and ineffective communications), research was undertaken amongst typical consumers. This revealed that the consumers differentiated between good bread and bad bread, and an increasing proportion aligned Hovis with bad bread. The relaunch campaign revived a famous Hovis ad that featured a small lad on a bike. This time the lad travelled through time, featuring significant world events. The 122 second ad was voted campaign of the year by the BBC and won the best marketing communications prize by the Marketing Society. The point of this story is that the ad was so well made, so memorable and so good that people like to talk about these quality communications. In Dichter's terms, this is message involvement, and is a potent source of word-of-mouth communication.

Source: Based on Reynolds (2010); Smith (2010)

Question

If WoM communication is so important why is it not a core activity within marketing communications for all brands?

Task

When you next visit a leisure or entertainment complex make a mental note of the ways in which the brand owner encourages visitors to talk about the complex.

These motivations to discuss products and their associative experiences vary between individuals and with the intensity of the motivation at any one particular moment. There are two main persons involved in this process of word-of-mouth communications: a sender and receiver. Research indicates that the receiver's evaluation of a message is far from stable over time and accuracy of recall decays (expectedly) through time. What this means for marketing communications is that those people who have a positive product experience, especially in the service sector, should be encouraged to talk as soon as possible after the event (Christiansen and Tax, 2000). For example, Pepsi Raw was launched in pubs and bars in order to reach young affluent consumers. The goal was to encourage this target audience to talk about the brand and in doing so imbue the brand with social group associations and then roll the brand out across supermarkets (Simms, 2007). Goldsmith and Horowitz (2006) found that risk reduction, popularity, reduced costs, access to easy information, and even inspiration from offline sources such as cinema, tv and radio were some of the primary reasons why people seek the opinions of others online.

According to Reichheld (2003) cited by Mazur (2004) organisations should measure word-of-mouth communication because those who speak up about a brand are risking their own reputation when they recommend a brand. Looking at the financial services sector, Reichheld argues that measures based on customer satisfaction or retention rates can mask real growth potential because they are measures of defection, and switching barriers may induce inertia. He found three particular groups based on their type of word-of-mouth endorsement: promoters, passively satisfied and detractors. In particular he identified a strong correlation between an organisation's growth rate and the percentage of customers who are active promoters.

Opinion leaders

Katz and Lazerfeld (1955) first identified individuals who were predisposed to receiving information and then reprocessing it to influence others. Their studies of American voting and purchase behaviour led to their conclusion that those individuals who could exert such influence were more persuasive than information received directly from the mass media. These opinion leaders, according to Rogers (1962), tend 'to be of the same social class as non-leaders, but may enjoy a higher social status within the group'. Williams (1990) uses the work of Reynolds and Darden (1971) to suggest that they are more gregarious and more self-confident than non-leaders. In addition, they have a greater exposure to relevant mass media (print) and as a result have more knowledge/familiarity and involvement with the product class, are more innovative and more confident of their role as influencer (leader) and appear to be less dogmatic than non-leaders (Chan and Misra, 1990).

Opinion leadership can be simulated in advertising by the use of product testimonials. Using ordinary people to express positive comments about a product to each other is a very well-used advertising technique.

The importance of opinion leaders in the design and implementation of communication plans should not be underestimated. Midgley and Dowling (1993) refer to *innovator communicators*: those who are receptive to new ideas and who make innovation-based purchase decisions without reference to or from other people. However, while the importance of these individuals is not doubted, a major difficulty exists in trying to identify just who these opinion leaders and innovator communicators are. While they sometimes display some distinctive characteristics, such as reading specialist media vehicles, often being first to return coupons, enjoying attending exhibitions or just involving themselves with new, innovative techniques or products, they are by their very nature invisible outside their work, family and social groups.

> ### Viewpoint 2.3 Digital influencers
>
> When Sony wanted to launch its BRAVIA LCD television it was a faced with an audience that was essentially cynical towards advertising and promotional messages and hard to reach with telling branded messages. The success of the launch was partly due to its use of a key part of the audience, digital influencers.
>
> Digital influencers are people who understand, appreciate and enjoy technology. They are effectively digital opinion leaders and they represent an important target audience. The key for Sony was to encourage these influencers to spread the word about BRAVIA to the early majority and reach the mass market.
>
> The original BRAVIA television ad was based round 250,000 coloured balls fired out of a cannon in San Francisco. During filming, local residents shot their own video footage. This found its way onto the Internet, which in turn provoked significant comment and interest. Quite transparently, Sony started to feed the digital influencers with blogging 'blog fodder', and they in turn used the material to develop conversations with other much broader audiences. Sony also slowly released official film that helped to create links from the Sony site to the original amateur images posted on Flickr. As the mainstream audiences, who are less technologically able than influencers, tuned into the BRAVIA interest so simpler content was made available, for example, screensavers and mobile phone wallpapers.
>
> *Source*: Based on Whitton and Ryan (2006)
>
> #### Question
> Do you believe the increasing use of opinion leaders is due to cost cutting or because it is superior form of communication?
>
> #### Task
> Think about buying a new laptop, make a note of who or what you would consult prior to purchase.

Opinion formers

Opinion formers are individuals who are able to exert personal influence because of their authority, education or status associated with the object of the communication process. Like opinion leaders, they are acknowledged and sought out by others to provide information and advice, but this is because of the formal expertise that opinion formers are adjudged to have. For example, community pharmacists are often consulted about symptoms and medicines, and film critics carry such conviction in their reviews that they can make or break a new production.

Popular television programmes, such as *EastEnders*, *Casualty* and *Coronation Street*, all of which attract huge audiences, have been used as vehicles to draw attention to and open up debates about many controversial social issues, such as contraception, abortion, drug use and abuse, and serious illness and mental health concerns.

The influence of opinion formers can be great. For example, the editor of a journal or newspaper may be a recognised source of expertise, and any offering referred to by the editor in the media vehicle is endowed with great credibility. In this sense the editor acts as a gatekeeper, and it is the task of the marketing communicator to ensure that all relevant opinion formers are identified and sent appropriate messages.

However, the credibility of opinion formers is vital for communication effectiveness. If there is a suspicion or doubt about the impartiality of the opinion former, then the objectivity of their views and comments are likely to be perceived as tainted and not believed so that damage may be caused to the reputation of the brand and those involved.

Many organisations constantly lobby key members of parliament in an effort to persuade them to pursue 'favourable' policies. Opinion formers are relatively easy to identify, as they need to be seen shaping the opinion of others, usually opinion followers.

Opinion followers

The vast majority of consumers can be said to be opinion followers. The messages they receive via the mass media are tempered by the opinions of the two groups of personal influencers just discussed. Some people actively seek information from those they believe are well informed, while others prefer to use the mass media for information and guidance (Robinson, 1976). However, this should not detract from the point that, although followers, they still process information independently and use a variety of inputs when sifting information and responding to marketing stimuli.

Ethical drug manufacturers normally launch new drugs by enlisting the support of particular doctors who have specialised in the therapy area and who are recognised by other doctors as experts. These opinion formers are invited to lead symposia and associated events to build credibility and activity around the new product. At the same time, public relations agencies prepare press releases with the aim that the information will be used by the mass media (opinion formers) for editorial purposes and create exposure for the product across the target audience, which, depending upon the product and/or the media vehicle, may be GPs, hospital doctors, patients or the general public. All these people, whether they be opinion leaders or formers, are active influencers or talkers (Kingdom, 1970).

Developing brands with word-of-mouth communication

So far in this chapter word-of-mouth communication (WoM) has been examined as naturally occurring, unplanned conversations. This is not necessarily correct as many organisations deliberately attempt to reach their audiences using WoM principles. The term word-of-mouth marketing (WoMM) refers to the electronic version of the spoken endorsement of a product or service, where messages are targeted at key individuals who then voluntarily pass the message to friends and colleagues. In doing so they bestow, endorse and provide the message with a measure of credibility. WoMM is a planned, intentional attempt to influence consumer-to-consumer communications using professional marketing methods and technologies (Kozinets et al., 2010) to prompt WoM conversations.

From this it can be assumed that there are a variety of methods that organisations use to influence their audiences, all in the name of WoM. Of these, three main forms of WoM can be identified; voluntary, prompted and managed.

- **Voluntary** WoM can be considered to be the most natural form of interpersonal conversation, free from any external influence, coercion or intent. This still occurs among genuine opinion leaders, formers and followers for reasons considered earlier.
- **Prompted** WoM occurs when organisations convey information to opinion leaders and formers, with a view to deliberately encouraging them to forward and share the information with their followers. The goal is to prompt conversations among followers based around the credibility bestowed on the opinion leader. This outward perspective can be counter-balanced by an inward view. For example, some organisations use various elements of social media, for example, blogs, online communities and forums, to prompt consumer-to-consumer conversations and to then listen, observe and revise their approaches to the market.
- **Managed** WoM occurs when organisations target, incentivise and reward opinion leaders for recommending their offerings to their networks of followers. In these situations opinion leaders lose their independence and objectivity within the communication process, and become paid representatives of a brand. As a result the credibility normally attached to these influencers diminishes and the essence of freely expressed opinions about products and brands is removed.

There is evidence that organisational use of contemporary marketing communications seeks to drive voluntary conversations, stimulated by positive product and service experiences. The prompted approach is used extensively and enables organisations to retain credibility and a sense of responsibility. PQ Media reported in 2010 that the managed approach is increasing as clients seek to move their communication budgets closer to where target audiences spend their time online. They expect this sector to grow very quickly. The organisations that exploit their audiences through managed WoM conversations are not acting illegally, but may be guilty of transgressing ethical boundaries and demonstrating disrespect for their audiences. Not a position for long term strength.

Traditionally brands were built partly through offline communications directed to opinion leaders, when they could be identified, and through opinion formers. Sporting and entertainment celebrities have been used as brand ambassadors for a long time. They are used to enable audiences to develop positive associations between the personality of the ambassador and a brand. McCracken (1989) believes that celebrity endorsement works through the theory of meaning transfer. Consumers make an overall assessment of what a celebrity 'represents' to them, based on their perception and interpretation of the celebrity's identity cues. These cues relate to their behaviour, comments, ability, and attributes that are of particular interest to the consumer. McCracken (1989: 315) refers to their public image as demonstrated in 'television, movies, military, athletics, and other careers'.

The meaning assigned to a celebrity is transferred from the celebrity endorser to the product when the two are paired in a commercial message. Gwinner and Eaton (1999) argue that when a consumer acquires/consumes the product, the meaning is transferred to the user and the process is complete.

Contemporary brand development now incorporates the use of social media, and bloggers in particular, who play an increasingly critical role in the dissemination of brand related information. More detailed information about these elements can be found in Chapter 14, but here it is important to establish the way in which brands can be developed through word-of-mouth marketing/communication.

Opinion formers such as journalists, receive information about brands through press releases. They then relay the information, after editing and reformatting, to their readers and viewers through their particular media. So, brands target brand-related information at journalists, with the intention that their messages would be forwarded to their end user audience.

Bloggers are now an important and influential channel of communication. However, they do not share the same characteristics as journalists. For example, the number of bloggers in any one market can be counted in terms of tens of thousands of people (Clark, 2010), in contrast to the relatively small, select number of opinion formers. The majority of bloggers have an informal interest in a subject, whereas opinion formers are deemed to have formal expertise. Bloggers however, are not tied to formal processes or indeed an editor. As a result bloggers do not have to be objective in their comments and are not constrained by any advertising messages. Most importantly, bloggers conduct conversations among themselves and their followers, whereas journalists receive little feedback. More information about blogging can be found in Chapter 14.

Viewpoint 2.4　Fashionable bloggers

In January 2010, fashion blogger Tavi Gevinson, aged 14, sat in the front row at the Christian Dior couture show in Paris, and in front of the *Grazia* journalist. Clark (2010) observes this as a reflection of the way key influencers are changing the branding process. No longer are glossy magazines the primary vehicle to reach consumers. Now it is word of mouth through social media, and blogging in particular, that is shaping the way the fashion industry operates. This change in emphasis is even recognised by many of the leading fashion magazines who have run features about fashion blogs. For example, Clark reports that WhatKatieWore.com has been featured in the *Sunday Times Style* magazine, *Marie Claire* and *Grazia*.

In an attempt to promote the island and reduce the average age of visitors, the Barbados Tourism Authority harnessed the power of bloggers and their propensity to communicate their experiences through social media and their networks. The initiative was supported by airlines and hotels who service the island.

Eight entrepreneurs were taken on a three-week tour to experience not only the holiday dimension but also both the business activities and opportunities.

There was no formal requirement to inform others but it was inevitable that the trip would trigger conversations. In addition to email and general comments, the entrepreneurs blogged regularly, made videos and posted these and their comments on various sites, including Facebook. The cost of the trip, the reach of these influencers and the credibility of their messages was deemed to be superior than a single ad in a national newspaper.

Source: Based on Clark (2010); Roberts (2010)

Question

To what extent is blogging a means of self expression or something else?

Task

Find three different blogs in fashion, travel and sport. Make a list of their similarities and differences.

Process of adoption

An interesting extension to the concept of opinion followers and the discussion on WoM communications is the process by which individuals become committed to the use of a new product. Rogers (1983) has identified this as the process of adoption and the stages of his innovation decision process are represented in Figure 2.5 on page 51. These stages in the adoption process are sequential and are characterised by the different factors that are involved at each stage (e.g. the media used by each individual).

Exhibit 2.3 A 1970's magazine ad for Mane, a hair loss treatment
Image courtesy of The Advertising Archives

1 Knowledge

The innovation becomes known to consumers, but they have little information and no well-founded attitudes. Information must be provided through mass media to institutions and people whom active seekers of information are likely to contact. Information for passive seekers should be supplied through the media and channels that this group habitually uses to look for other kinds of information (Windahl *et al.*, 1992).

> Bill washes his hair regularly, but he is beginning to notice tufts of hair on his comb. He becomes aware of an advertisement for Mane in a magazine.

2 Persuasion

The consumer becomes aware that the innovation may be of use in solving known and potential problems. Information from those who have experience of the product becomes very important.

> Bill notices that the makers of Mane claim that not only does their brand reduce the amount of hair loss but also aids hair gain. Mane has also been recommended to him by someone he met in the pub last week. Modelling behaviour predominates.

3 Decision

An attitude may develop and may be either favourable or unfavourable, but as a result a decision is reached whether to trial the offering or not. Communications need to assist this part of the process by continual prompting.

> Bill is prepared to believe (or not to believe) the messages and the claims made on behalf of Mane. He thinks that Mane is potentially a very good brand (or not). He intends trying Mane because he was given a free sample (or because it was on a special price deal).

4 Implementation

For the adoption to proceed in the absence of a sales promotion, buyers must know where to get it and how to use it. The product is then tested in a limited way. Communications must provide this information in order that the trial experience be developed.

> Bill buys 'Mane' and tests it.

5 Confirmation

The innovation is accepted or rejected on the basis of the experience during trial. Planned communications play an important role in maintaining the new behaviour by dispelling negative thoughts and positively reaffirming the original 'correct' decision. McGuire, as reported in Windahl *et al.* (1992), refers to this as post-behavioural consolidation.

> It works, Bill's hair stops falling out as it used to before he started using 'Mane'. He reads an article that reports that large numbers of people are using these types of products satisfactorily. Bill resolves to buy 'Mane' next time.

This process can be terminated at any stage (see Figure 2.5) and, of course, a number of competing brands may vie for consumers' attention simultaneously, so adding to the complexity and levels of noise in the process. Generally, mass communications are seen to be more effective in the earlier phases of the adoption process for products that buyers are actively interested in, and more interpersonal forms are more appropriate at the later stages, especially trial and adoption. This model assumes that the stages occur in a predictable sequence, but this clearly

Figure 2.5 Stages in the innovation decision process of adoption
Source: Reprinted with the permission of The Free Press, a division of Simon & Schuster, Inc., from *Diffusion of Innovations*, Third Edition by Everett M. Rogers. Copyright © 1962, 1971, 1983 by The Free Press. All rights reserved

does not happen in all purchase activity, as some information that is to be used later in the trial stage may be omitted, which often happens when loyalty to a brand is high or where the buyer has experience in the marketplace.

Process of diffusion

The process of adoption in aggregate form, over time, is diffusion. According to Rogers (1983), diffusion is the process by which an innovation is communicated through certain channels over a period of time among the members of a social system. This is a group process and Rogers again identified five categories of adopters. Figure 2.6 shows how diffusion may be fast or slow and that there is no set speed at which the process occurs. The five categories are as follows:

1 Innovators

These groups like new ideas and have a large disposable income. This means they are more likely to take risks associated with new products.

2 Early adopters

Research has established that this group contains a large proportion of opinion leaders and they are, therefore, important in speeding the diffusion process. Early adopters tend to be younger than any other group and above average in education. Internet activity and use of publications is probably high as they actively seek information. A high proportion of early adopters are active bloggers. This group is important to the marketing communications process because they can determine the speed at which diffusion occurs.

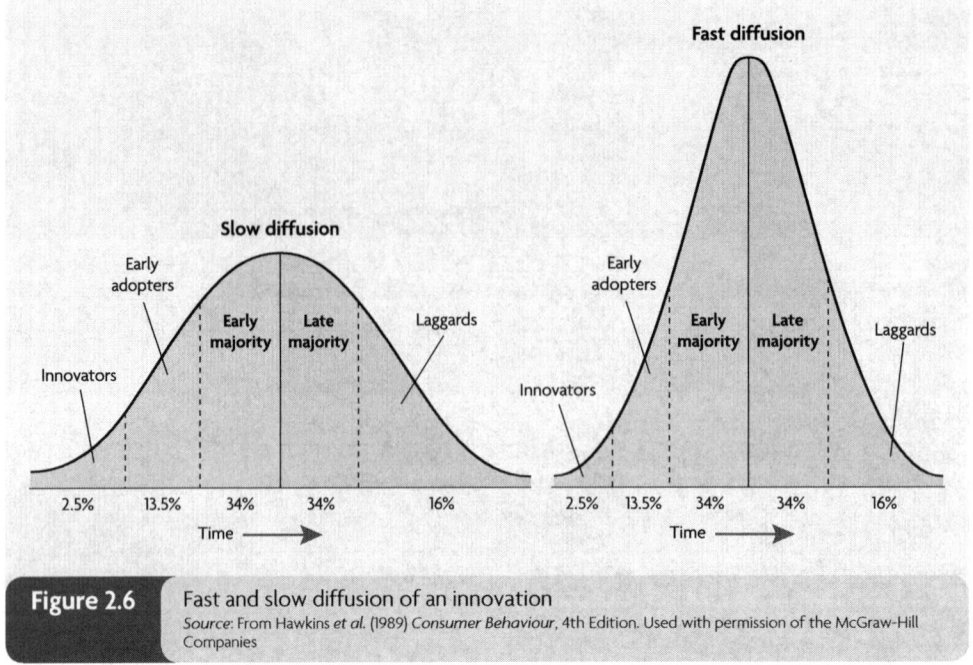

Figure 2.6 Fast and slow diffusion of an innovation
Source: From Hawkins *et al.* (1989) *Consumer Behaviour*, 4th Edition. Used with permission of the McGraw-Hill Companies

3 Early majority

The early majority are usually composed of opinion followers who are a little above average in age, education, social status and income. Although not capable of substantiation, it is probable that web usage is high and they rely on informal sources of information and take fewer publications than the previous two groups.

4 Late majority

This group of people is sceptical of new ideas and only adopts new products because of social or economic factors. They take few publications and are below average in education, social status and income. Their web usage may be below average.

5 Laggards

This group of people is suspicious of all new ideas and is set in their opinions. Lowest of all the groups in terms of income, social status and education, this group takes a long time to adopt an innovation.

This framework suggests that, at the innovation stage, messages should be targeted at relatively young people in the target group, with a high level of income, education and social status. This will speed word-of-mouth recommendation and the diffusion process. Mahajan *et al.* (1990) observe that the personal influence of word-of-mouth communications does not work in isolation from the other communication tools and media. Early adopters are more likely to adopt an innovation in response to 'external influences' and only through time will the effect of 'internal influences' become significant. In other words, mass media communications need time to work before word-of-mouth communications can begin to build effectiveness. However, digital developments circumnavigate the need to use mass media, which means that viral communications and social networks alone can lead to substantial WOM penetration.

Gatignon and Robertson (1985) suggest that there are three elements to the diffusion process, which need to be taken into account, particularly for the fast-moving consumer goods sector

1. the rate of diffusion or speed at which sales occur;
2. the pattern of diffusion or shape of the curve;
3. the potential penetration level or size of the market.

Care should be taken to ensure that all three of these elements are considered when attempting to understand the diffusion process. It can be concluded that if a campaign is targeted at innovators and the early majority, and is geared to stimulating word-of-mouth communications, then the diffusion process is more likely to be successful than if these elements are ignored.

Summary

In order to help consolidate your understanding of communication theory, here are the key points summarised against each of the learning objectives:

1 Understand the linear model of communication and appreciate how the various elements link together and contribute to successful communication

The linear or one-way communication process suggests that messages are developed by a source, encoded, transmitted, decoded and meaning applied to the message by a receiver. Noise in the system may prevent the true meaning of the messages from being conveyed, whilst feedback to the source is limited. The effectiveness of this communication process is determined by the strengths of the linkages between the different components.

2 Examine the impact of the media and personal influences on the communication process

There are two particular influences on the communication process that need to be considered. First, the media used to convey information has fragmented drastically as a raft of new media have emerged. Second, people influence the communication process considerably, either as opinion leaders, formers or as participants in the word-of-mouth process.

3 Demonstrate the characteristics of the influencer and interactional forms of communication

The influencer model depicts information flowing via media channels to particular types of people (opinion leaders and opinion formers; see pp 45–46) to whom other members of the audience refer for information and guidance. Through interpersonal networks, opinion leaders not only reach members of the target audience who may not have been exposed to the message, but may reinforce the impact of the message for those members who did receive the message.

Increasingly communication is characterised by attributing meaning to messages that are shared, updated and a response to other messages. These 'conversations' can be termed interactional and are an integral part of society. The interactional model of communication attempts to assimilate the variety of influences acting upon the communication process and account for the responses (interactions) people give to messages received from people and machines.

4 Explain the characteristics associated with opinion leaders, formers and followers

Opinion leaders are members of a peer group who have informal expertise and knowledge about a specific topic. Opinion formers have formal expertise bestowed upon them by virtue of their qualifications, experience and careers. Opinion followers value and use information from these sources in their decision-making processes. Marketing communications should therefore target leaders and formers as they can speed the overall communication process.

5 Examine the nature and characteristics associated with word-of-mouth communication

Word-of-mouth communication (WoM) is 'interpersonal communication regarding products or services where the receiver regards the communicator as impartial'. WoM is an increasingly important form of effective communication, one which is relatively cost free yet very credible.

6 Describe the processes of adoption and diffusion as related to marketing communications

The process of adoption in aggregate form, over time, is diffusion. It is a group process by which an innovation is communicated through certain channels over a period of time among the members of a social system. Five particular groups each with distinct characteristics can be identified.

The process of adoption in aggregate form, over time, is diffusion. According to Rogers (1983), diffusion is the process by which an innovation is communicated through certain channels over a period of time among the members of a social system.

Review questions

1. Name the elements of the linear model of communication and briefly describe the role of each element.
2. Make brief notes explaining why the linear interpretation of the communication process is not entirely satisfactory.
3. Draw the influencer model of communication.
4. Discuss the differences between the linear, influencer and interactional models of communications.
5. How do opinion leaders differ from opinion formers and opinion followers?
6. Why is word-of-mouth communication so important to marketing communications?
7. What are the three elements of word-of-mouth communication identified by Bone?
8. If voluntary is one form of WoM, what are the other two and how do they differ?
9. Using a product of your choice show how the stages in the process of adoption can be depicted.
10. Draw a graph to show the difference between fast and slow diffusion.

References

Arndt, J. (1967) Role of Product-Related Conversations in the Diffusion of a New Product, *Journal of Marketing Research*, 4 (August), 291–295.

Ballantyne, D. (2004) Dialogue and its role in the development of relationship specific knowledge, *Journal of Business and Industrial Marketing*, 19(2), 114–123.

Bone, P.F. (1995) Word of mouth effects on short-term and long term product judgments, *Journal of Business Research*, 21(3), 213–223.

Chan, K.K. and Misra, S. (1990) Characteristics of the opinion leader: a new dimension, *Journal of Advertising*, 19(3), 53–60.

Christiansen, T. and Tax, S.S. (2000) Measuring word of mouth: the questions of who and when, *Journal of Marketing Communications*, 6, 185–199.

Clark, N. (2010) How brands can reach bloggers, *Marketing*, 3 March, 24–26.

Dichter, E. (1966) How word-of-mouth advertising works, *Harvard Business Review*, 44 (November/December), 147–166.

Gatignon, H. and Robertson, T. (1985) A propositional inventory for new diffusion research, *Journal of Consumer Research*, 11, 849–867.

Goldsmith, R.E. and Horowitz, D. (2006) Measuring motivations for online opinion seeking, *Journal of Interactive Advertising*, 6(2), (Spring), 3–14. Retrieved 5 April 2010 from http://www.jiad.org/article76

Gwinner K.P. and Eaton, J. (1999) Building Brand Image Through Event Sponsorship: The Role of Image Transfer, *Journal of Advertising*, 28(4), (Winter), 47–57.

Hawkins, D.I., Best, R.J. and Coney, K.A. (1989) *Consumer Behaviour: Implications for Marketing Strategy*, Homewood, IL: Richard D. Irwin.

Helm, S. and Schlei, J. (1998) Referral potential – potential referrals: An investigation into customers' communication in service markets, Proceedings from 27th EMAC Conference, *Marketing Research and Practice*, 41–56.

Johnson, G.J., Bruner II, G.C. and Kumar, A. (2006) Interactivity and its facets revisited, *Journal of Advertising*, 35(4), (Winter), 35–52.

Katz, E. and Lazarfeld, P.F. (1955) *Personal Influence*. Glencoe, IL: Free Press.

Kingdom, J.W. (1970) Opinion leaders in the electorate, *Public Opinion Quarterly*, 34, 256–261.

Kozinets, R.V., de Valck, K., Wojnicki, A.C. and Wilner, S.J.S. (2010) Networked Narratives: understanding word-of-mouth marketing in online communities, *Journal of Marketing*, 74 (March), 71–89.

Lam, D., Lee, A. and Mizerski, R. (2009) The Effects of Cultural Values in Word-of-Mouth Communication, *Journal of International Marketing*, 17(3), 55–70.

Mahajan, V., Muller, E. and Bass, F.M. (1990) New product diffusion models in marketing, *Journal of Marketing*, 54 (January), 1–26.

Mallen, B. (1977) *Principles of Marketing Channel Management*. Lexington, MA: Lexington Books.

Mazur, L. (2004) Keep it simple, *Marketing Business* (March), 17.

Mazzarol, T., Sweeney, J.C. and Soutar, G.N. (2007) Conceptualising word-of-mouth activity, triggers and conditions: an exploratory study, *European Journal of Marketing*, 41(11/12), 1475–1494.

McCracken, G. (1989) Who is the Celebrity Endorser? Cultural Foundations of the Endorsement Process, *Journal of Consumer Research*, 16(3), 310–321.

Midgley, D. and Dowling, G. (1993) Longitudinal study of product form innovation: the interaction between predispositions and social messages, *Journal of Consumer Research*, 19 (March), 611–625.

Palmer, I. (2009) WoM is about empowering consumers in shaping your brand, *Admap*, 504 (April), retrieved 2 June 2010 from www.warc.com/admap

Patzer, G.L. (1983) Source credibility as a function of communicator physical attractiveness, *Journal of Business Research*, 11, 229–241.

PQ Media (2010) More brands start paid conversations online, *Warc News*, retrieved 17 May 2010 from www.warc.com/news/

Reichheld, F.F. (2003) The one number you need to grow, *Harvard Business Review* (December), 47–54.

Reynolds, J. (2010) Hovis embarks on first 'buzz marketing' drive, *Marketing*, 2 June, 3.

Reynolds, F.D. and Darden, W.R. (1971) Mutually adaptive effects of interpersonal communication, *Journal of Marketing Research*, 8 (November), 449–454.

Roberts, J. (2010) Mobilise the people to shape your brand, *Marketing Week*, 4 February, retrieved 23 June 2010 from www.marketingweek.co.uk/in-depth-analysis/cover-stories/mobilise-the-people-to-shape-your-brand/3009483.article

Robinson, J.P. (1976) Interpersonal influence in election campaigns: two step flow hypothesis, *Public Opinion Quarterly*, 40, 304–319.

Rogers, E.M. (1962) *Diffusion of Innovations*, 1st edn, New York: Free Press.

Rogers, E.M. (1983) *Diffusion of Innovations*, 3rd edn, New York: Free Press.

Santo, B (2006) Have you heard about *word of mouth?*, *Multichannel Merchant*, 2(2), (February), 28–30.

Schramm, W. (1955) How communication works, in *The Process and Effects of Mass Communications* (ed. W. Schramm), 3–26, Urbana, IL: University of Illinois Press.

Shannon, C. and Weaver, W. (1962) *The Mathematical Theory of Communication*. Urbana, IL: University of Illinois Press.

Simms, J. (2007) Bridging the gap, *Marketing*, 12 December 2007, 26–28.

Smith, N. (2010) Hovis: Marketing Society Award for Excellence, *Marketing*, 9 June, 15.

Stokes, D. and Lomax, W. (2002) Taking control of word of mouth marketing: the case of an entrepreneurial hotelier, *Journal of Small Business and Enterprise Development*, 9(4), 349–357.

Theodorson, S.A. and Theodorson, G.R. (1969) *A Modern Dictionary of Sociology*. New York: Cromwell.

Williams, K. (1990) *Behavioural Aspects of Marketing*. Oxford: Heinemann.

Windahl, S., Signitzer, B. and Olson, J.T. (1992) *Using Communication Theory*, London: Sage.

Whitton, F. and Ryan, L. (2006) Sony BRAVIA LCD TV-Balls, *IPA Effectiveness Awards*, Institute of Practitioners in Advertising, Retrieved 18 January 2008 from www.warc.com/ArticleCentre,/Default.asp?CType=A&AID=WORDSEARCH82662&Tab=A

Yuan, Y., Caulkins, J.P. and Roehrig, S. (1998) The relationship between advertising and content provision on the Internet, *European Journal of Marketing*, 32(7/8), 667–687.

Chapter 3
Audiences: attitudes, behaviour and decision-making

Understanding the way in which customers perceive their world, the way they learn, develop attitudes and respond to marketing communication stimuli is fundamental if effective communications are to be developed. In the same way, understanding the ways in which buyers make decisions and the factors that impact upon the decision process can affect the effectiveness of marketing communications.

Aims and learning objectives

The aims of this chapter are to first consider some of the ways information is processed by people and second to examine the key issues associated with purchase decision-making and their impact on marketing communications.

The learning objectives are to enable readers to:

1. explain the nature of perception and describe how marketing communications can be used to influence the way people perceive and position brands;
2. describe the key components of attitudes and explain ways in which marketing communications can be used to influence attitudes;
3. set out ideas concerning the nature of perceived risk and to relate ways in which marketing communications can be used to alleviate such uncertainty;
4. appreciate the nature of involvement and to explain how marketing communications can be used to reflect high and low involvement situations;
5. explain how marketing communications can be used to complement the purchase decision-making processes adopted by organisations.

Introduction

Marketing is about many things, but one of its central themes is the management of behaviour. Marketing communications is about making promises and so it makes sense therefore, to understand buyer behaviour, in order that these promises be realistic and effective. Understanding the ways in which buyers make decisions and the factors that impact upon the decision process can affect the effectiveness of marketing communications. In particular, it can influence message structure, content and scheduling. In this chapter, and indeed the book, reference is made to both buyers and audiences. This is because although all buyers constitute an audience, not all audiences are buyers.

Information processing

Marketing communications is an audience-centred activity so it is vitally important to understand the way in which audiences' process information prior to, during and after making product/service purchase decisions. Here three main information processing issues are considered; awareness, perception and attitudes.

Awareness

Awareness of the existence and availability of a product/service or an organisation is necessary before information can be processed and purchase behaviour expected. Much of marketing communications activity is directed towards getting the attention of the target audience, simply because of the vast number of competing messages and 'noise' in the marketplace. Many different techniques and approaches have been developed, first through advertising and now in most aspects of marketing communications. The goal is to get the undivided attention of the audience, to create awareness of the key messages and induce engagement opportunities. Awareness, therefore, needs to be created, developed, refined or sustained, according to the characteristics of the market and the particular situation facing an organisation at any one point in time (see Figure 3.1).

In situations where the audience experiences high involvement and is fully aware of a product's existence, attention and awareness levels need only be sustained, and efforts need to be applied to other communication tasks, which may be best left to the other elements of the communications mix. For example, sales promotion and personal selling are more effective at informing, persuading and provoking purchase of a new car once advertising has created the necessary levels of awareness.

Where low levels of awareness are found, getting attention needs to be a prime objective so that awareness can be developed in the target audience. Where low involvement exists, the decision-making process is relatively straightforward. With levels of risk minimised, buyers with sufficient levels of awareness may be prompted into purchase with little assistance of the other elements of the mix. Recognition and recall of brand names and corporate images are felt by some (Rossiter and Percy, 1987) to be sufficient triggers to stimulate a behavioural response. The requirement in this situation would be to refine and strengthen the level of awareness in order that it provokes interest and stimulates a higher level of involvement during recall or recognition.

Where low levels of awareness are matched by low involvement, the prime objective has to be to create awareness of the product in association with the product class. It is not surprising that organisations use awareness campaigns and invest a large amount of their resources in establishing their brand or corporate name. Many brands seek to establish 'top of mind awareness' as one of their primary objectives for their advertising spend. For example,

Figure 3.1 An awareness grid

	Involvement High	Involvement Low
Awareness High	Sustain current levels of awareness (deploy other elements of the promotional mix)	Refine awareness (inputs through the introduction of knowledge components)
Awareness Low	Build awareness quickly	Create association of awareness of product with product class need

Comparethemarket.com, a price comparison car insurance website, decided to differentiate themselves in an intensely competitive market. They decided to change the way their name was perceived because name familiarity is key (and their name was unmemorable), and their identity and name were very similar to their nearest competitor (gocompare). By adopting the name 'meerkat' and developing the comparethemeerkat.com site, brand name awareness rose considerably (Jukes, 2009).

Once awareness has been created in the target audience, it should not be neglected. If there is neglect, the audience may become distracted by competing messages and the level of awareness of the focus product or organisation may decline.

Perception

Perception is concerned with how individuals see and make sense of their environment. It is about how individuals select, organise and interpret stimuli, so that they can understand their world.

Selection

Individuals are exposed, each day, to a tremendous number of stimuli. De Chernatony (1993) suggested that each consumer is exposed to over 550 advertisements per day, while Lasn (1999) estimated that this should be 3,000 advertisements per day (cited by Dahl *et al.*, 2003). In addition there are thousands of other non-commercial stimuli that each individual encounters. To cope with this bombardment, our sensory organs select those stimuli to which attention is given. The nature of the stimuli, or external factors such as the intensity and size, position, contrast, novelty, repetition and movement, are factors that have been developed and refined by marketing communicators to attract attention. Animation is used to attract attention when the product class is perceived as bland and uninteresting, such as margarine or teabags. Unexpected camera angles and the use of music can be strong methods of gaining the attention of the target audience, as used successfully in the Bacardi Breezer and Renault commercials. Sexual attraction can be a powerful means of capturing the attention of audiences, and when associated with a brand's values can be a very effective method of getting attention (for example, the Diet Coke advertisement, see Exhibit 3.1).

Exhibit 3.1 Diet Coke
The hugely successful Diet Coke television ads depict office workers timing their work break to coincide with the presence of certain attractive males.
Images courtesy of The Advertising Archives

Organisation

These selected stimuli are organised in order to make them comprehensible and are then given meaning. Stimuli therefore need to be presented in ways that we can understand or create meaning. The use of contour (e.g. the Coke bottle), and grouping objects to convey meaning by association enable easier organisation of stimuli. For example, some products are shown next to fruit or vegetables so that we transfer the healthy association to the promoted product.

Interpretation

Once stimuli are organised they need to be interpreted so that meaning can be attributed. As Cohen and Basu (1987) state, by using existing categories meanings can be given to stimuli. These categories are determined from the individual's past experiences and they shape what the individual expects to see. These expectations, when combined with the strength and clarity of the stimulus and the motives at the time perception occurs, mould the pattern of the perceived stimuli. Stimuli, therefore, are selected, organised and interpreted.

Marketing communication and perception

The way in which individuals perceive, organise and interpret stimuli is a reflection of their past experiences and the classifications used to understand the different situations each individual frames every day. Individuals seek to frame or provide a context within which their role becomes clearer. Shoppers expect to find products in particular situations, such as rows, shelves or display bins of similar goods. They also develop meanings and associations with some grocery products because of the utility and trust/emotional satisfaction certain pack types evoke. The likelihood that a sale will be made is improved if the context in which a purchase transaction is undertaken does not contradict a shopper's expectations.

Marketing communications should attempt to present products (objects) in a frame or 'mental presence' (Moran, 1990) that is recognised by a buyer, such as a consumption or purchase situation. A product has a much greater chance of entering an individual's evoked set if the situation in which it is presented is one that is expected and relevant. However, a new pack design can provide differentiation and provoke people into reassessing their expectations of what constitutes appropriate packaging in a product category.

Javalgi *et al.* (1992) point out that perception is important to product evaluation and product selection. Consumers try to evaluate a product's attributes by the physical cues of taste, smell, size and shape. Sometimes no difference can be distinguished, so the consumer has to make a judgement on factors other than the physical characteristics of the product. This is the basis of branding activity, where a personality is developed for the product that enables it to be

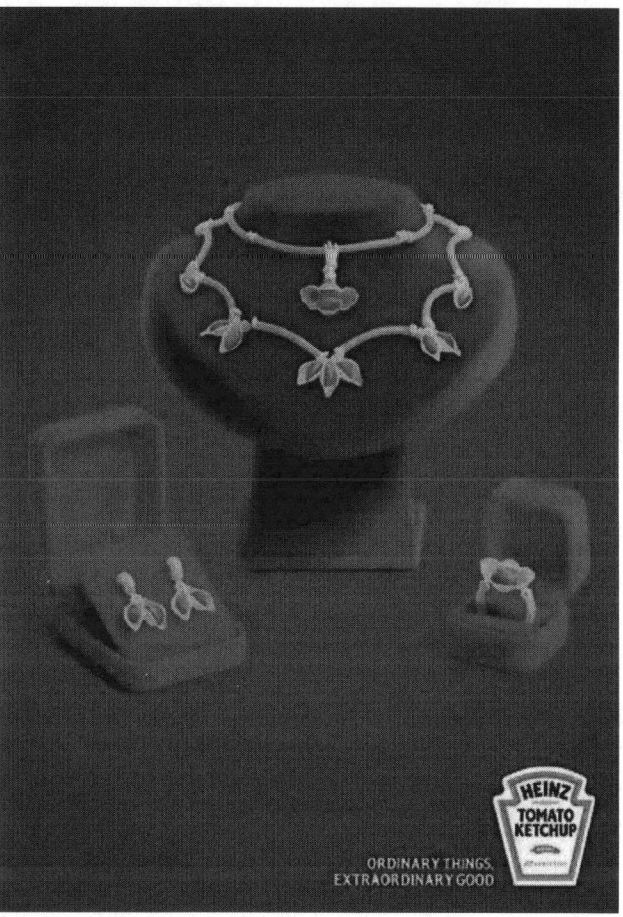

Exhibit 3.2 Heinz seek to position their tomato ketchup as a refinement in the Czech Republic
Image used with permission from MARK/BBDO in the Czech Republic

perceived differently from its competitors. The individual may also set up a separate category or evoked set in order to make sense of new stimuli or satisfactory experiences. Consumer perception of salon- and shop-based haircare products shows important differences and indicates the different roles that marketing communication needs to play: see Figure 3.2. Within each of these sectors many brands are developed that are targeted at different segments based upon demographic, benefit and psychographic factors.

Finally, individuals carry a set of enduring perceptions or images. These relate to themselves, to products and to organisations. The concept of positioning the product in the mind of the consumer is fundamental to marketing strategy and is a topic that will be examined in greater depth in Chapter 4. The image an individual has of an organisation is becoming recognised as increasingly important, judging by the proportion of communication budgets being given over to public relations activities and corporate advertising in particular.

Organisations develop multiple images to meet the positioning requirements of their end-user markets and stakeholders. They need to monitor and adjust their identities constantly in respect of the perceptions and expectations held by the other organisations in their various networks. For example, the level of channel coordination and control can be a function of the different perceptions of channel members. These concern the perception of the channel depth, processes of control and the roles each member is expected to fulfil. Furthermore, the perception of an organisation's product quality and its associated image (reputation) is becoming increasingly important.

Figure 3.2 A comparison of the different perceptions and beliefs of salon and shop haircare brands

Attitudes

Attitudes relate to an individual's predispositions, shaped through experience, to respond in an anticipated way to an object or situation. Attitudes are learned through past experiences and serve as a link between thoughts and behaviour. These experiences may relate to the product itself, to the messages transmitted by the different members of the channel network (normally mass media communications) and to the information supplied by opinion leaders, formers and followers.

Attitudes tend to be consistent within each individual: they are usually clustered and very often interrelated. This categorisation leads to the formation of stereotypes, which is extremely useful for the design of messages as stereotyping allows for the transmission of a lot of information in a short time period (30 seconds) without impeding learning or the focal part of the message.

Attitude components

Attitudes are hypothetical constructs, and they are considered to consist of three components: a cognitive or learning component, an affective or feeling element and a conative or action component (see Figure 3.3).

1 Cognitive component (learn)

This component refers to the level of knowledge and beliefs held by individuals about a product and/or the beliefs about specific attributes of the offering. This represents the learning aspect of attitude formation. Marketing communications are used to create attention and awareness, to provide information and to help audiences learn and understand the features and benefits a particular product/service offers.

2 Affective component (feel)

By referring to the feelings held about a product – good, bad, pleasant or unpleasant – an evaluation is made of the object. This is the component that is concerned with feelings, sentiments, moods and emotions about an object. Marketing communications are used to induce feelings about the product/service such that it becomes a preferred brand. This preference may

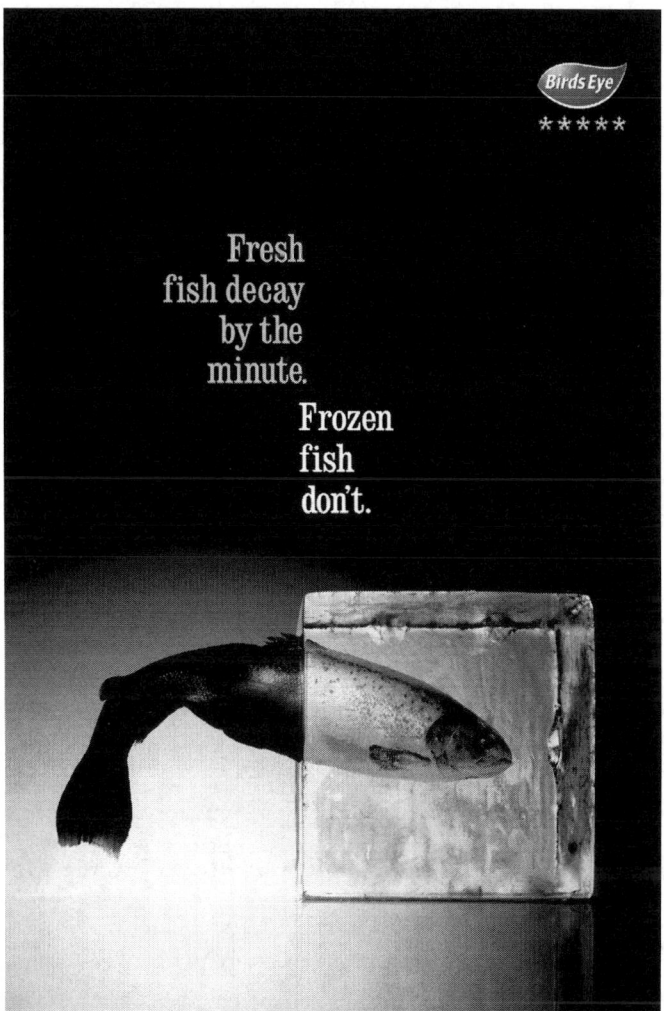

Exhibit 3.3	An ad by Birds Eye to change the way frozen food was perceived by consumers
	At a time when chiller sales were exceeding frozen foods, Bird's Eye launched a campaign where one of the messages was that Bird's Eye fish was frozen as soon as it was caught, unlike some wet fish sales where the fish can be up to 10 days old. Image courtesy of Birds Eye Ltd.

be based on emotional attachment to a brand, conferred status through ownership, past experiences and longevity of brand usage or any one of a number of ways in which people can become emotionally involved with a brand.

3 Conative component (do)

This is the action component of the attitude construct and refers to the individual's disposition or intention to behave in a certain way. Some researchers go so far as to suggest that this component refers to observable behaviour. Marketing communications therefore, should be used to encourage audiences to do something. For example, visit a website, phone a telephone number, take a coupon, book a visit, press red (on a remote control unit) for interactivity through digital television.

This three-component approach to attitudes is based upon attitudes towards an object, person or organisation. The sequence of attitude formation is learn, feel and do. This approach to attitude formation is limited in that the components are seen to be of equal strength.

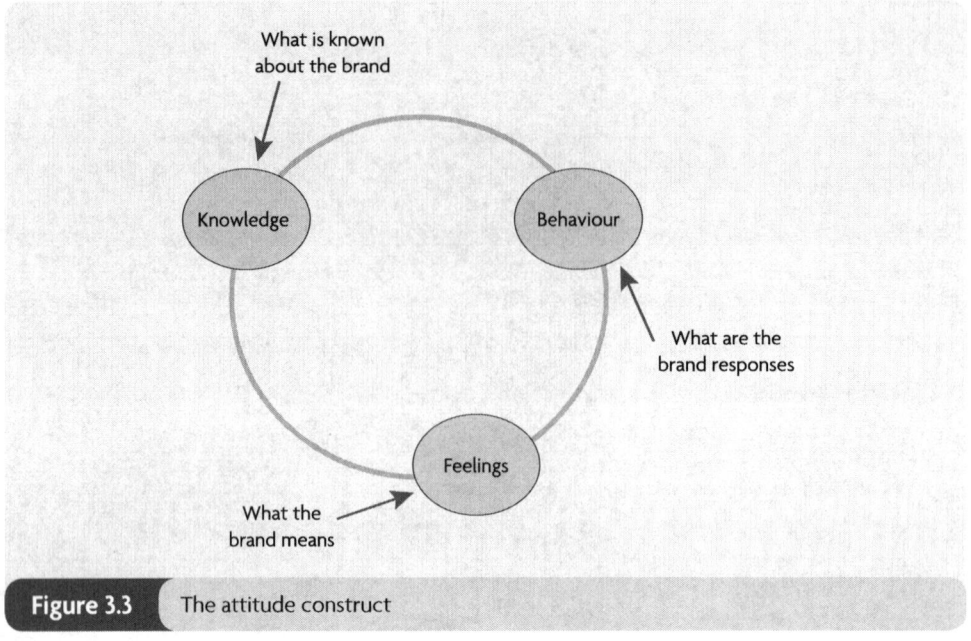

Figure 3.3 The attitude construct

A single-component model has been developed where the attitude only consists of the individual's overall feeling towards an object. In other words, the affective component is the only significant component.

Changing attitudes with marketing communications

Marketing communications is important to either maintain or change attitudes held by stakeholders. It is not the only way as product and service elements, pricing and channel decisions all play an important part in shaping the attitudes held. However, marketing communications has a pivotal role in conveying each of these aspects to the target audience. Branding (Chapter 6) is a means by which attitudes can be established and maintained in a consistent way and it is through the use of the tools of the communication mix that brand positions can be sustained. The final point that needs to be made is that there is a common thread between attributes, attitudes and positioning (Chapter 4). Attributes provide a means of differentiation and positions are shaped as a consequence of the attitudes that result from the way people interpret the associated marketing communications.

Viewpoint 3.1 Changing attitudes towards Weetabix

Weetabix is a premier brand among breakfast cereals. Many people have experienced the brand as a child, often as a baby, as the biscuit reduces to a mush when soaked with milk and becomes an ideal food for weaning. Weetabix is well established and market penetration rates of 40 per cent mean there is little room for growth and development. However, attitudes towards the brand were at best neutral, the biscuit being perceived to be bland. In addition, the breakfast market was experiencing change in the period 2003–05 and the blander products such as Cornflakes and Shredded Wheat were starting to lose share.

Weetabix commissioned qualitative research and asked a group of lapsed users to eat the brand for a week and keep a diary. Two of the more startling results were that many of the group soon reported health benefits (no snacking before lunch). In addition, others had started to add 'things' to the cereal to overcome the monotony of its blandness. Here lay the foundation for the advertising campaign, to reveal the variety, interest and added value by using different toppings. A 'Weetabix Week' advertising campaign was devised, which provided the basis for an event designed to stimulate and motivate people to use the brand. One of the goals was to change perceptions of the brand by encouraging consumers to experiment with different toppings. This was achieved by showing them ways other people topped off their daily Weetabix. The second goal was to motivate people to try the brand for three or four days, so that they started to feel the health benefits, before switching to their regular brand.

Television was the critical media because it allowed the audience to see the different toppings the participants used to decorate their Weetabix. The second benefit was that television enabled the audience to see 'real people' trying the Weetabix Week. These testimonials provided source credibility and opportunities to link consumption into lifestyle (e.g. children at breakfast, students late at night).

Source: Based on Okin and Robothan-Jones (2007)

Question
What might have been the impact had celebrities been used rather than normal consumers?

Task
Make a list of ideas that could be used to help consumers perceive the Weetabix brand differently.

Environmental influences on the attitudes people hold towards particular products and services are a result of many elements. First they are a reflection of the way different people interpret the marketing communications surrounding them. Second, they are a result of their direct experience of using them and third, a result of the informal messages received from family, friends and other highly credible sources of information. These all contribute to the way people perceive (and position) products and services and the feelings they have to them and to competing products. Managing attitudes (towards a brand) is therefore very important and marketing communications can play an important part in changing or maintaining attitudes. There are a number of ways in which attitudinal change can be implemented.

Change the physical product or service element

At a fundamental level, attitudes might be so ingrained that it is necessary to change the product or service. This may involve a radical redesign or the introduction of a significant new attribute. Only once these changes have been made should marketing communications be used to communicate the new or revised object. When VW bought Skoda it redesigned the total product offering before relaunch.

Change misunderstanding

In some circumstances people might misunderstand the benefits of a particularly important attribute and marketing communications is required to correct the beliefs held. This can be achieved through product demonstration of functionally based communications. Packaging and even the name of the product may need to be revised.

Build credibility

Attitudes towards a brand might be superficial and lack sufficient conviction to prompt conative behaviour. This can be corrected through the use of an informative strategy, designed to build credibility. Product demonstration and hands-on experience (e.g. through sampling) are effective strategies. Skoda supports a rally team to convey durability, speed and performance.

Change performance beliefs

Beliefs held about the object and the performance qualities of the object can be adjusted through appropriate marketing communications. For example, by changing the perceptions held about the attributes, it is possible to change the attitudes about the object.

Change attribute priorities

By changing the relative importance of the different attributes and ratings it is possible to change attitudes. Therefore, a strategy to emphasise a different attribute can change the attitude not only towards a brand but also to a product category. By stressing the importance of travel times, the importance of this attribute might be emphasised in the minds of potential holiday-makers. Dyson changed attitudes to carpet cleaning equipment by stressing the efficiency of its new cyclone technology rather than the ease of use, aesthetic design or generic name (Hoover) associations used previously.

Introduce a new attribute

Opportunities might exist to introduce a radically different and new (or previously unused) attribute. This provides a means for clear differentiation until competitors imitate and catch up. For example, by making prominent new service levels which are coupled with guaranteed refunds in the event of performance failure, this new attribute may lead to greater success.

Change perception of competitor products

By changing the way competitor products are perceived it is possible to differentiate your own brand. This could be achieved by using messages that distance a competitor's brand from your own. For example, an airline could highlight a key competitor's punctuality record, and this might help change the way its own performance level is perceived. In much the same way, Thomson Holidays used this approach when it used copy that read, 'We go there, we don't stay there'.

Change or introduce new brand associations

By using celebrities or spokespersons with whom the target audience can identify, it might be possible to change the way in which a brand is perceived. For example, a bread producer might use a well known athlete to represent their brand as a healthy food. Alternatively it may use children in its marketing communications to suggest that it is fun to eat and that all children love the brand.

Use corporate branding

By altering the significance of the parent brand relative to the product brand, it is possible to alter beliefs about brands and their overall value. In some situations there is little to differentiate competitive brands and little credible scope to develop attribute-based attitudes. By using the stature of the parent company it is possible to develop a level of credibility and brand values that other brands cannot copy, although they can imitate by using their parent brand. Procter & Gamble has introduced its name to the packs of many of its brands.

Change the number of attributes used

Many brands still rely on a single attribute as a means of providing a point of differentiation. This was popularly referred to as a unique selling proposition at a time when attribute and information based communications reflected a feature-dominated understanding of branding. Today, two or even three attributes are often combined with strong emotional associations in order to provide a point of differentiation and a set of benefit-oriented brand values.

> **Viewpoint 3.2**   **Branching out as NatWest change attitudes**
>
> The banking system is a classic example of market inertia. Customers see little reason to move or change their banks unless provoked by gross inefficiency or their accounts are mishandled. At the same time that many banks have closed a large proportion of their UK branch network and moved their call centres off shore to reduce costs, they have moved away from a human approach to customer service to one based on mechanics. There has since been a 'consumer backlash against foreign call centres [that] has led some companies to return operations to the UK' (Winterman, 2007).
>
> When the Royal Bank of Scotland bought NatWest in 2000 it reversed the strategy of closing branches and using overseas call centres. A policy of refurbishing all the branches has since been implemented, new branches opened and all call centre operations are now UK-based.
>
> As a result, NatWest have used this initiative as the backbone of their communication strategy. By positioning themselves against an attribute that had been discarded by competitors, NatWest have been able to establish a clear point of differentiation. By focusing their marketing and communications on their branch network in order to provide customers the opportunity for personal contact by just walking into a local branch, they have been able to add considerable value to the brand and given inert customers a reason to change to NatWest.
>
> *Source*: Based on Winterman (2007); www.natwest.com/
>
> **Question**
> As all banks provide a service, how feasible is it for them to use service as a basis for differentiation?
>
> **Task**
> Find two other banks and determine the attributes they use for differentiation.

Decision-making

Much of marketing communication activity has been oriented towards decision-making, and knowledge of a buyer's decision-making processes is vital if the correct type of information is to be transmitted at the right time and in the right or appropriate manner. There are two broad types of buyer: consumers and organisational buyers. First, consideration will be given to a general decision-making process and then an insight into the characteristics of the decision-making processes for consumers and organisational buyers will be presented. Figure 3.4 shows that there are five stages in the general process whereby buyers make purchase decisions and implement them. Marketing communications can impact upon any or all of these stages with varying levels of potential effectiveness.

Problem recognition

Problem recognition occurs when there is a perceived difference between an individual's current position and their ideal state. Marketing communications can be used to encourage 'problem recognition' by suggesting that the current state is not desirable, by demonstrating how consumers can tell whether they have a similar problem (e.g. 'Is your hair dull and lifeless?') or by suggesting that their current brand is inferior.

Figure 3.4 A general decision-making framework

Information search

Having identified a problem a prospective buyer will search for information in an attempt to resolve it. There are two main areas of search activity. The internal search involves a memory scan to recall experiences and knowledge, utilising the perceptual processes to see whether there is an 'off-the-shelf' solution. If there is no 'off-the-shelf' solution, the prospective buyer will resort to an external search. This will involve family and friends, reference sources and commercial guides and advertising.

Alternative evaluation

Potential solutions need to be evaluated in order that the optimum choice be made. Products considered feasible constitute the *preference set*, and it is from these seven or eight products that a smaller group of products is normally assembled. This is referred to as the *evoked set* (or repertoire) and it is from this that consumers make a choice. Attributes used to determine the sets are referred to as evaluative criteria. Very often these attributes are both objective and subjective in nature.

Purchase decision

Having evaluated various solutions, the buyer may develop a predisposition to make a purchase. This will involve matching motives and evaluative criteria with product attributes. This necessitates the use of the processes of learning and attitude formation.

Post-purchase evaluation

Direct experience of the product is an important part of the decision process. Feedback from use helps learning and attitude development and is the main contributor to long-run behaviour. Communication activity must continue to provide satisfaction and prevent the onset of cognitive dissonance. This is a state where, after the purchase decision has been made, a buyer might feel tension about a past decision either because the product fails to reach expectations or because the consumer becomes aware of a superior alternative.

Marketing communications, at this stage, should be aimed at reinforcing past decisions by stressing the positive features of the product, the emotional enhancement usage brings or by providing more information to assist its use and application. For example, much of the advertising undertaken by car manufacturers seeks to prevent the onset of tension and purchase dissatisfaction.

Types of consumer decision-making

Buyers do not follow the general decision sequence at all times. The procedure may vary depending upon the time available, levels of perceived risk and the degree of involvement a buyer has with the type of product. Perceived risk and involvement are issues that will be covered later. At this point three types of problem-solving behaviour (extended problem-solving, limited problem-solving and routinised response) will be considered.

Extended problem-solving (EPS)

Consumers considering the purchase of a car or house undertake a great deal of external search activity and spend a lot of time reaching a solution that satisfies, as closely as possible, the evaluative criteria previously set. This activity is usually associated with products that are unfamiliar, where direct experience and hence knowledge are weak, and where there is considerable financial risk.

Marketing communications should aim to provide a lot of information to assist the decision process. The provision of information through sales literature, such as brochures and leaflets, websites for determining product and purchase criteria in product categories where there is little experience, access to salespersons and demonstrations and advertisements, are just some of the ways in which information can be provided.

Limited problem-solving (LPS)

Having experience of a product means that greater use can be made of internal memory-based search routines and the external search can be limited to obtaining up-to-date information or to ensuring that the finer points of the decision have been investigated.

Marketing communications should attempt to provide information about any product modification or new attributes and convey messages that highlight those key attributes known to be important to buyers. By differentiating the product, marketing communications provides the buyer with a reason to select that particular product.

Routinised response behaviour (RRB)

For a great number of products the decision process will consist only of an internal search. This is primarily because the buyer has made a number of purchases and has accumulated a great deal of experience. Therefore, only an internal search is necessary, so little time or effort will be spent on external search activities. Low-value items that are frequently purchased fall into this category, for example toothpaste, soap, tinned foods and confectionery.

Some outlets are perceived as suitable for what are regarded as distress purchases. Tesco Express and many petrol stations position themselves as convenience stores for distress purchases (for example, a pint of milk at 10 o'clock at night). Many garages have positioned themselves as convenience stores suitable for meeting the needs of RRB purchases. In doing so they are moving themselves away from the perception of being only a distress purchase outlet.

Communicators should focus upon keeping the product within the evoked set or getting it into the set. Learning can be enhanced through repetition of messages, but repetition can also be used to maintain attention and awareness.

Perceived risk

An important factor associated with the purchase decision process is the level of risk perceived by buyers. This risk concerns the uncertainty of the consequences arising from a decision to purchase a particular brand.

Risk is perceived because the buyer has little or no experience of the performance of the product or the decision process associated with the purchase. Risk is related to not only brand-based decisions but also to product categories, an especially important aspect when launching new technology products, for example. The level of risk an individual experiences varies through time, across products, and is often a reflection of an individual's propensity to manage risk. Settle and Alreck (1989) suggest that there are five main forms of risk that can be identified; the purchase of a laptop demonstrates each element. These are set out in Table 3.1 with respect to the purchase of such a laptop.

A sixth element, time, is also considered to be a risk factor (Stone and Gronhaug, 1993):

> Using the laptop example, will purchase of the computer lead to an inefficient use of my time? Or can I afford the time to search for a good laptop so that I will not waste my money?

What constitutes risk is a function of the contextual characteristics of each situation, the individuals involved and the product under consideration.

A major task of marketing communications is to reduce levels of perceived risk. By providing extensive and relevant information a buyer's risks can be reduced substantially. Mass media, word-of-mouth, websites and sales representatives for example are popular ways to set out the likely outcomes from purchase and so reduce the levels of risk. Brand loyalty can also be instrumental in reducing risk when launching new products. The use of guarantees, third-party endorsements, money-back offers (some car manufacturers offer the opportunity to return a car within 30 days or exchange it for a different model) and trial samples (as used by many haircare products) are also well-used devices to reduce risk.

Many direct response magazine ads seek to reduce a number of different types of risk. Companies offering wine for direct home delivery, for example, try to reduce performance risk by providing information about each wine being offered. Financial risk is reduced by comparing their 'special' prices with those in the high street, social risk is approached by developing the brand name associations trying to improve credibility and time risk is reduced through the convenience of home delivery.

Table 3.1 Types of perceived risk

Type of perceived risk	Explanation
Performance	Will the unit reproduce my music clearly?
Financial	Can I afford that much or should I buy a less expensive version?
Physical	Will the unit damage my other systems or endanger me in any way?
Social	Will my friends and colleagues be impressed?
Ego	Will I feel as good as I want to feel when listening to or talking about my unit?

> **Viewpoint 3.3** Appealing to thoughtful car buyers
>
> In 2006 Hyundai had set a goal to sell 500,000 cars in the USA in 2009. Then the recession broke and changed the context and market conditions for selling cars. The cars had been made and were being shipped to the States. The only reasonable variable open to Hyundai to shift the cars out of the dealerships, was to revisit the marketing communications.
>
> The goals for the programme remained tough. The aim was to increase the brand based communications for the previous Jan–Feb results by 2 per cent, to maintain the previous period's number of shoppers (352,000) and to match the previous Jan–Feb's sales performance figures. In a market where only 9 per cent of consumers were looking to buy a new car, these were ambitious targets.
>
> Rather than focus on the car the campaign sought to focus on the consumer and their perceived risks, mainly financial. This was to be achieved by assuring consumer confidence by removing the financial risk from buying a new car.
>
> Research in 2007 found that there was a significant gap between the surprising truth of the cars' quality and the negative perceptions held by many individuals. Also, current Hyundai owners were more likely to be analytical, thoughtful decision-makers. Retail sales events followed the thoughtful theme, using a promotion that provided potential buyers access to investment experts who advised individuals about what to do with the money saved by buying a Hyundai.
>
> Research also showed that consumers would be worried about their ability to maintain the payments for a new car, if the economy got worse. This was overcome when an insurance company agreed to indemnify and protect the credit of any new Hyundai consumer.
>
> The transparent, upfront, matter-of-fact tone of the 'Assurance' campaign was thought to be important in order to be seen as sincere and understanding of the consumers' predicament. TV was used in order to be salient and reach as many people in the target market as quickly as possible. Large events such as the Super Bowl were used, as these stimulated both media and individual conversations.
>
> The results were startling. Sales at Chrysler, GM, Ford and Toyota each fell by anything from 32 per cent to 55 per cent. At Hyundai they were up 14 per cent. Not only did Hyundai reduce financial risk, they led a change in the way car companies communicated with their audiences.
>
> *Source*: Based on Anon (2010)
>
> ### Question
> What other risks might a car buyer have experienced when considering Hyundai? How might the Assurance campaign have helped overcome them?
>
> ### Task
> Flip through a newspaper or magazine, select three ads and determine whether there has been an attempt to reduce risk. If so how?

Involvement theory

Purchase decisions made by consumers vary considerably, and one of the factors thought to be key to brand choice decisions is the level of involvement (in terms of individual importance and relevance) a consumer has with either the product or the purchase process.

Involvement is about the degree of personal relevance and risk perceived by consumers when making a particular purchase decision (Rossiter et al., 1991). This implies that the level of involvement may vary through time as each member of the target market becomes more (or less) familiar with the purchase and associated communications. At the point of decision-making involvement is high or low, not some point on a sliding scale or a point on a continuum between two extremes.

High involvement

High involvement occurs when a consumer perceives an expected purchase that is not only of high personal relevance but also represents a high level of perceived risk. Cars, washing machines, houses and insurance policies are seen as 'big ticket' items, infrequent purchases that promote a great deal of involvement. The risk described is financial but, as we saw earlier, risk can take other forms. Therefore the choice of perfume, suit, dress or jewellery may also represent high involvement, with social risk dominating the purchase decision. The consumer, therefore, devotes a great deal of time to researching the intended purchase and collecting as much information as possible in order to reduce, as far as possible, levels of perceived risk.

Low involvement

A *low-involvement* state of mind regarding a purchase suggests little threat or risk to the consumer. Low-priced items such as washing powder, baked beans and breakfast cereals are bought frequently, and past experience of the product class and the brand cues the consumer into a purchase that requires little information or support. Items such as alcoholic and soft drinks, and chocolate are also normally seen as low involvement, but they induce a strong sense of ego risk associated with the self-gratification that is attached to the consumption of these products.

Two approaches to decision-making

From this understanding of general decision-making processes, perceived risk and involvement theory, it is possible to identify two main approaches to consumer decision-making.

High-involvement decision-making

If an individual is highly involved with the initial purchase of a product, EPS is the appropriate decision sequence, as information is considered to be processed in a rational, logical order. Individuals who are highly involved in a purchase are thought to move through the process shown in Figure 3.5. When high-involvement decision-making is present individuals perceive a high level of risk and are concerned about the intended purchase. The essential element in this sequence is that a great deal of information is sought initially and an attitude is developed before a commitment or intention to trial is determined.

Information search is an important part of the high-involvement decision-making process. Because individuals are highly motivated, information is actively sought, processed and

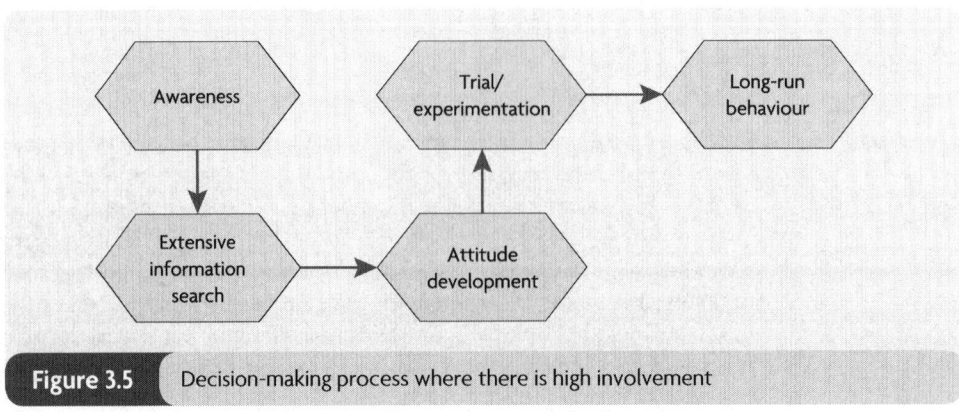

Figure 3.5 Decision-making process where there is high involvement

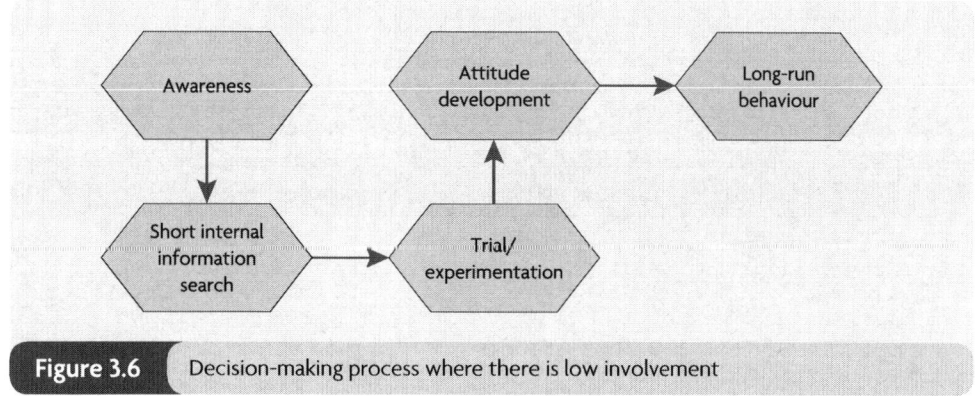

Figure 3.6 Decision-making process where there is low involvement

evaluated. Many media sources are explored, including the mass media, word-of-mouth communications, websites, and point-of-sale communications. As individuals require a lot of information, print media used to be the primary media where high involvement was identified. Today, websites are the primary source of large volumes of detailed information. Unlike print these sites can also be updated quickly but both types enable visitors to search and process information at a speed they can control.

Low-involvement decision-making

If an individual has little involvement with an initial purchase of a product, LPS is the appropriate decision process. Information is processed cognitively but in a passive, involuntary way. Processing occurs using right-brain thinking so information is stored as it is received, in sections, and this means that information is stored as a brand association (Heath, 2000). An advertisement for Andrex toilet tissue featuring the puppy is stored as the 'Andrex Puppy' without any overt thinking or reasoning. Because of the low personal relevance and perceived risk associated with this type of processing, message repetition is necessary to define brands and create meaningful brand associations. Individuals who have a low involvement with a purchase decision choose not to search for information and are thought to move through the process shown in Figure 3.6.

Communications can assist the development of awareness in the low-involvement decision-making process. However, as individuals assume a passive problem-solving role, messages need to be shorter than in the high-involvement process and should contain less information. Broadcast media are preferred as they complement the passive learning posture adopted by individuals. Repetition is important because the receiver has little or no motivation to retain information, and his or her perceptual selection processes filter out unimportant information. Learning develops through exposure to repeated messages, but attitudes do not develop at this part of the process (Harris, 1987).

Where low involvement is present, each individual relies upon internal, rather than external, search mechanisms, often prompted by point-of-purchase displays.

Impact on communications

Involvement theory is central to our understanding of the way in which information is processed and the way in which people make decisions about product purchases. We have established in the preceding section that there are two main types of involvement, high and low. These two types lead directly to two different uses of marketing communications. In decisions where there is high involvement, attitude precedes trial behaviour. In low-involvement cases this position is reversed.

Figure 3.7　Marketing communication approaches for the two levels of involvement

Where there is high involvement, consumers seek out information because they are concerned about the decision processes and outcomes. This can be because of the levels of uncertainty associated with the high costs of purchase and usage, inexperience of the product (category) often brought about due to the infrequency of purchases, the complexity of product and doubts about its operational usefulness. Because they have these concerns, people develop an attitude prior to behaviour. Informational ads that require cognitive processing are recommended.

Where there is low involvement, consumers are content to select any one of a number of acceptable products and often rely on those that are in the individual's evoked set. Low involvement is thought to be a comfortable state, because there are too many other decisions in life to have to make decisions about each one of them, so an opportunity not to have to seek information and make other decisions is welcome. See Figure 3.7 which indicates the marketing communication strategies best suited for each level within both involvement sequences. Emotional or transformational ads are recommended.

Planning communications based on involvement is not as straightforward as the preceding material might suggest. Various factors might influence the outcomes. For example, some individuals who are cognitively capable of processing information, may not always be able to process information in informational based ads because they are overloaded. In these circumstances they are more likely to develop positive attitudes towards affective or transformational based ads. Ranjbariyan and Mahmoodi (2009) also found that people under time pressure are more prone to use transformational ads as they will pick up visual cues to help their decision-making.

The material presented so far in this section is based on classical research, theoretical development and is supported by research. However, much of the knowledge has been developed in a non digital era and that raises questions about the depth of its validity in the contemporary world. Foley *et al.* (2009) undertook research that showed that people organise product categories according to the level of risk associated with brand choice decisions and the level of reward, the enjoyment people derive from the decisions they make. They also found that the types of categories people organise leads to different patterns of decision-making. Four main product categories were identified:

- **Routine** In this category people perceive low risk and low reward. Brand choice decision-making therefore characterised by inertia and decision-making is robotic.
- **Burden** People perceive high risk and low reward. Search is extensive and decision-making improved if someone can assist.
- **Passion** Risk is high and reward is high because people are emotionally engaged with these types of products and services. The symbolism and meaning attached to brands in the category is high, reflected in high ego and social risks.
- **Entertainment** People use this category where risk is low but reward can be high. This means that decision-making can be a pleasant, if brief experience.

Each of these categories has implications for the communications strategies necessary to reach people and be effective. For example, consideration of the type of website that best suits each of these categories provides immediate insight into how having an understanding or insight into the target audience can shape marketing communications.

Organisational buying decision processes

Organisational buying, according to Webster and Wind (1972), is 'the decision-making process by which formal organisations establish the need for purchased products and services and identify, evaluate and choose among alternative brands and suppliers'. Of particular significance is the relationship that develops between organisations involved as buyers or sellers.

One way of examining the context is to compare organisational decisions with those made in consumer markets. There are far fewer buyers in the organisational context than in the consumer market, although there can be a number of people associated with a buying decision in an organisation. Orders are invariably larger and the frequency with which they are placed is much lower. It is quite common for agreements to be made between organisations for the supply of materials over a number of years. Similarly, depending upon the complexity of the product (photocopying paper or a one-off satellite), the negotiation process may also take a long time.

Viewpoint 3.4 Healthy buying decisions

The purchase of medical supplies and equipment by hospitals is an important decision, if only because of the implications of the decisions made with regard to patient welfare. However, the wide variety of people involved in the process can lead to buying decisions becoming overly complex, sometimes over budget and delayed. For example, purchasing decisions regarding infusion pumps are influenced by various stakeholder groups including medical experts (such as doctors and consultants), administrators (such as general managers and purchasing administrators), those with financial responsibilities, purchasing agents and of course certain direct government representatives, primary care trusts and other influential stakeholders.

Question
What are the implications for manufacturers and suppliers in order that they communicate effectively with this range of influencers?

Task
Draw up a list of communication tools and media that you might use to communicate your infusion pumps. Prioritise them and justify your decisions.

Many of the characteristics associated with consumer decision-making processes can be observed in the organisational context. However, organisational buyers make decisions that ultimately contribute to the achievement of corporate objectives. To make the necessary decisions a high volume of pertinent information is often required. This information needs to be relatively detailed and is normally presented in a rational and logical style. The needs of the buyers are many and complex and some may be personal. Goals, such as promotion and career advancement within the organisation, coupled with ego and employee satisfaction, combine to make organisational buying an important and complex task, one that requires professional training and the development of expertise if the role is to be performed optimally.

Buyclasses

Organisational buyers make decisions that vary with each buying situation and buyclass. Buyclasses, according to Robinson *et al.* (1967), comprise three types: new task, modified rebuy and straight rebuy (Table 3.2).

New task

As the name implies, the organisation is faced with a first-time buying situation. Risk is inevitably high at this point, and partly as a consequence there are a large number of decision participants. Each participant requires a lot of information and a relatively long period of time is required for the information to be assimilated and a decision to be made.

Modified rebuy

Having purchased a product, the organisation may request through its buyer that certain modifications be made to future purchases, for example adjustments to the specification of the product, further negotiation on price levels or perhaps the arrangement for alternative delivery patterns. Fewer people are involved in the decision process than in the new task situation.

Straight rebuy

In this situation, the purchasing department reorders on a routine basis, very often working from an approved list of suppliers. No other people are involved with the exercise until different suppliers attempt to change the environment in which the decision is made. For example, they may interrupt the procedure with a potentially better offer.

Readers may have noticed the strong resemblance to the extended, limited and routinised response identified earlier with respect to the consumer market.

Table 3.2 Main characteristics of the buyclasses

Buyclass	Degree of familiarity with the problem	Information requirements	Alternative solutions
New buy	The problem is fresh to the decision-makers	A great deal of information is required	Alternative solutions are unknown, all are considered new
Modified rebuy	The requirement is not new but is different from previous situations	More information is required but past experience is of use	Buying decision needs new solutions
Rebuy	The problem is identical to previous experiences	Little or no information is required	Alternative solutions not sought or required

Reference has been made on a number of occasions to organisational buyers, as if these people are the only representatives of an organisation to be involved with the purchase decision process. This is not the case, as very often a large number of people are involved in the purchase decision. This group is referred to as either the decision-making unit (DMU) or the buying centre.

Buying centres vary in size and composition in accordance with the nature of each individual task. Webster and Wind (1972) identified a number of people who make up the buying centre.

Users are people who not only initiate the purchase process but will use the product, once it has been acquired, and evaluate its performance. *Influencers* very often help set the technical specifications for the proposed purchase and assist the evaluation of alternative offerings by potential suppliers. *Deciders* are those who make purchasing decisions. In repeat buying activities the buyer may well also be the decider. However, it is normal practice to require that expenditure decisions involving sums over a certain financial limit be authorised by other, often senior, managers. *Buyers* (purchasing managers) select suppliers and manage the process whereby the required products are procured. As identified previously, buyers may not decide which product is to be purchased but they influence the framework within which the decision is made. *Gatekeepers* have the potential to control the type and flow of information to the organisation and the members of the buying centre. These gatekeepers may be technical personnel, secretaries or telephone switchboard operators.

The size and form of the buying centre is not static. It can vary according to the complexity of the product being considered and the degree of risk each decision is perceived to carry for the organisation. Different roles are required and adopted as the nature of the buying task changes with each new purchase situation (Bonoma, 1982). It is vital for seller organisations to identify members of the buying centre and to target and refine their messages to meet the needs of each member of the centre.

The task of the marketing communications manager and the corresponding sales team is to decide which key participants have to be reached, with which type of message, with what frequency and to what depth contact should be made. Just as with individual consumers, each member of the buying centre is an active problem-solver and processes information so that personal and organisational goals are achieved.

Buyphases

The organisational buying decision process consists of several stages or buyphases (Robinson *et al.*, 1967). The following sequence of six phases or events is particular to the new task buyclass. Many of these buyphases are ignored or compressed when either of the other two buyclasses are encountered.

Need/problem recognition

Products or services are purchased because of two main events (Cravens and Woodruff, 1983). Difficulties may be encountered first as a result of a need to solve problems, such as a stock-out or new government regulations, and, secondly, as a response to opportunities to improve performance or enter new markets. Essentially, the need/recognition phase is the identification of a gap. This is the gap between the benefits an organisation has now and the benefits it would like to have. For example, when a photocopier breaks down or fails to meet the needs of the organisation, the communication benefits the copier offers are missed by the users. This gap can be bridged by getting the machine mended, by using a different machine on a temporary basis or by buying a new machine that provides the range of benefits required.

Product specification

As a result of identifying a problem and the size of the gap, influencers and users can determine the desired characteristics of the product needed to resolve the problem. This may take the form of a general description or may require a much more detailed analysis and the creation of a specification for a particular product. What sort of photocopier is required? What is it expected to achieve? How many documents should it copy per minute? Is a collator or tray required? This is an important part of the process, because if it is executed properly it will narrow the supplier search and save on the costs associated with evaluation prior to a final decision.

Supplier and product search

At this stage the buyer actively seeks organisations who can supply the necessary product. There are two main issues at this point. Will the product reach the required performance standards and will it match the specification? Secondly, will the potential supplier meet the other organisational requirements? In most circumstances organisations review the market and their internal sources of information and arrive at a decision that is based on rational criteria.

Organisations work wherever possible to reduce uncertainty and complexity. By working with others who are known, of whom the organisation has direct experience and who can be trusted, risk and uncertainty can be reduced substantially. This highlights another reason why many organisations seek relational exchanges and operate within established networks and seek to support each other.

The quest for suppliers and products may be a short task for the buyer; however, if the established network cannot provide a solution, the buying organisation has to seek new suppliers, and hence new networks, to be able to identify and short-list appropriate supplier organisations.

Evaluation of proposals

Depending upon the complexity and value of the potential order(s), the proposal is a vital part of the communication plan and should be prepared professionally. The proposals of the short-listed organisations are reviewed in the context of two main criteria: the product specification and the evaluation of the supplying organisation. If the organisation is already a part of the network, little search and review time need be allocated. If the proposed supplier is new to the organisation a review may be necessary to establish whether it will be appropriate (in terms of price, delivery and service) and whether there is the potential for a long-term relationship or whether this is a single purchase that is unlikely to be repeated.

Supplier selection

The buying centre will undertake a supplier analysis and use a variety of criteria depending upon the particular type of item sought. This selection process takes place in the light of the comments made in the previous section. A further useful perspective is to view supplier organisations as a continuum, from reliance on a single source to the use of a wide variety of suppliers of the same product.

Jackson (1985) proposed that organisations might buy a product from a range of different suppliers, in other words a range of multiple sources are maintained (a practice of many government departments). She labelled this approach 'always a share', as several suppliers are given the opportunity to share the business available to the buying centre. The major disadvantage is that this approach fails to drive cost as low as possible, as the discounts derived from volume sales are not achieved. The advantage to the buying centre is that a relatively small investment is required and little risk is entailed in following such a strategy.

At the other end of the continuum are organisations that only use a single-source supplier. All purchases are made from the single source until circumstances change to such a degree that the buyer's needs are no longer being satisfied. Jackson referred to these organisations as 'lost for good', because once a relationship with a new organisation has been developed, they are lost for good to the original supplier. An increasing number of organisations are choosing to enter alliances with a limited number or even single-source suppliers. The objective is to build a long-term relationship, work together to build quality and help each other achieve their goals. Outsourcing manufacturing activities for non-core activities has increased, and this has moved the focus of communications from an internal to an external perspective.

Evaluation

The order is written against the selected supplier and immediately the supplier is monitored and performance is evaluated against such diverse criteria as responsiveness to enquiries and modifications to the specification and timing of delivery. When the product is delivered it may reach the stated specification but fail to satisfy the original need. This is a case where the specification needs to be rewritten before any future orders are placed.

Organisational buying has shifted from a one-to-one dyadic encounter, salesperson to buyer, to a position where a buying team meets a selling team. The skills associated with this process are different and are becoming much more sophisticated, and the demands on both buyers and sellers are more pronounced. The processes of buying and selling are complex and interactive.

Readers are referred to the section at the end of Chapter 1 in which the differences between consumer and organisational marketing communications was highlighted. These differences reflect the various contextual issues that frame both the consumer and organisational environments. The nature of the environments, the tasks involved and the overall need of the recipients for particular types of information are some of the principal contextual issues.

Summary

In order to help consolidate your understanding of attitudes, behaviour and decision-making behaviour, here are the key points summarised against each of the learning objectives:

1 Explain the nature of perception and describe how marketing communications can be used to influence the way people perceive and position brands

Perception is concerned with how individuals see and make sense of their environment. It is about the selection, organisation and interpretation of stimuli by individuals so that they can understand their world. The effectiveness of marketing communications can be improved substantially if the elements of the marketing communications mix are designed to empathise with the perceptive view of buyers.

2 Describe the key components of attitudes and explain ways in which marketing communications can be used to influence attitudes

Attitudes are predispositions, shaped through experience, to respond in an anticipated way to an object or situation. Attitudes are learned through past experiences and serve as a link between thoughts and behaviour. Attitudes are hypothetical constructs, and they are considered to consist of three components: a cognitive or learning component, an affective or feeling element and a conative or action component.

Attitudes can be changed by using marketing communications to influence one or more of the three components.

3 Set out ideas concerning the nature of perceived risk and to relate ways in which marketing communications can be used to alleviate such uncertainty

Risk is perceived because the buyer has little or no experience of the performance of the product or the decision process associated with the purchase. Five main types of risk are normally observed, all which vary in intensity according to the individual, the product category and context. These are performance, social, ego, financial and functional risks.

A major task of marketing communications is to reduce levels of perceived risk. By providing extensive and relevant information a buyer's risks can be reduced substantially.

4 Appreciate the nature of involvement and to explain how marketing communications can be used to reflect high and low involvement situations

Involvement is about the degree of personal relevance and risk perceived by consumers when making a particular purchase decision. Involvement is about the way in which information is processed and the way in which people make decisions about product purchases. We have established in the preceding section that there are two main types of involvement, high and low. These two types lead directly to two different uses of marketing communications. In decisions where there is high involvement, attitude precedes trial behaviour. In low-involvement cases this position is reversed.

5 Explain how marketing communications can be used to complement the purchase decision-making processes adopted by organisations

Organisations can be observed to make purchase decisions in different ways, according to experience and product complexity. With many different people involved in organisational purchase decisions, a seller's marketing communications need to be adapted to suit the needs of the different participants and the experience the organisation has of purchasing in the product category.

Review questions

1. Name the dimensions of the awareness grid.
2. What are the three elements of perception used for processing stimuli?
3. Make brief notes about the characteristics of each of the attitude components.
4. Explain how marketing communications can be used to change attitudes.
5. What are buyclasses and buying centres?
6. What are EPS, LPS and RRB?
7. Describe the elements that constitute perceived risk.
8. Describe the high- and low-involvement decision-making processes.
9. Explain how marketing communications works with regard to attitude development in low and high involvement situations.
10. How might a salesperson utilise knowledge about the buying centre?

References

Anon (2010) North America Effies: Hyundai – Assurance, *Effie Worldwide*, retrieved 10 July 2010 from www.effie.org

Bonoma, T.V. (1982) Major sales: who really does the buying? *Harvard Business Review* (May/June), 113.

Cohen, J. and Basu, K. (1987) Alternative models of categorisation, *Journal of Consumer Research* (March), 455–472.

Cravens, D. and Woodruff, R. (1983) *Marketing*. Reading, MA: Addison-Wesley.

de Chernatony L. (1993) The seven building blocks of brands, *Management Today* (March), 66–67.

Dahl, D.W., Frankenberger, D. and Manchanda, R.V. (2003) Does it pay to shock? *Journal of Advertising Research*, 43(3), September, 268–280.

Foley, C., Greene, J. and Cultra, M. (2009) Effective ads in a digital age, *Admap*, 503 (March), retrieved 2 June 2010 from www.warc.com/articlecentre

Harris, G. (1987) The implications of low involvement theory for advertising effectiveness, *International Journal of Advertising*, 6, 207–221.

Heath, R. (2000) Low-involvement processing, *Admap* (March), 14–13.

Jackson, B. (1985) Build customer relationships that last, *Harvard Business Review*, 33(3), 120–128.

Javalgi, R., Thomas, E. and Rao, S. (1992) US travellers' perception of selected European destinations, *European Journal of Marketing*, 26(7), 45–64.

Jukes, M. (2009) Creative review: Comparethemarket.com *revolutionmagazine.com*, 26 February 2009, retrieved 3 November 2010 from www.brandrepublic.com/features/888761/Creative-review-Comparethemarketcom/?DCMP=ILC-SEARCH

Lasn, K. (1999) *Culture Jam: The Uncooling of America*. New York: Eagle Brook.

Moran, W. (1990) Brand preference and the perceptual frame, *Journal of Advertising Research* (October/November), 9–16.

Okin, G. and Robothan-Jones, R. (2007) Weetabix – The Weetabix Week: turning a barrier into a benefit, IPA Effectiveness Awards, 2007, retrieved 3 November 2010 from www.warc.com/ArticleCenter/Default.asp?CType=A&AID=WORDSEARCH86130&Tab=A

Ranjbariyan, B. and Mahmoodi, S. (2009) The Influencing Factors in Ad Processing: Cognitive vs. Affective Appeals, *Journal of International Marketing and Marketing Research*, 34(3), 129–140.

Robinson, P.J., Faris, C.W. and Wind, Y. (1967) *Industrial Buying and Creative Marketing*. Boston, MA: Allyn & Bacon.

Rossiter, J.R. and Percy, L. (1997) *Advertising Communications & Promotion Management*, 2nd edn. New York: McGraw-Hill.

Rossiter, J.R., Percy, L. and Donovan, R.J. (1991) A better advertising planning grid, *Journal of Advertising Research* (October/November), 11–21.

Settle, R.B. and Alreck, P. (1989) Reducing buyers' sense of risk, *Marketing Communications* (January), 34–40.

Stone, R.N. and Gronhaug, K. (1993) Perceived risk: further considerations for the marketing discipline, *European Journal of Marketing*, 27(3), 39–50.

Webster, F.E. and Wind, Y. (1972) *Organizational Buying Behavior*. Englewood Cliffs, NJ: Prentice-Hall.

Winterman, D. (2007) Just returning your call … to the UK, *BBC News Magazine* Wednesday, 14 February 2007. Retrieved 15 January 2008 from http://news.bbc.co.uk/1/hi/magazine/6353491.stm

Minicase 1.1 — Because it works!

Lynn Sudbury: Liverpool John Moores University

The array of beauty lotions and potions that claim to ward off wrinkles and other signs of ageing that women – and increasingly men – can choose from, is extensive. Indeed, in an overall industry reputed to be worth £25 billion world-wide and £6.2bn in Britain, Boots N°7 'Protect & Perfect' serum, retailing at £16.75 for 30ml and being on the shelves for three years already, was an unlikely contender for the title 'Magic Cream' that was to spark a wave of near hysteria that reached as far as the USA and Australia. Yet, that's exactly what happened after the product was featured on BBC's science programme *Horizon*.

The *Horizon* programme featured Lesley Regan, a 50-year-old professor of obstetrics and gynaecology at St Mary's Hospital in London, who went in search of 'The Holy Grail' – otherwise known as an anti-ageing product that scientifically worked. Her search led her to the cream perfected by scientist Steve Barton and his team in Nottingham. Mr Barton has been using the serum for several years, and had conducted his own trials with what he described as 'fantastic' results. However, it was only when the product was examined by a team of expert dermatologists at Manchester University that the claims became more believable. Professor Chris Griffiths, who heads the team at Manchester, explained that although they were initially sceptical, their independent research spanning 10 months and investigating a range of anti-ageing creams – many of which retail for far more than £17 – scientifically proved that N°7's Protect & Perfect actually worked. The cream was found to contain protecting and renewing agents associated with the production of collagen and elastin, as well as silicone and antioxidants, and was compared to prescription drugs used to treat severe acne and sun damage to skin. Professor Griffiths was reported to say 'At both basic science and clinical levels Boots N°7 Protect & Perfect has been shown scientifically to repair photo-aged skin and improve the fine wrinkles associated with photo-ageing.'

Boots had expected demand to rise once the programme had aired, and had prepared by shipping in 21 weeks supply of the product prior to the *Horizon* programme. Yet, despite the fact that the serum was only shown on camera for a few seconds, within 24 hours of the programme being aired, sales rose by 2,000 per cent, the shelves in Boots up and down the country were empty, waiting lists reportedly comprising four figures were opened, Boots' web store received 4,000 requests in one evening, and within days the product was being traded on eBay for up to £100. Some stores reported women charging behind counters, convinced that there would be hidden supplies there, others raced each other down aisles to get to the 'Magic Cream', and one store reported a near-riot when a single customer bought up their entire stock.

These events were only the beginning of the frenzy, however. While Boots switched most of their production to the Protect & Perfect line in an effort to cope with demand, the shortage fuelled further demand, as the news of the cream spread and more and more people wanted to buy it. The serum was a major conversation topic among mums outside schools and between friends. When stores received stock, they would telephone customers on the waiting lists telling them to be quick, and these customers would tell their friends, so stocks continued to disappear from shelves almost as fast as they could be filled, despite the product then being limited to one purchase per customer. Media reports of queues developing in the early hours outside Boots stores when stocks were expected fuelled even more demand. Many men also waited outside stores from 5a.m., some of them claiming to be under strict instructions from females to get their hand on the cream. Others, however, admitted to wanting to try the cream for themselves. Young girls queued up, some of them to buy for their mothers who had been trying to get hold of the cream for some time; others because they had heard from older friends that it actually worked.

Protect & Perfect was also big news on the web. Blogging gave individuals an outlet to share their thoughts, while an extraordinary number of online beauty forums such as 'Hey, Dollface!' focused on the serum. The 'Beauty Community Forum' of the magazine *Good Housekeeping*, for example, which has almost 44,000 members and can have many non-member guests online at any one time as well, contained entries from scores of women sharing their experiences, beliefs and knowledge about the product. Many asked for advice on how to get hold of the cream, and the magazine's Beauty Director was asking women to share their results with the forum after using the product for at least 8 weeks – the time she believed it took to see results. The product even featured on plastic surgery blogs, and on-line discussions about the brand could be found from doctors in Australia to beauty editors in America.

Not all communication about the brand was positive. Both the *Guardian* and the *Independent on Sunday* contained pieces from journalists pouring scorn on the women who queued half the night for the product, labelling their reaction as 'madness' and 'a case study of human perversity... another instance of the growing phenomenon we might call hysteria marketing'. Others, of course, might just call it word-of-mouth.

Questions

1. Discuss the reasons why in the first instance the *Horizon* programme caused such a reaction among consumers.
2. Identify the opinion formers and opinion leaders in the case.
3. Discuss the variables that influenced the word-of-mouth communications around *Protect & Perfect*.

Minicase 1.2 Unlocking the secrets of the male shopper

Richard Godfrey: School of Management, University of Leicester

Men have been a marketing afterthought for more than a century. Starting in the late 1800s, when *Good Housekeeping* and *Cosmopolitan* began teaching generations of women how to be Type A wives and mothers, brand managers painted a giant bull's-eye on the female consumer. They have taken relentless aim ever since. 'He makes. She buys.' That's the calculation that turned women into shoppers and men into providers.

(Byrne, 2006)

All this began to change following the Second World War, and has quickened apace in the last 30 years. Men are now actively forced/encouraged into a way of being in which they too have become increasingly objectified, measured through their own practices of consumption: by what they wear; their body image; their material possessions etc. This can be seen through the emergence and spread of men's magazines, High Street stores and forms of popular entertainment that encourage men to take greater interest in their appearance, to adopt consumption-led lifestyles.

The importance of men as (a market of) consumers has been marked by numerous attempts at classification and careful targeting by marketers. A recent issue of *Business Week* (4 September 2006) ran with the cover story 'Secrets of the Male Shopper' in which Nanette Byrne attempted to categorise male shopping habits into five distinct groups, based on a range of shared traits, attitudes and consuming behaviours. The first, the 'Metrosexual', who might be conceived of as the successor to the 1980s yuppie, is the quintessential 'feminised' male consumer. For him, consumption is all about style and the completion of self through designer brands and services. Against this she situates the 'Retrosexual', rejecting all things feminine, and reasserting a notion of masculinity through consumption of alcohol, sports (viewing) and junk food. There is also 'Modern Man', called by others 'New Man', who sits at something of a halfway point between the metro- and retrosexual. He has a vested interest in his appearance but does not subscribe to some of the vanity practices of the metrosexual: 'Moisturizer and hair gel are perfectly ordinary to him; a manicure is a tougher call' (Byrne, 2006). Then there is the 'Maturiteen' – the current cohort of teenagers – far more sophisticated in their consumption habits than previous teen generations and, thanks to their literacy with the Internet and other forms of telecommunications, far more influential over family decision-making than their predecessors. Finally, there is the 'Dad', for the most part something of a marketing undesirable but with new-found interest in fatherhood, increasingly the target of marketing communications. Byrne cites the example of the Bugaboo baby stroller, with its black and chrome frame, front and rear suspension and off-road wheels, as indicative of the targeted offerings now made towards such men.

Despite differences among these trait-based typologies, these men share a number of consuming habits. Perhaps one of the most significant of these is the increased attention paid to physical appearance. Most notably this occurs in relation to increased care and attention paid to one's body in terms of grooming, body modification and in the selection of clothing and accessories (of course, through these processes and practices, such body routines become 'masculinised'; that is to say, they become legitimate forms of masculine behaviour).

This changing attitude towards and among men has resulted in the rapid growth of a range of 'self-presentation' industries including fashion, cosmetic surgery and, markedly, in the market for men's grooming products, which was estimated to be worth more than £780 million in 2006. This market is now saturated with offerings all vying for a slice of this lucrative pie. Reflecting prevailing trends in the female grooming markets, many of the competitors in this industry position and communicate their brands using common (masculine) themes, such as use of sex appeal (especially at the higher end of the market), aspirational celebratory endorsers (such as Gillette's use, since 2004, of David Beckham), and, in the packaging of their goods, through the use of masculine colours and materials such as strong blues, black, red and brushed steel or silver. This makes for a cramped and, at times, undifferentiated drugstore shelf.

However, against this trend a number of competitors, recognising that not all men are alike, have started to move away from such standardised positioning in order to reflect the increasingly fragmented male audience. Lynx, for example, has focused on the social benefits of its brand. By combining sex with humour, campaigns over the last few years, such as the highly successful 'Pulse' campaign have sought to almost parody the communications activities of more exclusive brands. The Pulse ad demonstrated that even a 'nerdy' guy, with little going for him, can ooze sex appeal and get the girls, thanks to the 'Lynx effect'! The tongue-in-cheek ad, which sought to break down some of the established norms of communicating in this industry, not only proved a commercial success but also spawned a new dance craze and saw the track 'Make Luv', which was used in the ad, re-enter the singles chart at number one. The spread of the ad into popular culture was invaluable in helping to reposition a brand that had come to be associated, primarily, with the declining 'lad' culture of the 1990s.

Elsewhere, 'King of Shaves' has attempted to side-step many of the brands that adopt a more aspirational appeal by focusing on the functional (or technical) value of the brand. Playing on male traits that turn around the control and mastery of technology it deploys overt masculine language in its branding such as in the use of the slogan: 'The World's Best shaving and skincare "software"'. It offers brands such as the XCD Defender, where XCD stands for 'Enhance', 'Camouflage', 'Defend' and also offers a website offering 'expert' shaving tips and techniques.

A new entrant, Bulldog, launched in 2007, perhaps going after the 'Modern Man' or 'Dad's offers a range of grooming products using all natural ingredients but at supermarket prices. As noted in a recent edition of *Marketing Week*:

> They decided that they would not pitch their brand at an exclusive, niche market but instead aim Bulldog at mainstream consumers, giving them, they claim, a natural choice at a reasonable price for the first time. They gave the brand a strong masculine identity, taking a risk with the potentially polarising name Bulldog. Clean, white packaging with a bold typeface was chosen to make the range look markedly different from the market leaders such as Lynx, Nivea, Gillette and L'Oréal.
>
> (Jack, 2008)

With the spread of the tweenager phenomenon and boys as young as 10 or 12 now using grooming products, these consuming behaviours look set to continue well into the future.

References

Byrne, N. (2006) 'Secrets of the Male Shopper', *Business Week*, 4 September 2006. Last accessed on 14 March 2008.

Jack, L. (2008) 'Analysis: Bulldog aims to see off men's skincare competition', *Marketing Week*, 13 March 2008. Last accessed on 14 March 2008.

Questions

1. Identify the social and cultural changes that have led to the rise of the male shopper.
2. How might an understanding of 'perception theory' be used in the targeting of male consumers?
3. Identify the different male consumer typologies outlined in the case. What are their key personality traits? How could a marketing communicator use this information in order to position a brand?

Minicase 1.3 — Helping Hands

Charities such as Oxfam, Action Aid and Save the Children all provide aid on an international basis. Their mission is to provide a range of support services in areas that do not have sufficient resources, or where natural disasters such as floods and earthquakes cause large-scale poverty and starvation. All these charities rely mostly on voluntary donations to fund their activities.

Helping Hands is a worldwide charity (based in the UK) to promote the wellbeing of communities through education programmes about hygiene and diet. Helping Hands also aims to improve the lives and prospects of its beneficiaries through environmental development programmes.

In 2009–10, Helping Hands' voluntary income was £72.5 million. This was made up of money from the following sources:

Source of voluntary income	£m value
Emergency appeals	23.0
Donations/gifts	20.1
Government and other grants	13.3
Helping Hand Week	10.6
Legacies*	4.3
Other income	1.2
Total	£72.5m

* Money received from people after they have died.

Out of every £1 donated, approximately 20 per cent is spent driving fresh donations, with 10 per cent spent on administration and the remaining 70 per cent distributed across the various projects that are supported by the charity. Inevitably there are some tensions and negative attitudes between donors and charity managers concerning the distribution of the funds raised. The primary concern is that too much is spent on administration rather than supporting good causes.

Traditional charity supporters tend to be high-income women aged over 65, but there are indications that charity-giving has reached saturation. This is due partly to the demands arising from single disaster appeals, and partly to the need to support on-going projects around the world. Interestingly, there is a significant problem in encouraging younger people to donate regularly to charitable causes.

Charity-based marketing communications need to fulfil several goals, but two of the more important concern the maintenance of brand awareness (and associated brand values) and encouraging people to make donations.

Creating brand awareness

Maintaining brand awareness can be a problem, especially for a charity such as Helping Hands. The name suggests to some people, wrongly, that donations are spent on medical aid and equipment, or that aid only goes to poorer regions. To help overcome such misconceptions, the well-established annual event Helping Hands Week is used. This mass-market appeal is targeted at everyone in the UK and aims to raise awareness about Helping Hands and explain the work it does, as well as to collect donations.

Public relations and advertising are important parts of the charity's communications mix during this period. In 2009, Helping Hands spent over £2 million on media advertising. A well-known bank provided additional supportive press advertising. Helping Hands provides an online TV channel via their website, whilst celebrities are used to attract attention and provide publicity about overseas projects. Advertising messages are carefully designed to deliver key propositions, and television, press, radio and the Internet are the key media used to convey these messages to mass audiences, as well as to predetermined segments such as the youth market.

Driving donations

To drive donations, three main methods have traditionally been used: direct marketing, door-drops and street fund-raising. Income is also raised by selling branded merchandise such as bags, T-shirts, mugs, books, and other resource materials. These are promoted via a catalogue and can be purchased over the telephone or through the Helping Hands website.

Direct marketing, using direct mail and telemarketing, has been at the forefront of fund-raising activities. However, research by Nielsen in 2006 shows that 30 per cent of direct mail sent by charities is never opened, compared with the direct mail industry average of 22 per cent. An increasing number of people in the UK are signing up to the Mailing Preference Service in order to avoid receiving unsolicited direct mail. Some people are closing their letter boxes so that they cannot receive door-drops, whilst there appears to be growing public resistance to people waving collecting tins in the high street. Consumer resistance to the overuse of these techniques has become a problem, and because of the increasing number of charity appeals and demands made on individuals, 'compassion fatigue', a reluctance to make a charitable donation, is now quite common.

Emotionally based advertising appeals, based on guilt or humour, are well-used message approaches in many charity campaigns, but these can also have a negative effect on the target audience, however worthy the cause may be. In particular, younger audiences tend to switch off and disengage from charity-based communications. As a result of these developments, charities have been forced to consider fresh approaches to encourage donations.

One of the new and very successful initiatives is referred to as *ethical gift-giving*. This involves buying animals or farming equipment from a catalogue for a villager in a developing country, in the name of a friend or family member. One of the most popular charity Christmas gifts is a goat from the *Oxfam Unwrapped* catalogue and website. The *Lifetime Gift* scheme run by Helping Hands raised £1 million in 2004, £3 million in 2007 and over £3.5 million in 2009, at a time of recession and increasing hardship.

Activities that members of the youth market *do* like to support are major events such as music concerts supporting LIVE 8, and more recently, the Make Poverty History campaigns. These events represent 'added value' in the sense that those attending are being 'entertained' as well as supporting the charities or causes involved. This segment is also willing to engage with cause-related marketing, that is, making product or service purchases where a percentage of the payment goes to charity.

Sources: The above data has been based on a real-life organisation, but details have been changed for assessment purposes and do not reflect current management practices.

Questions

1. How might an understanding of engagement impact on any charity's marketing communications?
2. Using the DRIP framework, explain how charities such as Helping Hands, use marketing communications to carry out different communication tasks.
3. How can Helping Hands use marketing communications to try to change the attitudes of people who currently do not donate money to the charity?

Chapter 9
Integrated marketing communications

Integrated marketing communications are more likely to occur when organisations attempt to interact with their various internal and external audiences. The communication mix used in any interaction should be audience-centred and internally consistent with the organisation's objectives and strategies. Target audiences should perceive these communications and associated cues as relevant, likeable, timely and of value.

Aims and learning objectives

The aims of this chapter are to explore the nature and characteristics of integrated marketing communications and to understand the complexities associated with developing and implementing this form of marketing communications.

The learning objectives of this chapter are to:

1. introduce the concept of integrated marketing communications (IMC) and explore what it is that is integrated;
2. understand the different perspectives of IMC;
3. consider the background and reasons for the development and interest in IMC;
4. explore some of the issues associated with managing and implementing IMC;
5. explain variants of the IMC concept: media-neutral planning and open planning approaches;
6. consider how the structures and frameworks of advertising and communication agencies might need to change so that they are better able to work with IMC;
7. examine ideas concerning an incremental approach to IMC.

For an applied interpretation see J. Graham Spickett-Jones' MiniCase entitled *IMC – richer consumer engagement* at the end of this chapter.

Introduction

To appreciate the essence of integrated marketing communications (IMC) it is helpful to understand its origins and the key factors that have helped shape its development. For many years agencies and clients believed that to deliver messages to particular audiences it was necessary to use specific tools of the communications mix. At the time it was a common belief that to achieve specific communication effects *on* buyers it was necessary to use particular tools. So for example, clients were recommended to use advertising to create awareness, sales promotions to generate immediate sales uplifts and public relations to create interest and goodwill towards a brand. This view held that each tool has specific characteristics and particular communication abilities. As a result clients were required to deal with a variety of functionally different and independent agencies in order to complete their communication requirements with their various audiences.

> It was a common belief that to achieve specific communication effects *on* buyers it was necessary to use particular tools.

This 'specialisation' resulted in a proliferation of advertising agencies and the development of sales promotion houses. Public relations specialists stood off from any direct association with marketing. Personal selling had already evolved as a discrete function within organisations. This approach was also legitimised by the development of trade associations and professional management groups (for example, the Institute of Practitioners in Advertising (UK) and the Institute of Sales Promotion (UK)) that seek to endorse, advance, protect and legitimise the actions of their professions and members. One of the outcomes of this silo perspective and functional development of the marketing communications industry has been entrenchment and the inevitable opposition to change.

Now that clients have begun to re-orient their communications away from mass media approaches to increased levels of interaction with customers, the structural inadequacies of the marketing communication industry have served to constrain them. IMC has emerged partially as a reaction to this structural inadequacy and the realisation by clients that their communication needs can (and should) be achieved more efficiently and effectively than previously. In other words, just as power has moved from brand manufacturers to multiple retailers and now to consumers, so power is moving from agencies to clients.

This trend away from traditional communication strategies based on mass communications, directing generalised messages to huge segmented audiences has played a part in the development of IMC. Contemporary strategies are based more on personalised, customer-oriented and technology-driven approaches, and are often referred to as integrated marketing communications (IMC). Duncan and Everett (1993) recall that this new, largely media-oriented approach, has been referred to variously as *orchestration, whole egg* and *seamless communication*. More recent notions involve the explicit incorporation of corporate communications, reflected in titles such as integrated marketing and integrated communications (see Cornelissen (2000)).

> More recent notions involve the explicit incorporation of corporate communications.

It is interesting that the rapid development of direct marketing initiatives since the second half of the 1980s and the impact the Internet has made have coincided with a move towards what has become regarded as integrated marketing communications. A further significant development has been the shift in marketing philosophies, from transaction to relationship marketing, as introduced in Chapter 1 and considered in more detail in Chapter 7.

What is to be integrated?

The notion that some aspects of marketing communications should be integrated begs the question, what is it that needs to be integrated? While the origins of IMC might be found in

Figure 9.1 Elements for integration

the prevailing structural conditions and the needs of particular industry participants, an understanding of what elements should be integrated in order to achieve IMC needs to be established.

The problem with answering this question is that unless there is an agreement about what IMC is then identifying appropriate elements is far from easy, practical or in any one's best interests. Figure 9.1 shows some of the elements that need integrating.

The following represents some of the fundamental elements, but readers are advised to consider some of the other issues that have been raised in this chapter before confirming their views about this stimulating yet relatively young concept.

Communication tools

> The key visual triggers used in advertising should be replicated across the range of promotional tools used.

One of the early and more popular views of IMC was that the messages conveyed by each of the 'promotional' tools should be harmonised in order that audiences perceive a consistent set of meanings within the messages they receive. One interpretation of this perspective, is that the key visual triggers (design, colours, form and tag line) used in advertising should be replicated across the range of promotional tools used, including point of purchase and the sales force. At another level, integration is about bringing together the communication tools (Pitta *et al.* 2006). One such combination is the closer alliance of advertising with public relations. Increasing audience fragmentation means that it is more difficult to locate target audiences and communicate with them in a meaningful way. By utilising the power of public relations to get advertisements talked about, what the trade refer to as media equivalents, so a form of communications consistency, or integration to some, becomes possible.

The rapid development of direct marketing approaches has helped some organisations bring together the different tools such that they undertake more precise roles and reinforce each other. For example, the use of direct mail and telemarketing to follow through on an ad campaign is common place, but now web-enabled communications, customer care centres and sales promotions can be linked together through database applications, and all are designed to communicate the same core message.

Integrated crumbs

Two of McVitie's core brands are Hobnobs and Milk Chocolate Digestives and a campaign was required to reinforce the credentials of the McVitie's umbrella brand with consumers and to convey the message that their biscuits are made 100 per cent from UK wheat and oats.

To deliver this message they developed an integrated campaign based around the core message 'share the goodness'.

The campaign, which was advertising-led, consisted primarily of a £2m poster. In addition they used direct marketing to reinforce brand values. Public relations were used to support the campaign. Here the goal was to create media interest and comment about the brand. This was achieved through an art exhibition held at Leeds, Bristol and Birmingham city centres. The exhibition featured two 5ft bales of wheat covered with Milk Chocolate Digestives wrappers.

The events drew extensive broadcast and print media interest and the whole campaign saw sales rise a massive 9 per cent compared to the same period in the previous year.

Source: Cowlett (2007).

Question
Is this an example of integrated marketing communications or just good practice?

Task
Which other tools and media could have been used in the McVitie's campaign?

Messages

A further interpretation, at a deeper level, is that the theme and set of core messages used in any campaign should first be determined and then deployed as an integrated whole across the communication mix (sometimes referred to as synergy). One of the differences is the recognition that mass media advertising is not always the only way to launch consumer or business-to-business promotional activities, and that a consideration of the most appropriate mix of communication tools and media might be a better starting point when formulating campaigns.

> The theme and set of core messages used in any campaign should first be determined and then deployed as an integrated whole across the communication mix.

Another perspective of IMC, provided by Duncan and Moriarty (1998), is that stakeholders (including customers) automatically integrate brand messages. This suggests that as long as the gap between the different messages (in content and meaning) are acceptable, then management's task is to manage the process and seek to narrow these gaps that may be perceived.

What runs through both these approaches is the belief that above-the-line and below-the-line communications need to be moulded into one cohesive bundle, from which tools can be selected and deployed as conditions require.

Marketing mix

The elements of the marketing mix, however configured, also need to be integrated because they also communicate (Smith, 1996). The price and associated values, the product, in terms of the quality, design and tangible attributes, the manner and efficiency of the service delivery people and where and how it is made available, for example the location, web site, customer contact centres, retailer/dealer reputation and overall service quality need to be perceived by customers as a coordinated and consistent whole. These touch points with brands are aspects of a consumer's brand experience and are used to develop images that through

> The elements of the marketing mix, however configured, need to be integrated.

time may shape brand reputations. Traditionally the marketing mix was expected to deliver the brand proposition. Now it is expected that all these elements will be coordinated to maximise impact and enable customers to experience the brand through pre-, actual and post-product use.

Branding

> Brands are themselves a form of integration.

Brands are themselves a form of integration. This means that internally organisations need to be sufficiently coordinated so that the brand is perceived externally as consistent and uniform. However, this proposition is based on the view that a brand is prepared and delivered for a single target audience but audience and media fragmentation make this task more challenging. Audience sizes are shrinking, which means that in many situations a single audience is no longer economically viable. Brands therefore, need to appeal to a number of different audiences (White, 2000) and to do this it is necessary to develop brands that appeal to diverse consumer groups. White refers to these new brands as 'chameleon' brands. They are characterised by their ability to adapt to different situations (audiences and media) yet retain a core proposition that provides a form of continuity and recognition. For example, a top of the range music system may be seen by the owner as prestigious and technically superb, by a guest at a party as ostentatiously outrageous and overpriced and by a friend as a product of clever design and marketing. All three might have developed their attitudes through different sources (e.g. different print media, exhibitions, the Internet, retail stores, word-of-mouth) but all agree that the brand has a common set of values and associations that are important to each of them.

ViewPoint 9.2 Integration to promote conservation

When ZSL London Zoo launched Gorilla Kingdom in 2007 it used a wide range of communication tools and media and had to integrate their use if their sales and communication objectives were to be achieved.

Advertising, for example, outdoor such as billboards and London Underground poster sites.
Sales promotion, for example, included train promotion offers to encourage visitors from outside London.
Direct marketing, for example, direct mail to groups within the travel trade industry.
Public relations, for example, press releases, events, receptions for journalists and sponsorship of radio programme Magic FM.
Personal selling, for example, to people in the travel trade.

By integrating them within the new ZSL London Zoo brand and by timing and coordinating with each other, this marketing communications achieved significant impact and achieved its goals.

Question
How do we know a campaign is integrated?

Task
ZSL London Zoo subsequently launched the new Blackburn Aviary. Make brief notes about how would you use marketing communications to assist the launch.

The presentation of chameleon brands requires high levels of integration, a need to develop a series of innovative messages based around a core proposition. The use of a single ad execution needs to be replaced by multiple executions delivered through a variety of media, each complementing and reinforcing the core brand proposition. This means that the audience is more likely to be surprised or reminded of the brand (and its essence) through a series of refreshingly interesting messages, thereby raising the probability that the likeability factor (see Chapter 17) will be strengthened, along with the brand and all relevant associations.

A further dimension of the branding factor concerns the role of corporate brands and issues of corporate communications. Should these be integrated with product brand communications, and if so what are the branding strategies that should be followed?

Strategy

IMC is regarded by some as a means of using the tools of the communication mix in a more efficient and synergistic manner. At some level this can be true but IMC requires a deeper understanding of how and where messages are created. At a strategic level, IMC has its roots in the overall business strategy of an organisation. Using Porter's (1980) generic strategies, if a low-cost strategy (e.g. Asda) is being pursued, it makes sense to complement the strategy by using messages that either stress any price advantage that customers might benefit from or at least do not suggest extravagance or luxury. If using a differentiation focus strategy (e.g. Waitrose), price should not figure in any of the messages and greater emphasis should be placed on particular attributes that convey the added value and enable clear positioning. There is no right way (or formula) to establish IMC but there is a need to recognise that it is a developmental exercise and that it should have a strategic orientation as well as strategic outputs.

> There is no right way (or formula) to establish IMC.

Employees

The next element that should be integrated concerns the recognition that IMC cannot be sustained unless it is supported by all customer-facing employees. It is generally agreed that all employees should adopt a customer focus and 'live' the brand. While this can be achieved partially through the use of training courses and in-house documentation (including electronic forms), this usually requires a change of culture and that means a longer-term period of readjustment and the adoption of new techniques, procedures and ways of thinking and behaving.

Once the internal reorientation has begun (not completed), it is possible to take the message to external audiences. As long as they can see that employees are starting to act in different ways and do care about them as customers and do know what they are talking about in support of the products and services offered, then it is likely that customers (and other stakeholders) will be supportive. IMC should be concerned with blending internal and external messages so that there is clarity, consistency and reinforcement of the organisation's (or brand's) core proposition.

ViewPoint 9.3 'Try something integrated today'

The development and launch of Sainsbury's highly successful 'Try something new today' campaign, is regarded by many as a good example of a form of integrated marketing communications. The root of the campaign was in the business strategy, one which aimed to boost sales by £2.5bn by March 2008. At a store level this was translated into getting shoppers to put an extra £1.40 into their shopping baskets on each visit to a Sainsbury's store.

From this strategic goal the communications strategy took shape. From a positioning based on 'Making life taste better' to one which read, 'Try something new today', the £10m campaign, led by Jamie Oliver, sought to awake shoppers from what Sainsbury's referred to as 'Sleep Shopping', where people tend to buy the same products on a routine basis, to one where they are prepared to experiment a little.

The strength of the basic idea enabled the message to be used in various media, across channels and adapted for different target segments. Not only was the campaign rooted in business strategy but it also encouraged staff participation.

Staff were given two days' training and then provided with various ingredients and recipes so that they could try them out at home. The thinking was that they could pass ideas onto customers and in doing so provide credibility and enhance the in-store experience for shoppers.

Sources: Adapted from Anon. (2005); Brook (2005); Reed (2006); www.sainsburys.co.uk.

Question

Can IMC be achieved without having to incorporate a strategic orientation?

Task

Find out what each of the other main supermarkets regard as IMC.

Exhibit 9.1 Celebrity chef Jamie Oliver working with Sainsbury's to help us all 'try something new today'
Image courtesy of The Advertising Archives.

Technology

The interest and debate about IMC has been accelerated by developments in technology. The use of technology, and in particular database technologies, has enabled marketing managers a vastly improved view of customer behaviour, attitudes and feelings towards brands. This has allowed more precise and insightful communications to be generated and the subsequent feedback and measurement facilities have further developed the overall quality of customer communications. However, the mere presence of technology does not result in effective marketing communications. Technology needs to be integrated into not just the overall information systems strategy but also the marketing strategies of organisations. Technology is an enabler and to use it effectively requires integration. The effective use of technology can touch a number of areas within the IMC orbit. For example, technology can be used to develop effective web sites, extranets and intranets, customer contact centres, databases, advertising campaigns, fulfilment processes, CRM and sales force automation. If each of these applications is deployed independently of the others their impact will be limited. Developed within an integrated framework the potential for marketing and customer service can be tremendous.

> Technology needs to be integrated into not just the overall information systems strategy but also the marketing strategies of organisations.

Associated with the use of technology are issues concerning the measurement and evaluation of IMC activities. One of the criticisms of IMC is that no evaluation system has yet been proposed or implemented so that the claims made about IMC delivering superior returns can be validated (Swain, 2004). This is part of the planning process and so integration of all aspects of the campaign planning process is necessary.

Agencies

Reference has been made earlier and in Chapter 3 to some of the structural issues involving agencies in the marketing communications industry and with the development of IMC. Agencies play a critical role in marketing communications and if IMC is to be established it cannot be accomplished without the explicit involvement of all those working on the supply side.

Apart from questions concerning the range of promotional services offered by individual agencies and whether these are all delivered by a single agency or through a network of interacting agencies, two particular issues arise. The first concerns leadership and the other remuneration.

With regard to leadership should the agency or the client lead the process of developing IMC? The consensus appears to be that this is the client's role (Swain, 2004), mainly because clients are better positioned to make integration happen across their own organisation. However, Swain then points out that there is no agreement about who in the client organisation should be responsible for implementing IMC. Indeed, Kitchen *et al.* (2007) confirm the reluctance of both advertising and public relations agencies to provide for integrative working practices.

A similar question concerns the implementation of integrated campaigns. Most major brands operate with several agencies, each providing different skills. These are known as roster agencies simply because different agencies can be brought into different campaigns to provide support when necessary. Herein lies the problem for clients implementing an integrative programme: how best to manage an integrative approach? One way is to appoint a lead agency that assumes responsibility for integration. Another way, used by AOL, who work with 12 agencies, is for the client to drive the programme forward and to involve the roster agencies (Gray, 2007). However, many client organisations, such as Shell, prefer to appoint a lead agency and very often it is the generalist ad agency that is appointed.

The second issue, remuneration, should be regarded as interrelated to the measurement factor (Swain, 2004). This is because clients see reward as a derivative of performance. The traditional remuneration system is based on activities (Spake *et al.* (1999) cited by Swain). Commission earned from the use of media to gain awareness or change attitudes is not measured against revenue or profit performance, and is referred to as 'an activity'. Results- or 'outcome'-based systems are considered a performance measure. A move to IMC requires a change in agency performance measures and consequently, a change in their method of remuneration. Closer integration of agencies within the IMC process will, among other things, bring changes in structure, operations, performance measures, remuneration and new responsibilities within the client relationship.

> A move to IMC requires a change in agency performance measures.

This list of elements that need to be integrated is not exclusive. There are other influences that are particular to individual organisations that could have been included. However, consideration of these various elements suggests strongly that what is being integrated is far more than just the communication tools. Indeed, viewed holistically integration is a strategic concept that strikes at the heart of an organisation's marketing and business orientation.

The development of IMC

The word integration has been used in various ways and it is the interpretation of the word integration that determines whether integrated marketing communications is real, achievable or even practised. In many ways, reality suggests that the claims many organisations and the communications industry make in the name of IMC are simply a reflection of improved management and coordination of the communication tools. The recent interest in media-neutral planning (MNP) may be a good thing for the cause of improved communications and relationship development but MNP does not address the wider strategic issues, the importance of internal communications or the structural issues of IMC on both the client and agency sides.

As established above, early interpretations of IMC were constructed around the idea that what was to be integrated were the promotional tools and media. Scholars such as Shultz (1993) and Duncan and Everett (1993) led much of the IMC activity and many organisations were enthusiastic about the new ideas, driven by the desire to restructure internally, reduce costs and deliver consistent messages. Kitchen *et al.* (2004) refer to this as the inside-out IMC approach.

The next phase was characterised by an exploration of the nature, direction and content typified by definitions that introduced management, strategy and brand development into the IMC process. Shimp (2000) among others, supported the explicit introduction of these aspects to IMC.

The current interpretation has moved the IMC concept forward, this time as an audience- or customer-driven process, one that incorporates ideas concerning relationship marketing. Duncan and Mulhern (2004) cited by Reid (2005), Gronroos (2004) and Duncan (2002) have provided valuable insights into this dimension of IMC, one which Kitchen *et al.* (2004) refer to as the outside-in IMC approach.

It should be noted that while many writers, such as Kitchen and Shultz (1997 and 1998) and Duncan (2002), have written positively and consistently promoting ideas about IMC, other authors such as Cornelissen and Lock (2000), Percy *et al.* (2001) and Spotts *et al.* (1998), to name but a few, have been critical of the concept and have doubted the merits inherent in the concept. This dichotomy of views reveals the inherent instability of the IMC concept. Readers interested in a fuller appraisal of IMC are referred to Kitchen *et al.* (2004) and Cornelissen (2003).

As part of his critique Cornelissen (2003) distinguishes two different themes running through the IMC literature. The first is that IMC is regarded as a predominantly *process*-oriented concept and the second is that it is a *content*-oriented concept. These are examined in the following section.

> Unsurprisingly, there is no agreement about what IMC is, what it encompasses or how it should be measured.

Unsurprisingly therefore, there is no agreement about what IMC is, what it encompasses or how it should be measured. Indeed, there is no universally agreed definition and, apart from some anecdotal comment, there is little practical evidence of the application of a strategic, customer-oriented IMC programme. There are numerous claims of IMC practice but these are little more than coordinated promotional mix activities using themed messages (inside-out).

> IMC is a not a proven marketing theory – there is no empirical evidence to support the concept.

IMC is a not a proven marketing theory (Cornelissen, 2003). There is no empirical evidence to support the concept, yet the ideas inherent in the overall approach appear to hold value. Although Cornelissen refers to the IMC concept as only worthy of symbolic value, a view later refuted by Kitchen, it does appear that what is integration to one person (or agency) may be coordination or simply good professional practice to another.

Perspectives on IMC

Cornelissen argues that the literature indicates that there are two main interpretations of IMC: a content and a process perspective respectively.

The *content* perspective assumes that message consistency is the major goal in order to achieve the 'one voice, one look' position. IMC works when there is consistency throughout the various materials and messages. However, this is not a new practice as Cornelissen points out that practitioners having been doing this long before the term IMC surfaced. This view is also associated with the zero-based planning approach that holds that the choice of tools and media should be based on effectiveness criteria rather than the specialist functions for which the planners and managers are responsible. This means that the various agencies and personnel responsible for campaign design and deployment do so without prejudice or bias towards a preferred tool or media. This approach is discussed later in this chapter.

> The *content* perspective assumes that message consistency is the major goal in order to achieve the 'one voice, one look' position.

ViewPoint 9.4 Integrated toilet tissue

Velvet is a major toilet tissue brand bought by SCA Hygiene from Procter & Gamble. When SCA launched their Triple Velvet brand they referred to their integrated campaign. The £15m television campaign was supported with direct mail, sampling and touch-test panels in shopping centres, designed to help customers feel the softness of the brand.

Later that year SCA launched an interactive web site accompanied by an online campaign. This campaign extended the theme of the television ad as it features a virtual Velvet factory in which 'Baby MD' advises consumers about various product developments and promotions, while encouraging visitors to download various branded games. Aimed at mothers and children, the site is reported to replicate social networking experiences whose goal is to encourage return visits.

Source: Jones (2007).

Question
Is this primarily a process or content perspective of IMC?

Task
Visit the Velvet web site and comment on whether you believe the site appears to be part of an integrated approach. www.velvet-tissues.co.uk/.

The second interpretation offered by Cornelissen is referred to as a *process* perspective. Here the emphasis is on a structural realignment of the communication disciplines within organisations, even to the point of collapsing all communications into a single department. Even if this extreme interpretation is not a valid goal for an organisation, cross-functional systems and processes are regarded as necessary to enable integrated marketing communications.

The process perspective of IMC is rooted in the belief that real IMC can only be generated through an organisational structure that brings the various communication disciplines together in a single body or unit. By creating a single department out of which advertising, public relations and the other disciplines operate, so cross-functional coordination between the disciplines is enabled. Some argue that the process view needs to incorporate a series of intervening stages as systems, processes and procedures are brought together incrementally to enable the cross-functionality to work.

> The process perspective of IMC is rooted in the belief that real IMC can only be generated through an organisational structure that brings the various communication disciplines together.

Research suggests that organisations have made little attempt to restructure their marketing communications disciplines and that public relations and marketing remain as a clear divide. What has happened, however, is that there are much closer cross-functional relationships and systems and processes to support them. Some organisations are moving incrementally towards a process perspective of IMC.

ViewPoint 9.5 Integrated cigarettes

Imperial Tobacco Ltd (ITL) is Canada's largest tobacco manufacturer and its leading brand, Player's has experienced a growth in market share from 37 per cent in 1973 to over 68 per cent in 1998. The brand was targeted at males under 25 years old and used messages set in mountainous or aquatic settings using sports themes.

What is interesting about ITL is that they abandoned the brand management structure and adopted a brand planning process structure. This involves a cross-functional approach that is regarded as a more strategic approach to brand development and brand defence. The company also developed a detailed insight into product and image positioning.

The brand strategy was clearly articulated internally and it was used to provide a platform for a consistent approach to messages and media selection. Consistency across their marketing communications and brand imagery was also achieved through the division head of brand marketing who considered activities across all brands and functional areas.

Source: Dewhirst and Davis (2005).

Question
Is this primarily a process or content perspective of IMC?

Task
Read the paper by Dewhirst and Davis (2005) and learn more about ITL's approach to IMC.

In an attempt to develop our understanding of IMC, Lee and Park (2007) proposed a multidimensional model of IMC based on four key dimensions. These have been drawn from the literature and, unlike Cornelissen's work, represent an attempt to measure IMC. Their four dimensions are concerned with a single message, multiple customer groups, database marketing and the need to use IMC to build customer relationships. A fuller account of these dimensions can be seen in Chapter 15.

Kliatchko (2008) suggests that IMC has several distinctive attributes and he refers to them as the 'four pillars of IMC'. These are stakeholders, content, channels and results. Figure 9.2 sets out the constituent elements within each of the pillars.

His argument is that these four elements can be observed at different levels of IMC and that at each level one of the elements tends to dominate.

It may be that a suitable theoretical basis upon which to develop IMC is emerging through the relationship marketing literature. We know that a relationship orientation requires a multidisciplinary approach to trigger interaction and dialogue (Gronroos, 2004). So, it may be

Figure 9.2 The Elements of the four pillars of IMC
Source: Kliatchko (2008). Used with permission from WARC.

that a deeper understanding of relational theory will help to advance the IMC concept and provide researchers with a surer footing upon which to explore the topic.

However, whether a content or process perspective is adopted, the position remains that until there is empirical evidence to support a theoretical base upon which to build IMC strategy and operations, the phrase will probably continue to be misused, misunderstood and used in a haphazard and inconsistent way.

From this review and bearing in mind that no single form of IMC can be identified, the following general definition of IMC is offered:

IMC can represent both a strategic and tactical approach to the planned management of an organisation's communications. IMC requires that organisations coordinate their various strategies, resources and messages in order that they enable meaningful engagement with target audiences. The main purposes are to develop a clear positioning and encourage stakeholder relationships that are of mutual value.

This definition serves to link IMC with business-level strategies and relationships. The importance of coherence within the organisation is made, whether this be through systems or structural change. Implicit is the underpinning notion that IMC is necessary for the development of effective relationships and that not all relationships need be collaborative and fully relational, as is so often assumed to be the case in many contemporary interpretations.

> Implicit is the underpinning notion that IMC is necessary for the development of effective relationships.

Reasons for the developing interest in IMC

The explosion of interest in IMC has resulted from a variety of drivers. Generally they can be grouped into three main categories: those drivers (or opportunities) that are market-based, those that arise from changing communications, and those that are driven from opportunities arising from within the organisation itself. These are set out in Table 9.1.

The opportunities offered to organisations that contemplate moving to IMC are considerable and it is somewhat surprising that so few organisations have been either willing or able to embrace the approach. One of the main organisational drivers for IMC is the need to become increasingly efficient. Driving down the cost base enables managers to improve profits and levels of productivity. By seeking synergistic advantages through its communications and associated activities and by expecting managers to be able to account for the way in which they consume marketing communication resources, so integrated marketing communications becomes increasingly attractive. At the same time, organisation structures are changing more frequently and the need to integrate across functional areas reflects the efficiency drive.

From a market perspective, the predominant driver is the reorientation from transaction-based marketing to relationship marketing. The extension of the brand personality concept into brand relationships (Hutton, 1996) requires a customer consideration in terms of asking not only 'What do our customers want?', but also 'What are their values, do they trust us and are we loyal to them?' By adopting a position designed to enhance trust and commitment, an organisation's external communications need to be consistent and coordinated, if only to avoid information overload and misunderstanding.

> From a market perspective, the predominant driver is the reorientation from transaction-based marketing to relationship marketing.

From a communication perspective, the key driver is to provide a series of triggers by which buyers can understand the values a brand stands for and a means by which they can use certain messages to influence their activities within the relationships they wish to develop. By differentiating the marketing communications, often by providing clarity and simplicity, advantages can be attained.

Table 9.1 Drivers for IMC

Organisational drivers for IMC
- Increasing profits through improved efficiency
- Increasing need for greater levels of accountability
- Rapid move towards cross-border marketing and the need for changing structures and communications
- Coordinated brand development and competitive advantage
- Opportunities to utilise management time more productively
- Provide direction and purpose for employees

Market-based drivers for IMC
- Greater levels of audience communications literacy
- Media cost inflation
- Media and audience fragmentation
- Stakeholders' need for increasing amounts and diversity of information
- Greater amounts of message clutter
- Competitor activity and low levels of brand differentiation
- Move towards relationship marketing from transaction-based marketing
- Development of networks, collaboration and alliances

Communication-based drivers for IMC
- Technological advances (Internet, databases, segmentation techniques)
- Increased message effectiveness through consistency and reinforcement of core messages
- More effective triggers for brand and message recall
- More consistent and less confusing brand images
- Need to build brand reputations and to provide clear identity cues

An integrated approach should attempt to provide a uniform or consistent set of messages. These should be relatively easy to interpret and to assign meaning. This enables target audiences to think about and perceive brands within a relational context and so encourages behaviour as expected by the source. Those organisations that try to practise IMC understand that buyers refer to and receive messages about brands and companies from a wide range of information sources. Harnessing this knowledge is a fundamental step towards enhancing marketing communications.

It seems useful to itemise the advantages and disadvantages associated with IMC. These are set out in Table 9.2. General opinion suggests that the advantages far outweigh the disadvantages and that increasing numbers of organisations are seeking to improve their IMC resource. As stated earlier, database technology and the Internet have provided great impetus for organisations to review their communications and to implement moves to install a more integrated communication strategy.

Managing IMC

The development and establishment of IMC by organisations has not been as widespread as the amount of discussion around the subject has suggested. Recent technological advances and the benefits of the Internet and related technologies have meant that organisations have had a reason to reconsider their marketing communications and have re-evaluated their approach. Whatever route taken, the development of IMC requires change, a change in thinking, a change in actions and a change in expectations. The changes required to achieve IMC are large and the barriers are strong. What can be

> The development of IMC requires change, a change in thinking, a change in actions and a change in expectations.

Table 9.2 Advantages and disadvantages of IMC

Advantages of IMC
Provides opportunities to cut communication costs and/or reassign budgets
Has the potential to produce synergistic and more effective communications
Can deliver competitive advantage through clearer positioning
Encourages coordinated brand development with internal and external participants
Provides for increased employee participation and motivation
Has the potential to cause management to review its communication strategy
Requires a change in culture and fosters a customer focus
Provides a benchmark for the development of communication activities
Can lead to a cut in the number of agencies supporting a brand

Disadvantages of IMC
Encourages centralisation and formal/bureaucratic procedures
Can require increased management time seeking agreement from all involved parties
Suggests uniformity and single message
Tendency to standardisation might negate or dilute creative opportunities
Global brands restricted in terms of local adaptation
Normally requires cultural change from employees and encourages resistance
Has the potential to severely damage a brand's reputation if incorrectly managed
Can lead to mediocrity as no single agency network has access to all sources of communications

observed are formative approaches to IMC and that organisations have experimented and tried out various ideas within their resource and cultural contexts.

As with many aspects of change, there is nearly always resistance to the incorporation of IMC, and, if sanctioned, only partial integration has been achieved. This is not to say that integration is not possible or has not been achieved, but the path to IMC is far from easy and the outcomes are difficult to gauge with great confidence. However, it is the expectation (what level of IMC) that really matters, as it signals the degree of change that is required.

Resistance to integration

Resistance to change is partly a reflection of the experiences and needs of individuals for stability and the understanding of their environments. However, it is also a reflection, again, of the structural conditions in organisations and industry, which have helped determine the expectations of managers and employees.

Eagle and Kitchen (2000) set out four principal areas or themes concerned with barriers to IMC programmes:

- power, coordination and control issues;
- client skills, centralisation/organisation and cultural issues;
- agency skills/talent and overall time/resource issues;
- flexibility/modification issues.

While these provide a useful general overview, the following represent some of the more common, more focused reasons for the resistance to the incorporation of IMC.

Financial structures and frameworks

Resistance through finance-led corporate goals, which have dominated industry performance and expectations, has been particularly significant. The parameters set around it and the extent to which marketing communications is often perceived as a cost rather than an investment, have provided a corporate environment where the act of preparing for and establishing integrative activities is perceived negatively. Furthermore, the period in which communication activities are expected to generate returns is often too short and works against the principles of IMC and the time needed for the effects to take place.

Opposition/reluctance to change

The attitudes and opinions of staff are often predictable in the sense that any move away from tried and proven methods to areas that are unknown and potentially threatening is usually rejected. Change has long been regarded with hostility and fear, and as such is normally resisted. Our apparent need for stability and general security has been a potent form of resistance to the introduction of IMC. This is changing as change itself becomes a familiar aspect of working life. Any move towards IMC therefore, represents a significantly different approach to work, as not only are the expectations of employees changed but so also are the working practices and the associated roles with internal customers and, more importantly, those providing outsourcing facilities.

Traditional hierarchical and brand management structures

Part of the reluctance to change is linked with the structure and systems inherent in many organisations. Traditional hierarchical structures and systems are inflexible and slow to cope with developments in their fast-adapting environments. These structures can stifle the use of individual initiative, can slow the decision-making process and encourage inertia. The brand management system, so popular and appropriate in the 1970s and early 1980s, focuses upon functional specialisms, which is reflected in the horizontally and vertically specialised areas of responsibility. Brands now need to be managed by flexible teams of specialists, who are charged with responsibilities and the resources necessary to coordinate activities across organisations in the name of integration.

Attitudes and structure of suppliers and agencies

> Advertising agencies have maintained their traditional structures and methods of operating, while their clients have begun to adapt and reform themselves.

One of the principal reasons often cited as a barrier to integration is the relationship that clients have with their agencies, and in particular their advertising agencies. Generally, advertising agencies have maintained their traditional structures and methods of operating, while their clients have begun to adapt and reform themselves. The thinking behind this is that for a long time advertising agencies have tried to maintain their dominance of mass advertising as the principal means of brand development. In doing so they seek to retain the largest proportion of agency fee income, rather than having these fees diluted as work is allocated below the line (to other organisations).

The establishment of IMC threatens the current role of the main advertising agencies. This is not to say that all agencies think and act in this way. They do not, as witnessed by the innovative approaches to restructuring and the provision of integrated resources for their clients by agencies such as St Lukes. So, while clients have seen the benefits of integrated marketing communications, their attempts to achieve them have often been thwarted by the structures of the agencies they need to work with and by the attitudes of their main agencies.

Perceived complexity of planning and coordination

The complexity associated with integrating any combination of activities is often cited as a means for delaying or postponing action. Of greater significance are the difficulties associated with coordinating actions across departments and geographic boundaries. IMC requires the cooperation and coordination of internal and external stakeholder groups. Each group has an agenda that contains goals that may well differ from or conflict with those of other participants.

For example, an advertising agency might propose the use of mass media to address a client's needs, if only because that is where its specialist skills lie. However, direct marketing might be a more appropriate approach to solving the client's problem, but because there is no established mechanism to coordinate and discuss openly the problem/solution, the lead agency is likely to have its approach adopted in preference to others.

Implementing IMC

The restraints that prevent the development of IMC need to be overcome. Indeed, many organisations that have made significant progress in developing IMC have done so by instigating approaches and measures that aim to reduce or negate the impact of the barriers that people put up to prevent change. The main approaches to overcoming the barriers are as follows.

Adopting a customer-focused philosophy

The adoption of a customer-focused approach is quite well established within marketing departments. However, this approach needs to be adopted as an organisation-wide approach, a philosophy that spans all departments and results in unified cues to all stakeholders. In many cases, agencies need to adopt a more customer-oriented approach and be able and willing to work with other agencies, including those below the line.

Training and staff development programmes

A move towards IMC cannot be made without changes in the expectations held by employees within the client and agency sectors. Some of the key processes necessary for change need to be used. For example, the involvement and participation of all staff in the process is in itself a step towards providing motivation and acceptance of change when it is agreed and delivered.

> A move towards IMC cannot be made without changes in the expectations held by employees.

Appointing change agents

The use of change agents, people who can positively affect the reception and implementation of change programmes, is important. As IMC should span an entire organisation, the change agent should be a senior manager, or preferably director, in order to signal the importance and speed at which the new perspective is to be adopted.

Some organisations have experimented with the appointment of a single senior manager who is responsible for all internal and external communications.

Planning to achieve sustainable competitive advantage

In order to develop competitive advantages, some organisations have restructured by removing levels of management, introduced business reprocessing procedures and even set up outsourcing in order that they achieve cost efficiencies and effectiveness targets. Prior to the implementation of these delayering processes, many organisations were (and many still are) organised hierarchically.

Back in 1997 Brown foresaw that the emergence and establishment of IMC would only be successful once the industry matures, becomes market-oriented and leaves behind issues concerning client–agency complications. In addition, traditional brand management systems, most of which were designed to prevent the development of synergies or shared knowledge, need to be overhauled. These issues have not yet been fully resolved and IMC in practice remains ill-defined, and superficial. What is required therefore, is a restructuring and re-designation of who manages communications and this requires a planned approach. It is evident that current systems, processes, procedures and structures are not suitable to support and sustain a planned approach to enable the full development and delivery of IMC.

> IMC in practice remains ill-defined, and superficial.

Media-neutral planning

The media-neutral planning (MNP) approach emerged partly as a response to criticism of IMC and partly as an attempt to articulate the potential practice of IMC. For many MNP is integration under a different guise but one of the strengths of the concept is that it openly focuses on the needs of clients and agencies. It attempts to stimulate the use of a communication mix that is driven by the needs of a target audience and not those of the communication industry. This means that rather than keep recommending that clients use mass media communications, which have traditionally rewarded agencies through a more than generous commission system, a more balanced mix of tools and media should be adopted in order to be more effective and efficient.

One of the main reasons for the interest in IMC is the potential to reduce costs. The rise in some media costs, most notably television through the 1990s, the specialised and independent nature of the agency side of the industry, the proliferation of media opportunities and the splintering of audiences, the increasing clamour for measures of return on investment in communications have led to a reappraisal of the role and nature of marketing communications and the emergence of MNP ideas. As clients have tried to reduce costs they have made greater use of both through and below-the-line tools.

Agencies interested in preserving margins have attempted to maintain the prominence of advertising in their media plans but have reduced the emphasis on television advertising or have sought better deals through use of multiple television channel mixes, improved negotiation and more alliances. Some client organisations (e.g. Kraft, Kellogg's, Unilever and Procter & Gamble) have moved, if unintentionally, towards a form of coordinated marketing communication activity. These organisations have reduced their reliance on above-the-line media and have attempted to move towards the use of below-the-line tools in order to reduce costs and deliver consistent messages in an attempt to cut through the increasing clutter. Ray (2002) refers to organisations such as Nike, Reebok and Alliance & Leicester who have practiced MNP, however, he also refers to some of the problems, such as structures, areas of expertise and attitudes, faced by agencies attempting to offer a more neutral media approach for their clients.

ViewPoint 9.6 Boots use MNP

The launch by Boots of their Intelligent Colour Foundation was an important opportunity to support the contemporary, fashionable image of the No. 7 brand. The revolutionary product blends to the colour of an individual's skin and only requires the user to decide between three shades of light, medium and dark.

As part of the planning process, Boots decided to explore the use of MNP and formed a cross-disciplinary team to improve the level of interaction between departments and to optimise planning. The MNP team consisted of representatives of the brand, consumer insight, direct and relationship marketing (through the Advantage Card), PR and communication channel planning.

It was generally accepted that PR would play a critical role but rather than rely on television and magazine advertising, it was decided to augment the plan with direct mail using the Boots Advantage Card database. It was thought this would be more cost-effective than to invest further in other media, particularly television.

In order to measure the impact of this neutral approach, the planning team used two key measurement tools to avoid the misleading sales and awareness measures.

The first of these was a store-based model that could identify sales effect on a store-by-store basis thereby enabling the identification of stores by campaign area, e.g. with/without television, with/without mail, with/without in-store promotions etc. The second was a tracking study that would identify actual exposure to different media by means of a combination of viewing/reading questions together with the establishment of two matched samples to enable real comparisons of mailed versus non-mailed respondents. The tracking study measured awareness, product understanding, interest and image.

The detailed results are confidential but showed clearly that by including mail in the mix it also added value and Boots became more supportive of integrated communications and a media neutral approach.

For more information about this case readers should visit www.brandrepublic.com/think/.

Question
Is MNP just IMC under another name?

Task
Visit the www.brandrepublic.com/think/ and make a note of the key issues and MNP.

Exhibit 9.2 Boots Intelligent Colour foundation
Courtesy of Boots.

The drive behind the development of MNP appears to be concerned more with reducing the emphasis that television advertising plays in media plans, rather than the formulation of distinct media plans that deliver advertising messages in the most effective way, regardless of media selection. Many of those that support media-neutral approaches are often quoted using examples that involve a mix of tools and media.

> The drive behind the development of MNP appears to be concerned more with reducing the emphasis that television advertising plays in media plans.

MNP recognises that mass media advertising is not always the most appropriate way to launch or develop consumer or business-to-business promotional activities, and that a consideration of the most suitable mix of communication tools might be a better starting point when formulating campaigns. Advertising alone cannot carry the weight of a brand necessary to build and sustain the desired associations. Public relations, sales promotions and field marketing (merchandising) for example, have increasingly important roles to play in establishing and sustaining a brand. However, where advertising is used, the changing media landscape and the increasing penetration of new technology means that a greater use of cross-media planning approaches is likely to enhance the effectiveness of a campaign and reduce costs, especially if previous campaigns used television as the primary medium. The traditional model of media planning, whereby a primary medium and perhaps two or three secondary media are scheduled over a five-week campaign has now to be surpassed by a more contemporary mix that uses a cross-media plan combining new and old media and that is appropriate to target audience preferences and the context of the marketing communications activities.

Therefore, it might be interpreted that media-neutral mixes represent the response of the agency side of the marketing communications industry while IMC represents the client side approach to managing their marketing communications in a more effective and strategic manner. MNP should not be about mixing tools and media but should be regarded as an integral part of IMC. However, IMC is not the same as MNP.

The development and delivery of a marketing communications programme that repeatedly delivers significant value cannot be based solely on media-neutral planning or loose notions of IMC. What is necessary is the development of a strategic marketing communications approach that delivers a total brand experience (Tobaccowala and Kugel, 2001). This requires a co-ordinated approach to the selection and implementation of the right promotional tools and media that will deliver messages that are of significant value to the target audience. However, it also requires the integration of a cross-functional, multi-audience strategic approach to marketing communications, one that delivers a brand experience for the target audience.

> What is necessary is the development of a strategic marketing communications approach that delivers a total brand experience.

Open planning

In many ways media-neutral planning is an approach to planning where all media have equal probability of selection and those that are chosen are deemed the best vehicles to achieve the media plan's objectives. Although there are many benefits, such as changing attitudes and perhaps reducing some costs, the neutrality perspective seeks to address industry issues about the planning process and the thinking the incumbents undertake, rather than demonstrate direct concern with audience issues.

In an attempt to move thinking a step forward the open planning concept was developed by Jenkinson, who in 2002/03 coordinated a panel of leading marketers who shared a goal to simplify the media-neutral planning concept. The main goal was to reappraise the way organisations consider their processes and thinking about marketing communication activities with a view to optimising their communication potential. The MNP group argue that this requires rethinking the way communication disciplines (tools) and media are used, to develop new methods of evaluating communication activity and to accelerate the speed at which organisations are able to integrate their communications with their business and marketing strategies.

> The main goal was to reappraise the way organisations consider their processes and thinking about marketing communication activities with a view to optimising their communication potential.

The MNP group have proposed a series of new approaches based mainly on ideas concerning open planning. Open planning is concerned with eight action areas, each of which contributes to the process of MNP. These action areas are set out in Table 9.3. Readers wishing to know more should visit www.openplanning.org.uk.

Thinking in terms of these action areas should promote marketing communications that are audience-centred rather than promulgate the previous model that focused on the needs of the communication industry (see Figure 9.3).

Table 9.3 Action areas within the Open Planning approach

Action area	Explanation
Disciplines	Any promotional tool (i.e. discipline) can be used with any medium to achieve stated business and marketing objectives.
Media	Any medium can be used, by any tool (i.e. discipline), in almost all mixes. This means redefining media to mean anything that conveys a message to an audience. A salesperson becomes a medium.
Channels	Any mix of disciplines within a single medium becomes an open channel.
Process	All agencies (and others) should be involved with the thinking and planning process at the outset, to determine the message and goals before any resources are allocated (i.e. budgets).
Structure	The communication process should be driven by the communication preferences of a target audience (or community) rather than the silo structure-based functional specialisation present in much of the industry today.
Relationships	The relationship between client and agency should be open and functional. Agency remuneration should be based on the achievement of brand goals and not commission based on media choice.
Results	Defining more precise communication goals that enable a level playing field for all disciplines, media and agencies to maximise their contribution.
Tools	Use of media planning tools that embrace all touch points with customers.

Source: Adapted from Jenkinson and Sain (2004).

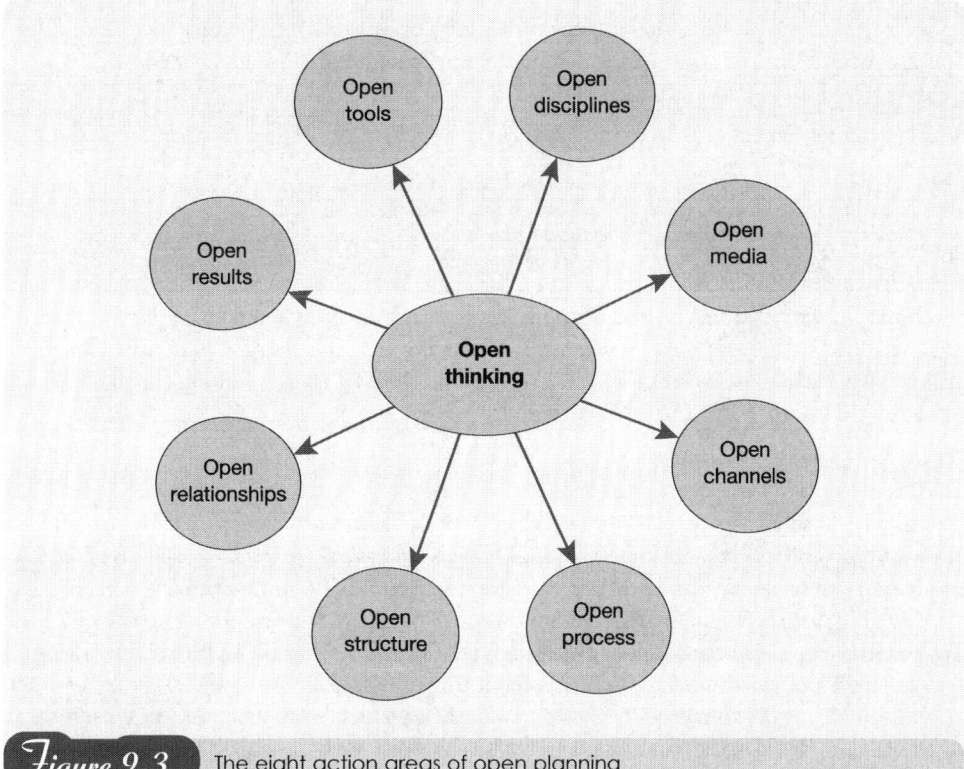

Figure 9.3 The eight action areas of open planning

Client structures and IMC

Clients have also embraced IMC and its influence on their structures. The hierarchical structures common in many organisations in the period up to the 1970s have been subject to attack. In search of survival in recession and increasing profits and dividends in times of plenty, organisations have sought to restructure and realign themselves with their environment. Hierarchies delivered a management structure that delegated authority in compartmentalised units. The brand management system that accompanied this structural approach provided a straitjacket and gave only partial authority to incumbents. At the same time, responsibility for pricing, channel management, personal selling and public relations activities was split off and allocated to a number of others. It follows from this that the likelihood of internal integration has been hampered by the structure of the organisation and the way in which structural units were assembled.

> The restructuring process has resulted in organisations that are delayered and leaner.

The restructuring process has resulted in organisations that are delayered and leaner. This means that the gap between senior management and those within the operating core (Mintzberg *et al.*, 2003) is both smaller and now capable of sustaining viable internal communications that are truly two-way and supportive.

Increasingly, organisations are operating in overseas or cross-border markets. For a deeper account of the issues concerning international marketing communications, readers are referred to Chapter 28. However, as organisations develop structurally, from international to multinational to global and transnational status, so the need to coordinate internally and to integrate internal communications becomes ever more vital to sustain integrated marketing communications (Grein and Gould, 1996). Internal marketing (Chapter 30) is becoming more popular with clients (and agencies) as it is realised that employees are important contributors to corporate identity programmes and invaluable spokespersons for the products they market. Internal communications can help not only to inform and remind/reassure but also to differentiate employees in the sense that they understand the organisation's direction and purpose, appreciate what the brand values are and so identify closely with the organisation as a whole. This is a form of integration from which marketing communications can benefit.

Reconsidering the IMC concept

The central ideas behind the IMC concept are sound and a logical step forward for marketing communications. IMC helps provide a strategic focus and the level of debate and interest about how best to use marketing communications has been advanced. The development of technology and more importantly, the relationship marketing concept, has given increased impetus to those who advocate the use of IMC. However, concerns about pinning down the exact meaning and interpretation of IMC remain.

IMC and transactional marketing

The discussion so far has been based largely on the assumption that exchanges are (or should be) essentially collaborative in character and that customers are willing and eager to enter into a wide range of relationships. However, it appears that some, if not the majority of exchanges,

> Buyers do not always wish to enter into a deep complex relationships with all suppliers.

are essentially transactional in character. Buyers do not always wish to enter into a deep complex relationships with all suppliers, nor do some consumers wish to enter into a relationship with the supplier of their favourite chocolate bar, dishwasher tablets or frozen peas. As a result these convenience-based exchanges are oriented towards a value based on the

Figure 9.4 The marketing mix communicates

product, its price and overall availability and convenience. Depending upon the product category, after-sales and service support will be important but, by definition, customers in transactional mode do not wish to enter into any serious interaction, let alone dialogue.

The target marketing process requires the development and implementation of a distinct marketing mix to meet the requirements of selected target markets. The elements are mixed together in such a way that they should meet the needs of the target segment. Each element of the marketing mix has a variable capacity to communicate (see Figure 9.4).

Therefore, it may be that traditional forms of marketing communications are sufficient to reach transactional customers. Messages that focus mainly on attributes, features and benefits, emotional values, price and availability will continue to be valid and improved if delivered though a coordinated mix of tools and media that are customer-oriented. By using communications that use a coordinated communications mix, which makes greater use of a range of tools and media that are neutral and seek to cut waste and improve efficiency, will be advantageous.

IMC and relationship marketing

As stated already, there is no universally agreed definition of IMC and the development of this relatively new, embryonic concept is strewn with attempts to pin it down and label it. What can be observed however is that the relationship marketing paradigm has developed at the same time as IMC and that there are areas where the two concepts intertwine and reinforce each other. One of the difficulties associated with the IMC view, and with its half-sister, media-neutral planning, is that successful marketing communications results from an entirely planned approach. Planning is an essential aspect of managing marketing communications but customers interact with products and services in different ways. They experience brands through their observation of others consuming them, through their own use, as well as through planned, unplanned and word-of-mouth communications. It is the totality of this communication experience that impacts on relationship development. IMC therefore has a critical role in the development of relationship marketing. This is because it is an important process, one that seeks to generate a response from customers, provoke interaction and then dialogue, which is a key characteristic of relationship marketing (Gronroos, 2004). These ideas are explored in greater depth in Chapter 7.

> The relationship marketing paradigm has developed at the same time as IMC.

Table 9.4 Duncan-Moriarty categories of relationship drivers

Relationship drivers	Explanation
Relationship development	Everything an organisation does and says is seen, heard and interpreted by stakeholders. The need is to provide a consistent relational focus through all messages
Processes	The need for a process and system to provide consistent strategic positioning and in doing so help support the identity and reputation
Organisational	Structural and cross-functional cohesion is necessary to support internal marketing and an unbiased use of all communication resources

Source: Derived from Reid (2005).

The Duncan and Moriarty IMC miniaudit has been designed to help assess an organisation's IMC relationship-building practices. It recognises the influence of organisational structure and marketing communication strategies and objectives and attempts to measure the strategic consistency of the brand messages. Many of the elements considered earlier in the section 'what is to be integrated' can be identified in the nine drivers identified by Duncan and Moriarty. These can be grouped into three categories, as presented in Table 9.4.

IMC therefore has a potentially greater role to play within collaborative transactions and with customers who wish to become involved within mutually rewarding relationships. To date IMC has been regarded as a concept that needs to be applied across an organisation's entire marketing communications and customer base. The suggestion is that aspects of IMC should be applied to both transactional and collaborative customers but greater emphasis on interaction and dialogue should be given to communication with current and potential relationship-driven customers and other stakeholders.

> Aspects of IMC should be applied to both transactional and collaborative customers.

An incremental approach to IMC

Integrated marketing communications means different things to different people. Opportunities to develop IMC appear to vary according to a variety of factors, including organisation size and development. Low (2000) suggests that IMC is more likely to be successful in smaller rather than large organisations. This is because they have fewer brands to be integrated, lower levels of hierarchical complexity and departmental formalisation and are inherently more adaptive. However, Reid (2005) found that large organisations were more likely to adopt IMC principles, suggesting this was due to their more sophisticated planning systems, greater number of formal mechanisms for managing customer data, and the fact that they are already experienced at managing internal functional groups and external agencies. He also found that the greater the level of market orientation within an organisation the more likely IMC practices would be successful. Both Low and Reid appear to agree that IMC is positively related to the intensity of competitive activity experienced by an organisation.

It is clear therefore, that the successful implementation of IMC needs to be founded on an audience-centred (outside-in) orientation. However, IMC also means different things to different organisations and the level of IMC implemented and experienced by organisations is bounded by their context. There

> The successful implementation of IMC needs to be founded on an audience-centred (outside-in) orientation.

Figure 9.5 An incremental approach to the establishment of IMC

is an emerging belief that although organisations should embrace the marketing mix and the communications mix in the name of IMC they should use cross-functional systems and processes to incorporate internal communications and all those outsourced providers who contribute to the overall marketing communication process. As Figure 9.5 demonstrates, all of these elements should be linked to the overall purpose of the organisation, normally encapsulated and framed in the strategy, philosophy and mission of the organisation.

It seems logical that moves towards the establishment of IMC must be undertaken in steps as it cannot be accomplished overnight, an incremental approach is required (Fill, 2001). Organisations experience an incremental approach to the implementation and establishment of IMC. What they achieve at any one moment is a function of their context, and may be recognised as forms of coordination. Different organisations have coordinated various aspects of their communications activities. Many organisations have focused upon their promotional activities and have tried to bring together their communications to provide consistency and thematic harmonisation. Others have developed more sophisticated systems and procedures to interlink their activities internally.

> Organisations experience an incremental approach to the implementation and establishment of IMC.

Stage 1
Therefore, it seems that the starting point in the move towards IMC needs to reflect the context within which exchanges occur. In the majority of cases these will be transactional, where the focus is on product and price. The move from this point will be towards coordinating the tools, media and messages of the mix and this will gradually take place both internally and externally with the organisation's various agencies.

Stage 2
In order to make this work and to move forward, organisations need to create a technology platform necessary to provide a stream of information upon which it is possible to interact coherently with customers. The technology will be used internally to provide an operational tie between the different departments and functional areas. This is an important part of the process as different sections of the organisation are introduced to the ideas of being market-oriented. To support this, the notion that internal marketing relationships and internal marketing communications play an important role in the overall orientation process is also introduced.

Stage 3
Organisations will begin to adopt media-neutral planning principles and/or develop fully coordinated, even integrated marketing communications. This will be characterised by data-driven communications, CRM and meaningful evaluation and measurement techniques. This stage will be complemented by the organisation moving towards a strong(er) customer orientation. This requires a *cultural shift* of values and beliefs, whereby organisational, brand identity and relationship issues become paramount. This can only be implemented at this stage, as the internal systems, procedures and employee mind set need to be in place if the strategy is to be credible to customers and other stakeholders.

Stage 4
The final IMC stage is reached when planned communications and brand experiences encourage continued interaction, dialogue and relationship development. At this stage all parties involved in IMC derive an enhanced value over and above the value that would have been achieved without the integration.

> The final IMC stage is reached when planned communications and brand experiences encourage continued interaction, dialogue and relationship development.

In order for these incremental stages to be undertaken and completed satisfactorily, managers must be clear and agreed about what it is they wish to achieve and communicate their intent to all those it involves, both inside and outside the organisation.

This sequential depiction sets out various incremental stages and does not require that they all be followed in strict order, and nor is it intended that all organisations should or do progress to the end. For many, perhaps small and medium-sized organisations, especially those with many transactional customers, promotional coordination or coordinated marketing communications stages may suffice.

One of the key issues encouraging the establishment of IMC has been the willingness of some public relations practitioners to move closer to the marketing department. When IMC began to emerge, Miller and Rose (1994) commentated that the previously held opposition to integration by public relations practitioners had begun to dissolve as the more enlightened agencies see it as 'a reality and a necessity'. Although this movement has not surged forward, many public relations agencies now proclaim that they provide IMC, particularly web and direct and database marketing services. Apart from this, the marketing communications industry has yet to come together and provide clients with the fully integrated services they desire.

Summary

In order to help consolidate your understanding of integrated marketing communications, here are the key points summarised against each of the learning objectives:

1. Introduce the concept of integrated marketing communications (IMC) and explore what it is that is integrated.

Integrated marketing communications (IMC) is concerned with the development, coordination and implementation of an organisation's various strategies, resources and messages. The role is to enable coherent and meaningful engagement with target audiences. In an age when consumers can touch brands across a range of channels it is important that each contact reinforces previous messages and facilitates the development of valued relationships. While the concept of IMC is attractive, to date the development of the approach in practical terms has not been very encouraging. There has been a great deal of debate about the meaning and value of an integrated approach and some attempt to coordinate the content and delivery of marketing communication messages. Most organisations have yet to achieve totally integrated marketing communications; only partial or coordinated levels of activity have so far been achieved.

A wide range of elements needs to be integrated. These include the communication tools, media and messages, plus the elements of the marketing mix, brands, strategy, employees, agencies and technology.

2. Understand the different perspectives of IMC.

Cornelissen identified two main perspectives of IMC running through the literature. He refers to one of these as a predominantly *process*-oriented concept and the second is that IMC is a *content*-oriented concept.

The *content* perspective holds that IMC works when there is a consistency throughout the various materials and messages. The *process* perspective of IMC is rooted in the belief that real IMC can only be generated through an organisational structure that brings the various communication disciplines together in a single body or unit.

3. Consider the background and reasons for the development and interest in IMC.

The interest in IMC has resulted from three main drivers. These include market-based drivers, those that arise from changing communications, and those that are driven from opportunities arising from within the organisation itself.

4. Explore some of the issues associated with managing and implementing IMC.

The management of IMC has been shown to be a challenging task and one that does not always result in a successful outcome. There is much resistance to the development of IMC, again based on a range of factors, some of them found in many situations regardless of what it is that is to be changed. There are several ideas concerning the best way to implement IMC but perhaps the most important point is that IMC can only be achieved by incremental change, not a one-off wholesale change.

5. Explain variants of the IMC concept: media-neutral planning and open planning approaches.

Media-neutral planning is an element of IMC but IMC is not the same as MNP. With increasing levels of fragmentation and rising media (television) costs the need for media-neutrality has increased. The main thrust of MNP is to reduce the emphasis on television and make increased use of other tools and media that are more audience-focused than traditional marketing communications practice has been to date.

Open planning is concerned with eight action areas, each of which contribute to the process of MNP. Working with action areas is designed to promote marketing communications that are audience-centred rather than perpetuate a focus on the communication industry.

6. Consider how the structures and frameworks of advertising and communication agencies might need to change so that they are better able to work with IMC.

Many organisations that have sought to develop IMC have had to restructure their organisations and provide new systems and processes to enable integration at a process level to develop. In much the same way, agencies have been faced with structural change in order to remain competitive to meet the needs of their clients. Their difficulty is that there is not an optimal structure. Agencies need to trade off between the need to provide expertise and the need to control and provide a central source of IMC.

7. Examine ideas concerning an incremental approach to IMC.

Integrated marketing communications means different things to different people. Opportunities to develop IMC appear to vary according to a variety of factors, including organisation size and development.

The development of IMC appears to be best achieved when an incremental approach is adopted. *Stage 1* considers the transactional elements and any move forward should be based on coordinating the tools, media and messages of the mix. This will gradually take place both internally and externally with the organisation's various agencies. *Stage 2* requires a technology platform necessary to provide a stream of information upon which it is possible to interact coherently with customers. *Stage 3* is characterised by data-driven communications, CRM and meaningful evaluation and measurement techniques. This stage is often complemented by a strong(er) customer orientation. This requires a *cultural shift* of values and beliefs, whereby organisational, brand identity and relationship issues become paramount. Finally, *Stage 4* is reached when planned communications and brand experiences encourage continued interaction, dialogue and relationship development.

Review questions

1. Discuss the main reasons for the development of IMC.
2. Prepare brief notes explaining four different elements that should be part of the integration process.
3. Explain how various definitions of IMC have evolved.
4. What are the reasons for interest in IMC and is it a valid concept?
5. Appraise the main reasons offered for the failure of organisations to develop IMC.
6. What is the incremental approach to establishing IMC?
7. Explain the ideas concerning media-neutral planning and what is open planning?
8. Explain the meaning of process and content perspectives of IMC.
9. Discuss the view that IMC is essentially the same as relationship marketing.
10. Prepare the outline for an essay arguing whether IMC is a strategic approach or just a means to correct internal operational difficulties and reduce media costs.

IMC – richer consumer engagement

J. Graham Spickett-Jones, University of Hull

IMC seeks to optimise the use of resources in the way campaign elements are combined, but it is not new or easy to describe. As communication technologies and agency skills advance, optimum campaign solutions may be both context specific and evolving. As early as the 1970s Stephen King (2007) recognised the power of a *coherent totality* in marketing propositions. He suggested this totality should be traced through the advertising, the pack and even the physical elements of a product to express an *integrated* brand personality. Back then, 'adverting was' often a primary means of encapsulating this brand personality. So advertising agencies liked to think of themselves as brand guardians, and they used processes that integrated advertising messages across different media platforms. Cost-effective advertising combinations, drawing on the relative strengths of outdoor, print and radio media, were often used to amplify television campaigns. However, as marketing communication disciplines have expanded and embraced new technology, the challenge of how to manage integration across the communication landscape has grown.

Debate remains over what IMC involves in practise, perhaps because IMC is a moving target. As the range of potential campaign resources expands and the media habits of consumers shift, the judgements about which campaign elements to integrate for optimal effectiveness may also change. One of the challenges of managing IMC remains the measurement of isolated elements within an integrated campaign framework. IMC requires ways to measure campaigns that can combine above-the-line and below-the-line activity and off-line and on-line channels. This is an area Google are keen to develop but their UK Managing Director, Mark Howe, regards this as a distant goal, 'It won't happen this year, but that is the Holy Grail' (McCormick, 2008).

An expanding range of potential campaign elements available to communication planners provides a creative palette for combining a range of contact points with different markets. This offers new and traditional 'touch points' as ways to reach people in different ways and with specific messages that suit each touch point. Intercepting people in ways that understand their responsiveness in different environments and particular media contexts can help to integrate campaign activity. It can help map an optimum *media journey* for different types of target groups so that a combination of touch points can be used to orchestrate the *brand journey* sought by a campaign. The tools may change but the task remains similar to one Stephen King would have recognised 30 years ago, the development of a *coherent totality* in the marketing proposition, and the coordinated effort to make cost-effective and optimal use of promotional resources.

What is different, however, is the growing complexity of the communication landscape, the ever more competitive pressure on organisations and the growing media literacy of the public. This means large IMC programmes may need to employ *communication planning* at an early stage of a campaign cycle to interpret the best type of campaign solution and the sort of communication agencies that might be needed to help. Often this communication planning service has been provided by one of the specialist media agencies but other large communication agencies have started to offer this service too, to try to retain a strong strategic campaign role. Communication planning can help develop a campaign brief, which may prepare to involve an integrated cocktail of professional communication services well before approaching these other agencies.

An example where communication planning was used early on to help coordinate a major integrated campaign can be seen in the work of the communication planning agency, Naked, for the directory enquiry service, 118 118. The service was launched in Britain in 2003 for the US directory enquiries provider, InfoNXX. The launch campaign involved a wide range of integrated communication activities and Naked worked on the campaign plan from an early stage, well ahead of the launch date, with the advertising agency WCRS, who developed the creative proposition used across the campaign.

The IMC campaign aimed to take people on a brand journey so that 118 118 would become the natural inheritor of the previous number associated with the directory enquiry service in the UK, 192. This was a time of forced market disruption because the telecommunications regulator at the time was keen to weaken the near monopoly on this lucrative service by the previously state-owned company, British Telecom (BT). To do this the established directory enquiry number was to be scrapped and replaced, and a number of companies had decided to enter the market. The challenge for all competitors would be similar, to become a *top of mind* number in a low involvement but potentially large and therefore lucrative market. Naked planned to take the market on a brand journey in stages. *Stage 1, Advertising*, starting to develop recognition of the brand. *Stage 2, Conversations*, planned to develop buzz so people would share information about the brand to give it legitimacy. *Stage 3, Experiential*, was designed to encourage participation and involvement with the brand. While *Stage 4, Personal*, was designed to create a sense of ownership, where the brand became a consumer's own service.

The media journey closely mapped these stages using carefully selected symbols to give continuity, a pair of men as spoof athletes decked out in running vests with the same 'competitor number' repeated on each vest: '118' and '118'. A zany personality for the two athletes was portrayed at Stage 1, using advertising across a wide range of platforms. This was anticipated to resonate with the UK public because of a love of nostalgia, humour and irreverence. The adverting helped establish the symbol (two wacky runners, each with a 118 vest) as a potential public icon. With the catch phrase, '*got your number*', this iconography was used as a vehicle to manage the rest of the brand journey. The media landscape employed both

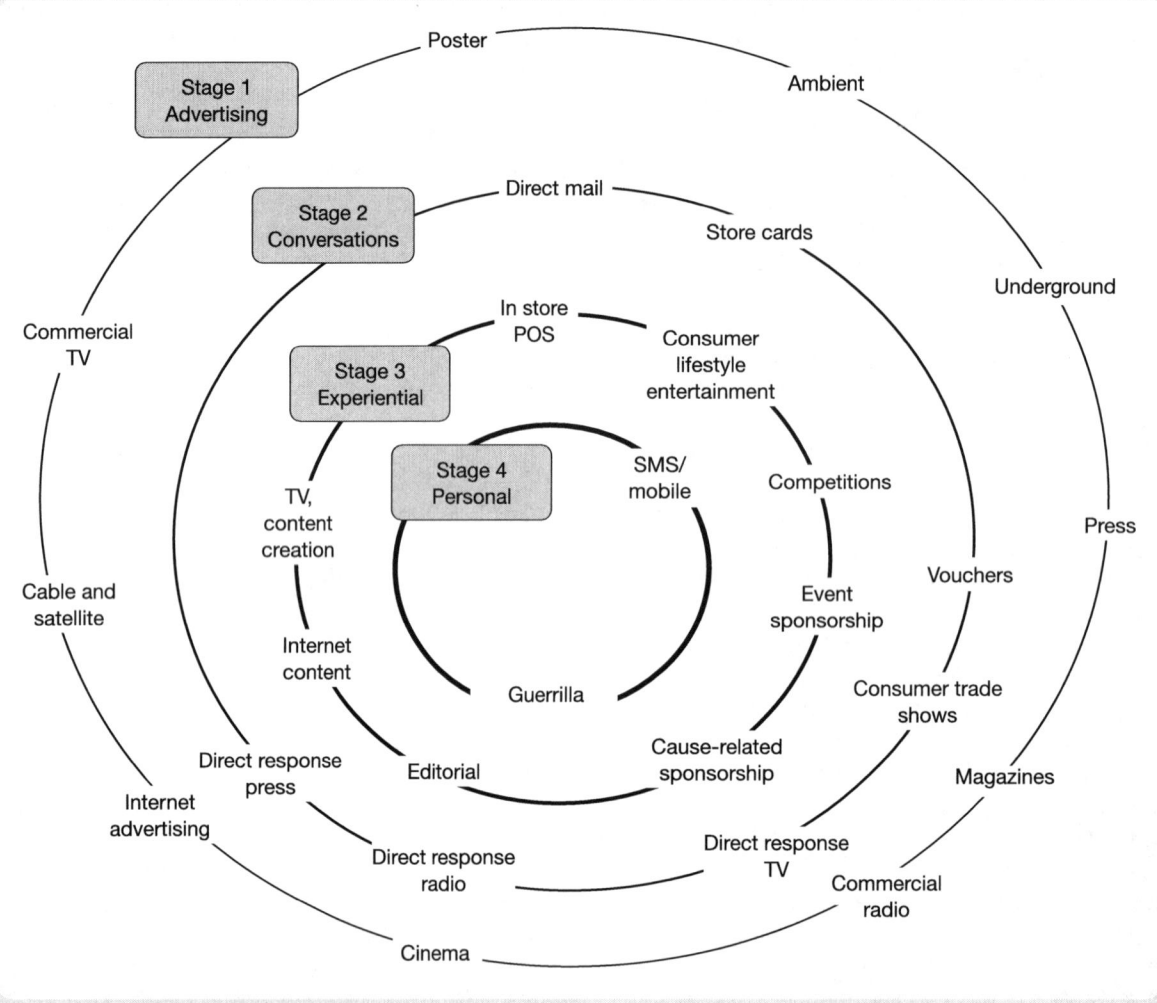

Figure 9.6 A media map of the launch campaign for '118 118'
Source: Adapted from presentation by agencies Naked, WCRS and Huge to D&AD's Xchange (2004) (London School of Fashion, 1 September 2004).

traditional channels and novel media spaces (e.g. fly-posting, street-hawkers [selling 118 shirts in the centre of major UK cities], washing-line stunts using 118 shirts and barber shop window promotions – seeming to advertise hair cuts like the spoof athletes used as brand symbols).

The campaign involved novel experiential elements, especially at Stage 3 of the programme. This made some of the tracking and measurement a particular challenge. However, the nature of the product behind the brand meant that the service requests could be tracked. Therefore the agencies involved agreed to work partly on a performance-based remuneration system, where they were rewarded for the success of the campaign measured by the volumes of traffic driven to use the directory enquiry service.

Within less than a year of the service going live 118 118 had a close to 50 per cent market share. This was achieved in an otherwise cluttered and competitive market that had been previously dominated by a near monopoly provider.

MiniCase references

King, S. (2007) What is a brand?. In *A Master Class in Brand Planning: The Timeless Works of Stephen King* (eds J. Lannon and M. Baskin), 27–40. London: John Wiley & Sons.

McCormick, A. (2008) Google looks for media's Holy Grail. *Media Week*, 12–19 February, 18.

MiniCase questions

1. In the campaign above, what might have been the role for consumer-driven content and social networks' websites?
2. In terms of the use of large-scale IMC, how might a launch campaign differ from the ongoing campaign activity needed to support a brand after launch?
3. Which participants involved in a campaign plan are best placed to coordinate IMC activity and why?
4. In what ways might IMC benefit from a network of service providers found in industry clusters, such as that found in Central London?

References

Anon. (2005) Sainsbury's polishes up its image, 19 September, retrieved 5 November 2007 from www.news.bbc.co.uk/1/hi/business/4259224.stm

Brook, S. (2005) Sainsbury's unveils new slogan, *MediaGuardian*, 19 September 2005. Retrieved 5 November 2007 from http://www.guardian.co.uk/media/2005/sep/19/business.advertising.

Brown, J. (1997) Impossible dream or inevitable revolution: an exploration of integrated marketing communications. *Journal of Communication Management*, **12**(1), 70–81.

Cornelissen, J. (2000) Integration in communication management: conceptual and methodological considerations. *Journal of Marketing Management*, **16**, 597–606.

Cornelissen, J.P. and Lock, A.R. (2000) Theoretical concept or management fashion? Examining the significance of IMC. *Journal of Advertising Research*, **50**(5), 7–15.

Cornelissen, J.P. (2003) Change, continuity and progress: the concept of integrated marketing communications and marketing communications practice. *Journal of Strategic Marketing*, **11** (December), 217–34.

Cowlett, M. (2007) Nexus gives biscuits a classic crunchy edge, *PR Week*, 16 May. Retrieved 19 February 2008 from http://www.prweek.com/uk/.

Dewhirst, T. and Davis, B. (2005) Brand strategy and integrated marketing communications (IMC): A case study of Player's cigarette brand marketing. *Journal of Advertising*, **34**(4), (Winter), 81–92.

Duncan (2002) *IMC: using advertising and promotion to build brands* (International edition). New York: McGraw-Hill.

Duncan, T. and Everett, S. (1993) Client perceptions of integrated marketing communications. *Journal of Advertising Research*, **3**(3), 30–9.

Duncan, T. and Moriarty, S. (1998) A communication-based marketing model for managing relationships. *Journal of Marketing*, **62** (April), 1–13.

Duncan, T. and Mulhern, F. (2004) *A white paper on the status, scope and future of IMC programs*. (From the IMC symposium by the IMC programs at Northwestern University and University of Denver.) New York: McGraw-Hill.

Eagle, L. and Kitchen, P. (2000) IMC, brand communications, and corporate cultures. *European Journal of Marketing*, **34**(5/6), 667–86.

Fill, C. (2001) Essentially a matter of consistency. *Marketing Review*, **1**(4), (Summer), 409–25.

Gray, R. (2007) Unity of purpose, *Marketing*, 13 December, 6.

Grein, A.F. and Gould, S.J. (1996) Globally integrated communications. *Journal of Marketing Communications*, **2**, 141–58.

Gronroos, C. (2004) The relationship marketing process: communication, interaction, dialogue, value. *Journal of Business and Industrial Marketing*, **19**(2), 99–113.

Hutton, J.G. (1996) Integrated relationship-marketing communications: a key opportunity for IMC. *Journal of Marketing Communications*, **2**, 191–9.

Jenkinson, A. and Sain, B. (2004) Open planning: media neutral planning made simple. Retrieved 14 November 2004 from www.openplanning.org/cases/openplanning/whitepaper.pdf.

Jones, G. (2007) Velvet makes digital debut, *Marketing*, 21 March, 14.

Kitchen, P.J. and Shultz, D.E. (1997) Integrated marketing communications in US advertising agencies: an exploratory study. *Journal of Advertising Research*, **37**(5), 7–18.

Kitchen, P.J. and Shultz, D.E. (1998) IMC – a UK ads agency perspective. *Journal of Marketing Management*, **14**(2), 465–85.

Kitchen, P., Brignell, J., Li, T. and Spickett-Jones, G. (2004) The emergence of IMC: a theoretical perspective. *Journal of Advertising Research*, **44** (March), 19–30.

Kitchen, P.J., Spickett-Jones, G. and Grimes, T. (2007) Inhibition of brand integration amid changing agency structures. *Journal of Marketing Communications*, **13**(2), 149–68.

Kliatchko, J. (2008) Revisiting the IMC construct: a revised definition and four pillars. *International Journal of Advertising*, **27**(1), 133–60.

Lee, D.H. and Park, C.W. (2007) Conceptualization and measurement of multidimensionality of integrated marketing communications. *Journal of Advertising Research*, (September), 222–36.

Low, G.S. (2000) Correlates of integrated marketing communications. *Journal of Advertising Research*, **40**(3), 27–39.

Miller, D.A. and Rose, P.B. (1994) Integrated communications: a look at reality instead of theory. *Public Relations Quarterly* (Spring), 13–16.

Mintzberg, H., Lampel, J.B., Quinn, J.B. and Ghoshal, S. (2003) *The Strategy Process*, 4th edn. Englewood Cliffs, NJ: Pearson Education.

Percy, L., Rossiter, J.R. and Elliot, R. (2001) *Strategic Advertising Management*, New York: Oxford University Press.

Pitta, D.A., Weisgal, M. and Lynagh, P. (2006) Integrating exhibit marketing into integrated marketing communications. *Journal of Consumer Marketing*, **23**(3), 156–66.

Porter, M.E. (1980) *Competitive Strategy: Techniques for Analyzing Industries and Competitors*. New York: Free Press.

Ray, A. (2002) How to adopt a neutral stance. *Marketing*, 27 June, 27.

Reed, D. (2006) Media rivalry barring integrated path. *Precision Marketing*, 25 August, 6.

Reid, M. (2005) Performance auditing of integrated marketing communication (IMC) actions and outcomes. *Journal of Advertising*, **34**(4) (Winter), 41–54.

Schultz, D. (1993) *Integrated Marketing Communications: Putting It Together and Making It Work*. Lincolnwood, IL: NTC Business Books.

Shimp, T.A. (2000) *Advertising Promotion: Supplemental Aspects of Integrated Marketing Communications*, 5th edn. Fort Worth, TX: Dryden Press, Harcourt College Publishers.

Smith, P. (1996) Benefits and barriers to integrated communications. *Admap* (February), 19–22.

Spake, D.F., D'Souza, G., Crutchfield, T.N. and Morgan, R.M. (1999) Advertising agency compensation: an agency theory explanation. *Journal of Advertising*, **28**(3), 53–72.

Spotts, H.E., Lambert, D.R. and Joyce, M.L. (1998) Marketing déjà vu: the discovery of integrated marketing communications. *Journal of Marketing Education*, **20**(3), 210–18.

Swain, W.N. (2004) Perceptions of IMC after a decade of development: who's at the wheel, and how can we measure success? *Journal of Advertising Research*, **44**(1) (March), 46–65.

Tobaccowala, R. and Kugel, C. (2001) Planning and evaluating cross-media programs. *Admap*, February, 33–6.

White, R. (2000) Chameleon brands: tailoring brand messages to consumers. *Admap*, (July/August), 8–40.

Chapter 10

Marketing communications: strategies, tactics and planning

A marketing communications strategy refers to an organisation's overall positioning orientation and their preferred approach to communicating with customers and stakeholders. Marketing communications strategies are contingent on the business and marketing strategies the organisation is pursuing. Tactics are concerned with the communication mix developed to deliver the positioning strategy.

Marketing communication plans are concerned with programmes and campaigns designed to articulate an organisation's marketing communication tactics and strategy.

Aims and learning objectives

The aims of this chapter are to explore the nature of strategy and marketing communications strategies in particular. The goal is to enable readers to appreciate the elements and concepts associated with marketing communication strategy, tactics and planning, and to introduce the marketing communications planning framework.

The learning objectives of this chapter are to:

1. establish the differences between strategy, tactics and planning;
2. appreciate the essence of marketing communications strategy;
3. consider three main marketing communication strategies: pull, push and profile;
4. explain the notion of strategic balance;
5. explore different approaches to Internet-based communication strategies;
6. present a planning framework and consider the different elements involved in the development of marketing communication plans;
7. highlight the importance of the linkages and interaction between the different elements of the plan.

For an applied interpretation see Angela Hall's MiniCase entitled *Ski Rossendale* at the end of this chapter.

Introduction

> In essence IMC represents a strategic approach to marketing communications.

This chapter follows on from the previous chapter that explored integrated marketing communications. In essence IMC represents a strategic approach to marketing communications, yet its application by many organisations is invariably more consistent with a tactical rather than strategic perspective. Various issues implicit in the previous discussion are relevant in this chapter and, although not developed further, should be considered by readers.

It is assumed by many that marketing communication strategy is simply the combination of tools of the communications mix. In other words, strategy is about the degree of direct marketing, personal selling, advertising, sales promotion and public relations that is incorporated within a planned sequence of communication activities.

This is important but this is tactical, and is not the essence of marketing communications strategy. From a strategic perspective, key decisions concern the overall direction of the programme and target audiences, the fit with marketing and corporate strategy, the key message and desired positioning the brand is to occupy in the market, the resources necessary to deliver the position and overall goals.

The chapter begins with a consideration of some fundamental ideas concerning the nature of strategy. From this a contextual and customer perspective is developed on which to build marketing communications strategy. This is used in preference to a production orientation, which is founded on the resource base. This customer orientation requires revisiting ideas concerning market segmentation and the characteristics and buying behaviour of the different target audiences. From here various dimensions of communications strategy are developed.

Understanding strategy

In order to appreciate the role and nature of communication strategy it is useful to appreciate the dimensions of the strategy concept. The management literature on strategy is extensive yet there seems to be little agreement or consensus about what it is, what it means or how it should be developed. A full discussion of this topic is beyond the scope of this book but what follows is a brief overview of some of the more general views about management strategy.

> The disparity of views about strategy is due to the multidimensional nature of the strategy concept.

Hambrick (1983) suggested that the disparity of views about strategy is due to the multidimensional nature of the strategy concept, that strategy is situational and that it varies according to industry and the environment in which it operates. In other words contextual issues determine the nature of strategy. This may be true but it does not help us understand what strategy is.

The one main area wherein most authors find agreement concerns the hierarchical nature of strategy within organisations (Kay, 1993; Johnson *et al.*, 2008; Mintzberg and Ghoshal, 2003). This refers to the notion that there are three main levels of organisational strategy; corporate, competitive and functional. Corporate strategy is considered to be directional and sets out the broad, overarching parameters and means through which the organisation operates in order to realise its objectives. Strategies at the functional level, for example, marketing, finance and production, should be integrated in such a way that they contribute to the satisfaction of the higher-level competitive strategies, which in turn should satisfy the overall corporate goals. Competitive-level strategies are important because not only do they set out the way in which the organisation will compete and use resources, but they should also provide clear messages about the way in which the organisation seeks to manage its environment.

Chaffee (1985) identifies several themes associated with the various strategic interpretations. The first is that strategy is used by organisations as a means of adjusting to changing environmental conditions and the second is that strategy is often referred to in terms of decision making, actions and implementation. Apart from the hierarchical element mentioned previously, one of her other significant observations concerned the point that strategy could take various forms, most notably, deliberate, emergent and realised formats.

Two main strategy schools of thought can be identified, namely the planning and the emergent approaches. The planning school is the pre-eminent paradigm and is based on strategy development and implementation, which is explicit, rational and planned as a sequence of logical steps. Andrews (1987) comments that strategy is concerned with a company's objectives, purpose and policies and its plans to satisfy the goals using particular resources with respect to a range of internal and external stakeholders. The organisation interacts with and attempts to shape its environment in pursuit of its goals. This perspective of strategy was first formulated in the 1950s and 1960s when the operating environments of most organisations were simple, stable and thus predictable. However, these conditions rarely exist in the twenty-first century and the validity of the rational model of strategy has been questioned.

> Two main strategy schools of thought can be identified, namely the planning and the emergent approaches.

The emergent school of thought considers strategy to develop incrementally, step-by-step, as organisations learn, sometimes through simple actions of trial and error. The core belief is that strategy is comprised of a stream of organisational activities that are continuously being formulated, implemented, tested, evaluated and updated. Chaffee suggests that strategy should be considered in terms of a linear, adaptive or interpretive approach, each one reflecting a progressively sophisticated perspective. While the linear approach reflects the more traditional and deliberate approach to strategy (Ansoff, 1965; Andrews, 1987), the adaptive strategy is important because it reflects the view that organisations flex and adjust to changing environments while the interpretive or higher-order point of view considers strategy to be a reflection of the influence of social order on strategic decision making.

> The emergent school of thought considers strategy to develop incrementally, step-by-step, as organisations learn, sometimes through simple actions of trial and error.

Two other strategic authors to be mentioned are Mintzberg (1994) and Whittington (1993). Mintzberg argues that strategy can be regarded as one or more of 5Ps of strategy. These are strategy as a Plan, Position, Perspective, Ploy and Pattern. Whittington (1993) offers four generic strategies: Classical, Evolutionary, Processual and Systemic (see Table 10.1).

Table 10.1 Views of strategy

Author	Type of Strategy	Explanation
Mintzberg	Plan	A predetermined, deliberate course of action, implementation and evaluation.
	Position	An attempt to locate an organisation within a market.
	Perspective	A collective view of the world, one that is ingrained within the organisation and its position within it.
	Ploy	A scheme or manoeuvre to sidestep or outwit competitors.
	Pattern	A stream of actions in which there are consistent patterns of behaviour.
Whittington	Classical	Planned, rational and deliberate.
	Evolutionary	Darwinian in outlook, this strategy perceives a manager's task as trying to survive by fitting as closely as possible to the prevailing environmental conditions.
	Processual	An essentially incremental perspective whereby strategy is concerned with learning from past actions and experience. Little emphasis is given to long-term planning and horizons.
	Systemic	Strategy is a reflection of the social systems in which strategists participate.

Sources: Whittington (1993); Mintzberg (1994).

There are a number of common points shared within these various views and perspectives of strategy. Chaffee, Mintzberg and Whittington all agree that strategy can be considered to be deliberate in nature as reflected in their respective linear, planned and classical approaches. They also agree that strategy can be emergent and can evolve from the actions of the organisation. This can be seen in their adaptive, pattern and processual approaches. They also develop views on the extent to which an organisation interacts with its environment or seeks to directly influence it. Chaffee refers to interpretive strategies, Mintzberg to strategy as a perspective and Whittington to systemic interpretations.

ViewPoint 10.1 Strategic Apples

According to Rumelt, an eminent US academic and strategy consultant, most corporate strategic plans are concerned with maintaining market share and rolling forward three- or five-year resource budgets. There is little strategy in the corporate strategies he sees.

For him, strategy is about exploiting change in the environment, change in terms of technological advances, resource prices, consumer tastes or competitive behaviour. Strategy is about how these changes are developed and the positions that firms adopt with regard to these changes. Rumelt refers to a discussion with Steve Jobs at Apple following his successful return to the company in 1998. Rumelt observed at the time that Apple, no matter how well they performed, were still operating in a small niche within the personal computer business. So, the question he posed was what was Jobs trying to achieve, what was the longer-term strategy? The unexpected answer was . . . 'I am going to wait for the next big thing'.

For Jobs, strategy is not about 'cutting costs and forming alliances', a disparaging phrase used by Rumelt when referring to common interpretations of corporate strategy. His role was to seize opportunities presented by the environment, evidenced through the subsequent success of Pixar, iPod and probably iPhone.

Source: Adapted from Lovallo and Mendonca (2007).

Question
How would you interpret Apple's approach to strategy – is it planning or emergent?

Task
Go to the web sites for Boeing and Airbus. What are their strategies?

> Strategy is about the means, speed and methods by which organisations adapt to and influence their environments.

Views on strategy have evolved as our understanding has developed. Strategy is not just about a deliberate, planned approach to business development, although it can be at the functional and competitive levels. Strategy is about the means, speed and methods by which organisations adapt to and influence their environments in order that they achieve their goals. What is also clear is that the demarcation between an organisation and its environment is less clear than it used to be. An imaginary line was once used to refer to a border between an organisation and its environment. This line is no longer deemed valid as organisations are now viewed as boundary-free. The implications of this borderless concept for marketing communications are potentially enormous. Not only do contemporary views of strategy amplify the significance of the interaction between strategy and an organisation's environment but they also stress the importance for strategy, at whatever level, to be contextually oriented and determined.

Market segmentation

The planned and deliberate perspective of strategy has had a long-term impact on marketing management. The process of market analysis and evaluation leading to planned strategies designed to meet prescribed and measurable goals is well established. It is argued that this approach enables finite resources to be used more efficiently as they can be directed towards markets that hold, potentially, greater value than other markets. Market segmentation is a part of this approach and is both a functional and competitive-level strategy. More importantly, the process of market segmentation is the means by which organisations define the broad context within which their strategic business units (SBUs) and products are offered.

Market segmentation is the division of a mass market into identifiable and distinct groups or segments, each of which has common characteristics, needs and display similar responses to marketing actions. Through this process specific target segments can be selected and marketing plans developed to satisfy the individual needs of the potential buyers in these chosen segments. The development, or rather identification, of segments can be perceived as opportunities, and, as Beane and Ennis (1987) suggest, 'a company with limited resources needs to pick only the best opportunities to pursue'. The most common bases upon which markets can be segmented are set out in Table 10.2.

This process of segmentation is necessary because a single product is unlikely to meet the needs of all customers in a mass market. If it were, then a single type of toothpaste, chocolate bar or car would meet all of our needs. This is not so, and there are a host of products and brands seeking to satisfy particular buyer needs. For example, ask yourself the question, 'Why do I use toothpaste?' The answer, most probably, is one of the following:

> Segmentation is necessary because a single product is unlikely to meet the needs of all customers in a mass market.

- You want dental hygiene.
- You like fresh breath and you do not want to offend others.

Table 10.2 Bases for segmenting markets

Segmentation base	Explanation
Demographic	Key variables concern age, sex, occupation, level of education, religion, social class and income characteristics, many of which determine, to a large extent, a potential buyer's ability to enter into an exchange relationship or transaction.
Geographic	In many situations the needs of potential customers in one geographic area are different from those in another area. For example, it is often said that Scottish beer drinkers prefer heavy bitters, Northerners in England prefer mild, drinkers in the West prefer cider, and in the South lager is the preferred drink.
Geodemographic	This type of segmentation is based on the assumption that there is a relationship between the type of housing people live in and their purchasing behaviours. At the root of this approach is the ability to use postcodes to send similar messages to similar groups of households, on the basis that where we live determines how we live. The most well-known commercial applications are Acorn (a classification of residential neighbourhoods), Mosaic and Pinpoint.
Psychographic	Through an analysis of consumers' activities, interests and opinions (AIO) it is possible to determine lifestyles or patterns of behaviour. These are a synthesis of the motivations, personality and core values held by individuals. These AIO patterns are reflected in the buying behaviour and decision-making processes of individuals. By identifying and clustering common lifestyles, a correlation with a consumer's product and/or media usage patterns becomes possible.
Behaviouristic	Usage and lifestage segments are derived from analysing markets on the basis of customer behaviour. Usage of soft drinks can be considered in terms of purchase patterns (two bottles per week), usage situations (parties, picnics or as an alcohol substitute) or purchase location (supermarket, convenience store or wine merchant). Lifestage analysis is based on the principle that people have varying amounts of disposable income and different needs at different stages in their lives. Their priorities for spending change at different trigger points and these points or lifestages do not occur at the same time.

Table 10.3 Benefit segments for the toothpaste market

Segment name	The sensory segment	The sociables	The worriers	The independents
Principal benefit sought	Flavour, product appearance	Brightness of teeth	Decay prevention	Price
Demographic strengths	Children	Teens, young people	Large families	Men
Special behavioural characteristics	Users of spearmint-flavoured toothpaste	Smokers	Heavy users	Heavy users
Brands disproportionately favoured	Colgate, Stripe	Macleans, Plus White, Ultra Brite	Crest, Sensodyne	Brands on sale
Personality characteristics	High self-involvement	High sociability	High hypochondriasis	High autonomy
Lifestyle characteristics	Hedonistic	Active	Conservative	Value oriented

Source: Haley (1968). Used with kind permission of the American Marketing Association.

- You want white, shining teeth to appear attractive and approachable.
- You like the fresh oral sensation.
- Other products (e.g. water, soap) are not so effective and do not taste very nice.

Whatever the reason, it is unlikely that given a choice everyone would all choose the same product. In what is now regarded as a classic study, Russell Haley (1968) undertook some pioneering research in this field and from it established four distinct types of customer. Even after over 35 years have elapsed this typology remains a potent practical example of market segmentation: those who bought toothpaste for white teeth (sociables); those who wished to prevent decay (worriers); those who liked the taste and refreshment properties (sensors); and finally those who bought on a price basis (independents). Each of these groups has particular demographic, behaviouristic and psychographic characteristics that can be seen in Table 10.3.

It is not surprising that a range of toothpaste products has been developed that attempts to satisfy the needs of different buyers, for example, Macleans for fresh breath, Crest for dental hygiene, Sensodyne for those sensitive to hot and cold drinks and numerous others promoted on special offers for those independent buyers looking for a low price. There are others who are not very interested in the product and have continued using a brand that others in their current or past households are comfortable with.

ViewPoint 10.2 Ethically Segmented

As the move towards ethical and environmental awareness grows, a study by Henley Centre reveals the extent to which the United Kingdom is becoming green. The report identifies five segments:

- Onlookers — Moderately concerned but have no intention of making small changes or living ethically, 26 per cent of the population.
- Conveniently conscious — Fairly concerned about the environment, think brands should act responsibly and they make easy lifestyle changes, 35 per cent of the population.
- Positive choosers — Highly aware, very concerned and try hard to live ethically, 31 per cent of the population.

> - Principled pioneers: The most committed group, happy to install alternative energy sources and calculate their carbon footprint, just 4 per cent of the population.
> - Vocal activists: Very similar to the positive choosers but they vocalise their concerns about unethical brands, 4 per cent of the population.
>
> This suggests there are opportunities for brands to develop strategies to appeal to these segments. In doing so, such ethical positioning appears to lead consumers to perceive brands to be of higher quality.
>
> Source: Tiltman (2007).
>
> ### Question
> How might this information affect an electronics manufacturer and a management consultancy?
>
> ### Task
> Using a search engine, locate a solar energy equipment supplier and see how they might segment their markets.

Therefore, target segments constitute the environment and the context for the marketing communications strategy and activities. It is the characteristics of the target segment and their perception that should shape an audience-centred marketing communication strategy.

Marketing communications strategy

Many organisations do not develop and implement a communication strategy. They may develop brand strategies, advertising strategies and indeed some form of integrated marketing communication strategies but there is little evidence of organisations developing corporate-led communication strategies. Steyn (2003) believes that this might be because practitioners do not fully understand the word *strategy*, while Moss and Warnaby (1998) suggest that academics have neglected the role of corporate communication in the strategy process. Holm (2006) reported that the programmes at two leading Swedish communication schools contained 90 per cent communication-related material and just 10 per cent on leadership matters. In contrast, the programme at Sweden's leading management school designed to deliver strategic education, devotes just 3 per cent of the time to communication issues. The general conclusion Holm draws is that those responsible for organisation, strategic leadership and decision making appear to lack insight, awareness and the skills regarding communication. Undoubtedly ideas concerning communication and strategy have not always been well articulated or taught together, are often tactical and there is certainly little agreement on what constitutes corporate communication and marketing communication strategies.

Marketing communications strategy is concerned with two key dynamics. The first dynamic is concerned with who, in broad terms, is the target audience? End-user customers need to derive particular benefits based on perceived value, from the exchange process. These benefits are very different from those that intermediaries expect to derive, or indeed any other stakeholder who does not consume the product or service. The second dynamic concerns the way in which an audience understands the offering they are experiencing either through use or through communications. The way in which people interpret messages and frame objects in their mind is concerned with positioning.

> The way in which people interpret messages and frame objects in their mind is concerned with positioning.

Marketing communications strategy therefore, is concerned with audiences and positioning.

Audiences

The prevailing approach to marketing communications (advertising) strategy has traditionally been founded upon the configuration of the 'promotional' mix. Strategy was an interpretation of the mix and hence the resources an organisation deployed. This represents a production rather than market orientation to marketing communications and is intrinsically misplaced. This inside-out form of strategy is essentially resource-driven. However, a market orientation to strategy requires a consideration of the needs of the audience first and then a determination of the various messages, media and disciplines to accomplish the strategy, an outside-in approach.

Consumer purchase decisions are characterised (very generally and see Chapter 6) by a single-person buying centre whereas organisational buying decisions can involve a large number of different people, fulfilling different roles and all requiring different marketing communication messages. It follows from this that the approach to communicating with these two very different target sectors should be radically different, especially in terms of what, where, when and how a message is communicated. Once communication objectives have been established, it is necessary to formulate appropriate strategies.

Communication objectives that are focused on consumer markets require a different strategy from those formulated to satisfy the objectives that are focused on organisational customers. In addition, there are circumstances and reasons to focus communications on the development of the organisation with a corporate brand and range of other stakeholders. Often, these corporate brands need to work closely with the development of product brands.

Positioning

> Positioning is the key strategic framework for an organisation's brand-based communications.

As noted in the earlier discussion about strategy, positioning is an integral concept, and for some the essence of strategy. Wind (1990) stated quite clearly that positioning is the key strategic framework for an organisation's brand-based communications, as cited by Jewell (2007).

All products and all organisations have a position in the minds of audiences. The task, therefore, is to actively manage the way in which audiences perceive brands. This means that marketing communications strategy should be concerned with achieving effective and viable positions so that the target audience understands what the brand does, what it means (to them) and can ascribe value to it. This is particularly important in markets that are very competitive and where mobility barriers (ease of entry into and exit from a market, e.g. plant and production costs) are relatively low.

Positioning is about visibility and recognition of what a product/service/organisation represents to a buyer. In markets where the intensity of rivalry and competition are increasing and buyers have greater choice, identification and understanding of a product's intrinsic values become critical. Channel members have limited capacities, whether this is the level or range of stock they can carry or for retailers, the amount of available shelf space that can be allocated. An offering with a clear identity and orientation to a particular target segment's needs will not only be stocked and purchased, but can warrant a larger margin through increased added value.

> Marketing communications strategy is essentially about positioning.

It is generally accepted that positioning is the natural conclusion to the sequence of activities that constitute a core part of the marketing strategy. Market segmentation and target marketing are prerequisites to successful positioning. It has also been established that marketing communications should be an audience-centred rather than product-centred activity. From this it can be concluded that marketing communications strategy is essentially about positioning. For new products and services, marketing communications needs to engage target audiences so that they can understand what the brand means, how it differs from similar offerings and as a result position it in their minds. For the vast majority of products and services that are already established, marketing communications strategy should be concerned with either maintaining a strong position or repositioning it in the minds of the target audiences. Chapter 11 provides more information about the positioning concept and the different strategies used by organisations to position their brands.

The 3Ps of marketing communications strategy

As a result of understanding the broad nature of the target audience and the way we want them to position the offering in their minds, it is possible to identify three main marketing communication strategies:

- Pull-positioning strategies – these are intended to influence end-user customers (consumers and b2b);
- Push-positioning strategies – these are intended to influence marketing (trade) channel buyers;
- Profile-positioning strategies – these are intended to influence a wide range of stakeholders, not just customers and intermediaries.

These are referred to as the 3Ps of marketing communications strategy. Push and pull relate to the direction of the communication to the marketing channel: pushing communications down through the marketing channel or pulling consumers/buyers into the channel via retailers, as a result of receiving the communications. They do not relate to the intensity of communication and only refer to the overall approach. Profile refers to the presentation of the organisation as a whole and therefore the identity is said to be 'profiled' to various other target stakeholder audiences, which may well include consumers, trade buyers, business-to-business customers and a range of other influential stakeholders. Normally, profile strategies do not contain or make reference to specific products or services that the organisation offers (see Table 10.4).

This may be blurred where the name of a company is the name of its primary (only) product, as is often the case with many retail brands. For example, messages about B&Q are very often designed to convey meaning about the quality and prices of its consumer products and services, however, they often reflect on the organisation itself, especially when its advertising shows members of staff in workwear, doing their work (see Exhibit 10.1).

All three of these strategies are intended to position the offering, in particular ways, in the minds of the target audience. Within each of these overall strategies, individual approaches should be formulated to reflect the needs of each particular case. So, for example, the launch of a new shampoo product will involve a push-positioning strategy to get the product on the shelves of the appropriate retailers. The strategy would be to gain retailer acceptance of the new brand and to position

> All three strategies are intended to position the offering, in particular ways, in the minds of the target audience.

Table 10.4 Marketing communications strategy options

Strategy	Target audience	Message focus	Communication goal
Pull	Consumers	Product/service	Purchase
	End-user b2b customers	Product/service	Purchase
Push	Channel intermediaries	Product/service	Developing relationships and distribution network
Profile	All relevant stakeholders	The organisation	Building reputation

Exhibit 10.1 B&Q use their staff in advertising campaigns as brand ambassadors. This serves to communicate brand values and to recognise the value of staff to the marketing programme
Courtesy of B&Q.

it as a profitable new brand to gain consumer interest. Personal selling supported by trade sales promotions will be the main marketing communications tools. A pull-positioning strategy to develop awareness about the brand will need to be created, accompanied by appropriate public relations work. The next step will be to create particular brand associations and thereby position the brand in the minds of the target audience. Messages may be primarily functional or expressive but they will endeavour to convey a brand promise. This may be accompanied or followed by the use of incentives to encourage consumers to trial the product. To support the brand, care lines and a web site will need to be put in place to provide credibility as well as a buyer reference point and an opportunity to interact with the brand.

> The degree to which these plans are developed varies.

In order that these strategies are implemented, it is normal procedure to develop a marketing communications plan. The degree to which these plans are developed varies across organisations and some rely on their agencies to undertake this work for them. However, there can be major benefits as a result of developing these plans in-house, for example, by involving and discussing issues internally and developing a sense of ownership.

As noted earlier, planning is not necessarily the same as strategy, although the two are often used interchangeably. Strategy is about the direction, positioning and implementation of an organisation's desired marketing communications (in this case) in order that it positions the brand in the minds of particular target audiences. Tactics are concerned with detail associated with campaigns to deliver the position. Planning, on the other hand, is usually about the formalisation of the strategy, tactics and ideas into a manageable sequence of activities that are linked, coherent and capable of being implemented in the light of the available resources. Marketing communications strategy is about the way an organisation positions its products and services in the minds of its customers and stakeholders. It must do this in the light of its business and marketing strategies and the prevailing contextual conditions, in order to encourage a degree of interaction and dialogue with selected stakeholders.

A marketing communications plan is concerned with the development and managerial processes involved in the articulation of an organisation's marketing communication strategy. This will be considered later in this chapter.

Figure 10.1 Drift in marketing communications strategy

There is little doubt that planning, tactics and strategy are interlinked but it is useful to consider strategy as something that needs to be attended to on a regular basis. With so many variables and an external environment that is subject to tremendous change, marketing communications strategy can be seen to drift, to move away from the original promises that framed its central message and lose the strength of the position gained. The only way to correct drift is to change the marketing communications strategy by at least an amount according to the degree to which messages have drifted. This might be best observed in Figure 10.1.

> Planning, tactics and strategy are interlinked.

Line B suggests that if current marketing communications remain as they are, then the size of the gap with the central theme of marketing communications will widen and any attempt to get back will be large and expensive. Line C depicts a brand that has adapted its marketing communications and positioning on a more frequent basis (than B) and as a result follows an emergent strategy, one that results in a more consistent message. This concept might be interpreted in terms of positioning and repositioning brands and the changing of agencies in order to revitalise and change the direction of the communications strategy currently being pursued.

A pull-positioning strategy

If messages designed to position a brand are to be directed at targeted, end-user customers, then the intention is invariably to generate increased levels of awareness, change and/or reinforce attitudes, reduce risk, encourage involvement and ultimately provoke a motivation within the target group. This motivation is to stimulate action so that the target audience expects the offering to be available to them when they decide to enquire, experiment or make a repeat purchase. This approach is a *pull-(positioning)* strategy and is aimed at encouraging customers to 'pull' products through the channel network (see Figure 10.2). This usually means that consumers go into retail outlets (shops) to enquire about a particular product and/or buy it, or to enter a similar transaction direct with the manufacturer or intermediary through direct mail or the Internet. B2b customers are encouraged to buy from dealers and distributors while both groups of consumers and b2b customers have opportunities to buy through direct marketing channels where there is no intermediary.

> A *pull-(positioning)* strategy is aimed at encouraging customers to 'pull' products through the channel network.

Figure 10.2 The direction of communication in a pull strategy

To accomplish and deliver a pull-positioning strategy, the traditional approach has been to deliver mass media advertising supported by below-the-line communications, most notably sales promotions. There has been greater use of direct marketing in non-fast-moving consumer goods sectors and use of the Internet presents opportunities to reach audiences in new ways, thereby reducing any reliance on the old formulaic approach to pull-based strategies. The decision to use a pull strategy has to be supported by a core message proposition. This will vary according to the outcomes of the context analysis and the needs of the target audience. However, it is probable that the core message will seek to differentiate (position), remind or reassure, inform or persuade the audience to think, feel or behave in a particular way. Agencies and clients have their own approach to this labelling activity.

ViewPoint 10.3 Probably the best pull strategy in the world

Carlsberg, just like many other consumer brands, are competing in a Western European market that is characterised by a proliferation of channels, media and customer segments. They use a wide communication mix, incorporating a full range of tools and media. For example, their consumer advertising uses television, outdoor, in-store, digital and print media. In addition, they use public relations, sponsorship and product placement, and they support local events and festivals to gain visibility.

As 10 per cent of their brands drive 80 per cent of their profits (that is one power brand in each of the ten European markets), so they have started to focus more of their resources on a reduced number of brands.

Pull strategies are configured around developing relationships with customers and Carlsberg refer to this development process as a 'funnel'. When building awareness they use sponsorship, festivals and events. When building on the awareness to generate increased loyalty they use media such as television as they believe they can communicate their messages more effectively this way. The final stage in the funnel process is to provide visibility in pubs and restaurants, and to activate brands in-store. This seemingly simple process can be complex because of the timing, costs and effectiveness associated with the move from one stage to another.

Source: Adapted from Riiber Knudsen (2007).

> **Question**
>
> How do Carlsberg position their brand?
>
> **Task**
>
> Find three drinks brands in the same category (e.g. alcohol, juice, water or carbonated) and determine how they want to be perceived.

Exhibit 10.2 This still from a Carlsberg ad uses humour to convey the message that if Carlsberg ran a football team it would probably provide the best goal celebration in the world.
Courtesy of Saatchi & Saatchi, London and Carlsberg UK. Director: Daniel Kleinman.

ASDA has developed a strong market share in the United Kingdom based mainly on price competition or on what is referred to as everyday low pricing (pull/price). Tesco runs everyday low pricing but uses sales promotions as a form of complementary positioning (pull/price/promotions). In their wake, Sainsbury's and Morrisons have used differing pull strategies to try and regain share, increase profitability and stave off takeover threats.

Although Sainsbury's uses EDLP (everyday low pricing) on 1,000 selected lines, it has adopted a classic branding campaign, based around the celebrity chef Jamie Oliver. Making heavy use of television, the brand is positioned around a quality proposition emphasised by the personality and the associated redesign of major stores.

The level and degree of involvement, explored at some depth in Chapter 5, has some implications for pull strategies. Marketing communication messages can be considered to be a stimulus that in some situations will have a strong impact on the level of involvement enjoyed by the target audience. A strategic response to this would be to adapt marketing communication messages so that they are effective at different levels of involvement, a form of differentiation.

Another approach would be to turn low-involvement decisions into high-involvement ones that, through communications, encourage members of the target audience to reconsider their perception of a brand or of the competition. Again, this represents a form of differentiation. A third approach is to segment the market in terms of the level of involvement experienced by each group and according to situational or personality factors, and then shape the marketing communication messages to suit each group.

A pull strategy therefore, refers to marketing communications (the use of tools, media and messages) designed to position an offering in the minds of particular end-user customer audience(s). This positioning can be achieved in many ways, and Chapter 11 considers a range of positioning techniques and opportunities.

A push-positioning strategy

A second group or type of target audience can be identified, based first on their contribution to the marketing channel, and second because these organisations do not consume the products and services they buy, but add value before selling the product on to others in the demand chain. The previous strategy was targeted at customers who make purchase decisions related largely to their personal (or organisational) consumption of products and services. This second group buys products and services, performs some added-value activity and moves the product through the marketing channel network. This group is a part of the b2b sector, and the characteristics and issues associated with trade channel marketing communications are explored in greater detail in Chapter 29.

Trade channel organisations, and indeed all b2b organisations, are actively involved in the development and maintenance of interorganisational relationships. The degree of cooperation between organisations will vary and part of the role of marketing communications is to develop and support the relationships that exist.

> The role of marketing communications is to develop and support the relationships that exist.

The 'trade' channel has received increased attention in recent years as the strategic value of intermediaries has become both more visible and questioned in the light of the Internet. As the channel networks have developed, so has their complexity, which impacts upon the marketing

ViewPoint 10.4 Makita use below-the-line branding

Black & Decker discovered that they were losing sales in the trade sector because their products were perceived to be more suitable for consumers and the do-it-yourself market. Their response was to develop a separate brand for this particular trade sector. They used a new name 'Makita', identified the product range through the colour, marine blue and made it available through different trade channels. The promotional materials and support documentation needed a different 'tone of voice' to reflect a more rugged and stronger position. The messages were integrated in order to reinforce the desired positioning and targeted at trade customers through intermediaries, such as ScrewFix and Toolsdirect that served to reinforce the new positioning.

Question
To what extent does this type of repositioning require the use of advertising?

Task
Find a competitor to Makita. How do they use marketing communications?

Figure 10.3 The direction of communication in a push strategy

communications strategies and tools used to help reach marketing goals. The expectations of buyers in these networks have risen in parallel with the significance attached to them by manufacturers. The power of multiple retailers, such as Tesco, Sainsbury's, Morrisons, Waitrose and ASDA, is such that they are able to dictate terms (including the marketing communications) to many manufacturers of branded goods.

A *push-positioning* communication strategy involves the presentation of information in order to influence other trade channel organisations and, as a result, encourage them to take stock, to allocate resources (e.g. shelf space) and to help them to become fully aware of the key attributes and benefits associated with each product with a view to adding value prior to further channel transactions. This strategy is designed to encourage resale to other members of the network and contribute to the achievement of their own objectives. This approach is known as a *push* strategy, as it is aimed at pushing the product down through the channel towards the end-users for consumption (see Figure 10.3).

> *Push-positioning* communication strategy involves the presentation of information in order to influence other trade channel organisations.

The channel network consists of those organisations with whom others must cooperate directly to achieve their own objectives. By accepting that there is interdependence, usually dispersed unequally throughout the network, it is possible to identify organisations that have a stronger/weaker position within a network. Communication must travel not only between the different levels of dependence and role ('up and down' in a channel context) and so represent bidirectional flows, but also across similar levels of dependence and role, that is horizontal flows. For example, these may be from retailer to retailer or wholesaler to wholesaler.

Marketing communications targeted at people involved in organisational buying decisions are characterised by an emphasis on personal selling. Trade advertising, trade sales promotions and public relations all have an important yet secondary role to play. Direct marketing has become increasingly important and the development of the Internet has had a profound impact on b2b communications and interorganisational relationships. However, personal selling has traditionally been the most significant part of the communication mix where a push strategy has been instigated.

Finally, just as it was suggested that the essence of a pull strategy could be articulated in brief format, a push strategy could be treated in a similar way. The need to consider the core message is paramount, as it conveys information about the essence of the strategy. Push/inform, push/position or push/key accounts/discount might be examples of possible terminology. Whether or not this form of expression is used, it is important that marketing communication strategy be referred to more than just push; what is to be achieved also needs to be understood.

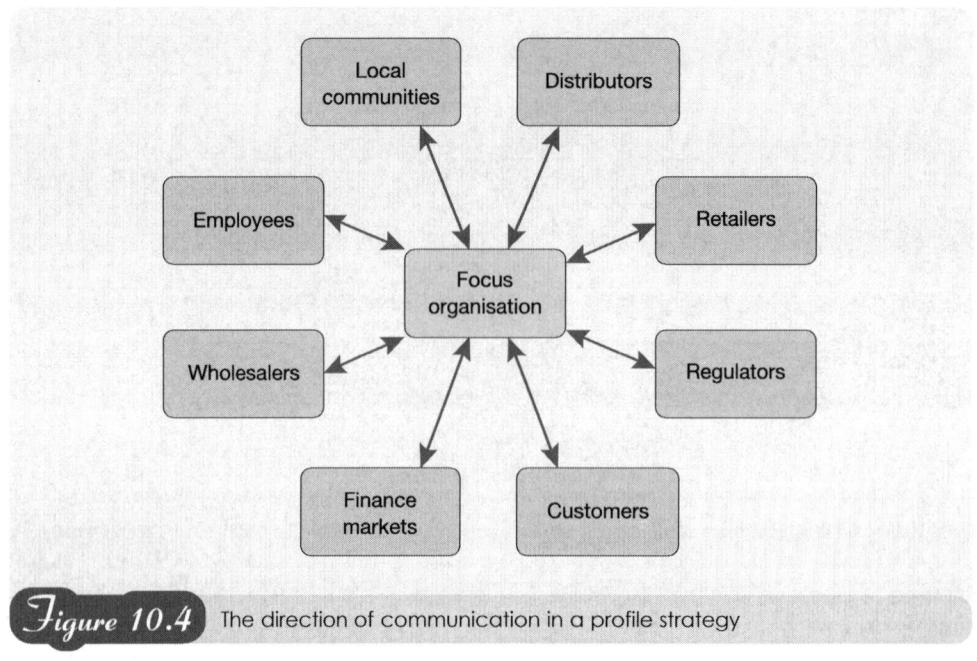

Figure 10.4 The direction of communication in a profile strategy

A profile-positioning strategy

The strategies considered so far concern the need for dialogue with customers (pull) and trade channel intermediaries (push). However, there is a whole range of other stakeholders, many of whom need to know about and understand the organisation rather than actually purchase its products and services (see Figure 10.4). This group of stakeholders may include financial analysts, trade unions, government bodies, employees or the local community. It should be easy to understand that these different stakeholder groups can influence the organisation in different ways and, in doing so, need to receive (and respond to) different types of messages. Thus, the financial analysts need to know about financial and trading performance and expectations, and the local community may be interested in employment and the impact of the organisation on the local environment, whereas the government may be interested in the way the organisation applies health and safety regulations and pays corporation, VAT and other taxes. It should also be remembered that consumers and business-to-business customers may also be more interested in the organisation itself and so help initiate an umbrella branding strategy, which is considered in Chapters 13 and 16.

Traditionally these organisational-oriented activities have been referred to as corporate communications, as they deal more or less exclusively with the corporate entity or organisation. Products, services and other offerings are not normally the focus of these communications. It is the organisation and its role in the context of the particular stakeholders' activities that is important. However, it should be noted that as more corporate brands appear, the distinction between corporate and marketing communications begins to become much less clear. Indeed, when considered in the light of the development and interest in internal marketing (and communications), it may be of greater advantage to consider corporate communications as an organisation's umbrella communications approach, with marketing communications activities a subpart of corporate communications (see Chapter 13 and van Riel, 1995).

> As more corporate brands appear, the distinction between corporate and marketing communications begins to become much less clear.

Communications used to satisfy this array of stakeholder needs and the organisation's corporate promotional goals are developed through what is referred to as a profile strategy, a major element of which is corporate branding, the subject of Chapter 13.

The awareness, perception and attitudes held by stakeholders towards an organisation need to be understood, shaped and acted upon. This can be accomplished though continual dialogue, which will normally lead to the development of trust and commitment and enable relationships to grow. This is necessary in order that stakeholders act favourably towards an organisation and enable strategies to flourish and objectives be achieved.

ViewPoint 10.5 So, who are we?

Organisations need to raise their profile for different reasons and at different times. These might reflect changing market conditions, trading circumstances, poor trading results, threat of takeover or a general repositioning.

G4S had to raise its profile because of a series of takeovers and mergers, which required the company to restructure, rebrand and reposition itself. Group 4 merged with Danish Falck in 2000, merged with Securicor in 2004, and then rebranded as G4S in 2006.

The first part of the rebranding incorporated staff. Through the use of a relaunch event day, 15,000 contracted staff were given information about the new company name, structure, board composition, new uniforms and livery. In addition, internal staff received information through desk drops, magazines, new letters and question–answer sessions.

Externally oriented communications revolved around the new logo. Fresh, clean and a break from the previous visual identity.

Source: Anon. (2008).

Question
What do you believe are the main differences between rebranding and raising profile?

Task
Make a list of all the reasons an organisation might choose to deliberately raise its profile.

To build corporate brands, organisations must develop modern integrated communication programmes with all of their key stakeholder groups. Audiences demand transparency and accountability and instant on-line access to news, developments, research and networks means that inconsistent or misleading information must be avoided. As if to reinforce this, a survey reported by Gray (2000) found that CEOs rated the reputation of their organisations as more important than that of their products. However, the leading contributor to the strength of the corporate brand is seen to be their products and services, followed by a strong management team, internal communications, PR, social accountability, change management and the personal reputation of the CEO.

Stakeholder analysis is used in the development of strategic plans, so if an organisation wants its communications to support the overall plan, it makes sense to communicate effectively with the appropriate stakeholders. Rowe *et al*. (1994) point out that, because of the mutual interdependence of stakeholders and the focus organisation, 'each stakeholder is in effect an advocate of any strategy that furthers its goals'. It follows, therefore, that it is important to provide all stakeholders with information that enables them to perceive and position the organisation, so as to generate the desired corporate image. This requires a communication strategy that addresses these particular requirements, even though there may not be any immediately recognisable shift in performance.

> It is important to provide all stakeholders with information that enables them to perceive and position the organisation.

However, it would be incorrect to perceive corporate communications as just a means of shaping or influencing the attitudes and behaviour of other stakeholders. Organisations exist within a variety of networks, which provide a context for the roles and actions of member organisations (Chapter 7). Bidirectional communication flows exist and organisations adapt themselves to the actions and behaviour of others in the network. Therefore, corporate communications provides a mechanism by which it can learn about the context(s) in which it exists and is itself shaped and influenced by the other stakeholders with whom it shares communications. Reference is made to the work of Grunig and Hunt (1984), considered in Chapter 19.

A *profile-positioning* strategy focuses an organisation's communications upon the development of stakeholder relationships, corporate image and reputation, whether that be just internally, just externally or both. To accomplish and deliver a profile strategy, public relations, including sponsorship and corporate advertising, become the pivotal tools of the marketing communications mix. Personal selling may remain a vital element delivering both product/service and corporate messages.

> A *profile-positioning* strategy focuses an organisation's communications upon the development of stakeholder relationships, corporate image and reputation.

Strategic balance

While the pull, push and profile strategies are important, it should be remembered that they are not mutually exclusive. Indeed, in most organisations it is possible to identify an element of each strategy at any one time. In reality, most organisations are structured in such a way that those responsible for communications with each of these three main audiences do so without reference to, or coordination with, each other. This is an example of how integrated marketing communications, which is examined in Chapter 9, needs to have one senior person responsible for all the organisational communications. Only through a single point of reference is it realistically possible to develop and communicate a set of brand values that are consistent and credible.

Recognising these limitations that organisations often place on themselves, the 3Ps should be considered as part of a total communication approach. Figure 10.5 depicts how the emphasis of a total communication strategy can shift according to changing contextual elements, for example, the needs of the various target audiences, resources and wider elements such as the environment and the competition. The marketing communications eclipse provides a visual interpretation of the balance between the three strategic dimensions. The more that is revealed

> The marketing communications eclipse provides a visual interpretation of the balance between the three strategic dimensions.

Figure 10.5 Marketing communication strategic eclipse

Table 10.5 Issues to be considered when developing marketing communications

Element	Issue
Target audiences	Which type of audience do we need to reach and why?
Channel strategies	How do we make our products/services available – direct or indirect?
Objectives	What do we need to achieve – what are our goals?
Positioning	How do we want to be perceived and understood?
Branding	How strong is our brand and what values and associations do stakeholders make with it?
Integration	How consistent are our communications, internally and externally?
Competitors	How do our communications compare with those of our key competitors?
Resources	What resources do we have and which do we need to secure?

of any one single strategy, the greater its role in any single campaign. Conversely, the less that is revealed, the smaller the contribution. In any one campaign, one or two of the three strategies might be used in preference to another and will often reflect branding approaches. For example, a brand manager's use of a profile strategy at Procter & Gamble or Mars will be virtually zero and will almost certainly be entirely pull in order to support the marketing channel or trade customers.

The role of each element of the marketing communications mix is important in communication strategy. Each tool has different strengths and should be used accordingly. For example, direct marketing and sales promotion are more likely to be effective in persuading consumer audiences, while personal selling is likely to be more effective in b2b situations. A profile strategy designed to change perception and understanding of the organisation is more likely to utilise public relations and corporate advertising.

Marketing communication strategy, regardless of the overall focus, is normally composed of a number of different elements. When considering strategy there are a number of key issues that need to be considered. These are shown in Table 10.5.

Strategy needs to be understood in terms of the answers given in response to several critical questions. First, how are the communication goals that have been set going to be achieved? Second, how are they going to be accomplished in terms of complementing the business and marketing strategies? Third, can current resources and opportunities support the strategy and do they encourage target audiences to respond to the communications?

Answers to these questions are not always easy to find and very often there will be conflicting proposals from different coalitions of internal stakeholders. In other words, there is a political element that needs to be considered and there may also be a strong overriding culture that directs the communication strategy and that may hinder innovation or the development of alternative methods of communication. Everyone who is involved with the development of marketing communications campaigns (internally and externally) should agree and prioritise necessary activities. The development of a marketing communications plan facilitates this process and enables the strategy to be articulated in such a way that the goals are achieved in a timely, efficient and effective manner.

Internet strategies

The development of Internet-based facilities is now quite commonplace for organisations and consumers. The function and speed of development of Internet facilities within organisations is a function of many factors, such as the size and core skills of the organisation. For example, it is normally easier for an IST organisation than a transport organisation to develop ecommerce facilities. Other factors include the nature of the product offering and the market and competitor conditions. It cannot, therefore, be concluded that there is a fixed pathway for the development and incorporation of the Internet within an organisation, nor should there be one, as the flexibility and adaptability to meet individual organisational requirements needs to be retained.

However, it is useful to understand the basic types of online facilities in order to appreciate the strategic thinking that needs to be undertaken. The Internet can become an integral part of the way an organisation operates, the way it sees its future and the way others see it, and not just be used to supplement the organisation's promotional programme. Having said that, it is this technology factor, more than any other, that has done so much to accelerate moves towards integrated marketing communications and to encourage managers to consider the totality of their activities rather than focus on an individual aspect.

> The Internet can become an integral part of the way an organisation operates, the way it sees its future and the way others see it.

The different Internet-related phases through which an organisation usually passes need to be considered alongside the technological platform that the organisation wishes to operate. Essentially the Internet provides web site access for everyone. An extranet platform enables an organisation to restrict access to a number of selected organisations/people. For example, end-user customers, intermediaries and suppliers all might use an extranet to provide benefits that all can share and through which the host might develop competitive advantage. An intranet platform enables the use of the same browser-based technology but access is restricted to the employees of an organisation.

The strategic choice of platform requires consideration of the different stakeholders and communities with which the organisation wishes to interact. The management of these groups is then necessary in order to ensure optimum usage and the development of suitable relationships. Management need to encourage stakeholder communities to grow and to interact with one another and this requires that users be empowered, encouraged to innovate and be reviewed on a regular basis.

While the ability to reach customers directly, avoiding channel intermediaries and reducing transaction costs is attractive, strategies must be decided upon for attracting customers to a web site (or TV-based 'shop'). Reliance on online communications alone is too limiting and unlikely to be successful, so a combination of off-line and on-line communications is necessary to attract sufficient traffic.

> Many online brands use television and outdoor advertising to promote not only the web site but, more importantly for them, the brand name to drive shareholder interest.

The variety of offline communications used by organisations varies according to their budgets and their overall strategy. Many online brands use television and outdoor advertising to promote not only the web site but, more importantly for them, the brand name to drive shareholder interest as these new entities seek stock market listings. As a result of this activity, outdoor advertising spend has grown substantially. Sponsorship is also used to promote web site addresses as well as a host of corporate literature such as company reports, brochures, calling cards and letterheads. Online communications vary from banner ads and pop-ups to viral marketing and public relations. However, research indicates that the most important factor driving first-time visits is word-of-mouth and recommendations by significant others. In other words, people are more disposed to having their web site behaviour directed by those they trust rather than risk time and effort seeking information based on communications that lack inherent credibility.

The balance between offline and online generated traffic will also vary depending upon the nature of the brand itself. If a brand is being developed by a bricks-and-mortar company as an additional distribution and communications channel, but there is to be no visible tie to the parent company (e.g. Egg and Citibank), then the offline branding development will need to be considerable. However, if the brand is to be tied in closely to the current channels (e.g. Argos), the initial branding can be constrained to converting current customers to the new product and to stimulating word-of-mouth recommendations, a much lower communications investment.

However, whatever the reason or branding strategy used to generate traffic, thought should be given to capitalising on the facilities to personalise the experience through the use of underlying data capture, storage, retrieval and processing abilities of integrated technologies. The ability to start with some knowledge of a customer's preferences, previous purchases, their already secure financial details and delivery address, for example, should be a major source of advantage. In addition, the interactive communications strategy needs to be thought through all points of customer interaction. Many companies have addressed the need to capture customers and even extract critical personal information but have failed to think through the total process and consider how the behaviour of the company communicates attitudes and degree of care. The use of email to confirm receipt and despatch details of a customer's order goes a long way to developing trust and positive customer attitudes, but unless the whole fulfilment exercise is compatible (and fulfilling), the whole of the investment in the front end of the exercise will be wasted.

Weltevreden *et al.* (2005) have determined a typology of Internet strategies used by retailers. In particular, they identify nine strategies employed by retailers with active web sites. These are shown at Table 10.6.

Four of these are 'information-only-strategies' where there are varying levels of product information available or services designed to assist customer relationships. The remaining five are referred to as 'online-sales-strategies' each tied in various ways to the organisation's physical outlets, or in one case not at all.

Weltevreden and Boschma (2008) conclude from a study of Danish retailers that adopting an Internet strategy invariably has positive effects on performance in terms of more customers, improved customer relationships, increased competitiveness and overall sales growth. They also found that adopting an Internet sales strategy was more beneficial for

> Adopting an Internet strategy invariably has positive effects on performance.

Table 10.6 Internet strategies used by retailers

Strategy	Explanation	Product information	Online sales
Billboard	Web site used to make customers aware of their existence	None	No
Brochure	Limited product information and services	Limited	No
Catalogue	Web site provides detailed product information but limited services	Extensive	No
Service	Web site used to provide additional services to improve relationships (e.g. help desks)	Limited/extensive	No
Export	Web site used to expand into new areas without affecting their physical outlets	Extensive	Yes
Mirror	Web site used as an additional virtual outlet but few linkages with physical outlets and no additional services	Extensive	Yes
Synergy	Customer interaction between web site physical outlets encouraged through cross-promotions, ordering/pick up, full availability	Extensive	Yes
Anti-mirror	Web site the dominant channel and the role of the physical outlets is to support the web site	Extensive	Yes
Virtual	Web site is the only organisational presence	Extensive	Yes

Source: Adapted from Weltevreden and Boschma (2008).

independent retailers than it was for multiple retailers. The researchers speculate that this may be due to the independents being able to reach a wider market than previously, whereas multiples already serve a wide market.

Developing a marketing communications plan

> The intended positioning can be missed if the marketing communication is not entirely effective.

The context in which a communication event is to occur shapes not only what and how messages are developed and conveyed, but also influences the interpretation and meaning ascribed to the communication. In other words the intended positioning can be missed if the marketing communication is not entirely effective. The development of marketing communication plans helps to minimise errors and provide for efficiency and effectiveness.

There are a number of contexts that influence or shape marketing communications. All marketing managers (and others) need to understand these contextual elements and appreciate how they contribute to and influence the development of marketing communication programmes. In addition, there are a number of other elements and activities that need to be built into a programme in order that it can be implemented. These elements concern the goals, the resources, the communication tools to be used and measures of control and evaluation. Just like the cogs in a clock, these elements need to be linked together if the plan is to work. The marketing communications planning framework (MCPF) aims to bring together the various elements that constitute marketing communications into a logical sequence of activities. The rationale for promotional decisions is built on information generated at previous levels in the framework. It also provides a checklist of activities that need to be considered.

To help students and managers comprehend the linkages between the elements and to understand how these different components complement each other, the rest of this chapter deals with the development of marketing communication plans. To that extent it will be of direct benefit to managers seeking to build plans for the first time or for those familiar with the activity to reconsider current practices. Second, the material should also be of direct benefit to students who are required to understand and perhaps prepare such plans as part fulfilment of an assessment or examination in this subject area.

> The MCPF represents a way of bringing together the different components in the communication process.

The MCPF represents a way of bringing together the different components in the communication process, of appreciating the way in which they relate to one another and is a means of writing coherent marketing communications plans for work or for examinations, such as those offered by the Chartered Institute of Marketing.

The marketing communications planning framework

It has been established (Chapter 1) that the principal tasks facing marketing communications managers are to decide:

1. Who should receive the messages.
2. What the messages should say.
3. What image of the organisation/brand receivers are expected to retain.
4. How much is to be spent establishing this new image.

5. How the messages are to be delivered.
6. What actions the receivers should take.
7. How to control the whole process once implemented.
8. What was achieved.

Note that more than one message is transmitted and that there is more than one target audience. This is important, as recognition of the need to communicate with multiple audiences and their different information requirements, often simultaneously, lies at the heart of marketing communications. The aim is to generate and transmit messages which present the organisation and their offerings to their various target audiences, encouraging them to enter into a dialogue. These messages must be presented consistently and they must address the points stated above. It is the skill and responsibility of the marketing communications planner to blend the communication tools and to create a mix that satisfies these elements.

A framework for integrated marketing communications plans

To enable managers and students to bring together the various promotional elements into a cohesive plan, which can be communicated to others, an overall framework is required.

The MCPF (Figure 10.6) seeks to achieve this by bringing together the various elements into a logical sequence of activities where the rationale for marketing communications decisions is built upon information generated at a previous level in the framework. Another advantage of using the MCPF is that it provides a suitable checklist of activities that need to be considered.

The MCPF represents a sequence of decisions that marketing managers undertake when preparing, implementing and evaluating communication strategies and plans. It does not mean that this sequence reflects reality; indeed, many marketing decisions are made outside any recognisable framework. However, as a means of understanding the different components, appreciating the way in which they relate to one another and bringing together various aspects for work or for answering examination questions such as those offered by the Chartered Institute of Marketing, this approach has many advantages and has been used by a number of local, national and international organisations.

Figure 10.6 The marketing communications planning framework

Marketing communications requires the satisfaction of communication objectives through the explicit and deliberate development of communication strategy. The MCPF will be used to show first, the key elements, second, some of the linkages and third, the integrated approach that is required.

> Marketing communications requires the satisfaction of communication objectives.

This framework reflects the deliberate or planned approach to strategy marketing communications. The process of marketing communications, however, is not linear, as depicted in this framework, but integrative and interdependent. To that extent, this approach is a recognition of the value of stakeholder theory and of the requirement to build partnerships with buyers and other organisations networked with the organisation.

Other 'decision sequences' have been advanced, in particular one by Rothschild (1987) and another by Engel et al. (1994). One of the difficulties associated with their frameworks is that they fail to bring strategy into the development of the promotional mix. Their frameworks rely on the objective and task approach, whereby plans are developed for each of the individual promotional tools, and then aggregated to form strategy.

Another more recent framework is the SOSTAC (situation, objectives, strategy, tactics, action, control) approach. This is essentially a sound system and moves closer than most of the others to achieving suitable marketing communication plans. However, as the framework is multipurpose and is intended for application to a variety of planning situations, there is a strong danger that the communication focus is lost at the situation analysis phase. This can lead to a reiteration of a SWOT (strengths, weaknesses, opportunities, threats) and/or a general marketing plan, with subsequent problems further down the line in terms of the justification and understanding of the communications strategy and promotional mixes that need to be deployed. In addition, the SOSTAC model does not give sufficient emphasis to the need to identify and understand the characteristics of the target audience, which is so important for the development of a coherent marketing communications plan.

The MCPF approach presented here is not intended to solve all the problems associated with the formulation of such plans, but it is robust enough to meet the needs of employers and examiners, and is recommended.

Elements of the plan

Marketing communications plans consist of the following elements. These elements will now be considered in turn.

- Context analysis
- Communication objectives
- Marketing communications strategy
- Coordinated promotional mix (methods, tools and media)
- Resources (human and financial)
- Scheduling and implementation
- Evaluation and control
- Feedback

Context analysis

Analysing the context in which marketing communication episodes occur is a necessary, indeed vital, first step in the planning process. The purpose is to understand the key market and communication drivers that are likely to influence (or already are influencing) a brand (or organisation) and either help or hinder its progress towards meeting its long-term objectives. This is different from a situation analysis, because the situation analysis considers a range of wider organisational factors, most of which

> The purpose is to understand the key market and communication drivers that are likely to influence a brand.

Table 10.7 The main elements of the context analysis

Context element	Dimensions
The customer context	Segment characteristics Levels of awareness, perception and attitudes towards the brand/organisation Level of involvement Types of perceived risk DMU characteristics and issues
The business context	Corporate and marketing strategy and plans Brand/organisation analysis Competitor analysis
The internal context	Financial constraints Organisation identity Culture, values and beliefs Marketing expertise Agency availability and suitability
The external context	Who are the key stakeholders and why are they important? What are their communication needs? Social, political, economic and technological restraints and opportunities.

are normally considered in the development of marketing plans (while the communication focus is lost). Duplication is to be avoided, as it is both inefficient and confusing.

The compilation of a context analysis (CA) is very important, as it presents information and clues about what the promotional plan needs to achieve. Information and market research data about target audiences (their needs, perception, motivation, attitudes and decision-making characteristics), the media and the people they use for information about offerings, the marketing objectives and time scales, the overall level of financial and other resources that are available, the quality and suitability of agency and other outsourced activities, and the environment in terms of societal, technological, political and economic conditions, both now and at some point in the future, all need to be considered.

At the root of the CA is the marketing plan. This will already have been prepared and contains important information about the target segment, the business and marketing goals, competitors and the time-scales in which the goals are to be achieved. The rest of the CA seeks to elaborate and build upon this information so as to provide the detail in order that the plan can be developed and justified.

The CA provides the rationale for the plan. It is from the CA that the marketing objectives (from the marketing plan) and the marketing communications objectives are derived. The type, form and style of the message are rooted in the characteristics of the target audience, and the media selected to convey messages will be based on the nature of the tasks, the media habits of the audience and the resources available. The main components of the context analysis are set out in Table 10.7.

Communication objectives

The role of promotional objectives in the planning process is important for a number of reasons. First, they provide a balance to the plan and take away the sole emphasis on sales that inevitably arises. Second, they indicate positioning issues, third, they highlight the required balance of the promotional mix, fourth, they

> Promotional objectives provide a balance to the plan and take away the sole emphasis on sales that inevitably arises.

provide time parameters for campaigns, and finally, they provide a crucial means by which particular marketing communication activities are evaluated.

Ideally, communication objectives should consist of three main elements:

Corporate objectives

These are derived from the business or marketing plan. They refer to the mission and the business area that the organisation believes it should be in.

Marketing objectives

These are derived from the marketing plan and are output-oriented. Normally these can be considered as sales-related objectives, such as market share, sales revenues, volumes, ROI and profitability indicators.

Marketing communication objectives

These are derived from an understanding of the current context in which a brand exists and the future context in the form of where the brand is expected to be at some point in the future. These will be presented as awareness levels, perception, comprehension/knowledge, attitudes towards and overall degree of preference for the brand. The choice of communication goal depends on the tasks that need to be accomplished. In addition, most brands need either to maintain their current brand position or reposition themselves in the light of changing contextual conditions.

These three elements constitute the promotional objectives and they all need to be set out in SMART terminology (see Chapter 11). What also emerges is a refinement to the positioning that managers see as important for success. Obviously, not all plans require express attention to positioning (e.g. government information campaigns) but most commercial and brand-oriented communication programmes need to communicate a clear position in their market. Thus, at this point the positioning intentions are developed and these will be related to the market, the customers or some other dimension. The justification for this will arise from the CA.

Marketing communications strategy

> It is imperative that the strategy be geared to the communication needs of the target audience.

The communication strategy should be customer- not method/media-oriented. Therefore, the strategy depends on whether the target audience is a consumer segment, a distributor or dealer network or whether other stakeholders need to be reached. In addition, it is imperative that the strategy be geared to the communication needs of the target audience that is revealed during the customer and business context analyses. This will show what the task is that marketing communications needs to fulfil. Having established who the audience is, push-, pull- or profile-dominated strategies can be identified. The next step is to determine the task that needs to be accomplished. This will have been articulated previously in the marketing communications objectives, but the approach at this stage is less quantitative and softer.

The DRIP tasks of marketing communications can be used to suggest the strategy being pursued. For example, if a new brand is being launched, the first task will be to inform and differentiate the brand for members of the trade before using a pull strategy to inform and differentiate the brand for the target, end-user customers. An organisation wishing to signal a change of strategy and/or a change of name following a merger or acquisition may choose to use a profile strategy and the primary task will be to inform of the name change. An organisation experiencing declining sales may choose to remind customers of a need or it may choose to improve sales through persuasion.

Coordinated communication mix

Having formulated, stated and justified the required position, the next step is to present the basic form and style of the key message that is to be conveyed. Is there to be a lot of copy or just a little? Is there to be a rational or emotional approach or some weighting between the two? What should be the tone of the visual messages? Is there to be a media blitz (e.g. a Microsoft-type day, as used for the launch of Windows 95, or Cable & Wireless yellow saturation)? It is at this point that those responsible for the development of these plans can be imaginative and try some new ideas. Trying to tie in the message to the strategic orientation is the important part, as the advertising agency will refine and redefine the message and the positioning.

From this the promotional mixes need to be considered *for each* of the strategies proposed, that is, a mix for the consumer strategy, a mix for the trade strategy and a distinct mix for the communications to reach the wider array of stakeholders.

The choice of promotional methods should clearly state the methods and the media to be used. A short paragraph justifying the selection is very important, as the use of media in particular is to a large extent dependent upon the nature of the goals, the target audience and the resources. The key is to provide message consistency and a measure of integration.

Resources

This is a vitally important part of the plan, one that is often avoided or forgotten about. The resources necessary to support the plan need to be determined and these refer not only to the financial issues but to the quality of available marketing expertise and the time that is available to achieve the required outcomes.

Gantt charts and other project planning aids are best used to support this part of the plan. The cost of the media and methods can either be allocated in a right-hand column of the chart, or a new chart can be prepared. Preferably, actual costs should be assigned, although percentages can be allocated if examination time is at a premium. What is important is the relative weighting of the costs and a recognition and understanding of the general costs associated with the proposed individual activities.

It must be understood that a television campaign cannot be run for less than £1.5 million and that the overall cost of the strategy should be in proportion to the size of the client organisation, its (probable) level of profitability and the size and dynamics of the market in which it operates.

Scheduling and implementation

The next step is to schedule the deployment of the methods and the media. This is best achieved by the production of a Gantt chart.

Events should be scheduled according to the goals and the strategic thrust. So, if it is necessary to communicate with the trade prior to a public launch, those activities tied into the push strategy should be scheduled prior to those calculated to support the pull strategy.

Similarly, if awareness is a goal then, if funds permit, it may be best to use television and posters first before sales promotions (unless sampling is used), direct marketing, point of purchase and personal selling.

Evaluation and control

Unless there is some form of evaluation, there will be no dialogue and no true marketing communications. There are numerous methods to evaluate the individual performance of the tools and the media used, and for examination purposes these should be stated. In addition, and perhaps more meaningfully, the most important measures are the communication objectives set in the first place. The success of a promotional strategy and the associated plan is the degree to which the objectives set are achieved.

Feedback

The planning process is completed when feedback is provided. Not only should information regarding the overall outcome of a campaign be considered but so should individual aspects of the activity. For example, the performance of the individual tools used within the campaign, whether sufficient resources were invested, the appropriateness of the strategy in the first place, any problems encountered during implementation and the relative ease with which the objectives were accomplished are all aspects that need to be fed back to all internal and external parties associated with the planning process.

This feedback is vitally important because it provides information for the context analysis that anchors the next campaign. Information fed back in a formal and systematic manner constitutes an opportunity for organisations to learn from their previous campaign activities, a point often overlooked and neglected.

> Feedback is vitally important because it provides information for the context analysis that anchors the next campaign.

Links and essential points

It was mentioned earlier that there are a number of linkages associated with different parts of the marketing communications plan. It is important to understand the nature of these links as they represent the interconnections between different parts of the plan and the rationale for undertaking the contextual analysis in particular. The contextual analysis (CA) feeds the items shown in Table 10.8. For example, research undertaken by Interbrand for Intercontinental Hotels to find out what influenced the brand experience of hotel guests, discovered that one of the key factors was the hotel concierge. As a result the role of the concierge became a central character in the communication strategy, influencing the campaign goals, positioning and message strategy (Gustafson, 2007). The promotional objectives derived from the CA feed decisions concerning strategy, tools and media, scheduling and evaluation.

The marketing communications strategy is derived from an overall appreciation of the needs of the target audience (and stakeholders) regarding the brand and its competitive position in the market. The communication mix is influenced by the previous elements and the budget that follows. However, the nature of the tools and the capacity and characteristics of the media influence scheduling, implementation and evaluation activities.

To help explain the MCPF and the linkages, a mini case study follows the chapter summary and review questions. You are required to prepare a marketing communications plan. It is

Table 10.8 Linkages within the MCPF

Objectives	From the marketing plan, from the customer, stakeholder network and competitor analysis and from an internal marketing review
Strategic balance between push, pull and profile	From an understanding of the brand, the needs of the target audiences, including employees and all other stakeholders, and the marketing goals
Brand positioning	From users' and non-users' perceptions, motivations, attitudes and understanding about the brand and its direct and indirect competitors
Message content and style	From an understanding about the level of involvement, perceived risk, DMU analysis, information-processing styles and the positioning intentions
Promotional tools and media	From the target audience analysis of media habits, involvement and preferences, from knowledge about product suitability and media compatibility, from a competitor analysis and from the resource analysis

suggested that you prepare one using the material in this chapter as a guide. An answer is available at the web site www.booknets/fillc that you can use to compare with your own response. The prepared answer is not the only possible answer – there are other plans that could be of equal significance and use.

Summary

In order to help consolidate your understanding of marketing communications strategy, here are the key points summarised against each of the learning objectives:

1. Establish the differences between strategy, tactics and planning.

Two main strategy schools of thought can be identified, namely the planning and the emergent approaches. The planning school is the pre-eminent paradigm and is based on strategy development and implementation, which is explicit, rational and planned as a sequence of logical steps.

The emergent school of thought considers strategy to develop incrementally, step-by-step, as organisations learn, sometimes through simple actions of trial and error. The core belief is that strategy is comprised of a stream of organisational activities that are continuously being formulated, implemented, tested, evaluated and updated.

Strategy should be considered to be about the means, speed and methods by which organisations adapt to and influence their environments in order to achieve their goals.

2. Appreciate the essence of marketing communications strategy.

Marketing communications strategy is concerned with two key dynamics. The first dynamic concerns who, in broad terms, is the target audience? End-user customers need to derive particular benefits based on perceived value from the exchange process. These benefits are very different from those that intermediaries expect to derive, or indeed any other stakeholder who does not consume the product or service. The second dynamic concerns the way in which an audience understands the offering they are experiencing either through use or through communications. The way in which people interpret messages and frame objects in their mind is concerned with positioning.

Marketing communications strategy is concerned with audiences and positioning.

3. Consider three main marketing communication strategies: pull, push and profile.

The 3Ps of marketing communications strategy are:

- Pull-positioning strategies – these are intended to influence end-user customers (consumers and b2b);
- Push-positioning strategies – these are intended to influence marketing (trade) channel buyers;
- Profile-positioning strategies – these are intended to influence a wide range of stakeholders, not just customers and intermediaries.

Push, pull and profile strategies can be combined in different ways to meet the needs of different communication tasks. In addition to the broad target, it is important to express strategy in terms of the differentiation (positioning), reminding/reassuring, informing and persuading of audiences.

4. Explain the notion of strategic balance.

The 3Ps are a part of a total communication approach. The pull, push and profile strategies are not mutually exclusive and it is possible to identify an element of each strategy operating at any one time.

The marketing communications eclipse provides a visual interpretation of the balance between the three strategic dimensions. The more that is revealed of any single strategy, the greater its role in any single campaign. Conversely, the less that is revealed, the smaller the contribution.

5. Explore different approaches to Internet-based communication strategies.

Internet communication strategies need to be developed on a variety of factors. These include the marketing strategy; whether the operation is a bricks extension or a pure play operation; the relationship to be held with any parent brand; the relationships with intermediaries; the methods to be used to drive site traffic; and perhaps the most important of these is probably the need to consider all points where customers interact with the brand.

6. Present a planning framework and consider the different elements involved in the development of marketing communication plans.

A marketing communications planning framework (MCPF) consists of the following elements.

- Context analysis
- Communication objectives
- Marketing communications strategy
- Coordinated communication mix (methods, tools and media)
- Resources (human and financial)
- Scheduling and implementation
- Evaluation and control
- Feedback.

The MCPF aims to bring together the various elements that constitute marketing communications into a logical sequence of activities. The rationale for promotional decisions is built on information generated at previous levels in the framework. It also provides a checklist of activities that need to be considered.

This framework reflects the deliberate or planned approach to strategic marketing communications. The MCPF represents a way of understanding the different promotional components, of appreciating the way in which they relate to one another and is a means of writing coherent marketing communications plans for work or for examinations.

7. Highlight the importance of the linkages and interaction between the different elements of the plan.

Just as the strength of the value chain lies in the internal linkages so the strength of a marketing communication plan is to be found within the various linkages that bind the components together. It is important to understand the nature of these links as they represent the interconnections between different parts of the plan and the rationale for undertaking the contextual analysis in particular.

Review questions

1. Write brief notes explaining some of the key approaches to understanding strategy.
2. Explain the role strategy plays in marketing communications.
3. Compare strategy with planning. In what ways might planning be the same as strategy?
4. What are the 3Ps of marketing communications strategy? Explain the differences between each of them and use the marketing communications eclipse to support your answer.
5. Explain the key characteristics associated with a pull strategy.
6. Draw two diagrams depicting the direction of communications in both the push and the pull strategies.
7. Describe what the 'core message' is and provide four examples.
8. Sketch the marketing communications planning framework – from memory.
9. Following on from the previous question, check your version of the MCPF with the original and then prepare some bullet-point notes, highlighting the critical linkages between the main parts of the framework.
10. Discuss the extent to which Internet strategies should be considered a part of marketing communication strategies as a whole.

MiniCase: 'Ski Rossendale'

Angela Hall: Manchester Metropolitan University Business School

Introduction

Ski Rossendale is located on a hillside in the Rossendale Valley, Lancashire, 20 miles north of Manchester. It has excellent travel links, just off the end of the M66 motorway, and with buses from Manchester every 15 minutes stopping within 1 mile.

Ski Rossendale's slopes are divided into three main areas. The main slope is 200m × 25m (with 2 button tows), the fun slope is 70m × 15m (with 1 button tow and big air and railslide feature), and the nursery slope is 35m × 40m (with 2 rope tows and a travelator lift). Currently the fun slope and nursery slope are made from SNOWFLEX virtual snow, the main slope was upgraded during the last year to incorporate part SNOWFLEX and also a half-pipe was added to the bottom of the main slope.

There is also an on-site cafe that is owned and run by Ski Rossendale, and this is open while the slope is open. The cafe offers drinks, breakfast, lunch and dinner. While no formal research has taken place on usage and views of the cafe, it is generally considered to be under-utilised by the users of the slope. Currently the cafe has a general seating area, the back section of which can be used as a separate small function area for children's parties, and an outside area where patrons can view the main slope while enjoying their refreshments.

Rossendale Leisure Trust (RLT) is a charitable trust and includes a number of business units within it. These take the form of five facilities: Haslingden Sports Centre, Haslingden Swimming Pool, Marl Pits Swimming Pool, Bacup Leisure Hall and Ski Rossendale. A sixth business unit operates under the title 'Lifestyles Team' and encompasses Sports Development, Arts Development and Healthy Communities.

Aims/objectives

Their vision is 'to establish Rossendale Leisure Trust as a benchmark organisation of its type in the UK' (www.rltrust.co.uk), with a mission of 'getting Rossendale on the move'. Seven trust values are presented:

- ensure every resident can access our services;
- help to bring our community together;

Exhibit 10.3 Ski Rossendale
Ski Rossendale.

- deliver better opportunities through partnership working;
- use resources effectively at all times;
- build on our achievements and learn from our mistakes;
- develop knowledge and understanding in sport and arts;
- provide a long-term legacy for the community of Rossendale.

No marketing objectives, or marketing communications objectives have been formalised by Ski Rossendale, and there are no formal marketing or marketing communications plans in place currently.

There is a business development manager at Ski Rossendale who took up position in July 2007. This person will develop business and focus on marketing activities, although they are from a sports science background, and currently has little marketing expertise.

Target audience

No detailed analysis of those using the slope has taken place. However, all those attending the slope are asked to give their postcode, this is recorded in paper form when hiring the equipment. Currently some very basic analysis of this is undertaken. The main geographical areas customers are from are Greater Manchester and Lancashire, with smaller numbers from Cumbria down to North Wales and into Yorkshire. Ski Rossendale would like to look at how to capture data on current users and build relationships with these people. Data on usage figures are available, but it is recognised that this information needs to be improved. Retaining existing customers and getting them to use the slope more is seen as a key objective in the immediate future. This is especially important bearing in mind competition from the Chill Factor e (a new indoor real snow development near the Trafford Centre, Manchester), which may well try to take customers away.

Potentially, anyone interested in keeping fit and interested in outdoor activities could be targeted. Research indicates that outdoor activity participants are sporting all-rounders, with many taking part in three or more sports overall (Mintel, 2004). There is a much higher interest in extreme sports (such as snowboarding and extreme skiing) among the 15–24 year olds (Mintel, 2003). Although 1.2 per cent of UK adults go on snowsports holidays (2003), some 3.7 per cent consider themselves leisure snowsports participants (Mintel, 2003). It is estimated that there will be a 7 per cent projected growth of 18–30 year olds between 2005 and 2010 who are seen as a key target audience (Mintel, 2005). While skiing and snowboarding are seen as minority sports, there are currently 1.6 million skiers and 0.5 million snowboarders aged 15+ within the United Kingdom (Mintel, 2006).

Ski Rossendale see one of their key target markets as being those people who are going on winter ski/snowboard holidays. The ski slope is at its busiest during the December to March period, as many people prepare themselves for their winter holiday, and lessons tend to be at full capacity during this peak period.

Currently Ski Rossendale acknowledges that they have poor links with local schools and consider this as an area for growth. However, one of the issues here is the cost of transporting children to the slope. The government has been encouraging further participation in sport with a number of plans (e.g. Plan for Sport March 2001, Game Place strategic view). Long term, the government see the promotion of sport in schools as especially important. The strengthening of links between schools and community sports clubs and the re-establishment of sport as an extra-curricular activity could be crucial in motivating schoolchildren to maintain their participation after they leave education, by introducing them to methods and venues for playing outside school. Also, increased sports participation in general is likely to encourage greater participation in extreme sports (Mintel, 2003). During the school summer holidays Ski Rossendale offered a number of holiday courses for children and this also allowed free use of the ski slope for the remainder of the school holidays.

Good links have been established with disabled groups, and the Uphill Ski Club is based at Ski Rossendale. Disabled groups are catered for much better than competitors, with disabled adaptive instruction, groups allowed to store specialist equipment there, and concessionary rates provided.

Saturday morning Kids' Club is popular, especially during the peak season. They cater for children from the age of 3 (Kindergarten classes run for 3–5 year olds). Two sessions 9.30 to 11a.m. and 11.30 to 1p.m. run every Saturday, but tend to be quieter and not running to full capacity outside the peak season. The summer Sunday race league is also aimed at children and getting them to engage with the ski slope on a more regular basis.

A key objective is to increase the level of usage of the slope at times outside peak season, especially with regard to lessons with instructors. The aim would be to offer incentives for individuals, families and other groups (e.g. schools) to increase their usage of the slope and lessons outside peak season. As the months of January and February are especially busy, they would also like to encourage people to start preparing for their holiday earlier.

Furthermore, the opening of the Chill Factor e at Trafford Park in Manchester is likely to take away some of Ski Rossendale's existing customers. Therefore, an increase in marketing communications in order to retain existing customers is also essential.

Children's parties have become increasingly popular for Ski Rossendale. This involves the use of large tubes that are sat on to come down the nursery slope, followed by a meal in the cafe. It is felt that there is potential for this to be developed further, especially during the summer months when the weather is better, and the slope quieter.

Adult parties are also starting to become popular. The use of the tubes is not restricted to the nursery slope, and therefore allows adults to go at a much faster speed. Party bookings allow for customers to bring their own alcohol and food. This allows the slope to be used outside normal opening times, and there appears to be potential to bring in increased revenue.

Prices 2008

Use of slope and hire of equipment only

Adult:	Standard Ticket (up to 2 hours)	£17
	Super Ticket (over 2 hours)	£19
Child:	Standard Ticket (up to 2 hours)	£10
	Super Ticket (over 2 hours)	£12
Adult Concession (students and over 60s)		
	Standard Ticket (up to 2 hours)	£10
	Super Ticket (over 2 hours)	£12

Special passes

Child:	Full year pass	£140
	Full year pass, direct debit	£13 per month
Adult:	Full year pass	£280
	Full year pass, direct debit	£25 per month

Ski lessons (including equipment hire)

Ski/board taster session (50 minutes)
Adult: £14
Child: £8
Ski/board lessons (1 hour 45 minutes, range of levels offered)
Adult: £25.00
Child: £17.50

A variety of full-day courses, ½ day courses, holiday courses etc. are offered in addition to the above. Instructors can also be hired for exclusive use by an individual or group. See www.ski-rossendale.co.uk for further information.

Ski/snowboard party
(includes equipment hire
and use of slope) 50 minute
lesson with an instructor,
followed by a party meal in
restaurant (minimum 6 in group)   £15.00 per person

Snow Tube party, with party meal   £10.00 per person

Competitors

At the moment, the main competitors are seen as Castleford, Sheffield and Halifax and the new facility next to the Trafford Centre in Manchester from November 2007.

Xscape Castleford (www.xscape.co.uk): This is the only real snow slope competitor currently, and therefore prices are much more expensive (e.g. 1 hour £21, 2 hours £31, lessons from £27 for 1 hour adult, and £23 per child). A wide range of facilities are available at the slope.

Sheffield Ski Village (www.sheffieldskivillage.co.uk): This is not seen as a main competitor, due to its distance, although facilities there are excellent, especially for skiing. A more complicated pricing structure exists here, although they offer a number of children's activities and 'piste & feast' events also.

Halifax (www.ridehalifax.co.uk): Closer than Sheffield, although the slope is smaller. It is more attractive to snowboarders, with a wide range of jumps (e.g. main 20ft kicker, side kicker, small learner jump, 10ft quarter pipe).

Manchester The Chill Factore (www.chilfactore.com) opened in November 2007. It is next to the Trafford Centre, Manchester, and is a ski complex offering snowboarding, skiing, ice wall for climbers, tobogganing facilities, along with a rock-climbing wall and a children's play area. There are three ski slopes, the longest being 180 metres long. There is also an après-ski area with alpine-themed bars and restaurants. This is Britain's biggest indoor ski slope. Prices are £22 per adult and £18 for children at peak times for $1\frac{1}{2}$ hours, and £17 adult/£14 children at off-peak times (although these prices do not cover hire of equipment, unlike Ski Rossendale).

Marketing communications

Ski Rossendale has recently out-sourced the production of a web site, which contains basic information concerning opening times, courses and costs, and allows for electronic queries to be raised.

Generally, little marketing communications is undertaken. A variety of leaflets is produced and these are available at the ski slope or at the other organisations within the trust. Some leaflets have been inserted into local newspapers, and some leaflet drops have been undertaken in some of the local areas, but this only happens very occasionally. Some local newspaper advertising has been undertaken, as well as limited PR through a small number of press releases. Representatives from Ski Rossendale also attend the annual Ski Show in Manchester, which takes place in October, and run ski lessons on the ski slope at the event. Some mutually beneficial marketing communications has been undertaken with Jaguar at Bolton and Blackburn, which involved Ski Rossendale banners and information being put up in its showrooms, while Jaguar brought demonstration cars to Ski Rossendale for a weekend. The first annual open day is being held this October where use of the facilities will be free for the day. The Marketing Manager feels that far more marketing communications could be undertaken. Innovative ideas are sought that will help to stretch the budget of £40,000 per annum. Although small, this is a substantial increase in the £10,000 available two years ago.

There is an opportunity to build relationships with existing customers, although at the moment, they do not have a full, useable database of these existing customers. Very few PR activities have been undertaken, and with such a small budget there is potential here to stretch this. Over the next year the key groups to target are: existing customers (retain them and increase their usage); better links and usage by schools; increase in use as a party destination (children and adults). In the longer term more users need to be attracted and usage for corporate events increased (although at the moment, they do not have the facilities to cater for this market).

MiniCase references

Mintel (2003) *Extreme Sports – UK* – November.
Mintel (2004) *Snow Sports – UK* – September.
Mintel (2005) *Extreme Sports – UK* – October.
Mintel (2006) *Snow Sports – UK* – September.

MiniCase questions

Your brief

The assignment is based on the Ski Rossendale case study. You are to take on the role of a marketing communications consultant to the Trust. Your task is to provide an analysis of the marketing communications problems and issues, set objectives and develop a new communications strategy for the club. This is to be implemented over the next 12 months.

Tasks

1. Analysis
You should provide a thorough, logically structured analysis of the facts as reported in the case, using other information to support your analysis. You will need to consider internal and external influences and use the figures, where appropriate, to provide evidence to support your analysis. This should include a summary of what you believe the key issues are that the Trust faces. These should be focused on areas that come under your remit as a consultant in marketing communications.

2. Objectives
These should be specific; they should relate to the 12-month period; you may include longer-term objectives. You should include some numerate objectives.

3. Marketing communications strategy
The final part of your report will provide strategic direction for the organisation. Define target segments. How should the organisation position itself? Which elements of the communications mix should be utilised and to what purpose? You should include a schedule of the methods and media to be used. You should also present an outline budget indicating the cost and allocation of budget to your communications proposals. Sources should be clearly quoted for all costs.

4. Evaluation of the marketing communications plan
Discuss how you would measure the effectiveness of the plan, and how this would be monitored and evaluated. Ensure you refer to appropriate theory in this area.

References

Andrews, K. (1987) *The Concept of Corporate Strategy*. Homewood, IL: Richard D. Irwin.

Anon. (2008) Guarding her patch. *The Marketer*, February, 27–9.

Ansoff, H.I. (1965) *Corporate Strategy*. New York: McGraw-Hill.

Beane, T.P. and D.M. Ennis (1987) Market segmentation: a review. *European Journal of Marketing*, **21**(5), 20–42.

Chaffee, E. (1985) 'Three models of strategy'. *Academy of Management Review*, **10**(1), 89–98.

Engel, J.F., Warshaw, M.R. and Kinnear, T.C. (1994) *Promotional Strategy*, 8th edn. Homewood, IL: Richard D. Irwin.

Gray, R. (2000) The chief encounter. *PR Week*, 8 September, 13–16.

Grunig, J. and Hunt, T. (1984) *Managing Public Relations*. New York: Holt, Rineholt & Winston.

Gustafson, R. (2007) Best of all worlds. *Marketing: Brands by Design*, 14 November, 11.

Haley, Russell I. (1968) Benefit segmentation: a decision-oriented research tool. *Journal of Marketing*, **32** (July), 30–5.

Hambrick, D.C. (1983) High profit strategies in mature capital goods industries: a contingency approach. *Academy of Management Journal*, **26**, 687–707.

Holm, O. (2006) Integrated marketing communication: from tactics to strategy, *Corporate Communications: An International Journal*, **11**(1), 23–33.

Jewell, R.D. (2007) Establishing effective repositioning communications in a competitive marketplace. *Journal of Marketing Communications*, **13**(4), 231–41.

Johnson, G., Scholes, K. and Whittingham, R. (2008) *Exploring Corporate Strategy*, 8th edn. Harlow: Pearson Education.

Kay, J. (1993) The structure of strategy. *Business Strategy Review*, **4**(2) (Summer), 17–37.

Lovallo, D.P. and Mendonca, L.T. (2007) Strategy's strategist: an interview with Richard Rumelt, *McKinsey Quarterly*, **4**. Retrieved 30 September 2007 from www.mckinseyquarterly.com/strategy/strategic-thinking/Strategys

Mintzberg, H. (1994) *The Rise and Fall of Strategic Planning*. Englewood Cliffs, NJ: Prentice-Hall.

Mintzberg, H. and Ghoshal, S. (2003) *Strategy Process: Concepts, Context and Cases*. Global edn. Englewood Cliffs, NJ: Financial Times/Prentice-Hall.

Moss, D. and Warnaby, G. (1998) Communications strategy? Strategy communication? Integrating different perspectives. *Journal of Marketing Communications*, **4**(3), 131–40.

van Riel, (1995) *Principles of Corporate Communication*, Harlow: Financial Times/Prentice-Hall.

Riiber Knudsen, T. (2007) Confronting proliferation . . . in beer: an interview with Carlsberg's Alex Myers, *McKinsey Quarterly*. Retrieved 28 July 2007 from www.mckinseyquarterly.com/marketing/confronting-proliferation

Rothschild, M. (1987) *Marketing Communications*. Lexington, MA: DC Heath.

Rowe, A.J., Mason, R.O., Dickel, K.E., Mann, R.B. and Mockler, R.J. (1994) *Strategic Management: A Methodological Approach*, 4th edn. Reading, MA: Addison-Wesley.

Steyn, B. (2003) From strategy to corporate communication strategy; a conceptualisation, *Journal of Communication Management*, **8**(2), 168–83.

Tiltman, D. (2007) Who is the ethical consumer? *Marketing*, 11 July, 28–30.

Weltevreden, J.W.J., Atzema, O.A.L.C. and Boschma R.A. (2005) The adoption of the Internet by retailers: a new typology of strategies. *Journal of Urban Technology* **12**(3), 59–87.

Weltevreden, J.W.J. and Boschma, R.A. (2008) Internet strategies and performance of Dutch retailers. *Journal of Retailing and Consumer Services*, **15**(3) (May), 163–78.

Whittington, R. (1993) *What is Strategy and Does it Matter?* London: Routledge.

Wind, Y.J. (1990) Positioning analysis and strategy. In *The Interface of Marketing and Strategy* (eds G. Day, B. Weitz and R. Wensley), 387–412 (Greenwich, CT: JAI Press).

Chapter 7
Agencies: practice, regulation and international communications

Communication agencies provide clients with access to the media, research materials, creative teams and the production facilities necessary for them to communicate with a range of audiences. However, there are certain practices, processes and procedures plus regulations that need to be understood in order for a client's message to be implemented, whether in domestic or international markets.

Aims and learning objectives

The aim of this chapter is to introduce the communications industry, the various organisations involved and some of the issues and practices, including international communications, associated with the operation of the industry.

The learning objectives of this chapter are to:

1. provide an introductory understanding of the communications industry, including the nature and role of the main types of organisations;
2. consider the processes associated with selecting an agency;
3. explore the key operations used by clients and agencies in the development of campaigns;
4. examine the methods of remuneration used to reward agencies;
5. review the regulation, including ethical issues, associated with marketing communications;
6. explain the principal ideas and strategies involved with international marketing communications practice.

Introduction

The marketing communications industry consists of four principal actors. These are the media, the clients, the agencies (historically, the most notable of which are advertising agencies) and finally the thousands of support organisations, such as production companies and fulfilment houses, that enable the whole communication process to function. It is the operations and relationships between these organisations that not only drive the industry but also form an important context within which marketing communications can be understood. Figure 7.1 sets out the main actor organisations in the industry.

There is an argument that organisations should manage and develop their marketing communications 'in-house', that is, do it themselves. This could enable better control and lower costs. However, this argument is now very weak due to the increasing complexity and diversity of communication activities and the restructuring of organisations aimed at de-layering and hollowing out their organisations. It can only be through outsourcing that organisations experience increased levels of flexibility and gain access to the special skills and expertise necessary to engage audiences in competitive environments.

One of the many decisions an organisation has to make is whether to employ people on a permanent basis, recruit temporary workers as demand requires or use specialists on a continuous or ad hoc basis. Most organisations use a mixture of these different types and adjust the balance between them according to trading and other environmental factors.

With regard to marketing communications, organisations can do-it-themselves and develop what is called an in-house facility. This provides a good level of control over the tools, messages and media used, and can improve on the speed of decision-making, compared to using an outside agency. On the other hand it increases fixed costs, reduces flexibility and introduces political dimensions, often around budgets, which tend to deflect from objectivity and creativity. Perhaps the most critical dimension concerns the lack of access to expertise. In an age where integration is a popular concept, it is important to have access to experts in the various communication disciplines. It is extremely unlikely that such experts can be readily found in-house. Having said this, many retail and business-to-business organisations choose to use in-house facilities, if only because of a lack of resources.

An alternative route is to use freelancers or self-employed consultants. Although each individual's skills may have been developed within a particular discipline, such as public relations or advertising, freelancers can provide flexibility and access to some experts through their network of personal contacts. However, it should be remembered that the use of freelancers

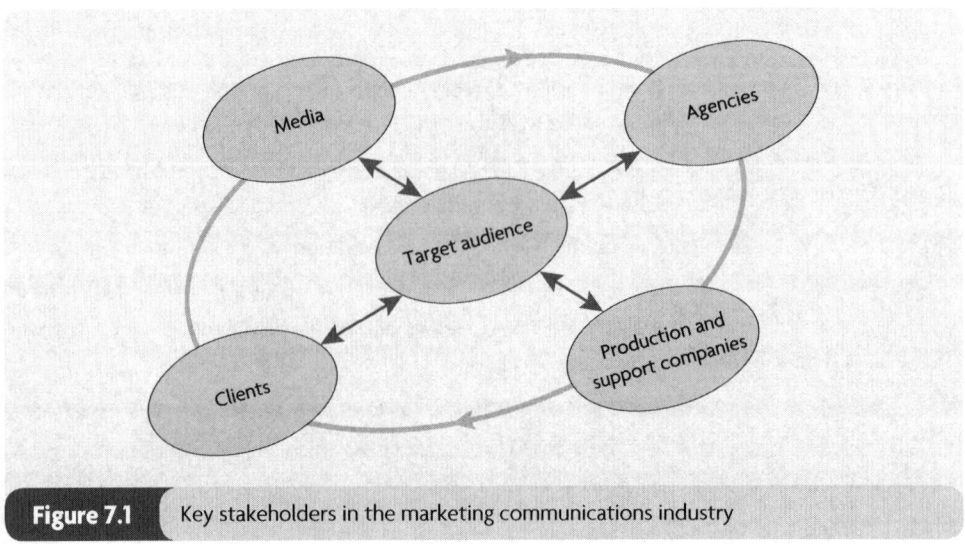

Figure 7.1   Key stakeholders in the marketing communications industry

and in-house facilities requires use of the client organisation's resources, if only to manage the freelancers. Crowdsourcing, the use of the public to generate creative advertising content, is an attempt by clients to circumnavigate the agency sector in order to find new material and cut costs. This form of user generated content is explored in more detail in Chapter 15.

The use of agencies is popular because they can provide objectivity, access to expertise and specialist technologies whilst at the same time allow the client to concentrate on their core business activities. Indeed, this is the route taken by the vast majority of organisations who regard the use of communication agencies in the same way as they do accountants, consultants, lawyers and other professionals. By outsourcing these activities, organisations buy experts whose specialist services can be used as and when required. This flexibility has proved to be both efficient and effective for both client and agency. However, the decision to use an agency leads to further decisions concerning, which type of agency and what do we want them to do, how many agencies should we use and what role should the client play in the relationship with the agency?

These may sound to be strange questions but consider the question of strategy. Should the client decide on the marketing communications, branding and positioning strategies or is this a part of the agency's tasks? Different client organisations will adopt different positions depending upon their experience, size and the nature of the task that needs to be undertaken. Another question concerns whether a single agency is required to deliver integrated marketing communication activities, whether a single agency should manage the integration process and subcontract tasks to other specialist or group-based agencies (and in doing so act as lead agency) or should a series of specialist agencies be appointed, each reporting to the client?

Agency types and structures

The marketing communications industry consists of a number of different types of organisations whose purpose is to enable clients to communicate effectively and efficiently with their target audiences. Essentially, clients appoint agents to develop and implement campaigns on their behalf. To accomplish this advertising agencies buy media time and space from media owners, public relations agencies place stories with the media for their client's representation, and other agencies undertake a range of other communications activities on behalf of their clients.

Originally, advertising agents undertook two main roles, creative message design and media planning and buying. The media component has subsequently been spun off to specialist agencies. However, the interest and drive towards integrated marketing communications has helped agents assume new, more independent roles in the communications industry. The development of digital media has had a profound impact on the public relations industry and the development of integrated marketing communications. For example, agencies that can form teams of specialists who can work across different audiences, yet provide an integrated approach are much sought after by clients (Wilson, 2009). Ideally these teams should consist of 12 members. Too many and ineffectiveness becomes an issue, too few and creativity is sacrificed. The real difficulty that Wilson identifies is how to ensure all 12 are client focused.

In addition to this White (2007) identifies several pressures working on agencies. These are the growth in importance of direct marketing, the increasing range of media and the need among large organisations for quasi-global ad networks. The result of this development is that a number of different types of agencies have emerged, all of which seek to fulfil particular roles.

Full-service agencies

The first and most common type of agency (advertising) is the full-service agency. This type of organisation offers the full range of services that a client requires in order to advertise its products and services. Agencies such as J. Walter Thompson and Leo Burnett offer a full service consisting of strategic planning, research, creative development, production, interactive and media planning and buying. Very often these services are offered on a global basis but this does not mean a full service agency needs to be large, employing thousands of people. Some mid-size agencies employing a couple of dozen people can offer a full service. Whatever the size, some of these activities may be subcontracted, but overall responsibility rests with the full-service agency.

Boutiques

A derivative of this type of agency is the boutique or creative shop, which often forms when creative personnel (teams) leave full service agencies to set up their own business. Boutiques provide specialist or niche services for clients such as copyrighting, developing creative content and other artistic services. These agencies provide clients with an alternative source of ideas, new ways of thinking about a problem, issue or product. Clients choose to use them because they either wish to use particular styles and approaches for their creative work or they want to generate a raft of creative ideas.

Viewpoint 7.1 It's not advertising, it's communication

Many aspects of the marketing communications industry have changed and are continuing to change. Some of these concern the nature and size of agencies with many large dominant groups emerging. For example, four major organisations pitched for Samsung's worldwide branding account; Interpublic (using its Fraftfcb operation), Omnicom (using BBDO agency), WPP (using J. Walter Thompson and Red Cell) and Publicis Groupe (using Leo Burnett and Saatchi & Saatchi).

The fact that WPP won the account is not the point. These organisations evolve as advertising agencies but now they have transformed themselves into 'communication partners'. This reflects the increasing attention given to relationship marketing, the development of integrated marketing communications and the relative decline in the dominance of advertising within the communications mix. Organisations now seek to communicate different messages and this involves using a variety of (neutral) media. The term 'communication agencies' or partners, suggests variety and flexibility and reflects a change in core business.

Apart from structural and name change the industry launched Social Professional in September 2007. This is a social network site designed specifically for all people working in the marketing communications industry. The free-to-use site was developed so that the industry had a facility in which to collaborate, network and communicate in a secure, moderated environment.

Among the main features are forums on a wide range of topics, including advertising, direct marketing, branding, sponsorship, reverse chronological ordering of blogs, an option to create an alter ego to encourage more honest debate and an RSS feed service to help users keep up-to-date with market developments.

Source: Based on Donohue (2007) plus various

Question
Is use of the term 'communication partners' disingenuous when advertising continues to be core business?

Task
Visit the website of one of the big four and determine the spread of their business activities.

Media specialists

Similarly, media specialists provide clients with media services expertise. These organisations deliver media strategy and consulting services for both client advertisers as well as agencies.

Their core business however, is focused on the planning, scheduling, buying and monitoring of a client's media schedule. Child (2007) reports that advertisers believe the role of strategic media planning is 50 per cent more important today than it was seven years ago. The key advantage of using a media specialist is that they have the capacity to buy media time and space at rates far lower than a client or advertising agency can procure them. This is because of the sheer volume of business that media specialists buy. Child also believes that there are some indications that clients believe it is more important to have a global media network rather than a global advertising agency.

Two main forms of media specialist have emerged: media independents, where the organisation is owned and run free of the direction and policy requirements of a full service agency, and media dependents, where the organisation is a subsidiary of a creative or full service organisation. The largest dependent in Britain is ZenithOptimedia, owned originally by Saatchi & Saatchi, and the largest independent is Carat.

Digital media

Digital media agencies have developed as a result of the rapid growth of the digital media industry. The growth has come from two main areas. The first concerns the surge of online brands that hit the market full of expectation of transforming the way business is conducted. The second concerns established offline brands seeking to reach customers by adding interactive capabilities to their marketing channels.

The provision of Internet facilities has been the main area of work, mainly communication and business operations activities. This has been followed by WAP technology activity, Web 2.0 and interactive television.

À la carte

Partly in response to the changing needs of clients and consumers, many organisations require greater flexibility in the way their advertising is managed. Consequently these clients prefer to use the services of a range of organisations. So, the planning skills of a full service agency, the creative talent of a particular boutique and the critical mass of a media-buying independent provide an *à la carte* approach. This approach requires the client advertiser to manage the entire marketing communication process, an 'in-house' arrangement. This process enables improved flexibility yet demands strong management coordination and control as the process is more complex and problematic.

Other communication agencies

The agencies and organisations set out so far have their roots and core business firmly set within the advertising part of the communications industry. In addition to these there is a swathe of other agencies, each specialising in a particular aspect of the marketing communications industry. So, there are agencies that provide sales promotion, public relations, sponsorship, field marketing, events, experiential marketing and direct marketing. Their structure and operations reflect the needs of their market specialism but they are based on the principles through which advertising agencies operate.

Direct marketing agencies

Direct marketing has become a significant and influential part of the marketing communications industry. Direct marketing and direct response agencies create and deliver campaigns through direct mail, telemarketing or through a variety of offline and online media, which is referred to as direct response media.

One of the distinguishing elements of a direct marketing agency is the database. These agencies maintain large databases that contain mailing lists. This data can be merged and reconstructed to reflect a client's target market. The agency helps to develop promotional materials and then implements the campaign through the data list. Direct agencies will either own or have access to a fulfilment house. These organisations fulfil customer orders, that is, process the order and take payment resulting from the direct marketing campaign, send out the ordered products and deal with after sales services as necessary.

Selecting an agency

The process of selecting an agency that is set out below appears to be rational and relatively straightforward. Readers should be aware that the reality is that the process is infused with political and personal issues, some of which can be contradictory. Logically the process commences with a *search*, undertaken to develop a list of potential candidates. This is accomplished by referring to publications such as *Campaign Portfolio* and the *Advertising Agency Roster*, together with personal recommendations. The latter is perhaps the most potent and influential of these sources. As many as 10 agencies could be included at this stage although six or seven are to be expected.

Viewpoint 7.2 Better to pitch the relationship

When Rob Murray was appointed as Marketing Director for Wickes, the building and DIY supplies store, he had to appoint an advertising agency to help bring about the changes he had determined needed to happen. In his previous position at Ryvita he had used the agency MWO who had proved successful for all parties.

Murray appointed MWO to the Wickes account, worth £10 million a year, without a pitch, and just a little bit of support from procurement consultants. Based on the successful relationship and the known operations and processes, Murray felt the strength of the relationship was important and was not something that could be replicated by the many other agencies, all of whom could also produce good ads.

Martin Glenn at Birds Eye Iglo is reported to have appointed Abbot Mead Vickers BBDO with whom he worked when at PepsiCo, while Jim Hytner appointed Walker Media when at Channel 5 and Barclays. Agency–client relationships do matter.

Source: Based on Charles (2008)

Question
Should it be mandatory that all agency appointments be made as a result of a fair and equal pitching process?

Task
Pick two brands of your choice, go to their websites and find out how long their current agency has been with the brand.

Next, the client will visit each of the short-listed candidates in what is referred to as a *credentials presentation*. This is a crucial stage in the process, as it is now that the agency is evaluated for its degree of fit with the client's expectations and requirements. Agencies could develop their websites to fulfil this role, which would save time and costs. The agency's track record, resources, areas of expertise and experience can all be made available on the Internet from which it should be possible to short-list three or possibly four agencies for the next stage in the process: the pitch.

In the PR industry agencies are selected to pitch on the basis of the quality and experience of the agency people, its image and reputation and relationships with existing clients. In addition, Pawinska (2000) reports that the track record of the agency and the extent of its geographical coverage are also regarded as important.

To be able to make a suitable bid the agencies are given a brief and then required to make a formal presentation (the *pitch*) to the client some 6–8 weeks later. This presentation is about how the agency would approach the strategic and creative issues and the account is awarded to whichever produces the most suitable proposal. Suitability is a relative term, and a range of factors need to be considered when selecting an organisation to be responsible for a large part of a brand's visibility. A strategic alliance is being formed and therefore a strong understanding of the strategic objectives of both parties is necessary, as is an appreciation of the structure and culture of the two organisations. The selection process is a bringing together of two organisations whose expectations may be different but whose cooperative behaviour is essential for these expectations to have any chance of materialising. For example, agencies must have access to comprehensive and often commercially confidential data about products and markets if they are to operate efficiently. Otherwise, they cannot provide the service that is expected.

However, it should be noted that pitches are not mandatory, and as Jones (2004) reports, nearly one-third of clients move their accounts without involving pitches. One of the reasons for this is the increasing cost involved in running the whole process, as much as £50,000 according to Jones. Indeed Wethey (2006) questions the whole validity and efficacy of the pitching process. He argues that many pitches are a waste of resources (time and money), that too many agencies devote too much of their resources chasing new business, that pitches do not solve client problems and that the whole process is often unrealistic.

The immediate selection process is finalised when terms and conditions are agreed and the winner is announced to the contestants and made public, often through press releases and the use of trade journals such as *Campaign*, *Marketing* and *Marketing Week*.

This formalised process is now being questioned as to its suitability. The arrival of new media firms and their need to develop communication solutions in one rather than eight weeks has meant that new methods have had to be found. In addition, agencies felt that they were having to invest a great deal in a pitch with little or no reward if the pitch failed. Their response has been to ask for payment to pitch which has not been received well by many clients. The tension that arises is that each agency is required to generate creative ideas over which they have little control once a pitch has been lost.

The pitching process also fails to give much insight into the probable working relationships and is very often led by senior managers who will not be involved in the day-to-day operations.

Agency operations

Most communications agencies are generally organised on a functional basis. There have been moves to develop matrix structures utilising a customer orientation, but this is very inefficient and the low margins prohibit such luxuries. There are departments for planning, creative and media functions coordinated on behalf of the client by an account handler or executive.

The account executive fulfils a very important role in that these people are responsible for the flow of communications between the client and the agency. The quality of the communications between the two main parties can be critical to the success of the overall campaign and to the length of the relationship between the two organisations. Acting at the boundary of the agency's operations, the account executive needs to perform several roles, from internal coordinator and negotiator to presenter (of the agency's work), conflict manager and information gatherer. Very often account executives will experience tension as they seek to achieve their clients' needs while trying to balance the needs of their employer and colleagues. These tensions are similar to those experienced by salespersons and need to be managed in a sensitive manner by management.

> ### Viewpoint 7.3 Google tools assist agencies
>
> Google's strategy is very different to that pursued by others in or related to the media industry. For many, innovation is about closed, payment-based systems. In contrast Facebook and Google follow an open, collaborative systems approach. This means that developers can develop innovative applications using the Google platform, without having to pay for the access to the underpinning technology. This helps ensure that the innovations and applications are compatible and based on a common platform.
>
> In another dimension, communication agencies can benefit from the stream of ideas and applications from Google. Boyd (2010) considers the Google Wonder Wheel, a tool which simplifies and arranges search results, similar to a mind map. Sketchup, a new 3D modelling facility, and Google Insight, a tool that enables keyword research, provides trend data on keyword searches and permits the data to be filtered by location. All of these have high potential usage by agencies. Edge (2010) refers to the range of free tools that can be used to track campaign performance, ad development and testing, using YouTube (which is owned by Google). In the same article Rebelo (2010) refers to the power of the Google tools to assist the creativity process and to move the way agencies operate, forward.
>
> *Source:* Based on Rebelo (2010); Edge (2010); Boyd (2010).
>
> #### Question
> To what extent do these advancements assist marketing communications?
>
> #### Task
> Find out two other recent innovations by Google and make notes about how they might help agencies do a better job for their clients.

Once an account has been signed, a client brief is prepared that provides information about the client organisation. It sets out the nature of the industry it operates in together with data about trends, market shares, customers, competitors and the problem that the agency is required to address. This is used to inform agency personnel. In particular, the account planner will undertake research to determine market, media and audience characteristics and make proposals to the rest of the account team concerning how the client problem is to be resolved.

Briefing is a process that is common across all client–agency relationships in the communication industry. Regardless of whether working in direct marketing, sales promotion, advertising, public relations, media planning and buying or other specialist area, the brief has a special importance in making the process work and the outcomes significant. However, the importance of preparing a brief of suitable quality has for some been underestimated. With agencies having to brief themselves and some briefs insufficiently detailed, a recent joint industry initiative sought to establish common working practices. The outcome of the process was a briefing template intended to be used by all across the communications agencies in the industry. Eight key headings emerged from the report and these can be seen in Figure 7.2.

In addition to the role of account handler, which might be regarded as one of traffic management, is the role undertaken by account planners (or creative planners). The role of the account planner was the subject of a flurry of debate (Collin, 2003; Grant *et al.*, 2003; Zambarino and Goodfellow, 2003). The general conclusion of these papers is that the role of account planner, which has been evolving since the beginning of the 1960s, has changed as the communications industry has fragmented and that a new role is emerging in response to integrated marketing communication and media neutral planning initiatives.

The traditional role of the account planner, which began in full-service agencies, was to understand the client's target consumers and develop strategies for the creative and media departments. As media broke away from full-service agencies so the role of the account planner shifted to the creative aspect of the agency work. Media planners assumed the same type of

Project management – Provide basic project details, e.g. timescales, contacts and people, project numbers

Where are we now? – Describe current brand details, e.g. background, position, competitors, key issues

Where do we want to be? – What needs to be achieved in terms of goals, e.g. sales, market share, ROI, shareholder value, awareness, perception, etc.

What are we doing to get there? – What is the context in terms of the marketing strategy, overall communication strategy and campaign strategy?

Who do we need to talk to? – What is understood about the audiences the communications are intended to influence?

How will we know if we have arrived? – What will be measured, by whom, how and when to determine whether the activity has been successful?

Practicalities – Budgets, timings and schedules, creative and media imperatives

Approvals – Who has the authority to sign off the brief and the agency work?

Figure 7.2 Briefing template

work in media companies although their work focused on planning the right media mix to reach the target audience.

Creative teams comprise a copywriter and an art director, supported by a service team. This team is responsible for translating the proposal into an advertisement. In a full-service agency, a media brief will also be generated, informing the media planning and buying department of the media and the type of media vehicles required. However, the vast majority of media planning work is now undertaken by specialist media agencies, media independents, and these will be briefed by the client, with some support from those responsible for the creatives.

In recent years, partly as a response to the growth of new media, a raft of small entrepreneurial agencies has emerged, to exploit the new opportunities arising from the digital revolution. Many of these are run without the control and structures evident in large, centralised agencies. While dedicated teams might theoretically be the best way to manage a client's project, the reality in many cases is the use of project teams comprising expert individuals working on a number of projects simultaneously. This is not a new phenomenon, but as a result many people are multi-tasking and they assume many roles with new titles. For example, the title *Head of Content* has arisen to reflect the significance of content issues in the new media market. Project managers assume responsibility for the implementation phase and the coordination of all aspects of a client's technological facilities. In addition, there are positions such as head of marketing, mobile (increasing focus on WAP technology), production and technology. The result is no hierarchies, flat structures and flexible working practices and similar expectations.

Agency remuneration

There are three main ways in which agencies are paid. These are *commission*, *fees* and *payment by results* (PBR). These are often supplemented by retainers and bonuses (see Figure 7.3). Very rarely is a single method used within a contract.

Figure 7.3 Methods of agency remuneration

Traditionally, advertising agencies were paid a commission by media owners for selling space in their publications. A fee of 15 per cent of the value of the media bought emerged as the norm. However, as relationships between agencies and clients strengthened, it seemed only reasonable that the clients should feel that agencies should act for them (and in their best interests), and not for the media owners. A number of questions were raised about whether the agency was actually being rewarded for the work it did and whether it was being objective when recommending media expenditure. As media independents emerged, questions started to be asked about why media agencies received 3 per cent and the creative agency received 12 per cent.

Fees became more popular, and there were some experiments with payment by results. The use of bonuses is widespread but whereas the intention is to reward excellent work, some agencies see bonuses as a means by which fees are reduced and as some clients refuse to pay, the impact on relationships can be far from positive (Child, 2007). Fees have been around for a long time, either in the form of retainers or on a project-by-project basis. Indeed, many agencies charge a fee for services over and above any commission earned from media owners.

For many, payment by results seems a good solution. In 2009 Coca-Cola introduced a new way by which their agencies were to be remunerated. Referred to as a value-based compensation model, Tylee (2010) argues that it extends the PBR model. Agencies are promised profit mark ups of 30 per cent if specific targets are met. If they are not, then only their costs are covered. At the time of writing it is uncertain whether this model will be adopted by other clients. Procter & Gamble have also adopted a similar value based reward programme, and as Williams (2010) indicates, value-based systems can be based on a variety of factors, as long as they are not timesheets based on hours and costs.

However, agencies have no control over the other marketing activities of the client, which might determine the degree of success of the campaign. Indeed, this raises the very thorny question of what 'success' is and how it might be measured. Despite these considerations, it appears that PBR is starting to become an established form of remuneration with over 30 per cent of agency–client contracts containing an element of PBR.

Regulating marketing communications

Just as organisations send messages about their identity through both formal and informal ways, so organisations send messages, partially through marketing communications, about

Table 7.1 Some of the ethical issues in marketing communications

Ethical theory	Distinctive characteristic	Example
Duties or principles	Good or bad is evident in the act itself, irrespective of the consequences	'Never tell lies'
Consequences	Whether an act is good or bad depends on what happens as a result of the act	Utilitarianism: 'take the action that results in the greatest good for the greatest number'
Virtues	Virtues are good qualities in a person's character that lie between undesirable extremes	'Study and imitate the behaviours of those who are judged to be good'
Teleological	Goodness or badness judged against the purpose of the organisation	'A business should not do things that are not consistent with the business purpose'

their attitude and stance on ethical issues. As ethical issues are becoming increasingly prominent, so organisations are attempting to become more actively involved in addressing the ethical consequences of their marketing communications (Christy, 2009: 88).[1]

Issues about matters that may be right or wrong are manifest in a wide range of marketing communications activities. The way an organisation attends to its duties and responsibilities, the extent to which it plans and considers the consequences of its actions before acting provides a broad measure of its overall attitude towards to all of its stakeholders and associated environments. This is referred to as corporate and social responsibility (CSR) and is fast becoming a key agenda item for many organisations.

There are three main theoretical approaches to CSR, each of which reflects an organisation's perspective of to whom it is primarily responsible. The shareholder approach suggests that an organisation's actions should be considered in terms of its ability to satisfy shareholders. The stakeholder approach recognises the influence of a wider array of stakeholders or constituencies, whilst the societal approach accepts the role organisations play in the fabric and expectations of society. Whichever of these approaches are adopted, the role of marketing communications within CSR is still wide and its use therefore should be carefully considered (managed) especially in an era of integrated marketing communications. Some of the different ways in which ethical issues can be considered in this context are listed in Table 7.1.

The importance of context

The importance of context in judging ethical behaviour can be seen in the debate in the UK over the problems arising from the selling of private pensions during the 1980s. In many cases customers were persuaded by salespeople to switch out of existing pension schemes into new schemes whose subsequent performance left them worse off. In these cases the complex nature of the services, together with the unfamiliarity of many of the customers with the various types of product and how to choose between them, led them to place an unusually great reliance on the advice provided by the salesperson. Put another way, the extent to which the buyer was foreseeably able to 'beware' in these cases was very limited, which in turn should have placed a greater than normal ethical duty on the salesperson to ensure that the customers were properly informed of the consequences and implications of the switch. The fact that these ethical standards were clearly not met in a large number of cases has caused a great deal of loss, anxiety and inconvenience for the customers who lost out, but also a great deal of difficulty, expense and embarrassment for the pensions industry as a whole.

---

[1] The author wishes to acknowledge the work of Richard Christy from whose chapter in Fill (2009) much of this material on ethics has been adapted.

> ### Viewpoint 7.4 Pension confusion
>
> Diacon and Ennew (1996) point out that marketing transactions in financial services have greater than normal potential for ethical complications. The unavoidable complexity of many financial services products is heightened by the fact that the evaluation may depend upon individual calculations carried out for the customer by the salesperson; also, risk for the customer may be significant, in that the actual benefits received will often depend upon the performance of the economy over a long period. The authors highlight a number of other ethical issues relevant to insurance selling, including:
>
> - the issue of 'fitness for purpose' in both the design of the products and the way in which they are matched to customer needs;
> - the transparency of the price for these products, such that any commissions payable to the intermediary organisation or individual salesperson are clearly visible;
> - the need for truth in promotion, not only in terms of strict factual correctness, but also in terms of what the consumer might be expected to understand from a phrase;
> - the effect of the sales targeting and reward systems of the selling organisation on the behaviour of salespeople, particularly in view of the important advisory component of this type of selling.
>
> The serious problems arising from personal pension selling during the 1980s provide an example of how important it is for businesses to maintain an active awareness of the likely effects of their actions. It is difficult to escape the conclusion that a more enlightened assessment of the long-term interests of the business on the part of financial service providers would have helped to avert many of the problems, to the great benefit of all involved. This is easy to conclude with hindsight: the effective ethical businesses are those that manage to cultivate this type of foresight.
>
> *Source*: Based on Diacon and Ennew (1996)
>
> #### Question
> To what extent could the recent failure of the financial services industry and the recession that was triggered, be traced to any of the four items highlighted in this viewpoint?
>
> #### Task
> Choose a financial services company, go to its website and consider the transparency of its communications.

A further critical contextual element concerns the relationship between buyer/seller. In relational exchanges value for all parties is rooted in the maintenance of trust and commitment. So, the communications and associated expectations used in relational exchanges will be different to those used in transactional exchanges. A customer might, for example, feel upset if a car salesperson with whom he had dealt for many years failed to tell him that the model he was buying was about to be superseded, because that would seem to be inconsistent with the trust built up over the years. The same customer might not be at all upset to find the same thing happen with a personal computer bought from a discount store in London, not only because computers are known to date more quickly than models of cars, but also because there was no long-term relationship to be brought into question.

Regulating marketing communications

It should be clear that a range of marketing communications activities have ample opportunity to mislead, offend or, at another level, individuals might be subject to more severe distress such as physical injury, psychological suffering or perhaps financial loss. It is important therefore to have in place a system that provides a measure of control over the industry, one which regulates marketing communications activities in order to protect and serve society in ways in which are regarded as appropriate.

Regulation is managed through a blend of two main approaches. One is based on legislation, that is the use of law to provide a legal boundary on what is and what is not permitted. The second approach is based on a set of voluntary codes and processes, run by members of the marketing industry. Although the voluntary codes are used to manage day-to-day questions, Harker's (1998) review of approaches to regulation in five countries suggests that a combination of both legal and voluntary approaches can work effectively to regulate the marketing communications industry.

In the UK, the Advertising Standards Authority has responsibility for advertising content regulation in both broadcast and non-broadcast advertising (the former by delegation from Ofcom, the general regulator for the communications industry and the latter by continuance of the ASA's former role). The ASA, which is funded by levies from advertising, administers a set of codes of advertising practice for the various types of advertising (see www.asa.org.uk for further details). The system aims to provide clear arrangements for consumers, as well as a consistent structure for dealing with the increasingly diverse range of communications media that has developed in recent years.

Although Ofcom retains backstop powers over the regulations for managing the arrangements for broadcast advertising, the system remains effectively self-regulatory in approach, building on the ASA's experience as the regulator of non-broadcast advertising content. Strictly speaking, the system is co-, rather than self-regulatory, in that Ofcom, with its statutory powers, has delegated the responsibility for maintaining and applying codes of practice approved by the regulator (see www.ofcom.org.uk).

Self-regulation

In the UK, a range of specialised codes have been developed to provide guidance on the production of acceptable marketing communications in particular circumstances. The website of the Advertising Standards Authority (ASA) (http://www.asa.org.uk) provides access to full-text versions of these codes. The ASA's main code for non-broadcast advertising (the Code of Advertising, Sales Promotion and Direct Marketing, published by the Committee of Advertising Practice) begins with a set of general principles. The first two in particular set the tone for the whole code:

> All marketing communications should be legal, decent, honest and truthful. All marketing communications should be prepared with a sense of responsibility to consumers and to society.
> (ASA Code of Advertising, Sales Promotion and Direct Marketing (2003: 6))

The general rules of the Code discuss the requirements of legality, decency, honesty and truthfulness in more detail and also provide guidance on, for example, the protection of privacy, the use of testimonials and endorsements, on competitor comparisons and product availability.

Later sections of the main Code focus on sales promotion (sections 27 to 40) and direct marketing (sections 41 to 45), with guidance on specific issues such as free offers and free trials (section 32) and the increasingly important area of database practice (section 43). The Code also offers detailed guidance on specific marketing communications contexts, such as: alcoholic drinks, children, motoring, health and beauty products and therapies, weight control, financial products and tobacco.

Besides the advice and guidance, it defines the processes through which advertisers should comply with the Code and the sanctions that can be applied. A key aim of the Code is to help those in the industry to produce 'marketing communications that are welcomed and trusted' (p. 3). Since the broadening of its responsibilities in 2004, the ASA also now maintains a range of Codes on broadcast advertising:

- the Radio Advertising Standards Code;
- the TV Advertising Standards Code;
- the Alcohol Advertising Rules;
- Advertising Guidance Notes (concerning, for example, the identification of programmes likely to appeal to children and young people);
- Rules on the Scheduling of Advertising;
- Code for Text Services;
- Guidance on Interactive TV.

As can be seen from this list, the self-regulatory regime is required to encompass the technology-fuelled proliferation of broadcast entertainment and information services. Keeping up to date with this rapid development, as well as remaining sensitive to changes in public sensitivity or taste is a major challenge for any organisation and the ASA's library of advertising codes can be expected to continue to evolve in future.

International marketing communications

The differences between operating within home or domestic markets, compared with overseas or international markets are many and varied. Most of these differences can be considered within an economic, cultural, legal, technological and competitive framework. If the core characteristics of a home market (such as prices, marketing channels, finance, knowledge about customers, legislation, media and competitors) are compared with each of the same factors in the international markets in which an organisation might be operating, the degree of complexity and uncertainty can be easily illuminated. Management might be conversant with the way of doing business at home but, as they move outside the country/regional borders/areas that represent their domain of knowledge, understanding and to some extent security, so levels of control decline and risk increases.

Key variables

There are a large number of variables that can impact on the effectiveness of marketing communications that cross international borders. Many of these are controllable by either local or central management. However, there are a large number that are uncontrollable, and these variables need to be carefully considered before communications are attempted. The following variables (culture and media) are reviewed here because of their immediate and direct impact on organisations and their communication activities.

Culture

The values, beliefs, ideas, customs, actions and symbols that are learned by members of particular societies are referred to as culture. The importance of culture is that it provides individuals with identity and the direction of what is deemed to be acceptable behaviour. Culture is acquired through learning. If it were innate or instinctive, then everyone would behave in the same way. Human beings across the world do not behave uniformly or predictably. Therefore different cultures exist, and from this it is possible to visualise that there must be boundaries within which certain cultures, and hence behaviours and lifestyles, are permissible or even expected. These boundaries are not fixed rigidly, as this would suggest that cultures are static. They evolve and change as members of a society adjust to new technologies, government policies, changing values and demographic changes, to mention but a few dynamic variables. From a marketing communications perspective, the prevailing culture in a region must be respected, otherwise it is likely that a brand and or an organisation will be rejected. For example, the Dove ads in which happy women of all shapes and sizes pose in their underwear have had to be shown in different ways to meet the needs of different cultures. In Brazil the women are depicted hugging each other yet in the United States they stand slightly apart from each other, as body contact in the United States is not part of the culture (Laurance, 2007).

Culture is passed from generation to generation. This is achieved through the family, religion, education and the media. These conduits of social behaviour and beliefs serve to provide consistency, stability and direction. The extent to which the media either move society forward or merely reflect its current values is a debate that reaches beyond the scope of this book. However, there can be no doubt as to the impact that the media have on society and the important part that religion plays in different cultures around the world.

Culture has multiple facets, and those that are of direct relevance to marketing communications are the values and beliefs associated with *symbols*, such as language and aesthetics, *institutions* and *groups*, such as those embracing the family, work, education, media and religion, and finally *values*, which according to Hofstede *et al.* (1990) represent the core of culture. These will be looked at in turn.

Symbols

Language, through both the spoken and the non-spoken word, permits members of a society to enter into dialogue and to share meaning. Aesthetics, in the form of design and colour, forms an integral part of packaging, sales promotions and advertising. Those involved in personal selling must be aware of the symbolic impact of formal and informal dress codes and the impact that overall personal appearances and gestures (for example when greeting or leaving people) may have on people in different cultures. Advertisers need to take care that they do not infringe a culture's aesthetic codes when designing visuals or when translating copy into the local language.

Institutions and groups

The various institutions that help form the fabric of societies and particular cultures provide a means by which culture is communicated and perpetuated through time. These groups provide the mechanisms by which the process of socialisation occurs. Of these groups, the family plays an important role. The form of the *family* is evolving in some Western cultures, such that the traditional family unit is declining and the number of single-parent families is increasing. In many developing economies the extended family, with several generations living together, continues to be a central, stable part of society. Marketing communication messages need to reflect these characteristics. The impact and importance of various decision-makers need to be recognised and the central creative idea needs to be up to date and sensitive to the family unit.

Work patterns vary across regions: not all cultures expect a 9-to-5 routine. This is breaking down in the UK as delayering pressurises employees to work increased hours, while in Asia-Pacific Saturday morning work is the norm.

Literacy levels can impact heavily on the ability of target audiences to understand and to ascribe meanings to marketing communication messages. The balance between visual and non-visual components in messages and the relative complexity of messages should be considered in the light of the education levels that different countries and regions have reached. In addition to these factors, some target audiences in more developed economies have developed a high level of advertising sophistication. The meaning given to messages is in some part a reflection of the degree to which individuals understand commercial messages and what the source seeks to achieve. This high level of interaction with messages or advertising literacy suggests that advertisers need to create a dialogue with their audiences that recognises their cognitive processing abilities and does not seek to deceive or misinform.

Religion has always played an important part in shaping the values and attitudes of society. Links between religion and authority have been attempted based on the highly structured nature of religion and the role that religion can play in the family, forming the gender, decision-making roles and nurturing the child-rearing process. While the results of research are not conclusive, there appears to be agreement that religion plays an important part in consumer buying behaviour and that marketing communications should take into account the level of religious beliefs held by the decision-maker (Delner, 1994).

Similarly, mass communication technologies provide audiences with improved opportunities to understand and appreciate different religious beliefs and their associated rituals and artefacts, so care needs to be taken not to offend these groups with upsetting or misinformed marketing communications.

Values

One of the most important international, culturally oriented research exercises, was undertaken by Hofstede (1980, 1991). Using data gathered from IBM across 53 countries, Hofstede's research has had an important impact on our understanding of culture (Hickson and Pugh, 1995). From this research, several dimensions of culture have been discerned. The first of these concerns the individualist/collectivist dimension. It is suggested that individualistic cultures emphasise individual goals and the need to empower, to progress and to be a good leader. Collectivist cultures emphasise good group membership and participation. Consequently, difficulties can arise when communications between these two types of culture have meanings ascribed to them that are derived from different contexts. To avoid the possible confusion and misunderstanding, an adapted communication strategy is advisable.

In addition to these challenges, comprehension (ascribed meaning) is further complicated by the language context. In high-context languages, information is conveyed through who is speaking and their deportment and mannerisms. Content is inferred on the basis that it is implicit: it is known and does not need to be set out. This is unlike low-context languages, where information has to be detailed and 'spelled out' to avoid misunderstanding. Not surprisingly, therefore, when (marketing) communications occur across these contexts, inexperienced communicators may be either offended at the blunt approach of the other (of the low-context German or French, for example) or intrigued by the lack of overt information being offered from the other (from the high-context Japanese or Asians, for example). Referring to advertising creative strategy, Okazaki and Alonso (2003) assert that the Japanese prefer a more subtle, soft approach. In contrast, North Americans prefer a more direct, hard-sell strategy with direct, explicit messages.

A further cultural dimension concerns the role that authority plays in society. Two broad forms can be identified. In high-power-distance cultures, authority figures are important and guide a high proportion of decisions that are made. In low-power-distance cultures, people prefer to use cognitive processing and make reasoned decisions based on the information available. What might be deduced from this is that expert advice and clear, specific recommendations should be offered to those in high-power-distance cultures, while information provision should be the goal of marketing communications to assist those in low-power-distance cultures (Zandpour and Harich, 1996).

People in different cultures can exhibit characteristics that suggest they feel threatened or destabilised by ambiguous situations or uncertainty. Those cultures that are more reliant on formal rules are said to have high levels of uncertainty avoidance. They need expert advice, so marketing communications that reflect these characteristics and are logical, clear and provide information directly and unambiguously (in order to reduce uncertainty) are likely to be more successful.

From the adaptation/standardisation perspective, this information can be useful in order to determine the form of the most effective advertising messages. Zandpour and Harich used these cultural dimensions, together with an assessment of the advertising industry environment in each target country. The results of their research suggest that different countries are more receptive to messages that have high or low levels of logical, rational and information-based appeals (think). Other countries might be more receptive to psychological and dramatically based appeals (feel).

Research concerning the effectiveness of advertising strategies in the USA and Australia (Frazer and Sheehan, 2002) found that safety appeals were more frequently used in Australia than the USA. This may well reflect varying cultural values regarding concern for safety-related issues, concern for the environment and varying regulatory requirements.

Media

The rate of technological change has had a huge impact on the form and type of media that audiences can access. However, media availability is far from uniform, and the range and types of media vary considerably across countries. These media developments have been accompanied by a number of major structural changes to the industry and the way in which it is regulated. Many organisations (client brands, media and agencies) have attempted to grow through diversification and the development of international networks (organic growth and alliances), and there has been an increase in the level of concentration as a few organisations/individuals have begun to own, and hence control, larger proportions of the media industry. For example, Rupert Murdoch, Ted Turner, Time-Warner, Bertelsmann and Silvio Berlusconi now have substantial cross-ownership holdings of international media. This concentration is partly the result of the decisions of many governments to deregulate their control over the media and to create new trading relationships. As a result, this cross-ownership of the media (television, newspapers, magazines, cable, satellite, film, publishing, advertising, cinema, retailing, recorded music) has created opportunities for client advertisers to have to go to only one media provider, which will then provide access to a raft of media across the globe. For example, the Time-Warner/AOL merger was intended to take the concentration and cross-industry collaboration a stage further as positions for future markets are adopted. This facility, known as one-stop shopping, has been available in North America for some time, and was attempted by Saatchi & Saatchi and WPP in the 1980s from a European base, but it is only since the 1990s that this opportunity has been offered elsewhere. The failure of the Time-Warner/AOL merger is symptomatic of other cultural and business-related problems.

Deregulation has had a profound impact on media provision in nearly all parts of the world. This often manifests itself in terms of the growth in types of the media available and the number of media vehicles.

International communication strategy

The degree to which organisations should adapt their external messages to suit local or regional country requirements has been a source of debate since Levitt (1983) published his seminal work on global branding. The standardisation/adaptation issue is unlikely to be resolved, yet is an intuitively interesting and thought-provoking subject. The cost savings associated with standardisation policies are attractive and, when these are combined with the opportunity to improve message consistency, communication effectiveness and other internally related efficiencies such as staff morale, cohesion and organisational identity, the argument in favour of standardisation seems difficult to renounce. However, in practice there are very few brands that are truly global. Some, such as McDonald's, Coca-Cola and Levi's, are able to capitalise on the identification and inherent brand value that they have been able to establish across cultures. The majority of brands lack this depth of personality, and because individual needs vary across cultures, so enterprises need to retune their messages in order that their reception is as clear and distinct as possible.

Adaptation

The arguments in favour of adapting messages to meet the needs of particular local and/or regional needs are as follows:

- Consumer needs are different and vary in intensity. Assuming there are particular advertising stimuli that can be identified as having universal appeal, it is unlikely that buyers across international borders share similar experiences, abilities and potential either to process information in a standardised way or to ascribe similar sets of meanings to the stimuli they perceive. Ideas and message concepts generated centrally may be inappropriate for local markets.
- The infrastructure necessary to support the conveyance of standardised messages varies considerably, not only across but often within broad country areas.
- Educational levels are far from consistent. This means that buyers' ability to give meaning to messages will vary. Similarly, there will be differing capacities to process information, so that the complexity of message content has to be kept low if universal dissemination is to be successful.
- The means by which marketing communications are controlled in different countries is a reflection of the prevailing local economic, cultural and political conditions. The balance between voluntary controls through self-regulation and state control through legislation is partly a testimony to the degree of economic and political maturity that exists. This means that what might be regarded as acceptable marketing communications activities in one country may be unacceptable in another. For example, cold calling is not permissible in Germany but, although not popular with either sales personnel or buyers, is allowed in the Netherlands and France.
- Local management of the implementation of standardised, centrally determined messages may be jeopardised because of a lack of ownership. Messages crafted by local 'craftsmen' to suit the needs of local markets may receive increased levels of support and motivation.

The localised communication strategy used by McDonald's in India reflects the company's sensitivity to local culture. On entry to the Indian market the global brand values were amended to position McDonald's as supportive of Indian family values. This appeal was targeted at middle class families, designed to encourage the younger generation to perceive McDonald's as a key part of their social identity. Once this had been established communications were used to present the brand as inexpensive and accessible to a wide range of other consumers (Anon, 2010). Coca-Cola recognise that they are a local business and the need to differentiate in India and China is paramount.

Standardisation

Just as the arguments for adaptation appear convincing at first glance, then so do those in favour of standardisation:

- Despite geographical dispersion, buyers in many product categories have a number of similar characteristics. This can be supported by the various psychographic typologies that have been developed by advertising agencies for their clients. As brand images and propositions are capable of universal meaning, there is little reason to develop a myriad of brand messages.
- Many locally driven campaigns are regarded as being of poor quality, if only because of the lack of local resources, experiences and expertise (Harris, 1996). It is better to control the total process and at the same time help exploit the opportunities for competitive advantage through shared competencies.
- As media, technology and international travel opportunities impact on increasing numbers of people, so a standardised message for certain offerings allows for a strong brand image to be developed.
- Just as local management might favour local campaigns, so central management might prefer the ease with which they can implement and control a standardised campaign. This frees local managers to concentrate on managing the campaign and removes from them the responsibility of generating creative ideas and associated issues with local advertising agencies.

- Following on from this point is one of the more enduring and managerially appealing ideas. The economies of scale that can be gained across packaging, media buying and advertising message creation and production can be enormous. In addition, the prospect of message consistency and horizontally integrated campaigns across borders is quite compelling. Buzzell (1968) argued that these economies of scale would also improve levels of profitability.

Fielding (2000) and Hite and Fraser (1988) argue that the evidence indicates that, although organisations pursued standardisation strategies in the 1970s, the trend since then has been towards more local adaptation. Harris (1996) makes the point that, although the operation of a purely standardised programme is considered desirable, there is no evidence to suggest that standardisation actually works. There appears to have been little research to compare the performance of advertising that has been developed and implemented under standardisation policies with that executed under locally derived communications.

However, while a few organisations do operate at either end of the spectrum, the majority prefer a contingency approach. This means that there is a degree of standardisation, where for example creative themes, ideas and campaign planning are centrally driven and other campaign elements such as language, scenes and models are adapted to the needs of the local environment. The cosmetic manufacturer L'Oréal used to distribute its Studio Line of hair care products aimed at 18–35-year-olds, across 50 countries. 'These are the same products with the same formulation with the same attitudinal message of personal choice' (Sennett, in Kaplan, 1994). All the advertisements have the same positioning intentions, which are developed centrally, but the executions (featuring different hairstyles) are produced locally to reflect the different needs of different markets.

It is too easy to consider the internationalisation debate in terms of packaged goods companies when other sectors have approached the task in different ways. Bold (2000) refers to pharmaceutical companies that have generally made the product, as opposed to brands, the centre of their communication strategy. Drugs are launched in different countries using different names and different strategies targeted at the medical professionals. He comments that while this approach was prevalent, the structure of pharmaceutical companies tended to be nation-focused, even to the extent that there would be separate regionalised budgets. The merger and consolidation activity, together with the rapid rise in patient involvement in health care (e.g. AIDS), has resulted in the formation of centralised marketing departments and the development of multinational brands.

The argument for some form of standardisation is twofold. First, there is an increasing need for improved levels of internal efficiency (and accountability) in terms of the use of resources. Second, there is an increasing awareness of the benefits that standardised advertising may have on organisational identity, employee morale and satisfaction. The pressure to make cost savings and to develop internal efficiencies, therefore, appears to override the needs of the market.

However, those who argue in favour of standardisation need to be aware that the information content will often need to be correspondingly low. Mueller (1991) observes that the greater the amount of information the greater the opportunity for buyers to discriminate among alternative purchases. Conversely, the emphasis with uninformative advertising is to use imagery and indirect (peripheral) cues. Multinational organisations prepare individual marketing mixes for individual countries/areas. Products and prices will be different, so comparisons are difficult. Likewise, key attributes will vary across countries/areas, so this means that organisations need to decide whether high levels of standardisation and low levels of information are preferable to adapted campaigns with higher levels of information content.

The criteria by which organisations should decide whether to adapt or standardise their marketing (communications) activities is normally the impact that the different strategies are likely to have on profit performance (Buzzell, 1968). The basis for these financial projections has to be a suitably sensitive segmentation analysis based on a layering of segment information. Country-only or arbitrary regional analysis is unlikely to be suitable. Cross-cultural and psychographic data need to be superimposed to provide the richness upon which to build effective communications.

Organisations rarely decide on a polarised strategy of total adaptation or complete standardisation. In practice, a policy of 'glocalisation' seems to be preferred. Under this approach, organisations develop standard messages centrally, but expect the local country areas to adapt them to meet local cultural needs by adjusting for language and media components. There are, of course, variations on this theme. For example, head office might decide on the strategic direction and thrust of the campaign and leave the local country management to produce its own creatives.

Viewpoint 7.5 Beat the international cravings

Pharmaceutical brands tend to be country-specific due mainly to cultural attitudes towards healthcare, medicine and related activities. Regulations also pose problems as they vary across countries and restrict what messages can and cannot be said. Therefore, the task of converting a pharmaceutical brand into a global entity requires lateral thinking, something that Nicorette undertook in their quest to be a billion dollar brand by 2010.

The answer lay in repositioning Nicorette as a consumer brand, one imbued with emotion rather than one that conveyed rational, information health-dominated messages. This meant that rather than convey messages about how Nicorette could help a smoker give up completely, messages were designed to support smokers through each cigarette not smoked and overcoming the cravings.

The creative instrument used across the campaign was 'Cravings Man'. A 2.5 metre cigarette with a face, legs and arms. Each ad showed a smoker literally beating the craving for a cigarette. This creative idea travelled across all countries as the same underlying feelings are experienced by all smokers (see Exhibit 7.1).

Source: Based on Horry and Miller (2006)

Exhibit 7.1 Nicorette cravings ad
Image courtesy of The Advertising Archives

Question
How might 'Cravings Man' be used in other tools and media?

Task
Find one of Nicorette's competitors and compare the basic messages they convey with Nicorette's.

Summary

In order to help consolidate your understanding of the marketing communication industry, here are the key points summarised against each of the learning objectives:

1 Provide an introductory understanding of the communications industry, including the nature and role of the main types of organisations

The structure of the industry is similar in most countries but the relationships and operations will inevitably vary. However, the marketing communication industry in Britain has evolved slowly, with large agencies seeking to bring a range of communication skills and facilities together within a single group. Mid-size and small agencies still maintain a functional orientation (e.g. advertising, promotion, public relations or digital), although there are many attempting to provide an integrated service.

The agencies broker or facilitate the communication needs of clients, while media houses plan, buy and monitor media purchases for their clients. Production facilitators ensure the processes work by making videos, providing fulfilment or staging events. All deliver specific value to the industry and have different roles to play.

2 Consider the processes associated with selecting an agency

The process commences with a *search*, undertaken to develop a list of potential candidates. The client should then visit each of the short-listed candidates in what is referred to as a *credentials presentation*. This is a crucial stage in the process, as it is now that the agency is evaluated for its degree of fit with the client's expectations and requirements.

Selected agencies are given a brief and then required to make a formal presentation (the *pitch*) to the client some 6–8 weeks later. This presentation is about how the agency would approach the strategic and creative issues and the account is awarded to whichever produces the most suitable proposal. The winning agency is invited to discuss terms and conditions, and the winner is announced to the contestants and made public.

3 Explore the key operations used by clients and agencies in the development of campaigns

Once the client–agency relationship is established, the operational procedures are based on briefings, and there are three main ones: the client, creative and media briefs.

4 Examine the methods of remuneration used to reward agencies

Relationships between clients and agencies are of critical importance and part of their trust and commitment is reflected in the remuneration agencies receive for their contribution to their client's business. There are three keys methods: commission, payment by results and fees. These are normally combined within a contract.

5 Review the regulation, including ethical issues, associated with marketing communications

The regulation of marketing communications is generally undertaken through a blend of statutory measures, imposed by a government, or voluntary codes, coordinated and implemented by the industry itself, otherwise referred to as self-regulation.

Ethical issues are becoming increasingly prominent and many organisations are attempting to become more actively involved in addressing the ethical consequences of their marketing communications activities. Concern about telling the truth, their attitude towards vulnerable groups, respect and concern for individual privacy, ensuring all communications are tasteful and decent and that the use of inducements to clients, sales personnel and others are transparent and appropriate are some of the more obvious areas towards which organisations should direct their attention.

6 Explain the principal ideas and strategies involved with international marketing communications practice

There are a large number of variables that need to be carefully considered before communications are attempted in an international or global arena. Two of the more important ones are culture and media availability.

Organisations that operate in an international environment need to consider whether their messages should be adapted to meet the needs of country or regional audiences or whether they should be standardised and use a single message that is delivered to all audiences.

Review questions

1. Who are the main types of organisation that make up the marketing communication industry?
2. Identify some of the issues that prevail in the industry.
3. Write notes for a presentation explaining the different types of agency available to clients.
4. What factors should be taken into consideration and what procedures might be followed when selecting an agency?
5. What are the basic dimensions for the development of good agency–client relationships?
6. Write short notes about the briefing system.
7. Prepare some brief notes explaining how culture impacts on an organisation's marketing communications.
8. Select two countries of your choice. Compare the significance of cultural symbols and provide examples of how these are used.
9. You have been asked to make a presentation to senior managers on the advantages and disadvantages of standardising the marketing messages delivered for your brand throughout the world. Prepare notes for each of the slides you will use.
10. Your client is currently following an adapted strategy, but is considering changing to a standardised approach. What might be the impact of this move on your agency?

References

Anon (2010) McDonald's takes localised approach in India, *Exchange4Media and Warc*. Retrieved 12 May 2010 from www.warc.co./news/

Bold, B. (2000) Unlocking the global market, *PR Week*, 11 August, 13–14.

Boyd, M. (2010) Google shows adland the new tools of its trade, *Campaign*, 25 June, 11.

Buzzell, R. (1968) Can you standardise multinational marketing? *Harvard Business Review*, 46 (November/December), 102–113.
Charles, G. (2008) The buddy system, *Marketing*, 6 February, 16.
Child, L. (2007) How to manage your relationship, *Marketing Agency*, (December), 4–7.
Christy, R. (2009) Ethics in Marketing Communications. In *Marketing Communications: interactivity, communities and content*, 5th edn. (ed. C. Fill) 99–127. Harlow: FT/Prentice Hall.
Collin, W. (2003) The interface between account planning and media planning – a practitioner perspective. *Marketing Intelligence and Planning*, 21(7), 440–445.
Delner, N. (1994) Religious contrast in consumer decision behaviour patterns: their dimensions and marketing implications. *European Journal of Marketing*, 28(5), 36–53.
Diacon, S.R. and Ennew. C.T. (1996) Can Business Ethics Enhance Corporate Governance? Evidence from a Survey of UK Insurance Executives, *Journal of Business Ethics*, 15(6), 623–634.
Donohue, A. (2007) Social networking site for marketing professionals launches. *Brand Republic*, 28 September. Retrieved 8 October 2007 from www.brandrepublic.com/News/741288/Social-networking-site-marketing-professionals-launches/
Edge, M. (2010) Google shows adland the new tools of its trade, *Campaign*, 25 June, 11.
Fielding, S. (2000) Developing global brands in Asia, *Admap* (June), 26–29.
Frazer, C.F. and Sheehan, K.B. (2002) Advertising strategy and effective advertising comparing the USA and Australia, *Journal of Marketing Communications*, 8, 149–164.
Grant, I., Gilmore, C. and Crosier, K. (2003) Account planning: whose role is it anyway? *Marketing Intelligence and Planning*, 21(7), 462–472.
Harris, G. (1996) International advertising: developmental and implementational issues, *Journal of Marketing Management*, 12, 551–560.
Hickson, D.J. and Pugh, D.S. (1995) *Management Worldwide*. London: Penguin.
Hite, R.E. and Fraser, C. (1988) International advertising strategies of multinational corporations. *Journal of Advertising Research*, 28 (August/September), 9–17.
Hofstede, G. (1980) *Culture's Consequences: International Differences in Work Related Values*. Thousand Oaks, CA: Sage.
Hofstede, G. (1991) *Cultures and Organisations*. London: McGraw-Hill.
Hofstede, G., Neuijen, B., Ohayv, D.D. and Sanders, G. (1990) Measuring organisational cultures: a qualitative and quantitative study across twenty cases, *Administrative Science Quarterly*, 35(2), 286–316.
Horry, T. and Miller, J. (2006) Sold not dispensed – the power of consumer brands vs pharmaceutical brands, *Advertising Works*, 15, 333–334. Henley: NTC Publications.
Jones, M. (2004) 10 things agencies need to know about clients, *Admap*, 39(5) (May), 21–23.
Kaplan, R. (1994) Ad agencies take on the world, *International Management* (April), 50–52.
Laurance, B. (2007) Unilever learns to join the dots, *Sunday Times*, 18 March, 11.
Levitt, T. (1983) The globalization of markets, *Harvard Business Review* (May/June), 92–102.
Mueller, B. (1991) An analysis of information content in standardised vs. specialised multinational advertisements, *Journal of International Business Studies* (First Quarter), 23–39.
Okazaki, S. and Alonso, J. (2003) Right messages for the right site: online creative strategies by Japanese multinational corporations, *Journal of Marketing Communications*, 9, 221–239.
Pawinska, M. (2000) The passive pitch, *PR Week*, 12 May, 14–15.
Rebelo, M. (2010) Google shows adland the new tools of its trade, *Campaign*, 25 June, 11.
Tylee, J. (2010) Will others follow Coke's remuneration model?, *Campaign*, 19 February, 17.
Wethey, D. (2006) The shocking truth about the pitch, *The Marketer*, September, 7–8.
White, R. (2007) Structuring the (ad) agency, *Admap*, March, 14–15.
Williams, T. (2010) Why agencies should call time on selling time, *Campaign*, 16 July, 12.
Wilson, S. (2009) The purpose of integration, *PRWeek-Thought Leader* (December), 15.
Zambarino, A. and Goodfellow, J. (2003) Account planning in the new marketing and communications environment (has the Stephen King challenge been met?), *Marketing Intelligence and Planning*, 21(7), 424–434
Zandpour, F. and Harich, K. (1996) Think and feel country clusters: a new approach to international advertising standardization, *International Journal of Advertising*, 15, 325–344

Chapter 8
Shaping relationships with marketing communications

The importance of relationship marketing is now recognised as a central aspect of both consumer and business marketing. The role that marketing communications can play in establishing and nurturing key relationships is pivotal, yet the ways in which marketing communications might best be deployed depend to a large extent on the context in which both the relationship and the communications are configured.

Aims and learning objectives

The aim of this chapter is to explore concepts and ideas concerning marketing relationships and to consider the role marketing communications can play in developing and sustaining relationships with customers, employees and agencies.

The learning objectives of this chapter are to:

1. examine ideas associated with perceived customer value;
2. consider the theoretical concepts underpinning relationship marketing, including marketing exchanges and value creation;
3. explain the concepts of trust and commitment and how they can be used to develop loyalty and retention programmes;
4. consider the customer development cycle and the role of marketing communications in developing customer relationships;
5. appraise the role of marketing communications in the development of employee relationships;
6. examine the characteristics associated with client/agency relationships.

Introduction

Relationship marketing has become a key aspect of both consumer and business marketing. There are a number of dimensions associated with organisational and consumer relationships, many of which encompass established concepts such as trust, commitment and loyalty. The role that marketing communications can play in establishing and nurturing key relationships can be pivotal, yet the ways in which marketing communications might be best deployed depends to a large extent on the context in which both the relationship and the communications are configured.

Value has become an increasingly significant concept, to both marketing practitioners and academics. Indeed, many believe that the only viable marketing strategy should be to deliver improved shareholder value (Doyle, 2000) whilst others believe value creation represents the only viable interpretation about how marketing works (Vargo and Lusch, 2004). However, the importance of providing value for customers is not a new idea. Concepts of differentiation, unique and emotional selling propositions (USPs and ESPs) and positioning are founded on the idea that superior perceived value is of primary significance to customers.

It has been understood for a long time that customers buy benefits not features, that they buy products and services as solutions which enable them to achieve their goals. The majority of women buy lipstick because of a mixture of both tangible and intangible attributes or even features and benefits. They buy particular brands because they feel different as a result of using them. What they buy varies from person to person, but in terms of tangible attributes they prefer to buy colour and smudge-free lips (no 'bleed'), that the lipstick stays on the lips, prevents dryness, is long lasting and smooth (Puth *et al.*, 1999). However, among the intangible attributes are self-confidence, a coordinated fashion accessory, trust, perhaps an alter ego or, as Revlon once claimed, 'hope'.

The same principle applies to organisational marketing. Business customers buy solutions to business problems, not just stand-alone products. These benefits and solutions constitute potential added value for customers, and represent the reason why one offering is selected in preference to another. For both consumers and business customers, value is determined by the net satisfaction derived from a transaction, not the costs incurred to obtain it.

So, if customers seek to satisfy their needs through their purchase of specific products and services then it can be said that the satisfaction of needs is a way of delivering value. Kothandaraman and Wilson (2001) argue that the creation of value is dependent upon an organisation's ability to deliver high performance on the benefits that are important to the customer and this in turn is rooted in their competency in technology and business processes, or core competences. According to Doyle (2000) the creation of customer value is based on three principles:

- Customers will choose between alternative offerings and select the one that (they perceive) will offer them the best value.
- Customers do not want product or service features, they want their needs met.
- It is more profitable to have a long-term relationship between a customer and a company rather than a one-off transaction.

Value is the customer's estimate of the extent to which a product or service can satisfy their needs. However, normally there are costs associated with the derivation of benefits such that a general model of value would identify the worth of the benefits received for the price paid (Anderson and Narus, 1998). Therefore, value is relative to customer expectations and experience of competitive offerings within a category and can be derived from sources other than products, such as the relationships between buyers and sellers (Simpson *et al.*, 2001).

Figure 8.1 A continuum of value-oriented exchanges
Source: Adapted from Day (2000)

Development of the relationship marketing concept

Interaction between customers and sellers is based around the provision and consumption of perceived value. However, the quality, duration and level of interdependence between customers and sellers can vary considerably. The reasons for this variance are many and wide-ranging but at the core are perceptions of shared values and the strength and permanence, referred to as connectedness, of any relationship that might exist. Relationship value can be visualised as a continuum (see Figure 8.1).

At one end of the continuum are market exchanges, characterised by short-term, product or price oriented exchanges, between buyers and sellers coming together for one-off exchanges independent of any other or subsequent exchanges. Both parties are motivated mainly by self-interest. Movement along the continuum represents the acceptance and desire for increasingly valued relationships. Interactions between parties are closer and stronger. The focus moves from initial attraction to retention and mutual understanding of each other's needs.

At the other end of the continuum are relational exchanges or what Day (2000) refers to as collaborative exchanges. These are characterised by a long-term orientation, where ultimately there is complete integration of systems and processes and where the relationship is motivated by partnership and mutual support. Trust and commitment underpin these relationships and these variables become increasingly important as relational exchanges become established.

Perceived value may take many forms and be rooted in a variety of attributes, combined in different ways to meet segment needs. However, the context in which an exchange occurs between a buyer and a seller provides a strong reflection of the nature of their relationship. If the exchange is focused on the product (and the price) then the exchange is considered to be essentially transactional or market. If the exchange is focused around the needs of the customer and the seller then the exchange is considered to be collaborative, truly relational. The differences between market and collaborative exchanges are set out in Table 8.1 and provide an important starting point in understanding the nature of relationship marketing. The table provides a more comprehensive list of fundamental differences between market and collaborative-based marketing.

Although market exchanges focus on products and prices, there is still a relational component, if only because interaction requires a basic relationship between parties for the transaction to be completed (Macneil, 1980).

Table 8.1 Characteristics of market and collaborative exchanges

Attribute	Market exchange	Collaborative exchange
Length of relationship	Short term Abrupt end	Long term A continuous process
Relational expectations	Conflicts of goals Immediate payment No future problems (there is no future)	Conflicts of interest Deferred payment Future problems expected to be overcome by joint commitment
Communication	Low frequency of communication Formal, mass media communication predominates	Frequent communication Informal, personal, interactive communication predominates
Cooperation	No joint cooperation	Joint cooperative projects
Responsibilities	Distinct responsibilities Defined obligations	Shared responsibilities Shared obligations

Viewpoint 8.1 Added value OnAir

As part of its customer development Airbus has developed facilities for airlines to offer a range of consumer communications while in flight. The system enables passengers to use email and text messages, send and receive voice messages and browse the web all through the use of their own phones, laptops and PDAs.

Airbus has identified a major opportunity in the market and believes the system, branded as OnAir, represents significant added value for major premium travel airlines to offer their passengers. It is expected that Boeing will offer a similar system with both manufacturers recognising the need for their customers to offer passengers additional value in what is a highly competitive market.

Question
Consider the view that the speed at which Boeing nullified Airbus' OnAir system suggests that added value has to be protected and, in the long term, be of significance.

Task
Make a note of two ways in which a rail operator might provide added value to attract and retain travellers.

The role of collaboration in relationship marketing is important. However, many organisations maintain a variety of relationships with their different customers and suppliers, some highly collaborative and some market oriented or, as Spekman and Carroway (2006: 10) suggest, 'where they make sense'. Relationship marketing is characterised by the frequency and intensity of the exchanges between customers and sellers. As these exchanges become more frequent and more intense so the strength of the relationships between buyers and sellers improves. It is this that provided the infrastructure for this perspective of marketing, one based on relationships (Spekman, 1988; Rowe and Barnes, 1998), rather than the objects of a transaction, namely products and prices.

Relationships expressed as value creation

Just as ideas about relationships have evolved, so have those associated with perceived value. Rather than consider relationships as a function of exchange, an emerging view, driven by the service-dominant logic (SDL) group (Vargo and Lusch, 2004; Vargo, 2009), is to consider relationships as a function of value, or what is known as, value-in-use.

The conventional view is that sellers create value for their customers who select suppliers on the basis of their perception of the optimal value offered to them. Grönroos (2009) argues that value can only be realised by customers when utilised through the use of their own processes, resources and capabilities. Grönroos considers that value should be considered to consist of two fundamental elements; value propositions and value creation. Suppliers develop *value propositions* and these are essentially suggestions or promises of value that are embedded in their offerings. Customers fulfil *value creation* when they incorporate these products and services into their processes. Suppliers can assist their customers by creating opportunities to engage with their value generating processes. The level of interaction between the parties might vary from zero to full participation, co-creation.

So, an alternative to the spectrum of exchange relationships presented earlier would be a spectrum of value propositions, or more importantly, a spectrum of interaction leading to various forms of value creation. Movement along the relationship continuum can be interpreted as a change in the way value is created. Ribeiro *et al.* (2009) identify four core value strategies. These are exchange (or commodity) value, added value, performance value and value co-creation strategies.

Market exchange relationships are characterised by an exchange of basic resources. Sellers provide a core service but it is buyers who assume full responsibility and resources, to create the value they require out of the essential service resource that is transacted.

The role for marketing communications is to convey brand promises, or value propositions. Communications should be concerned not just with features and benefits associated with their products but with an overall service solution that buyers can incorporate into their own systems to resolve their problems. The promise is to provide buyers with the resources necessary to help them create the value they require. This approach is referred to as an 'added value' strategy and examples include providing training, financial assistance or installation support.

Following these interactions buyers and sellers become stronger and closer, so that the original value perceived in the exchange of products and prices gradually gives way to a focus on the relationship which itself becomes of value. Further along the continuum some organisations provide 'performance value' strategies. Here value is created by the activities of buyers and sellers working together for mutual benefit, but value is still passed from one to another. Examples include joint product development and projects to enhance the buyer's software systems and processes and initiatives designed to improve manufacturing efficiencies.

Viewpoint 8.2 Performance value crisps

A campaign launched in July 2008 by Walkers sought to forge stronger bonds with their customers. By actively integrating them with the campaign not only did the brand get extensive product exposure but also the relationship between consumers and the brand was developed. The campaign, called 'Do Us a Flavour' challenged the public to think up a unique flavour of crisp.

The campaign involved all of Walkers' agencies to work together, as different stages required different contributions. The first stage began with a TV push created by AMV, with the goal of stimulating members of the public to come up with flavour ideas. Simultaneously, a PR drive led by Freud, had the goal of creating excitement among TV hosts and radio presenters. This was achieved partly by Freud devising bespoke flavours for different presenters. For example, the flavour for Chris Moyles was 'meat and two veg'.

The *Sun* newspaper generated a great deal of PR as did a substantial cross-section of the media. Underpinning it all was the drive to encourage people to visit a dedicated website. At the end of this first stage, customers sent in over 1.2 million entries. Stage 2 was about a judging panel, led by chef Heston Blumenthal, picking the top six entries. These were Cajun Squirrel, Crispy Duck & Hoisin, Fish & Chips, Builder's Breakfast, Chilli & Chocolate and Onion Bhaji.

Stage 3 was the period ending May 2009 during which the crisps could be bought individually or in a special multipack containing all six flavours. Votes could be cast on the Walkers website, through Facebook, and through Yahoo!, which hosted a 'do us a flavour' channel. In addition to all the multichannel activity it was the well-established technique of the on-pack promotion that worked well for many contestants, including one of the six finalists.

Builders Breakfast won the most votes and the person behind it won £50,000, in addition to the £10,000 that each finalist was awarded. Better still, the winner was set to receive one per cent of profits from all future sales of their flavour, an estimated £50,000+ a year.

One of the points this campaign illustrates is the way the brand and its customers worked together to create value that both parties enjoyed consuming, either physically or emotionally. Here real performance value emerged through the parties to the relationship working together.

Source: Based on Nettleton (2009); Anon (2009); Angear and Sambles (2009); White *et al.* (2010)

Question

Identify the key elements that support the relationship between Walkers and their customers. Is this form of the relationship sustainable?

Task

Write notes explaining how this example demonstrates trust and commitment in a relationship.

Exhibit 8.1 The finalists in Walkers' 'Do Us a Flavour' campaign

Here are the six finalists, whose recipes were subjected to a public vote. From left to right: Martyn Wright, Staffordshire – Cajun Squirrel; Vicky Howard, Northwich – Crispy Duck & Hoisin sauce; Jane Hallam, Sheffield – Fish & Chips; Carole Wood, Durham – Onion Bhaji; Catherine Veitch, High Wycombe – Chilli & Chocolate; Emma Rushin, Derbyshire – Builder's Breakfast.

Image courtesy of Freud Communications (Photographer: Iain Lewis)

Table 8.2 Value strategies and defining characteristics

Defining characteristics	Value strategies			
	Commodity	Value added	Performance	Value co-creation
Value-generating drivers	Product quality Delivery performance Market price	Services support Personal interactions Product and service quality	The know-how of others Time to market Performance from both (costs, revenues, productivity)	Joint and radical innovation Leveraging new competencies
Management intention	Attract and satisfy	Customer retention (implicit: profit, satisfaction, loyalty, risk reduction, etc.)	Interactions to establish, develop and facilitate cooperative relationship and mutual benefit	Coordinating relationships among companies in a network to seek new resources and value networks
Duration	Discrete	Continuous, but discrete hiring	Continuous and long-term contracts	Continuous, mutual cooperation contracts
Adaptation	Little or no adaptation	Process adaptations	Process adaptations	Adaptations and business creation
Description of value offering	'We offer good products and competitive prices'	'We offer excellence'	'We customize, we build on order for the customer'	'Our customers, suppliers and other partners got us here and will take us wherever it need be to generate value'
Management structure	Functional hierarchical: mkt., sales, R&D, etc.	Processes and functions like: customer service manager. CRM manager	Customer and market managers/cross-functions and levels	Business managers
Capabilities	Production 　Delivery 　　Promoting-communicating 　　　Process leveraging 　　　　Relationship 　　　　　Mastery and integration into the customer's business model 　　　　　　Radical innovation 　　　　　　　Setting up networks			

Source: Ribeiro *et al.* (2009), adapted from: Möller and Törrönen (2003); Coviello *et al.* (1997); Ulaga and Eggert (2006); Möller *et al.* (2005); Prahalad and Ramaswamy (2004). Used with permission

Collaborative relationships are characterised by value that is created by both parties as a form of co-production or through 'value co-creation' (Sheth and Uslay, 2007). This is a situation where both organisations work together for mutual benefit, and value is generated together, not traded by a supplier to a buyer, as in performance value. More information about these different value strategies is given in Table 8.2.

Trust, commitment and loyalty

Embedded within these exchange and service ideas and concepts associated with relationship marketing, are three core concepts, trust, commitment and loyalty (and retention). These are considered in turn.

Trust

Many writers contend that one of the crucial factors associated with the development and maintenance of both personal and interorganisational relationships is trust (Morgan and Hunt, 1994; Doney and Cannon, 1997). Trust is an element of personal, intraorganisational and interorganisational relationships, and is both necessary for and results from their perpetuation of others. As Gambetta (1988) argues, trust is a means of reducing uncertainty in order that effective relationships can develop.

Cousins and Stanwix (2001) suggest that, although trust is a term used to explain how relationships work, often it actually refers to ideas concerning risk, power and dependency, and that these propositions are used interchangeably. From their research of vehicle manufacturers it emerges that b2b relationships are about the creation of mutual business advantage and the degree of confidence that one organisation has in another.

Interorganisational trust is based on two main dimensions: credibility and benevolence. Credibility concerns the extent to which one organisation believes (is confident) that another organisation will undertake and complete it's agreed roles and tasks. Benevolence is concerned with goodwill, and that the other organisation will not act opportunistically, even if the conditions for exploitation should arise (Pavlou, 2002). In other words, interorganisational trust involves judgements about another organisation's reliability and integrity.

Institutional trust is clearly vital in b2c markets where online perceived risk is present and known to have prevented many people from purchasing online. In the b2b market, institutional trust is also important but more in terms of the overall reputation of the organisation. The development and establishment of trust is valuable because of the outcomes that can be anticipated. Three major outcomes from the development of trust have been identified by Pavlou, namely satisfaction, perceived risk and continuity.

- **Satisfaction** can reduce conflict and the threat of opportunism and that in turn enhances the probability of buyer satisfaction, an important positive outcome of institutional trust.
- **Perceived risk** is concerned with the expectation of loss and is therefore tied closely with organisational or brand performance. Trust that a seller will not take advantage of the imbalance of information between buyer and seller effectively reduces risk.
- **Continuity** is related to business volumes, necessary in online b2b marketplaces, and the development of both on and offline enduring relationships. Trust is associated with continuity and when present is therefore indicative of long-term relationships. Ryssel *et al.* (2004: 203) recognise that trust (and commitment) have a 'significant impact on the creation of value and conclude that value creation is a function of the atmosphere of a relationship rather than the technology employed'.

Trust within a consumer context is equally important as a means of reducing uncertainty. Brands are an important means of instilling trust mainly because they are a means of condensing and conveying information so that they provide sufficient information for consumers to make calculated purchase decisions in the absence of full knowledge. In a sense consumers transfer their responsibility for brand decision-making, and hence brand performance, to the brand itself. Through extended use of a brand, purchasing habits develop or what is termed routinised response behaviour emerges. This is important not just because complex decision-making is simplified but because the amount of communication necessary to assist and provoke purchase is considerably reduced.

The establishment of trust can be based around the existence of various components. Morrison and Firmstone (2000) identify reputation, familiarity/closeness, performance and accountability as four critical elements. According to Young and Wilkinson (1989) the presence of trust within a relationship is influenced by four other factors. These are the duration of the relationship, the relative power of the players, the presence of cooperation and various environmental factors that may be present at any one moment. Extending these ideas into what is now regarded by many as a seminal paper in the relationship marketing literature,

Morgan and Hunt (1994) argued, and supported with empirical evidence, that the presence of both commitment and trust leads to cooperative behaviour and this in turn is conducive to successful relationship marketing.

Commitment

Morgan and Hunt regard commitment as the desire that a relationship continue (endure) in order that a valued relationship be maintained or strengthened. They postulated that commitment and trust are key mediating variables between five antecedents and five outcomes (see Figure 8.2).

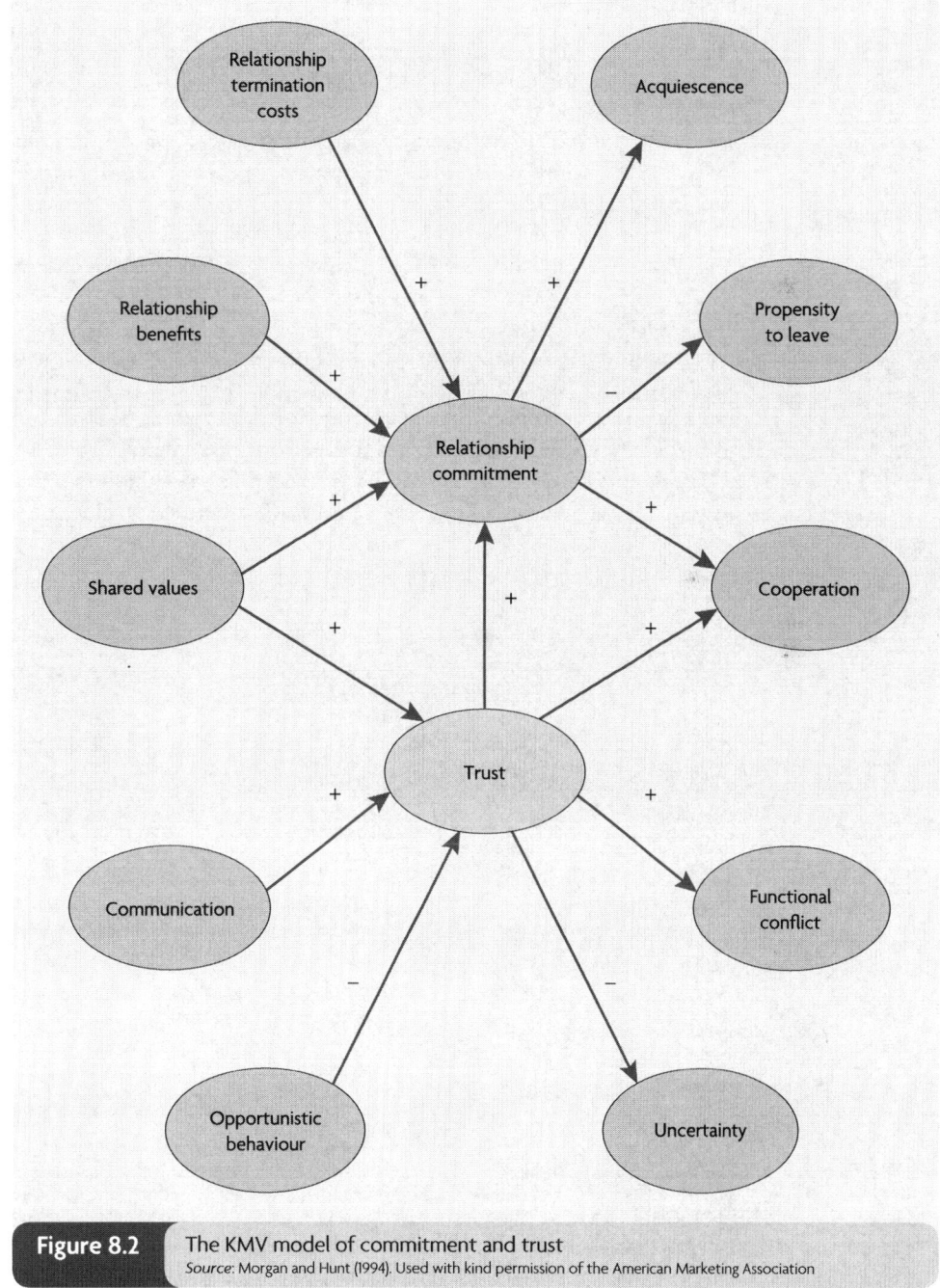

Figure 8.2 The KMV model of commitment and trust
Source: Morgan and Hunt (1994). Used with kind permission of the American Marketing Association

According to the KMV model the greater the losses anticipated through the termination of a relationship the greater the commitment expressed by the exchange partners. Likewise, when these partners share the same values commitment increases. Trust is enhanced when communication is perceived to be of high quality but decreases when one organisation knowingly takes action to seek to benefit from the relationship, which will be to the detriment of the other.

The centrality of the trust and commitment concepts to relationship marketing has thus been established and they are as significant to marketing channel relationships as to other b2b relationships (Achrol, 1991; Goodman and Dion, 2001).

Customer loyalty and retention

Implicit within ideas about customer relationships is the notion that retained customers are loyal. However, this can be misleading as 'loyalty' may actually be a term used to convey convenience or extended utility. Loyalty, however presented, takes different forms, just as there are customers who are more valued than others. Christopher *et al.* (2002) depict the various types of relationships as stages or steps on a ladder, the relationship marketing ladder of loyalty (see Figure 8.3).

A prospect becomes a purchaser, completed through a market or discrete exchange. Clients emerge from several completed transactions but remain ambivalent towards the seller organisation. Supporters, despite being passive about an organisation, are willing and able to enter into regular transactions. Advocates represent the next and penultimate step. They not only support an organisation and its products but actively recommend it to others by positive, word-of-mouth communications. Partners, who represent the top rung of the ladder, trust and support an organisation just as it trusts and supports them. Partnership status is the embodiment of relational exchanges and interorganisational collaboration.

The simplicity of the loyalty ladder concept illustrates the important point that different customers represent different value to sellers. The perceived value (or worth) of a customer

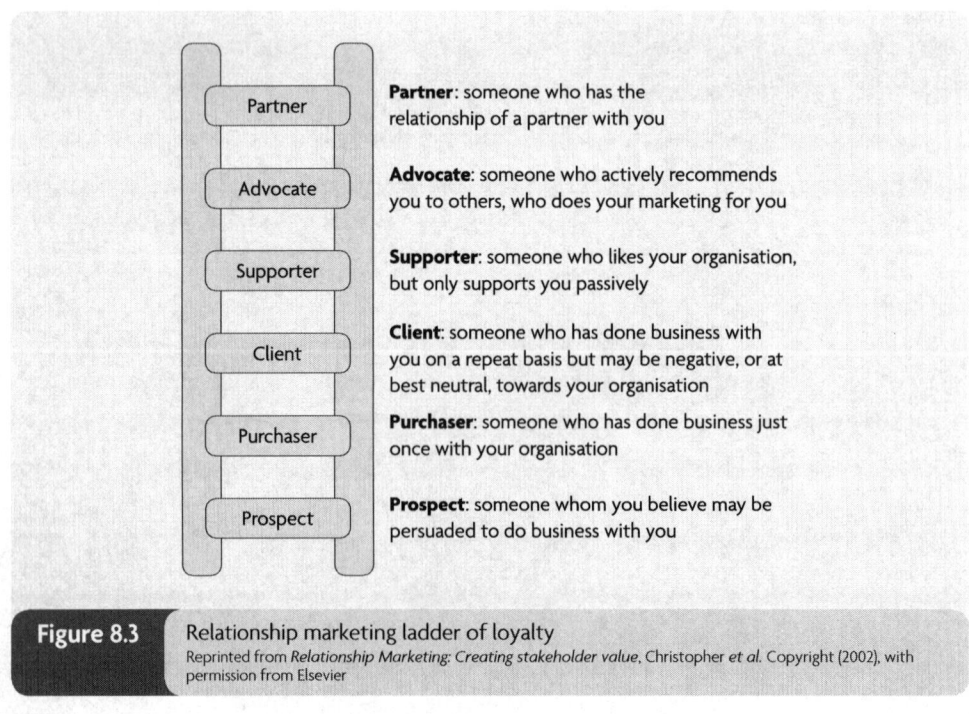

Figure 8.3 Relationship marketing ladder of loyalty
Reprinted from *Relationship Marketing: Creating stakeholder value*, Christopher *et al.* Copyright (2002), with permission from Elsevier

Table 8.3 Types of loyalty

Emotional loyalty	This is a true form of loyalty and is driven by personal identification with real or perceived values and benefits.
Price loyalty	This type of loyalty is driven by rational economic behaviour and the main motivations are cautious management of money or financial necessity.
Incentivised loyalty	This refers to promiscuous buyers: those with no one favourite brand who demonstrate through repeat experience the value of becoming loyal.
Monopoly loyalty	This class of loyalty arises where a consumer has no purchase choice owing to a national monopoly. This, therefore, is not a true form of loyalty.

may or may not always be fully reciprocated, understood or recognised, so it is not surprising that that there is a wide variety and complexity of relationships. What the ladder does not reveal is the dynamic nature of relationships.

Types and levels of loyalty

In addition to the popularity of the loyalty concept shown by organisations, manifest in the increasing number of loyalty based schemes, the term loyalty has attracted much research attention. As a result there are a variety of interpretations, definitions and depictions of the concept. According to Oliver (1997: 392) loyalty is a deeply held sense of commitment to continue buying a preferred product or service on a consistent basis for the foreseeable future. As Evanschitzky and Wunderlich (2006) phrase it, 'thereby causing repetitive same-brand or same brand-set purchasing, despite situational influences and marketing efforts that have the potential to cause switching behavior'.

Table 8.3 represents some of the more general types of loyalty that can be observed.

These hierarchical schemes suggest that consumers are capable of varying degrees of loyalty. Loyalty at one level can be seen to be about increasing sales volume, or fostering loyal purchase behaviour. High levels of repeat purchase, however, are not necessarily an adequate measure of loyalty, as there may be a number of situational factors determining purchase behaviour, such as brand availability (Dick and Basu, 1994).

At another level, loyalty can be regarded as an attitudinal disposition. O'Malley (1998) suggests that customer satisfaction has become a surrogate measure of loyalty. However, she points out that there is plenty of evidence to show that many satisfied customers buy a variety of brands and that polygamous loyalty, as suggested by Dowling and Uncles (1997), may be a better reflection of reality.

At whichever level of loyalty, customer retention is paramount and neither behavioural nor attitudinal measures alone are adequate indicators of true loyalty. O'Malley suggests that a combination of the two is of greater use and that the twin parameters, relative attitudes (to alternatives) and patronage behaviour (the recency, frequency and monetary model), as suggested by Dick and Basu, when used together offer more accurate indicators of loyalty.

Principles of retention

Reference to customer retention is a central concept to relationship marketing, whether considered a function of exchange or service value. Marketing has been characterised by its potential to influence and attract customers. Indeed, early ideas considered marketing to be a social anathema due to the perception that it persuaded and manipulated people into purchasing goods and services they did not want. While these fears and misgivings have generally been overcome, a further fallacy concerned the notion that all customers are good customers. As most commercial organisations will now agree, some customers are far more attractive than other customers, on the grounds that some are very profitable, others are marginally profitable but offer great potential and others offer little and/or incur losses.

Through the use of relationship cost theory it was possible to identify the benefits associated with stable and mutually rewarding relationships. Such customers avoid costly switching costs that are associated with finding new suppliers, while suppliers experience reduced quality costs incurred when adapting to the needs of new customers. Reichheld and Sasser (1990) identified an important association between a small (e.g. 5 per cent) increase in customer retention and a large (e.g. 60 per cent) improvement in profitability. Therefore, a long-term relationship leads to lower relationship costs and higher profits. Since this early work there has been general acceptance that customers who are loyal not only improve an organisation's profits but also strengthen its competitive position (Day, 2000) because competitors have to work harder to dislodge or destabilise their loyalty. It should be noted that some authors suggest the link between loyalty and profitability is not that simple (Dowling and Uncles, 1997), while others argue that much more information and understanding is required about the association between profitability and loyalty, especially when there may be high costs associated with customer acquisition (Reinartz and Kumar, 2002).

By undertaking a customer profitability analysis it is possible to identify those segments that are worth developing, and hence build a portfolio of relationships, each of varying dimensions and potential. These relationships provide mutually rewarding benefits and offer a third dimension of the customer dynamic, namely customer development.

Loyalty and retention programmes

Dowling and Uncles (1997) developed a conceptual framework in which they identified the primary characteristics of loyalty programmes. They highlighted three main dimensions, each with bipolar elements; the type of rewards (direct versus indirect), the timing of the rewards (immediate or delayed) and the tangibility of rewards (tangible versus intangible). So, where there is low involvement decision-making, as in the purchase of grocery products, the key rewards preferred by customers were identified as direct, immediate and tangible.

Despite questions about the nature and meaning of the term loyalty, the growth of loyalty programmes has been a significant development in recent years. Often developed inappropriately in the name of relationship marketing, loyalty schemes have received a great deal of attention. One of the more visible and successful schemes has been the Clubcard offered by Tesco. This has been partly responsible for Tesco dominating the UK retail market.

The use of loyalty schemes was encouraged through the use of swipe cards. Users are rewarded with points each time a purchase is made. This is referred to as a 'points accrual programme', whereby loyal users are able to build up the necessary points, which are stored (often) on a card, and 'cashed in' at a later date for gifts or merchandise. The benefit for the company supporting the scheme is that the promised rewards motivate customers to accrue more points and in doing so increase their switching costs, effectively locking them into the loyalty programme and preventing them from moving to a competitor brand. Swipe cards were then developed technologically into smart cards (a card that has a small microprocessor attached) which can record enormous amounts of information, and is updated each time a purchase is made. The applications for this are much greater and of increased benefit to customers.

Some frequent flyer loyalty schemes, such as BA Executive Club and Virgin Freeway, have been very successful (Brownsell, 2009) and the cards are also used to track individual travellers. Airlines are able to offer cardholders particular services, such as special airport lounges and magazines; the card through its links to a database also enables a traveller's favourite seat and dietary requirements to be offered. In addition, the regular accumulation of air miles fosters continuity and hence loyalty, through which business travellers reward themselves with leisure

Viewpoint 8.3   Cantrell retains customers

The office products division of the Cantrell Corporation had been an important part of the company's overall performance with 40 per cent of its revenue derived online. However, office products customers rely on flawless ecommerce performance from their suppliers to help reduce their administrative overheads, and as a result competition within this sector is strong.

One of the challenges facing Cantrell was that their website was not integrated with customer account information, so customers with questions about order status or account balances flooded the call centres. Costs were rising, customers were leaving and performance targets were being missed with increased regularity. Cantrell resolved to

Exhibit 8.2   Viking Direct – an office supplies company
Using an offline catalogue and online store in combination, Viking Direct drive traffic and provide business customers with different channels to access and buy their office supplies. See www.viking-direct.co.uk/
Images courtesy of Viking Direct

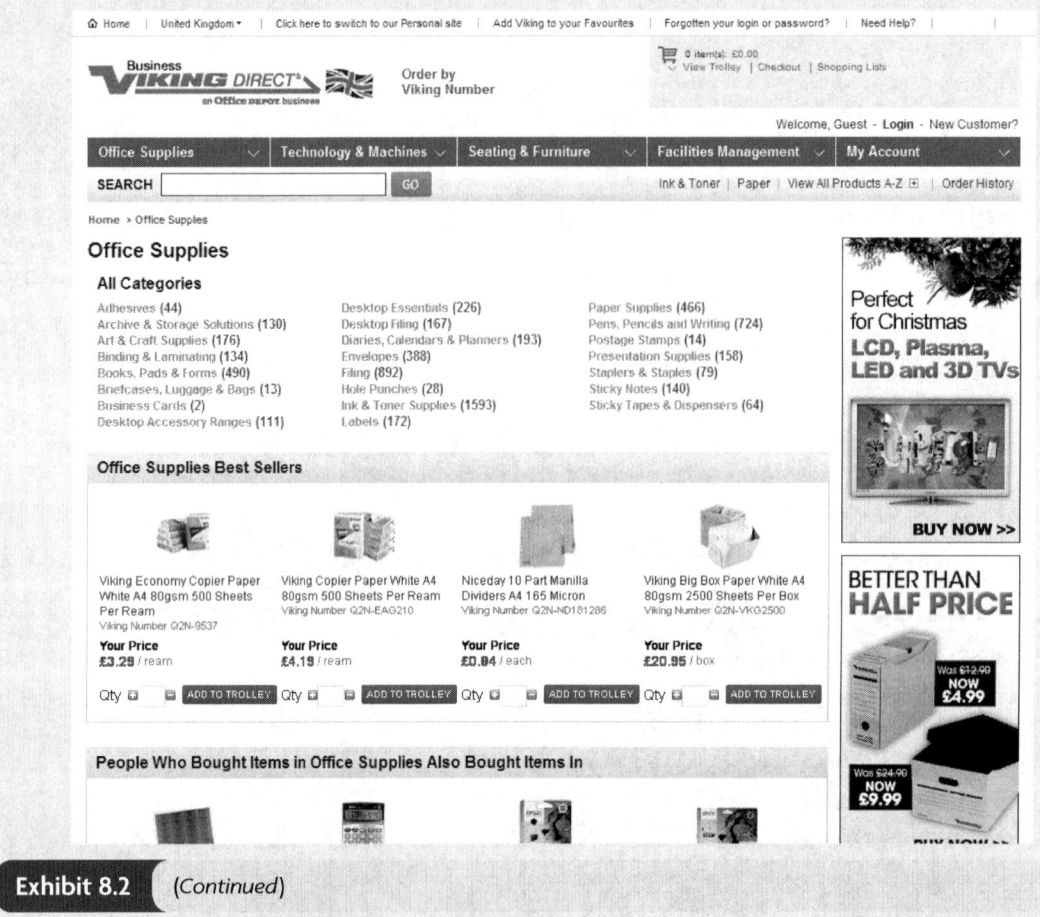

Exhibit 8.2 (Continued)

reassert their prominence in the market. To do this they had to create a world-class shopping experience, with CRM capabilities, automatic fulfilment and integration with their largest customers. The company developed a new website and as a result customers are now able to research their questions online, and the company no longer needs to fund an additional call centre.

Customers can now shop online for office supplies, order online training courses and read online newsletters that are customised for them. They can quickly and efficiently find the items they need in the online catalogue, order them and check stock. Cantrell's order fulfilment system now reads web orders just as if they had been generated from the call centre, and fulfils them automatically. As a result, instead of customers leaving, new accounts are being registered at record levels, order fulfilment cycles have been reduced and costs lowered, all in the name of using technology to improve customer management and retention.

Question

To what extent do you believe customer retention is function of the trade-off between trust and the switching costs associated with finding and establishing a relationship with a different supplier?

Task

List and prioritise the top four attributes you believe the supplier of office equipment must possess.

travel. However, the airlines' desire to develop relationships with their customers might not be fully reciprocated as customers seek only convenience.

Perhaps the attention given to loyalty and retention issues is misplaced because marketing is either about the identification, anticipation and satisfaction of customer needs (profitably), or it is about customer management. Either way, if marketing strategies are successful, it might be reasonable to expect that customers would return anyway, reducing the need for overt 'loyalty' programmes. The absence of any loyalty card at ASDA suggests that they do not see such investment as a suitable (profitable) way of achieving competitive advantage and differentiation. There is an argument that these schemes are important not because of the loyalty aspect but because they allow for the collection of up-to-date customer information and which can be used to make savings in the supply chain. Research indicates strongly that owners of store loyalty cards tend to be more store loyal than those who do not hold a card. Furthermore, when card holders are satisfied with the reward scheme associated with the card programme, they demonstrate greater loyalty and become less price sensitive than card holders who are dissatisfied with the scheme (Demoulin and Zidda, 2008). However, the use of loyalty cards does not appear to influence customer loyalty, for example, by enhancing performance or satisfaction. The one element that loyalty programmes appear to achieve is a strengthening of the relationship between an individual's intention to buy and their actual buying behavior (Evanschitzky and Wunderlich, 2006).

That information has not been updated, but what was one of the main logistical problems concerning the management and analysis of the huge volumes of data collected has largely been overcome. Some organisations use less than half the data they collect and then it was argued that the data actually used can be bought in at a much lower cost than these loyalty schemes cost to run. This may be partly true but vastly improved data-mining and warehousing techniques have led to more effective use of customer data.

There has been a proliferation of loyalty cards, reflecting the increased emphasis upon keeping customers rather than constantly finding new ones and there is evidence that sales lift by about 2 or 3 per cent when a loyalty scheme is launched. Schemes do enable organisations to monitor and manage stock, use direct marketing to cross and up-sell customers, and manage their portfolio in order to consolidate (increase?) customer's spending in a store. Whether loyalty is being developed by encouraging buyers to make repeat purchases or whether the schemes are merely sales promotion techniques that encourage extended and consistent purchasing patterns is debatable. Customer retention is a major issue and a lot of emphasis has been given to loyalty schemes as a means of achieving retention targets.

Hallberg (2004) reports a major study involving in excess of 600,000 in-depth consumer interviews. The study identifies different levels of loyalty and concludes that significant financial returns are gained only when the highest level of loyalty is achieved. These levels of loyalty are set out in Figure 8.4.

Figure 8.4 Levels of loyalty: the brand emotional loyalty pyramid
Source: Hallberg (2004). Used with permission of Palgrave Macmillan

Hallberg refers to the impact of emotional loyalty, a non-purchase measurement of attachment to a brand:

- At the 'No Presence' level consumers are unaware of a brand and so there is no emotional loyalty.
- At the 'Presence' level there is awareness but emotional loyalty is minimal.
- At the 'Relevance and Performance' level the consumer begins to feel that the brand is acceptable in terms of meeting their needs.
- At the 'Advantage' level consumers should feel that the brand is superior with regard to a particular attribute.
- At the 'Bonding' level emotional loyalty is at its highest because consumers feel the brand has several unique properties. They love the brand.

Loyalty schemes are exponentially effective when the consumers reach the bonding stage. Although sales generally increase the further up the pyramid consumers move it is only at the bonding stage that sales start to reflect the emotional attachment people feel towards the brand. Hallberg refers to the success and market leadership that Tesco has achieved but the principles established through this study should apply to loyalty programmes regardless of category or sector.

The role of marketing communications in relationships

Having considered ideas about relationship marketing and retention, and established its centrality within contemporary marketing thought, it now remains to explore ways in which marketing communications can contribute to relationship marketing. As a general guide, transaction marketing, where the focus is product and price, uses mass, formal based, relatively infrequent communications, where persuasion (promotion) is a central element. With relationship marketing, and its focus on the relationship between the participants, communications are characterised as personal, informal and relatively frequent, which leads to individual communication behaviours that encourage interaction and dialogue. This is compatible with the concepts of integrated marketing communications (IMC).

Grönroos (2004) suggests that although IMC cannot be synonymous with relationship marketing, it is an important aspect. He develops the view that there are two main types of message that customers receive, process and use to determine the extent to which a relationship delivers value. The first of these types is the planned marketing communication message, which is predetermined and delivered through various media and tools of the communication mix. Planned messages set out an organisation's promises. The second are messages generated through the product and service aspects of the interaction that occurs between organisations and their customers. The degree to which these two streams of messages support or counter each other will influence the type of unplanned communications that ensue, and the nature of word-of-mouth communications that arise. (See Figure 1.1 for a graphical representation of these types of marketing communication message.)

The greater the degree that the two sets of messages support or reinforce one another, the more favourable the unplanned communication that should result in positive word-of-mouth communication (Grönroos and Lindberg-Repo, 1998). This can lead to the establishment of two-way communication, an increasing propensity to share information, a process of reasoning and ultimately dialogue. Reasoning is important because it enables a sharing of values and a deeper understanding of the other party's needs and position. Through shared meaning, trust increases. Grönroos (2004) argues that relationship marketing develops not from planned marketing communications, but through the interaction and personal experience of products and services and the degree to which these two sets of messages and meanings complement the

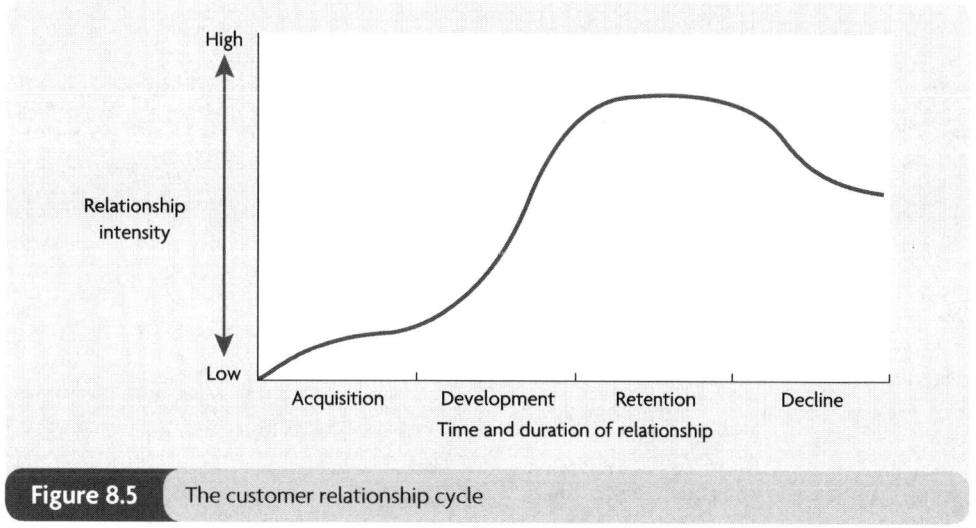

Figure 8.5 The customer relationship cycle

promises and messages transmitted previously. He suggests that when these two processes come together a single communication process emerges. Put precisely he says, 'the two processes merge into a relationship dialogue' (2004: 107).

Marketing communications can play an important role throughout all relationship phases and at all stages of the customer lifecycle. Indeed, marketing communications should be used to engage with audiences according to the audiences' needs, whether transactional and remote or whether relational and close. According to Ryssel *et al.* (2004) the use of information systems and technology, which enables communication to be timely, accurate and direct, has a positive impact on trust.

Customer relationships can be considered in terms of a series of relationship development phases; customer acquisition, development, retention and decline. Collectively these are referred to as the customer lifecycle. The duration and intensity of each relationship phase in the lifecycle will inevitably vary and it should be remembered that this representation is essentially idealistic. A customer relationship cycle is represented in Figure 8.5.

Customer acquisition

The acquisition phase is characterised by three main events: search, initiation and familiarisation (see Table 8.4).

The logical sequence of acquisition activities moves from search and verification through the establishment of credentials. The length of this initiation period will depend partly on the importance of the buying decision and the complexity of the products, and partly upon the nature of the introduction. If the parties are introduced by an established and trusted source then certain initiation rites can be shortened.

Table 8.4 Customer acquisition events

Acquisition event	Explanation
Search	Buyers and sellers search for a suitable pairing
Initiation	Both parties seek out information about the other before any transaction occurs
Familiarisation	The successful completion of the first transaction enables both parties to start revealing more information about themselves

Once a transaction occurs the buyer-sellers start to become more familiar with each other and gradually begin to reveal more information about themselves. The seller receives payment, delivery and handling information about the buyer, and as a result is able to prepare customised outputs. The buyer is able to review the seller's products and experience the service quality of the seller.

During the acquisition phase marketing communications needs to be geared towards creating awareness and providing access to the brand. Included within this period will be the need to help potential customers become familiar with the brand and to help them increase their understanding of the key attributes, possible benefits from use and to know how the brand is different and represents value that is superior to the competition. Indeed, marketing communications has to work during this phase because it needs to fulfil a number of different roles and it needs to be targeted at precise audiences. Perhaps the main overriding task is to create a set of brand values that are relevant and which represent significant value for the target audience. In DRIP terms, differentiation and information will be important and, in terms of the communications mix, advertising and direct marking in the b2c market and personal selling and direct marketing in the b2b market.

Customer development

The development phase is characterised by the seller attempting to reduce buyer risk and enhancing credibility. This is achieved by encouraging cross-selling whereby the buyer consumes other products, by improving the volume of purchases, by engaging the buyer with other added-value services and by varying delivery times and quantities. The buyer's acquiescence is dependent upon their specific needs and the degree to which the buyer wishes to become more involved with the supplier. Indeed, it is during this phase that the buyer is able to determine whether or not it is worth developing deeper relationships with the seller.

The main goals during the development phase are for the sellers to reduce buyer-perceived risk and to simultaneously enhance their own credibility. In order to reduce risk a number of messages will need to be presented through marketing communications. The selection of these elements will depend upon the forms of risk that are present either in the market sector or within individual customers. Marketing communications needs to engage by communicating messages concerning warranties and guarantees, finance schemes, third-party endorsements and satisfied customers, independent testing and favourable product performance reports, awards and the attainment of quality standards, membership of trade associations, delighted customers, growth and market share, new products and alliances and partnerships, all of which seek to reduce risk and improve credibility.

In DRIP terms information and persuasion will be important and in terms of the communications mix, public relations, sales promotion and direct marking in the b2c market and personal selling, public relations and direct marketing in the b2b market.

Viewpoint 8.4 Integrated, luxurious communications by Fabergé

Fabergé's re-entry into the luxury jewellery market is remarkable for many reasons, but of these one stands out, the brand's use of marketing communications to build relationships.

The average price of a piece of Fabergé jewellery is over £100,000, so issues concerning security, access, positioning, and service and support are critical. The traditional channel strategy is to establish a small number of prestigious retail stores where all of these factors can be managed. However, the downside is that this product oriented strategy fails to maximise customer convenience.

Fabergé's solution was to develop customer relationships based on an integrated online/offline strategy. Customers can visit the website and inspect jewellery in their own time, from any part of the world. Using high-quality photography it is possible for customers to see jewellery in greater depth than they can physically in store.

Help is provided by online sales assistants. Using voice, video, and text according to the customer's choice customers are able to refine their preferences. However, purchasing is not carried out online. Once an item is selected, a sales assistant flies out to meet the customer to allow them to see, touch and try on the product, as necessary. Experience suggests that a purchase is made on most occasions once the product is seen physically.

Source: Based on Murphy (2009); www.faberge.com

Question

List the ways the elements of the marketing communications mix have been used to build customer relationships at Fabergé.

Task

Visit the Fabergé website (www.faberge.com/) and find the bell!

Exhibit 8.3 The Poppy Ring – a thing of beauty
The *Poppy Ring* epitomises Fabergé's positioning in the luxury jewellery market.
Image courtesy of Fabergé

Customer retention

The retention phase is the most profitable, where the greatest level of relationship value is experienced. The retention phase will generally last as long as both the buyer and seller are able to meet their individual and joint goals. If the relationship becomes more involved greater levels of trust and commitment between the partners will allow for increased cross-buying and product experimentation and, for b2b relationships, joint projects and product development. However, the very essence of relationship marketing is for organisations to identify a portfolio of customers with whom they wish to develop a range of relationships. This requires the ability to measure levels of retention and also to determine when resources are to be moved from acquisition to retention and back to acquisition.

The length of the retention phase will reflect the degree to which the marketing communications is truly interactional and based on dialogue. Messages need to be relational and reinforcing. Incentive schemes are used extensively in consumer markets as a way of retaining customers and minimising customer loss (or churn, defection or attrition). They are also used to cross-sell products and services and increase a customer's commitment and involvement with the brand. Through the use of an integrated programme of communications value can be enhanced for both parties and relational exchanges are more likely to be maintained. In business markets personal contact and key account management are crucial to maintaining interaction, understanding and mutual support. Electronic communications have the potential to automate many routine transactions and allow for increased focus on one-to-one communications.

In DRIP terms reinforcement and information will be important and, in terms of the communications mix, sales promotion and direct marking in the b2c market and personal selling (and key accounts), public relations and direct marketing in the b2b market.

Customer decline

Customer decline is concerned with the closure of a relationship. Termination may occur suddenly as a result of a serious problem or episode between the parties. The more likely process is that the buying organisation decides to reduce their reliance on the seller because their needs have changed, or an alternative supplier who offers superior value has been found. The buyer either formally notifies the established supplier or begins to reduce the frequency and duration of contact and moves business to other, competitive organisations.

The termination process therefore may be sharp and sudden or slow and protracted. Marketing communications plays a minor role in the former but is more significant in the latter. During an extended termination, marketing communications, especially direct marketing in the form of telemarketing and email, can be used to deliver orders and profits. These forms of communication are beneficial because they allow for continued personal messages but do incur the heavy costs associated with field selling (b2b) or advertising (b2c).

In DRIP terms reinforcement and persuasion will be important and, in terms of the communications mix, direct marketing in both markets and sales promotion in the b2c will be significant.

This cycle of customer attraction (acquisition), development, retention and decline represents a major difference to the four Ps approach. It is, above all else, customer focused and more appropriate to marketing values. The car manufacturer Audi developed the Audi Customer Journey. This is used to chart the ownership cycle and then superimpose optimised brand communications for each owner. This approach is reflected in Audi's loyalty rate which has grown consistently since the Journey was introduced.

However, even this approach is questionable as, although the focus of analysis is no longer the product but the relationship, the focus tends to be oriented towards the 'customer relationship' rather than the relationship per se. In other words there is a degree of asymmetry inherent in the relationship marketing concept.

Employee relationships and marketing communications

Traditionally, external stakeholders (customers, intermediaries and financiers) are the prime focus of marketing communications. However, recognition of the importance of internal stakeholders as a group who should receive marketing attention has increased, and the concept of *internal marketing* emerged in the 1980s.

Today the role of the employee within the branding process, and through their interface with customers and other stakeholders, is recognised as critically important. Now employees are recognised as brand ambassadors (Freeman and Liedtka, 1997 and Hemsley, 1998). This is particularly important in service environments where employees represent the interface between an organisation's internal and external environments and where their actions can have a powerful effect in creating images among customers (Schneider and Bowen, 1985; Balmer and Wilkinson, 1991).

Employees are important to external stakeholders not only because of the tangible aspects of service and production that they provide but also because of the intangible aspects, such as attitude and the way in which the service is provided: 'How much do they really care?' Images are often based more on the intangible than the tangible aspects of employee communications. Toyota's reassurance-based communications following the well publicised safety issues was anchored in its use of employees. Their campaign entitled 'Your Toyota is my Toyota' was used to present the human face of the car manufacturer and involved selected employees pledging their support to customers (Brownsell, 2010).

Management is responsible for the allocation of resources and the process and procedures used to create value. Its actions effectively constrain the activities of the organisation and shape the nature and form of the communications the organisation adopts, either consciously or unconsciously. Each organisation is a major influence upon its own marketing communications and can influence the perception others have of the character and personality of the organisation.

Purpose of internal marketing communications

Research by Foreman and Money (1995) indicates that managers see the main components of internal marketing as falling into three broad areas, namely development, reward and vision for employees. These will inevitably vary in intensity on a situational basis.

All of these three components have communication as a common linkage. Employees and management (members) need to communicate with one another and with a variety of non-members, and do so through an assortment of methods. Communication with members, wherever they are located geographically, needs to be undertaken for a number of reasons. These include the DRIP factors (Chapter 1), but these communications also serve the additional purposes of providing transaction efficiencies and affiliation needs; see Table 8.5.

The values transmitted to customers, suppliers and distributors through external communications need to be reinforced by the values expressed by employees, especially those who interact with these external groups. Internal marketing communications are necessary in order that internal members are motivated and involved with the brand such that they are able to present a consistent and uniform message to various stakeholders. This is an aspect of integrated marketing communications and involves product and organisation centred messages.

Table 8.5 The roles of internal marketing communications

DRIP factors	To provide information
	To be persuasive
	To reinforce – reassure/remind
	To differentiate employees/groups
Transactional	To coordinate actions
	To promote the efficient use of resources
	To direct developments
Affiliation	To provide identification
	To motivate personnel
	To promote and coordinate activities with non-members

If there is a set of shared values then internal communications are said to blend and balance the external communications. This process whereby employees are encouraged to communicate with customers helps ensure that what is promised by an organisation is realised and delivered, sometimes referred to as 'living the brand'.

Organisational culture

According to Beyer (1981), organisational identity is a subset of the collective beliefs that constitute an organisation's culture. Indeed, internal marketing is shaped by the prevailing culture, as it is the culture that provides the context within which internal marketing practices are to be accomplished.

Corporate culture, defined by Schein (1985), is 'the deeper level of basic assumptions and beliefs that are shared by members of an organisation, that operate unconsciously and define in a basic taken for granted fashion an organisation's view of its self and its environment'. A more common view of organisational culture is 'the way we do things around here'. It is the result of a number of factors, ranging through the type and form of business the organisation is in, its customers and other stakeholders, its geographical position, and its size, age and facilities. These represent the more tangible aspects of corporate culture. There are a host of intangible elements as well. These include the assumptions, values and beliefs that are held and shared by members of the organisation. These factors combine to create a unique environment, one where norms or guides to expected behaviour influence all members, whatever their role or position.

Internal engagement

Ideas about engagement, explored elsewhere in this book, have their roots in employee-based communications. It is generally accepted that employees need to buy-in to their workplace values in order that they be fully motivated and effective (Thomson and Hecker, 2000). This buy-in or process of engagement, consists of two main components; an intellectual and an emotional element (Hardaker and Fill, 2005). The intellectual element is concerned with employees buying-in and aligning themselves with the organisation's strategy, issues and overall direction. The emotional element is concerned with employees taking ownership of their contribution and becoming committed to the achievement of stated goals. Engagement is not passive as Starling (2008) believes, it has learning, understanding and action elements, not all of which need to be implemented at the same time, for all people.

Viewpoint 8.5 Explosive employee engagement at TNT

Most CEOs know how important it is that employees understand the organisation's strategy, mission and values. One of the standard ways of communicating these elements is to cascade the message through levels of management to employees. This is often coupled with question and answer sessions, newsletters and email. However, this sequential process suffers from information loss and deviance as messages are relayed in wave, each successively distanced from the perceived source.

TNT overcame this problem by developing a Virtual CEO office, called 'In Touch with Peter', on the firm's intranet. The site contains the CEO Agenda which details the strategic priorities for the coming year. Every two months there is a 90-minute online chat session, based around one the strategic agenda items. A transcript of the chat is posted and actions arising are also made available. The CEO blogs once every two weeks and his response to the employees' responses are also posted. Participation in the blogging process is often undertaken by those employees who are already engaged. TNT believes that reaching out to the disengaged can be achieved successfully by responding openly and respectfully to negative postings. What is more, those who are engaged can be expected to share their engagement with the disengaged, through dialogue.

Source: Based on van Harmelen (2008)

Question
To what extent are electronic communications between management and employees a poor substitute for face-to-face communication?

Task
Write a list of all the ways managers and employees might communicate with one another. Prioritise this list in terms of the effectiveness of the communication methods.

Exhibit 8.4 Peter Bakker (CEO), who features in the 'In Touch with Peter' interface
Image © 2010 TNT N.V.

Communication strategies should be based on the information processing styles of employees and access to preferred media. Ideally these communications should reflect a suitable balance between the need for rational information to meet intellectual needs, and expressive types of communication to meet the emotional needs of a workforce. It follows that the more effective the communication, the higher the level of engagement.

The development of brands based around employees, can be accomplished effectively and quickly by simply considering the preferred information processing style of an internal audience. By developing messages that reflect the natural processing style and using a diversity of media that best complements the type of message and the needs of each substantial internal target audience, the communication strategy is more likely to be successful.

Client–agency relationships

There are a vast number of relationships that form between various clients and agencies, disciplines, and within individual organisations. The nature of the relationships that exist in the marketing communications industry undoubtedly shapes and influences the strategies and operations of its member organisations. These are of course business-to-business relationships and require marketing communications that reflect the personal, often face-to-face nature of the way these two parties interact.

There are a number of agency–client relationships that have flourished over a very long period of time, and some for several decades. However, these appear to be in the minority, as many relationships appear to founder as clients abandon agencies and search for better, fresher solutions, because a contract expires, the client needs change or because of takeovers and mergers between agencies, which require that they forfeit accounts that cause a conflict of interest.

From a contextual perspective these buyer/seller relationships can be seen to follow a pattern of formation, maintenance and severance, or pre-contract, contracting process and post-contract stages (Davidson and Kapelianis, 1996). Clients and agencies enter into a series of interactions (West and Paliwoda, 1996) or exchanges through which trust and commitment are developed. Hakansson (1982) identified different contexts or atmospheres within which a relationship develops. These contexts had several dimensions: closeness/distance, cooperation/conflict, power/dependence, trustworthiness and expectations. Therefore, the client–agency relationship should be seen in the context of the network of organisations and interactions (or exchanges) that occur in a system. It is through these interactions that the tasks that need to be accomplished are agreed, resources made available, strategies determined and goals achieved.

The quality of an agency/client relationship is a function of trust, which is developed through the exchanges which fosters confidence. As discussed earlier, commitment is derived from a belief that the relationship is worth continuing and that maximum effort is warranted at maintaining the relationship (Morgan and Hunt, 1994). The development of new forms of remuneration, based around payment by results, also signifies a new client focus and a willingness to engage with clients and to be paid according to the success and contribution the agency can provide (Lace and Brocklehurst, 2000).

Poor relationships between agencies and clients are likely to result from a lack of trust and falling commitment. As it appears that communication is a primary element in the formation and substance of relational exchanges, clients might be advised to consider the agencies in their roster as an extended department of the core organisation and to use internal marketing communication procedures to assist the development of identity and sense of belonging.

In many ways agencies are an extension of the internal perspective discussed earlier. If this notion is accepted then it is important to involve, engage and embrace agencies in the same way as employees. However laudable this might be, practice suggests many agencies are kept at a distance and are treated on a need-to-know basis.

Traditionally communications have been based on face-to-face meetings and telephone conversations, supported by contact reports and briefing documents. Increasingly digital media plays a central role in the communications between clients and agencies. Often this can be through a portal and FTP sites through which briefs, contact reports, creative ideas and market knowledge can be shared globally, 24/7.

The agency–client relationship is based on the value clients can generate through the services provided their selected an agency. Therefore, agencies are keen to demonstrate their willingness and potential to generate value as frequently as possible, normally in the way in which the client is serviced. One of the issues that can arise from this client–agency dynamic is the 'over-servicing' that can occur as agencies strive to please their clients. Essentially this involves giving extra time to the client, free of charge, rather than charge lower rates. Blyth (2009) identifies two forms of over-servicing, observed in the PR industry. The first is the *deal-based* over-service, where an agreement between senior managers on both sides to promote a new product, is reached without any planning and costing. The result is that the client rarely gets what they expect, and the agency over works to deliver the desired outcomes and the account loses money.

The second form is *client-induced* over-servicing. This can occur when the client encourages the account team to put in more time and the agency managers fail to prevent the team responding. Again the result can be reduced margins, not only on this account but also on others in the portfolio as the account team's time is spread more thinly.

Summary

In order to help consolidate your understanding of the way marketing communications can shape relationships, here are the key points summarised against each of the learning objectives:

1 Examine ideas associated with perceived customer value

Value is the customer's estimate of the extent to which a product or service can satisfy their needs. According to Doyle (2000) the creation of customer value is based on three principles:

- Customers will choose between alternative offerings and select the one that (they perceive) will offer them the best value.
- Customers do not want product or service features, they want their needs met.
- It is more profitable to have a long-term relationship between a customer and a company rather than a one-off transaction.

2 Consider the theoretical concepts underpinning relationship marketing, including marketing exchanges and value creation

Relationship value can be visualised as a continuum. At one end of the continuum are transactional exchanges, characterised by short-term, product or price oriented exchanges, between buyers and sellers coming together for one-off exchanges. At the other end of the continuum are relational exchanges. These are characterised by a long-term orientation, where ultimately there is complete integration of systems and processes and where the relationship is motivated by partnership and mutual support.

An alternative view considers a spectrum of value propositions, which depict various forms of value creation. Movement along the relationship continuum can be interpreted as a change in the way value is created. Ribeiro *et al.* (2009) identify four core value strategies. These are exchange (or commodity) value, added value, performance value and value co-creation strategies.

3 Explain the concepts of trust and commitment and how they can be used to develop loyalty and retention programmes

Trust is a means of reducing uncertainty in order that effective relationships can develop. Commitment is a desire to continue and strengthen a valued relationship. Loyalty arises from these two concepts and can be considered from a behavioural (increasing sales) and/or an attitudinal (customer satisfaction) perspective. Loyalty is a deeply held sense of commitment to continue buying a preferred product or service on a consistent basis for the foreseeable future.

4 Consider the customer development cycle and the role of marketing communications in developing customer relationships

Customer relationships can be considered in terms of a series of relationship development phases; customer acquisition, development, retention and decline. Collectively these are referred to as the customer lifecycle. The duration and intensity of each relationship phase in the lifecycle will inevitably vary and it should be remembered that this representation is essentially idealistic.

Relationship marketing develops through a combination of planned marketing communications, the interaction and personal experience of products and services and the degree to which these two sets of messages and meanings complement the promises and messages transmitted previously. When these two processes come together a single communication process emerges and a relationship dialogue ensues.

5 Appraise the role of marketing communications in the development of employee relationships

Internal marketing communications are necessary in order that employees, managers and outsourced agencies providing client interfaced activities (e.g. subcontractors, call centres), are sufficiently motivated and involved with the brand such that they are able to present a consistent and uniform message to various stakeholders.

Communication strategies should be based on the information processing styles of employees and their access to preferred media. Ideally these communications should reflect a suitable balance between the need for rational information to meet intellectual needs and expressive types of communication to meet emotional needs of the workforce. It follows that the more effective the communication, the higher the level of engagement.

6 Examine the characteristics associated with client/agency relationships

The quality of an agency/client relationship is a function of trust, which is developed through the exchanges and that fosters confidence and commitment. This is derived from a belief that the relationship is worth continuing and that maximum effort is warranted at maintaining the relationship. Today, the client/agency relationship might be seen in terms of the current and potential value created by the two parties working together.

The development of new forms of remuneration, based around payment by results, plus the use of digital technology to cut production costs, increase communication speed and enhance responsiveness and signifies a willingness by agencies to engage with clients and improve the relationship outcomes.

Review questions

1. Discuss the view that the notion of customer value is too abstract to be of worth to organisations when loyalty is so hard to establish.
2. Identify the three principles Doyle established for the development of customer value.
3. Without looking back, draw the figure depicting the range of value oriented exchanges.
4. Make a list of the main differences between transactional and relationship marketing.
5. What is the link between trust and commitment?
6. Prepare brief notes defining loyalty and then find two different commercial loyalty programmes and consider the marketing communications used to support them.
7. Draw the customer relationship lifecycle and show how marketing communications is used at the different stages.
8. Discuss ways in which marketing communications can be used to develop relationships with customers.
9. What is employee engagement from a communication perspective?
10. Explain the term 'over-servicing' and suggest ways in which it might be managed.

References

Achrol, R.S. (1991) Evolution of the marketing organisation: new forms for turbulent environments. *Journal of Marketing*, 55(4), 77–93.

Anderson, J.C. and Narus, J.A. (1998) Business marketing: understand what customers value, *Harvard Business Review*, 76 (June), 53–65.

Angear, B. and Sambles, M. (2009) How Walkers used co-creation to get the UK to do it a flavour, *Admap*, 508 (September). Retrieved 6 November 2010 from www.warc.com/ArticleCenter/Default.asp?CType=A&AID=WORDSEARCH89872&Tab=A

Anon (2009) Cajun squirrel among crisp flavours tested by Walkers, *The Telegraph*. Retrieved 1 March 2010 from www.telegraph.co.uk/foodanddrink/4206310/Cajun-squirrel-among-crisp-flavours-tested-by-Walkers.html

Balmer, J.M.T. and Wilkinson, A. (1991) Building Societies: change, strategy and corporate identity, *Journal of General Management*, 17(2), 22–33.

Beyer, J.M. (1981) Ideologies, values and decision making in organisations. In *Handbook of Organisational Design* (eds P. Nystrom and W. Swarbruck). London: Oxford University Press.

Blyth, A. (2009) Calling time on over-servicing, *PRWeek-Thought Leader* (December), 4–5.

Brownsell, A. (2009) Not just the ticket, *Marketing*, 9 December, 14.

Brownsell, A. (2010) Toyota's road to recovery, *Marketing*, 12 May, 17.

Christopher, M., Payne, A. and Ballantyne, D. (2002) *Relationship Marketing: Creating Stakeholder Value*. Oxford: Butterworth Heinemann, Elsevier.

Cousins, P. and Stanwix, E. (2001) It's only a matter of confidence! A comparison of relationship management between Japanese and UK non-owned vehicle manufacturers, *International Journal of Operations and Production Management*, 21(9), October, 1160–1180.

Davidson, S. and Kapelianis, D. (1996) Towards an organisational theory of advertising: agency–client relationships in South Africa, *International Journal of Advertising*, 15, 48–60.

Day, G. (2000) Managing market relationships, *Journal of the Academy of Marketing Science*, 28(1), Winter, 24–30.

Demoulin, N.T.M. and Zidda, P. (2008) On the impact of loyalty cards on store loyalty: Does the customers' satisfaction with the reward scheme matter? *Journal of Retailing and Consumer Services*, 15(5) (September), 386–398.

Dick, A.S. and Basu, K. (1994) Customer loyalty: toward an integrated framework, *Journal of the Academy of Marketing Science*, 22(2), 99–113.

Doney, P.M. and Cannon, J.P. (1997) An examination of the nature of trust in buyer–seller relationships, *Journal of Marketing*, 62(2), 1–13.

Dowling, G.R. and Uncles, M. (1997) Do customer loyalty programmes really work?, *Sloan Management Review* (Summer), 71–82.

Doyle, P. (2000) *Value Based Marketing*. Chichester: John Wiley.

Evanschitzky, H. and Wunderlich, M. (2006) An Examination of Moderator Effects in the Four-Stage Loyalty Model, *Journal of Service Research*, 8(4) (May), 330–345.

Foreman, S.K. and Money, A.H. (1995) Internal marketing: concepts, measurements and application, *Journal of Marketing Management*, 11, 755–768.

Freeman, E. and Liedtka, J. (1997) Stakeholder capitalism and the value chain, *European Management Journal*, 15(3), 286–296.

Gambetta, D. (1988) *Trust: Making and Breaking Co-operative Relations*. New York: Blackwell.

Goodman, L.E. and Dion, P.A. (2001) The determinants of commitment in the distributor–manufacturer relationship. *Industrial Marketing Management*, 30(3) (April), 287–300.

Grönroos, C. (2004) The relationship marketing process: communication, interaction, dialogue, value, *Journal of Business and Industrial Marketing*, 19(2), 99–113.

Grönroos, C. (2009), Marketing as promise management: regaining customer management for marketing, *Journal of Business and Industrial Marketing*, 24(5/6), 351–359.

Grönroos, C. and Lindberg-Repo, K. (1998) Integrated marketing communications: the communications aspect of relationship marketing, *The IMC Research Journal*, 4(1), 3–11.

Hakansson, H. (1982) *International Marketing and Purchasing of Industrial Goods: An Interaction Approach*. Chichester: John Wiley.

Hallberg, G. (2004) Is your loyalty programme really building loyalty? Why increasing emotional attachment, not just repeat buying, is key to maximizing programme success, *Journal of Targeting Measurement and Analysis for Marketing*, 12(3), 231–241.

Hardaker, S. and Fill, C. (2005) Corporate Service Brands: the intellectual and emotional engagement of employees, *Corporate Reputation Review: an International Journal*, 7(4) (Winter), 365–376

Hemsley, S. (1998) Internal affairs, *Marketing Week*, 2 April, 49–53.

Kothandaraman, P. and Wilson, D. (2001) The future of competition: value creating networks, *Industrial Marketing Management*, 30(4) (May), 379–389.

Lace, J.M. and Brocklehurst, D. (2000) You both win when you play the same game, *Admap*, October, 40–42.

Macneil, I.R. (1980) *The New Social Contract*. New Haven, CT: Yale University Press.

Morgan, R.M. and Hunt, S.D. (1994) The commitment-trust theory of relationship marketing, *Journal of Marketing*, 58 (July), 20–38.

Morrison, D.E. and Firmstone, J. (2000) The social function of trust and implications of e-commerce, *International Journal of Advertising*, 19, 599–623.

Murphy, D. (2009) Structural Change, *Revolution*, December, 38–39.

Nettleton, K. (2009) Close-Up: Walkers' 'do us a flavour' is engaging the nation, *Campaign*, 23 January, retrieved 1 March 2010 from www.campaignlive.co.uk/news/features/875884/close-up-walkers-do-us-flavour-engaging

Oliver, R.L. (1997) *Satisfaction: A Behavioral Perspective on the Consumer*. New York: McGraw-Hill.

O'Malley, L. (1998) Can loyalty schemes really build loyalty?, *Marketing Intelligence and Planning*, 16(1), 47–55.

Pavlou, P.A. (2002) Institution-based trust in interorganisational exchange relationships: the role of online b2b marketplaces on trust formation, *The Journal of Strategic Information Systems*, 11(3–4) (December), 215–243.

Puth, G., Mostert, P. and Ewing, M. (1999) Consumer perceptions of mentioned product and brand attributes in magazine advertising, *Journal of Product Brand Management*, 8(1), 38–50.

Reichheld, F.F. and Sasser, E.W. (1990) Zero defections: quality comes to services, *Harvard Business Review* (September), 105–111.

Reinartz, W.J. and Kumar, V. (2002) The mismanagement of customer loyalty, *Harvard Business Review* (July), 86–94.

Ribeiro, A.H.P., Brashear, T.G., Monteiro, P.R.R. and Damázio, L.F. (2009) Marketing relationships in Brazil: trends in value strategies and capabilities, *Journal of Business and Industrial Marketing*, 24(5/6), 449–459.

Rowe, W.G. and Barnes, J.G. (1998) Relationship marketing and sustained competitive advantage, *Journal of Market-Focused Management*, 2(3), 281–289.

Ryssel, R., Ritter, T. and Gemunden H.G. (2004) The impact of information technology deployment on trust, commitment and value creation in business relationships, *Journal of Business and Industrial Marketing*, 19(3), 197–207.

Schein, E.H. (1985) *Organisational Culture and Leadership*. San Francisco, CA: Jossey-Bass.

Schneider, B. and Bowen, D. (1985) Employee and customer perceptions of service in banks: replication and extension, *Journal of Applied Psychology*, 70, 423–433.

Sheth, J.N. and Uslay, C. (2007) Implications of the Revised Definition of Marketing: From Exchange to Value Creation, *Journal of Public Policy & Marketing*, 26(2) (Fall) 302–307.

Simpson, P.M., Sigauw, J.A. and Baker, T.L. (2001) A model of value creation; supplier behaviors and their impact on reseller-perceived value, *Industrial Marketing Management*, 30(2)

(February), 119–34.

Spekman, R. (1988) Perceptions of strategic vulnerability among industrial buyers and its effect on information search and supplier evaluation, *Journal of Business Research*, 17, 313–326.

Spekman, R.E. and Carraway, R. (2006) Making the transition to collaborative buyer–seller relationships: An emerging framework, *Industrial Marketing Management*, 35, 10–19.

Starling, J. (2008) Why engagement is no longer enough, *Strategic Communication Management*, 12(1) (December/January), 7.

Thomson, K. and Hecker, L.A. (2000) The business value of buy-in. In *Internal Marketing: Directions for Management* (eds R.J. Varey and B.R. Lewis), 160–172. London: Routledge.

van Harmelen, R. (2008) Inviting TNT's employees into the CEOs virtual office, *Strategic Communication Management*, 12(1) (December/January), 12.

Vargo, S.L. (2009) Toward a transcending conceptualization of relationship: a service-dominant logic perspective, *Journal of Business & Industrial Marketing*, 24(5/6), 373–379.

Vargo, S.L. and Lusch, R.F. (2004) Evolving a New Dominant Logic for Marketing, *Journal of Marketing*, 68 (January), 1–17.

West, D.C. and Paliwoda, S.J. (1996) Advertising client–agency relationships, *European Journal of Marketing*, 30(8), 22–39.

White, T., Wassef, S. and Angear, B. (2010) Walkers – Embracing the unfamiliar: Walkers do us a flavour, *IPA Effectiveness Awards 2010*. Retrieved 6 November from www.warc.com/ArticleCenter/Default.asp?CType=A&AID=WORDSEARCH92547&Tab=A

Young, L.C. and Wilkinson, I.F. (1989) The role of trust and co-operation in marketing channels: a preliminary study, *European Journal of Marketing*, 23(2), 109–122.

Minicase 2.1

'Get on your bike!'
Mountain biking tourism in the Cairngorms National Park (CNP)

Andrew Turnbull: Aberdeen Business School, Robert Gordon University

Interest in mountain biking is currently undergoing rapid growth in Scotland and mountain biking tourism offers a means to use the Scottish landscape to attract several, largely untapped, target audiences, including thrill seekers, mountaineers, mountain bike owners, holidaymakers and families. These groups represent a small but growing proportion of the nearly 20 million visitors each year to Scotland from the UK, as well as those from abroad. The question is, however, how can these audiences, with their differing requirements, be engaged and what communications strategies might be employed to reach them most cost effectively?

Areas in Scotland such as the CNP can potentially benefit significantly from successful diversification and provision of facilities for the sport, but a number of stakeholders will need to be satisfied in the process, not least those concerned about the effects on the environment. Certainly mountain biking fits in well with some of the principal aims of the park, for example to promote understanding and enjoyment of the special qualities of the area and to contribute to the social development of the area's communities. The issue is whether this can be successfully linked to the promotion of sustainable use of the park's natural resources. For the long term, it is critical that any new mountain biking facilities do not have a detrimental impact upon fragile landscapes or rare wildlife.

Before considering how to communicate, profiles of the receivers must be drawn up. The interest groups here can be summarised as users, divided into the sub-segments above, environmentalists, the media and both local authorities and the Scottish Executive. It is not enough simply to communicate with actual and potential customers when considering such a high profile and environmentally sensitive location. A clear conflict in each group's desires and objectives represents a major obstacle to a successful communications plan.

So the strategy put forward, which stems from primary research activity, included a mix of communications tools taking into account potential resources, the complexity of the messages to be conveyed and the diversity of the audiences, as well as the nature, size and location of the market. Above all, it should be realised that mountain biking trails in the Cairngorms are in their infancy, so awareness creation is the key.

To start with however, advertising will be limited, in part because the audiences are geographically spread and in part because of the expense. Specialist publications such as *Cycling World* and *Men's Health* can be used, however, and other titles will be considered in or immediately pre-season, including local press in the CNP area. Inserts, as a form of direct marketing, also represent an option and information leaflets, including sales promotional offers, will be distributed to all visitor centres, attractions and accommodation outlets, including Guest Houses, B&Bs, hostels and hotels. These can be targeted not just within the CNP area, but in any location within a two-hour drive time.

Cinema, in all the major cities in Scotland, is a medium that has potential when the right films are on screen, as the cost is significantly lower than broadcast media, the impact is high and audiences can be easily matched to the mountain biker user profiles identified above. The disadvantage, of course, is that unlike press ads and leaflets, no direct response is possible, only the inclusion of a web address.

The importance of new media, in particular the Internet, cannot be underestimated given the young, educated and well-off customer profile. Dialogue allows interactivity and feedback can give competitive advantage! Websites (such as http://cycling.visitscotland.com/mountain_biking/mb_centre/mountain_biking_cairngorms) providing maps and giving information regarding the newest facilities, the latest trails and access routes will be vital too, in encouraging word-of-mouth among a close-knit group who will frequently communicate between themselves. Receivers in such a market will be easily influenced by opinion and style leaders.

Inevitably, in a campaign with limited finances, publicity gained through public relations activities are expected to form the central part of the communications strategy involving traditional media. Apart from the use of press releases concerning events such as mountain biking championships, advertorials and competitions will be placed in relevant press titles and stands reserved at selected UK exhibitions. Costs can be shared by entering alliances with bike manufacturers and other joint promotional activities are potentially available with equipment and clothing providers, retail outlets and even the ordnance survey map producers. All these organisations are in a position to help each other and combined activity through the pooling of resources will prove mutually beneficial.

Joining forces with other businesses looking to serve the mountain bike community will also assist with presenting a united front to the environmental lobby and the authorities. A socially responsible, environmentally aware message that nevertheless emphasises the financial benefits to the area, allows the media too to support mountain biking initiatives, rather than seek to find fault and take issue with the influx of new people and new activities that potentially conflict with more traditional pursuits such as hill walking and climbing.

An evaluation focus is always critical when measuring the reaction to initiatives targeted so precisely at niche audiences. As with all communications activities, measurement involves both 'hard' factors, which can be precisely quantified, and 'soft' factors, that must then be interpreted to assess their value.

So, for example, the number of new mountain bike trails is known exactly, the number of visitors using them can be estimated and expenditure associated with each visitor group can also be calculated from market research. The share of visits that mountain bikers represent to the area can also be determined as can uplift of, and response to, leaflets left in accommodation establishments and 'hits' on web sites, together with pages viewed and time spent browsing. Visitors to exhibition stands, as well as numbers leaving contact details, are further measures of success. Where media are utilised, then cover, reach and frequency, as well as a profile of the media user, give a good indication of who has been reached and how often.

Nevertheless, it is not just quantifiable measures that demonstrate effectiveness of a campaign. Qualitative measures, including attitudes towards the messages conveyed, the imagery associated with the creative execution, and values expressed, will all contribute to the overall impact.

The way is clear to allow CNP to diversify into mountain biking tourism. Given a good product, with the establishment of trails and facilities, then a focused communications campaign should overcome conservative values and capitalise on the opportunities this relatively new sport provides. The region's economy will benefit, Scotland's reputation will grow and a country that breathes history will further embrace the modern tourist marketplace.

Questions

1. For any marketing communications programme to work, it is essential that the messages sent reach the target audience(s). Summarise all the audiences identified in the case and consider the segmentation criteria that have been applied.
2. Critically analyse the communications process in the case, in the context of at least two models identified earlier in the text book. For example, the process of adoption model and the original Schramm *et al.* linear model.
3. Identify and critically examine the choice and balance of communications activities and media planned and determine first, the reasons for their selection and second, how well you believe they will work together.

Minicase 2.2 The Thoroughly Delicious Ice Cream Company

Ice cream is made from a mixture of milk, fat and sugar, which is cooled and whipped to create a light, airy texture. Flavours, such as fruit or chocolate, are added before the blend is frozen again and then packaged. Premium and super premium ice creams were developed in the 1980s and 1990s and these contain a much higher concentration of milk and cream.

People consume ice cream at one of two main locations. One of these is 'at home', having purchased the product from a supermarket or other retail outlet. This purchase is often planned, as part of a shopping event. The 'at-home' market is worth approximately 33 per cent of the total ice cream market. The other type of location is at a restaurant or café, or when relaxing on a beach or in the countryside. This is referred to as the 'out-of-home' market and is very often the result of an impulse, or unplanned purchase. This market constitutes approximately 66 per cent of the total. Apart from good distribution, there is one critical success factor that applies to all producers in the ice cream market and that is the need to be innovative and have proven new product development processes.

Unilever and Nestlé are the world's leading ice cream companies with brands that are established in many countries around the world. The UK ice cream market is led by Unilever, with brands such as Magnum, Carte D'Or, and Cornetto. Baskin-Robbins, the US ice cream brand, entered the UK market in 2010 with a range of premium ice cream tubs. Häagen-Dazs and Unilever's Ben & Jerry's have established themselves as the leading brands in the global super premium market.

The ice cream sector is facing a number of interrelated challenges. Consumers are beginning to be concerned with health issues such as obesity and allergies. As a result they are now much more interested in the ingredients of the foods they are eating, with purity and freshness key elements. Related to this are trends towards consuming more locally produced foods in preference to mass-produced factory products. Green issues are also much more prevalent in the sector than they used to be and the rapid development of 'Fairtrade' brands is testimony to the recent success of these brands in some developed economies. Ben & Jerry's have always been positioned on an ethical platform demonstrated by their policy not to use eggs from caged birds. However, their Classic Vanilla brand, launched in August 2006, was the first UK Fairtrade ice cream brand. Another successful brand, Green & Black's ice cream, has been positioned on their pure organic content.

The final major issue concerns the growing trend towards smaller households (one to two people). This means that the traditional family unit is changing and this requires that ice cream producers adapt their 'at home' products to meet the needs of smaller, different family units.

The Thoroughly Delicious Ice Cream company (TDIC) is a medium-sized family owned company and is typical of a growing number of smaller, local, European premium ice cream producers. Their rapid development owes much to the founder's need to diversify away from milk production when government regulations and milk quotas began to make the milk business unprofitable in the mid-1990s. TDIC's extensive range of ice cream products uses fresh milk, double cream and is free of artificial flavourings, preservatives or colours, all of which are to be found in global brands.

Many people choose the TDIC brand because they know where it is made, what goes into it and there is no complicated supply chain. TDIC's product innovation abilities are well established and have drawn substantial media attention. Their range of subtle and bold flavours appeal to different market segments, have widespread appeal and are even used by many top chefs.

Unlike national and global ice cream brands such as Unilever and Nestlé, TDIC differentiates itself by selling its ice cream through its own ice cream stores or parlours. Here customers not only buy their favourite TDIC brands but can also consume them within a specialist ice cream environment, one which is dedicated to indulgence and luxury. TDIC own 12 stores but they have started to franchise an increasing number of retail outlets. These are developed in clusters and located around major towns and cities.

National brands make extensive use of mass media communications and use national advertising to create awareness and emotional brand values. Smaller companies such as TDIC do not have the budget or the necessity to reach such broad audiences. They use regional and local advertising to reach highly targeted audiences. They also make extensive use of public relations, and their press coverage can be found regularly in leading magazines and newspapers. TDIC have also won several awards, often in recognition of their product development and branding. Vanessa Burridge is the Marketing Manager for TDIC and she has established some key relationships with journalists attached to both local and national newspapers. However, she is aware that the new franchise development strategy requires a new approach to TDIC's marketing communications.

Sources: This case is drawn from a number of sources, including those listed below. It is based partly on a real ice cream company, one that has been anonymised. This case is to be used for teaching and learning purposes and is not intended to infer good or bad management practice; www.icecreamprofits.com/articles/ice-cream-franchise-advertising.asp; Cowlett, M. (2010) Don't blame it on the weather, *Marketing*, 25 July, 26–27; Lewis, H. (2006) Market is heating up for premium, natural, convenient and green ice cream, *Just-Food*, 23 November. Retrieved, 18 January 2007 from www.just-food.com/article.aspx?id=96729

Questions

One of tasks facing Vanessa Burridge is to find ways of developing the TDIC brand and at the same time support the emerging franchise network. As a marketing communications expert and friend of the family, she has asked you for advice in response to the following issues.

Having spent some time considering the issues you should prepare a hand-written, formal response outlining your views with regard to the following questions:

1. Explain the key differences between the marketing communications used to support national brands and those used to support local brands of ice cream.

2. Identify the main relationship issues that might concern the TDIC franchisees, and then explain how TDIC might use marketing communications to manage these issues.

3. Explain how an understanding of customer buyer behaviour might influence the marketing communications used by ice cream companies.

4. Examine ways in which online and digital marketing communications might be used by companies such as TDIC.

Minicase 2.3 — Seaport Communications

It could be argued that the importance of marketing communications in the development and competitive positioning of seaports around the world has never been as strong as it is now. This is due mainly to advances in technology, alternative forms of transport and changing seaport customer preferences. These have all served to influence the volume, nature and frequency of freight and passenger traffic using seaports, and in recent years often creating excess or under-utilised port capacity.

The role of marketing communications in the seaport context can be understood in the light of stakeholder management theory. All ports have a number of different stakeholders, each of whom derives different benefits from their stake in the port's activities. Typical stakeholders include ferry and cargo operators, logistics and freight handlers, ferry passengers, employees, the local community, financial services providers and local companies who support the port's infrastructure. Many of these stakeholders are interdependent and few operate successfully without the support of others. An example of these stakeholder interdependencies can be seen through the problems faced by a major European port. Having sustained a thriving port business for many years, based partly on the full utilisation of its ferry berths, difficulties arose when one of the two main ferry companies using the port decide to withdraw its services. This was forced upon them by severe competition from low cost airlines. The withdrawal of the ferry operator resulted in excess capacity, an increase in local unemployment, a fall in income to the local government and a subsequent impact on the provision of some of the local community services, due to budget revisions.

Most seaports play a major role in the economic and social environment of their hinterland, or local region that supports the port. Marketing communications can be used to reach different stakeholders, many of whom are to be found in this area. Once identified, it is important to communicate different messages to different stakeholders using different media. Of course, the choice of communications mix depends largely on the goal of each campaign. Port users, such as a ship owners and freight managers are key stakeholders, so as well as seeking new customers, communications targeted at these stakeholders are often geared to operational issues, providing information about port procedures, fees and access.

The local community derives both an economic and social benefit. For example school children can learn about ports, their facilities, commerce, role and relationship with other countries and companies. Very often these marketing communications can be used to reach parents in order to educate and inform them about recent port developments and its overall significance to the local community. Apart from the benefits of social cohesion and local identity, this can be important for example when a port seeks support for development or investment opportunities. Sponsorship and funding of local community projects can also be used to build community relations.

Communications with ferry passengers are also important as these stakeholders often have an opportunity to sail from alternative ports or forms of transport. Public relations and advertising are often used to develop a port's identity and enable passengers to develop favourable images of the seaport and immediate area. This can create opportunities for passengers to stay in the town before the outward trip or after the return journey.

Although all the tools of the communications mix are used by seaports to communicate with various stakeholders, sales promotions are the least used and personal selling is mainly deployed to create contracts with seaport cargo carriers. Word of mouth communications are vitally important, especially as seaports are largely service providers and there is little tangible evidence of the facilities offered. Word of mouth communications between prospective and established seaport customers can be critical. The use of opinion leaders and opinion formers is therefore necessary to stimulate positive comment and develop relationships.

Questions

1. Explain how marketing communications might be used to change the attitudes of international freight and transportation companies, so that they use your local seaport rather than a competitor seaport, 35 miles (55 km) along the coast.

2. Determine a suitable position for the port and then explain how the port's positioning might be communicated to freight carriers.

Chapter 16
Advertising and strategy

An attempt to understand how advertising might work must be cautioned by an appreciation of the complexity and contradictions inherent in this commercial activity. Understanding how advertising might work, with its rich mosaic of perceptions, emotions, attitudes, information and patterns of behaviour, has been a challenge for many eminent researchers, authors and marketing professionals.

Aims and learning objectives

The aims of this chapter are to explore the different views about advertising strategy and to consider the complexities associated with understanding how clients can best use advertising.

The learning objectives of this chapter are to:

1. consider the role advertising plays in both consumer and business-to-business markets;
2. appraise the use of emotion in advertising and consider concepts associated with shock advertising;
3. explain the principal frameworks by which advertising is thought to influence individuals;
4. appraise the strong and weak theories of advertising;
5. consider ways in which advertising can be used strategically;
6. examine ideas concerning the use of advertising to engage audiences.

For an applied interpretation see Lorna Stevens' MiniCase entitled *Tapping into a new zeitgeist: women consumers, lifestyle trends and the Red experience* at the end of this chapter.

Introduction

The purpose of an advertising plan is to provide the means by which appropriate messages are devised and delivered to target audiences who then act in appropriate ways. This may be to buy a product, to enquire about a product or simply memorise a single aspect for future action. Guidelines for the content and delivery of messages are derived from an understanding of the variety of contexts in which the messages are to be used. For example, research might reveal a poor brand image relative to the market leader, or the different or changing media habits of target consumers. The nature of the messages and the problems to be addressed will be specified in the promotional objectives and strategy.

An advertising plan is composed, essentially, of three main elements:

- the message – what is to be said;
- the medium – how the message will be conveyed;
- the timing – manner in which the message will be carried.

This chapter is the first of two about advertising and several others in the next part of the book, about media. This chapter explores two main advertising issues, the first is about the way advertising might work, and consideration is given to some of the principal models and frameworks that have been devised to best describe the process by which advertising works. The second issue focuses on the strategic use of advertising, and the chapter is used to introduce a number of concepts and frameworks that have contributed to our understanding.

The chapter builds on the ideas about how marketing communications might work (Chapter 8) and shares some common thoughts. Chapter 17 considers the content of advertising messages, or what is to be said. In addition to these, Chapters 24–27 consider the media and ways in which advertising messages can be delivered.

The role of advertising

The role of advertising in most marketing communications campaigns is important. Advertising, whether it be on an international, national, local or direct basis, has the potential to engage audiences, albeit on a short-term basis. Engagement is enabled either by changing perceptions and building brand values or by encouraging a change in behaviour, often delivered through a call-to-action.

Advertising can reach huge audiences with simple messages that present opportunities to allow receivers to understand what a product is, what its primary function is and how it relates to all the other similar products. This is the main function of advertising: to communicate with specific audiences. These audiences may be consumer- or organisation-based, but wherever they are located, the prime objective is to build or maintain awareness of a product or an organisation.

Advertising cannot be said to have a single task as it can be used to achieve a number of DRIP-based outcomes. In can be used to differentiate and position brands, it can be used to reinforce brand messages, and it can easily inform and even persuade audiences to think and behave about and around products, services, brands and organisations. However, apart from its ability to reach large audiences, the key strengths of advertising have been to develop brand awareness, values and associations.

> The key strengths of advertising have been to develop brand awareness, values and associations.

Management's control over advertising messages is strong; indeed, of all the elements in the communications mix, advertising has the greatest level of control. The message, once generated and signed off by the client, can be transmitted in an agreed manner and style and at times that match management's requirements. This means that, should the environment change unexpectedly, advertising messages can be 'pulled' immediately. For example, had a BA image campaign designed to build the reputation of the airline been planned for April 2008 in the United Kingdom, it would have had to have been 'pulled' (stopped) following the chaotic transfer to and opening of the new Terminal 5 building at Heathrow in March. Difficulties associated with redirecting over 15,000 pieces of lost baggage, clearing the check-in queues and restoring normal flight schedules, plus the wider debate concerning what caused the problem, and the potential of further 'disruption', would have prevented BA's messages from being received and processed normally. It is more likely that there would have been a negative effect had the planned advertising been allowed to proceed.

ViewPoint 16.1 Easy advertising

Rather than concentrate on differentiation or the development of brand awareness, the role of advertising at easyJet appears to be essentially about reinforcement. The airline undertakes substantial levels of in-house public relations. This is used to drive awareness levels, and is accomplished by the successful television docu-soap called 'Airline'. This reality television programme, which has drawn audiences of over 8 million, is about the everyday working life of easyJet's staff and customers at Luton airport.

All tickets are booked online so advertising's role is partly to drive site traffic. This is typified by the use of sales promotions, which are all linked to the Internet. This means customers must go online if they wish to take advantage of promotional fares.

Exhibit 16.1 easyJet use their aircraft to communicate their identity in a bold way
AFP/Getty Images.

The advertising strategy, therefore, is intended to reinforce the easyJet brand values that are based around the idea of 'consumer champion' and to drive customers to its web site. The advertising also serves to position the easyJet brand based slightly on anarchy as well as price and value for money. Interestingly, the media used are essentially press, outdoor and radio plus use of its own aircraft as flying billboards. Television is not used partly because of the positive exposure generated by the docu-soap, partly because of the targeting and costs, and partly because of the effectiveness of the media used.

Question
Would you increase or decrease easyJet's advertising in a recession. Why?

Task
Compare the advertising messages used by Ryanair and easyJet.

Advertising costs can be regarded in one of two ways. On the one hand, there are the absolute costs, which are the costs of buying the space in magazines or newspapers or the time on television, cinema or radio. These costs can be enormous, and they impact directly on cash flow. For example, the rate card cost of a full-page (colour) advertisement in the *Daily Mail* was £45,612 (April 2008). To show a 30-second ad each day for one week in the 365-seater Screen 6 at the Sheffield Vue Cinema multiplex, costs £175 (April 2008).

On the other hand, there are the relative costs, which are those costs incurred to reach a member of the target audience with the key message. So, if an audience is measured in hundreds of thousands, or even millions on television, the cost of the advertisement spread across each member of the target audience reduces the cost per contact significantly. This aspect is developed further in Chapter 27.

> The cost of the advertisement spread across each member of the target audience reduces the cost per contact significantly.

The main roles of advertising are to build awareness, induce engagement (if only on a cognitive basis) and to (re)position brands, by changing either perception or attitudes. The regular use of advertising, in cooperation with the other elements of the communication mix, can be important to the creation and maintenance of a brand personality. Indeed, advertising has a significant role to play in the development of competitive advantage. In some consumer markets advertising is a dominant form of promotion. Advertising can become a mobility barrier, deterring exit and, more importantly, deterring entry to a market by organisations initially attracted by the potential profits of the industry. Many people feel that some brands sustain their large market share by sheer weight of advertising; for example, the washing powder brands of Procter & Gamble and Unilever.

Advertising can create competitive advantage by providing the communication necessary for target audiences to frame a product. By providing a frame or the perceptual space within which to pigeonhole a product, target audiences are able to position an offering relative to their other significant products much more easily. Therefore, advertising can provide the means for differentiation and sustainable competitive advantage. It should also be appreciated, however, that differentiation may be determined by the quality of execution of the advertisements, rather than through the content of the messages.

Advertising in the business-to-business market is geared, primarily, to providing relevant factual information upon which 'rational' decisions can be made. Regardless of the target audience, all advertising requires a message and a carrier to deliver the message to the receiver. This text concentrates on these two main issues, while acknowledging the wider role that advertising plays in society.

Emotion in advertising

The preceding material, if taken at face value, suggests that advertising only works by people responding to advertising in a logical, rational and cognitive manner. It also suggests that people only take out the utilitarian aspect of advertising messages (cleans better, smells fresher). This is obviously not true and there is certainly a strong case for the use of emotion in advertising in order to influence and change attitudes through the affective component of the attitudinal construct (Chapter 6).

ViewPoint 16.2 An emotional M&S revival

In the late 1990s and early twenty-first century M&S experienced subsiding financial performance and a wealth of negative press comment. This in particular contributed to the public's loss of confidence in the brand.

The new CEO, Stuart Rose, revised the product range to make it more stylish and fashionable. He lowered some of the opening price points to be in line with the competition, improved service and started the process of refurbishing and redesigning the layout of stores. Only once these actions had been put in place could communications be used to re-engage customers with the brand and to rebuild their confidence. One of the first tasks that communications needed to achieve was to counter the negative public relations and give a reason for lapsed customers to reappraise and revisit the store. Food and womenswear were key to the revival, the former contributes 50 per cent of M&S turnover and the latter drives brand perceptions.

The strapline 'Your M&S' encapsulated the move to be audience-centred, was meaningful and could apply to a range of audiences. The choice of high visibility media was critical to conveying ideas about conviction and critical mass. The 'Your M&S' campaign sought to reassure customers, many of whom could identify with Twiggy, who fronted the womenswear ads. The food ads were underscored by the line 'This is not just food, this is M&S Food', which was backed by emotional, sultry music by Santana.

The success of the communications campaign can be demonstrated at various levels. For example, a blouse worn by Twiggy in one ad sold more in a single week than any other product in the whole history of M&S. The power of M&S' communications spawned press coverage said to worth an additional £6 million pounds in advertising space. The ROI on clothing was estimated at £2.61 for every £1 spent on media while the share price zoomed up to 595p, nearly 50 per cent above the price offered by Phillip Green when he attempted to buy the company in July 2004.

Sources: Sweney, *et al.* (2006); Thompson, *et al.* (2006).

Question
Discuss the view that once the M&S product range was corrected there was no real reason to use mass communications as word-of-mouth would have kicked in.

Task
Go to Youtube, find the 'This is not just food, this is M&S Food' ad. How else could food be conveyed emotionally?

Most advertised brands are not normally new to consumers as they have some experience of the brand, whether that be through use or just through communications. This experience affects their interpretation of advertising as memories have already been formed. The role of feelings in the way ads work suggests a consumerist interpretation of how advertising works rather than the rational, which is much more a researchers' interpretation (Ambler, 1998). Consumers view advertising in the context of their experience of the category and memories of the brand. Aligned with this approach is the concept of likeability, where the feelings evoked by advertising trigger and shape attitudes to the brand and attitudes to the advertisement (Vakratsas and Ambler, 1999). Feelings and emotions play an important role in advertising especially when advertising is used to build awareness levels and brand strength.

> Consumers view advertising in the context of their experience of the category and memories of the brand.

Most of the models presented later in this chapter are developed on the principle that individuals are cognitive processors and that ads are understood as a result of information processing. The best examples of these are the hierarchy of effects or sequential models where information is processed step by step. This view is not universally accepted. Researchers such as Krugman (1971), Ehrenberg (1974), Corke and Heath (2004) and Heath and Feldwick (2007) dispute the importance of information processing, denying that attention is necessary for people to understand ads and that the creativity within an ad is more important in many circumstances, than the rational message the ad purports to deliver.

Shock strategy

Advertising strategy may also be considered in terms of the overall response a target audience might give on receipt of particular messages. Some organisations choose a consistent theme for their campaigns, one that is often unrelated to their products or services. One such strategy is the use of shock advertising. Shock advertising according to Venkat and Abi-Hanna (1995) 'is generally regarded as one that deliberately, rather than inadvertently, startles and offends its audience'.

> Shock advertising is generally regarded as one that deliberately, rather than inadvertently, startles and offends its audience.

Dahl *et al.* (2003) suggest that shock advertising by definition is unexpected and audiences are surprised by the messages because they do not conform to social norms or their expectations. They argue that audiences are offended because there is 'norm violation, encompassing transgressions of law or custom (e.g., indecent sexual references, obscenity), breaches of a moral or social code (e.g., profanity, vulgarity), or things that outrage the moral or physical senses', for example gratuitous violence and disgusting images (p. 268). The clothing company French Connection's use of the FCUK slogan and the various Benetton campaigns depicting a variety of incongruous situations (for example a priest and a nun kissing and of a man dying of AIDS) are contemporary examples of norm violation. Shock advertising is not only used by commercial organisations such as Diesel, Egg and Sony Entertainment but is also used by not-for-profit organisations such as the government (anti-smoking), charities (child abuse) and human rights campaigners (Amnesty International) (see Viewpoint 16.3).

ViewPoint 16.3 Problem? What problem?

In a campaign designed to raise awareness and to shock the public into being less complacent about domestic violence, Amnesty International used posters in the style of cosmetics advertising, featuring models using make-up to hide the damage and injuries caused by violence.

The posters, used in over 100 tube stations, depict 'Cachez', a fictional cosmetics brand, and use the slogan 'Gentle skincare for bruising relationships'. The powerful messages show a smiling model with different injuries – a black eye, a cut cheek, a scar below her breast and three red marks on her shoulder. The aim is to address the complacency that exists about the issue and to make people think about the horror of domestic violence. Through the use of cosmetics to symbolically cover up the issue, Amnesty tried to shock people into not accepting this (or any) form of violence (see Exhibit 16.2).

Source: www.amnesty.org.

Question

Do you believe that the use of advertising to shock people into a change of behaviour is morally wrong.

Task

Find an ad that uses shock techniques. What are the elements in the ad that generate the shock impact?

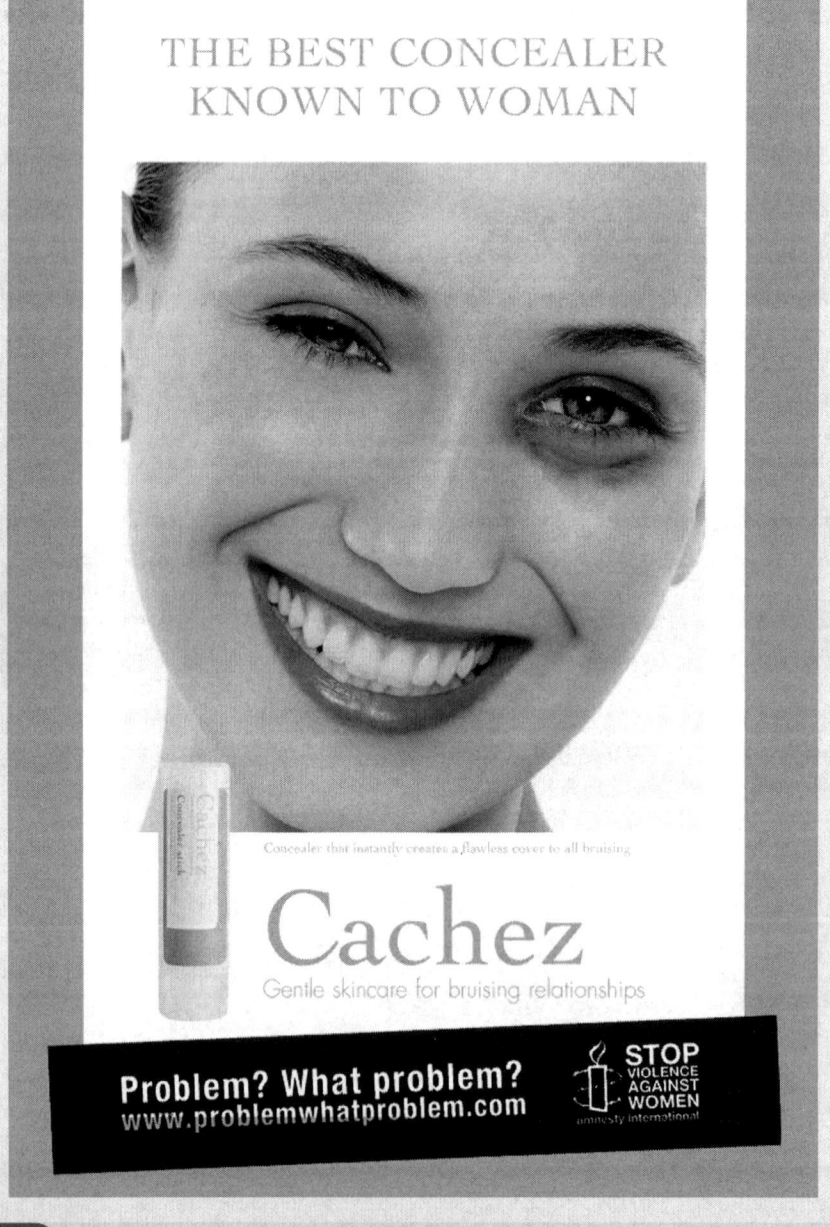

Exhibit 16.2   Amnesty International – Problem? What problem?

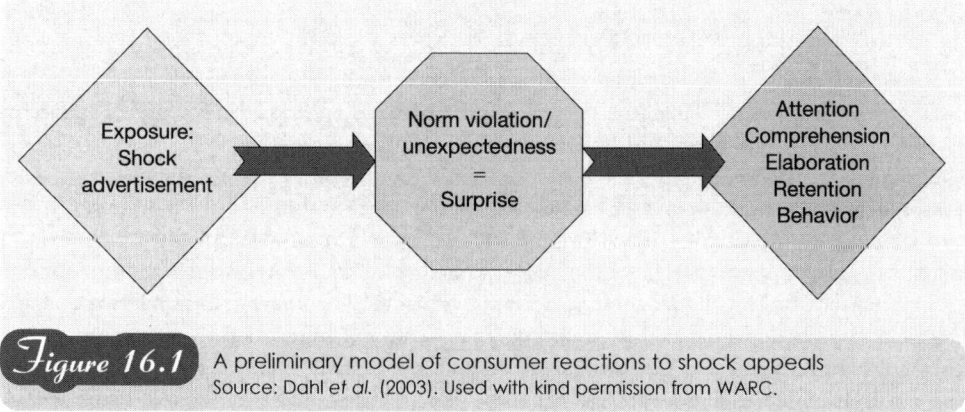

Figure 16.1 A preliminary model of consumer reactions to shock appeals
Source: Dahl et al. (2003). Used with kind permission from WARC.

The main reason for using a shock advertising strategy is that it is a good way to secure an audience's attention and achieve a longer-lasting impact than through traditional messages and attention-getting devices. The surprise element of these advertisements secures attention, which is followed by an attempt to work out why an individual has been surprised. This usually takes the form of cognitive engagement and message elaboration in order that the message be understood. Through this process a shocking message can be retained and behaviour influenced. This process is depicted in Figure 16.1.

Shocking ads also benefit from word-of-mouth communication as these messages provoke advertisement-related conversations (Dichter, 1966). The credibility of word-of-mouth communication impacts on others who, if they have not been exposed to the original message, often seek out the message through curiosity. Associated with this pass-along impact is the generation of controversy, which can lead to additional publicity for an organisation and its advertisements. This 'free' publicity, although invariably negative, is considered to be desirable as it leads to increased brand awareness without further exposure and associated costs. This in turn can give the organisation further opportunities to provide more information about the advertising campaign and generate additional media comment.

> Shocking ads benefit from word-of-mouth communication as these messages provoke advertisement-related conversations.

The use of shock tactics has spread to viral marketing, a topic discussed in more detail in Chapter 26. Virals delivered through email communications have an advantage over paid-for advertising because consumers perceive advertising as an attempt to sell product, whereas virals are perceived as fun, can be opened and viewed (repeatedly) at consumer-determined times. Furthermore, virals are not subject to the same regulations that govern advertising, opening opportunities to convey controversial material. For example, a Volkswagon viral showed a suicide bomber exploding a device inside a car but the vehicle remained in one piece ('small but tough'). Another for Ford Ka showed a cat being decapitated by the sunroof. As Bewick (2006) suggests, joking with terrorism and pets is a sure-fire way of generating shock, and with that comes publicity.

Advertising models and concepts

In Chapter 7 a series of sequential models is presented. These models, essentially hierarchy of effects frameworks, were the first attempts to explain how advertising works (AIDA). The sequential nature of these early interpretations was attractive because they were easy to comprehend, neatly mirrored the purchase decision process and provided a base upon which campaign goals were later assigned (Dagmar). However, as our knowledge of buyer behaviour increased and as the significance of the USP declined so these hierarchy of effects models also declined in terms of our understanding about advertising. Now they are insignificant and are no longer used as appropriate interpretations of how advertising works.

In their place a number of new frameworks and explanations have arisen, all of which claim to reflect practice. In other words these new theories about how advertising works are a reflection of practice, of the way advertising is considered to work, or at least used by advertising agencies and interpreted by marketing research agencies. These are examples of information processing models, mentioned earlier in this chapter. The first to be considered here were developed by O'Malley (1991) and Hall (1992) and they suggest that there are four main advertising frameworks (Figure 16.2).

1. The sales framework
   This framework, oriented mainly to direct-response work, is based on the premise that the level of sales is the only factor that is worth considering when measuring the effectiveness of an advertising campaign. This view holds that all advertising activities are aimed ultimately at shifting product – generating sales. Advertising is considered to have a short-term direct impact on sales. This effect is measurable and, while other outcomes might also result from advertising, the only important factor is sales. On sales alone will the true effect of any advertising be felt.

   > Advertising is considered to have a short-term direct impact on sales.

2. The persuasion framework
   The second framework assumes advertising to work rationally, because messages are capable of being persuasive. Persuasion is effected by gradually moving buyers through a number of sequential steps. These hierarchy of effects models assume that buyer decision-making is rational and can be accurately predicted. As discussed earlier, these models have a number of drawbacks and are no longer used as the basis for designing advertisements, despite great popularity in the 1960s and 1970s.

Figure 16.2 Four advertising frameworks
Source: After O'Malley (1991) and Hall (1992).

Persuasive mobiles

The use of advertising to persuade audiences can be key when launching new brands, when the competition becomes intensive or when the audience experiences high involvement.

In 2008 Sony Ericsson implemented a campaign designed to offset the threat of Apple and the iPhone, plus the push from market leaders Nokia. Sony Ericsson used campaigns to support its latest handsets, Cyber-Shot, Walkman, clamshell and touch-screen handsets. Included within this activity was support for their first sub-brand, Xperia and the first handset, X1.

Samsung were also experiencing pressure and used a £16m pan-European awareness campaign to introduce Soul, its key handset for 2008. Motorola meanwhile sought to back its Z10 kick-slider phone using television to demonstrate key attributes.

Source: Jones (2008).

Question
Why did Motorola use television to demonstrate the key attributes of their Z10 brand?

Task
Visit www.sonyericsson.com/x1/?lc=en&cc=gb. Watch the film for X1. Good?

3. The involvement framework
   Involvement-based advertisements work by drawing members of the target audience into the advertisement and eliciting a largely emotional response. Involvement with the product develops as a consequence of involvement with the advertisement. Yellow Pages developed a highly successful series of television commercials that centred upon a fictional character called J.R. Hartley. This elderly gentleman was shown using Yellow Pages as a means of resolving a number of problems and served to provide warmth and character that involved people not only with J.R. Hartley but also helped establish brand values.

   > Involvement-based advertisements work by drawing members of the target audience into the advertisement.

   Another example of this approach can be observed in the Nescafé Gold Blend coffee advertisements. During the late 1980s and early 1990s, UK viewers witnessed the development of a relationship between an aspirational couple with a mutual liking for the Gold Blend brand of coffee. Each advertisement presented particular events in the development of the couple's relationship. Each ad was eagerly anticipated by audiences, many of whom were obsessive about the unfolding drama. By involving the target in the drama, the brand became part of the involvement, a crucial part of each of the ritualistic playlets. Later, the couple were reincarnated as a younger couple and presented in a more adventurous context. Again, the theme was romance, which was allowed to unfold over a series of different advertisements.

4. The salience framework
   This interpretation is based upon the premise that advertising works by standing out, by being different from all other advertisements in the product class (see Exhibit 16.4). The launch of Radion, a soap powder that used the twin propositions of cleaning and removing odours, was remarkable because of its ability to 'shout' at the audience through the use of lurid colours and striking presentations. Cillit Bang, Injurylawyers4u, and Sheila's Wheels are some of the ads consumers report that they find irritating.

ViewPoint 16.5   The day Cillit went bang

Cillit Bang is a brand of household cleaner, owned by Reckitt Benckiser and introduced to the market in 2004. Since then the brand has been supported by a heavyweight ad campaign that features a fictional spokesperson, Barry Scott. The message is delivered through demonstration of the power of the brand to clean various surfaces, including a 1p coin dipped into the fluid. 'Members of the public' provide testimonials to the power of the cleaners and Barry Scott constantly repeats the brand name loudly, supported by heavy music, to the point that the message becomes annoying and for many, exceedingly irritating.

These ads are designed as if they are spoofing 1960s commercials. Yet despite the old-fashioned approach the brand became a market leader with a 12 per cent share (Mintel) and the ads have spawned a wave of look-alikes and remixes.

Sources: Various including Tiltman (2008).

Question
Why has an ad that irritates the audience so much become a market leader?

Task
Use Google to find some of the remixes of the Cillit Bang ads.

Acceptance of the persuasion and salience frameworks is based on the assumption that the audience are active, rational problem-solvers and are perfectly capable of discriminating among brands and advertisements. Furthermore, the models bring to attention two important points about people and advertising. Advertisements are capable of generating two very clear types of response: a response to the featured product and a response to the advertisement itself. As discussed earlier in Chapter 8, the cognitive responses that people make when exposed to marketing communication messages, in this case advertisements, and the elaboration likelihood model (ELM) are important means of understanding how different motivations affect decision-making.

The strong and the weak theories of advertising

The explanations offered to date are all based on the premise that advertising is a potent marketing force, one that is persuasive and which is done *to* people. More recent views of advertising theory question this fundamental perspective. Prominent among the theorists are Jones, McDonald and Ehrenberg, some of whose views will now be presented. Jones (1991) presented the new views as the strong theory of advertising and the weak theory of advertising.

The strong theory of advertising

All the models presented so far are assumed to work on the basis that they are capable of affecting a degree of change in the knowledge, attitudes, beliefs or behaviour of target audiences. Jones refers to this as the strong theory of advertising, and it appears to have been universally adopted as a foundation for commercial activity.

Exhibit 16.3 Cillit Bang
This brand uses a hard hitting, loud, and repetitive message to get attention and maintain awareness levels. Typical of the strong theory's persuasive approach.
Photo courtesy of Cillit Bang and Reckitt Benckiser.

According to Jones, exponents of this theory hold that advertising can persuade someone to buy a product that they have never previously purchased. Furthermore, continual long-run purchase behaviour can also be generated. Under the strong theory, advertising is believed to be capable of increasing sales at the brand and class levels. These upward shifts are achieved through the use of manipulative and psychological techniques, which are deployed against consumers who are passive, possibly because of apathy, and are generally incapable of processing information intelligently. The most appropriate theory would appear to be the hierarchy of effects model, where sequential steps move buyers forward to a purchase, stimulated by timely and suitable promotional messages.

> Under the strong theory, advertising is believed to be capable of increasing sales at the brand and class levels.

The weak theory of advertising

Increasing numbers of European writers argue that the strong theory does not reflect practice. Most notable of these writers is Ehrenberg (1988, 1997), who believes that a consumer's pattern of brand purchases is driven more by habit than by exposure to promotional messages. The framework proposed by Ehrenberg is the awareness–trial–reinforcement (ATR) framework. Awareness is required before any purchase can be made, although the elapsed time between awareness and action may be very short or very long. For the few people intrigued enough to want to try a product, a trial purchase constitutes the next phase. This may be stimulated by retail availability as much as by advertising, word-of-mouth or personal selling stimuli. Reinforcement follows to maintain awareness and provide reassurance to help the customer to repeat the pattern of thinking and behaviour and to cement the brand in the repertoire for occasional purchase activity. Advertising's role is to breed brand familiarity and identification (Ehrenberg, 1997).

> Advertising's role is to breed brand familiarity and identification.

Following on from the original ATR model (Ehrenberg, 1974), various enhancements have been suggested. However, Ehrenberg added a further stage in 1997, referred to as the nudge. He argues that some consumers can 'be nudged into buying the brand more frequently (still as part of their split-loyalty repertoires) or to favour it more than the other brands in their consideration sets' (p. 22). Advertising need not be any different from before; it just provides more reinforcement that stimulates particular habitual buyers into more frequent selections of the brand from their repertoire.

According to the weak theory, advertising is capable of improving people's knowledge, and so is in agreement with the strong theory. In contrast, however, consumers are regarded as selective in determining which advertisements they observe and only perceive those that promote products that they either use or have some prior knowledge of. This means that they

ViewPoint 16.6 Nudging chocolate

Our choice of preferred chocolate brands is fairly clear cut and considering that the amount we eat each year is so large, it is difficult to see how the volume of purchases or the frequency of consumption could be improved. The role of advertising in this market is not to inform or improve awareness, as these are high enough already. The real task in this market is to assist those who are lapsed brand users to try the brand again, in other words to nudge them back to the brand.

So, rather than build brand values the focus is on consolidating or changing behaviour. Consumer buying of chocolate has also changed as impulse buying has declined and been replaced by mass purchasing at supermarkets. Consumers get cost savings and control consumption through a single weekly purchase. This pressurises advertising into helping to secure the trade listings necessary to get product on to the supermarket shelves.

Question
Do you agree with this nudging perspective or does advertising really persuade us to buy more than we would normally purchase?

Task
Find out who the target market is for three different brands of chocolate.

---

already have some awareness of the characteristics of the advertised product. It follows that the amount of information actually communicated is limited. Advertising, Jones continues, is not potent enough to convert people who hold reasonably strong beliefs that are counter to those portrayed in an advertisement. The time available (30 seconds in television advertising) is not enough to bring about conversion and, when combined with people's ability to switch off their cognitive involvement, there may be no effective communication. Advertising is employed as a defence, to retain customers and to increase product or brand usage. Advertising is used to reinforce existing attitudes, not necessarily to drastically change them.

Unlike the strong theory, this perspective accepts that when people say that they are not influenced by advertising they are in the main correct. It also assumes that people are not apathetic or even stupid, but capable of high levels of cognitive processing.

In summary, the strong theory suggests that advertising can be persuasive, can generate long-run purchasing behaviour, can increase sales and regards consumers as passive. The weak theory suggests that purchase behaviour is based on habit and that advertising can improve knowledge and reinforce existing attitudes. It views consumers as active problem-solvers.

These two perspectives serve to illustrate the dichotomy of views that has emerged about this subject. They are important because they are both right and they are both wrong. The answer to the question 'How does advertising work?' lies somewhere between the two views and is dependent upon the particular situation facing each advertiser. Where elaboration is likely to be high if advertising is to work, then it is most likely to work under the strong theory. For example, consumer durables and financial products require that advertising urges prospective customers into some form of trial behaviour. This may be a call for more information from a sales representative or perhaps a visit to a showroom. The vast majority of product purchases, however, involve low levels of elaboration, where involvement is low and where people select, often unconsciously, brands from an evoked set.

New products require people to convert or change their purchasing patterns. It is evident that the strong theory must prevail in these circumstances. Where products become

> Where elaboration is likely to be high if advertising is to work, then it is most likely to work under the strong theory.

established their markets generally mature, so that real growth is non-existent. Under these circumstances, advertising works by protecting the consumer franchise and by allowing users to have their product choices confirmed and reinforced. The other objective of this form of advertising is to increase the rate at which customers reselect and consume products. If the strong theory were the only acceptable approach, then theoretically advertising would be capable of continually increasing the size of each market, until everyone had been converted. There would be no 'stationary' markets.

Considering the vast sums that are allocated to advertising budgets, not only to launch new products but also to pursue market share targets aggressively, the popularity and continued implicit acceptance of the power of advertising suggest that a large proportion of resources are wasted in the pursuit of advertising-driven brand performance. Indeed, it is noticeable that organisations have been switching resources out of advertising into sales promotion activities. There are many reasons for this (Chapter 18), but one of them concerns the failure of advertising to produce the expected levels of performance: to produce market share. The strong theory fails to deliver the expected results, and the weak theory does not apply to all circumstances. Reality is probably a mixture of the two.

The alphabetical model

Prue (1998) presents a framework entitled the alphabetical model, based upon the premise that advertising should be interpreted from a customer orientation. His model is an attempt to return to the simplicity inherent in the AIDA and other sequential models (see Figure 16.3). This is not so much a theory as a rather wide depository for all known interpretations of how advertising might work.

Using advertising strategically

There are many varied and conflicting ideas about the strategic use of advertising. For a long time the management of the tools of the communication mix was considered strategic. Indeed, many practitioners still believe in this approach. However, ideas concerning integrated marketing communications and corporate identity (Chapters 9 and 13) have helped provide a fresh perspective on what constitutes advertising strategy, and issues concerning differentiation,

Figure 16.3 The alphabetical model of advertising
Source: Adapted from Prue (1998) An all-embracing theory of how advertising works?, *Admap*, February, pp. 18–23. Reproduced with permission of the publisher.

brand values and the development of brand equity have helped establish both strategic and a tactical or operational aspect associated with advertising.

One of the first significant attempts to formalise advertising's strategic role was developed by Vaughn when working for an advertising agency, Foote, Cone and Belding. These ideas (see below) were subsequently debated and an alternative model emerged from Rossiter and Percy. Both frameworks have been used extensively by advertising agencies, and although their influence has now subsided the underlying variables and approach remain central to strategic advertising thought.

The FCB matrix

> Brain specialisation theory suggests that the left-hand side of the brain is best for handling rational, linear and cognitive thinking.

Vaughn (1980) developed a matrix utilising involvement and brain specialisation theories. Brain specialisation theory suggests that the left-hand side of the brain is best for handling rational, linear and cognitive thinking, whereas the right-hand side is better able to manage spatial, visual and emotional issues (the affective or feeling functions).

Vaughn proposed that by combining involvement with elements of thinking and feeling, four primary advertising planning strategies can be distinguished. These are informative, affective, habitual and self-satisfaction (see Figure 16.4). According to Vaughn, the matrix is intended to be a thought provoker rather than a formula or model from which prescriptive

Figure 16.4 FCB grid
Source: Vaughn (1980). Used with kind permission from WARC.

solutions are to be identified. The FCB matrix is a useful guide to help analyse and appreciate consumer/product relationships and to develop appropriate communication strategies. The four quadrants of the grid identify particular types of decision-making and each requires different advertising approaches. Vaughn suggests that different orderings from the learn–feel–do sequence can be observed. By perceiving the different ways in which the process can be ordered, he proposed that the learn–feel–do sequence should be visualised as a continuum, a circular concept. Communication strategy would, therefore, be based on the point of entry that consumers make to the cycle.

Some offerings, generally regarded as 'habitual', may be moved to another quadrant, such as 'responsive', to develop differentiation and establish a new position for the product in the minds of consumers relative to the competition. This could be achieved by the selection of suitable media vehicles and visual images in the composition of the messages associated with an advertisement. There is little doubt that this model, or interpretation of the advertising process, has made a significant contribution to our understanding of the advertising process and has been used by a large number of advertising agencies (Joyce, 1991).

The Rossiter–Percy grid

Rossiter *et al.* (1991), however, disagree with some of the underpinnings of the FCB grid and offer a new one in response (revised 1997) (Figure 16.5). They suggest that involvement is not a continuum because it is virtually impossible to decide when a person graduates from high to low involvement. They claim that the FCB grid fails to account for situations where a person moves from high to low involvement and then back to high, perhaps on a temporary basis, when a new variant is introduced to the market. Rossiter *et al.* regard involvement as the level of perceived risk present at the time of purchase. Consequently, it is the degree of familiarity buyers have at the time of purchase that is an important component.

A further criticism is that the FCB grid is an attitude-only model. Rossiter *et al.* quite rightly identify the need for brand awareness to be built into such grids as a prerequisite for attitude development. However, they cite the need to differentiate different purchase situations. Some brands require awareness recall because the purchase decision is made prior to the act of purchasing. Other brands require

> Some brands require awareness recall because the purchase decision is made prior to the act of purchasing.

Figure 16.5 The Rossiter–Percy grid
Source: Adapted from Rossiter and Percy (1997). Used with kind permission.

awareness recognition at the point of purchase, where the buyer needs to be prompted into brand choice decisions. Each of these situations requires different message strategies, and these are explored in Chapter 17.

The other major difference between the two grids concerns the 'think–feel' dimension. Rossiter *et al.* believe that a wider spectrum of motives must be incorporated, as the FCB 'think–feel' interpretation fails to accommodate differences between product category and brand purchase motivations. For example, the decision to use a product category may be based on a strictly functional and utilitarian need. The need to travel to another country often designates the necessity of air transport. The choice of carrier, however, particularly over the North Atlantic, is a brand choice decision, motivated by a variety of sensory and ego-related inputs and anticipated outputs. Rossiter *et al.* disaggregate motives into what they refer to as informational and transformational motives. By detailing motives into these classifications, a more precise approach to advertising tactics can be developed (Chapter 17). Furthermore, the confusion inherent in the FCB grid, between the think and involvement elements, is overcome.

It should be understood that these 'grids' are purely hypothetical, and there is no proof or evidence to suggest that they are accurate reflections of advertising. It is true that both models have been used as the basis for advertising strategy in many agencies, but that does not mean that they are totally reliable or, more importantly, that they have been tested empirically so that they can be used in total confidence. They are interpretations of commercial and psychological activity and have been instrumental in advancing our level of knowledge. It is in this spirit of development that these models are presented in this text.

There are parts in both of these frameworks that have a number of strong elements of truth attached to them. However, for products that are purchased on a regular basis, pull strategies should be geared to defending the rationale that current buyers use to select the brand. Heavy buyers select a particular brand more often than light users do from their repertoire. By providing a variety of consistent stimuli, and by keeping the brand alive, fresh buyers are more likely to prefer and purchase a particular brand than those that allow their brands to lose purchase currency and the triggers necessary to evoke memory impressions.

> For products purchased on an irregular basis, marketing communications need only touch the target audience on a relatively low number of occasions.

For products purchased on an irregular basis, marketing communications need only touch the target audience on a relatively low number of occasions. Strategies need to be developed that inform and contextualise the purchase rationale for consumers. This means providing lasting impressions that enable consumers to understand the circumstances in which purchase of a particular product/brand should be made once a decision has been made to purchase from the product category. Here the priorities are to communicate messages that will encourage consumers to trust and bestow expertise on the product/brand that is offered.

Advertising to engage

Advertising has traditionally been used to develop brand identities by stimulating awareness and perception. Marketing communications have evolved such that identity and values are insufficient. The growth of direct marketing and one-to-one, preferably interactive, communications have become paramount, and marketing budgets have swung more towards establishing a call-to-action, a behaviour rather than attitudinal response. The issue that remains is what is the role for advertising and what strategies should be used? One approach would be to maintain current advertising strategies on the grounds that awareness and perception are always going to be key factors. The other extreme approach would be to call for advertising to be used solely for direct-response work. Neither of these two options seems appropriate or viable in the twenty-first century.

In an age where values and response are both necessary ingredients for effective overall communication, advertising strategy in the future will probably need to be based on engagement. Customers will want to engage with the values offered by a brand that are significant to them individually. However, there will also be a need to engage with them at a behavioural level and to encourage them to want to respond to the advertising. Advertising strategy should therefore reflect a brand's context and be adjusted according to the required level of engagement regarding identity development and the required level of behavioural response. Advertising will no longer be able to rightly assume the lead role in a campaign and will be used according to the engagement needs of, first, the audience, second, the brand, and third, the communication industry, in that order.

> Advertising strategy should reflect a brand's context.

ViewPoint 16.7 Ding Dong attacking advertising

Following BSkyB's share purchase of 18 per cent of ITV in 2007 a dispute erupted with its arch rival Virgin Media. Virgin claimed it was a move designed to prevent them from buying the organisation. Not long after this Sky and Virgin agreed to disagree about a fee for the Sky Basics TV package, which led to those channels being unavailable to Virgin Media viewers.

The dispute has two sides. Sky claim the dispute is about Virgin's refusal to pay the asking price to continue carrying the channels. Virgin on the other hand believe that Sky is trying to compel Virgin's customers into switching providers by denying them access to the basic channels (BBC).

Since then the two companies entered into a public spat and used advertising to make allegations and claims designed to inform the public of the real situation as each side saw it.

For example, Virgin Media used a print campaign to compare the TV, broadband and phone services of the two companies. Called 'The Real Deal' the campaign sought to show their superior service. However, Sky brought six complaints about the ads, claiming them as misleading or untrue. These were upheld by the Advertising Standards Authority (Sweney, 2007).

In November 2007 Virgin announced that it was to cease its campaign against Sky, after having spent £32 million on the advertising. James Kidd, Managing Director of Marketing at Virgin Media is reported to have said 'There's no point in spending any more time or money whacking the crap out of each other' (Jones, 2007).

Sources: BBC (2007); Jones (2007); and Sweney (2007).

Question
What value might Virgin have generated from this £32 million spend?

Task
Find two other brands that have been engaged in a public spat and what was the outcome?

Cohen (2003) refers to the gap between advertising used to develop brand identity and the need to encourage audience responses. He develops an OPC model where O refers to the offer, P to the product and C to the call-to-action. Advertising therefore should attempt to bring these elements together in a single, significant presentation. Key to his model is the brand/response (B/R) ratio, which relates to the relative levels of emphasis on the brand and response elements. The ratio refers to a line or spectrum of effects between these two elements. Traditional brand-based advertising equates with a B/R of 100/0 and direct response has a B/R of 0/100 where the sole intention is to maximise the likelihood of a response. The strategic claim behind this approach may be in need of elaboration to be operationally robust, but the principle of moving the focus of advertising strategy to one that recognises the need to incorporate brand experiences is essentially sound.

Summary

In order to help consolidate your understanding of advertising strategy, here are the key points summarised against each of the learning objectives:

1. Consider the role advertising plays in both consumer and business-to-business markets.

The role of advertising in most marketing communications campaigns is to engage audiences. Engagement is enabled either by informing, changing perceptions and building brand values or by encouraging a change in behaviour.

Advertising can reach huge audiences with simple messages that present opportunities to allow receivers to understand what a product is, what its primary function is and how it relates to all the other similar products. This is the main function of advertising: to communicate with specific audiences. These audiences may be consumer- or organisation-based, but wherever they are located the prime objective is to build or maintain awareness of a product or an organisation.

2. Appraise the use of emotion in advertising and consider concepts associated with shock advertising.

Advertising does not always work through rational information processing. Feelings and emotions play an important role, especially when advertising is used to build awareness levels and brand strength.

Audiences are offended by shock advertising because there is 'norm violation, encompassing transgressions of law or custom, breaches of a moral or social code, or things that outrage the moral or physical senses', for example gratuitous violence and disgusting images. The main reason for using a shock advertising strategy is that it is a good way to secure an audience's attention and achieve a longer-lasting impact than through traditional messages and attention-getting devices.

3. Explain the principal frameworks by which advertising is thought to influence individuals.

The hierarchy of effects frameworks (e.g. AIDA), were the first attempts to explain how advertising works. The sequential nature of these early interpretations was attractive because they were easy to comprehend, neatly mirrored the purchase decision process and provided a base upon which campaign goals were later assigned (Dagmar). However, as our knowledge of buyer behaviour increased and as the significance of the USP declined so these hierarchy of effects models also declined in terms of our understanding about advertising. Now they are insignificant and are no longer used as appropriate interpretations of how advertising works.

In their place a number of new frameworks and explanations have arisen, all of which claim to reflect practice. In other words these new theories about how advertising works are a reflection of practice, of the way advertising is considered to work, or at least used by advertising agencies and interpreted by marketing research agencies. The first of these information processing models were developed by O'Malley (1991) and Hall (1992) and they suggest that there are four main advertising frameworks: persuasion, sales, salience and involvement.

4. Appraise the strong and weak theories of advertising.

The strong theory of advertising reflects the persuasion concept, and has high credibility when used with new brands. However, the contrasting view is that advertising should be regarded as a means of defending customers' purchase decisions and for protecting markets, not building them. Reality suggests that the majority of advertising cannot claim to be of significant value to most people and that the strong and the weak theories are equally applicable, although not at the same time nor in the same context.

5. Consider ways in which advertising can be used strategically.

Advertising, once considered the prime form of mass persuasion, is now subject to many different views. Those who are sceptical of advertising's power to persuade consumers to change their purchasing habits now explore ideas concerning advertising's strategic role in reinforcing brand messages and repositioning brands.

The FCB and Rossiter–Percy grids represent formalised attempts to interpret the strategic use of advertising. Intended to provide agencies with a method that might ensure consistency, meaning and value with respect to their clients' brands, these are no longer considered by agencies to be sufficiently flexible, rigorous or representative of how contemporary advertising performs.

A more current perspective of advertising strategy suggests that advertising should become more engaged with the customer's experience of the brand and not be rooted just in the development of brand values.

6. Examine ideas concerning the use of advertising to engage audiences.

In an age where values and response are both necessary ingredients for effective overall communication, future advertising strategy will probably need to be based on engagement. Advertising strategy should therefore reflect a brand's context and be adjusted according to the required level of engagement regarding identity development and the required level of behavioural response. Advertising will no longer be able to rightly assume the lead role in a campaign and will be used according to the engagement needs of, first, the audience, second, the brand, and third, the communication industry, in that order.

Review questions

1. Find two advertisements and write notes explaining how they depict the roles of advertising.
2. Write brief notes outlining the difference between absolute and relative costs.
3. Name the three elements in advertising, identified by Dahl *et al.* (2003), which cause audiences to be offended. Find an example of each.
4. What are the essential differences between the involvement and salience frameworks of advertising? Find four advertisements (other than those described in the text) that are examples of these two approaches.
5. Write a short presentation explaining the differences between the strong and weak theories of advertising.
6. Select an organisation of your choice and find three ads it has used recently. Are the ads predominantly trying to persuade audiences or are they designed to reinforce brand values?
7. Evaluate the contribution of Prue's alphabetical model of advertising.
8. Draw the FCB grid and place on it the following product categories: shampoo, life assurance, sports cars, kitchen towels, box of chocolates.
9. Prepare a report explaining the differences between the Rossiter–Percy and FCB grids.
10. Write brief notes outlining the strategic role advertising plays within an organisation's overall promotional activities.

MiniCase: Tapping into a new zeitgeist: women consumers, lifestyle trends and the *Red* Experience

Lorna Stevens: University of Ulster

In 1998, EMAP Elan launched a new woman's magazine called *Red* onto the already crowded UK women's monthly magazine market. The decision was based on the EMAP Elan's belief that there was an emerging sensibility in women in their thirties and forties that was not being catered for. This new 'zeitgeist' (spirit of the age) was the notion that age was a state of mind, and that contemporary women were taking youthful values and behaviours into their 30s and beyond. These 'middle-youth' women wanted a lively and vibrant magazine that helped them escape from their busy, day-to-day lives. EMAP Elan would offer women readers 'the precious experience of time to oneself' in a 'time poor world' (Rainey et al., 1999).

The challenge for the *Red* team was to entice women in their 30s and 40s to buy the new magazine, and to do so they reckoned they would need to stress the pleasurable *experience* of consuming it. The advertising campaign revolved around three television ads, called 'Defining Moments', 'The Strip' and 'Me-Time'. Each of these advertisements made a direct appeal to the experiential aspects of consumption, namely the emotions and sensory feelings associated with the act of consumption (Holbrook and Hirschman, 1982).

Women's monthly magazines, while they are undeniably rich in information and advice for women, also have very strong experiential appeals for women. The editorial team at *Red* was convinced that women's magazines needed to provide an oasis of calm and pleasure in the midst of 'time-poor' everyday lives. Instead of addressing women in their 30s and 40s according to their numerous roles in life, then, the *Red* team decided that their unique proposition would be to focus on *Red* magazine as a self-indulgent, pleasurable *experience* that enabled women consumers to take time out from the demands of their daily, juggling lives. The name '*Red*' was chosen because it was considered 'quite sexy, quite glamorous, quite modern' (Anne-Marie Lavin, EMAP Elan). It also conjures up passion, warmth, feistiness, challenge, readability and simplicity. The focus of the marketing strategy would be on attitude and lifestyle, encapsulated by the core concept '*Red* Time is Me Time'.

The first television ad, 'Defining Moments' comprised a series of fleeting and evocative images, filmed in black-and-white, of a woman at work and at play, with soothing, classical music in the background. Its emphasis was on lifestyle rather than demographics. A female voiceover relates the following lines as the various scenes unfold:

'If you think life's too short for communal changing rooms/If you're madly in love with your garden/If you buy things and hide the receipts/If you're having an affair, or not/If you've grown up without growing old/And you don't want to have it all, you just want to have what you want/Then it's probably time you saw *Red*.

The ad has an almost documentary quality as we see a quick succession of scenes from the woman's life. She is slim and attractive, dressed simply in a white shirt and dark trousers. We see her dining with friends, out of doors with her red setter dog; driving her car; dancing in a glamorous cocktail dress. We see her pensively looking out the window at bare winter branches, and a man leaving the house – an illicit lover or a devoted husband? Then we see her at a drawing board, talking on the phone; having her back scrubbed in a bath tub; on a bicycle with a child. The final image is the front cover of *Red*'s first issue, with the caption 'Go on, treat yourself.'

The advertisement's attractive and evocative cinematic style and its romantic images are clearly designed to appeal to women consumers' senses and emotions. By the end of the ad nothing is known about the magazine's contents, but the ad is designed to enable the target market to recognise aspects of themselves in the series of so-called 'defining moments'. Anne-Marie Lavin, the then marketing manager of *Red*, observes: 'I think you can launch a magazine quite easily, but it's more difficult to launch a brand, and everything that we do – and that's everything in the magazine used to market it – reflects those values.'

The second advertisement in the series is called 'The Strip', which was launched a year after 'Defining Moments'. This ad caused considerable debate at its inception stage, as it shows a woman doing a striptease. The *Red* team were somewhat anxious about this concept, and were worried that if the ad was too sexually suggestive it might alienate the target market. They therefore worked closely with the ad agency to ensure that the ad portrayed the woman in a humorous way, as a likeable, human subject, rather than an objectified sex object.

An attractive 30-something woman enters a dark room wearing a black coat and high-heeled shoes. She switches on a lamp, and picks up a red note from the console table. Grinning, she tosses the note away from her, and her bag. Next she slowly removes her coat, shoulder by shoulder, and we realise she is doing a striptease. A woman's smoky voice sings *'I dreamt that I was chasing – the monster out of me'*. There are several cream sofas in the room, with scarlet cushions. The woman strikes various exaggerated, humorous poses as she gradually strips off to her underwear. At one point she kicks off one of her shoes, and it flies through the air, knocking over a tall vase of white lilies. She pulls a face, but continues to smile. We notice a bright green toy on the floor behind her. One of her stockings drifts onto a console table beside a framed photograph of a man, and she blows an exaggerated kiss at it. She walks over towards a sofa, tripping over the soft toy as she does so. She laughs and makes a face at herself in the mirror, and snatches some clothing from the back of the sofa. The next scene is of her reclining on the cream sofa, surrounded by rich red cushions, dressed in tracksuit bottoms and a fleecy top, smiling and reading a copy of *Red* magazine. A woman's voice now says *'Red* magazine – drop everything'*, underlining the humour that pervades the ad. Despite its somewhat risky and indeed risqué marketing strategy, the ad worked, and indeed sales of the magazine increased by 30,000 on the previous month.

The third advertisement, 'Me-Time', was launched a year after 'The Strip'. This ad was very different from the two previous ads, but once again there was a clear focus on the concept of 'me-time'. The ad focuses on ideal reading scenarios, and gives centre stage to a red sofa, which is used in every frame in the ad to symbolise the concept of 'me-time'. An elegant scarlet sofa is shown in a variety of idyllic places: a lush, flower-filled summer meadow, complete with butterflies; a sandy beach by moonlight; the sofa surrounded by a circle of candles; a sunny Mediterranean terrace; a rugged, mountain landscape overlooking a still lake, against a backdrop of a blue and white streaked sky. The final image is of a woman sitting on the sofa in an Italianate-style terrace, complete with elegant columns, urns and a water fountain. She sits, her bare feet drawn up beside her, absorbed in a copy of *Red* magazine,

smiling. At the end of the ad a woman's voice says '*Red* magazine – your sofa awaits.' We are then shown the current issue of *Red*, against a luxurious red satin background, underlining its magical and precious qualities, and its associations with sensuous pleasure and relaxation. 'Your sofa awaits' clearly recalls the famous line from the Cinderella fairytale 'Your carriage awaits'. And just as a pumpkin can become a glass carriage, a sofa can become a magic carpet when combined with a very special ingredient, *Red* magazine. In short, it can carry its readers off to better places!

The *Red* marketing campaign was a great success: against the odds, the magazine was able to squeeze its way into the crowded women's magazine market, and more importantly, hold its own there, a feat it has continued to perform in the 10 years since its launch. Much of *Red*'s success is down to the clear focus of EMAP Elan's marketing strategy, and its memorable TV ads, all of which were based on the concept of 'me-time'. The *Red* case is testimony to the fact that consumers are very receptive to ads that appeal to their emotions, feelings and senses. *Red* magazine's development team recognised that it was not just about getting the contents of the magazine right; it was about creating the right ambiance around the magazine, and developing a strong and appealing brand image and personality for *Red*. It was also about understanding its market, and positioning the brand in such a way as to reflect current lifestyle trends. By creating a brand that encapsulated the notion of me-time and self-indulgence, *Red* appealed to 'middle-youth' women in their 30s and 40s who wanted a lively and pleasurable read, *and* the chance to put their feet up and indulge in some 'me-time'!

MiniCase questions

1. Can you think of other marketing campaigns that have recognised a new consumer trend or 'zeitgeist' and developed their campaign around this?
2. Do you think that experiential appeals have become more commonplace than informational ones in advertising? If so, why do you think this is the case?
3. The women's magazine market is holding its own in the face of increased competition from the Internet, TV and newspapers, and in fact magazine readership is rising, with Keynote predicting that this trend will continue. Why do you think women's magazines continue to appeal to women?

References

Ambler, T. (1998) Myths about the mind: time to end some popular beliefs about how advertising works. *International Journal of Advertising*, **17**, 501–9.

BBC (2007) *Q&A: Sky and Virgin Media TV row*, 24 May. Retrieved from http://news.bbc.co.uk/1/hi/business/6390655.stm.

Bewick, M. (2006) Pushing the boundaries. *The Marketer*, September, 25.

Cohen, A. (2003) Closing the brand/response gap. *Admap*, (September), 20–2.

Corke, S. and Heath, R.G. (2004) The hidden power of newspaper advertising. *Media Research Group Conference*, Madrid, (November).

Dahl, D.W., Frankenberger, K.D. and Manchanda, R.V. (2003) Does it pay to shock? Reactions to shocking and nonshocking advertising content among university students. *Journal of Advertising Research*, **43**(3) (September), 268–81.

Dichter, E. (1966) How word-of-mouth advertising works. *Harvard Business Review*, **44** (November/December), 147–66.

Ehrenberg, A.S.C. (1974) Repetitive advertising and the consumer. *Journal of Advertising Research*, **14** (April), 25–34.

Ehrenberg, A.S.C. (1988) *Repeat Buying*, 2nd edn. London: Charles Griffin.

Ehrenberg, A.S.C. (1997) How do consumers come to buy a new brand? *Admap* (March), 20–4.

Hall, M. (1992) Using advertising frameworks. *Admap* (March), 17–21.

Heath, R. and Feldwick, P. (2007) 50 years using the wrong model of TV advertising. *Admap*, (March), 36–8.

Jones, G. (2008) Handset manufacturers plot response to iPhone. *Marketing*, 13 February, 1.

Jones, J.P. (1991) Over-promise and under-delivery. *Marketing and Research Today* (November), 195–203.

Jones, G. (2007) Virgin Media pulls ads attacking rival Sky service. *Marketing*, 7 November, 3.

Joyce, T. (1991) Models of the advertising process. *Marketing and Research Today* (November), 205–12.

Krugman, H.E. (1971) Brain wave measurement of media involvement. *Journal of Advertising*, **11**(1), 3–9.

O'Malley, D. (1991) Sales without salience? *Admap* (September), 36–9.

Prue, T. (1998) An all-embracing theory of how advertising works? *Admap* (February), 18–23.

Rossiter, J.R. and Percy, L. (1997) *Advertising Communications & Promotion Management*, 2nd edn. New York: McGraw-Hill.

Rossiter, J.R., Percy, L. and Donovan, R.J. (1991) A better advertising planning grid. *Journal of Advertising Research* (October/November), 11–21.

Sweney, M. (2006) A successful ad campaign has revived the fortunes of Marks & Spencer. *The Guardian*, Monday, 6 November. Retrieved 15 January 2008 from www.guardian.co.uk/retail/story/0,,1940204,00.html.

Sweney, M. (2007) Sky wins ad wrangle with Virgin. *The Guardian*, 1 August. Retrieved 4 December 2007 from http://www.guardian.co.uk/media/2007/aug/01/advertising.news.

Thompson, M., Neal, J., Threadgould, S. and Lema Trillo, S. (2006) Marks & Spencer, This is not just advertising, this is M&S advertising: how confident communications helped restore public confidence in M&S. *Institute of Practitioners in Advertising*, www.ipa.co.uk, Retrieved 25 September 2007 from www.warc.com.

Tiltman, D. (2008) People's choice: most irritating ads of 2007. *Marketing*, 8 January. Available at www.brandrepublic.com/Marketing/News/774978/Peoples-choice-irritating-ads-2007/.

Vakratsas, D. and Ambler, T. (1999) How advertising works: what do we really know? *Journal of Marketing*, **63** (January), 26–43.

Vaughn, R. (1980) How advertising works: a planning model. *Journal of Advertising Research* (October), 27–33.

Venkat, R. and Abi-Hanna, N. (1995) *Effectiveness of Visually Shocking Advertisements: Is it Context Dependent?* Administrative Science Association of Canada Proceedings, **16**(3), 139–46.

Chapter 27
Media planning and behaviour: delivering the message

Media planning is essentially a selection and scheduling exercise. The selection concerns the choice of media vehicles to carry the message on behalf of the advertiser. With media fragmentation, audiences are switching between media with greater regularity, which impacts on media scheduling. Decisions regarding the number of occasions, timing and duration that a message is exposed, in the selected vehicles, to the target audience have become increasingly critical.

Aims and learning objectives

The aims of this chapter are to introduce the fundamental elements of media planning and to set out some of the issues facing media planners.

The learning objectives of this chapter are to:

1. explain the role of the media planner and highlight the impact of media and audience fragmentation;
2. consider various theories concerning the content of different media and related media switching behaviours;
3. examine the key concepts used in media selection: reach and cover, frequency, duplication, rating points and CPT;
4. appreciate the concept of repetition and the debate concerning effective frequency and recency planning;
5. understand the concepts of effectiveness and efficiency when applied to media selection decisions;
6. introduce media source effects as an important factor in the selection and timing of advertising in magazines and television programmes;
7. explore the different ways in which advertisements can be scheduled.

For an applied interpretation see Yasmin Sekhon's MiniCase entitled *Targeting the 'brown pound' – an untapped market* at the end of this chapter.

Introduction

Once a message has been created and agreed, a media plan should be determined. The aim of the media plan is to devise an optimum route for the delivery of a message to the target audience. This function is normally undertaken by specialists, either as part of a full-service advertising agency or as a media independent whose primary function is to buy air time or space from media owners (e.g. television contractors or magazine publishers) on behalf of their clients, the advertisers. This traditional role has changed since the mid 1990s, and many media independents now provide consultancy services, particularly at the strategic level, plus planning and media research and auditing services.

> The aim of the media plan is to devise an optimum route for the delivery of a message.

Media departments are responsible for two main functions. These are to 'plan' and to 'buy' time and space in appropriate media vehicles. There is a third task – to monitor a media schedule once it has been bought – but this is a function of buying. Planners define the target audience and choose the type of medium. Buyers choose programmes, frequencies, spots and distribution and assemble a multichannel schedule (Armstrong, 1993). In the past the media planner has been pre-eminent, but the role of the buyer is changing. Some feel the role of the buyer is in the ascendancy, but there are others who feel that the role is capable of increased automation and that many software packages already fulfil many functions of the media buyer. Such a move has implications for the type of person recruited. In the United States, for example, many semi-skilled people have been recruited on a part-time basis to do many parts of the traditional media planner's job.

As mentioned earlier, media planning is essentially a selection and scheduling exercise. The selection refers to the choice of media vehicles to carry the message on behalf of the advertiser. Scheduling refers to the number of occasions, timing and duration that a message is exposed, in the selected vehicles, to the target audience. However, there are several factors that complicate these seemingly straightforward tasks. First, the variety of available media is huge and increasing rapidly. This is referred to as media fragmentation. Second, the characteristics of the target audience are changing equally quickly. This is referred to as audience fragmentation. Both these fragmentation issues are discussed later in this chapter. The job of the media planner is complicated by one further element: money. Clients have restricted financial resources and require the media planner to create a schedule that delivers their messages not only effectively but also efficiently, which means within the parameters of the available budget.

> Scheduling refers to the number of occasions, timing and duration that a message is exposed.

The task of the media planner, therefore, is to deliver advertising messages through a selection of media that match the viewing, reading or search habits of the target audience at the lowest possible cost. In order for these tasks to be accomplished, three sets of decisions need to be made about the choice of media, vehicles and schedules.

Decisions about the choice of media are complex. While choosing a single one is reasonably straightforward, choosing media in combination and attempting to generate synergistic effects is far from easy. Advances in technology have made media planning a much faster, more accurate process, one that is now more flexible and capable of adjusting to fast-changing market conditions.

One of the key tasks of the media planner is to decide which combination of vehicles should be selected to carry the message to the target audience. In addition, McLuhan (1966) said that the medium is the message, that is, the choice of medium (or vehicle) says something about the brand and the message itself. He went on to say that the medium is the *massage*, as each medium massages the recipient in different ways and so contributes to learning in different ways. For example, Krugman (1965) hypothesised that television advertising washes over individuals. He said that viewers, rather than participate actively with

> The medium is the *massage*.

television advertisements, allow learning to occur passively. In contrast, magazine advertising requires active participation if learning is to occur. Today, online and interactive advertising actively promotes involvement and participation.

The various media depicted in Table 27.1 have wide-ranging characteristics. These, and the characteristics of the target audience, should be considered when deciding on the optimal media mix. It should be clear that simply deciding on which media to use is fraught with difficulties, let alone deciding on the optimal combination – how much of each media should be used – before even considering the cost implications.

Table 27.1 A summary of media characteristics

Type of media	Strengths	Weaknesses
Print		
Newspapers	Wide reach High coverage Low costs Very flexible Short lead times Speed of consumption controlled by reader	Short lifespan Advertisements get little exposure Relatively poor reproduction, gives poor impact Low attention-getting properties
Magazines	High-quality reproduction that allows high impact Specific and specialised target audiences High readership levels Longevity High levels of information can be delivered	Long lead times Visual dimension only Slow build-up of impact Moderate costs
Television	Flexible format, uses sight, movement and sound High prestige High reach Mass coverage Low relative cost, so very efficient	High level of repetition necessary Short message life High absolute costs Clutter Increasing level of fragmentation (potentially)
Radio	Selective audience, e.g. local Low costs (absolute, relative and production) Flexible Can involve listeners	Lacks impact Audio dimension only Difficult to get audience attention Low prestige
Outdoor	High reach High frequency Low relative costs Good coverage as a support medium Location-oriented	Poor image (but improving) Long production time Difficult to measure
Digital media	High level of interaction Immediate response possible Tight targeting Low absolute and relative costs Flexible and easy to update Measurable	Segment-specific Slow development of infrastructure High user set-up costs Transaction security issues
Transport	High length of exposure Low costs Local orientation	Poor coverage Segment-specific (travellers) Clutter
In-store POP	High attention-getting properties Persuasive Low costs Flexible	Segment-specific (shoppers) Prone to damage and confusion Clutter

Media switching behaviour

The range of media has grown dramatically in the past 30 years and is continuing to grow as technology, in particular, advances. However, even before digital media started to change the media landscape, researchers had recognised that different media have different capabilities and that media were not completely interchangeable. In other words, different tasks can be accomplished more effectively using particular media. This implies that there is a spectrum of media depending on the content they carry.

Daft and Lengel (1984) were the first to propose that this content issue concerned the richness of the information conveyed through each medium. As a result, the tasks facing managers should be considered according to the degree of fit with the most appropriate media based on the richness of the information. Communication media help resolve ambiguity and facilitate understanding in different ways and to different degrees. They established that there were four main criteria that determined what level of richness a medium possessed:

> The tasks facing managers should be considered according to the degree of fit with the most appropriate media based on the richness of the information.

- the availability of instant feedback;
- the capacity to transmit multiple cues;
- the use of natural language;
- the degree of personal focus.

Media richness theory (MRT) holds that there is a hierarchy or spectrum of media ranging from personal or face-to-face encounters as the richest media through to single sheets of text-based information as lean media at the other end. Rich media facilitate feedback, dialogue iteration and an expression of personal cues such as tone of voice, body language and eye contact that in turn help establish a personal connection. In descending order of richness the other media are telephone, email, letter, note, memo, special report, fliers and bulletins. At this end of the richness scale numeric and formal written communication is slow, often visually limited and impersonal.

> Rich media facilitate feedback, dialogue iteration and an expression of personal cues.

MRT suggests that rich media reduce ambiguity more effectively than others, but are more resource-intensive than lean media. If rich media allow for more complex and difficult communications, then lean media are more cost-effective for simple or routine communications. McGrath and Hollingshead (1993) developed a matrix showing the levels of richness required to perform certain tasks successfully and efficiently. Their media richness grid identifies the level of fit between the information richness requirements of the tasks and the information richness capacity of the media (see Table 27.2).

Social influence theory (SIT) was developed by Fulk *et al.* (1990). This is intended to complement MRT as it also assumes that the relatively objective features of media do influence how individuals perceive and use media. However, these researchers argue that SIT has a strong social orientation because different media properties (such as ability to transmit richness) are subjective and are influenced by attitudes, statements and the behaviour of others. This approach recognises that members of groups influence other people in terms of their perceptions of different media. The main difference between MRT and SIT is that MRT identifies rich media as inefficient for simple or routine communication whereas SIT suggests rich media can be just as appropriate for simple messages as it is for ambiguous communication.

A third approach, the technology acceptance model (TAM) relates to the utility and convenience a medium offers. The perceived usefulness and perceived ease of use are regarded as the main issues that are considered when selecting media (King and Xia, 1997). Perceived usefulness refers to the user's subjective assessment

> The technology acceptance model (TAM) relates to the utility and convenience a medium offers.

Table 27.2 Media richness grid

	Computer text systems	Audio systems	Video systems	Face-to-face communication
Generating ideas and plans	Good fit	Marginal fit: medium too resource-intense	Poor fit: medium too resource-intense	Poor fit: medium too resource-intense
Choosing correct answer: intellective tasks	Marginal fit: medium too constrained	Good fit	Good fit	Poor fit: medium too resource-intense
Choosing preferred answer: judgement tasks	Poor fit: medium too constrained	Good fit	Good fit	Marginal fit: medium too resource-intense
Negotiating conflicts of interest	Poor fit: medium too constrained	Poor fit: medium too constrained	Marginal fit: medium too constrained	Good fit

Source: Adapted from McGrath and Hollingshead (1993).

Table 27.3 Factors influencing the choice of technology

Factor	Explanation
Experience and familiarity	With virtual operations the amount of experience using a particular interactive medium
Permanence	The degree to which users need an historical record of team interactions or decisions
Symbolic meaning	The subjective meanings attached to the use of a particular medium
Time constraints	The amount of time available to the user to use a medium in order to execute their tasks
Access to technology and/or support	The number of and access to available media influences media choice

that using a specific computer application will improve their job performance. Perceived ease of use addresses the degree to which a user expects the identified application to be free of effort.

Influential factors for media selection

In addition to these richness, social and utility issues of media selection, other factors are also important. Duarte and Snyder (2001) propose a list of factors influencing technology selection (see Table 27.3).

Switching behaviour

It is clear that different media have different properties and that people switch between media according to their tasks, social environment, familiarity and access to different media. What is important, therefore, is to understand switching behaviour and the decision-making process that people use. Decisions are made through *rational* and *systematic* processes or alternatively there are unaccountable factors that 'bound' decision-making. The classic, eight-stage rational–linear decision-making model (situation analysis, objectives setting, through to choosing and

Table 27.4 Reasons for moving to richer or leaner media

Movement	Reasons
Towards a richer medium	Message complexity
	Increased comfort
	Time pressure
	Timely discussion required
	Need to rest from computer-based medium
Towards a leaner medium	Desire for written record
	Reducing cost
	Convenience (of being asynchronous or distant)
	Share individual written work (attachment)
	External pressure or requirement

evaluating alternatives, making the decisions, evaluation and consequences) is well known and its criticisms well documented. Simon (1972, 1987) showed that people make decisions within 'bounded rationality', performing limited searches and accepting the first acceptable alternative, what is regarded as 'satisficing behaviour'.

Srinavasan (1996) developed a satisfaction–loyalty curve whereby an individual's level of satisfaction is the biggest determinant of their switching behaviour. As their satisfaction increases, so does loyalty, and the reverse is equally true. For each person there is a point at which decreasing satisfaction intersects with the decreasing loyalty levels. This is the point at which switching occurs and the current brand is abandoned in favour of another.

> For each person there is a point at which decreasing satisfaction intersects with the decreasing loyalty levels.

Keaveney (1995) distinguishes between involuntary, simple and complex switching behaviours. Involuntary switching may be due to factors beyond an individual consumer's control (e.g. business liquidated), whereas simple switching is characterised by individual events where consumers can identify a single incident or factor causing the switch, for example a price change. Complex switching behaviour occurs when a customer's loyalty has decreased due to a variety of factors, which might include core product failure, price changes and poor service. It should be noted that switching is very often a routine behaviour influenced by the expectations of the context in which the media decision is made. For example, when sending text-based documents to team members, most people would select email and use file attachments.

As a final comment on media switching behaviour it is useful to return to MRT and to consider the reasons why individuals move towards rich or lean media. These are set out in Table 27.4. Therefore, movement between media is based on a range of criteria and will vary according to the context and individual skills and preferences.

Vehicle selection

The discussion so far has explored unpaid media, and increasingly the Internet and the use of email communications fit this range. However, organisations need to use media that are owned by others in order to convey their messages. These paid-for media have particular characteristics and ability to deliver rich or lean content. The discussion now moves on to consider different paid-for media and the ways in which organisations develop a media mix to meet their communications needs.

Increasingly, organisations are required to prove how advertising adds value to the bottom line. While this is not a new question, it is one that is being asked more often and in such a way that answers are required. As advertisers attempt to demonstrate effectiveness, contribution and return on investment, senior managers are increasingly haunted by questions concerning the choice of media, how much should be spent on message delivery and how financial resources are to be allocated in a multichannel environment.

ViewPoint 27.1 Media vehicles for 'You & Us'

When UBS launched their 'You & Us' global campaign, advertising played an important role in communicating what UBS stands for to its clients. The aim was to help support their efforts to build stronger client relationships, and help them to make more confident financial decisions, hence the phrase 'You & Us'. With television and print their aim was to increase relevance in specific markets. Regional variations are also being created.

The television spot, titled 'Everywhere', emphasises the global/personal dimension and follows meetings between two people that occur in interesting, unusual locations around the world. This speaks of the benefits that accrue from being able to access the resources of a global financial firm through a strong, personal relationship.

The advertising focuses on two key themes: globality and understanding. Both strands of communication support the core message of proactively finding solutions to our customers' needs, but each does so in a slightly different way that makes the overall message accessible.

The print advertising reflects the visual tones and style used in the television work, and places an increased graphic emphasis on 'You & Us'. Importantly, the new press ads were designed to enable the reader to project themselves into the situation depicted, thus fostering empathy.

In order to deliver these messages a media plan was established. This set out the specific types of media the campaign was to use and where possible certain types of media and specific vehicles. One of the first

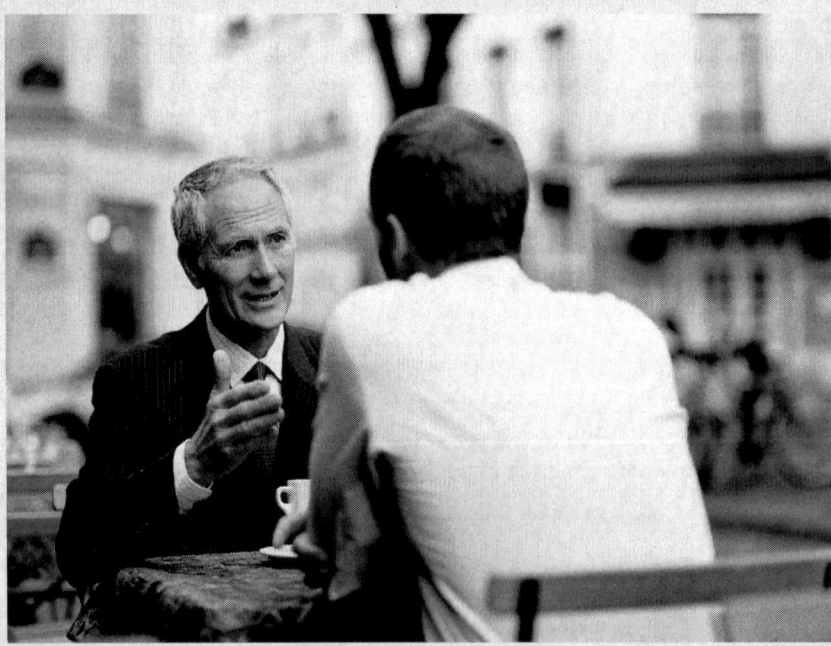

Exhibit 27.1 Although this is not an actual shot used by UBS, this picture represents the essence of the core message that the 'You & Us' campaign sought to deliver. See the UBS web site for actual pictures used in their campaign
© Michael Prince/Corbis.

decisions was whether television, a class of media, had a role to play. Once the answer was yes, particular television channels in the target countries, such as the USA, UK, Germany, France, Italy and in Asia were selected. This was then followed by the selection of print and outdoor media and particular vehicles were then determined.

Question
Why do you believe UBS used television in order to reach high net worth individuals and businesses?

Task
Visit the site www.ubs.com and follow the links through 'About Us' and then 'You & Us'. View the campaign detail and see the television and print ads. Make notes on what impresses you and what you might have done differently.

Management's attention towards media decision-making has increased as the media have become more visible and significantly more important. For example, Brech (1999) reports that companies need to make choices about the split between the Internet, mass media, digital TV, outdoor and print media. Companies such as BT, IKEA and ScottishPower need to use media strategically in order that they reach the right audience, in the right context, at the right time and at an acceptable cost. To help organisations achieve these goals a variety of approaches have been adopted. For example, New PHD is an agency retained by BT to advise about strategic (media) planning and budget allocation. However, ZenithOptimedia implements decisions for press and radio and the Allmond Partnership manages television and cinema, while Outdoor Connections handles poster-buying. This division provides objectivity, reduces partisan approaches and can deliver more effective media plans. Cost per response is certainly one way of measuring effectiveness, but the communication impact, or share of mind, is also important. There has also been a move away from volume of media to one where media decisions are made by looking at media in the context of the brand's total communications.

> Cost per response is certainly one way of measuring effectiveness.

A further problem facing clients and media concern the integrated media experience. For a long time, some organisations have used above-the-line media to reach audiences of 20 million people. With fragmented media it is difficult to generate consistent levels and types of impact. Increasingly, media management is being outsourced so there are fewer in-house areas of expertise. All this means that, to forge appropriate solutions, advertisers and media agencies need to work closely together so that the relationship becomes so close that it acts more as an extension to the marketing department. Decisions regarding which vehicles are to carry an advertiser's message depend on an understanding of a number of concepts: reach and coverage, frequency, gross rating points, effective frequency, efficiency and media source effects.

Media planning concepts

There are several fundamental concepts that underpin the way in which traditional media should be selected and included in the media plan. These are reach, frequency, gross rating points, duplication and effective frequency.

Reach and coverage

Reach refers to the percentage of the target audience exposed to a message at least once during the relevant time period. Where 80 per cent of the target audience has been exposed to a message, the figure is expressed as an '80 reach'.

Coverage, a term often used for reach, should not be confused or used in place of reach. Coverage refers to the size of a potential audience that might be exposed to a particular media vehicle. For media planners, therefore, coverage (the size of the target audience) is very important. Reach will always be lower than coverage, as it is impossible to reach 100 per cent of a target population (the universe).

Building reach within a target audience is relatively easy, as the planner needs to select a range of different media vehicles. This will enable different people in the target audience to have an opportunity to see the media vehicle. However, there will come a point when it becomes more difficult to reach people who have not been exposed. As more vehicles are added, so repetition levels (the number of people who have seen the advertisement more than once) also increase.

Frequency

> Frequency refers to the number of times a member of the target audience is exposed to a media vehicle.

Frequency refers to the number of times a member of the target audience is exposed to a media vehicle (not the advertisement) during the relevant time period. It has been stated that targets must be exposed to the media vehicle, but to say that a target has seen an advertisement simply because they have been exposed to the vehicle is incorrect. For example, certain viewers hop around the channels as a commercial break starts. This has been referred to as 'channel grazing' by Lloyd and Clancy (1991). Individuals have different capacities to learn and to forget, and how much of a magazine does a reader have to consume to be counted as having read an advertisement? These questions are still largely unanswered, so media planners have adopted an easier and more consistent measure – opportunities to see (OTS).

This is an important point. The stated frequency level in any media plan will always be greater than the advertisement exposure rate. The term OTS is used to express the reach of a media vehicle rather than the actual exposure of an advertisement. However, a high OTS could be generated by one of two different events. First, a large number of the target audience are exposed once (high reach) or second, a small number are exposed several times (high frequency).

This then raises the first major issue. As all campaigns are restricted by time and budget limitations, advertisers have to trade off reach against frequency. It is impossible to maximise both elements within a fixed budget and set period of time.

ViewPoint 27.2 Haier than the weather

Haier, the major Chinese global manufacturer of consumer durables, uses television in China to reach its main audiences. In a country where it is estimated that over 250 million Chinese families watch CCTV programmes, Haier sponsors the weather forecast, which is the highest-rated programme in China. Guaranteeing large audiences on a repeat basis ensures Haier achieves high OTS based on a large frequency.

Source: Adapted from unpublished student coursework and www.zaobao.com/.

Question

As there is little natural fit between Haier and the weather forecast is this a good use of marketing communications?

Task

Pick a leading brand in a country of your choice and find out if it is involved in any sponsorship arrangements. If they are, what do you think the goal might be, reach or frequency, or indeed something else?

To launch a new product, it has been established that a wide number of people within the target audience need to become aware of the product's existence and its salient attributes or benefits. This means that reach is important but, as an increasing number of people become aware, so more of them become exposed a second, third or fourth time, perhaps to different vehicles. At the outset, frequency is low and reach high, but as a campaign progresses so reach slows and frequency develops. Reach and frequency are inversely related within any period of time, and media planners must know the objective of a campaign: is it to build reach or develop frequency?

> Reach and frequency are inversely related within any period of time.

Gross rating point

To decide whether reach or frequency is the focus of the campaign objective, a more precise understanding of the levels of reach and frequency is required. The term gross rating point is used to express the relationship between these two concepts. GRPs are a measure of the total number of exposures (OTS) generated within a particular period of time. The calculation itself is simply reach × frequency:

reach × frequency = gross rating point

Media plans are often determined on the number of GRPs generated during a certain time period. For example, the objective for a media plan could be to achieve 450 GRPs in a burst (usually four or five weeks). However, as suggested earlier, caution is required when interpreting a GRP, because 450 GRPs may be the result of 18 message exposures to just 25 per cent of the target market. It could also be an average of nine exposures to 50 per cent of the target market.

Rating points are used by all media as a measurement tool, although they were originally devised for use with broadcast audiences. GRPs are based on the total target audience (e.g. all women aged 18–34, or all adults) that might be reached, but a media planner needs to know, quite rightly, how many GRPs are required to achieve a particular level of effective reach and what levels of frequency are really required to develop effective learning or awareness in the target audience. In other words, how can the effectiveness of a media plan be improved?

Effective frequency

There are a number of reasons why considering the effectiveness of a media plan has become more important in recent years. First, there is the combination of media and audience fragmentation plus increasing media costs. Second, there is short-termism, increased managerial accountability and intensifying competition. This last point about competition refers to the media planning industry itself and the restructuring and concentration of media buying points (centralisation) in response to clients' globalisation strategies and their need for more cost-effective ways of buying media.

Frequency refers to the number of times members of the target audience are exposed to the vehicle. It says nothing about the quality of the exposures and whether any impact was made. Effective frequency refers to the number of times an individual needs to be exposed to an advertisement before the communication is effective. Being exposed once or possibly twice is unlikely to affect the disposition of the receiver. But the big question facing media planners is, how many times should a message be repeated for effective learning to occur? The level of effective frequency is generally unknown, but there has been some general agreement following work by Krugman (1972) that, for an advertisement to be effective (to make an impact), a target should have at least three OTS, the three-hit theory. The first exposure provokes a 'What is this?' reaction, the second reaction is 'What does this mean to me?' The reaction to the third is 'Oh, I remember'

> The big question facing media planners is, how many times should a message be repeated for effective learning to occur?

(du Plessis, 1998). The three-exposure theory is based on messages that first provide understanding, second, provide recognition and third, actually stimulate action. More than 10 exposures is regarded as an ineffective plan and hence a waste of resources.

Determining the average frequency partially solves the problem. This is the number of times a target reached by the schedule is exposed to the vehicle over a particular period of time. For example, a schedule may generate the following:

10 per cent of the audience is reached ten times ($10 \times 10 = 100$)
25 per cent of the audience is reached seven times ($25 \times 7 = 175$)
65 per cent of the audience is reached once ($65 \times 1 = 65$)
Total = 340 exposures

Average frequency = 340/100 = 3.4

This figure of average frequency is misleading because different groups of people have been reached with varying levels of frequency. In the example above, an average frequency of 3.4 is achieved but 65 per cent of the audience is reached only once. This means that the average frequency, in this example, may lead to an audience being underexposed.

Members of the target audience do not buy and read just one magazine or watch a single television programme. Consumer media habits are complex, although distinct patterns can be observed, but it is likely that a certain percentage of the target audience will be exposed to an advertisement if it is placed in two or more media vehicles. Those who are exposed once constitute unduplicated reach. Those who are exposed to two or more are said to have been duplicated. Such overlapping of exposure, shown in Figure 27.1, is referred to as duplicated reach.

> Media plans need to specify levels of duplicated and unduplicated reach.

Duplication provides an indication of the levels of frequency likely in a particular media schedule. Duplication also increases costs, so if the objective of the plan is unduplicated reach, duplication brings waste and inefficiency. So media plans need to specify levels of duplicated and unduplicated reach.

Figure 27.1 Duplication

> ### ViewPoint 27.3 Optimising media schedules
>
> Multi-media optimisers (MMO) are software programs that plan and schedule the placing of advertising campaigns across more than one medium. MMOs use single-source or fused database information rather than survey-based information, which is prone to inaccuracies.
>
> MMOs take into account duplication rates when deciding which combination of media vehicles to use (not types such as television and magazines). They also facilitate media-neutral planning (see Chapter 9).
>
> However, MMOs work on responses, and this can pose problems in terms of agreeing what form of response is valid, while audiences have to be converted to ad exposures/impacts in order to base evaluation on equivalent measures. Accounting for decay rates and adstock features (ad impact retention) by medium, through time is also problematic.
>
> Sources: Adapted from Jarvis and McElroy (2004) and www.fipp.com/sadmin/1418.
>
> #### Question
> If media planning software works just on responses can this be an effective planning tool?
>
> #### Task
> Find out the training necessary to become a media planner.

Nevertheless, it is generally agreed that a certain level of GRPs is necessary for awareness to be achieved. It is also accepted that increased GRPs are necessary for other communication effects to be achieved. These levels of GRPs are referred to as weights, and the weight of a campaign reflects the objectives of the campaign. For example, a burst designed to achieve 85 per cent coverage with eight OTS would make a 680 rating, which is considered to be heavy. Such high ratings are often associated with car launches and, for example, products that are market leaders in their class, such as Nescafé or Pantene. An average rating would be one set to achieve a 400 rating, through 80 per cent coverage and five OTS over the length of a five-week period.

Our understanding about how learning works can assist the quest for effective frequency levels. The amount of learning in individuals increases up to a certain point, after which further exposure to material adds little to our overall level of knowledge. The same applies to the frequency level and the weightings applied to exposures.

Coverage and reach figures only show the numbers of people who are exposed to the vehicle. Effective reach measures those that are aware of the message. This ties in with the previous discussion on effective frequency levels. Essentially, media planners recognise that effective advertising requires that, in addition to the other aspects of advertising planning, a single transmission (reach) of an advertisement will be unproductive (Krugman, 1975; Naples, 1979). A minimum of two exposures and a reach threshold of 45 per cent of the target audience are required for reach to be regarded as effective (Murray and Jenkins, 1992).

Recency planning

A relatively new perspective to counter the effective frequency model has emerged from the United States. This is known as recency planning, and developed at a time when the weak theory of advertising started to gain greater acknowledgement as the most acceptable general interpretation of how advertising works. There is also a growing general acceptance that advertising is not the all-powerful communication tool it was once thought to be, and that the timing and presentation of advertising messages needs to be reconsidered in the light of the way advertising is currently thought to work.

If it is accepted that consumer decision-making is more heavily influenced by 'running out' of particular products (opening empty fridges and store cupboards), than by exposure to

Table 27.5 The differences between effective frequency and recency planning

Recency planning model	Effective frequency model
Reach goal	Frequency goal
Continuity	Burst
One-week planning cycle	Four-week planning cycle
Lowest cost per reach point	Lowest cost per thousand
Low ratings	High ratings

Source: Adapted from Ephron (1997). Used by permission of WARC.

advertising messages that are repeated remorselessly, then it follows that advertising needs to be directed at those people who are actually in the market and prepared to buy (Ephron, 1997).

As many fast-moving consumer goods products are purchased each week, Jones (1995) argues that a single exposure to an advertising message in the week before a purchase is to be made is more important than adding further messages, thereby increasing frequency. Recency planning considers reach to be more important than frequency.

> The strategy requires reaching as many consumers as possible in as many weeks as possible.

The goal of this new approach is to reach those few consumers who are ready to buy (in the market). To do this the strategy requires reaching as many consumers as possible in as many weeks as possible (as far as the budget will extend). This requires a lower weekly weight and an extended number of weeks for a campaign. Advertising budgets are not cut; the fund is simply spread over a greater period of time. According to Ephron, this approach is quite different from effective frequency models and quite revolutionary (see Table 27.5).

This approach has been greeted with a number of objections. It has not been universally accepted, nor has it been widely implemented in the UK market. Gallucci (1997), among others, rejected the notion of recency planning because effectiveness will vary by brand, category and campaign. He claims that reaching 35 per cent of the Indonesian cola market once a week will not bring about the same result as reaching 65 per cent four times a week.

The development of banner advertising on the Internet raises interesting questions concerning effective frequency in new media. Is the frequency rate different and, if so, how many times is exposure required in order to be effective? Research into this area is in its infancy and no single, accepted body of knowledge exists. Broussard (2000) reports that, in a limited study concerning the comparison of a direct-response and a branding-based campaign on the Internet, the lowest cost per lead in the direct-response campaign was achieved with low frequency levels. Results from the branding campaign suggest that up to seven exposures were necessary to improve brand awareness and knowledge of product attributes.

The debate concerning the development of recency planning and effective frequency will continue. What might be instrumental to the outcome of the debate will be a better understanding of how advertising works and the way buyers use advertising messages that are relevant to them.

Media usage and attitudes

A large number of people have a negative attitude towards advertising, and TV ads in particular. Advertising is regarded as both intrusive and pervasive. Beale (1997) developed a four-part typology of personality types based upon respondents' overall attitudes towards advertising

Table 27.6 Advertising attitudes for media determination

Cynics (22 per cent)
This group perceives advertising as a crude sales tool. They are resentful and hostile to advertisements, although they are more likely to respond to advertisements placed in relevant media.

Enthusiasts (35 per cent)
Enthusiasts like to get involved with advertising and creativity is perceived as an important part of the process. Apart from newspapers, which are regarded as boring, most types of media are acceptable.

Ambivalents (22 per cent)
While creativity is seen as superfluous and irrelevant, ambivalents are more disposed to information-based messages or those that promise cost savings. The best advertisements are those that use media that reinforce the message.

Acquiescents (21 per cent)
As the name suggests, this group of people has a reluctant approach to advertising. This means that they see advertising as unavoidable and an inevitable part of their world. Therefore, they are open to influence through a variety of media.

Source: Adapted from Beale (1997). Used with kind permission.

(see Table 27.6). Through an understanding of the different characteristics, it is possible to make better (more informed) decisions about the most appropriate media channels to reach target audiences.

It is common for advertisers and media planners to discuss target markets in the context of heavy, medium, light and non-users of a product. It is only now that consideration is being given to the usage levels of viewers and readers. ZenithOptimedia has determined that television audiences can be categorised as heavy, medium and light users based on the amount of time they spend watching television. One of the implications of this approach is that if light users consume so little television, then perhaps it is not worthwhile trying to communicate with them and resources should be directed to the medium and heavy user groups. The other side of the argument is that light users are very specific in the programmes that they watch, therefore it should be possible to target messages at them and a heavy number of GRPs should be used. However, questions still remain about the number of ratings necessary for effective reach in each of these categories.

> Light users are very specific in the programmes that they watch.

A more contemporary study by Schultz *et al.* (2006) sought to discover how media consumption is determined by an individual's need to access media. Using criteria based on the amount of time spent with all forms of media, the amount of simultaneous media usage, the need to provide or receive information and the speed at which a medium delivers the information, four clusters were identified. These were:

- Zeros – this group consists of people who are not active media consumers.
- Traditionals – this group use media sequentially, one form of media at a time.
- Information hounds – this group are heavy media users and information providers.
- Network creators – this group are heavy users but primarily use slow media and use the information largely for their own purposes.

The researchers believe this media consumption model should be used to enhance the media planning process by being used in addition to the general demographic-, geographic- and psychographic-based approaches. Further research was based around three key dimensions: media usage, media influence and simultaneous media usage.

Ostrow (1981) was the first to question how many rating points should be purchased. He said that, rather than use average frequency, a decision should be made about the minimum level of frequency necessary to achieve the objectives and then maximise reach at that level. Ostrow (1984) suggested that consideration of the issues set out in Table 27.8 would also assist.

Table 27.7 The SIMM database – media usage dimensions

Media dimension	Explanation
Media usage	Average usage of media, based on minutes, for both weekday and weekend consumption. Includes, newspaper, direct mail, magazines, radio, television and the Internet.
Media influence	The self-reported average for each media category across eight product groups: electronics, apparel, groceries, home improvement, cars, medicines, telecom services and eating out.
Simultaneous media usage	This is an average of all pairs of media that were reported as 'used simultaneously'. If a pair is reported as regularly consumed then it was assumed to be 70 per cent of the time. If reported as occasional, then it was defined as 30 per cent of the time.

Source: Schultz et al. (2006).

Table 27.8 Issues to be considered when setting frequency levels

Issues	Low frequency	High frequency
Marketing issues		
Newness of the brand	Established	New
Market share	High	Low
Brand loyalty	Higher	Lower
Purchase and usage cycle times	Long	Short
Message issues		
Complexity	Simple	Complex
Uniqueness	More	Less
Image versus product sell	Product sell	Image
Message variation	Single message	Multiple messages
Media plan issues		
Clutter	Less	More
Editorial atmosphere	Appropriate	Not appropriate
Attentiveness of the media in the plan	Holds	Fails to hold
Number of media in the plan	Less	More

Source: Adapted from Ostrow (1984).

The traditional approach of using television to reach target audiences to build awareness is still strong. For example, Procter & Gamble, Unilever, Nestlé, Kellogg's and BT all spend in excess of 70 per cent of their budgets on television advertising. However, many major advertisers have moved from a dominant above-the-line approach to a more integrated and through-the-line approach as a more effective way of delivering messages to target audiences. Nescafé now uses 48-sheet posters and Unilever, traditionally a heavy user of television, has begun to use radio and posters as support for its television work.

Efficiency

> All promotional campaigns are constrained by a budget.

All promotional campaigns are constrained by a budget. Therefore a trade-off is required between the need to reach as many members of the target audience as possible (create awareness) and the need to repeat the message to achieve effective learning in the target audience. The decision about whether to emphasise reach or frequency is assisted by a consideration of the costs involved in each proposed schedule or media plan.

There are two main types of cost. The first of these is the *absolute cost*. This is the cost of the space or time required for the message to be transmitted. For example, the cost of a full-page, single-insertion, black-and-white advertisement, booked for a firm date in the *Sunday Times*, is £56,150 (November 2004). Cash flow is affected by absolute costs.

> The cost of a full-page, single-insertion, black-and-white advertisement, booked for a firm date in the *Sunday Times*, is £56,150 (November 2004).

In order that an effective comparison be made between media plans the *relative costs* of the schedules need to be understood. Relative costs are the costs incurred in making contact with each member of the target audience.

Traditionally, the magazine industry has based its calculations on the cost per thousand people reached (CPT). The original term derived from the print industry is CPM, where the 'M' refers to the Roman symbol for thousand. This term still has limited use but the more common term is CPT: CPT = space costs (absolute) × 1,000/circulation. The newspaper industry has used the milline rate, which is the cost per line of space per million circulation.

Broadcast audiences are measured by programme ratings (United States), and television audiences in Britain are measured by television ratings or TVRs. They are essentially the same in that they represent the percentage of television households that are tuned to a specific programme. The TVR is determined as follows:

TVR = number of target TV households tuned into a programme
× 100/total number of target TV households

A single TVR, therefore, represents 1 per cent of all the television households in a particular area that are tuned into a specific programme.

A further approach to measuring broadcast audiences uses the share of televisions that are tuned into a specific programme. This is compared with the total number of televisions that are actually switched on at that moment. This is expressed as a percentage and should be greater than the TVR. Share, therefore, reveals how well a programme is perceived by the available audience, not the potential audience. The question of how to measure relative costs in the broadcast industry has been answered by the use of the rating point or TVR. Cost per TVR is determined as follows:

Cost per TVR = time costs (absolute costs)/TVR

Intra-industry comparison of relative costs is made possible by using these formulae. Media plans that only involve broadcast or only use magazine vehicles can be evaluated to determine levels of efficiency. However, members of the target audience do not have discrete viewing habits; they have, as we saw earlier, complex media consumption patterns that involve exposure to a mix of media classes and vehicles. Advertisers respond to this mixture by placing advertisements in a variety of media, but have no way of comparing the relative costs on an inter-industry basis. In other words, the efficiency of using a *News at Ten* television slot cannot be compared with an insertion in *The Economist*. Attempts are being made to provide cross-industry media comparisons, but as yet no one formula has yet been provided that satisfies all demands. The television and newspaper industries, by using CPT in combination with costs per unit of time and space respectively, have attempted to forge a bridge that may be of use to their customers.

Finally, some comment on the concept of CPT is necessary, as there has been speculation about its validity as a comparative tool. There are a number of shortcomings associated with the use of CPT. For example, because each media class possesses particular characteristics, direct comparisons based on CPT alone are dangerous. The levels of wastage incurred in a plan, such as reaching people who are not targets or by measuring OTS for the vehicle and not the advertisement, may lead to an overestimate of the efficiency that a plan offers.

> There are a number of shortcomings associated with the use of CPT.

Similarly, the circulation of a magazine is not a true representation of the number of people who read or have an opportunity to see. Therefore, CPT may underestimate the efficiency unless the calculation can be adjusted to account for the extra or pass-along readership that occurs in reality. Having made these points, media buyers in the United Kingdom continue to use CPT and cost per rating point (CPRP) as a means of planning and buying time and space. Target audiences and television programmes are priced according to the ratings they individually generate. The ratings affect the cost of buying a spot. The higher the rating, the higher the price to place advertisements in the magazine or television programme.

Planning, placing and measuring ads online

The decision to place online ads is complicated not just by deciding which of the various formats discussed previously should be used, but also by where and when the ads need to be placed. Table 27.9 sets out the various options available for placing online ads.

Longhurst (2006) argues that much of the online media planning work is based on dividing the expenditure (investment) by the anticipated response (click-throughs) to determine a cost

Table 27.9 Online ad placement opportunities

Location for ad placement	Explanation
Portals	Major portals such as Google, Yahoo and MSN attract the majority of online ads. Smaller portals enable more specific targeting of messages to reach defined target audiences. For example, airlines or ferries on a travel portal.
Community web sites	Social networking sites consist of communities of people who share common pastimes, health issues, geographic location or other interests. These represent ideal opportunities to reach specific target audiences.
Search engines	Pay-per-click ads based on users searching on particular key words constitute a major source of revenue for each search engine. See p. 782 for more information.
Shopping comparison sites	Ads placed on sites where a comparison of shopping products has been requested is going to reach a high proportion of a target audience.
Chat rooms	In return for providing software and hosting, companies can place ads on relevant pages.
Online forums	Ads can be targeted to meet the needs and interests of the topics and subjects being discussed.
Blogs	Blog sites are provided for bloggers to write, but in order to sustain the site ads need to be placed, again targeted to the principle subjects under discussion.
Podcasts	Opportunities to place ads around specific podcasts are currently limited but will increase as podcasting becomes more mainstream.
RSS aggregators	These enable subscribers to receive specific information and short news updates from organisations that bring information together (aggregators) and feed it out. Some RSS aggregators are beginning to sell ad space on the various news feeds.
Mobile devices	Opportunities to reach audiences on the move increase as technology improves.
Newsletters	The content or theme of a newsletter will attract appropriate advertisers.
Online magazines	Whether a manufacturer or an association produces these they still provide good opportunities to reach audiences with specific interests.

Source: Based on Gay et al. (2007).

per response. This figure is then used to compare with other media combinations. The problem is that this approach is not market-oriented and the investment sum is all too often simply determined by taking a preset percentage of the main budget.

The media planning concepts referred to previously in this chapter (reach, frequency, etc.) evolved to help manage traditional media. The interruption model has been the main way traditional media has been used. This is predicated on the idea that the media manages audiences, influences what they see, when they see it and shapes the pattern of their media behaviour. Advertisers therefore, interrupted an audience's viewing or reading to deliver product messages, for which, according to the advertiser's segmentation analysis, they were suitable recipients.

However, technological advances have brought about huge changes in the types of available media and the way in which people now use media. As Moore (2007) rightly points out, people use traditional media for information and entertainment. Now they can be active participants as opportunities to be interactive enables user-generated-content (Chapter 2) through search, downloading, sharing, publication and involvement in virtual communities. Advertisers should not try to interrupt participants but facilitate interaction. Moore (2007), media manager for the drinks-based group, Diageo in the United Kingdom, suggests that, in addition to the need for information and entertainment, media now need to satisfy four new consumer motivations: to discover, participate, share and express (themselves). What he does not say is that these do not apply to all consumers in the same way. Most people consume a mixture of traditional and new media, with particular audiences skewed more to one rather than the other. The argument that mass media advertising is in permanent decline is a fallacy, proved by the continuing investment by a range of brands in television advertising. There has certainly been a readjustment of media budgets to reflect contemporary media usage, but the new is not going to wipe out the old.

> Most people consume a mixture of traditional and new media.

The early years of digital and online media saw attempts to use the established methods of measurement and evaluation. However, it became clear that these methods were not entirely suitable, simply because digital media are used differently. Instead of measuring how often a message is delivered or the share of audience reached with a message, it becomes more important to measure a consumer's expectations of a brand and their interaction with brands. Put another way these might be considered as dwell time (the amount of time consumers spend with a brand), dwell quality (a consumer's perceived richness resulting from brand interaction) and dwell insight (what motivates a consumer to spend time with a brand).

Media source effects

CPT is a quantitative measure, and one of its major shortcomings is that it fails to account for the qualitative aspects associated with media vehicles. Before vehicles are selected, their qualitative aspects need to be considered on the basis that a vehicle's environment may affect the way in which a message is perceived and decoded.

An advertisement placed in one vehicle, such as *Cosmopolitan*, may have a different impact on an identical audience to that obtained if the same advertisement were placed in *Options*. This differential level of 'power of impact' is caused by a number of source factors, of which the following are regarded as the most influential:

- *vehicle atmosphere* – editorial tone, vehicle expertise, vehicle prestige;
- *technical and reproduction characteristics* – technical factors, exposure opportunities, perception opportunities;
- *audience and product characteristics* – audience/vehicle fit, nature of the product.

Vehicle atmosphere

Editorial tone

This refers to the editorial views presented by the vehicle and the overall tone of the material contained. Understandably, some clients do not want to be associated with particular television shows or certain specialist magazines that are characterised by sex or violence.

Vehicle expertise

Magazines and journals can reflect a level of expertise and represent source credibility. Readers who regard particular magazines, especially some of the consumer SIMs (e.g. *Golf Monthly*), business-to-business magazines (e.g. *Fire & Rescue*) and academic journals (e.g. *Harvard Business Review*), as important sources of credible information are more relaxed and open to persuasion.

Vehicle prestige

The message strategy adopted for each advertisement should be appreciated, as this can have a strong effect upon the scheduling. The prestige of a vehicle is important to some products, especially when targeted at audiences where vehicle status is important, for example *Country Life*. Transformational advertisements have been shown to be more effective in prestige-based vehicles than in expertise-based vehicles (and vice versa for information-based advertisements).

> Transformational advertisements have been shown to be more effective in prestige-based vehicles.

Technical and reproduction characteristics of a vehicle

Technical factors

The technical characteristics of the vehicle, such as its visual capability, may influence the impact of the message. The use of colour, movement and sound may be necessary for the full effectiveness of a message to be realised. Other messages may need only a more limited range of characteristics, such as sound. For example, the promotion of inclusive tour holidays benefits from the communication of an impression (photograph/drawing) of the destination resort. This is important, as each destination needs to be differentiated, in the minds of the target audience, from competing destinations.

Exposure opportunities

The possibility that an advertisement will be successfully exposed to the target increases as more consideration is given to the likelihood of successful communication. Each vehicle has a number of time slots or spaces that provide opportunities for increased exposure. The back pages of magazines or facing matter often command premium advertising rates, just as prime-time spots or film premieres on television always generate extra revenue for the television contractors.

Perception opportunities

Being exposed to the message does not mean that the message is perceived. A reader may not perceive an advertisement when searching for the next page of an article. Similarly, a car driver may not 'hear' a radio message because their attention may be on a passing car or a strange engine noise. The solution is to use strong attention-grabbing materials, such as loud or distinctive music or controversial headlines. In addition, new, imaginative ways of attracting attention are being developed. Car dealers have used incentives to attract audiences to test drive a car and receive vouchers for a free video film or have free subscriptions to particular magazines.

ViewPoint 27.4 Digital perception at Terminal 5

When Heathrow airport opened Terminal 5 in March 2008, a raft of new advertising technology was released. Over 200 digital screens have been built into the infrastructure of the airport, all with strategic placement. Here the advertising panels have been sited alongside the path that passengers take from check-in to their flight. Some giant displays are referred to as 'global gateways' some dominating the security area. Some digital ads are incorporated into the flight-information screens.

The digital screens enable ad continuity so that a passenger may see a seemingly endless line of the same ads. This opportunity to reach a mass of people in this way is a first for this part of the advertising industry. Now the industry has the opportunity to use digital technology to deliver moving, interactive, responsive and time-specific advertising. This means that interactive ads can be changed for morning, noon and afternoon customers, unlike the traditional outdoor poster sites that need two weeks, several rolls of paper and a bucket of paste. Visa have taken four giant lightboxes that measure 29m × 36m and should be seen by all passengers as they move through to the departure areas.

Digital and interactive screens have been installed at other airports following the T5 launch, in the London Underground, in and around various new shopping centres and maybe even a bus shelter near you.

Sources: Bainbridge (2008); Bokaie (2008).

Question
To what extent are these digital screens and their location likely to aid the exposure and perception opportunities (to reach travellers with effective messaging)?

Task
Next time you visit an air or rail terminal look out for digital screens and make a note of which brands are using them.

Exhibit 27.2 T5 Visa's digital screens
Courtesy of JCDecaux Airport.

Audience/product characteristics

Audience/vehicle fit

The media plan should provide the best match between the target market and the audience reached by the vehicles in the media schedule. The more complex the target market description or consumer profile, the greater the difficulty of matching it with appropriate vehicles.

ViewPoint 27.5 Monday is Horlicks night

Horlicks is a rich milky drink made with malt that contains high levels of calcium and other vitamins. Traditionally, it is associated with older people and helps relaxation and inducing sleep. MediaCom was given the task of finding a new target audience and repositioning the brand. Planning and research identified women aged 35+ who were stressed trying to manage both their careers and their family. MediaCom also identified Mondays as the night when they were most likely to have a poor night's sleep.

This information enabled MediaCom to target the Monday night schedule, and the end of evening section, or the 'wind-down ritual' in particular. With a 13-week concentration Horlicks was able to target its customers at a time when they would be most receptive and as a result a new market was won. It was reported that sales climbed 28 per cent in the first four weeks of the campaign.

Source: Adapted from Grimshaw (2004).

Question

Although sales rose during the first four weeks, does this measure provide sufficient long-term optimism for the brand? If not, why not?

Task

Think of a product that you use, consider when you use it and try to identify communications that reflect your usage.

Exhibit 27.3 Horlicks
Horlicks, part of GSK Nutritional Healthcare U.K.

Weilbacher (1984) argues that media evaluation based on product usage may be better than using demographics and psychographics. These may be inappropriate and inefficient when matching markets with audiences. As advertising is directed at influencing consumer behaviour, product usage is a more logical measure of media evaluation. This view is supported by media planners targeting heavy, medium and light users.

This perspective contrasts with the view of Rothschild (1987). He regards demographic and psychographic factors as relatively stable and enduring factors, and thus suitable influences on the media selection decision. By contrast, the dynamic factors (those that vary within an individual with respect to brand choice, purchase behaviour and time of adoption between products) are seen as being more suitable for influencing media strategy.

Nature of the product

In addition to this, consideration needs to be given to the nature of the product itself. Audiences have particular viewing patterns, therefore it does not make sense to advertise when it is known that the target audience is not watching (for example, promoting children's sweets late at night or photocopiers in consumer-interest magazines).

Prime television spots such as *Coronation Street* or major sporting occasions such as the Olympic Games attract many major competitive brands. It may be wise to avoid competing for time and look for other suitable programmes.

Vehicle mood effects

The mood that a vehicle creates can also be an important factor. Aaker *et al.* (1992) report on the work of a number of studies in this area. These suggest that food advertisements using transformational appeals are more effective when placed in situation comedies than in thrillers and mystery programmes. Advertisements for analgesics work better in both adult westerns and situation comedies (Crane, 1964).

These qualitative, vehicle-related source effects need to be considered as support for the quantitative work undertaken initially. They should not be used as the sole reason for the selection of particular media vehicles, if only because they are largely subjective.

Scheduling

This seeks to establish when the messages are transmitted in order that the media objectives be achieved at the lowest possible cost. The first considerations are the objectives themselves. If the advertising objectives are basically short term, then the placements should be concentrated over a short period of time. Conversely, if awareness is to be built over a longer term, perhaps building a new brand, then the frequency of the placements need not be so intensive and can be spread over a period so that learning can occur incrementally.

The second consideration is the purchasing cycle. It has been noted before that the optimum number of exposures is thought to be between three and ten, and this should occur within each purchasing cycle. Obviously, this is only really applicable to packaged goods, and is not as applicable to white or brown goods or, indeed, the business-to-business sector. However, the longer the cycle, the less frequency is required.

> The optimum number of exposures is thought to be between three and ten.

The third consideration is the level of involvement. If the objective of the plan is to create awareness, then when there is high involvement few repetitions will be required compared with low involvement decisions. This is because people who are highly involved actively seek information and need little assistance to digest relevant information. Likewise, where there is low involvement, attitudes develop from use of the product, so frequency is important to maintain awareness and to prompt trial.

Finally, the placement of an advertisement is influenced by the characteristics of the target audience and their preferred programmes. Selecting compatible 'spots' is likely to improve message delivery considerably.

Timing of advertisement placements

The timing of placements is dependent on a number of factors. One of the overriding constraints is the size of the media budget and the impact that certain placement patterns can bring to an organisation's cash flow. Putting cost to one side, many researchers have identified and labelled different scheduling patterns. Govoni *et al.* (1986), Sissors and Bumba (1989), Burnett (1993) and Kotler (1997) all suggest different approaches to scheduling. Figure 27.2 and the following are presented as a synthesis of the more common scheduling options.

Continuity patterns

Continuous patterns involve regular and uniform presentation of the message to the target audience. Over the long term, a continuous pattern is more appropriate for products and services where demand is crisis led, e.g. plumbing, or where there is a long purchase cycle. These continuous patterns are often used for mature products, where reminder advertising is appropriate. A rising pattern is used when activity centres around a particular event, such as the FA Cup Final, the Olympic Games or a general election. A fading pattern may follow an initial burst to launch a new product or to inform of a product modification.

> A rising pattern is used when activity centres around a particular event.

Flighting patterns

> Flighting allows advertisers the opportunity to spread their resources across a longer period of time.

Flighting allows advertisers the opportunity to spread their resources across a longer period of time. This may improve the effectiveness of their messages. A flighting pattern may be appropriate in situations where messages need to reflect varying demand, such as that experienced by the retail sector throughout the year. Flighting is also adopted as a competitive response to varying advertising weights applied by rivals. These schedules are used for specific events, such as support for major sales promotions and responses to adverse publicity or one-off market opportunities.

Flighting patterns can also be used in short and often heavy periods of investment activity. Because of the seasonality of the product (e.g. for inclusive tour operators), advertising at other times is inappropriate and a waste of resources. This approach can also be used to respond quickly to a competitor's potentially damaging actions, to launch new products or to provide unique information, such as the announcement of a new organisation as a result of merger activity, or to promote information about a particular event such as an impending share offer.

Pulsing patterns

Pulsing seeks to combine the advantages of both the previous patterns. As a result, it is the safest of all the options, but potentially the most expensive. It allows advertisers to increase levels of message activity at certain times of the year, which is important for times when sales traditionally increase, as with fragrance sales in December and ice-cream in June.

Whereas flighting presents an opportunity for individuals to forget messages during periods of no advertising, pulsing helps to prevent the onset of forgetting, to build high levels of awareness and to provide a barrier that holds back competitor attack.

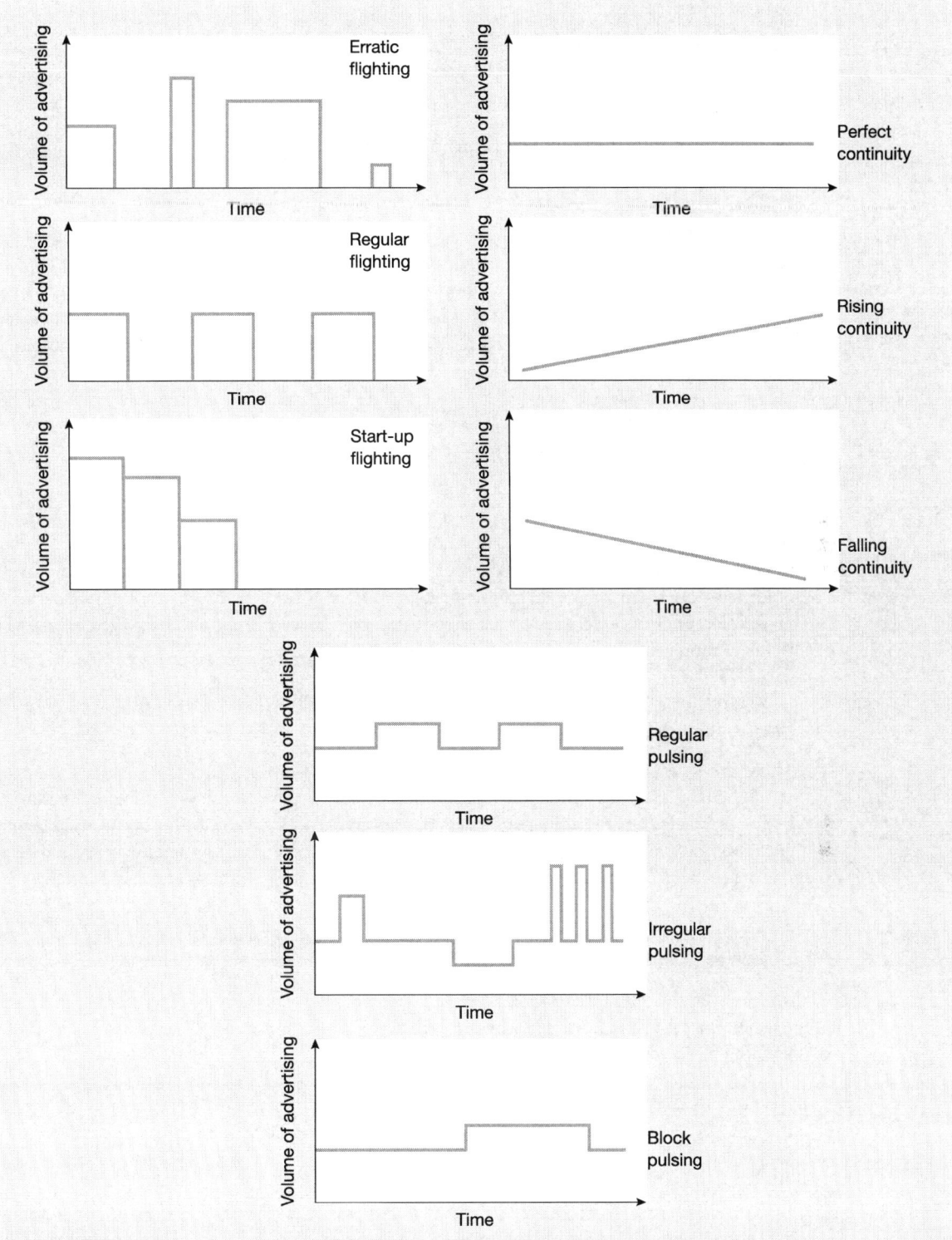

Figure 27.2 Media scheduling patterns

Summary

In order to help consolidate your understanding of media planning, here are the key points summarised against each of the learning objectives:

1. Explain the role of the media planner and highlight the impact of media and audience fragmentation.

Media planning is concerned with the selection and scheduling of media vehicles designed to carry an advertiser's message. The variety of media is rapidly increasing and is referred to as media fragmentation. This makes the media planner's task increasingly complicated because the size of audience available to each media reduces, making the number of media required to reach a target market increasingly large.

2. Consider various theories concerning the content of different media and related media switching behaviours.

Consideration was given to media richness theory (MRT), which holds that there is a hierarchy of media ranging from the richest media such as personal or face-to-face encounters through to lean media typified by single sheets of text-based information.

Social influence theory (SIT) complements MRT as it also assumes that the relatively objective features of media do influence how individuals perceive and use them. The technology acceptance model (TAM) relates to the perceived usefulness and perceived ease of use as the main issues that are considered when selecting media.

3. Examine the key concepts used in media selection: reach and cover, frequency, duplication, rating points and CPT.

There are several fundamental concepts that underpin they way in which media should be selected and included in the media plan. These concepts refer to the percentage of the target audience reached, the number of times they receive a message, the number of media they are exposed to and various measures associated with the efficiency with which media deliver messages.

4. Appreciate the concept of repetition and the debate concerning effective frequency and recency planning.

The greater the number of exposures the more likely an individual is to learn about the message content. The question is how many times should a message be repeated for effective learning to occur, i.e. what is the effective frequency?

Recency planning is a reach-based model and argues that a single exposure to an advertising message in the week before a purchase is more important than adding further messages, thus increasing frequency. Recency planning considers reach to be more important than frequency.

5. Understand the concepts of effectiveness and efficiency when applied to media selection decisions.

The efficiency of a schedule refers to the costs involved in delivering messages. There are two main types of cost. The first of these is the *absolute cost*, which is the cost of the space or time required for the message to be transmitted. The second concerns the costs incurred in making contact with each member of the target audience. These are refereed to as the *relative costs* and are used to compare different media schedules.

The magazine industry uses calculations based on the cost per thousand people reached (CPT). Broadcast audiences are measured by television ratings or TVRs. These represent the percentage of television households that are tuned to a specific programme.

6. Introduce media source effects as an important factor in the selection and timing of advertising in magazines and television programmes.

Different media impact on audiences in different ways because of three main factors. These are the *vehicle atmosphere* – editorial tone, vehicle expertise, vehicle prestige; their *technical and reproduction characteristics* – technical factors, exposure opportunities, perception opportunities; and finally their *audience and product characteristics* – audience/vehicle fit, nature of the product.

7. Explore the different ways in which advertisements can be scheduled.

The scheduling of a media plan seeks to establish when the messages are transmitted in order that the media objectives be achieved at the lowest possible cost. Various factors affect the schedule: the campaign objectives; the purchasing cycle; the level of involvement; and the characteristics of the target audience and their preferred programmes. The selection of compatible 'spots' is likely to improve message delivery considerably.

Review questions

1. Compare media richness theory, social influence theory and the technology adoption model.
2. What are the main tasks facing media planners?
3. If the rate at which information decays within individuals is known, then the task of the media planner is simply to place messages at suitable intervals in the path of decay. Discuss.
4. Why is it important that a media planner knows whether reach or frequency is the main objective of a media plan?
5. Why are frequency levels so important? Explain the concept of effective frequency.
6. How does recency planning differ from effective frequency?
7. What is a TVR and how does it relate to GRPs?
8. How does planning for digital media differ from that for traditional media?
9. Write a brief report outlining the principal characteristics of media source effects.
10. What are the main ways in which media plans can be scheduled?

Targeting the 'brown pound' – an untapped market

Yasmin Sekhon: Bournemouth University

The fundamental aim of media planning is to formulate a strategy that will allow marketing communication messages to reach the target audience. This involves 'buying' time and space and utilising the appropriate media vehicles. However, for a media plan to work it has to be effective and efficient, having the relevant impact and getting the message across.

One key issue, as yet not properly resolved, concerns ways in which marketers can make the right decisions when targeting the 'brown pound'. That is, how to use the right media to reach ethnic markets, especially when these markets are generally under-researched and remain untouched.

Background

The combined disposable income of ethnic minorities in the United Kingdom is in the region of £32bn, according to the Institute of Practitioners in Advertising (IPA). However, businesses are generally guilty of not effectively promoting to these audiences and paying little or no attention to them. Often labelled as the 'hard-to-reach groups' it seems to be a self-fulfilling prophecy, it is hard to reach them so why bother?

The 'brown pound', and the ethnic communities that constitute it, have some key characteristics that must be understood and targeted accordingly. In planning to target these audiences once the appropriate message has been devised, the relevant media vehicle has to be chosen. This will involve choosing the right media and scheduling them according to the target market needs.

Characteristics

Based on the last census, South Asians represented 3 per cent of the UK population, which is approximately 1.6 million people. This segment consists of not only actual immigrants, but also second- and third-generation Asians born in this country. In the main, these group are highly educated, professional and some are business-owning individuals. The audience profile of this segment varies from male to female and young to old, with varying amounts of disposable income.

Distinguishing between the different generations is important. The first generation may have a greater affiliation with their home country – their cultural roots – and so consumption decisions are made according to their own level of acculturation in Britain. While the second generation, born and bred in the United Kingdom, will live a more bi-cultural lifestyle, mixing both Eastern and Western value systems.

So what is the optimal solution for reaching this diverse but potentially rich group? Many of the campaigns aimed at this audience are neither planned nor do they demonstrate consideration of the media and channels, which means that the right media space is not being bought, so it remains an untapped market.

The role of media

The choice of media has to meet the target audience's needs. Essentially, those targeting ethnic audiences have a plethora of media to choose from, encompassing radio or television stations, newspapers, magazines and also web sites.

However, when making decisions about which media to choose it may be more favourable to use a combination that will result in synergistic results. There are a number of media vehicles that can be selected to carry a company's promotional message. However, choices have to take account of the generation, the age, level of disposable income and levels of affiliation with the home and host countries.

Reaching and communicating to this audience, ethnic minority media often uses community-based methods of distribution, but organisations are really not tapping into these communities' related opportunities. Punjab Radio for instance, targets Britain's Punjabi community. Also, particular television programmes such as Zee TV and specialist magazines, for example, *Asiana*, *Asian Women* and *Asian Bride* are media where potential messages can reach ethnic audiences in a concentrated manner.

However, when selecting and scheduling media, organisations also need to think beyond the sole use of concentrated media. What about the more traditional and mainstream media? The integration of both would have a greater impact and allow a number of different touch points for the potential customer.

Companies that wish to tap into the 'brown pound' have a number of choices to make when planning their marketing communications campaigns. First, the objectives of the campaign have to be understood – what do you want to say to the consumers and what tools will be most effective for the message? In addition, issues concerning reach and frequency are important.

However, to tap into the 'brown pound' it may be a case of not only understanding the differences, but also recognising the similarities between consumers of an ethnic background compared to the indigenous population. Also, the message has to be relevant to the segment and how you can influence ethnic consumers: directly, indirectly, through reference groups or opinion leaders? Finally, the timing and scheduling of campaigns, in order to develop a consistent message and deliver it at times relevant to the target audience, is all-important in targeting what marketers have labelled as 'select audiences'.

The 'brown pound' still remains a fairly untapped market, it is worth millions, so planning the right message, and delivering it through the right media, at the right time, could bring lucrative returns for many companies.

MiniCase questions

1. Using a company or brand of your choice, plan an outline marketing communications campaign aimed at one specific ethnic group. Pay particular attention to media choice and the campaign schedule.
2. Which particular factors might need to be taken into account when planning campaigns to reach ethnic groups?
3. When planning a media mix to reach ethnic audiences, what do you believe might be the critical factors?

References

Aaker, D., Batra, R. and Myers, J.G. (1992) *Advertising Management*, 4th edn. Englewood Cliffs, NJ: Prentice-Hall.

Armstrong, S. (1993) The business of buying: time, lads, please. *Media Week*, 3 September, 26–7.

Bainbridge, J. (2008) Now ad campaigns can take off. *The Independent*, 17 March 2008, 10.

Beale, C. (1997) Study reveals negativity towards ads. *Campaign*, 28 November, 8.

Bokaie, J. (2008) Gateway to Britain. *Marketing*, 19 March, 16.

Brech, P. (1999) When the media buck stops with you. *Media Week*, 19 November, 22–3.

Broussard, G. (2000) How advertising frequency can work to build online effectiveness. *International Journal of Market Research*, **42**(4), 439–57.

Burnett, J. (1993) *Promotion Management*. New York: Houghton Mifflin.

Crane, L.E. (1964) How product, appeal, and program affect attitudes towards commercials. *Journal of Advertising Research*, **4** (March), 15.

Daft, R.L. and Lengel, R.H. (1984) Information richness: a new approach to managerial behavior and organizational design. In *Research in Organizational Behavior*, **6** (eds L.L. Cummings and B.M. Straw), 191–233. Homewood, IL: JAI Press.

Duarte, D.L. and Snyder, N.T. (2001) *Mastering Virtual Team*, 2nd edn. San Francisco, CA: Jossey-Bass.

Ephron, E. (1997) Recency planning. *Admap* (February), 32–4.

Fulk, J., Schmitz, J.A. and Steinfield, C.W. (1990) A social influence model of technology use. In *Organizations and Communication Technology* (eds J. Fulk and C. Steinfield). Newbury Park, CA: Sage.

Gallucci, P. (1997) There are no absolutes in media planning. *Admap* (July/August), 39–43.

Gay, R., Charlesworth, A. and Esen, R. (2007) *Online Marketing: A Customer Led Approach*. Oxford: Oxford University Press.

Govoni, N., Eng, R. and Galper, M. (1986) *Promotional Management*. Englewood Cliffs, NJ: Prentice-Hall.

Grimshaw, C. (2004) MediaCom – media agency of the year. *Marketing Agency*, December, 7.

Jarvis, T. and McElroy, B. (2004) Can optimisers provide a lifeline for media? *Admap*, **39**(2) (February), 32–5.

Jones, P. (1995) *When Ads Work: New Proof that Advertising Triggers Sales*. New York: Simon & Schuster, Free Press/Lexington Books.

Keaveney, S.M. (1995) Consumer switching behavior in service industries: an exploratory study. *Journal of Marketing*, **59**(2), 71–82.

King, R.C. and Xia, W. (1997) Media appropriateness: effects of experience on communication media choice. *Decision Sciences*, **28**(4), 877–909.

Kotler, P. (1997) *Marketing Management: Analysis, Planning, Implementation and Control*, 9th edn. Englewood Cliffs, NJ: Prentice-Hall.

Krugman, H.E. (1965) The impact of television advertising: learning without involvement. *Public Opinion Quarterly*, **29** (Fall), 349–56.

Krugman, H.E. (1972) How potent is TV advertising? Cited in du Plessis (1998).

Krugman, H.E. (1975) What makes advertising effective? *Harvard Business Review* (March/April), 96–103.

Lloyd, D.W. and Clancy, K.J. (1991) CPMs versus CPMis: implications for media planning. *Journal of Advertising Research*, **31**(4) (August/September), 34–44.

Longhurst, P. (2006) Budgeting for online: is it any different? *Admap*, November, 36–7.

McGrath, J.E. and Hollingshead, A.B. (1993) Putting the 'group' back into group support systems: some theoretical issues about dynamic processes in groups with technological enhancements. In *Group Support Systems: New Perspectives* (eds L.M. Jessup and J.S. Valacich, 78–9). New York: Macmillan.

McLuhan, M. (1966) *Understanding Media: The Extensions of Man*. New York: McGraw-Hill.

Moore, L. (2007) 21st century media: let your brand lose control. *Marketing*, 5 December, 10–11.

Murray, G.B. and Jenkins, J.R.G. (1992) The concept of effective reach in advertising. *Journal of Advertising Research*, **32**(3) (May/June), 34–42.

Naples, M.J. (1979) *Effective Frequency: The Relationship Between Frequency and Advertising Effectiveness*. New York: Association of National Advertisers.

Ostrow, J.W. (1981) What level of frequency? *Advertising Age* (November), 13–18.

Ostrow, J.W. (1984) Setting frequency levels: an art or a science? *Marketing and Media Decisions*, **24**(4), 9–11.

Plessis, E. du (1998) Memory and likeability: keys to understanding ad effects. *Admap* (July/August), 42–6.

Rothschild, M.L. (1987) *Marketing Communications*. Lexington, MA: D.C. Heath.

Shultz, D.E., Pilotta, J.P. and Block, M.P. (2006) Media consumption and consumer purchasing, ESOMAR, Worldwide Multi-media Measurement, Shanghai, Retrieved 12 March 2008 from http://www.bigresearch.com/esomar2006.pdf.

Simon, H. (1972) Theories of bounded rationality. In *Decision and Organisation* (eds C.B. McGuire and R. Radner), 161–76. London: North-Holland.

Simon, H. (1987) Bounded rationality. In *The New Palgrave* (eds J. Eatwell, M. Milgate and P. Newman). London: Macmillan.

Sissors, J.Z. and Bumba, L. (1989) *Advertising Media Planning*, 3rd edn. Lincolnwood, IL: NTC Business Books.

Srinivasan, M. (1996) New insights into switching behaviour: marketers can now put a numerical value on loyalty. *Marketing Research*, **8**(3), 26–34.

Weilbacher, W. (1984) *Advertising*, New York: Macmillan.

Chapter 24
Traditional media

The use of particular media is required in order that client messages are delivered to specific target audiences. The array of available media is continually growing but each has strengths and weaknesses that impact on the quality, effectiveness and the meaning attributed to the message by the audience. This chapter focuses on the nature and characteristics of traditional, offline media.

Aims and learning objectives

The aim of this chapter is to establish the principal characteristics of each type of offline media. This will assist understanding of the management processes by which media are selected and scheduled to deliver advertiser's messages. Digital media are explored in the following chapter and media planning and scheduling processes are looked at in Chapter 27.

The learning objectives of this chapter are to:

1. determine the variety and types of traditional media;
2. explain the main criteria used to evaluate media and their use;
3. establish the primary characteristics of each type of medium;
4. examine the strengths and weaknesses of each type of medium;
5. provide a brief summary of the main UK trends in advertising expenditure on each type of medium;
6. consider the dynamics associated with direct response media;
7. explore ways in which media can be integrated.

For an applied interpretation see Nicola Robinsonova's MiniCase entitled *For different types of wood: the Pila Pasak (Shepherd's Sawmill) campaign* at the end of this chapter.

Introduction

Organisations use the services of a variety of media in order that they can deliver their planned messages to target audiences. Of the many available media, six main *classes* can be identified. These are broadcast, print, outdoor, digital, in-store and other media classes. Within each of these classes there are particular *types* of media. For example, within the broadcast class there are television and radio, and within the print class there are newspapers and magazines.

> Six main classes can be identified: broadcast, print, outdoor, digital, in-store and other media.

Within each type of medium there are a huge number of different media *vehicles* that can be selected to carry an advertiser's message. For example, within UK television there are the terrestrial networks (Independent Television Network, Channel 4 and Channel 5) and the satellite (BSkyB) and cable (e.g. Virgin Media) networks. In print, there are consumer and business-oriented magazines and the number of specialist magazines is expanding rapidly. These specialist magazines are targeted at particular activity and interest groups, such as *Amateur Photographer*, *Golf World* and the infamous *Sponge Divers Gazette*! This provides opportunities for advertisers to send messages to well-defined homogeneous groups, which improves effectiveness and reduces wastage in communication spend. Table 24.1 sets out the three forms of media – classes, types and vehicles – with a few examples.

Table 24.1 Summary chart of the main forms of media

Class	Type	Vehicles
Broadcast	Television	*Coronation Street*, *X Factor*
	Radio	Virgin Radio, Classic FM
Print	Newspapers	The *Sunday Times*, *The Mirror*, *The Daily Telegraph*
	Magazines: Consumer Business	*Cosmopolitan*, *Woman*, *The Grocer*, *Plumbing News*
Outdoor	Billboards	96-, 48- and 6-sheet
	Street furniture	Adshel
	Transit	London Underground, airport buildings, taxis, hot-air balloons
Digital media	Internet	Web sites, email, intranets
	Digital television	Teletext, SkyText,
	CD-ROM	Various including music, educational, entertainment
In-store	Point-of-purchase	Bins, signs and displays
	Packaging	The Coca-Cola contour bottle
Other	Cinema	Pearl & Dean
	Exhibitions	Ideal Home, The Motor Show
	Product placement	Films, TV, books
	Ambient	Litter bins, golf tees, petrol pumps
	Guerrilla	Flyposting

Evaluative criteria

One of the key marketing tasks is to decide which combination of vehicles should be selected to carry the message to the target audience. The means by which this decision is reached is the subject of Chapter 27. First, however, it is necessary to consider the main characteristics of each type of media in order that media planning decisions can be based on some logic and rationale. The fundamental characteristics concern the costs, the richness of the communication, the interactive properties and audience profile associated with a communication event.

Costs

One of the important characteristics that needs to be considered is the costs that are incurred using each type of medium. There are two types of cost: absolute and relative. Absolute costs are the costs of the time or space bought in a particular media vehicle. These costs have to be paid for and directly impact upon an organisation's cash flow. Relative costs are the costs of contacting each member of the target audience. Television, as will be seen later, has a high absolute cost but, because messages are delivered to a mass audience, when the absolute cost is divided by the total number of people receiving the message the relative cost is very low.

Communication richness

> The use of sight, sound and movement can generate great impact with a message.

The way in which a message is delivered and understood by a target audience varies across types of media. Certain media, such as television, are able to use many communication dimensions, and through the use of sight, sound and movement can generate great impact with a message. Other types of media have only one dimension, such as the audio capacity of radio or the written word on a page of text. The number of communication dimensions that a media type has will influence the choice of media mix. This is because certain products, at particular points in their development, require the use of different media in order that the right message be conveyed and understood. A new product, for example, may require demonstration in order that the audience understands the product concept. The use of television may be a good way of achieving this. Once understood, the audience does not need to be educated in this way again and future messages need to convey different types of information that may not require demonstration, so radio or magazine advertising may suffice (see Chapter 27, where media richness theory is explored).

Interactive properties

Following on from the previous element is the important issue of interactive communications. The development of digital media has enabled interaction, which we know can lead to dialogue, and this in turn enables relationship development (Ballantyne, 2004). However, there are some circumstances in which interaction is not required due to the nature of the market, the product or the objectives of the campaign. In these circumstances the mix will need to consist of media that primarily deliver messages through a one-way, or monologic, communication format.

> Those that deliver a call-to-action will need to use media that enable interaction.

Marketing communications that seek to engage audiences through interaction, in particular those that deliver a call-to-action, will need to use media that enable interaction and to be used where support facilities are in place to facilitate interactive communications.

Audience profile

The profile of the target audience (male, female, young or old) and the number of people within each audience that a media type can reach are also significant factors in media decisions. For example, 30 per cent of adults in the socioeconomic grade A read the *Sunday Times*. Only

4 per cent of the C2 group also read this paper. Messages appropriate to the A group would be best placed in the *Sunday Times* and those for the C2 group transmitted through the *News of the World*, which 34 per cent of the C2 group read. It is important that advertisers use media vehicles that convey their messages to their target markets with as little waste as possible. Newspapers enable geographically dispersed audiences to be reached. The tone of their content can be controlled, but the cost per target reached is high. Each issue has a short lifespan, so for positive learning to occur in the target audience a number of insertions may be required.

A large number of magazines contain specialised material that appeals to particular target groups. These special-interest magazines (SIMs) enable certain sponsors to reach interested targets with reduced wastage. General-interest magazines (GIMs) appeal to a much wider cross-section of society, to larger generalised target groups. The life of these media vehicles is generally long and their 'pass along' readership high. It should not be forgotten, however, that noise levels can also be high owing to the intermittent manner in which magazines are often read and the number of competing messages from rival organisations.

Television reaches the greatest number of people, but although advertisers can reach general groups, such as men aged 16–24 or housewives, it is not capable of reaching specific interest groups and it incurs high levels of wastage. This blanket coverage offers opportunities for cable and satellite operators to offer more precise targeting, but for now television is a tool for those who wish to talk to mass audiences. Television is expensive from a cash-flow perspective but not in terms of the costs per target reached.

Radio offers a more reasonable costing structure than television and can be utilised to reach particular geographic audiences. For a long time, however, this was seen as its only real strength, particularly when its poor attention span and non-visual dimensions are considered. Although radio will never overtake television in terms of usage and overall popularity, radio has been shown to be capable of generating a much closer personal relationship with listeners, witnessed partly by the success of Classic FM and local radio stations, than is possible through posters, television or print.

The interesting point about outdoor and transit advertising is that exposure is only made by the interception of passing traffic. Govoni *et al.* (1986) make the point that such interception represents opportunistic coverage. Consequently the costs are low, at both investment and per contact levels.

The use of direct marketing has grown in recent years, as technology has developed and awareness has increased. The precise targeting potential of direct mail and its ability to communicate personally with target audiences is impressive. In addition, the control over the total process, including the costs, remains firmly with the sponsor.

The size of the industry should not be underestimated as UK advertising expenditure reached £19.1 billion in 2006 (see Table 3.1 in Chapter 3).

Print media

Of the total amount spent on advertising, across all media, most is spent on the printed word. Newspapers and magazines are the two main types of media in this class. They attract advertisers for a variety of reasons, but the most important is that print media are very effective at delivering a message to a target audience.

> Print media are very effective at delivering a message to a target audience.

Most people have access to either a newspaper or a magazine. They read in order to keep up to date with news and events or to provide themselves with a source of entertainment. People tend to have consistent reading habits and buy or borrow the same media vehicles regularly. For example, most people read the same type of newspaper(s) each day and their regular choice of magazine reflects either their business or leisure interests, which are normally quite stable. This means that advertisers, through marketing research, are able to build a database of the main characteristics (a profile) of their readers. This in turn allows advertisers to buy space in those media vehicles that will be read by the sort of people they think will benefit from their product or service.

The printed word provides advertisers with the opportunity to explain their message in a way that most other media cannot. Such explanations can be in the form of either a picture or a photograph, perhaps demonstrating how a product is to be used. Alternatively, the written word can be used to argue why a product should be used and detail the advantages and benefits that consumption will provide the user. In reality, advertisers use a combination of these two forms of communication.

> The print media are most suitable for messages designed when high involvement is present in the target market.

The print media are most suitable for messages designed when high involvement is present in the target market. These readers not only control the pace at which they read a magazine or newspaper, but also expend effort to read advertisements because they care about particular issues. Where elaboration is high and the central processing route is preferred, messages that provide a large amount of information are best presented in the printed form.

Magazines are able to reach quite specialised audiences and tend to be selective in terms of the messages they carry. In contrast, newspapers reach a high percentage of the population and can be referred to as a mass medium. The messages that newspapers carry are usually for products and services that have a general appeal.

Print media is often regarded as a secondary medium to television. There are several reasons for this, but one of them is linked to the perceived 'emotional power' of television. However, Heath and McDonald (2007) report research by OTX using the CEP®Test, which demonstrates that emotive power of print and television ads are basically the same. Their research suggests strongly that press is just as effective as television in building brands and is, in fact, superior with regard to attention-getting and communicating information. What this means is that advertisers can seriously reduce their media costs simply by switching some of their budget out of television and into print and still achieve the same impact.

Newspapers

In general, newspaper readership is in decline and has been falling since the mid 1980s. This is most starkly visible among the young as they gather their news from other sources, most notably the television and now the Internet. The biggest shift has been away from the popular press with some movement towards the quality press. As a result advertising expenditure has not grown in this medium. In 2006, expenditure on national newspaper advertising reached £1.9 billion, down from the £2.3 billion in 2003 (Advertising Association, 2007).

> Newspapers are repositioning themselves as multi-platform publishing entities.

Faced with a declining market newspapers are repositioning themselves as multi-platform publishing entities. In addition to the change from broadsheet to compact formats and the provision of online papers, innovation in the newspaper sector is critical. This is reflected in the growth of free papers, the growing interest in local news and a cross-media orientation (WARC, 2007). This requires major structural change and some risk in anticipating consumer needs.

Strengths

Readers are in control when reading a newspaper and as a result newspaper advertisements are seen positively. This means that readers choose which advertisements are read, how long they consider them (dwell time) and how often they are read. This facilitates 'comparison shopping' and is useful when readers experience high involvement. Newspapers provide wide exposure for advertisements, and market coverage in local, regional or national papers can be extensive. These media vehicles are extremely flexible as they present opportunities for the use of colour and allow advertisements of variable sizes, insertions and coupons.

Weaknesses

The combination of a high number of advertisements and the small amount of genuine reading time that many readers give to newspapers, means that most newspaper advertisements receive little exposure. Statistics show that newspaper circulation has fallen behind population growth; furthermore, teenagers and young adults generally do not read newspapers.

Advertising costs have risen very quickly and the competition to provide news, not just from other newspapers, but also from other sources such as cable, satellite and terrestrial television, means that newspapers are no longer one of the main providers of news. Printing technologies advanced considerably during the 1980s and 1990s, but the relatively poor quality of reproduction means that the impact of advertisements can often be lost.

Magazines

For some time the circulation of monthly magazines was larger than weekly magazines. This has changed as weeklies now have the dominant share of the circulation. Magazine advertising revenue has been fairly static at around £812 million in 2006 (Advertising Association, 2008), whereas advertising in business magazines fell by 7 per cent in 2006. However, business magazines attract substantially more advertising revenue than the consumer sector, despite being highly fragmented and complex.

Strengths

The visual quality of magazines is normally very high, a result of using top-class materials and technologies. This provides advertisers with great flexibility with the visual dimension of their messages. The visual element of magazines is a real strength as it can be used to create impact and demand the attention of readers.

The large number and wide range of specialised titles means that narrow, specific target audiences can be reached much more successfully than with other media vehicles. For example, messages concerning ski equipment, clothing and resorts will be best presented in specialist ski magazines on the basis that they will be read by those who have an interest in skiing, rather than, for example, knitting, snooker or fishing. Magazines can provide a prestigious and high-quality environment, with the editorial providing authority, reassurance and credibility to the advertising that they contain.

Magazines are portable, can be read nearly anywhere and some have the potential to bestow status on the reader. Magazines are often passed along to others to read once the original user has finished reading it. This longevity issue highlights the difference between circulation (the number of people who buy or subscribe to a magazine) and readership (the number of people who actually read the vehicle, perhaps as a friend or partner at home, in a doctor's waiting room or at the instigation of a department head or workplace superior).

> Magazines are often passed along to others to read.

Weaknesses

Magazine audience growth rates have fallen behind the growth in advertising rates. Therefore the value of advertising in magazines has declined relative to some other types of media. The long period of time necessary to book space in advance of publication dates and to provide suitable artwork means that management has little flexibility once it has agreed to use magazines as part of the media schedule. Apart from specialist magazines, a single magazine rarely reaches the majority of a market segment. Several magazines must be used to reach potential users. Having reached the target, impact often builds slowly, as some readers do not read their magazine until some days after they have received it. The absolute and relative costs associated with magazines are fairly high, particularly costs associated with general-interest magazines. Special-interest magazines, however, allow advertisers to reach their target audiences with little waste and hence high levels of efficiency.

ViewPoint 24.1 Land Rover's adventurous publications

The psychological issues associated with owning a 4 × 4 are probably quite complex. At one level the rationale for ownership is that they are practical, roomy and safe. At another more emotional level, owners gain a spirit of adventure and perhaps feel that this type of car enables them to project a slightly different dimension of their personality.

Loyalty towards the Land Rover brand is strong, with many customers purchasing these vehicles for many years. At the heart of Land Rover's loyalty programme are two publications. **Onelife** is a customer-focused publication, mailed to existing Land Rover owners. It provides an introduction to Land Rover's world of adventure and features expeditions and more local outdoor activities closer to home. This is a biannual magazine that generates a 6.8 per cent response rate.

The other publication is sent to dealers. This is a communication pack that contains sets of letters, postcards and mailing materials all designed to help Land Rover dealers manage their particular customers through each of the stages of their vehicle ownership. Both publications are supported by the Land Rover web site, which develops the adventures theme with the G4 Challenge and Go Beyond. The latter pages enable people to upload their own adventures, which do not necessarily feature Land Rover.

Land Rover's customer loyalty programme provides an unrivalled ownership experience. All of Land Rover's marketing communications develop their customers' thirst for adventure and knowledge about their vehicles. They also encourage them to become life-long advocates of the brand. Not surprising then that Land Rover has one of the highest repurchase rates of any vehicle manufacturer.

Question
Why do you think print media are so effective in this context?

Task
Get a copy of any customer magazine sent direct to a household, and compare the content with a consumer magazine bought off the shelf of a retail store.

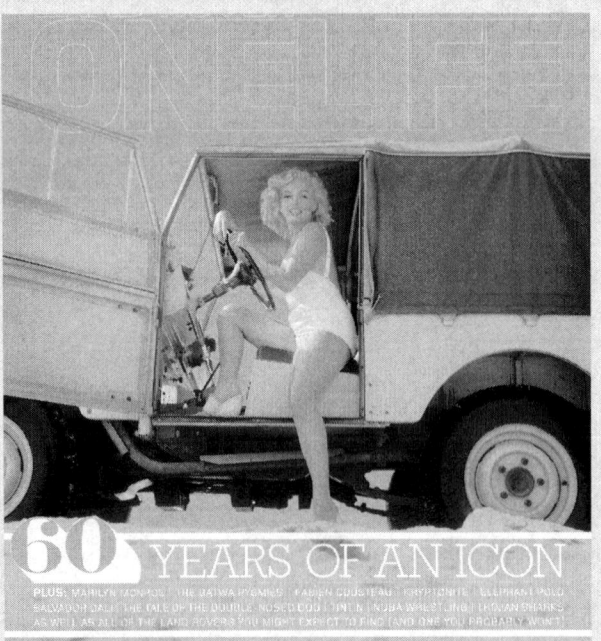

Exhibit 24.1 OneLife is Land Rover's customer magazine that is sent twice a year, to encourage engagement with the brand and eventual repurchase
Courtesy of Land Rover.

Customer magazines differ from consumer magazines because they are sent to customers direct, often without charge, and contain highly targeted and significant brand-related material. These have made a big impact in recent years and, partly because of high production values, have become a significant aspect of many direct marketing activities.

The number of customer magazines has grown in recent years across a variety of sectors. *M&S Magazine*, Waitrose's *Food Illustrated*, Honda's *Dream* and Boots' *Health and Beauty* are just some of the more prevalent titles. In Spring 2005, the NSPCC, in a co-branding alliance with Woolworths, launched *Your Family*. This is a quarterly magazine and is part of the charity's positive parenting campaign. Distributed free through Woolworths' stores, the magazine is funded through advertising and competes against paid-for consumer magazine titles such as *Practical Parenting* and *BBC Parenting*.

One final form of print media yet to be discussed concerns directories. Advertising expenditure on directories has continued to increase. One of the largest consumer directories is Yellow Pages, or Yell as they are now called, as they have diversified across new media (e.g. Yell.com).

Broadcast media

Fundamentally, there are two main forms of broadcast media, television and radio. Advertisers use this class of media because it can reach mass audiences with their messages at a relatively low cost per target reached.

> Advertisers can reach mass audiences with their messages at a relatively low cost per target reached.

Approximately 99 per cent of the population in the United Kingdom has access to a television set and a similar number have a radio. The majority of viewers use television passively, as a form of entertainment; however, new technological applications, such as digitalisation, indicate that television will be used proactively for a range of services, such as banking and shopping. Radio demands active participation, but can reach people who are out of the home environment.

Broadcast media allow advertisers to add visual and/or sound dimensions to their messages. The opportunity to demonstrate or to show the benefits or results that a particular product can bring gives life and energy to an advertiser's message. Television uses sight, sound and movement, whereas radio can only use its audio capacity to convey meaning, but it does stimulate a listener's imagination and thus can involve audiences in a message. Both media have the potential to tell stories and to appeal to people's emotions. These are dimensions that print media find difficulty in achieving effectively within the time allocations that advertisers can afford.

Advertising messages transmitted through the broadcast media use a small period of time, normally 60, 30 or 20 seconds, that are bought from the owners of the medium. The cost of the different time slots varies throughout a single transmission day and with the popularity of individual programmes. The more listeners or viewers that a programme attracts, the greater the price charged for a slice of time to transmit an advertising message. This impacts on the costs associated with such advertising. The time-based costs for television can be extremely large. For example, as at April 2008, the rate card cost of a nationwide 30-second spot in the middle of *Coronation Street* was £95,042 (www.itvsales.com). However, this large cost needs to be put in perspective. The actual cost of reaching individual members of the target audience is quite low, simply because all the costs associated with the production of the message and the purchase of time to transmit the message can be spread across a mass of individuals, as discussed earlier.

The costs associated with radio transmissions are relatively low when compared with television. This reflects the lack of prestige that radio has and the pervasiveness of television. People are normally unable, and

> The costs associated with radio transmissions are relatively low when compared with television.

usually unwilling, to become actively involved with broadcast advertising messages. They cannot control the pace at which they consume such advertising and as time is expensive and short, so advertisers do not have the opportunity to present detailed information. The result is that this medium is most suitable for low involvement messages. Where the need for elaboration is low and the peripheral processing route is preferred, messages transmitted through electronic media should seek to draw attention, create awareness and improve levels of interest.

As the television and radio industries become increasingly fragmented, so the ability to reach particular market segments has become more difficult, as the target audience is often dispersed across other media. This means that the potential effectiveness of advertising through these media decreases. These media are used a great deal in consumer markets, mainly because of their ability to reach large audiences, but there is often considerable wastage and inefficiency. The result is that advertisers are moving their advertising spend to other media, most notably, online.

Television

For a number of years there was above inflation growth in television advertising expenditure, but annual growth since 2003 has been moderate. When the dot-com bubble burst, revenue growth stopped abruptly and station average prices have been falling by anything up to 30 per cent, causing major difficulties for the various station owners. The value of television advertising in 2006 was £4,594 million and showing little growth. This has prompted a review of the capacity of television advertising. The current regulations allow for a maximum of 12 minutes advertising an hour. However, the overall average must be seven minutes an hour, with a specific average of eight minutes an hour between 6p.m. and 11p.m. Ofcom are about to change this, although at the time of writing it is not clear whether the average will be increased by one or two minutes. The change is designed to bring the public service broadcasters (ITV1, Channel 4, Five, GMTV and S4C) into line with EU rules, which govern multi-channel television stations. Such a change will reduce prices and provide better opportunities for smaller business to use the medium.

The number of households connected to cable networks represented 13.0 per cent of all homes by December 2006. This is now a static figure even though cable television is now more established, stable and attractive to advertisers, who are able to target their audiences easily and communicate with less wastage. More importantly, the percentage of homes with a satellite dish is now 32 per cent.

Strengths

From a creative point of view, this medium is very flexible and the impact generated by the combination of sight and sound should not be underestimated. Consumer involvement and likeability of an advertisement is dependent upon the skill of the creative team. The prestige and status associated with television advertising is higher than that of other media: in some cases, the credibility and status of a product or organisation can be enhanced significantly just by being seen to be advertising on television.

The prestige and status associated with television advertising is higher than that of other media. The costs of reaching members of large target segments are relatively low, so the medium is capable of a high level of cost efficiency.

Weaknesses

> Because the length of any single exposure is short, messages have to be repeated on television.

Because the length of any single exposure is short, messages have to be repeated on television in order to enhance learning and memory. This increases the absolute costs of producing and transmitting television commercials, which can be large, making this medium the most expensive form of advertising.

Television audiences are increasingly fragmented as the number of entertainment and leisure opportunities expands. For example, terrestrial television networks are suffering from the competition from cable and satellite broadcasters plus video recorders and other sources of entertainment. This proliferation of suppliers has led to television clutter. In order to keep viewers, programmes are now promoted vigorously by television companies and a variety of techniques are being used to prevent viewers from channel grazing (switching).

The trend towards shorter messages has led to increased clutter. Management flexibility over the message is frustrated, as last-minute changes to schedules are expensive and difficult to implement. The only choices open to decision-makers are either to proceed with an advertisement or to 'pull' it, should circumstances change in such a way that it would be inappropriate to proceed.

Technological developments, most notably the development of interactive television (iTV), have been slow to be adopted. However, this is changing as iTV is increasingly recognised as the way forward (see Chapter 25 for more on iTV). However, as technology advances to create better, more commercially viable interactive opportunities so it also develops disruptive potential to benefit viewers who dislike advert interruptions. First, there was TiVo, a device to blank out ads when recording programmes, which was slow to catch on but is now gathering momentum. Now there are personal video recorders (PVRs) that enable viewers to pause live programmes, 'time-shift' programming to suit their own lifestyles and convenience and to fast forward through commercial breaks in six seconds (Sherwin, 2004). He reports that advertisers are developing 'intelligent' ads that impart information, so that they are recognised when the fast forward button is activated.

ViewPoint 24.2 — Eating Weetabix with the help of television

Weetabix is a premier brand among breakfast cereals. Many people have experienced the brand as a child, often as a baby, as the biscuit reduces to a mush when soaked with milk and becomes an ideal food for weaning. Weetabix is well established and market penetration rates of 40 per cent mean there is little room for growth and development. In addition, the breakfast market was experiencing change in the period 2003–05 and the plainer products such as Cornflakes and Shredded Wheat were losing share.

Weetabix commissioned qualitative research and asked a group of lapsed users to eat the brand for a week and keep a diary. Two of the more startling results were that many of the group soon reported health benefits (no snacking before lunch). In addition, others had started to add 'things' to the cereal to overcome the monotony of its blandness. Here lay the foundation for the advertising campaign, to reveal the variety, interest and added value by using different toppings. A 'Weetabix Week' advertising campaign was devised, which provided the basis for an event designed to stimulate and motivate people to use the brand. First, to encourage them to experiment with different toppings by showing them ways others approached their Weetabix. Second, to provide motivation for people to try the brand for long enough (3/4 days) so that they started to feel the health benefits.

Television was the critical media because it allowed the audience to see the different toppings the participants used to decorate their Weetabix. The second benefit was that television enabled the audience to see 'real people' trying the Weetabix Week. These testimonials provided source credibility and opportunities to link consumption into lifestyle (e.g. children at breakfast, students late at night).

Source: Okin and Robothan-Jones (2007).

Question
What might have been the impact had celebrities been used rather than normal consumers?

Task
Which tools and media would you have used to support the Weetabix Week?

Radio

There has been a rapid increase in the number of commercial radio services offered in the United Kingdom since 1973. Advertising expenditure on radio reached £582 million in 2003, a growth of 6.8 per cent on the previous year, but has since fallen back to £534 million in 2006. This renewed interest in radio is possibly due to a trend away from television and a recognition of the versatility of what is often regarded as a secondary medium.

Strengths

> Radio permits specialised programming, which in turn attracts selective audiences.

Radio permits specialised programming, which in turn attracts selective audiences. Radio is a mobile medium (that is, one that can travel with audiences), so that messages can be relayed to them, for example, even when shoppers are parking their cars near a shopping precinct. The production costs are low and radio has great flexibility, which management can use to meet changing environmental and customer needs. If it is raining in the morning, an advertiser can implement a promotional campaign for umbrellas in the afternoon.

From a creative point of view the medium needs the active imagination of the listener. Radio has a high level of passive acceptance and the messages that are received are more likely to be retained than if they were delivered via a different medium. This combination of features makes radio an excellent support medium.

Weaknesses

Because there is an absence of visual stimuli, the medium lacks impact and the ability to hold and enthuse an audience. Levels of inattentiveness can be high, which means that a high number of messages are invariably ignored or missed. When this is combined with low average audiences, high levels of frequency are required to achieve acceptable levels of reach.

Outdoor media

The range of outdoor media encompasses a large number of different media, each characterised by two elements. First, they can be observed at locations away from home. For this reason some refer to this medium as 'out-of-home'. Second, they are normally used to support messages that are transmitted through primary media: broadcast and print. Outdoor media can therefore, be seen to be a secondary but important support media for a complementary and effective communications mix.

One of the common strands that bind these diverse media together is that they are all used to reach consumers who are themselves in transit, moving from one place to another, even if this is a shopping trip, going to/from work or taking a holiday. Fitch (2007) comments that this class of media is not associated with any particular content. Advertising in television, radio, magazines, newspapers, cinema and the Internet media involves interrupting or accompanying editorial, informational or entertainment material. This is not the case with outdoor media.

There is a balance to be achieved between reaching people and enriching their landscape and annoying those who do not like to see commercial messages on every available space. In Fitch's view, the use of outdoor media must take into account the following variables: 'the length of the ad exposure (viewer "dwell time" in relation to the ad), the ad's intrusiveness on the surrounding environment, and the likely mood and mindset of the consumers who will encounter the ad'. It is the interaction of these variables that shape each individual's experience of outdoor media and hence the effectiveness of each communication.

Media spend on outdoor advertising declined in the early 1990s after steady growth in the 1980s. Growth returned once again to the sector as the UK economy moved out of recession

ViewPoint 24.3 A laddering brand

The use of large or intriguing outdoor media simply to attract the attention of passers-by is a technique that has been employed by advertisers over the years. One of the more noticeable advertisers in recent years has been hosiery manufacturer Pretty Polly. In 2007, the brand wanted to stir a little bit of controversy and at the same time re-establish its credentials as a fashion brand for women.

Using an internationally recognised fashion photographer (Georges Antoni) they developed an eye-catching image of a model's long legs on a ladder. Referred to as 'Stairway to Heaven', the image was used in a variety of places: the web site, buses, billboards, in-store, through direct marketing and to support retailers.

In order to attract real media attention the image was placed on a temporary 64 ft high tower that was placed on the Chiswick Tower roundabout, a very busy traffic route to the west of London. The stunt achieved placement in several London newspapers, three national women's magazines, one national newspaper and several fashion web sites.

Source: Cowlett (2007).

Question
Is the use of this type of outdoor media likely to cause accidents rather than promote brand recall?

Task
Choose a brand and think of interesting ways in which outdoor media might be used to attract attention.

Exhibit 24.2 'Stairway to Heaven' for the Pretty Polly brand and Britain's largest billboard
Courtesy of Pretty Polly.

and has since grown consistently. In 2007, steady growth helped advertising revenues to £1,084 million (Advertising Association, 2008).

> Outdoor media consist of three main formats.

Outdoor media consist of three main formats: street furniture (such as bus shelters); billboards (consisting primarily of 96-, 48- and 6-sheet poster sites); and Transit (which covers the Underground, buses and taxis). Outdoor media accounted for approximately 5.7 per cent of total advertising expenditure in 2006, and has been taking an increasing percentage of organisations' media spend. Recent growth has been due to a 34 per cent increase in the growth of 6-sheet posters (Advertising Association, 2007).

Other reasons for the growth in outdoor expenditure are that it can reinforce messages transmitted through primary media, act as a substitute media when primary media are unavailable (e.g. tobacco organisations deprived of access to television and radio) and provide novelty and interest (electronic, inflatable and three-dimensional billboards), which can help avoid the clutter caused by the volume of advertising activity.

Billboards and street furniture

These are static displays and, as with outdoor media generally, are unable to convey a great deal of information in the short period of time available in which people can attend to the messages. However, advances in technology permit precise targeting of poster campaigns on a national, regional or individual audience basis, or by their proximity to specific outlets, such as banks, CTNs (confectioner, tobacconist and newsagent) and off-licences. There are two key developments in the industry that concern the replacement of the traditional bucket-and-paste production process. The first is the use of biodegradable one-sheet posters. The second concerns the use of high definition (HD) billboards, which are glue-less vinyl posters that can be clipped in and out of a frame, reused and eventually recycled (Gray, 2008). Evaluation using the POSTAR system allows for measurement of not only the size and type of audience but also the traffic flows, travel patterns and even how people read posters.

Strengths

One of the main advantages of this medium springs from its ability to reach a large audience. This means that most members of a target audience are likely to have an opportunity to see the message, so the cost per contact is very low. It is generally recognised that outdoor media can provide tremendous support to other tools in the media mix, particularly at product launch, as back-up and when attempting to build brand name recognition.

The medium is characterised by its strong placement flexibility. Messages can be placed geographically, demographically or by activity, such as on the main routes to work or shopping. The potential impact is high, as good sites can draw the eye and make an impression. Gross rating points (GRPs; see Chapter 27) can be developed quickly by reaching a large percentage of the target audience many times in a short period.

Weaknesses

Messages transmitted by this medium do not allow for the provision of detailed information. Posters are passed very quickly and the potential attention span is therefore brief. This means that the message must be short, have a high visual impact and be capable of selling an idea or concept very quickly. Printing and production lead times are long; therefore, while control over message content is high, the flexibility in delivery once showings are agreed can be a limiting factor. The final disadvantage of outdoor media to be mentioned is that the effectiveness of message delivery is very difficult to measure, and in an age when accountability is becoming an increasingly important factor, this drawback does not help to promote the usage of this medium.

Transit

The names, signs and symbols that are painted on the sides of lorries and taxis can best represent transit or transport advertising. These moving posters, which travel around the country, serve to communicate names of organisations and products to all those who are in the vicinity of the vehicle. Indeed, transport advertising includes all those vehicles that are used for commercial purposes. In addition to lorries and taxis, transit media include buses, the Underground (trains, escalators and walkways), airplanes, blimps and balloons, ferries and trains, plus the terminals and buildings associated with the means of transport, such as airports and railway stations. For example, at Milan airport, the walls of terminal 1 are dominated by huge advertisements for the Giorgio Armani brand. The difference between outdoor and transport media is arbitrary, although the former are media static and the latter are media mobile.

> The difference between outdoor and transport media is arbitrary.

Transit, and in particular taxi advertising, has been found to have very good reach and that its main role should be as a support medium (Veloutsou and O'Donnell, 2005). Messages can be presented as inside cards, where the messages are exposed to those using the vehicle. An example of this would be the small advertising messages displayed on the curvature of the roof of London Underground trains. Outside cards are those that are displayed on the exterior of taxis, buses and other commercial vehicles.

Strengths

The exposure time given to messages delivered via transport media can be high, but is dependent upon the journey time of the reader. The high readership scores that are recorded are due, possibly, to the boredom levels of travellers. The cost is relatively low, mainly because no extra equipment is necessary to transmit the message. Local advertisers tend to benefit most from transport advertising, as it can remind buyers of particular restaurants, theatres and shops.

Weaknesses

The medium fails to cover all market segments, as only particular groups use transportation systems. In comparison with other media it lacks status, is difficult to read (particularly in the rush hour) and suffers from the high level of clutter associated with inside cards.

In-store media

As an increasing number of brand choice decisions are made during the shopping experience, advertisers have become aware of the need to provide suitable in-store communications. The primary objective of using in-store media is to direct the attention of shoppers and to stimulate them to make purchases. The content of messages can be easily controlled by either the retailer or the manufacturer. In addition, the timing and the exact placement of in-store messages can be equally well controlled.

As mentioned previously, both retailers and manufacturers make use of instore media although, of the two main forms (point-of-purchase displays and packaging), retailers control the point-of-purchase displays and manufacturers the packaging. Increasingly, there is recognition of the huge potential of retail stores becoming an integrated media centre, with retailers selling and managing media space and time. Attention is given here to in-store media and the retail media format, while a consideration of packaging issues can be found in Chapter 23.

Point-of-purchase (POP)

There are a number of POP techniques, but the most used are window displays, floor and wall racks to display merchandise, posters and information cards, plus counter and checkout displays. The most obvious display a manufacturer has at the point of purchase is the packaging used to wrap and protect the product until it is ready for consumption. This particular element is discussed in Chapter 23.

Supermarket trolleys with a video screen attached have been trialled by a number of stores. As soon as the trolley passes a particular infrared beam a short video is activated, promoting

> Indirect messages can play a role in in-store communications.

brands available in the immediate vicinity of the shopper. Other advances include electronic overhead signs, in-store videos at selected sites around the store and coupons for certain competitive products dispensed at the checkout once the purchased items have been scanned. Indirect messages can also play a role in in-store communications: for example, fresh bread smells can be circulated from the supermarket bakery at the furthest side of the store to the entrance area, enticing customers further into the supermarket. Some aroma systems allow for the smell to be restricted to just 45 cm (18 inches) of the display.

End-of-row bins and cards displaying special offers are POP media that aim to stimulate impulse buying. With over 75 per cent of supermarket buying decisions made in store, a greater percentage of communication budgets will be allocated to POP items.

ViewPoint 24.4 Thorntons keep it in-store

Valentine's Day is an important day for chocolate manufacturers and retailers. For Thorntons, who have 600 retail outlets, Valentine's Day in 2008 was approached without any advertising work. Apart from product-oriented PR work, all the communications were kept in-store with a heavy emphasis on merchandising.

Thorntons use email to deliver catalogues to b2b customers, while their web site is used to support the flowers, champagne and hamper ranges that complement their gift portfolio.

Source: Jacob (2008).

Question
Why do you think Thorntons have pulled out of any above-the-line work for Valentine's Day?

Task
Think of another gift-oriented brand, and find out what communications are used to support it.

Exhibit 24.3 A Thorntons store
Courtesy of Thorntons.

Strengths

Point-of-purchase media are good at attracting attention and providing information. Their ability to persuade is potentially strong, as these displays can highlight particular product attributes at a time when shoppers have devoted their attention to the purchase decision process. Any prior awareness a shopper might have can be reinforced.

From management's point of view, the absolute and relative costs of POP advertisements are low. Furthermore, management can easily fine tune a POP ad to reflect changing conditions. For example, should stock levels be high and a promotion necessary to move stock out, POP displays can be introduced quickly.

> The absolute and relative costs of POP advertisements are low.

Weaknesses

These messages are usually directed at customers who are already committed, at least partly, to purchasing the product or one from their evoked set. POP messages certainly fail to reach those not actively engaged in the shopping activity.

There can be difficulties maintaining message continuity across a large number of outlets. Signs and displays can also be damaged by customers, which can impact upon the status of a product. Shoppers can therefore be negatively influenced by the temporary inconvenience of damaged and confusing displays. Unless rigorously controlled by store management, the large amount of POP materials can lead to clutter and a deterioration in the perception shoppers have of a retail outlet.

Retail media centres

Traditionally retailers allow their stores to be used in a variety of ways by a variety of organisations to communicate messages to their audiences. These audiences are jointly owned, not necessarily in equal proportion, by the branded food manufacturers that use stores for distribution purposes, and the retailers that try to build footfall or store traffic through retail branding approaches. As a result, the management of the media opportunities and the messages that are communicated are uncoordinated, inconsistent and the media potential, to a large extent, ignored. In the past, retailers will have argued that their core business rests with retailing, not selling and managing media. However, the media world has developed considerably in recent years, often in tandem with developments in technology. For a long time, retailers have built databases using customer information and developed sales promotion-based loyalty programmes as a result.

Street furniture has been used in the immediate vicinity of supermarkets and shopping centres and malls to drive local traffic. In-store radio has been used, first as background and now, in many cases, as a radio station based on entertainment. In-store posters, promotions, merchandising and various ambient media opportunities have been used haphazardly or, at best, in an uncoordinated way. All of these have been managed by a variety of specialists, typical of the way in which the marketing communications industry has developed (see Chapter 3). However, as Reid (2004) pointed out, Tesco and Asda-Walmart installed various in-store plasma television screens. The intention was to sell television time according to product category, some of which equates directly with particular aisles and store space. In addition, Asda has created its own media (or sales) centre through which media activities are coordinated. Tesco understands the media potential of each of its stores and the opportunities that advertisers value by reaching the 27 per cent of all UK shoppers who visit Tesco each week. Indeed, some of the time sold on the Tesco television channels has been sold to advertisers that are not stocked in store (e.g. finance, travel and cars). It was hoped that this retail channel would grow in volume, value and media presence. However, the experiments are reported not to have been entirely successful and in some cases the screens have been removed.

Cinema

> There has been a revival in the level of expenditure on cinema advertising, reflecting the trends in audience sizes.

There has been a revival in the level of expenditure on cinema advertising, reflecting the trends in audience sizes. In 2007 cinema advertising was worth £203 million (Esposito, 2008) or approximately 1 per cent of total advertising spend. Advertisers used to be reluctant to use this medium, but as the number of people visiting cinemas in the United Kingdom grew considerably since 1998 reaching 167 million in 2003. However, attendances have fallen back since then and although they were 156 million in 2007 (CAA/EDI), this was partly because of the wet summer which served to boost cinema attendance. The growth in attendances was linked to the increase in multiplex cinemas (multiple screens at each site) and as Esposito reports, the appalling summer weather in 2007 that drove many people into the cinema for their entertainment. Advertisers have followed the crowds but have also listened to the research that shows that cinema audiences remember more detail than television audiences and as a captive audience there are no distractions.

With customer satisfaction levels improving, advertisers have consistently increased the adspend in this medium. Advertising messages transmitted in a cinema have all the advantages of television-based messages. Audio and visual dimensions combine to provide high impact. However, the audience is more attentive because the main film has yet to be shown and there are fewer distractions or noise in the communication system. The implication is that cinema advertising has greater power than television advertisements. This power can be used to heighten levels of attention and, as the screen images are larger than life and because they appear in a darkened room that is largely unfamiliar to the audience, the potential to communicate effectively with the target audience is strong.

Strengths

> The mood of the audience is generally positive, particularly at the start of a show.

The mood of the audience is generally positive, particularly at the start of a show. This mood can be carried over into the commercials. Furthermore, the production quality of cinema messages is usually very high and transmission is often assisted by high-quality audio (digital surround-sound systems) that is being installed in the new multiplex arenas.

The production and transmission costs are quite low, which makes this an attractive media vehicle. The attention-getting ability and the power of this medium contribute to the high recall scores that this medium constantly records, often four times higher than the average recall scores for television commercials.

Weaknesses

The costs associated with reaching local audiences are low; however, if an advertiser wishes to reach a national audience, the costs can be much higher than those for television. The audience profile for UK cinema admissions indicates that approximately 80 per cent of visitors are aged 15 to 34. With an increasing proportion of the population aged over 55 (the grey market), cinema advertising is limited by the audience profile and the type of products and services that can be realistically promoted.

The third and final weakness is, to some, the most important. The irritation factor associated with viewing advertising messages when customers have paid to see a film has been found to be very high. Some respondents, to a number of studies, have expressed such an intensity of feeling that they actively considered boycotting the featured products. So despite the acclaim and positive reasons for using cinema advertising, advertisers are advised to be careful about the films they select to run their commercials against (audience profile will also be affected) and whether they should use this medium.

> Advertisers are advised to be careful about the films they select to run their commercials against.

ViewPoint 24.5 Orange cinemas?

Orange are the only mobile operator to work with cinema (at the time of writing). In addtion to their considerable £13.5m spend on cinema advertising in 2007 they also sponsored the Bafta film awards. The reason for this activity is that the main cinema audience is the 16- to 34-year-old demographic and that matches Orange's target market. Interestingly they do not use cinema for product-based communications, but use the medium to develop a strong link between Orange and the cinema. Research indicates that Orange are perceived to be the number-one brand associated with film in the United Kingdom.

Mobile brand Orange have used a cinema campaign called 'The Film Board'. For several years 'The Film Board' has occupied the 'gold spot' – the last ad spot before the main feature film begins. The Board is a fictional panel, obsessed with product placement, who listen to famous people and celebrities pitch their ideas for movies. For example, John Cleese pitched his idea for a dramatic war film, but he is not taken seriously by the Board, who even get one of their executives to watch the pitch on their Orange 3G Mobile phone.

Sources: Esposito (2008); www.visit4info.com/details.cfm?adid=24648.

Question
Although Orange have developed strong associations with cinema could it be said that they 'own the medium' as they do not use the medium to promote products?

Task
Next time you visit the cinema make a note of the Film Board spot and consider how prominent Orange is.

Exhibit 24.4 Vue Entertainment has 63 state-of-the-art multiplex cinemas with over 615 screens and 136,000 seats. Vue alone attracts over 32 million customers every year
Freud Communications.

Ambient media

Ambient media are a fairly recent innovation and represent a non-traditional alternative to outdoor media. Ambient media are regarded as out-of-home media that fail to fit any of the established outdoor categories. Ambient media can be classified according to a variety of factors (see Table 24.2). Of these, standard posters account for the vast majority of ambient activity (59 per cent) with distribution accounting for 24 per cent and the four remaining categories just 17 per cent.

Guerrilla tactics

Guerrilla media tactics are an attempt to gain short-term visibility and impact in markets where the conventional media are cluttered and the life of the offering is very short.

Traditionally, flyposting was the main method, practised most often by the music business. Now the term refers to a range of activities that derive their power and visibility from being outside the jurisdiction of the paid-for media. Sabotage is a stronger interpretation, as the tactics require the hijacking of conventional media events. Lanigan (1996) reports on the use of spray paint to sabotage other advertisers' posters, while the launch of the *Blah Blah Blah* music magazine involved sticking speech bubbles over posters carrying messages for other advertisers.

> Sabotage is a stronger interpretation of guerrilla tactics.

Table 24.2 Ambient media categories

Ambient category	Explanation
Standard posters	Washrooms, shopping trolleys, phone boxes
Distribution	Tickets, receipts, carrier bags
Digital	Video screens, projections, LED screens
Sponsorships	Playgrounds, golf holes, petrol pump nozzles
Mobile posters	Lorries, barges, sandwich boards
Aerials	Balloons, blimps, towed banners

Source: Advertising Association (2003) *Advertising Statistics Yearbook*. Used by permission of WARC.

Direct response media

This chapter on the media would not be complete without reference to direct response media. The principal use of the media is to convey one of two types of message: one is oriented towards the development of brands and attitudes; the other is aimed at provoking a physical (and mental) response. It follows that attitude and response-based communications require different media.

Conventional media (television, print or radio) once used just to develop brands and attitudes are now used as a mechanism or device to provoke a response, through which consumers/buyers can follow up a message, enter into an immediate dialogue and either request further information or purchase goods. The main difference with new media is the time delay or response pause between receiving a message and acting on it. Through direct response mechanisms, the response may be delayed for as long as it takes to make a telephone call, press a button or fill out a reply coupon. However, the response pause and the use of a separate form of communication highlight the essential differences.

Estimates vary, but somewhere between 30 per cent and 40 per cent of all television advertisements now carry a telephone number or web address. Direct response television (DRTV) is attractive to those promoting service-based offerings and increasingly travel brands and some FMCG brands are using it. Reid (1996) argues that DRTV can be likened to a video game. Level 1 is viewing the commercial, while level 2 requires the respondent to phone in and receive more information and derive greater entertainment value. Only at level 3 will there be an attempt to sell directly to the respondent. The main purpose for advertisers using this route is to extract personal information for the database and subsequent sales promotion and mailing purposes.

One aspect that is crucial to the success of a direct response campaign is not the number of responses but the conversion of leads into sales. This means that the infrastructure to support these promotional activities must be thought through and put in place, otherwise the work and resources put into the visible level will be wasted if customers are unable to get the information they require – the provision of the infrastructure alone is not sufficient – the totality of the campaign should support the brand. Indeed, this is an opportunity to extend brand opportunities and provide increased brand experiences.

Integrated media

This chapter has considered the merits of different media and has considered them as single media as if they operate in environments unaffected by each other, or indeed aloof from any other influence. Obviously, this is far from reality, and in a world of integrated marketing communications, media neutral planning and open planning approaches each medium needs to be considered in the light of its effectiveness when deployed with other media.

There is a growing body of evidence that shows that the effectiveness of the media increase considerably when media are used in combination. Just as it was shown in Chapter 20 that the impact of sponsorship improves when advertising is used before, during and after the sponsored event, so the impact of particular media can improve when they are used collectively within a campaign. Of course, the possible number of media combinations is huge and too numerous for each to be considered here.

> The effectiveness of the media increase considerably when media are used in combination.

ViewPoint 24.6 Golfing media

Sports events often represent prime promotional opportunities, if only because of the television coverage. For example, major golf tournaments attract huge global television audiences and as a result attract advertisers. The placement of billboards and posters around a golf course are restricted but the tees, where golfers drive off for each hole, are prime points for advertisers. Sometimes these are restricted to the sole use of the tournament's sponsors but it is possible to see a wide array of brands as the camera focuses on the golfers preparing to play. In some cases flowers on the surrounding grassy banks can be used to remind audiences of the location, and the perimeter boards reinforce brand messages or the main sponsors of the event. Very often a clock is used to remind viewers just who is sponsoring the event, while the caddies' bibs carry advertising messages and even the waste bins receive financial support.

All of these are different types of media and they are used to deliver a variety of messages.

Question
To what extent are this cluster of messages likely to cut through or are there just too many?

Task
Choose a sporting event of your choice and note the various promotional opportunities.

It is now commonly accepted that online advertising in general works best with offline media. The main reason for this is that it is necessary to drive people to a particular web site. To date, there is no firm evidence to show that any one type of offline media is best suited to this task and a great deal depends on the nature of the product or service, as well as the audience's involvement in the category.

Snoddy (2007) reports on research referred to as 'brain fingerprinting' (see Chapter 12 for more details). This technical study claims to have scientifically proven that when newspaper advertising is used with television ads, the brand impact scores rise by 72 per cent. As a result, the Newspaper Marketing Agency claims that newspapers provide a complementary impact for, and improve, the impact and response to television ads.

Catalogues, once a popular way of buying clothes and household items, is no longer a fashionable marketing channel and has faded with the development of the Internet and online shopping. While the huge bulky catalogues have all but disappeared, they have been replaced with newer, slimmer and highly targeted catalogues. The product scope is narrow and the aim is to drive people to the brand's web site. The new slim-line catalogues contain a fraction of the products available, but provide a preview and an incentive to visit the web site. Referred to as 'flick-to-click' this approach reflects changing consumer behaviour. Research reported by Murphy (2007) found that 66 per cent of consumers prefer the combination of catalogue to view and online to buy. The most popular categories were clothing, travel, cosmetics and gardening. It is suggested that this behaviour is a function of time-poor customers who prefer to read something offline, at a time convenient to them, perhaps late at night when relaxing (not in front of a computer screen).

> The new slim-line catalogues contain a fraction of the products available, but provide a preview and an incentive to visit the web site.

Outdoor has long been seen as an important support for television and print media, often used to reinforce brand messages or to create attention. What is key of course is to understand how, when and which media people use. Before the arrival of digital media individuals used a limited media mix. This was often based around a few television channels, a Sunday and a weekday paper, maybe a couple of magazines and perhaps cinema. This mix has been transformed so that today research indicates that adults consume a portfolio of media that embraces 10–15 television channels, 10–15 web sites and a similar number of magazines. This does not account for a wealth of other media such as radio and cinema. In addition, people are consuming media through time and place shifting and using their portfolio of media in an integrated format (WARC, 2007).

Summary

In order to help consolidate your understanding of traditional media, here are the key points summarised against each of the learning objectives:

1. Determine the variety and types of traditional media.

Of the many available media, six main classes can be identified. These are broadcast, print, outdoor, new, in-store and other media classes. Within each of these classes there are particular types of media. For example, within the broadcast class there are television and radio, and within the print class there are newspapers and magazines.

Within each type of medium there are a huge number of different individual media vehicles that can be selected to carry an advertiser's message.

2. **Explain the main criteria used to evaluate media and their use.**

Understanding of the key characteristics of each type of media assists media selection and planning. The fundamental characteristics concern the costs, the richness of the communication, the interactive properties and audience profile associated with a communication event.

3. **Establish the primary characteristics of each type of medium.**

The rich array of characteristics that each type of media possesses serve to engage audiences in different ways.

4. **Examine the strengths and weaknesses of each type of medium.**

These were detailed in the chapter and represent opportunities for organisations to make sure they use the right media to deliver against different goals.

5. **Provide a brief summary of the main UK trends in advertising expenditure on each type of medium.**

The overall trend in media spend is that organisations are increasingly moving funds from offline to online media. Digital media spend is increasing and is increasing at a rate far faster than any other type or class of media. Although digital spend is greater than print, most of the large grocery firms allocate less than 1 per cent of their total budget to online resources.

6. **Consider the dynamics associated with direct response media.**

The principal use of the media is to convey one of two types of message: one is oriented towards the development of brands and attitudes; the other is aimed at provoking a physical (and mental) response. It follows that attitude- and response-based communications require different media. One aspect that is crucial to the success of a direct response campaign is not the number of responses but the conversion of leads into sales.

7. **Explore ways in which media can be integrated.**

There is a growing body of evidence that shows that the effectiveness of the media increases considerably when media are used in combination. The possible number of media combinations is huge and too numerous for each to be considered here. It is important to understand how, when and which media people use. Before the arrival of digital media, individuals used a limited media mix. This was often based around a few television channels, a Sunday and a weekday paper, maybe a couple of magazines and perhaps cinema. This mix has been transformed so that today research indicates that adults consume a portfolio of media that embraces 10–15 television channels, 10–15 web sites and a similar number of magazines. This does not account for a wealth of other media such as radio and cinema. In addition, people are consuming media through time and place shifting and using their portfolio of media in an integrated format.

Review questions

1. Explain the differences between media classes, types and vehicles. Give two examples of each to support your answer.
2. Describe the main characteristics of the print media. Find examples to illustrate your points.
3. Compare and contrast newspapers and magazines as advertising media.

4. What do you think will be the impact on broadcast television of the growth in penetration by cable television? How will this affect advertisers?
5. If radio is unobtrusive, why should advertisers use it?
6. What are the strengths and weaknesses of outdoor advertising media? Why is it sometimes referred to as the last true broadcast medium?
7. Why are the relative costs of each medium different?
8. Under what conditions might cinema be used as the primary medium?
9. List the main types of ambient media.
10. Explain the role of primary and secondary media. Is this a valid demarcation in a period of media-neutral planning?

**For different types of wood:
The Pila Pasak (Shepherd's Sawmill) campaign**

Nicola Robinsonova: Freelance Marketing Consultant

The Sawmill

Pila Pasak is a small, but growing sawmill based in the Czech Republic. The company was established in the 1940s and was nationalised during the communist era, before being restituted to a descendant of the founder in 1994. When Pasak first started renting the sawmill, the only advertising consisted of hand-painted signs. There are competitors to Pila Pasak located in the same geographical area. Potential customers need to know about Pila Pasak and actively choose to purchase from the sawmill in preference to a competitor.

Lubos Pasak bought the sawmill in 2003. It now has a staff of 43 (unusually for the industry type, more than 50 per cent of the workforce is female). The sawmill is located in South Bohemia, a landscape of forests and lakes, close to the E55 (European motorway) linking Prague with Linz in Austria. Wood arrives at the plant as tree trunks, and leaves in a variety of forms. There is no waste, tree bark is sold to garden centres, the wood-chip is bought by a wood pellet manufacturer. Any other waste is sold as fuel for wood-burning stoves.

The product itself is essentially a commodity and not capable of differentiation. Pila Pasak would claim to have a higher quality of product than its competitors, but this would be hard to justify. There is not a lot of difference between one sawmill and another. The tree trunks are bought from the same central supplier. The Czech forestry is state owned and state operated, and sets the price and quantity of wood for each year. Wood prices can vary in response to supply and demand – for example the price fell in 2007 partly because of strong storms that blew down many trees.

Pila Pasak's customers are mainly from the building trade, with a limited number of private purchasers. A notable recent customer was the producer of the movie Oliver Twist. Antique timber from Pila Pasak featured in the film, which was filmed partly in the Czech Republic.

About Czech media

Since communism ended in 1989, there has been a rapid transformation of the Czech media industry. Previously, no advertising was allowed, whereas now there is a range of newspapers and magazines (*Tyden* 150k daily readership and *Respekt* 70k) and an active trade press. Broadcast media includes four national television stations and a range of local and national radio stations. There is less regulation of outdoor media, so many prominent adverts, including huge (aesthetically challenging) 3-D sculptures appear beside the major roads of the country. The Czech parliament is now debating the safety issues of such advertising structures.

Ice hockey is the national sport and so billboard ads surround ice hockey pitches in the same way as can be observed at football matches in the United Kingdom. Transport advertising is well established, one notable example being the Zappa cement factory, which uses a highly original livery for their vehicles, as well as a quite extraordinary level of decoration on the plant itself.

The infrastructure supporting Internet use in the Czech Republic is very developed, and so the Internet (and Internet marketing) is a normal part of life. Instore media, such as point-of-purchase and packaging is perhaps somewhat less prominent than in more consumerist societies (or countries with a longer consumerist history), and most Czechs prefer to spend weekends in their country cottages rather than shopping. Other media such as cinema, exhibition and ambient advertising can all be found in the Czech Republic, though product placement is not quite so common in the film industry.

One option used by retail advertisers in the Czech Republic is a weekly broadsheet delivered to the door of every customer, seemingly from every supermarket and chain store.

These free-sheets contain only limited amounts of product- and price-based information. However, people in the Czech Republic do not complain about it, not because they are unsophisticated about advertising, or naive about the purpose of free-sheets, but because many homes in this region are still heated by log-burning stoves, and stoves need fire-lighters, and what better way to acquire them than to have them delivered by a free 'just-in-time' mechanism.

Marketing communications and Pila Pasak

Pila Pasak has a web site (www.pasak.cz), which is visited by around 1,200 people a month. It is a brochure site, with no online shop or additional functionality. Pasak estimates that only 10 per cent of his customers have Internet access and he feels that so far the site has not been of great interest to his customers.

The current marketing communications strategy of Pila Pasak aims to differentiate and remind customers. The marketing budget is 0.7 per cent of turnover, reflecting the growth of the company since a more standard 2–3 per cent budget was set in 2003. Regional advertising agencies are used, but only to print and position the billboard adverts, which are produced in-house.

The campaign was launched in November 2007. The main strap line of the advertising campaign translates as 'For different types of wood' and features three women, each of different size, shape and skin tone, and there is a great deal of exposed flesh (see Exhibit 24.5). Pasak selected four billboard locations within 10 kilometres of the premises to display Eurotype 5.4 × 2.8 m print ads (see Exhibit 24.5).

Media choices

For reasons of cost and practicality, there are no press or radio adverts, and the web site has not been made a part of the campaign. The monthly cost of the billboard equals that of a one-eighth of a page ad in a regional daily, with an estimated readership of 20,000 people. The only point of sale is the sawmill itself, and there is no packaging. Newspaper ads are comparatively expensive when considered alongside billboards.

The sawmill is passed by 30,000 vehicles daily and is on the main road between Prague and Austria. For Pila Pasak, the one clear advantage of this position is that advertising can be created over time by trial and error. The ads can be changed regularly and the effects measured. For example, 'normal'-looking women are used in this campaign because more glamorous models were not so effective. Pasak explains that the more glamorous models did not attract as many new customers because they were not seen as a potentially realistic part of the life of the average Pila Pasak customer.

Exhibit 24.5 Outdoor advertising used by Pila Pasak

Promotional materials

The campaign was not carried over to the corporate gifts distributed over the Christmas period by Pila Pasak. The calendar, which was sent out to key business contacts, featured a collection of historic photos of moustaches. The 'different kinds of wood' calendar cards were given to customers at the payment counter. A more special corporate gift was a bottle of Borovicka, a locally produced spirit flavoured with Juniper berries. The text on the labels had been amended to read 'Pasakova Borovicka'.

Some measures of campaign success include awareness levels among potential customers. For example, people from outside the geographical area of South Bohemia recall the campaign when the name Pila Pasak is mentioned to them. The campaign also received coverage in the national press. For example, a full-page article in *Respekt* with a half-page image of the Pila Pasak advert. When customers visit the premises of Pila Pasak, they can see images from previous adverts over the last 15 years, perhaps a form of strategic brand reinforcement.

MiniCase questions

1. If the Shepherd's Sawmill was based in the United Kingdom, how would you redesign this marketing campaign?
2. What reaction would you imagine if you were to run the campaign as it stands in the United Kingdom?
3. Find out what 'Pasak' means (both literally and in Czech slang), how does this impact on perceptions of the campaign?

References

Advertising Association (2004) *Advertising Statistics Year Book*. Henley: NTC. Also at www.adassoc.org.uk/inform/.

Advertising Association (2007) *Advertising Statistics Year Book*. Henley: NTC. Also at www.adassoc.org.uk/inform/.

Advertising Association (2008) *Advertising Statistics Year Book*. Henley: NTC. Also at www.adassoc.org.uk/inform/.

Ballantyne, D. (2004) Dialogue and its role in the development of relationship specific knowledge. *Journal of Business and Industrial Marketing*, **19**(2), 114–23.

Cowlett, M. (2007) Pretty Polly replicates success of 'Hello Boys', Campaign, 14 March. Retrieved 25 January 2008 from www.prweek.com/uk/search/article/643525/.

Esposito, M. (2008) Cinema advertising: stars of the silver screen. *Marketing*, 9 January. Retrieved 19 January from www.brandrepublic.com/InDepth/Features/775594/Cinema-advertising-Stars-silver-screen/.

Fitch, D. (2007) Outdoor advertising. Retrieved 20 January 2008 from www.millwardbrown.com/Sites/MillwardBrown/Content/News/EPerspectiveArticles.aspx?id=%2f200711010001.

Govoni, N., Eng, R. and Galper, M. (1986) *Promotional Management*. Englewood Cliffs, NJ: Prentice-Hall.

Gray, R. (2008) Green credentials on display. *Marketing*, 9 April, 33–4.

Heath, R. and McDoanld, S. (2007) Press advertising: equal to TV in building brands. *Admap*, (April) 482, 34–6.

Jacob, R. (2008) How personalisation has helped build Thorntons. *UtalkMarketing.com*. Retrieved 26 Februray 2008 from www.utalkmarketing.com/Pages/Article.aspx?ArticleID=4353&Title.

Lanigan, D. (1996) Guerrilla Media. *Campaign*, 5 April, 26–7.

Murphy, D. (2007) Off the page, on to the web, *The Marketer*, (October) 31–3.

Okin, G. and Robothan-Jones, R. (2007) Weetabix – The Weetabix Week: turning a barrier into a benefit. *Institute of Practitioners in Advertising*, IPA Effectiveness Awards. Retrieved 18 April 2008 from www.ipa.co.uk.

Reid, A. (1996) FMCG advertisers are starting to wise up to DRTV. *Campaign*, 26 April, 15.
Reid, A. (2004) Asda leads charge as retail media comes of age. *Campaign*, 2 July, 15.
Sherwin, A. (2004) Instant adverts to counter digital TV viewers. *The Times*, 24 July, 15.
Snoddy, R. (2007) A potent brain wave for newspapers, *Marketing*, 2 May, 18.
Veloutsou, C. and O'Donnell, C. (2005) Exploring the effectiveness of taxis as an advertising medium. *International Journal of Advertising*, **24**(2), 217–39.
WARC (2007) WARC Media report the newspaper market in 2007. Retrieved 21 January 2008 from www.warc.com.

Chapter 14
Interactive marketing communications

For many organisations the use of digital, interactive marketing communications has become an important channel to reach and communicate effectively with specific audiences. Digital media based communications enable individual targeting, personalised messages, interactivity and opportunities to cultivate dialogue, share information and develop relationships.

Aims and learning objectives

The aims of this chapter are to explore the key tools and applications used by organisations in order that they communicate interactively with their audiences.

The learning objectives of this chapter are to:

1. appraise the nature and characteristics of interactive marketing communications;
2. consider some of the issues relating to the way in which each of the tools of the communications mix can be used interactively;
3. evaluate search engine marketing and distinguish the main features of both pay-per-click and search engine optimisation;
4. discuss the features of email marketing communications for both customer acquisition and retention;
5. evaluate the role of electronic word-of-mouth communications, and consider applications such as viral marketing communications, podcasting, Twitter, RSS feeds and web logs;
6. identify the characteristics of online communities and consider how social networks and affiliate marketing can be used to develop marketing communications opportunities.

Introduction

The title of this chapter is *interactive* marketing communications. The use of the word interactive is important as it denotes the key characteristic of this form of marketing communications. It is key because it signifies the functionality that is available, namely the ability of all participants in a communication network to respond to messages, share knowledge and create content. This is not a feature of most offline marketing communications media such as radio, billboards or magazines. It is also key because it indicates that this type of communication environment is open, that is, more democratic than conventional marketing communications. The latter tend to be one-sided and driven primarily by organisations and the satisfaction of their more overt needs. The word interactive suggests that all parties to a communication event are enabled to communicate. Finally, the word interactive is used to cover a wide spectrum of electronic environments, one that is not limited or defined by the Internet. For example, mobile communications do not operate online, yet can be used to reach people digitally wherever they are and engage them, potentially interactively.

Perhaps the strongest characteristic of interactive marketing communications is that it enables communications to move from one-way and simple two-way models to one that is literally 'interactive'. Interactivity normally precedes the establishment of dialogue between participants in the communication process. This in turn enables all participants to contribute to the content that is used in the communication process. This is referred to as user-generated-content, as demonstrated by people uploading videos to YouTube or even emailing comments to radio and television programmes. This symbolises a shift in the way in which marketing communications has developed, especially in the online environment. So, when the maintenance of 'relationships' is a central marketing activity it is possible to conclude that interactive marketing communications has an important role to play. Table 14.1 sets out some of the interactive properties associated with each of the primary tools of the marketing communications mix. The chapter then continues to consider some of the specific digital applications and facilities used by organisations to communicate with other organisations.

Search engine marketing

Websites need visitors and the higher the number of visitors the more effective the website is likely to be. Many people know of a particular site and simply type in the address or use a bookmark to access it. However, the majority of people arrive at sites following a search using particular key words and phrases to search for products, services, news, entertainment and the information they need. They do this through search engines and the results of each search are displayed in rank order. It is understandable therefore, that those ranked highest in the results lists are visited more often than those in lower positions.

Therefore, from a marketing perspective it is important to undertake marketing activities to attain the highest possible ranking position, and this is referred to as search engine marketing (SEM). There are two main search engine marketing techniques; search engine optimisation (SEO) and pay-per-click (PPC) with the latter outweighing the former quite substantially (Jarboe, 2005).

Search engine optimisation

Search engine optimisation (SEO), or as it used to be referred, organic search, is a process used to get a high ranking position on major search engines and directories. To achieve top-ranking positions, or least a first page listing, it is necessary to design webpages and create links with other quality websites, so that search engines can match closely a searcher's key words/phrases with the content of registered webpages.

Table 14.1 The interactive dimensions of the tools of the marketing communications mix

Marketing communications tool	Format	Comment
Interactive advertising	Banner ads	Over 50 per cent all web ads are banner ads, responsible for over 90 per cent of all Internet ad awareness. Although effective as a stand-alone ad, banner ads are linked through to an advertiser's chosen destination and therefore can act as a gateway to other websites. The aim of banner ads is to attract attention and stimulate interest, but the problem is that click-through rates are very low, at just 0.18 per cent (Mathews, 2007). Today, banners are not highly regarded but they continue to be used with many incorporating Flash, rich media, multipurpose units and sky-scrapers (very tall banner ads) as these formats generate better recall scores than the standard banner.
	Pop-ups	Also known as transitional online ads, pop-ups appear in separate browser windows, usually when webpages are being loaded or closed. With high speed loading, pop-ups are now generally regarded as intrusive.
	Microsites	This type of site is normally product or promotion-specific, and is often run as a joint promotion with other advertisers. Creating a separate site avoids the difficulty of directing traffic to either of the joint partners' sites. Microsites are much less expensive to set up than a traditional site and are particularly adept at building awareness as click-throughs to microsites are higher than through just banners.
	Online video	The development of YouTube has changed the perception of online video advertising. Online video ads can be used in a number of different ways apart from simply showing ads at the beginning or end of programmes. Online video content normally plays in an unstoppable loop, so the ads are unavoidable. In addition, advertisers are able to place ads within video streams, another reason preventing users from avoiding them. Also, video ads can be embedded within webpages and online articles, relating closely to the site content. A growth area.
	Advergames	The use of custom made online games designed to provide both entertainment and communicate a brand message, has grown considerably in recent years. Messages can be embedded as in integral part of the game, or they can be positioned passively, such as a billboard in Second Life. The messages may be designed to promote a brand or educate an audience. For example, banks have developed short games followed by messages about a new credit card. An alternative approach is to educate audiences as used in health campaigns to reach children to inform about diet and obesity issues. In all cases advergaming allows people to develop positive brand experiences through play.

Interactive sales promotions	Used to provoke a behavioural response, they can also be used in a mobile context, and not be restricted to an online context. The main aims of using interactive sales promotion are first, that they can either attract or retain customers, and second, that they provide interest and involvement with the brand by encouraging interaction and return visits. In reality, sampling, free gifts, e-coupons, price deals and competitions are the main incentives used interactively.

The Internet enables sampling to occur very well. Music and software can be downloaded for trial purposes, while services such as photo processing can be tested risk-free through introductory offers. Another area experiencing growth is the rather oddly termed 'e-coupons'. Downloaded coupons can be redeemed online using a code at checkout, or printed off and used offline in-store. |
| Interactive direct marketing | Used to integrate a range of activities, but underpins the majority of communication activities in the online environment. There are some branding-based communications, but the majority of activity is wrapped up as direct marketing, whether that be in the form of direct response advertising (e.g. banners or rich media), sales promotion (e-coupons or sampling) or public relations (e.g. sponsorship, blogs and podcasts). Used to converge different media in order to convert warm prospects.

Offline direct marketing is used to drive traffic to a website. This might be undertaken by branding or by providing incentives. For example, many insurance companies use direct response television ads to inform consumers of their low cost/high value insurance deals to be found at their website. Email and viral marketing are used extensively. |
| Interactive public relations | Used extensively to present the organisation (and its products and services) in a positive manner to a range of stakeholders. The goal is to create 'mentions' in both traditional media and online on other websites, which is important for establishing links and achieving higher search engine rankings. Newsletters and white papers are reputation-driven with a diverse range of content concerning organisational and/or technical-related material. These communications can be an essential part of the 'stick ness' that good websites seek to develop. Recipients who find these communications of value either anticipate their release or return to the host's website to search in archived files for past copies and items of interest.

Statements concerning an organisation's position on an issue of public interest, corporate social responsibility or environmental matters can be published, while investor relations and public affairs issues are easily accommodated. Sponsorship activities are an important part of interactive online marketing communications, whether they be in the form of a partnership deal or direct sponsorship of a social networking site. Websites can also play an important role in terms of crisis management. In the event of an organisational crisis or disaster, up-to-date information can be posted quickly, either providing pertinent information or directing visitors to offline information and associated facilities. |
| Interactive personal selling | Face-to-face personal communications are, by definition, always interactive. However, the online application for the purposes of buying and selling remains the one part of the mix that cannot be easily addressed. Video conferencing does provide this facility but costs and logistics limit the practical application of this tool to conferencing and non-sales meetings. Although the Skype telephone software enables people to talk over the Internet using their PCs free of charge, using next-generation peer-to-peer software, the online environment is an impersonal medium and, as such, does not allow for direct personal communication. |

Each search engine, such as Google, MSN Search and Yahoo, uses an algorithm to compare the content of relevant site pages with the key words/phrases used to initiate the search. Search engines use robotic electronic spiders to crawl around registered sites and from this compile an index of the words they find, placed there by the designer of each website. When a search is activated, it is the database housing these keyword/phrases that is searched, not the millions of world-wide webpages.

In order to get a high ranking it is important for a site to be registered, which is normally achieved by adding the URL of a site directly into a search engine. Some sites are automatically registered if there are links with another company that is already registered. Once registered, a high ranking is best achieved by attaining a match between the search words/phrases entered by the searcher and the words/phrases on the pages stored in the index. Achieving a good match can be helped by understanding, if not anticipating, the words and phrases that are likely to be used by individual searchers. Through web analytics, the study of website visitors' behaviour, it is possible to analyse the search terms used by current visitors. This can also help improve the matching process. However, there are some fundamental activities that can influence ranking positions.

The first important factor is referred to as 'keyphrase density', which refers to the number of times a key phrase is repeated in the text of a webpage. The next concerns the number of inbound links from what are regarded as good-quality sites. The greater the number of quality links, the higher the ranking is likely to be. Two further factors that affect a page's ranking concern the use of tags. The use of keywords in the *title tag* of a webpage and the *meta tags*, which signify the content and describe what searchers will find when they click on the site, are embedded by webpage designers and read by some search engine spiders. When key words and phrases used by searchers match those in these tags, it is likely that the site will have a higher ranking. For example, the airline easyJet, who sell more than 98 per cent of its seats via the www.easyjet.com website, use search engine optimisation to drive traffic to its websites across Europe. It is vital that easyJet appears when the search phrases associated with the discount airlines business are used.

Viewpoint 14.1 Searching the market for meerkats

Comparethemarket.com, a price comparison site for car insurance, was ranked fourth in the market and lacked the resources its main competitors could bring, especially in terms of advertising budgets, necessary to drive awareness, web visits and click through. Their name was instantly forgettable, their identity and name were very similar to their nearest competitor (gocompare), they had no single point of differentiation and they were last to the market. The task was to find a strong point of differentiation.

In this market it is easy to get people to remember 'compare'-led brand names but very difficult to get them to remember how one is different to the other. Fortunately the one element that distinguished this brand from the competition was the word 'market' in their name. It was reasoned that rather than use a rational attribute-based positioning like their competitors, who were perceived to be irritating and disliked, the key was to differentiate through entertainment.

In search terms the word market was expensive. At the time it was worth £5 per click so the task was to find a cheaper term or phrase that could be used by people as a substitute for 'market'.

The word 'meerkat' costs only 5p and so a campaign was built around a Russian meerkat called Aleksandr Orlov. He was portrayed as founder of www.comparethemeerkat.com, a site for comparing meerkats, and as someone who is frustrated by the confusion between Comparethemarket.com and Comparethemeerkat.com. The joke caught the imagination of the target audience and the site quickly assumed number one position. Orlov was an instant success, and quickly spawned tens of thousands of Facebook followers and instant recognition.

Source: Based on Jukes (2009); VCCP (2009); Ramsay (2009)

Question
To what extent is the success of SEO a function of second guessing the keywords people are likely to use?

Task
Identify three brands of coffee, submit the word coffee, and note the position of each of your brands in the listing.

Exhibit 14.1 Comparethemeerkat's Aleksandr Orlov from a Comparethemarket.com ad
Image courtesy of The Advertising Archives

Pay-per-click searches

Pay-per-click (PPC) is similar to display advertising found in offline print formats. Ads are displayed when particular search terms are entered into the search engine. These ads appear on the right-hand side of the results page and are often referred to as sponsored links. However, unlike offline display ads, where a fee is payable in order for the ad to be printed, here a fee is only payable once the display ad is clicked, and the searcher is taken through to the company's webpage. See Exhibit 14.2 for an example of these sponsored links displayed as a result of the keyphrase 'cheap airline tickets' input to Google.

It is important for organisations to maintain high visibility, especially in competitive markets, and they cannot rely on their search engine optimisation skills alone. PPC is a paid search list and once again, position in the listings (on the right-hand side of the page) is important. The position in the list is determined mainly through a bidding process. Each organisation bids an amount they are willing to pay for each searcher's click, against a particular key word or phrase. Unsurprisingly, the higher the bid the higher the position on a page. To place these bids, brokers (or PPC ad networks) are used and their role is to determine what a competitive cost per click should be for their client. They achieve this through market research to determine probable conversion rates, and from this deduce what the purchase and lifetime value of customers are likely to be. Consideration needs to be given to the quality of the landing page to which searchers are taken (not the home page), and whether the call-to-action is sufficiently strong.

Search engine marketing is important if only because of the relative ineffectiveness of other online marketing activities. The goal of SEM is to drive traffic to websites, and ranking on the search-results page is achieved in two fundamentally different ways. In SEO ranking searches are based on content while the PPC approach relies entirely on price as a ranking mechanism.

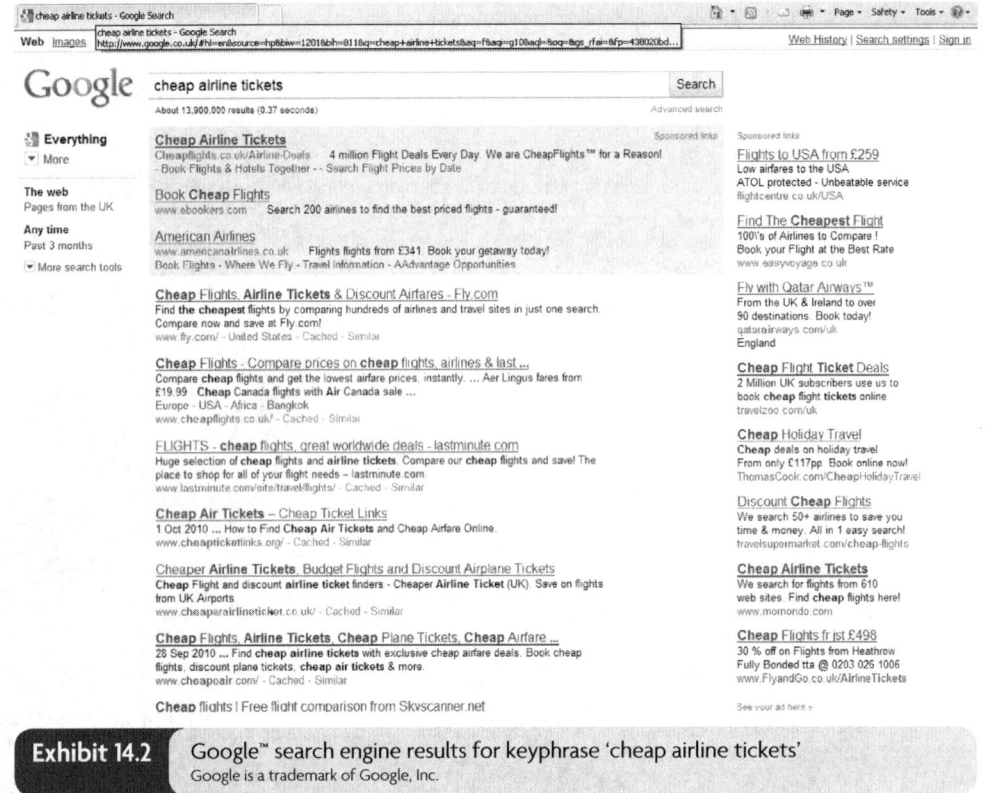

Exhibit 14.2 Google™ search engine results for keyphrase 'cheap airline tickets'
Google is a trademark of Google, Inc.

Of these two main approaches, research indicates that the PPC model attracts far more investment (by advertisers) than the SEO model. This indicates that paid ads or sponsored links have low credibility and do not carry high levels of trust. Added to this is the overwhelming research that shows that SEO is more effective in terms of recall and driving site traffic (Jansen and Molina, 2006). However, Kimberley (2010) reports that research undertaken by IAB has found that brands are failing to exploit the potential offered by search engine marketing.

Viewpoint 14.2 Searching for quality chocolate

Luxury chocolate retailer Hotel Chocolat began as a mail-order business. However, the company's marketing strategy involved the development of a multichannel approach. This was realised through the launch of an online store and then through the opening of various offline stores.

The design and opening of its online store required that the company consider its search engine marketing and in particular SEO. In order to determine the key search words and phrases that customers for high quality chocolates would use, rather than just chocolate, they used a mind mapping process. Phrases such as 'Gifts for Christmas' and 'Gifts for Valentines' emerged, complementing their peak sales periods.

The company has bought a cocoa plantation in the West Indies and both text and video content was added to the site. This material was reflected in the site's tags so that a range of related ethical key phrases was built into its SEO work and Hotel Chocolat's search ratings improved.

Question
Why do people search for chocolate – don't we know where to buy our preferred chocolate?

Task
Choose a product category you are interested in and list some of the keywords that should assist SEO.

Email marketing

There are two key characteristics associated with email communications. First, it can be directed at clearly defined target groups and individuals. Second, email messages can be personalised and refined to meet the needs of individuals. In this sense email is the antithesis of broadcast communications, which are scattered among a mass audience and lack any sense of individualisation, let alone provide an opportunity for recipients to respond. In addition, email can be used with varying levels of frequency and intensity, which is important when building awareness, reinforcing messages or when attempting to persuade someone into a trial or purchase.

Organisations need to manage two key dimensions of email communications; outbound and inbound email. Outbound email concerns messages sent by a company often as a part of a direct marketing campaign, designed to persuade recipients to visit a website, to take a trial or make a purchase. The inbound dimension concerns the management of email communications received from customers and other stakeholders. These may have been stimulated either by an individual's use of the website, exposure to a news item about the product or organisation, or through product experience, which often entails a complaint. Managing inbound email represents a huge opportunity not only to build email lists for use in outbound campaigns, but also to provide high levels of customer service interaction and satisfaction. If undertaken properly and promptly this can help to build trust and reputation, which in turn can stimulate word-of-mouth communication, all essential aspects of marketing communication. Activity-triggered email that incorporates the interests of the target audience and which follow up on audience behaviour are deemed to be more successful and good practice, if only because of the higher conversion rates and return on investment.

Viewpoint 14.3 Email haven

Email marketing can not only stimulate a response but can also be used to develop brand experiences. For example, Haven, the holiday company, embedded video in their emails. In order to capture attention, these were designed to play automatically when the email is opened, rather than require the recipient to click on a link.

The facility appealed to two main audiences. Previous visitors could relive the Haven experience and have their beliefs reinforced, key to securing another booking. Potential visitors could feel the Haven experience virtually, provide a point of differentiation and build anticipation. The email also linked to the main website enabling recipients to access further information, offers and booking online.

The campaign successfully raised the conversion rate by 50 per cent.

Source: Based on Fletcher (2009).

Question
What might be the reasons for declining levels of email marketing?

Task
Find an online source of business mailing lists. Review the website and make a list of the sorts of questions you might ask.

The use of email to attract and retain customers has become a main feature of many marketing communications campaigns. Using appropriate email lists is a fast, efficient and effective way to communicate regularly with a market. Email-based marketing communication enables organisations to send a variety of messages concerning public relations-based announcements, newsletters and sales promotions, to distribute online catalogues and to start and manage permission-based contact lists. Many organisations build their own lists using data collected from their CRM system. By acquiring email responses and other contact mechanisms, addresses and contact details can be captured for the database and then accessed by all customer support staff. The use of email to attract and retain customers has become a main feature of many organisations' marketing communications campaigns. Indeed, email can be used to deliver messages at all points in the customer relationship lifecycle.

Short message services (SMS)

Although different in format, short message services (SMS), or 'texting', can be regarded as an extension of email communication. SMS is a non-intrusive but timely way of delivering information and as Doyle (2003) points out, the Global System for Mobile Communication (GSM) has become a standard protocol, so that users can send and receive information across geographic boundaries. Apart from pure text, other simple applications consist of games, email notifications, and information-delivery services such as sports and stock market updates.

Yaobin *et al.* (2010) undertook a study into the reasons why consumers use SMS. The research was based in China, where SMS is used extensively and the results highlighted three main reasons for use. These concern the perceived utilitarian value of SMS, the level of intrinsic enjoyment and the satisfaction derived from the involvement in communication. The third reason was the relatively low costs of use.

For some time organisations were relatively slow at adopting SMS despite the low costs and high level of user control (target, content and time). However, as organisations recognise these benefits so SMS has become an integral part of the media mix for many organisations. However, marketers also need to consider the potential concerns of consumers, most notably security and privacy. Just as with email, there is the potential for unwanted messages (i.e. spam) and Internet service providers (ISP) need to manage the increasing numbers of unsolicited messages through improved security systems as SMS becomes more widespread. Given that most consumers pay for SMS functionality, marketers should realise that invading personal privacy greatly reduces the potential value and effectiveness of SMS.

Apps

An app is a mobile application, a piece of software that is downloaded and runs on mobile devices such as smartphones. Apps enable users to do things such as find a cinema, restaurant, bank or other destination, read news, update a grocery list, track a team's score, play games, remember where the car is parked, all on a mobile phone (Sullivan, 2010). Procter & Gamble launched an app to support its Pampers brand, called *Hello Baby*, which allows pregnant women to track the development of their baby.

From a marketing communication perspective, apps enable a brand to be connected with a user as they move around. Some apps can become an integral part of a user's life, some can strengthen brand awareness, and others offer opportunities for more frequent interaction and brand engagement.

Most of the 140,000 available apps have been developed for Apple's iPhone and iPod Touch. Unsurprisingly, people prefer free apps, which is significant in terms of the limited opportunities brands have to recover the approximately £55,000 to $65,000 necessary to develop a mainstream app.

Goddard (2010) suggests that apps can be categorised into four types:

- **Campaign based** apps have high brand value content but little everyday utility. This means they will attract attention in the short term but will not serve to retain users.
- **Popular gimmick** apps are characterised by having low brand value, and are not very useful. Their value lies in supporting short term campaigns or events, but can become obsolete

when the campaign finishes. A brewer launched an app resembling a pint of beer that poured out when the mobile device was tilted. Good for entertainment purposes but once seen there is little value in repeating.
- **Straight utilities** are apps that serve as everyday tools. Location finders, currency converters, and recipe and menu directories can be useful but competition is high and standout opportunities are rare.
- **Branded utilities** are both highly useful and develop the brand promise. These are considered to be the most powerful types of mobile apps, simply because engagement occurs through the functionality which is tied to the essential value of the brand.

Apps enable brands such as Chanel, Ford, Pepsi, Visa, Lynx and many others, opportunities to provide users with branded content, which as Yuill (2010) suggests, can be anywhere at anytime to suit the user.

Widgets

Widgets are stand-alone applications that enable users to interact with the owner of the widget. As Chaffey (2008) suggests, the applications can provide functionality such as a calculator or real-time information, as in travel updates or weather forecasts. Widgets sit on a desktop, are relatively cheap to develop, easy to manage and ideally are distributed virally.

The real benefit of widgets is that they provide a way of advertising a brand, delivering online public relations or even driving direct response sales via affiliate marketing.

Blythe (2008) sees the real potential of widgets as sponsored entities on social networking sites. To date, attempts by brands to derive commercial benefit from social networking sites have been thwarted by the prevailing network culture that is essentially one that rejects advertising and outright commercialism. Sponsored widgets might provide a means of overcoming these difficulties as widgets offer benefits that might appeal to social network users. For example, the group Jamiroquai use a widget that allows their fans to keep up-to-date on video releases, tour dates and tracks. Cadbury have created a game called 'Room with a Goo'. In it players are required to stop Creme Eggs being smashed, blended and splattered. A widget on the Bebo site enables users to destroy or rebuild others Cadbury's Creme Eggs by either hugging or karate-chopping the eggs, virtually. A whole range of widget applications can be seen at www.directory.snipperoo.com.

Affiliate marketing

Associated with the concepts of communities and networks, affiliate marketing has become an essential aspect of online marketing communications and ecommerce. Walmsley (2010) estimates that affiliate marketing is worth approximately £4 billion in sales in the UK. Affiliate schemes are based on a network of websites on which advertisements or text links are placed. Those who click on them are taken directly to the host site. If this results in a sale, only then will the affiliate receive a commission (payment for the ad). Cookies, information generated by a web server and stored in the user's computer, ready for future access (http://www.cookiecentral.com/c_concept.htm), are used to track, monitor and record transactions and pay commission plus any agreed charges. As with many online marketing schemes, management can be undertaken in-house or outsourced. If the latter approach is adopted then many of the relationship issues discussed earlier, need to be considered and managed.

Amazon is probably one of the best examples of affiliate marketing schemes. Amazon has thousands of affiliates who all drive visitors to the Amazon website. If a product is sold to the visitor as a result of the click-through, then the affiliate is rewarded with a commission payment. Affiliate schemes are popular because they are low-cost operations, paid on a results-only basis and generating very favourable returns on investment.

McCormick (2010) reports on the use of affiliate marketing by Lastminute.com. This organisation considers its affiliate network as a team and an integral part of its marketing programme. Affiliates receive emails twice a week advising about key performing products and offers in their key sales areas. Blogs are used to provide up to date information. Lastminute.com also provide their affiliates with advice and facilities to generate increased income. For example, these include bespoke banners for placement by the key affiliate partners and templates and designs for email newsletters. Even quiet or underperforming affiliates are reached with communications that flag relevant offers to get them operating once again.

Review sites constitute a large proportion of affiliate activity and so these are targeted with specific offers to be run against each relevant review. Feedback is encouraged and analysis shows that clicks through from affiliates rose in 2009 by 22.4 per cent.

Augmented reality

Glasses Direct enable customers to see online how they look with different frames. The 'online mirror' technologies behind this facility are referred to as augmented reality (AR). By mixing the real world with digitally generated information or images, AR opens opportunities for both business and consumer-oriented interactive marketing communications (Clawson, 2009). So, augmented reality will allow people to see what they look like in different clothes, without having to get changed into them and with developments in mobile technology, without a change of location.

At the time of writing AR based technologies are developing but they are increasingly used in mobile applications in connection with location facilities. For example, they can be used as virtual wardrobes, shop fronts, store layouts and as a means of locating shops, tube stations, restaurants, pubs and theatres with a mobile phone (Benady, 2009).

Viewpoint 14.4   E.On augment their sponsorship of the FA Cup

E.On's sponsorship of the FA Cup involved two trophy tours. One was the conventional nationwide tour enabling fans to physically get close to the famous cup. The other was a virtual tour enabled through augmented reality (AR). Fans of the two finalists were able to go online and using a webcam and capture an image of themselves lifting the FA Cup.

Marketing communications used to support the activities involved a national print campaign and viral video seeded across a range of targeted websites. They were both intended to raise awareness and the former intended to drive traffic to the website where there were instructions on how to use the AR facility, and of course, register with E.On.

The press work included an augmented reality marker, so that people with enabled phones could access the virtual FA Cup online, straightaway.

The digital campaign lasted just one week and over 90,000 users visited the site in that period whilst the seeded content prompted three times the normal click-throughs.

Source: Based on Dundas (2010)

Question
How might augmented reality assist marketing communications?

Task
Identify two non-football activities that would benefit from the use of augmented reality technology.

Bring your family and The FA Cup together in 4 easy steps.

1. Visit familyfootball.co.uk and select The Virtual FA Cup.

2. Hold the black symbol in the centre up to your webcam.

3. Experience that moment of glory felt by Chelsea yesterday.

4. Email a video or picture of your celebrations to your friends and family.

Exhibit 14.3 Virtual entertainment with AR
Image for this past campaign is used courtesy of E.ON UK plc

Word-of-mouth communication

It was established in Chapter 2 that people use word-of-mouth recommendations to provide information and to support and reinforce their purchasing decisions. The impact of personal influences on the offline communication process can be important if communication is to be successful. Opinion leaders and formers were identified as significant personal influencers, simply because organisations target these individuals with messages knowing that they will transmit messages onwards to the organisation's target audience. The same principle is true of digital communications where the popular term 'word-of-mouse' is used to reflect personal, electronic recommendation and endorsement. However, the role of opinion formers is much diminished in the online world, especially with the predominant 18–25-year-old user group. For them expert opinion, as represented by opinion formers, is rejected in favour of peer group recommendation. For example, www.last.fm, a social music platform, tracks individual music preferences based on what people play on their computers or iPods, locates individuals in neighbourhoods who share similar tastes and then wait for them to interact. People share views, interests and favourite music and then make recommendations to others in their neighbourhood, based on shared preferences (Crow, 2007). Although there is a hint of social engineering, the power of peer group and opinion leader recommendation has seen this model copied by others, including book libraries.

Five main aspects of electronic word-of-mouth communication are considered here: viral marketing, podcasts, web logs (or blogs), Twitter and RSS feeds.

Viral marketing

Viral marketing involves the use of email to convey messages to a small part of a target audience where the content is sufficiently humorous, interesting or persuasive that the receiver feels emotionally compelled to send it on to a friend or acquaintance. For example, football matches between teams from the same city are always full of tension, grit and passion, and that is just the fans. One such cup match was played between Everton and Liverpool in February 2009. The match was being screened live but there was a technical error with the automated advertising system, just as the match went into extra time. So as fans watched a Tic Tac ad interrupt the match, unknown to them the winning goal was scored by Everton.

Once the inevitable arguments died down, the agency WCRS, who developed the ad for Tic Tac, decided to use the event to make a 20-second viral for a little bit of fun. The aim was to re-create Dan Gosling's goal, but instead they used two teams dressed as orange and lime Tic Tac men. Filmed on a winter's day on the Hackney Marshes, the viral not only poked fun at the issue but also provided entertainment around the Tic Tac brand (Nettleton, 2009).

Viral can also be used to support product launches, as demonstrated by the launch of Google Wave. Essentially a collaboration tool which allows users to swap messages, pictures, video, and gadgets and merges them into a single, user friendly application, it was important to demonstrate the features of the new product. This was achieved using a viral based on a scene from the film *Pulp Fiction*. The visual effects are performed through a remote user clicking on Google Wave, and the audio was just the dialogue from the film. The viral was viewed 500,000 times in the first two weeks, posted on 335 blogs and featured in over 4,600 tweets (GoViral, 2009).

The term, 'viral marketing' was developed by a venture capital company, Draper Fisher Juvertson (Juvertson and Draper, 1997). It was used to describe the Hotmail email service, one of the first free email address services offered to the general public and one that has grown enormously. According to Juvertson (2000: 12) they defined the term simply as 'network-enhanced word-of-mouth'. However, although the literature contains a variety of terminology used to explain what viral marketing is, for example *stealth marketing* (Kaikati and Kaikati,

Exhibit 14.4 Old Spice ads prove to be viral hits
Image courtesy of The Advertising Archives

2004), *interactive marketing* (Blattberg and Deighton, 1991) and *referral marketing* (de Bruyn and Lilien, 2004), viral marketing (communications) is the term used here.

Porter and Golan (2006: 33) suggest that viral advertising is 'unpaid peer-to-peer communication of provocative content originating from an identified sponsor using the Internet to persuade or influence an audience to pass along the content to others'. They argue that these materials are usually seeded through the Internet, are often distributed through independent third-party sites, are usually personal, more credible than traditional advertising and humour is almost unanimously employed in executions. Kirby, a leading viral marketing consultant, agrees indicating that there are three key elements associated with viral marketing (2003):

- *content*, which he refers to as the 'viral agent' is the quality of the creative material and whether it is communicated as text, image or video;
- *seeding*, which requires identifying websites or people to send email to in order to kick start the virus;
- *tracking*, or monitoring, the impact of the virus and in doing so provide feedback and a means of assessing the return on the investment.

However, although these qualities might be present, it is necessary that receivers of viral messages are predisposed to open the message, derive value from the message and be sufficiently engaged to become a part of the virus campaign by sending it on to others.

There is no doubt that viral marketing is difficult to control and can be very unpredictable, yet despite these characteristics organisations are incorporating this approach within their marketing communications in order to reach their target audiences. Increasingly organisations are using word-of-mouth communications to generate conversations before the official launch. Kellogg's used social media for six months before officially launching Special K Crackers with traditional media. Ford in America used social media to encourage word-of-mouth communication for a year before running tv ads for the latest edition Fiesta (Anon, 2010). The key reasons for this approach are that it helps identify interested communities and consumer groups and it also encourages feedback, in a similar way to test marketing.

Social media

The terms social media and social networks have become increasingly prevalent. Although similar, they do not mean the same yet are often used interchangeably, and mistakenly. Kaplan and Haenlein (2009: 61) define social media as 'a group of Internet based applications that build on the ideological and technological foundations of Web 2.0 and that allow the creation and exchange of User Generated Content'. In other words social media refers to a broad range of web based applications and social networking sites are one of the many applications that are available. Others include weblogs, content communities (e.g. YouTube), collaborative projects (e.g. Wikipedia), virtual game worlds (e.g. World of Warcraft) and virtual social worlds (e.g. Second Life).

Social networks

One particular interpretation of online communities is the rapid development of social networks. Social networks are about people using the Internet to share lifestyle and experiences. The participants in these networks not only share information and experiences, but they can also use the interactive capacity to build new relationships. The critical aspect of social networks is that the content is user-generated and this means users own, control and develop content according to their needs, not those of a third party.

Social networks concern the Internet's ability to enable people to share experiences. Typical sites include MySpace, Bebo, YouTube and Facebook, each of which has experienced rapid growth in recent years. These sites provide certain segments of the population, mainly the 16–25-year-old group, an opportunity to use online networks to reach their friends, generate new ones and share experiences, information and insights. The activity might also be regarded as a supplement to their offline social networks. Some sites encourage ranking and rating of content that has been added to the site by others, for example Digg and Flickr. What is happening is that social networks are helping to re-engineer the way in which parts of society link together and share information (Walmsley, 2007).

The results of a European-wide study undertaken by Forrester Research reveal that there are six key characteristics that typify the dominant usage by online consumers of social media (Pinkerfield, 2007). There are those whose core activity on these sites is to publish content (9 per cent); those who prefer to comment (18 per cent); networkers (1 per cent); those who gather information (12 per cent); people who prefer to listen and observe interaction (19 per cent); and finally a large group who ignore all these activities (41 per cent).

When these data are aggregated on a country by country basis, it is revealed that the Dutch are the most active users publishing the most blogs and webpages. The Spanish prefer to comment, while the Italians actively gather information. French users are most likely to read blogs and reviews (are listeners), while UK users prefer to visit social media sites and make comments, typical of networkers. The study found that the Germans tend to ignore most social media.

The growth of MySpace and Facebook is partly a reflection of the relative investment made in them. MySpace has seen little investment and has attracted widespread criticism, whereas Facebook is perceived to be innovative and eager to meet the needs of its target audience. For example, as part of its strategic development in 2007, Facebook allowed its users to build and install applications within the social network. The more obvious marketing strategy would have been to charge developers the opportunity to access Facebook's users. However, by opening the site up in this way, and free of charge, huge numbers of people switched to the site and within a couple of months over 1,700 new applications, such as SuperPoke, which encourages users to 'slap, chest-bump or headbutt', photo slideshows and online data storage, had been developed, integrated and accessed by site visitors.

The relative immaturity of the social networking arena and the way in which content is developed raises challenges about how organisations can best use social media as part of their marketing communications to reach their target audiences. It has been mentioned earlier that site users are less than loyal as many have own multiple sites, so the challenge is to persuade users to visit their sites as often as possible and to encourage them to attract new users. The key therefore, is to create sites that are 'sticky', that is, contain sufficient content and facilities that engage users and give them reason to stay on the site for longer periods of time and also give them reason to return on a regular basis. If this works and the number of users increases then this should attract advertisers who are willing to pay premium rates.

However, questions then arise about the effectiveness of online ads in a social networking environment. Many users do not like brand advertising and prefer to take advice from their online peers in these communities when deciding what to buy, rather than listen to advertisers. Social networking is becoming a media channel in its own right and it is one that is reflecting the voice of consumers instead of those of brand owners.

An understanding of social media reveals that brand communications should not be invasive, intrusive or interruptive. In order to work, marketing communications need to become part of the context in which site users interact. Online advertising will continue to form a major revenue stream for the owners of these social networking sites, but increasingly this needs to be supplemented with the use of a mixture of sponsorship, product placement and public relations. For example, sponsored groups, such as Apple's 'Apple Students' group, with 400,000 members, have been developed (Hicks, 2007).

Asda approached Mumsnet.com, a parenting online community, for advice about the extent to which its clothing products encouraged the sexualisation of children. This followed the well publicised outcry concerning Primark's sales of padded bikini tops for young children (Charles, 2010).

See also Viewpoint 14.5 for two examples of the way in which brands are beginning to be involved with social networks.

Viewpoint 14.5 Kodak snaps into social media

Although more companies are using social media as part of their consumer communications, the role of social media within the business market is less well established. Kodak is one of the more advanced organisations, placing social media as a central element of their b2b programme.

The head of marketing at Kodak started using Twitter within his family but soon gained a following of over 27,000 'Kodak families', a substantial proportion of whom were also working through Facebook. Among these were commercial photographers and printers with whom Kodak were able to communicate directly, without any filters. As a result Kodak are able to gauge which products are being discussed and in what context. Automated tweet responses are enabled in many cases, but perhaps the major point is that Kodak has set up a Chief Listener. This person listens to the social media conversations and helps shape and route the dialogue so that Kodak are in a better position to learn from their business customers and consumers and in doing so are able to develop products and services that meet the needs of their markets more accurately.

Source: Based on Turner (2010)

Question
What are the key difficulties faced by brands attempting to use social networks to reach their target markets?

Task
Ask your networked friends what they feel about brands using social networks to reach them.

Web logs

Web logs, or blogs as they are commonly known, are personal online diaries. Although personal issues are recorded and shared, a large proportion of blogs concern organisations and public issues, and they are virtually free. As Wood *et al.* (2006) conclude, blogging represents a simple, straightforward way of creating a web presence.

Even if the quality and content of some blogs varies considerably, their popularity has grown enormously. The informality of blogs enables information to be communicated in a much more relaxed manner than most other forms of marketing communication. This is typified by the use of podcasting and the downloading of blogs to be 'consumed' at a later, more convenient time or while multi-tasking. Blogs represent user-generated-content (for more on UGC see Chapter 15) and are often a key indicator of the presence of an opinion leader or former.

Blogs can be understood using a number of criteria, other than the basic consumer or corporate demarcation. Typically, the content and the type of media are the main criteria. A blog can be categorised by its content or the general material with which it is concerned. The breadth of content is only limited by the imagination, but some of the more mainstream blogs tend to cover topics such as sport, travel, music, film, fashion and politics. Blogs can also be categorised according to the type of media. For example, 'vlogs' contain video collections, whereas a 'photoblog' is a collection of photos and a 'sketchblog' contains sketches.

Nardi *et al.* (2004), as cited by Jansen *et al.* (2009) found five reasons why people choose to blog:

- documenting their lives;
- providing commentary and opinions;
- expressing deeply held emotions;
- articulating ideas through writing;
- forming and maintaining communities.

These appear to be a list of outward facing reasons. What is not mentioned here are inner directed reasons, such as the need for feedback or psychological issues relating to the need for self-esteem, reassurance and reinforcement of an individual's identity.

Business-related or corporate blogs represent huge potential as a form of marketing communications for organisations. This is because blogs reflect the attitudes of the author, and these attitudes can influence others. As consumers write about their experiences with brands, opportunities exist for organisations to identify emerging trends, needs and preferences, and to also understand how brands are perceived. Sony used blogging as an integral part of its campaign to establish the Handycam and Cybershot brands. When shooting the ad in Miami, dubbed as 'Sony Foam City', Sony invited 200 visitors, mainly bloggers. Each was equipped with a Sony camera and encouraged to capture the soapy event which involved covering parts of Miami with foam. Clips of the ad and the making of the ad were then leaked onto the Internet in advance of the launch of the ad being released and in doing so created a buzz around the brands.

Organisations can set up *external* corporate blogs to communicate with customers, channel partners and other stakeholders. Many major organisations use external blogs to provide information about company issues and other organisations use blogs to launch brands or attend to customer issues. The other form of corporate blog is the *internal* blog. Here the focus is on enabling employees to write about and discuss corporate policies, issues and developments. Some organisations encourage interaction between their employees and customers and the general public. Although problems can arise through inappropriate comments and observations, blogging is an informal communication device that can serve to counter the formality often associated with planned marketing communications.

Therefore, enabling people to blog, perhaps by creating dedicated web space, facilitates interaction and communication through people with similar interests. There is also an added attraction in that communities of bloggers can attract advertisers and form valuable revenue streams. Blogs can be used by organisations as a form of public relations in order to communicate with a range of stakeholders. For example, a blog on an intranet can be used to support internal communications, on an extranet to support distributors and on the Internet to reach and influence consumers.

Microblogging

Microblogging or nanoblogging as it is sometimes referred to, is a short format version of blogging. It is a form of eWoM and uses web social communication services (Jansen *et al.*, 2009) of which Twitter is probably the best known. A microblog, or tweet, consists of a short comment, a post of 140 characters, which is shared with a network of followers. This makes production and consumption relatively easy in comparison to blogs.

These posts can be distributed through instant messages, email, mobile phones or the web. Therefore, as Jansen *et al.*, put it, people can share brand-related thoughts at any time, and more or less anywhere, with people who are connected via web, cell phone or IM and email, on an unprecedented scale.

Viewpoint 14.6 All of a twitter

The longer term impact of twittering is debated by many but there are several examples where the effectiveness of microblogging is clearly demonstrated. When *Daily Mail* journalist Jan Moir published a controversial article about the death of Boyzone singer, Stephen Gately, Scott Pack tweeted about a 'vile piece of journalism'. Soon various people had led responses and a twitterstorm emerged. The huge volume of activity, within a few hours, led the # janmoir story (# a twitter method of uniting all related tweets) to become the top topic. The effect of this activity was to make the *Mail* change its website headline, Marks and Spencer withdrew their advertising on the webpage, whilst the Press Complaints Commission received a record number of 1,000 complaints, a figure that was to rise to 22,000.

Twitter announced in April 2010 that they were to enable advertisers to purchase 'promoted tweets'. These ads are intended to be compatible with the conversations they accompany.

Source: Based on Henley (2009); www.bbc.co.uk

Question
To what extent does twittering represent a marketing opportunity for organisations?

Task
Find two twitter conversations, one led by a politician and the other by a celebrity. How does the content differ?

It is already understood that WoM has a particularly significant impact on purchasing decisions, but eWoM can take place close to or even during a purchase process. Although eWoM may be less personal than face2face WoM, it has substantially greater reach and has greater credibility because it is in print and accessible by others (Hennig-Thurau *et al.*, 2004). The implication of this is that microblogging offers huge potential to marketers. Twitter recognise this potential and in April 2010 announced that they were to allow advertising on their site. However these are not conventional adverts. These ads are tweets, and are an integral part of the conversations, referred to as 'Promoted Tweets'. These messages, limited to 140 characters, appear at the top of the page when a user has searched for that word, and will only show up in search results (Steele, 2010).

Jansen *et al.* explore the commercial potential and find that of all microblogs (in their sample), 19 per cent mention an organisation, product or service. Of these, '20 per cent express a sentiment or opinion concerning that company, product or service' (2009: 2184). They also find that the ratio of positive to negative tweets is approximately 50 per cent to 35 per cent. This last point is interesting as it is generally accepted that in offline WoM a positive brand experience is likely to be shared with three people whereas a negative experience is usually shared with nine others.

Podcasting

Podcasting emerged as a major new form of communication in 2005 and has grown significantly since then. This is mainly because of the huge growth in the adoption of MP3 players and the desire for fresh, up-to-date or different content.

Podcasting is a process whereby audio content is delivered over the Internet to iPods, MP3 players and computers, on demand. A podcast is a collection of files located at a feed address, which people can subscribe to by submitting the address to an aggregator. When new content becomes available it is automatically downloaded using an aggregator or feed reader which recognises feed formats such as RSS (see below).

In many ways podcasting is similar to radio broadcasts, yet there are a couple of major differences. First, podcast material is pre-recorded and time-shifted so that material can be listened to at a user's convenience, that is, on demand. The second difference is that listeners can take the material they have chosen to listen to, and play it at times and locations that are convenient to them. They can listen to the content as many times as they wish simply because the audio files can be retained.

Podcasting is relatively inexpensive and simple to execute. It opens up publishing to a host of new people, organisations as well as individuals, and it represents a new media channel for audio content. Users have control over what they listen to, when they listen to it and how many times they listen to the content.

RSS

RSS stands for 'really simple syndication' and refers to the distribution of news content on the web. Rather than trawl all relevant webpages to find new content and updates, RSS allows for specific content to be brought together and made available to an individual without their always having to return to numerous sites. Just checking the RSS feed to see whether something new has been posted online can save huge amounts of time.

Originally email was the preferred way of notifying people of breaking news and information updates. The problem with email is that not only has the user to sort out and organise the separate strands of information, they also have to contend with increasing amounts of spam and unwanted material that accompanies it. In addition, RSS feeds allow content updates to be read in a reader, not online.

From a publisher's point of view RSS feeds enable information to reach a wide audience. This is because of syndication. Once content has been created, RSS feeds allow the content to be grouped (syndicated) with websites that publish similar content. These are referred to as aggregator websites. Each feed consists of brief information about headlines, a summary of the content and a link to the article on the requisite website.

From a marketing perspective RSS feeds act as a media channel delivering a variety of information about news stories, events, headlines, project updates and even corporate information, often as press releases. This information is delivered quickly and efficiently to audiences who have signed up and effectively given express permission to be sent the information.

Interactive online communities

Armstrong and Hagel (1996) were two of the first researchers to propose the benefits of virtual communities. They also saw that the development of these communities is one of the key elements that differentiate interactive from traditional media. Communities of people who share a common interest(s), who interact, share information, develop understanding and build relationships all add value, in varying degrees, through their contribution to others involved with the website. In a sense, user groups and special interest groups are similar facilities, but the key with all these variations is the opportunity to share information electronically, often in real time.

Chaffey *et al.* (2006) refer to Durlacher (1999), who argues that there are four main types of community defined by their purpose, position, interest and profession (see Table 14.2). Communities can be characterised by several determining elements. Muniz and O'Guinn (2001) identify three core components:

- consciousness of kind: an intrinsic connection that members feel towards one another;
- the presence of shared rituals and traditions that perpetuate the community's history, culture and consciousness;
- a sense of moral responsibility, duty or obligation to the community as a whole and its individual members.

Within these online or virtual communities five particular characteristics can be identified. The first concerns the model of communication, which is essentially visitor-to-visitor and in some cases customer-to-customer. Second, communities create an identity that arises from each individual's involvement and sense of membership and belonging. The more frequent and intense the interaction, the stronger the identity the participants feel towards the community. Third, relationships, even close friendships develop among members, which in turn can facilitate mutual help and support. The fourth characteristic concerns the language that the community adopts. Very often specialised languages or codes of (electronic) behaviour emerge that have particular meaning to members. The fifth and final characteristic refers to the methods

Table 14.2 Four types of virtual community

Type of community	Explanation
Purpose	Those attempting to achieve the same goal or who are experiencing a similar process
Position	Those experiencing particular circumstances. These might be to do with life-stage issues (the old or the young), health issues or perhaps career development opportunities
Interest	Those sharing a hobby, pastime or who are passionately involved with, for example, sport, music, dance, family trees, jigsaws, gardening, film, etc.
Profession	Those involved with the provision of b2b services. Often created by publishers these portals provide information about jobs, company news, industry issues and trading facilities (e.g. auctions).

Source: Durlacher (1999). Used with permission

used to regulate and control the behaviour and operations of the community. Self-regulation is important in order to establish acceptable modes of conduct and interaction among the membership.

The role that members assume within these communities and the degree to which they participate also varies. There are members who attend but contribute little, those who create topics, lead discussion, those who summarise and those who perform brokerage or intermediary roles among other members.

According to Jepsen (2006) the number of consumers undertaking product information search within virtual communities can be expected to develop simply because the number of experienced Internet users will grow. The provision and form of online communities will inevitably develop and frameworks will emerge in order that understanding about the way they operate (effectively) is disseminated. Szmigin and Reppel (2004) have offered their customer bonding triangle framework, which is built on interactivity, technical infrastructure and service value elements (see Figure 14.1). It is argued by the authors of this framework that it is the fit between the elements that determines the level of bonding between community members. Further work is required in this area, but this framework provides an interesting conceptualisation of the elements that characterise this approach.

The knowledge held in virtual communities can be expected to be of significant value when searching for product information. In 1999, Kozinets presented four segments related to virtual communities, based around two dimensions. The four segments identified by Kozinets, are referred to as insiders, devotees, minglers and tourists. Insiders have strong social ties to other members of the community and consumption is central to their self-image. Devotees only have ties to the product, minglers are tied to the members and tourists do not have ties to the product or other members. Jepsen speculates that information provided by the virtual community may be sufficiently strong for insiders that it replaces information from offline sources. This is probably not the case for any of the other three segments.

As a final comment, how should marketers manage all of this activity? Well apart from developing an integrated approach to marketing communications, strategy and tactics and learning to listen to social media rather than invade and interrupt it, Coca-Cola have developed a 4Rs model to assist their approach to this important issue. The 4Rs are regarded as pillars of their social media strategy; reviewing, responding, recording and redirecting.

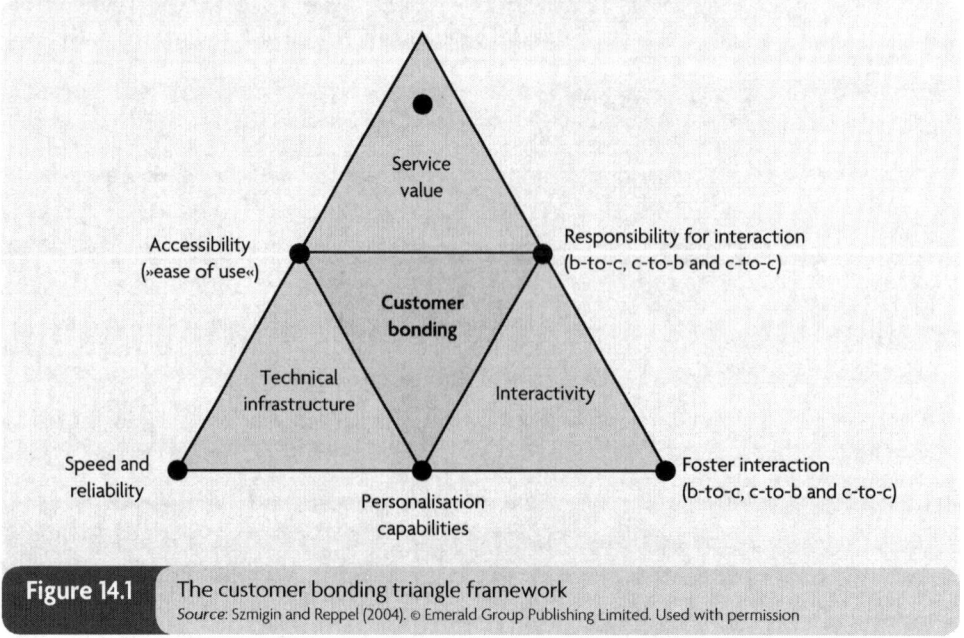

Figure 14.1 The customer bonding triangle framework
Source: Szmigin and Reppel (2004). © Emerald Group Publishing Limited. Used with permission

Fawkes (2010) explains that conversations around the various Coke brands are tracked by specialist service companies. This review provides insight into the nature of the conversations and the overall sentiment being expressed about the brands. The response is enabled in two ways. Subject matter experts from a variety of departments inside the organisation respond to the specific or unusual queries and questions. A 'blog squad' of social media power users deal with the more general and orthodox questions posed by individuals.

The recording element refers to the development of blogs, podcasts and video material designed to entertain their audiences with compelling content. The redirecting pillar concerns the way Coca-Cola enables people to find and connect with the content that they create. This is achieved by interconnecting links through Google, Facebook and other major interfaces and search engines, through to MyCokeRewards. See also www.coca-cola.com.

Summary

In order to help consolidate your understanding of interactive marketing communications, here are the key points summarised against each of the learning objectives:

1 Appraise the nature and characteristics of interactive marketing communications

Interactive marketing communications allows participants in the communication process to interact with one another. Rather than passive one-way communication that characterises much of offline marketing communications, interactivity is inclusive, engages audiences and can lead to dialogue and the development of meaningful relationships.

2 Consider some of the issues relating to the way in which each of the tools of the communications mix can be used interactively

As offline revenues from television and print advertising decline, so money is being switched into interactive and online advertising. Direct response advertising is the primary approach used in this environment as advertisers seek to encourage users to click-through to destination webpages and microsites. Banner ads and sponsored link ads form the backbone of advertising in this fast-growing environment but online video advertising is set to grow.

Interactive based sales promotions, public relations and direct marketing all have key roles to play in a converging multimedia environment. Sales promotions and direct marketing provide incentives and motivation for people to become interactive and to become involved with a campaign or brand. Personal selling has the least application of all the traditional tools in an online environment.

3 Evaluate search engine marketing and distinguish the main features of both pay-per-click and search engine optimisation

There are two types of search engine marketing techniques: search engine optimisation (SEO) and pay-per-click (PPC). The latter outweighs the former quite substantially in terms of investment but the former is superior in terms of quality of results.

4 Discuss the features of email marketing communications for both customer acquisition and retention

Email communications can be directed at clearly defined target audiences, even individuals; they can be personalised and refined to meet the needs of individuals. In addition, email can be used with varying levels of frequency and intensity, which is important when building awareness, reinforcing messages or when attempting to persuade someone into a trial or purchase. It is a particularly useful way of provoking responses and can be used for customer acquisition and retention.

5 Evaluate the role of electronic word-of-mouth communications, and consider applications such as viral marketing communications, podcasting, RSS feeds, Twitter, and web logs

Word-of-mouth communications in an online environment is fast becoming a major form of communication. Viral marketing, podcasting, blogging and twittering are key ways in which word-of-mouth is being used.

6 Identify the characteristics of online communities and consider how social networks and affiliate marketing can be used to develop marketing communications opportunities

The development of online communities of people who share a common interest(s), interact, share information, develop understanding and build relationships has been a major characteristic of what is referred to as Web 2.0. In particular, social networks such as Facebook, MySpace and Bebo have millions of registered users and present major opportunities for communicating brands. The problem, however, is that conventional offline marketing communications, and advertising in particular, do not work in these environments. Alternative, more subtle and supportive communication strategies are required, such as sponsorship, product placement and public relations.

Review questions

1. Define interactive marketing communications and explain its key characteristics.
2. What might go wrong with the use of interactive marketing communications?
3. Identify reasons why organisations use interactive online advertising.
4. Name three types of online ad formats.
5. To what extent is online public relations just online advertising?
6. Explain the basic principles underpinning the way in which both search engine optimisation and pay-per-click systems operate.
7. Write a report examining the use of email as a form of marketing communications. Find examples to support the points you make.
8. Discuss the three key elements that Kirby associates with successful viral marketing.
9. Make brief notes concerning the ways in which marketing communications should be used within online communities.
10. Appraise the concept of word-of-mouth communication and consider its use within social networks.

References

Anon (2010) Brands use social media to drive pre-launch buzz, *Brand Week*. Retrieved 25 May 2010 from www.warc.com/news/

Armstrong, A. and Hagel III, J. (1996) The real value of on-line communities, *Harvard Business Review*, 74(3) (May/June), 134–141.

Benady, D. (2009) The future of shopping, *Revolution*, December, 48–51.

Blattberg, R.C. and Deighton, J. (1991) Interactive marketing: exploiting the age of addressability, *Sloan Management Review*, 33(1), 5–14.

Blythe, A. (2008) How can brands exploit widgets? *Revolution* (April), 13.

de Bruyn, A. and Lilien, G.L. (2004) A multi-stage model of word-of-mouth through electronic referrals, *eBusiness Research Centre Working Paper*, February.

Chaffey, D., Ellis-Chadwick, F., Johnston, K. and Meyer, R. (2006) *Internet Marketing*. 3rd edn. Harlow: Pearson Education.

Chaffey, D. (2008) Using branded widgets, gadgets and buttons for web marketing. Retrieved 8 April 2008 from www.davechaffey.com/Internet-Marketing/C8-Communications/E-tools/Online-PR/Using-Widgets-Marketing

Charles, G. (2010) Asda calls in Mumsnet to approve kids clothes, *Marketing*, 21 April, 1.

Clawson, T. (2009) Don't believe the hype, *Revolution*, December, 44–47.

Crow, D. (2007) Talking about my generation, *The Business*, 28 July, 18–20.

Doyle, S. (2003) The big advantage of short messaging. Retrieved 16 May from www.sas.com/news

Dundas, C. (2010) Digital makes the brand connection, *Admap* (April). Retrieved 2 June 2010 from www.warc.com/ArticleCenter

Durlacher (1999) UK on-line community, *Durlacher Quarterly Internet Report*, Q3, 7–11, London.

Fawkes, F. (2010) Coca-Cola's Approach To Social Media, *FSFK*, 17 May. Retrieved 9 June 2010 from http://www.psfk.com/2010/05/brand-news-coca-cola%E2%80%99s-approach-to-social-media.html

Fletcher, M. (2009) Why data adds up, *Revolution – The Email Handbook*, September, 16–21.

Goddard, M. (2010) Sizing up a proposed app, *ABA Bank Marketing*, 42(4) (May) 20–23.

GoViral (2009) Viral View: Social Technographics: Are you keeping up with your online audience? Campaignlive, 6 November. Retrieved 14 June 2010 from http://www.brandrepublic.com/News/964382/Viral-View-Social-Technographics-keeping-online-audience/?DCMP=ILC-SEARCH

Henley, J. (2009) The power of tweets, *The Guardian*. Retrieved 3 November 2009 from www.guardian.co.uk

Hennig-Thurau, T., Gwinner, K.P. Walsh, G. and Gremle, D.D. (2004) Electronic word of mouth via consumer-opinion platforms: What motivates consumers to articulate themselves on the Internet?, *Journal of Interactive Marketing*, 18(1), 38–52.

Hicks, R. (2007) All About... Facebook, *Media Asia*, 3 August. Retrieved 13 August 2007 from http://www.brandrepublic.com/News/675228/About-Facebook/

Jansen, B.J. and Molina, P.R. (2006) The effectiveness of web search engines for retrieving relevant e-commerce links, *Information Processing and Management*, 42(4) (July), 1075–1098.

Jansen, B.J., Zhang, M., Sobel, K. and Chowdury, A. (2009) Twitter Power: Tweets as Electronic Word of Mouth, *Journal of the American Society for Information Science and Technology*, 60(11), 2169–2188.

Jarboe, G. (2005) Why does search engine marketing look like a penny-farthing bicycle?, *Internet Search Engine Database*, 11 January. Retrieved 27 July 2007, from www.isedb.com/news/article/1086/

Jepsen, A.L. (2006) Information search in virtual communities: is it replacing use of offline communication?, *Journal of Marketing Communications*, 12(4) (December), 247–261.

Jukes, M. (2009) Creative review: Comparethemarket.com, 26 February. Retrieved 20 September from www.brandrepublic.com/InDepth/Features/930643/APG-Creative-Strategy-Awards—Comparethemarketcom-meerkat-campaign-VCCP

Juvertson, S. (2000) *What is Viral Marketing?*, Draper Fisher Juvertson website. Retrieved 12 March 2006 from http://www.dfj.com/cgi-bin/artman/publish/printer_steve_may00.shtml

Juvertson, S. and Draper, T. (1997) *Viral marketing*, Draper Fisher Juvertson website. Retrieved 12 March 2006 from http://www.dfj.com/cgi-bin/artman/publish/printer_steve_tim_may97.html

Kaikati, A.M. and Kaikati, J.G. (2004) Stealth marketing: how to reach consumers surreptitiously, *California Management Review*, 46(4), 6–22.

Kaplan, A.M. and Haelein, M. (2010) Users of the world unite! The challenges and opportunities of social media, *Business Horizons*, 53, 59–68.

Kimberley, S. (2010) Search marketing fails to deliver full potential, *Marketing*, 30 June, 7.

Kirby, J. (2003) The message should be used as a means to an end, rather than just an end in itself, *VM-People*, 16 October. Retrieved 31 August 2007 from www.vm-people.de/en/vmknowledge/interviews/interviews_detail.php?id=15

Kozinets, R.V. (1999) E-tribalized marketing?: the strategic implications of virtual communities on consumption, *European Management Journal*, 17(3), 252–264.

Mathews, K. (2007) Is branding best and are click throughs through?, *Internet Advertising Bureau*. Retrieved 31 August 2007 from http://www.iabuk.net/en/1/isbrandingbestandareclickthroughsthrough.mxs

McCormick, A. (2010) Digital Report: Keep your affiliates onside, *Marketing*, 28 April, 41–43.

Muniz Jr, A.M. and O'Guinn, T.C. (2001) Brand community, *Journal of Consumer Research*, 27(4), 412–432.

Nardi, B.A., Schiano, D.J., Gumbrecht, M., and Swartz, L. (2004) Why we blog, *Communications of the ACM*, 47(12), 41–46.

Nettleton, K. (2009) Men dressed as Tic Tacs re-enact missed Everton goal, *Campaign*, 11 February. Retrieved 14 June 2010 from http://www.campaignlive.co.uk/news/880522/Men-dressed-Tic-Tacs-re-enact-missed-Everton-goal/?DCMP=ILC-SEARCH

Pinkerfield, H. (2007) New social media user types unveiled, *Revolution*, 28 June 2007. Retrieved 13 August 2007 from http://www.brandrepublic.com/News/667634/New-social-media-user-types-unveiled/

Porter, L. and Golan, G.J. (2006) From subservient chickens to brawny men: a comparison of viral advertising to television advertising, *Journal of Interactive Advertising*, 6(2), 30–38.

Ramsay, F. (2009) Building on Animal Magic, *Marketing*, 19 August, 20–21.

Steele, F. (2010) Twitter unveils advert Tweets in bid for profits, *Times Online*, 13 April. Retrieved 13 April 2010 from http://business.timesonline.co.uk/tol/business/industry_sectors/media/article7095914.ece

Sullivan, E.A. (2010) *Marketing App*-titude, *Marketing News*, 44(3), 15 March, 6.

Szmigin, I. and Reppel, A.E. (2004) Internet community bonding: the case of macnews.de, *European Journal of Marketing*, 38(5/6), 626–640.

Turner, C. (2010) How Kodak is using social media to convert users into consumers. Retrieved 20 March 2010 from www.utalkmarketing.com

VCCP (2009) Comparethemarket.com 'meerkat campaign', *campaignlive.co.uk*. Retrieved 17 September 2009 from http://www.brandrepublic.com/InDepth/Features/930643/APG-Creative-Strategy-Awards—Comparethemarketcom-meerkat-campaign-VCCP

Walmsley, A. (2007) Social networks are here to stay, *Marketing*, 27 June, 15.

Walmsley, A. (2010) Make your affiliations pay, *Marketing*, 5 May, 13.

Wood, W., Behling, R. and Haugen, S. (2006) Blogs and business: opportunities and headaches, *Issues in Information Systems*, V11(2), 312–316.

Yaobin, L., Deng, Z. and Bin, W. (2010) Exploring factors affecting Chinese consumers' usage of short message service for personal communication, *Information Systems Journal*, 20(2), 183–208.

Yuill, M. (2009) Smartphones and app stores driving mobile media, Admap, 503 (March). Retrieved 2 June 2010 from www.warc.com/articlecenter/

Chapter 25
Digital media

The development of digital-based technologies and web-enabled communications has had a profound effect on marketing communications. However, the full potential of these new technologies has yet to be realised as customer behaviour adapts and learns new ways of incorporating these facilities. Interactivity and rapid two-way communications enabled by technology require the development of new communication strategies and a fresh understanding of how best to communicate with target audiences.

Aims and learning objectives

The aim of this chapter is to consider the nature and characteristics of digital media. The intention is to examine the many aspects and features of digital media and to consider its potential to assist marketing communications. It is recommended that this chapter be read prior to Chapter 26 where the application of these tools and devices is considered in greater detail.

The learning objectives of this chapter are to:

1. explain the key forms of digital media;
2. understand what digital media enables users to do;
3. examine some of the issues arising from the design and use of web sites;
4. explain the key differences between traditional and digital media;
5. consider future technologies and their impact on marketing communications;
6. explain what convergence means and how it influences marketing communications.

For an applied interpretation see Matt King's MiniCase entitled *Integrating traditional and digital media* at the end of this chapter.

Introduction

The dramatic impact that digital technologies have had on people does not need amplification here. However, digitisation has provided marketers with the opportunity to develop new ways of communicating with a variety of audiences. This chapter starts by setting out the main types of digital media. It then proceeds to explain what they are and examines the generic benefits that each of these types of digital media can bring, that is, what it enables users to do. Part of this enabling concerns the creation of web sites, and this chapter explores their design and marketing functionality, before comparing some of the key characteristics of traditional and digital media. The chapter concludes with a consideration of the future of digital media, the associated convergence issues that are evolving and how these might impact on marketing communications in the future.

Chapter 26 then explores the various ways in which marketers have used digital media to communicate effectively with their various audiences.

Key forms of digital media

As suggested above, the range of digital media is vast and is growing rapidly. However, the following section considers some of the key types or forms of digital media and should not be considered comprehensive.

The Internet

The Internet provides a wide variety of activities, including electronic mail, global information access and retrieval systems, discussion groups, multiplayer games and file transfer facilities, all of which not only help to transform the way we think about marketing communications, but also impact on business strategy, marketing channel structures, interorganisational relationships and the configuration of the marketing communications mix.

The Internet impacts upon marketing in two main ways: distribution and communication. The first concerns distribution and marketing channels. The Internet provides a new, more direct route to customers, which can either replace or supplement current distribution/channel arrangements. The second element concerns the Internet as a communication medium. It provides a means of reaching huge new audiences and enabling the provision of vast amounts of information. These two elements, distribution and communication, combine as ebusiness and ecommerce to provide benefits for both buyers and sellers.

The Internet is an important way of providing product and service information and can enable organisations to provide frequent and intensive levels of customer support. With it come doubts about its ability to deliver competitive advantage and whether it could offer suitable levels of privacy, security and measures of advertising effectiveness.

The Internet is not a panacea for a manager's marketing communications problems. It is a relatively new and different means of communication, one that should be integrated into the marketing communications mix. Offline communications are used to raise site awareness and interest among a wide audience and to provide them with the site address. Once at the web site, in-depth product information can be exchanged for customer-specific details to refresh the database and fuel future communication activities. It is this holistic perspective of the new media that should be developed.

Traditional marketing communications strategies employ a mix of tools and normally involve an emphasis on one type of communication device, depending on the context. Broadly speaking, it has been the norm to weight advertising over the other tools when dealing with consumer markets, and to weight personal selling when operating in the b2b sector. This reflects advertising's ability to raise awareness and develop brands and personal selling's prime skill at provoking behavioural action and closing orders. These general approaches have begun to be relaxed as audience and media fragmentation gathers speed and new ways of doing business (e.g. ecommerce) are developed.

> The Internet is the fastest growing advertising medium.

The Internet is the fastest growing advertising medium, attracting revenues from a range of sources, some of which are investments previously devoted to television. Online advertising now equates to 10.6 per cent of total adspend and grew at 47.5 per cent in 2006 (Advertising Association, 2008). To demonstrate this extraordinary growth, online advertising attracted £153 million in 2000. By 2006 this figure had reached £2,016 million.

> Advertising online takes one of two main forms.

Advertising online takes one of two main forms, display advertising, which includes, banners, interruptive, sponsorships, tenancies and display on email. Classified advertising is principally concerned with paid for search (see later in this chapter), but also includes recruitment and classifieds (including b2b).

The development of Web 2.0 or social media has added a new and critical dimension to the Internet. Web 2.0 represents a step change in the development and use of the Internet and even at the time of writing, Web 3.0 looms. Constantinides and Fountain (2008) argue that there are three main principles associated with Web 2.0:

- there is a focus on service-based, simple, open source solutions as online applications;
- it represents continual and incremental application development which requires users to participate and interact in new ways. So, from a position of consuming media, users are now contributors, reviewers and content editors;
- Web 2.0 also represents a new service business model that has created new opportunities to reach small, individual business customers with low-volume products.

Many of the applications associated with Web 2.0 (social networks, RSS (Really Simple Syndication), Viral marketing etc.) are explored in Chapter 26.

The prime benefit of the Internet, as a hybrid medium, is that it is good at all of these activities, but it is not as good for any one task as a single communication tool might be. Interestingly, it excels as a part of the communication and decision-making process that the established communication tools fail to properly address, namely the search for, and retrieval of, information pertinent to purchase behaviour. It might be said, therefore, that the Internet provides a complementary facility to the marketing communication tools and as such should be used with, and not instead of, the established means of marketing communication. Above all else, the Internet is a medium, not a tool.

> The Internet provides a complementary facility to the marketing communication tools and as such should be used with the established means of marketing communication.

Database technologies

A marketing database is a collection of records that can be related to one another in multiple ways and from which information, usually customer-related, can be obtained in a variety of formats. This can be analysed to determine appropriate segments and target markets and used to stimulate and record individual responses to marketing communications. It therefore plays a role as a storage, sorting and administrative device to assist direct, personalised communications.

When customer-related transactional and response data are combined with additional information from external sources, such as a list broker, the database can become a potent source for marketing communication activities. Indeed, the increasing sophistication of information retrieval from databases enables much more effective targeting and communications.

Databases provide a means of monitoring changes in customer behaviour, identifying new target markets, and cross-selling products and services. The purpose of cross-selling is to reduce customer churn and increase switching costs (Kamakura *et al.*, 2003). While increasing a customer's potential switching costs may not be compatible with relationship marketing principles, the result of successful implementation may be improved levels of customer retention and satisfaction where relationships are more discrete and transactional rather than collaborative in nature.

There are many potential operational problems associated with interrogating and processing information within live databases. Ryals and Payne (2001) point out that the transaction processing performance may be slowed down when interrogating customer information and the structure of the database itself is constantly changing in response to the large volume of transactions. Many organisations use data warehouses (and smaller data marts). These are integrated stores of data collected from a variety of sources (e.g. customer contact centres, the sales force and market research) and are updated at intervals, making it non-volatile and easier for interrogating customer information.

Multimedia

The term multimedia has not achieved universal agreement. Strictly speaking, the term refers to any presentation of information or material that uses two or more media. However, the term multimedia has only gained prominence since the advent of digital technologies. So, multimedia is generally assumed to refer to the integration of text, audio and images in order to enhance the user interface with computer-based applications. As a result 'streaming' of video and 'audio over the Internet' typify multimedia applications. As hardware and communications technology evolve, so new systems and applications develop to provide delivery of personalised email and marketing communication messages.

> Multimedia is generally assumed to refer to the integration of text, audio and images in order to enhance the user interface.

Mobile technologies

Mobile phone technologies have advanced considerably and have enjoyed huge commercial success. Wireless application protocol, or WAP, phones possess the usual email and text information services, but they also have an Internet browser facility. As a result, messages can be not only location- but also time-specific. For example, a message can be sent when someone is in a town centre at lunch time, promoting a cafe, restaurant or shop. However, market growth in WAP technologies has been far less than originally expected, partly because of the text input facilities and the need for improved information displays.

New and faster technologies, such as general packet radio service (GPRS) and third-generation (3G) services enabling sound and image transfers, are expected to herald a successful relaunch of m-commerce. For example, in September 2007, Mazda used mobile advertising to drive awareness of their new Mazda2 model and to position the car as a stylish, bold new car. Video ads over 3 and T-Mobile networks were used to reach their core market, 25–34-year-old adults (Utalkb, 2007).

A further important development has been Bluetooth, the name given to a short-range radio technology that enables any kind of electronic equipment to be connected. Bluetooth's founding members include Ericsson, IBM, Intel, Nokia and Toshiba and their goal is to let Bluetooth's radio communications take the place of wires for connecting peripherals, telephones and computers.

Mobile marketing communications (to give it its full title) involves the delivery of direct marketing messages to mobile devices using wireless technologies. The prevailing usage is built around short message services (SMS), multimedia messaging services (MMS – which combines text with simple graphics and sound), wireless application protocol (WAP) mobile Internet and WAP push services and full multimedia third-generation (3G) services for both product promotion and entertainment purposes (MMA, 2007).

The more common title for this activity is mobile marketing, while some in the industry refer to it as proximity marketing. These titles are misleading because marketing is more than just communications, if only because this is primarily a communications medium, nothing more. In view of this discrepancy and to avoid misunderstanding, the phrase mobile communications is used here.

Apart from the sheer volume of users, 150 million in the European Union alone (www.bbc.co.uk) there are several reasons why the use of mobile communications has grown in recent years:

- *Interactivity*: the use of SMS provides recipients with the opportunity to respond directly to incoming requests. Simple yes/no answers are quick and easy to execute while opportunities to encourage interaction with brands exist 24/7, whether that be in- or out-of-home.
- *Personalisation*: mobile communications can enable messages that are customised to the personal needs of users. This means information can be highly targeted and contain relevant information.
- *Ubiquity*: the portability of mobiles means that it is possible to reach users at virtually any location, at any time and send them location-specific information.
- *Integration*: the effectiveness of mobile communications is optimised when it is used as a part of an integrated communications campaign.
- *Accountability*: the volume and nature of SMS responses can be measured, which is important from an investment perspective. In addition, it is possible to measure the contribution that different media make to drive responses. This in turn helps organisations to optimise their offline media spend and pursue integrated communications.
- *Cultural expectations*: as the number of mobile phones in circulation reaches saturation point, and as technology develops enabling more efficient communication, so peer group pressure and the entertainment industry encourage use of mobile phones. For example, presenters of television and radio programmes encourage their audiences to engage with them through text and mobile facilities in response to news items, quizzes and general topics of current interest. For many this form of communication and involvement has become a normal element of their leisure and entertainment expectations.

The key attributes of mobile communications are that it is a personal channel, one which enables direct, targeted and interactive communications and which can occur at any time and any place. SMS communications have underpinned its growth and are used not just for brand awareness-based advertising, but also as an effective way of delivering sales promotions, such as announcing special offers and 'text and win' events. This again reflects the contemporary role of mobile communications. However, as with email, it is also important to consider the potential privacy concerns of customers, especially as the receipt of unwanted messages (i.e. spam) may well increase.

> It is also important to consider the potential privacy concerns of customers.

One of the difficulties facing the mobile communications industry has been how to provide a direct link between the offline and online environments. One possible solution is to use quick response or QR codes. These are two dimensional barcodes as represented at Exhibit 25.1.

By taking a picture of a QR code with a camera phone with a built in QR code reader, consumers can access further brand-related material that is linked to the code. Used with great success in Japan, some believe the use of QR codes will transform mobile marketing in Europe. Murphy (2008) reports that others are not so positive, citing differences in the Japanese technology infrastructure, which serves to facilitate this type of use and Britain's less than favourable disposition towards the use of Java software.

The potential to develop mobile communications is enormous, simply because the channel can deliver direct marketing messages related to advertising, sales promotion and public relations to individuals regardless of location. These messages can be used to develop brand awareness, support product launches, incentivise customers through competitions and promotions and promote trade and distributor involvement, as well as provide branded entertainment.

> The potential to develop mobile communications is enormous.

ViewPoint 25.1 Mobile health

A large number of Health and Fitness Clubs, such as LA Fitness, Bannatynes, Greens, Village, Aquaterra and Esporta use mobile communications regularly. For example, Cannons Health Clubs, who manage 67 sites across the United Kingdom serving 165,000 members, have used mobile and email communications for customer acquisition and retention. In particular, they have found it very effective as part of their CRM programme by providing an effective delivery channel for time-sensitive issues, such as appointment reminders.

The effectiveness of mobile communications is demonstrated by Cannon's use of it for customer acquisition and their response rate is said to be 10 per cent. Text campaigns cost approximately £2 per response and they have found that text-only-generated new members regularly drive revenues exceeding £500 per member.

Mobile communications are used to reduce the number of no-shows and so increase conversion rates. Health Clubs can send SMS reminders to advise prospective members of gym tours, remind new joiners of induction training and members of classes and events. The gym manager, personal trainer or receptionist will book a text message reminder for the time required at the point of initial contact. This also gives the customer the opportunity to cancel in advance, thereby allowing the Club to fill the space.

SMS campaigns can be used to convert prospects once they have been informed by local offline media. By sending them a message using the keywords 'Offer' or 'Join' it is possible to track which offline media they might have been exposed to and from this data set switch their advertising between local press, radio and poster media according to which generates the highest response levels.

Source: Thurner (2007).

Question
Why have organisations been slow to develop mobile communication opportunities?

Task
Think about those organisations that contact you through SMS. How do you react and why?

Exhibit 25.1 A QR code
Source: Murphy (2008). Reproduced from *Marketing* magazine with the permission of the copyright owner, Haymarket Business Publications Limited.

Business applications

The phrase 'information systems and technology' (IST) is used to embrace the wide variety of new technologies that have been developed to improve the quality of life for the people who use IST and for those who benefit from their deployment. Ryssel *et al.* (2004: 197) refer to information technology as a term that embraces 'all forms of technology utilized to create, capture, manipulate, communicate, exchange, present and use information in its various forms (business data, voice conversations, still images, motion pictures, multimedia presentations and other forms, including those not yet conceived)'. They conceptualise the range of IST in terms of where the IST are used (internal or external) and across which broad functions (information, communication and decision support) (see Figure 25.1).

However, it is not the intention to provide a detailed examination of each of these systems or of the various technologies, as that is beyond the scope of this book. Readers interested in this aspect of technology are referred to Chaffey *et al.* (2006) or Rayport and Jaworski (2004).

A raft of increasingly sophisticated application programmes have evolved to meet the needs of the market. Initially electronic data interchange (EDI) via public networks, and now the Internet, managed the direct transmission between different companies' computer systems of data relating to business transactions. The applications tended to focus on systems designed by suppliers to assist customers in their purchasing procedures, processes and overall decision-making. The level of sophistication and scope of these applications now embrace a network of transactions and flow of information between a number of organisations. Radjou (2003: 25) refers to 'supply network processes', which encompass the following categories:

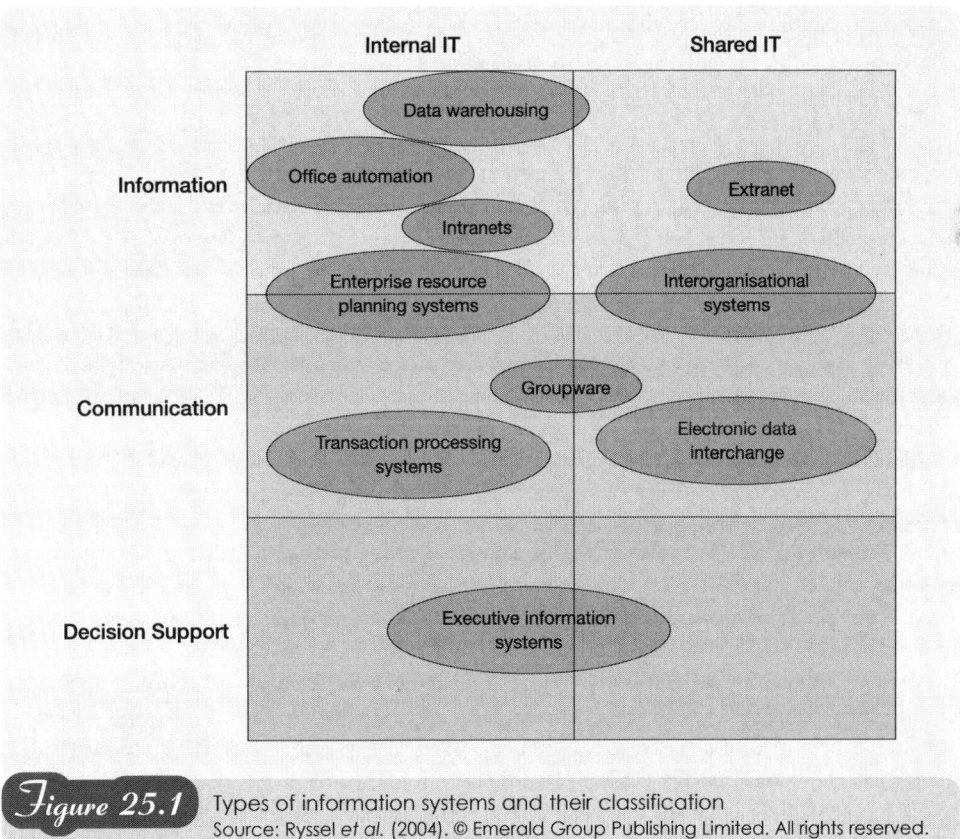

Figure 25.1 Types of information systems and their classification
Source: Ryssel *et al.* (2004). © Emerald Group Publishing Limited. All rights reserved.

- product lifecycle management;
- supply chain management;
- enterprise asset management;
- production network management;
- continuous demand management;
- order fulfilment and distribution management;
- aftermarket service management.

These applications serve to reduce costs, speed up processes, improve accuracy and provide added value for end-user customers. In terms of the relationships between organisations and their customers, these applications can serve to improve collaboration, both internally and externally. For example, enterprise-wide solutions such as complete enterprise resource planning (ERP) systems attempt to integrate all business processes across an organisation's accounting, manufacturing, sales and human resource departments. Further downstream, electronic point of sale (EPOS), which involves computerised tills linked back to a company's central computer(s), enables the data of every retail sale to be transmitted back to the organisation to facilitate sales and inventory management and, in a marketing context, can be used to better understand customer demand and buying behaviour. As networks, including the Internet, have extended to connect multiple businesses in the supply chain, sophisticated point-of-sale data have enabled collaborative marketing. For example, the leading supermarkets have systems that enable selected suppliers to 'find out information such as the repeat purchase rate of individual products, profiles of customers purchasing particular products and the most appropriate tools to attract customers' (Thomas, 2003).

> These applications serve to reduce costs, speed up processes, improve accuracy and provide added value for end-user customers.

Interorganisational use of network technologies to share business information and coordinate supply chain activities has been termed 'ecollaboration' and represents a major area of development, particularly for high-technology-based companies.

Interactive television

Another important technological development is digital broadcasting and the opportunities for interactive television. Digital television and interactive services are two related but different facilities. Digital television is well established, but full interactivity has yet to be delivered to the majority of the population. Potential advantages are consumer familiarity, the full-screen, high-quality sound and picture format, fast channel and picture/text 'hopping', combining entertainment and shopping. The disadvantages include the current high cost of the sets to consumers and of broadcasting for companies. Also, it cannot deal with individual customers until TV-based email is widely established. Penetration rates will rise as analogue services in the United Kingdom are phased out.

Digital services provide many benefits for consumers, one of which will be the opportunity to screen out current intrusive advertising. Interactive, or red button advertising has to be driven by consumers who decide which advertisements they want to watch, when, and how long they will stay involved. The creative possibilities are far ranging, but in order to retain audiences it will become increasingly important to develop creative ideas based on a sound understanding of the target audience and their interactive and buying patterns. In January 2008, Andy Duncan, Channel 4's CEO, is reported to have claimed that red button technology is 'slow', 'basic' and 'clunky' (Jones, 2008). Their exit was followed in April 2008 by Channel 5. They announced it was abandoning its interactive red button advertising facility, citing that it was too costly (the return was poor) and that it did not fit the organisation's strategy.

> Digital services provide many benefits for consumers.

Currently on UK teletext there are pages about holiday bargains that direct potential users to the Internet (www.teletext.co.uk/holidays) where they will find a searchable database, plus weather reports, resort reviews and advice. This service claims a choice of preferred operators, competitive pricing, confidence – full financial protection, up-to-date offers and human interaction at the point of sale. It states that, in the future, customers will be able to access the full functionality of the web site via digital television and/or mobile phone.

> Digital television and interactive marketing communications are unlikely to thrive in isolation from other methods of communication.

The point is that digital television and interactive marketing communications are unlikely to thrive in isolation from other methods of communication. Just as online facilities need offline drivers, and just as bricks and clicks appear to be a more profitable format than clicks only, so an integrated perspective is required if digital television and interactive advertising are to be successful.

The BBC iPlayer and 4Odemand are hybrid applications (databases, television content, interactivity and broadband) that have quickly become popular forms of access to entertainment content material. These facilities enable people to watch recently transmitted television programmes (usually a week old) on their computers.

Video conferencing

There are currently two main types of video conferencing systems: PC-based and room-based. PC-based, or desktop, systems are suitable for a small number of people, for short time periods. The cameras are usually fixed focus, with small field capability, and viewing screens are also small. Transmission speeds are limited by modem and telephone line capabilities. An advantage is that software applications and files can be shared and viewed jointly.

Room-based systems use large, sophisticated (pan–tilt–zoom) cameras and wide television screens, which means that more people can participate. Transmission via ISDN (integrated services digital network), including satellite links, facilitates better picture/sound quality. Video conferencing can be used in marketing communications for research (audience polling), product promotion/launch, training, employee and/or channel member briefings and sales negotiations. The advantages of video conferencing include speed and convenience as travel costs, carbon footprints and time away from core tasks are minimised; there is potential to reduce message ambiguity as there is joint and simultaneous viewing of materials and instant feedback; and relationships with customers and stakeholders can be improved through increased, more personal communication.

One of the disadvantages is that all participants have to be available at the same time, which can be difficult across time zones. The connections are not always reliable and room time-slots often cannot be extended beyond the original booking. Some people are uneasy in front of cameras, which may impair effectiveness.

> The use of video conferencing has increased because the cost of the equipment has plummeted and there have been major technical advances.

The use of video conferencing has increased because the cost of the equipment has plummeted and there have been major technical advances, which have improved the clarity and reliability of many commercial systems. In addition, there have been periods of major global crisis, and an increasing number of messages about global warming, all of which have led some organisations to reduce their volume of air travel, and spurred the use of video conferencing.

Kiosks

Electronic kiosks are terminals that can be accessed by the public for information and services. Very often, kiosks are operated via touch-screens and video displays and incorporate card readers, coupon printers and other devices specific to their application. Increasingly, electronic kiosks provide not only multimedia facilities but also enable access to the Internet (www.scala.com).

ViewPoint 25.2 — REI in kiosks

The outdoor climbing, hiking and mountain biking clothes made by REI require a high degree of touch and trial as well as significant information prior to purchase. REI has exploited these characteristics by building in-store climbing walls as well as hiking boot and mountain bike test areas. Due to limited retail floor space, REI installed web kiosks through which customers research 68,000 items as well as 45,000 web pages of product information.

By exploiting the fundamental nature of its products and through the instalment of kiosks in its stores, REI has effectively engaged its customers in a multi-channel experience. Kiosk implementation has allowed it to dedicate floor space to test areas while simultaneously attending to its breadth of inventory. Customers can utilise the strength of each channel and have consequently increased their spending. According to Jupiter Communications, existing REI customers who shopped online for the first time increased their store spending by 22 per cent and customers shopping on more than one channel spent overall more than in the previous year.

Question
If kiosks free up floor space for customer experience should not all shops move in this direction?

Task
Think of a product category that you are interested in, and make notes about how kiosks might enhance customers' experiences.

What digital media enables users to do

The various technologically-driven facilities referred to above can influence an organisation's marketing communications in many different ways. The implementation and benefits derived from technology will vary across organisations. This is because the level of strategic significance afforded to these investments, the culture, managerial skills, resources and degree to which the organisation has a true customer orientation differ widely. This section considers some of the generic ways in which digital media can influence marketing communications, but readers should be aware that the intensity of the influence is variable and far from uniform.

Interactivity

Digital technology allows for true interactively based communications, where messages can be responded to more or less instantly. Although there has been considerable media attention given to the development and potential of interactive services, the reality is that only a relatively small proportion of the public has become immersed in interactive environments, measured in terms of advertising space sold, usage and attitude research, and the number of transactions undertaken interactively. The development of interactive services may well be best served by the identification of those most likely to adopt such services and who will encourage others in their social orbits to follow their actions. This strategy would require communication with innovators and early adopters to speed the process of adoption (Rogers, 1983). This is quite crucial, as the infrastructure and associated heavy costs require an early stream of cash flows (Kangis and Rankin, 1996). The cost of equipment and time taken to learn and utilise interactive services does represent a barrier to adoption. These barriers might be substantial, depending on the background characteristics, education, personality, propensity to take risks and willingness to develop new skills and patterns of behaviour. This reinvention process can take individuals varying amounts of time to accomplish and hence impact on the speed of adoption.

> Digital technology allows for true interactively based communications.

Technological advances have enabled a range of other interactive communication opportunities. So far, emphasis has been placed on the Internet, but there have been many other imaginative and exciting developments and applications. One area where interactivity has been subject to experimentation is television, and some organisations have experimented with interactive messages, most notably the very first interactive advertisement for Chicken Tonight, plus Dove, Mazda and Tango.

One of the biggest factors accelerating the consumer use of digital television will be the variety of entertainment possibilities that the Internet can provide. The development of the BBC iPlayer facility has helped stimulate computer-based viewing of television programmes, which in turn may change consumer behaviour with regard to the consumption of this form of entertainment. This in turn may assist online shopping behaviour.

> Home shopping represents a significant change in buyer behaviour.

Home shopping represents a significant change in buyer behaviour that may affect a range of ancillary activities. Several UK supermarket operators have invested heavily in shopping channels and they have had to learn new fulfilment operations and new processes and procedures to meet customer expectations. Although Tesco appears to have been particularly successful, there is little evidence to suggest that retailers will give up their high street presence, as predicted in the later 1990s. The physical shopping experience provides many consumers with significant entertainment and social interaction satisfactions and these are unlikely to be discarded for total virtual shopping.

The financial services sector can be expected to undergo further change as home banking in particular becomes a secure and more convenient transaction context. Entertainment possibilities will be even more attractive, as interactive games and interactive viewing through pay-per-view, video on demand and time shifting (which is, as Rosen pointed out as long ago as 1997, the option to view yesterday's programmes today) become easily accessible.

The new technology and the new communication infrastructure offer increasing numbers of people the opportunity to experience interactive marketing communications. This may impact on their expectations and bring changes to the way in which people lead their lives.

Intuitive software is used to monitor a visitor's movement around a site, store it and then adjust the site to meet the preferred pattern each time that visitor enters the site. The implications for targeting advertising are enormous. However, despite all these developments, it appears that Cohen (1995) was quite prophetic when he commented that there was 'great uncertainty as to the level of consumer demand' (p. 8). In 1995, technology and demand were uncertain, but even at the beginning of the twenty-first century online profitability remains elusive to many virtual traders. The reality must be that technological advances and changes in buyer behaviour are more severely lagged than originally realised. While some consumers are ready and eager to take advantage of the new opportunities, many are not, and the process of diffusion needs to move forward in order that an increasing proportion of customers has the means and motivation to participate in the interactive environments.

Multichannel marketing

Although not entirely responsible, new technology has enabled organisations to reach new markets and different segments using more than a single marketing channel. Database-generated telemarketing, direct mail, email and Internet channels now complement field sales, retail and catalogue selling and have allowed organisations to determine which customers prefer which channels, and which are the most profitable. This in turn enables organisations to allocate resources far more effectively and to spread the customer base upon which profits are developed. A multichannel strategy should accommodate customers' account channel preferences, their usage patterns, needs, price sensitivities and preferred point of product and service access. So, as Stone

> A multichannel strategy should accommodate customers' account channel preferences, their usage patterns, needs and price sensitivities.

and Shan (2002) put it, the goal is to manage each channel profitably while optimising the attributes of each channel so that they deliver value for each type of customer.

Multichannel strategies have added new marketing opportunities, and enabled audiences to access products and services in ways that best meet their own lifestyle and behavioural needs. For organisations this has reduced message wastage, used media more efficiently and, in doing so, reduced costs and improved communication effectiveness.

ViewPoint 25.3 Multichannel NME

NME is a long-term music brand launched in magazine format in 1953 (as *New Music Express*). Among its claims are that it helped develop the careers of many bands and artists, including the Stones, Beatles, Bowie and the Sex Pistols. However, as the magazine market as whole continues to slide so NME was not immune especially as many of the readership are digital natives and generally averse to magazines.

Part of the remedy was to launch new media channels. The first of these was NME.com which now draws 1.8 million unique users. The web site is used to complement the magazine, although it provides increased depth and covers content not always suitable for the print version and enables blogging from music events.

A further channel, NMETV, was launched in 2007. Available to 9 million homes, the programme content includes video and interviews, and can be used to enhance material in the magazine channel.

NME Radio was launched in the summer of 2008 and is available on a number of national digital broadcast platforms.

Each of the media channels offers different opportunities, but NME have been able to integrate them so that each one reinforces the other. The television channel draws a different audience to the magazine, the former claiming 25–34-year-olds and the latter 15–24-year-olds. The obvious remaining question is, which of these channels is the most profitable?

The answer is magazines, even though circulation fell 12 per cent in the second half of 2007.

Source: Turner (2008).

Question
Is there an optimum number of channels that brands should use?

Task
Choose a grocery brand and find out how many channels are used to reach you.

Retailers are faced with particular problems that concern the amount of property/freehold they possess and the as yet unknown pattern of consumer shopping behaviour in the light of multichannel opportunities. The Arcadia Group (which owns Dorothy Perkins, Miss Selfridge, Wallis, Topshop, etc.) made a significant attempt to make its own name synonymous with online shopping through the development of Zoom, an online shopping mall. Some people might think that retailers should dispose of their fixed assets and move into the Internet or perhaps reconfigure their store layouts. In most cases, the optimum solution is to develop a multichannel solution whereby a range of media and experiences is offered to consumers. So, some prefer the Internet, some traditional shopping, some will use interactive television and some will prefer catalogue shopping. Many prefer a mix of these. This approach puts customers' needs first by determining their preferred marketing channels and also enables organisations to reconfigure their cost structures.

What may happen is that shopping activities become divided into categories that reflect particular channel options. So routine, unexciting purchases may be consigned to online and interactive channels, and the more explorative, stimulating and perhaps socially important purchases are prioritised for shopping expeditions. Many stores have recognised the

> Unexciting purchases may be consigned to online and interactive channels, and the more explorative, stimulating and perhaps socially important purchases are prioritised for shopping expeditions.

need to adapt themselves to provide more value (than a current product focus). Related benefits and enhanced services are important as they help differentiation and attract customers. For example, the bookstore Waterstones provides coffee bars and comfortable seating, an environment in which customers are encouraged to relax and consider their possible purchases. Larger stores and mainstream brands may need to establish themselves as 'destination' stores where the attraction for consumers is bound by excitement, entertainment and a brand experience. In some destination stores it is possible to test products in simulated but related environments. For example, attending cookery classes in supermarkets or test driving a range of cars in the countryside.

In the United States these types of store are now relatively common, and experience shows that High Street shopping is not about to die, but take a revised shape, form and role. Mercedes has a cafe on the Champs-Elysées in Paris but its role is to remind, differentiate and bring the brand into people's consciousness away from the traditional frame of reference. There is no persuasion as cars cannot be bought (or sold), but the brand is reinforced. See Chapter 21 for more on multichannel strategies.

Personalisation

For the first time, digital technology has empowered organisations to personalise messages and communicate with stakeholders on a one-to-one basis, on a scale that is commercially viable. This has driven the dramatic development of direct marketing, reshaped the basis on which organisations target and segment markets, stimulated dialogue, brought about a raft of new strategies and challenged the conventional approach to mass marketing and branding techniques.

The use of email communications is now extensive and viral marketing campaigns are gaining increasing acceptance. As with all forms of communication, the successful use of email requires an understanding of the recipient's behaviour. Email communication enables a high degree of personalisation, and in order to personalise messages it is necessary to understand the attitudinal and behavioural characteristics of each email audience (Chaffey, 2003). He suggests that the following need to be considered:

> The successful use of email requires an understanding of the recipient's behaviour.

- How many recipients read their emails from home and at work?
- Which times of the day and days of the week do they read their email?
- How soon after receipt is email read?
- How do recipients configure their email readers?

Understanding the email behaviour of different audiences can influence the degree of personalisation that is given to email communications and web site welcome messages. However, email communication that is based on an understanding of the audience's email behaviour should influence the message content, the time when it should be sent and, most importantly, the keys to encouraging recipients to open the email and not delete it. These keys are the 'header' of the email, which contains the subject matter, and the 'from' address, which signifies whether the sender is known and hence strongly determines whether the email is perceived positively at the outset. If it is, then there is a stronger chance that the email will be opened and hence a greater opportunity for response and interactivity. A deeper consideration of email communication can be found in Chapter 26.

However, many people now expect a high level of personalisation and virtual recognition as opportunities arising through 'personalisation' reach beyond email communication. Personalisation is a sensitive area, often twinned with privacy issues. Indeed there appears to be little agreement about what constitutes personalisation and to that end Vesanen (2007) identifies five types of personalisation. These are shown at Table 25.1.

> Personalisation is a sensitive area, often twinned with privacy issues.

Table 25.1 Types of personalisation

Type of personalisation	Segment marketing	Adaptive personalisation	Cosmetic personalisation	Transparent personalisation	Collaborative customisation
Typical actor	Reader's Digest	Yahoo.com	Google.com	Amazon.com	Hairdresser
Basic idea	To match customer preferences better than with mass-marketing	To let customers choose from different options	The organisation changes the package of standard good	The organisation changes the content of a good with a standard look	The organisation and customer are together building the product
When to use	Little customer knowledge, cheap	A lot of choices to choose from	Customer sacrifice is due to presentation	Customer contacts are repetitive	Determining either-or choices
Customer information	Purchase-/demographic information	Direct choice by customer	Purchase-/demographic-/behavioural information	Purchase-/demographic-/behavioural information	Direct interaction
Learning opportunity	Low	Medium	Medium	Medium	High
Customer interaction	None	High	Low	Low	High
Change in presentation	Possibly	No	Yes	No	Likely
Variation of product	Possibly	No	No	Yes	Likely

Source: Reprinted by permission of Harvard Business School Press. From *The Experience Economy: Work is theatre and every business is a stage* by J. Pine and J. Gilmore. Boston, MA 1999. Copyright © 1999 by the Harvard Business School Publishing Corporation; all rights reserved.

Personalisation should be an integral aspect of relationship marketing, especially in b2b markets. The degree of personalisation will inevitably vary over the customer lifecycle and become more intimate as a relationship matures.

> Personalisation should be an integral aspect of relationship marketing.

Mobility

Digital technologies now support a range of devices and applications that enable mobile communications. Mobile commerce (or mcommerce) refers to the use of wireless devices such as mobile phones for transactional activities; and because the wireless facility enables transactions to be undertaken in real time and at any location, a feature referred to as 'ubiquity', the impact on marketing communications could be huge. Because of the reachability, the opportunity to keep in touch, increased convenience, localisation and personalisation opportunities offered by this new technology, theoretically it will soon be possible to track people to particular locations. Then the delivery of personalised and pertinent information plus inducements and promotional offers in order to encourage specific purchase behaviour can have greater impact.

SMS communications are used increasingly not just for brand awareness-based advertising but also as an effective way of delivering sales promotions, such as announcing special offers. This again reflects the increasing ubiquity of contemporary mobile communications. However, as with email, it is also important to consider the potential privacy concerns of customers, especially as the receipt of unwanted messages (i.e. spam) may well increase.

Speed

IST has enabled aspects of marketing communications to be conducted at much faster, indeed electronic speeds. This impact is manifest in direct communications with end-users and in the production

> IST has enabled aspects of marketing communications to be conducted at much faster, indeed electronic speeds.

process itself. Draft documents, film and video clips, contracts, address lists and research and feedback reports, to name but a few, can all now be transmitted electronically, saving processing time and reducing the elapsed production time necessary to create and implement marketing communication activities and events.

Efficiency

Efficiency is a broad term used to encompass a wide array of issues. New technology helps organisations to target their messages accurately to discrete groups or audiences. Indeed, one-to-one marketing is possible, and when compared with mass communications and broad audiences it is clear that IST offers huge opportunities for narrow casting and reduced communication waste. Rather than shower audiences with messages that some of them do not wish to receive, direct marketing should, theoretically, enable each message to be received by all who are favourably disposed to the communication.

This principle of narrow casting applies equally well to communication costs. Moving away from mass media to direct marketing and one-to-one communications reduces the absolute costs associated with campaigns. The relative costs may be higher but these richer communications facilitate interactive opportunities with a greater percentage of the target audience than previously experienced in the mass broadcast era.

> A further type of efficiency can be seen in terms of the accuracy and precision of the messages that are delivered.

A further type of efficiency can be seen in terms of the accuracy and precision of the messages that are delivered. Marketing communications delivers product information, specifications and service details, contracts, designs, drawings and development briefs when customising to meet customer needs. The use of IST can help organisations provide customers with precise information and reduce opportunities for information deviance.

Enhanced relationships

As mentioned previously, new technology is now used by organisations to gather and use information about customers in order to better meet their needs. Through the use of the database, organisations now seek to develop longer-term relationships with customers, with programmes and strategies that are dubiously termed as customer loyalty schemes. While there may be doubt about the term loyalty, there can be no doubt that IST has helped develop new forms of sales promotion and influenced customer relationships. What should also be clear is that the existence of IST in an organisation or relationship is no guarantee that additional value will be created (Ryssel et al., 2004).

Some customer service interface functions have been replaced with technology in the name of greater efficiency, cost savings and improved service. Financial services organisations are able to inform customers of their bank balances automatically without human intervention. Meyronin (2004: 222) refers to this as an 'infomediation' strategy and suggests that this neglect of the human interaction in the creation of joint value in service environments may be detrimental.

Relationships with intermediaries have also been affected by new technology. The development of ecommerce has given rise to channel strategies that either result in channel functions and hence members being discarded, or give rise to opportunities for new functions and members. These processes, disintermediation and reintermediation respectively, are both dynamic and potentially destabilising for organisations and their channel partners.

Strategic implications

Organisations have had to adapt to new technologies as a means of delivering value to their stakeholders. The strategic implications are very significant although it should be noted that not all organisations have recognised or responded adequately to the strategic challenge, witnessed by the problems associated with customer relationship management (CRM) systems. IST has not changed the value propositions or the assumptions of the value chain itself (Porter, 1985). Apart from enabling organisations to adopt a customer focus, what IST has done is change the way in which the primary and support activities work in order that value be generated. New technology has enabled organisations to reach new markets, work with different channel partners and provide value and satisfaction for a range of new audiences.

Web sites

Web sites are the cornerstone of Internet activity for organisations, regardless of whether they are operating in the b2b, b2c or not-for-profit sectors and whether the purpose is merely to offer information or provide fully developed embedded ecommerce (transactional) facilities. The design characteristics of a web site can be crucial in determining the length of stay, activities undertaken and the propensity for a visitor to return to the site at a later time. When the experience is satisfactory, then both the visitor and the web site owner might begin to take on some of the characteristics associated with relationship marketing.

To understand the characteristics associated with web site interaction, consideration will first be given to their strengths and weaknesses, then the issues associated with the development of a web site will be identified and finally the processes involved in attracting and managing web site activity will be examined.

Web sites can be used for a variety of purposes but essentially they are either product-oriented or corporate-oriented. Product-oriented web sites aim to provide product-based information such as brochureware, sales-based enquiries, demonstrations and endorsements through to online transactions and ongoing technical support as the main activities.

Corporate-oriented web sites aim to provide information about the performance, size, prospects, financial data and job opportunities relating to the organisation. They also need to relate to issues concerning the ethical expectations and degree of social responsibility accepted by the company, if only to meet the needs of prospective investors and employees. The demarcation is not necessarily as clear cut as this might suggest, but the essence of a site's orientation is largely derived from the organisation's approach to branding.

The strengths and weaknesses of web site facilities are set out in Table 25.2; however, it should be remembered that these are generalised comments and that some organisations have attended to these issues and have been able to develop the strengths and negate some of the weaknesses such that their web sites are particularly attractive, user friendly and encourage repeat visits.

Strengths

Any www user can create a web site, consisting of a home page and a number of linked pages. Business pages can carry advertising, product catalogues, descriptions, pricing, special offers, press releases – all forms of promotional material. They can link to online order pages, so that potential customers can order directly, or to email facilities for requesting further information or providing feedback. Consumer interest and activity can be monitored easily, allowing for timely market research, rapid feedback and strategy adaptation.

Barriers to entry are low, it is relatively inexpensive to create/maintain a site and share of voice is theoretically equal for all participants, although in practice this is clearly not the case. Large organisations can buy banner ads and have a better chance of appearing in the first few results presented by search engines (see Chapter 26 for more detail on Search). Good design can add to brand appeal and recognition.

> Barriers to entry are low, it is relatively inexpensive to create/maintain a site and share of voice is theoretically equal for all participants.

Table 25.2 Strengths and weaknesses of web site-based communications

Strengths	Weaknesses
Quick to set up and easy to maintain	Slow access and page downloading speeds, but increasing broadband access has reduced this type of problem
Flexibility	Huge variability in web site design and user friendliness
Variety of information	Attract large amounts of unsolicited email
High level of user involvement	Security and transaction privacy issues
Potentially high level of user convenience (and satisfaction)	Variable levels of Internet penetration across UK households
Range of service facilities	Inconsistent fulfilment standards (online transactions only)
Global reach and equal access opportunities	Variability and speed of technology provision
Open all hours – reduced employment costs	Lack of regulation concerning content and distribution
Very low relative costs (per person reached)	Online search time costs prohibitive for many users
Can provide cost efficiencies in terms of marketing research	

Potential customers actively seek products and services, which is both time- and cost-effective from a company's point of view, and indicative of positive attitudes, perception and involvement. Channel communications can also be swift and supportive. Coverage is global, without the need for huge investment or expensive staff to be employed around the clock. Savings can be made in advertising budgets, travel, postage and telephone costs. Different time zones no longer matter in the virtual environment, and language barriers are less of an issue.

Weaknesses

For some the disadvantages are that the speed of access, page location and loading are still too slow for many users, especially from home PCs. However, as broadband penetration increases, so these problems disappear. Perversely however, even broadband and the extra bandwidth brings other difficulties. The launch of the BBC iPlayer in 2008 resulted in over 17 million users in the first seven weeks (BBC Radio) and people are downloading greater and greater volumes of material such that the infrastructure was, even then, starting to creak.

Potential customers are easily put off by slow or unreliable connections and this frustration can result in negative images of the company or product. Poorly designed web sites, which confuse rather than clarify, also create a poor impression, one that can deter a return visit.

Unsolicited email is extremely annoying to many users and may be counterproductive. Worries over the security of financial details and transactions online, while not discouraging people from seeking information, may still be a barrier to full ecommerce. Fulfilment issues, principally delivery problems (such as long delays), wrong items, incorrect billing, plus the associated inconvenience of returning products or otherwise seeking resolution, may deter repeat purchase.

Some regard ecommerce as transactional web sites or extended enterprises, but it is more to do with information/communication management and the impact on relationships.

ecommerce should be aimed at building new relationships with established customers and providing potential customers with a reason to change. The idea that ecommerce provides process efficiencies is correct but these features need to be transformed into benefits for customers.

Web site design

The design and functionality of a web site is now recognised as an important integral aspect of an organisation's communication strategy. Indeed many organisations now update their sites on a regular basis. What constitutes a suitable web site has also been the subject of much debate and speculation, marked by a lack of substantial empirical work to determine a common framework. Of the many ideas available two are featured here, if only because of their currency at the time of writing and the background of the researchers involved.

> The design and functionality of a web site is now recognised as an important integral aspect of an organisation's communication strategy.

Karayanni and Baltas (2003) suggest that web sites have four main characteristics. These are set out in Table 25.3 and were presented in the context of b2b markets.

This breakdown is useful because it indicates the main facilities that a successful site should provide. However, what it does not provide is a depth of insight and balance that would help organisations design their sites more appropriately. Rayport and Jaworski (2004) offer a 7Cs framework, which they subsequently develop into a map that can be used to analyse sites and to design sites more effectively.

The 7Cs of the customer interface design are intended to cover the range of elements necessary for good web site design. These are set out in Table 25.4.

> The 7Cs of the customer interface design are intended to cover the range of elements necessary for good web site design.

Table 25.3 Four aspects of web site design

Web site characteristic		Explanation
Interactivity		The provision of solutions in response to the provision of personal information and the ability of users to customise preferences. This can be delivered through memory storage/organisation and response to individual needs.
Navigability		The structure and organisation of the site combined with the ease with which information can be retrieved.
Multimedia design		The Internet offers all the facilities that each of the other media provide individually. This provides opportunities for stimulation as well as flexibility and visitor involvement with a site.
Content	Company content	Information relating to the organisation, its markets, culture and values are important to establish credibility and reduce risk.
	Customer content	This concerns both the provision of information, for example a *frequently asked questions* facility, and the collection of information about customers and the market.

Source: Karayanni and Baltas (2003) © Emerald Group Publishing Limited. All rights reserved.

Table 25.4 The 7Cs of the customer interface

Type of community	Explanation
Context	Layout and design of web site
Content	Text, sound, pictures and video material
Community	Site-enabled, user-to-user communication
Customisation	Site facilities to tailor itself to user needs
Communication	The ways in which two-way communication is enabled
Commerce	Ability to enable commercial transactions
Connection	The number of other linked sites

Source: Rayport and Jaworski (2004).

Context

The context of a site is concerned with the balance between the functional and aesthetic look and feel. Some sites will be designed such that their functionality dominates the aesthetic and will try to provide text-based information rather than emphasising the visual elements of the site. Conversely other sites attempt to provide warm feelings for visitors and use multimedia facilities to create an emotional engagement with the site, often at the expense of long loading times. The balance between the functional and emotional can be termed balanced (although Rayport and Jaworski call it integrated). In this approach, visitors experience a site that provides a suitable level of information, is easy to navigate and yet is interesting and stimulating in terms of the emotional satisfaction derived from using the site. This need not be the optimal site design for all organisations, as the context should reflect the values and purpose of the organisation itself. At one extreme, high fashion and luxury brands will focus on aesthetic styled sites while the Driving Vehicle Licensing Agency would be expected to be predominately functional.

Content

This refers to what is presented on the site in terms of audio, text, graphics, images and video. The content can be considered in terms of the following:

- *offering mix* – the balance between information, products and services;
- *appeal mix* – the balance between functional (attribute and benefits) and the emotional (feelings and brand engagement) appeals;
- *multimedia mix* – the selected combination of audio, text, graphics, images and video;
- *timeliness mix* – the time sensitivity of the information determines how often a site needs to be updated. For example, www.BBC.co.uk/news has to be updated on a frequent and regular basis, whereas a site dealing with largely historical or archive data (e.g. family trees) needs less regular attention.

Community

The increasing role and significance of online communities indicates that site design should reflect the needs and significance of these communities to organisations. Online communities are about the interaction between the users of a site, not between the site and users. These interactions may be one-to-one (email) or among many (chat rooms) but are significant to organisations as they can be a source of information about customer feelings and attitudes that may be strong or weak. A deeper consideration of these communities can be found at the end of this chapter.

> ### ViewPoint 25.4 Gorilla games
>
> When ZSL London Zoo developed their campaign to launch Gorilla Kingdom in 2007 they used a variety of media to reach their target audience. These included outdoor, especially the London Underground sites, radio, using sponsorship of the Travel and Transport element of Magic FM, and digital in the form of both web and email.
>
> Gorilla Kingdom was a major investment project and so it was important to attract visitors to the 'new green oasis within London'. In addition to strong branding, work with the travel trade and several important joint promotions and partnerships plus heavy public relations activities and events, the ZSL web site had an important role to play as the fulcrum for the launch.
>
> The web site carried a microsite for Gorilla Kingdom. This held information about gorillas, pictures and visuals about the development of the new exhibit through the various phases of construction and video interviews with the keepers. Email banners were developed and all staff were encouraged to incorporate them in their electronic signatures.
>
> However, one particular development attracted considerable attention. Radio presenter and celebrity Chris Evans apparently spent seven minutes on his Radio 2 programme discussing the merits of their 'gorilla game'. This required players to download a virtual gorilla and then look after it for three weeks. The three people who looked after their gorilla best won the opportunity to meet the real gorilla behind the scenes.
>
> Source: Winner of the Best Marketing Project at the BIAZA awards 2007.
>
> ### Question
> To what extent did the emotional element of the gorilla game complement the more informative aspects of the ZSL web site?
>
> ### Task
> Make a list of some of the other ways a web site can be used to attract, retain and encourage visitors to return.

Customisation

This is concerned with the extent to which a site is capable of being adapted to the individual needs of visitors. When customisation is initiated by customers it is referred to as personalisation, but when driven and managed by the organisation it is called tailoring. Obviously, different sites will provide varying levels of customisation, from low through medium to high levels, and this will be reflected in the users' site experience.

Communication

The type of communication provided by a site is to some extent a reflection of the type of relationship offered by the organisation. The communication may be broadcast (content update reminders or mass mailings), in which case one-way communication prevents user response and with it opportunities for dialogue. Alternatively, interactive communication (user ratings or feedback) enables user response that can lead to dialogue.

> The type of communication provided is to some extent a reflection of the type of relationship offered by the organisation.

Connection

Connection is concerned with the degree to which a site is linked or connected to other sites. These links may be located on other web pages and, when clicked, take the user to another site. If a transaction then occurs a commission is payable to the affiliate site. Outside links make it

Table 25.5 7Cs framework map

Context	Aesthetically dominant		Functionally dominant	Integrated
Content	Product-dominant		Information-dominant	Service-dominant
Community	Nonexistent		Limited	Strong
Customisation	Generic		Moderately customised	Highly customised
Communication	One-to-many, nonresponding user	One-to-many, responding user	One-to-one, nonresponding user	One-to-one, responding user
Connection	Destination		Hub	Portal
Commerce	Low		Medium	High

Source: Rayport and Jaworski (2004).

difficult for the user to return to the original page and are therefore not used a great deal. Framed links attempt to overcome this problem. Pop-up windows present a new site within the original site but can be annoying to users.

Commerce

The ability of a site to support financial transactions is an important feature of product-dominated web sites. Apart from the need to provide a secure and risk-free trading environment, the key activities associated with these sites are: registration, shopping carts, credit card approval, one-click shopping, orders through affiliate sites, configuration facilities (different combinations of products and services), order tracking and delivery options. All of the 7Cs can be mapped and a site analysed against this criteria (see Table 25.5). Use of this mapping approach, that is the identification of which element applies to a web site, can enable web site designers to better understand how their site appears to visitors and enables sites to be developed according to the planned needs of organisations.

> There is little empirical research that shows how different web site design features impact on visitor responsiveness.

To conclude this section it should be noted that there is little empirical research that shows how different web site design features impact on visitor responsiveness. Indeed Kent *et al.* (2003) make the point that there is a gulf between what many organisations expect of a web site capability to foster relationships and the actual web sites that are designed to facilitate these relationships. They argue that there is an inconsistency in what is thought to be possible through a web site and practice, that it is generally recognised that web sites are all too often poorly used dialogic tools, and that the actual design of a web site can have a strong impact on the way in which visitors perceive the organisation and hence influence its relationship-building potential.

Web sites – visitor behaviour

It is possible to deconstruct users' web site behaviour into a number of discrete activities, but the resultant list would be far too complex to be of any practical assistance. However, several authors have tried to discriminate among Internet users and segment the market accordingly. For example, Lewis and Lewis (1997) were one of the first and they segmented the Internet on the basis of people who use the Internet. Later Forsyth *et al.* (2000) grouped users on the basis of those who are active online consumers, a behavioural approach to segmentation.

> The design of web sites should account for the needs of different types of users.

The design of web sites should account for the needs of these different types of users and also the different stages each has reached in terms of their experience in using the Internet, their stage in the adoption

Table 25.6 Online segments

	Group of Internet users	Explanation
Lewis and Lewis (1997)	Directed information seekers	Experienced users who know what information they require and where to find it.
	Undirected information seekers	Inexperienced users (generally) who surf looking for information or who browse for leisure and pleasure.
	Directed buyers	Experienced users who are online with the express intention of purchasing specific goods/services.
	Bargain hunters	Users in search of free offers and sizeable discounts.
	Entertainment seekers	Users whose intentions are primarily to exploit sales promotions and competition opportunities and use chat rooms.
Forsyth et al. (2000)	Simplifiers	Simplifiers like readily available product information, reliable customer service and easy returns, and they respond positively to any evidence conveyed through advertising or on-site messages.
	Surfers	Surfers move quickly among sites, continually seeking new online experiences. Sites must offer a strong online brand, cutting-edge design and features, constant updates, and a rich variety of products and services.
	Bargainers	Bargainers care mainly about getting a good deal and enjoy the search for a good price, control over transactions, and the sense of community that sites such as eBay offer.
	Connectors	Connectors tend to be novices who use the Internet mainly to relate to other people through chat services.
	Routiners	Routiners use the Internet for news and financial information and spend more than 80 per cent of their online time surfing through their 10 favourite sites.
	Sportsters	Sportsters behave like Routiners but gravitate to sports and entertainment sites. They view content as entertainment, so sites must be fresh, colourful and interactive to attract them.

process (see Chapter 2) and different stages users have reached in the buying process. For the purposes of the rest of this text, reference is made to two broad categories, active (goal-directed) and passive (experiential) information seekers.

The initial goal is to generate awareness of the web site and this needs to be understood in the knowledge that there are many web users who have no interest in a particular (your) web site and those who do are said to have a potential interest. The task is therefore to drive awareness levels among those who might find the site useful.

The second phase is to encourage the potential segment to actually visit the site. The problem is that there are two types of information seeker, passive and active. Passive seekers have no intention of hitting any particular site, whereas active seekers do have the express intention of visiting a particular site. Part of the communication strategy must therefore be geared to facilitating active seekers and attracting passive information seekers.

The next phase is to ensure that active seekers, once on the web site, are able to find the information they need quickly and efficiently so that they are inclined to revisit. This entails good site access and, once found, good site design so that navigation is easy, simple and fast. This normally means that the design of the site is simple and is user-, rather than technology-oriented. Passive information seekers, on the other hand, need to be made curious and stimulated to want to know more about the site and the products and services available. Here the objective is to convert hitters into visitors. A site registration book, supported perhaps with sales promotion devices, or a site design that is sufficiently intriguing, may allow these goals to be met. Research suggests that there are three main elements that strongly influence the perceived quality of a web site visit (Oxley and Miller, 2000):

- all are content-oriented and refer to whether the site material is relevant to the needs of the visitor;
- the degree to which the content (and design) encourages curiosity to explore the site;
- whether the content is presented in an interesting way.

These three points correlate strongly with the idea of 'likeability', that advertising effectiveness improves when an individual assigns significant value (represented by relevance, curiosity and interest) to any particular form of marketing communication discipline, but advertising in particular in this case (Chapters 8 and 16). Therefore, the main factors that might influence the way an individual perceives a web site may be similar to the way they process and evaluate other marketing communications and, in particular, advertising messages. Goldsmith and Lafferty (2002) have made similar observations and consider theories concerning attitudes towards the ad as developed by Lutz *et al.* (1983) and Bruner and Kumar (2000). Attitudes developed towards advertisements can also impact on attitudes towards the brand and hence are better indicators of purchase intentions (see Chapter 5). Goldsmith and Lafferty also refer to ad brand recall and the fact that those consumers who have strong emotional feelings towards a brand (a positive attitude) are more likely to be able to recall it. Therefore, investment in marketing communications that seeks to establish top-of-mind awareness of a brand and also creates positive attitudes are more likely to be successful.

> Attitudes developed towards advertisements can impact on attitudes towards the brand.

Key differences between traditional and digital media

Having considered the characteristics of traditional media in the previous chapter, this appears to be the right point at which to bring traditional and digital media together. In comparison with traditional media, the Internet and digital media facilities provide an interesting contrast (see Table 25.7). Space (or time) within traditional media is limited and costs rise as demand for the limited space/time increases. On the Internet, space is unlimited so absolute costs remain very low and static, while relative costs plummet as more visitors are recorded as having been to a site. Another aspect concerns the focus of the advertising message. Traditionally, advertisers tend to emphasise the emotional rather than information aspect, particularly within low-involvement categories. Digital media allow focus on the provision of information and so the emotional aspect of advertising messages tends to have a lower significance. As branding becomes a more important aspect of Internet activity, it is probable that there will be a greater use of emotions, especially when the goal is to keep people at a web site, rather than driving them to it.

> Digital media allow focus on the provision of information and so the emotional aspect of advertising messages tends to have a lower significance.

Apart from the obvious factor that digital media, and the Internet in particular, provide interactive opportunities that traditional media cannot provide, it is important to remember

Table 25.7 Comparison of new and traditional media

Traditional media	New media
One-to-many	One-to-one and many-to-many
Greater monologue	Greater dialogue
Active provision	Passive provision
Mass marketing	Individualised marketing
General need	Personalised
Branding	Information
Segmentation	Communities

that opportunities-to-see are generally driven by customers rather than by the advertiser that interrupts viewing or reading activities. People drive the interaction at a speed that is convenient to them; they are not driven by others.

Management control over internet-based marketing communications is relatively high, as not only are there greater opportunities to control the position and placement of advertisements, promotions and press releases, but it is also possible to change the content of these activities much more quickly than is possible with traditional media. The goals outlined above indicate the framework within which advertising needs to be managed.

In addition to considering the attributes of the two different forms of media, it is also worth considering the content of the information that each is capable of delivering. These are set out in Table 25.8.

As mentioned earlier, digital media are superior at providing rational, product-based information whereas traditional media are much better at conveying emotional brand values. The former have a dominant cognition orientation and the latter an emotional one. There are other differences, but the predominant message is that these types of media are, to a large

Table 25.8 Comparison of information content

Web sites/Internet	Traditional media
Good at providing rational, product-based information	Better at conveying emotional brand values
More efficient as costs do not increase in proportion to the size of the target audience	Costs are related to usage
Better at prompting customer action	Less effective for calling to action except point-of-purchase and telemarketing
Effective for short-term, product-oriented brand action goals and long-term corporate identity objectives	Normally associated with building long-term values
Poor at generating awareness and attention	Strong builders of awareness
Poor at managing attitudes	Capable of changing and monitoring attitudes
Measures of effectiveness weak and/or in the process of development	Established methodologies, if misleading or superficial (mass media); direct marketing techniques are superior
Dominant orientation – cognition	Dominant orientation – emotion

extent, complementary, suggesting that they should be used together, not one independently of the other.

Future technologies and marketing communications

The Internet lies at the heart of current and future marketing applications of new technology but Karnell (2004) suggests that future developments will be based around three main themes: wireless networking, smart devices and intelligent communications services.

Wireless networking refers to communication between computers and related devices that does not require the use of cables and wires. It works through the use of low-powered radio frequency and infrared waves. Protocols such as Wi-Fi (wireless fidelity) means that wireless-enabled computers or personal digital assistants (PDAs) can connect to the Internet if they are within 15 metres of an access point.

Radio frequency identification (RFID) tags contain chips and work on the basis that a radio signal, received by an antenna, activates the chip, which in turn transmits a unique code identifying the object to which the tag is attached (Blau, 2003). In addition to security applications, retail staff are able to use handheld devices to check stock and to assemble orders in the established way, but these tags are also used to trigger screens within changing rooms, enabling customers to view video clips of the merchandise. Using video cameras and plasma screens, in place of mirrors, customers are able to see themselves from behind (Dean, 2003).

RFID tags do not need line-of-sight reading, as with barcodes, which means that hundreds of tags can be read in a second, saving considerable amounts of time. In addition, these radio tags are capable of providing not only the universal product codes as used in barcodes, but also a unique identifying code. This means that promotions can be based on particular groups of items purchased and changed very quickly in response to changing market or competitive conditions. Consumers can use this technology to sample games and music CDs.

ViewPoint 25.5 Store into the future

The building used by the Metro Future Store in Germany is completely covered by a wireless network. Through this network, various mobile devices such as personal shopping assistants (PSAs) and personal digital assistants (PDAs) and static devices such as electronic shelf labels (ESLs), check-out points and flat-screen displays for product promotion are all interlinked.

PSAs are for the use of shoppers whose shopping trolleys have a touch screen mini-computer linked to the network and an integrated scanner. This is referred to as a PSA and allows shoppers to scan their own purchases, and the data to be transmitted to the checkout in advance of the shopper.

The PDAs are also linked to the network and are used by store employees to check stock by directly accessing Metro's merchandise management system at any time and at any point in the store. Using VoIP (Voice over Internet Protocol) technology, it is planned for the PDAs to receive 'soft phone' functionality, enabling staff to make calls in addition to sending messages or downloading information.

Source: Adapted from Fill (2005).

Question
Is this use of technology of real value to customers?

Task
Find one piece of new technology that has a retail application.

Barcode technology is a mature technology and will gradually be replaced by radio tags as the cost of the embedded chips decreases. RFID technology is being used to develop electronic labelling systems and smart shelves. Connected to the store network, smart shelves have readers embedded in them that will enable the main system to be informed when merchandise is removed, and will then automatically trigger a request for shelf replenishment.

Out-of-store applications of wireless technologies will grow as the Internet becomes an information utility where corporations, individuals and governments will access and interact with information anywhere, anytime and, most importantly, with any device. For marketers, this increased access means greater scope for targeted and personalised delivery of timely marketing communications messages and increased opportunities for co-branding and marketing alliances.

> Out-of-store applications of wireless technologies will grow as the Internet becomes an information utility.

Smart devices, or information-powered devices, have continuous Internet access and can be incorporated within furniture and furnishings, clocks and watches, carpets, refrigerators and freezers, and lighting and security systems. These devices can process information, signals, graphics, animation, video and audio and have the ability to exchange such information with another smart device. These devices, which will be able to receive up-to-date news, traffic, weather and sports information, have the potential to radically change the way consumers interact with brands. In addition to obvious above-the-line communications, this technology opens up opportunities for sponsorship and promotional programmes.

Intelligent communication services are smart devices that are integrated with the Internet. This will enable them to detect changes in their environment and in doing so prompt users to act in particular ways. Karnell suggests that this will enable marketers to track products and consumers and deliver intelligent real-time, proximity-specific and ultra-personalised information. So, as a freezer senses that the last pizza (previously tagged) has been removed it will prompt, via text, visuals or voice that a new pizza is required. This may in time be remotely linked through to a specified store, which will automatically add the item to the consumer's standing order for home delivery.

These devices could be used in-store enabling retailers and brand owners to interact with consumers while they are shopping or they might be used to make purchasing and brand choice decisions in the home. Used as the ultimate form of personalised marketing communications, messages can be delivered, at the appropriate time in the consumption cycle, about products and services, lower prices or promotional offers (e.g. time-based electronic coupons); all driven by each customer's individual consumption patterns and transaction history, they have the potential to transform the shopping experience.

> These devices could be used in-store enabling retailers and brand owners to interact with consumers while they are shopping.

Biometrics

The film *Minority Report* contains a sequence in which Tom Cruise enters a futuristic store, at which point his iris/retina is scanned, checked, cross-referenced and a stream of products and services related to his preferences are then presented to him. While this futuristic view of technology-enabled, personalised marketing communications has yet to be commercially resolved and implemented, the concept and use of biometric technology applications are currently being developed. At present a range of applications are available or are at an advanced stage of development. Das (2004) refers to hand geometry, fingerprint, voice/speech, iris/retinal and face recognition facilities with earlobe, brain mapping, odour and gait recognition at an early stage of development. For example, the WatchPad uses a fingerprint sensor to identify the owner of a watch, thus replacing the need for passwords, improving security and with it trust, and reducing perceived risk and reasons not to buy.

Many of these biometric technologies have been used within security-related environments to identify and authenticate individuals. Some voice recognition technologies have been used successfully in back-office situations and are currently considered to be best used to gather simple information such as names, addresses and/or supporting applications such as voicemail account management through a preset menu of choices (Rockwell, 2004).

Although these voice recognition technologies have the potential to reduce customer contact centre costs there are difficulties associated with dialects and regional accents (Rockwell, 2004). In addition, it is not yet possible to induce real-time dialogue with smart devices in order to communicate personalised product offers. Although in development it should be remembered that the advent of these facilities will also prompt a series of privacy- and personal freedom-related issues.

Industry issues

New technology has led to changes in the balance of the tools used by many organisations. Most notably, those operating in the FMCG sector that spend vast sums on above-the-line media in order to develop brand values have begun to spend more below-the-line in an effort to impact on behaviour rather than just brand development. Direct marketing has also impacted on the advertising spend, and with the development of IMC and related concepts such as media-neutral planning, the balance of the communications spend has moved towards either sales promotions and/or direct marketing.

The content of many marketing communication messages has therefore swung, and with it the work of advertising agencies. Agencies have had to adapt to a new environment, one in which clients expect their agencies to present strategies that involve a much broader range of tools and media and to offer new skills and resources. This has been achieved mainly through acquisition and the development of international networks of agencies, from all disciplines, pooling their talents in order to secure domestic and international business.

Tapp and Hughes (2004) refer to the impact of IST on the company–customer interface and on the internal processes and marketing resources within client companies. They report on the major impact IST has had internally, and the struggle organisations have experienced coping with the disruption new technology has stimulated. In terms of marketing communications, this disruption is potentially enormous. With web sites becoming the focus of much internal communication activity; forces propelling ideas concerning the desire to integrate marketing communications and planning; and strategy processes having to accommodate uncertain industry, media and audience expectations, marketing communications has been severely buffeted by IST.

However, while the changes driven by new technology might bring about an unwelcome internal production focus, these changes should be seen positively, as a primary means of moving organisations forward. New technology can help organisations communicate more effectively and more efficiently, both internally and externally. By adopting a stronger customer focus, organisations can deliver improved levels of customer value and be better placed to meet their marketing goals and improve shareholder value.

> New technology can help organisations communicate more effectively.

Convergence in marketing communications

Ideas concerning the nature and characteristics of the concept of integrated marketing communications, previously explored in Chapter 9, continue to be discussed. There can be little doubt that there are genuine benefits for organisations and their stakeholders by striving to achieve the principles of IMC. More recently, however, there is a growing body of thought concerning media convergence. At one level convergence refers to a technological 'bringing

Table 25.9 Dimensions of media convergence

Convergence dimension	Explanation
Media technology	Digitalisation and a reduction in number of technological devices necessary to send and receive a variety of streams of information
Media content	Almost all media content can now be produced, edited, distributed and stored digitally. This negates any need to keep media (and devices) separate
Media economics	The increasing horizontal concentration of media ownership, typified by the mergers of different media companies across different sectors, plus the re-organisations experienced by several media organisations.

together' of digital devices. So, information in different formats such as audio, text, search, still and moving pictures, which previously required multiple devices to receive, such as an individual computer, television, radio or newspaper, is accessed through a single (converged) device. However, at another level convergence refers to what Murdock (2000), cited by Herkman (2007) sees as three different dimensions, or what Murdock refers to as levels. These are media technology, media forms (and contents) and media economics. These are explained in Table 25.9.

> At one level convergence refers to a technological 'bringing together' of digital devices.

New technology has driven the IMC concept not only through the development of direct marketing opportunities but also through ecommerce. Guens argues that IMC provides the *opportunity* for organisations to integrate their communications and that ecommerce has provided the *ability* for organisations to integrate their communications (2005). The proposition is that these two streams converge at the organisation's web site. The web site has become a central point for an organisation's digital communications. It is a point at which the complexity of messages that arise from different functional areas and departments can be integrated and managed together with the array of messages emanating from a variety of external stakeholders.

It may be that centralising marketing communications in this way has not helped to draw the offline and online communications into an integrated whole. Indeed, it appears that if marketing communications is to be audience-centred then it is crucial that the apparent focus on the technology and digitisation gives way to a more considered understanding of the meaning and interpretation that audiences give to the array of branded messages they receive, whether they be channelled through offline or online media.

ViewPoint 25.6 Integrated travel?

WAYN (Where Are You Now?) is a social network for travellers around the world. The network has over 8 million unique users, many of whom are young travellers and backpackers.

WAYN introduced streamed video ads in June 2007, partly to add value and partly to supplement their existing online ad strategy, including banner ads, skyscrapers and text ads. The aim is to enable users to view each other's video clips and click-on streaming ad 'tickers' with targeted travel and lifestyle products, services, deals and competitions. It is hoped that the integrated approach to site advertising will help WAYN's advertising partners provide relevant content without disrupting the viewing experience and flow of the social network.

However, WAYN also entered into a short-term sponsorship deal with the travel company Thomas Cook, who in return received exclusive branding rights on the network in exchange for providing competitions and special discounts. At first glance, the fit between the two organisations is quite clear and makes sense. However, in reality backpackers are not interested in the niceties of organised travel and prefer to make their own arrangements, picking and choosing deals off the Internet, many of which are more advantageous than those offered by Thomas Cook. What this experience makes abundantly clear is the need to ensure there is a tight fit between the sponsor and the needs of the target audience.

Sources: Anon (2007); Crow (2007).

Question

What value does WAYN bring to the site's users?

Task

The sponsorship with Thomas Cook was not a success. Which brand might be more successful in this type of arrangement?

At a macro level, media convergence and integrated marketing communications present an interesting context. Convergence should propel integration but evidence suggests that truly integrated marketing communications is not taking place at a level or consistency that some popular commentators suggest is happening or necessary. Apart from the technological, content and economic convergence, integrated marketing communications needs to adopt an audience-centred approach, one that accounts for the meaning different audiences bestow on the messages they receive.

Summary

In order to help consolidate your understanding of digital media, here are the key points summarised against each of the learning objectives:

1. Explain the key forms of digital media.

The range of digital media is vast and is growing rapidly but consideration was given to some of the key types or forms of digital media. The Internet, databases, multimedia, mobile phone technologies, business applications (software), interactive television, video conferencing and electronic kiosks were examined.

2. Understand what digital media enables users to do.

The benefits arising from using digital media are many, but consideration has been given to interactivity, multichannel marketing, personalisation, speed, mobility, efficiency, enhanced relationships and issues relating to strategy.

3. Examine some of the issues arising from the design and use of web sites.

The web site has become the fulcrum for many organisations and their marketing communications. The design characteristics of a web site can therefore be crucial in determining the length of stay, activities undertaken and the propensity for a visitor to return to the site at a later time. The 7Cs framework by Rayport and Jaworski provides a useful design checklist.

When the experience is satisfactory, then both the visitor and the web site owner might begin to take on some of the characteristics associated with relationship marketing.

4. Explain the key differences between traditional and digital media.

Space is unlimited on the Internet, so absolute costs remain very low and static, while relative costs plummet as more visitors are recorded as having been to a site. Digital media are superior at providing rational, product-based information, whereas traditional media are much better at conveying emotional brand values. The former have a dominant cognition orientation and the latter an emotional one. There are other differences, but the predominant message is that these types of media are, to a large extent, complementary, suggesting that they should be used together, rather than independently of each other.

5. Consider future technologies and their impact on marketing communications.

The Internet lies at the heart of current and future marketing applications of new technology, but as Karnell (2004) suggests, future developments are likely to be based around three main themes: wireless networking, smart devices and intelligent communications services. In addition, biometrics and issues arising within the industry will also impact significantly on the shape of future marketing communications.

6. Explain what convergence means and how it influences marketing communications.

At one level convergence refers to a technological 'bringing together' of digital devices. This means that information, in different formats such as audio, text, search, still and moving pictures, which previously required multiple devices, such as an individual computer, television, radio or newspaper are accessed through a single (converged) device. At another level convergence refers to media technology, media forms (and content) and media economics.

It is also argued that IMC provides the *opportunity* for organisations to integrate their communications and that digital media, albeit in the form of ecommerce or emarketing, provides the *ability* for organisations to integrate their communications, and in doing so converge systems, processes, structures and messages.

Review questions

1. Prepare brief notes explaining how the database has influenced marketing communications.
2. Discuss ways in which use of the Internet has assisted organisations to develop their marketing communications.
3. Identify different ways in which multimedia applications might be configured.
4. Why has the use of mobile communications been slow but is now about to increase rapidly?
5. Why is interactivity so important in contemporary marketing communications?
6. How would you advise a web site be designed from a marketing perspective?
7. To what extent does multichannel marketing assist marketing?
8. Prepare notes identifying how digital media have affected the structure of the marketing communications industry.
9. Explain the meaning of biometrics and consider how biometrics and wireless technologies might affect marketing communications in the future.
10. What is convergence and how might this affect marketing communications?

MiniCase: Integrating traditional and digital media

Matt King: Co-founder and Director of Media Safari

Introduction

The days when a marketing campaign ran a set number of times a year, in a pre-agreed format and through a pre-determined channel are long gone. Customers have moved on, and now prefer interactive communications and an ongoing dialogue that contains a sequence of personalised messages delivered in a way that is convenient to them. This process usually involves a combination of offline and online media, otherwise referred to as 'traditional' and 'digital' media, to engage and educate consumers and ultimately influence their purchase decisions.

The volume of competition, the limited shelf space retailers have to maximise their revenues and the short attention spans of many consumers, mean that bringing a product to market successfully does not happen by chance. It requires a meticulously planned and well-executed campaign, which involves close working relationships with all parties in the channel, to ensure that every aspect is brought together at exactly the right time.

Two cases are considered. Media Safari works with Avanquest Software (www.avanquest.com), a leading developer and publisher of personal and professional software for the global PC market. Avanquest markets a product called 'Radiotracker', a software title that legally downloads music from Internet radio stations to MP3 players, for free.

Ascaron Entertainment (www.ascaron.com) is one of the leading European 'boutique' developers and publishers of games. Ascaron launched a new game for PCs called 'Hard to be a God' and Media Safari managed the launch campaign.

The brief – setting objectives

Having established the product's target 'street date', i.e. launched to UK consumers in retail, e.g. PC World or Game, and online e.g. www.Amazon.co.uk or www.Play.com, the key task was to develop a marketing communications strategy and plan, incorporating a variety of tools, tactics and media. This included advertising, (full-colour, half-page ads) public relations (news releases) and direct marketing (e-shots), all delivered in a selection of target print and online magazines.

Achieving the right balance and mix of tools, tactics and media generally depends on the target audience and available budget, but will include both 'push' and 'pull' activity to satisfy trade and end-user needs. It is also at this stage that particular communications objectives are set, for example, the number of news releases and e-shots in the campaign, the levels of expected coverage in certain magazines or the anticipated number of downloads of a trial version or 'demo' directly from the company's web site.

Campaign commencement – creating awareness

Activity for the 'Hard to be a God' campaign began 17 weeks from its target street date. This gave Media Safari sufficient time to build the hype within the gaming industry, educate buyers within key retailers and to distribute the game's 'assets'. The 'assets' are the elements of the game, like the box shot, screen shots or trailers that are drip-fed to the Press to create excitement and anticipation for the launch of the game.

At this early stage, PR and 'media relations' play a crucial element in most launches, with advertising in key trade titles providing support. Particular magazines such as PC Gamer and www.gamespot.com (online) were targeted, offering them a 'preview' of the product. Preview coverage serves several important purposes. First, it assists the sales team to sell the game into the channel. The size of the pre-order gives the publisher an early indication of how many copies it is likely to sell. Second, it acts as a tool to sell into other media including the national newspapers and consumer lifestyles. Finally, it begins to populate gaming web sites and seeds consumer demand.

The third element is an essential part of any campaign and confirms the interdependence of traditional and online media. As consumers move to an increasing reliance on search engines as 'fact finding' tools, it is necessary to feed relevant web sites with 'optimised' news releases. 'Optimised' refers to the way a news release is written in order to enhance its chances of being picked up by the leading search engines.

The advantage of this in the context of 'Hard to be a God' is that when a consumer heard or read about the game and wanted to find out more, they searched

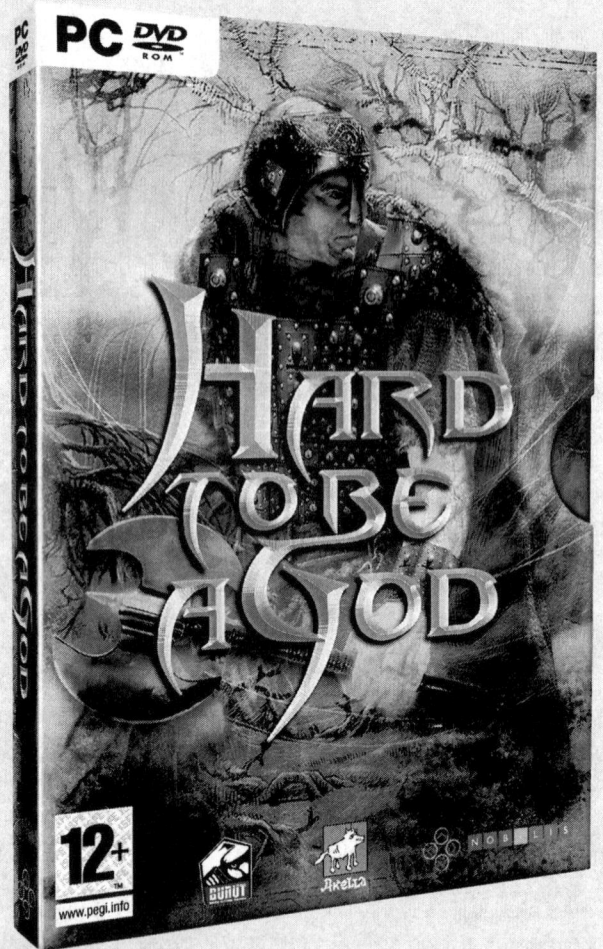

Exhibit 25.2 'Hard to be a God'

for the game and were presented with a selection of links that connect with sites carrying the previews and reviews. Online coverage of this kind also found its way into online gaming forums that helped stimulate word-of-mouth communication and viral marketing.

At this stage, consumers would also be likely to supplement their understanding by buying a gaming magazine. So the PR coverage and advertising in 'traditional' gaming magazines is used to support the 'digital' online coverage. Working with the editorial teams within the magazines to secure a review, Media Safari also provided them with a relevant and specific web address. Consumers were then guided to a web page containing additional information, opportunities to download screen savers and trailers etc., plus links to where it could be pre-ordered and purchased.

Engaging the consumer

Initial interest was therefore generated with the use of PR and advertising in both traditional and online media, the focus being to generate awareness and drive consumer traffic to a specific web site. At that stage, the balance of activity moved towards educating end-users to ensure that the resellers and retailers actually sold the product that they committed to stocking and promoting in-store or online.

In the case of 'Radiotracker', the PR and advertising coverage aimed to drive consumers to a particular space on the web. Once there, the emphasis shifted to engaging the consumer, capturing their information for use in future campaigns and to maintain the current dialogue. This was achieved by offering the customer

Exhibit 25.3 'Radiotracker'

access to similar or related products for free, a trial download lasting a set period of time and discounts on future purchases, all in return for registering and opting into the Avanquest database. This process of capturing customer data is continuous and serves to convert 'prospects' into 'customers'. It is the ability to segment the database and target specific groups with particular offers via email, a cost-effective and highly targeted method of direct marketing, that demonstrates the power of the digital environment.

Having registered and opted in, Avanquest then used these data to email the prospective customers regular updates on 'Radiotracker' containing specific offers to purchase the product. Avanquest continues to send regular e-newsletters containing information about other related products. The use of sales promotion here is used to drive the sale, as well as cross-sell or up-sell other products within the Avanquest range.

All correspondence includes reference codes to trace the sale and links to a support page, in case the transaction online becomes problematic or the consumer has any last minute questions.

Evaluation

With an ever-increasing need for consultancies to demonstrate a return on investment, evaluation of the communications activity and its relationship with sales is essential. Historically, traditional media would have to carry response codes, but this relied on the individual remembering where they saw the information and customer services asking for that code. This was invariably inconclusive, meaning that it was difficult to relate the sale to any meaningful marketing activity.

The Internet has changed all this. Now both traditional print PR and advertising activity carry specifically created URLs that drive traffic to particular pages on the web. So a news piece or promotion for 'Radiotracker' organised in a music magazine might use www.avanquest.co.uk/Mojo or www.radiotracker.co.uk/Mojo. This allows hit rates to be monitored, customer registrations to be counted, downloads to be assessed and click-through rates to ecommerce sites to be tracked. These are critical data and are used to demonstrate the effectiveness of the communications activity.

Last words

The interdependence of offline and online activity has become increasingly pronounced, with the digital environment being central to what Media Safari now does. By using PR and advertising to increase awareness and capture customer data, we can drive sales using direct marketing and sales promotion. Traditional and digital media can obviously operate in isolation, but by integrating the two environments, and allowing them to work off each other rather than in competition with each other, the potential for greater penetration and more effective evaluation will be greatly enhanced.

Media Safari is a marketing communications consultancy specialising in the technology sector. It provides the communications plans and activities for a number of global software developers and games publishers in the United Kingdom.

Source: www.mediasafari.co.uk.

MiniCase questions

1. What benefits do Avanquest achieve from building a customer database?
2. In the case of 'Radiotracker', what areas of media would you suggest targeting?
3. What methods can be used to evaluate the success of marketing communications activity and what new ways of evaluation could you look to introduce using digital media?

References

Advertising Association (2008) *Advertising Statistics Year Book*. NTC. Also at www.adassoc.org.uk/inform/.

Anon. (2007) WAYN streams ads through VideoEgg. *Revolution UK*, 4 June. Retrieved 15 August from http://www.brandrepublic.com/News/662000/WAYN-streams-ads-VideoEgg/.

Blau, J. (2003) Supermarket tunes into wireless. Retrieved 19 April 2004 from www.computerweekly.com/articles/.

Bruner, G.C. and Kumar, A. (2000) Web commercials and advertising hierarchy of effects. *Journal of Advertising Research*, January/April, 35–42.

Chaffey, D. (2003) E-marketing insights: what's new in marketing. Retrieved 27 August 2004 from www.wnim.com/archive/issue1903/emarketing.htm.

Chaffey, D., Mayer, R., Johnston, K. and Ellis-Chadwick, F. (2003) *Internet Marketing*. 2nd edn. Harlow: Pearson.

Chaffey, D., Mayer, R., Johnston, K. and Ellis-Chadwick, F. (2006) *Internet Marketing Strategy, Implementation and Practice*, 3rd edn. Harlow: Pearson Education.

Cohen, R. (1995) Interactive demand is not as high as believed. *Precision Marketing*, 25 September, 8.

Constantinides, E. and Fountain, S.J. (2008) Web 2.0: Conceptual foundations and marketing issues. *Journal of Direct, Data and Digital Marketing Practice*, **9**, 231–44.

Crow, D. (2007) Sponsorship can take online advertising to the next level. *The Business*, 30 June, 32.

Das, R. (2004) The application of biometric technologies: 'The Afghan Girl-Sharbat Gula'. Available online at: http://technologyexecutivesclub.com/articles/artbiometricsapplications.htm.

Dean, A. (2003) High street: the new technological battleground. Retrieved 18 April 2004 from www.raeng.org.uk/news/publications/ingenia/issue18.

Fill, C. (2005) Recent developments in below-the-line communications. In *Marketing Communication: New Approaches, Technologies and Styles* (ed. A. Kimmel). Oxford: Oxford University Press.

Forsyth, J.E., Lavoie, J. and McGuire, T. (2000) Segmenting the e-market. *The McKinsey Quarterly*, **4**. Retrieved 10 November 2004 from www.mckinseyquarterly.com/article.

Goldsmith, R.E. and Lafferty, B.A. (2002) Consumer response to web sites and their influence on advertising effectiveness. *Internet Research: Electronic Networking Applications and Policy*, **12**(4), 318–28.

Guens, T.W. (2005) Current and future developments in electronic commerce. In *Marketing Communication: Emerging Trends and Developments* (ed. A. Kimmel). Oxford: Oxford University Press.

Herkman, J. (2007) Current Trends in Media Research. Retrieved 18 January 2008 from www.nordicom.gu.se/common/pub1_pdf/261.

Jones, G. (2008) iTV returns will be worth the wait. *Marketing*, 9 April, 21.

Kamakura, W.A., Wedel, M., de Rosa, F. and Mazzon, J.A. (2003) Cross-selling through database marketing: a mixed factor analyzer for data augmentation and prediction. *International Journal of Research in Marketing*, **20**(1) (March), 45–65.

Kangis, P. and Rankin, K. (1996) Interactive services: how to identify and target the new markets. *Journal of Marketing Practice: Applied Marketing Science*, **2**(3), 44–67.

Karayanni, D.A. and Baltas, G.A. (2003) Web site characteristics and business performance: some evidence from international business-to-business organizations. *Marketing Intelligence and Planning*, **21**(2), 105–14.

Karnell, I. (2004) Tech watch: the future of one-to-one marketing. Retrieved 3 May 2004 from www.the-dma.org.

Kent, M.L., Taylor, M. and White, W.J. (2003) The relationship between web site design and organisational responsiveness to stakeholders. *Public Relations Review*, **29**(1) (March), 63–77.

Lewis, H. and Lewis, R. (1997) Give your customers what they want. Cited in Chaffey *et al.* (2003).

Lutz, J., Mackensie, S.B. and Belch, G.E. (1983) Attitude toward the ad as a mediator of advertising effectiveness. *Advances in Consumer Research*, **10**. Ann Arbor, MI: Association for Consumer Research.

Meyronin, B. (2004) ICT: the creation of value and differentiation in services. *Managing Service Quality*, **14**(2/3), 216–25.

MMA (2007) Mobile Marketing, *Alumni Briefing Paper*, May, Cambridge: Cambridge Marketing Colleges.

Murdock, G. (2000) Digital Futures: European Television in the Age of Convergence. In *Television Across Europe: A Comparative Introduction* (eds J. Wieten, G. Murdock and P. Dahlgren), 35–8. London: Sage.

Murphy, D. (2008) Crack the code. *Marketing*, 6 February, 30–1.

Oxley, M. and Miller, J. (2000) Capturing the consumer: ensuring website stickiness. *Admap* (July/August), 21–4.

Porter, M.E. (1985) *Competitive Advantage: Creating and Sustaining Superior Performance*. New York: Free Press.

Radjou, N. (2003) Supply chain processes replace applications: 2003 to 2008. In *Achieving Supply Chain Excellence through Technology* (ed. N. Mulani), 24–8. San Francisco, CA: Montgomery Research.

Rayport, J.F. and Jaworski, B.J. (2004) *Introduction to E-Commerce*. Boston, MA: McGraw-Hill/Irwin.

Rockwell, M. (2004) Can voice recognition answer the call? Retrieved 17 April 2004 from www. wirelessweek.com/article/.

Rogers, E.M. (1983) *Diffusion of Innovations*, 3rd edn. New York: Free Press.

Rosen, E.M. (1997) Digital TV will soon overtake the Internet. *Revolution* (July), 6–7.

Ryals, L. and Payne, A. (2001) Customer relationship management in financial services: towards information-enabled relationship marketing. *Journal of Strategic Marketing*, **9**, 3–27.

Ryssel, R., Ritter, T. and Gemunden, H.G. (2004) The impact of information technology deployment on trust, commitment and value creation in business relationships. *Journal of Business and Industrial Marketing*, **19**(3), 197–207.

Stone, M. and Shan, P. (2002) Transforming the bank branch experience for customers. *What's New in Marketing*, **10** (September). Retrieved 23 August 2004 from http://www.wnim.com/archive/.

Tapp, A. and Hughes, T. (2004) New technology and the changing role of marketing. *Marketing Intelligence and Planning*, **22**(3), 284–96.

Thomas, D. (2003) Sainsbury's boosts supplier collaboration. *ComputerWeekly.com*, 24 October 2003. Retrieved 10 November 2003 from http://www.computerweekly.com/articles/.

Thurner, R. (2007) *FitPr*, Retrieved 18 August 2007 from www.incentivated.com/PDFs/Feature_FitPro0707.pdf.

Turner, C. (2008) How NME achieved multi-platform success. *Utalk Case Studies*. Retrieved 28 February 2008 from www.utalkmarketing.com/pages/.

Utalkb (2007) Mazda2 mobile marketing campaign, *Utalk Case Studies*. Retrieved 9 November from www.utalkmarketing.com/pages/.

Vesanen, J. (2007) What is personalization? A conceptual framework. *European Journal of Marketing*, **41**(5/6), 409–18.

Chapter 10
Public relations and sponsorship

Public relations is a management process that is used to shape the attitudes and opinions held by an organisation's stakeholders. Through interaction and dialogue organisations aim to develop relationships that are of significant value to all parties. Sponsorship is used by organisations, partly to cut through the communications clutter and partly to establish awareness of corporate values and associations.

Aims and learning objectives

The aims of this chapter are to explore the role and characteristics of public relations and sponsorship, and to examine how organisations can use these tools to profile their corporate identity and their products.

The learning objectives of this chapter are to:

1. explain the nature, characteristics and audiences for public relations;
2. consider the issues relating to corporate responsibility and cause-related marketing;
3. provide an overview of some of the main tools used by public relations, including media relations, lobbying, corporate advertising and crisis management;
4. consider reasons for the use of sponsorship and the types of objectives that might be set;
5. appreciate the variety and different forms of sponsorship activities;
6. understand the role of sponsorship in the communications mix.

Introduction

The increasing emphasis given to public relations over recent years is testimony to its power and effectiveness. All organisations in the public, hybrid, not-for-profit and private sectors can use this tool to raise visibility, generate interest and build relationships.

Traditionally, public relations has been perceived as a tool that dealt with the manner and style with which an organisation interacted with its major 'publics'. It sought to influence other organisations and individuals through public relations, projecting an identity that would affect the image that different publics held of the organisation. By spreading information and improving the levels of knowledge that people held about particular issues, organisations use public relations to advance itself in the eyes of those it saw as influential. This approach is reflected in the definition of public relations provided by the Institute of Public Relations: 'Public Relations practice is the planned and sustained effort to establish and maintain goodwill and mutual understanding between an organisation and its publics.' However, Jacques (2009) observes some difficulties associated with defining public relations. First he refers to Harlow, who reported 472 different definitions of public relations, in 1976. Then, at the turn of the century, Cropp and Pincus (2001) state that definitions continue to proliferate.

One such 'new' definition, by Bruning and Ledingham (2000), is important as it serves to change the perspective of public relations. Now it becomes an instrument of relationship management. They say, public relations is the management of relationships between organisations and their stakeholders (publics).

Public relations is concerned with the development and communication of corporate and competitive strategies. Public relations provides visibility for an organisation, and this in turn, it is hoped, allows it to be properly identified, positioned and understood by all of its stakeholders. What some definitions do not emphasise or make apparent is that public relations should also be used by management as a means of understanding issues from a stakeholder perspective. Good relationships are developed by appreciating the views held by others and by 'putting oneself in their shoes'.

Through this approach to planned communication, a dialogue can be developed that is not frustrated by punctuated interruptions (anger, disbelief, ignorance and objections). Public relations is a management activity that attempts to shape the attitudes and opinions held by an organisation's stakeholders. It attempts to identify its policies with the interests of its stakeholders and formulates and executes a programme of action to develop mutual goodwill and understanding, and in turn develop relationships that are in the long-term interests of all parties.

Characteristics of public relations

Public relations should therefore, be a planned activity, one that encompasses a wide range of events. However, there are a number of characteristics that single out this particular tool from the others in the marketing communications mix. For example, the use of public relations does not require the purchase of airtime or space in media vehicles, such as television or magazines. This makes a major saving on a communication budget.

The decision about whether an organisation's public relations messages are communicated or not rests with those charged with managing the media resource, not the source of the message. Messages that are selected are perceived by stakeholders to be endorsements or the views of parties other than management. The outcome is that these messages usually carry greater perceived credibility than those messages transmitted through paid media, such as advertising.

The degree of trust and confidence generated by public relations singles out this tool from others in the marketing communications mix as an important means of reducing buyers' perceived risk. However, while credibility may be high, the amount of control that management is able to bring to the transmission of the public relations message is very low. For example, a press release may have been carefully prepared in-house, but as soon as it is passed to the editor of a magazine or newspaper, a possible opinion former, all control is lost. The release may be destroyed (highly probable), printed as it stands (highly unlikely) or changed to fit the available space in the media vehicle (almost certain, if it is decided to use the material). This means that any changes will not have been agreed by management, so the context and style of the original message may be lost or corrupted.

The costs associated with public relations also make this an important tool in the marketing communications mix. The absolute costs are minimal, except for those organisations that retain an agency, but even then their costs are low compared with those of advertising. The relative costs (the costs associated with reaching each member of a target audience) are also very low. The main costs associated with public relations are the time and opportunity costs associated with the preparation of press releases and associated literature. If these types of activity are organised properly, many small organisations could develop and shape their visibility much more effectively and in a relatively inexpensive way.

A further characteristic of this tool is that it can be used to reach specific audiences in a way that paid media cannot. With increasing media fragmentation and finer segmentation (customisation) of markets, the use of public relations represents a cost-effective way of reaching such markets and audiences.

Viewpoint 10.1 — Kittens in need

The KittenAid appeal in 2007, run by the Cats Protection charity, was designed to generate funds from the donors on the charity's database. The number of kittens delivered to the charity was exceptionally large in 2007 due to un-neutered cats breeding in the warm weather.

The campaign was started with a vismail teaser, showing video clips of the charity's kittens and announcing the arrival of kitten season. This was sent to the charity's 18,000 e-subscribers. This activity was then followed by direct mail activity, this time targeted at their 94,000 donors. The mailer was used to tell the story of the recovery of two very ill kittens, now in the care of the charity. The charity's magazine *The Cat* ran the story while their 29 adoption centres and 252 branches actively discussed the story and associated issues with local media.

As a result of this public relations campaign, the appeal generated 40 items of coverage in the media. On the morning of the first broadcast, the KittenAid message reached 1.5 million people and featured on various BBC Radio programmes. After just six weeks the donations reached £244,000, 15 per cent up on the whole of the previous year's fund raising.

Source: Based on Anon. (2007)

Question
What role did the vismail play in generating donations?

Task
Identify the direct marketing and public relations activities in the KittenAid example.

New technology has played a key role in the development and practice of public relations. Gregory (2004) refers to the Internet and electronic communication 'transforming public relations'. With regard to the use of the Internet by public relations practitioners she identifies two main schools. One refers to those who use the Internet as an extension to traditional or pre-Internet forms of communication. The second sees opportunities through the Internet to develop two-way, enhanced communication. There can be little doubt that new technology has assisted communication management in terms of improving the transparency, speed and reach of public relations messages, while at the same time enabling interactive communication between an organisation and its specific audiences. For example, in March 2010, Greenpeace released a viral campaign alleging that Nestlé were planting palm oil trees on land that had been reclaimed from the rain forests and in doing so were endangering the natural habitat of orangutans in Indonesia. Nestlé use palm oil in their KitKat brand and the viral depicted the oil running out of a KitKat as if it was blood. This was a powerful use of digital public relations, one that reached millions, before it was taken down off YouTube (Utalk, 2010).

So, the main characteristics of public relations are that it represents a very cost-effective means of carrying messages to stakeholder audiences, with a high degree of credibility. However, the degree of control that management is able to exert over the transmission of these messages can be limited.

Who are the audiences?

Although stakeholder groups are not static and new groups can emerge in response to changes in the environment, the core groups tend to be the following.

Employees (employee relations)

The employees of an organisation are key stakeholders and represent a major opportunity to use word-of-mouth communications. It has long been established that employees need to be motivated, involved and stimulated to perform their tasks at a high level. Their work as external communicators is less well-established, but they play a critical role providing external cues as part of an organisation's corporate identity.

Financial groups (financial or investor relations)

Shareholders require regular information to maintain their continued confidence in the organisation and to prevent them changing their portfolios and reducing the value of the organisation.

In addition to the shareholders, there are those individuals who are either potential shareholders or who advise shareholders and investors. These represent the wider financial community, but nevertheless have a very strong influence on the stature, strength and value of an organisation. Financial analysts need to be supplied with information in order that they be kept up to date with the activities and performance outcomes of organisations, but also need to be advised of developments within the various markets that the organisation operates.

Organisations attempt to supply financial analysts with current information and materials about the organisation and the markets in which they are operating, to ensure that the potential and value of publicly quoted organisations is reflected in the share price.

Customers (media relations)

The relationships that organisations develop with the media are extremely important in ensuring that their messages reach their current and potential customers. Customers represent a major stakeholder audience and are often the target of public relations activities, because although members of the public may not be current customers the potential they represent is significant. The attitudes and preferences towards the organisation and its products may be unfavourable, in which case it is unlikely that they will wish to purchase the product or speak positively about the organisation. By creating awareness and trust it is possible to create goodwill and interest, which may translate into purchase activity or favourable word-of-mouth communications. This is achieved through media relations.

Of all the media, the press is the most crucial, as it is always interested in newsworthy items and depends to a large extent on information being fed to it by a variety of corporate press officers. Consequently, publicity can be generated for a range of organisational events, activities and developments.

Organisations and communities (corporate public relations)

There are a variety of public, private, commercial and not-for-profit organisations and communities with whom organisations need to communicate and interact on a regular basis. Corporate public relations are used to reach this wide spectrum of audiences and cover a range of activities. Each audience has a particular set of issues and characteristics that lead to individual forms of public relations practice:

- public affairs – government and local authorities;
- community relations – members of local communities;
- industry relations – suppliers, associations and other trade stakeholders;
- issues management – various audiences concerning sensitive industries (e.g. tobacco or pharmaceuticals).

Organisations should seek to work with, rather than against, these stakeholder groups. As a result, public relations should be aimed at informing audiences of their strategic intentions and seeking ways in which the objectives of both parties can be satisfied.

Corporate responsibility

One major reason for the development of public relations in recent years has been the rise in importance of corporate responsibility and the use of cause-related marketing activities. Following increasing interest in sustainability and accountability issues, several high-profile financial disasters (e.g. Enron), technical disasters (e.g. BP) and the irresponsibility demonstrated by some organisations when the financial crisis broke in 2007/08 (e.g. Lehmann Brothers), corporate responsibility is now an important agenda item for a large number of organisations. There is now a need to be perceived as credible, transparent, responsible and ethically sound. This is now seen as an opportunity to differentiate organisations, especially where price, quality and tangible attributes are relatively similar. Being able to present corporate brands as contributors to the wider social framework, a role beyond that of simple profit generators, has enabled many organisations to achieve stronger, more positive market positions.

One of the avenues available to organisations to express their values and attitudes towards their need to be responsible is cause-related marketing. This is a commercial activity through which profit-oriented and not-for-profit organisations form partnerships to exploit, for mutual benefit, their association in the name of a particular cause.

The benefits from a properly planned and constructed cause-related campaign can accrue to all participants. Cause-related marketing helps improve corporate reputation, enables product differentiation and appears to contribute to improved customer retention through enhanced sales. In essence, cause-related marketing is a means by which relationships with stakeholders can be developed. As organisations outsource an increasingly larger part of their business activities and as the stakeholder networks become more complex, so the need to be perceived as (and to be) socially responsible becomes a critically important dimension of an organisation's image.

Viewpoint 10.2 Pouring water on troubled Coke

Although WWF and the Coca-Cola Corporation had been working together for several years on a number of projects to conserve water and address water efficiency in the company's operations, the announcement of a formal agreement between the two organisations marked a critical point for Coke.

The vast amount of water consumed by the Coca-Cola Corporation had led to widespread comment and criticism. In an attempt to change the perception held by the company's stakeholders, the announcement in 2007 that they were pledging to invest $20 million in WWF freshwater schemes, wherever they had a bottling plant, represented a public commitment to change.

Neville Isdell, then Chairman of Coca-Cola, stated:

> Our goal is to replace every drop of water we use in our beverages and their production. For us that means reducing the amount of water used to produce our beverages, recycling water used for manufacturing processes so it can be returned safely to the environment, and replenishing water in communities and nature through locally relevant projects.

As part of the deal WWF provide Coca-Cola with advice on a range of related environmental topics, including water conservation, usage and recycling in manufacturing, how to cut its energy and carbon footprint, and how the organisation can replenish water in local communities. In addition, the agreement involves joint communications programmes and campaigns, framing the relationship under cause for water conservation.

This scheme enables Coca-Cola to be seen as a more environmentally aware and socially responsible company. The scheme helps WWF achieve its goals and move towards encouraging other leading companies to become involved in similar schemes.

Source: Based on Bokaie (2007); Kleinman (2007); WWF Pressroom, www.panda.org/news_facts/newsroom/index.cfm?uNewsID=104940

Question

To what extent is this scheme a cynical ploy to soften Coke's reputation?

Task

Find out how Pepsi are meeting the environmental challenge.

Exhibit 10.1 WWF visual representing the drive to save freshwater ecosystems
Image courtesy of Getty Images/Brent Stirton

A framework of public relations

Communications with such a wide variety of stakeholders need to vary to reflect different environmental conditions, organisational objectives and forms of relationship. Grunig and Hunt (1984) have attempted to capture the diversity of public relations activities through a framework. They set out four models to reflect the different ways in which public relations is, in their opinion, considered to work. These models, based on their experiences as public relations practitioners, constitute a useful approach to understanding the complexity of this form of communication. The four models are set out in Figure 10.1.

The press agentry/publicity model

The essence of this approach is that communication is used as a form of propaganda. That is, the communication flow is essentially one way, and the content is not bound to be strictly truthful as the objective is to convince the receiver of a new idea or offering. This can be observed in the growing proliferation of media events and press releases.

The public information model

Unlike the first model, this approach seeks to disseminate truthful information. While the flow is again one way, there is little focus on persuasion, more on the provision of information. This

	Model			
Characteristic	**Press agentry/publicity**	**Public information**	**Two-way asymmetric**	**Two-way symmetric**
Purpose	Propaganda	Dissemination of information	Scientific persuasion	Mutual understanding
Nature of communication	One way; complete truth not essential	One way; truth important	Two way; imbalanced effects	Two way; balanced effects
Communication model	Source → Rec.*	Source → Rec.*	Source ⇌ Rec.* Feedback	Group ⇌ Group
Nature of research	Little; 'counting house'	Little; readability, readership	Formative; evaluative of attitudes	Formative; evaluative of understanding
Leading historical figures	P.T. Barnum	Ivy Lee	Edward L. Bernays	Bernays, educators, professional leaders
Where practised today	Sports, theatre, product promotion	Government, not-for-profit associations, business	Competitive business, agencies	Regulated business, agencies
Estimated percentage of organisations practising today	15%	50%	20%	15%

*Receiver.

Figure 10.1 Models of public relations
Source: Grunig and Hunt (1984). Used with kind permission

can best be seen through public health campaigns and government advice communications in respect of crime, education and health.

The two-way asymmetric model

Two-way communication is a major element of this model. Feedback from receivers is important, but as power is not equally distributed between the various stakeholders and the organisation, the relationship has to be regarded as asymmetric. The purpose remains to influence attitude and behaviour through persuasion.

The two-way symmetric model

This represents the most acceptable and mutually rewarding form of communication. Power is seen to be dispersed equally between the organisation and its stakeholders and the intent of the communication flow is considered to be reciprocal. The organisation and its respective publics are prepared to adjust their positions (attitudes and behaviours) in the light of the information flow. A true dialogue emerges through this interpretation, unlike any of the other three models, which see an unbalanced flow of information and expectations.

The model has attracted a great deal of attention and has been reviewed and appraised by a number of commentators (Miller, 1989). As a result of this and a search for excellence in public relations, Grunig (1992) revised the model to reflect the dominance of the 'craft' and the 'professional' approaches to public relations practices. That is, those practitioners who utilise public relations merely as a tool to achieve media visibility can be regarded as 'craft'-oriented.

Those organisations whose managers seek to utilise public relations as a means of mediating their relationships with their various stakeholders are seen as 'professional' practitioners. They are considered to be using public relations as a longer term and proactive form of planned communication. The former see public relations as an instrument, the latter as a means of conducting a dialogue.

These models are not intended to suggest that those responsible for communications should choose among them. Their use and interpretation depend upon the circumstances that prevail at any one time. Organisations use a number of these different approaches to manage the communication issues that exist between them and the variety of different stakeholder audiences with whom they interact. However, there is plenty of evidence to suggest that the press/agentry model is the one most used by practitioners and that the two-way symmetrical model is harder to observe in practice.

These models have been subjected to further investigation and Grunig (1997) concluded that these four models are not independent but coexist with one another. Therefore, as Yun (2006) suggested, it is better to characterise public relations as dimensions of communication behaviour.

Public relations: methods and techniques

The range of public relations cues or methods available to organisations is immense. Different organisations use different permutations in order that they can communicate effectively with their various stakeholder audiences. For the purposes of this text a general outline is provided of the more commonly used methods.

The range of public relations activities is diverse and categorisation problematic. The approach adopted here is that public relations consists of a range of communication activities, of which media relations, publicity and event management appear to be the main ones used by practitioners.

Media relations

Media relations consist of a range of activities designed to provide media journalists and editors with information. The intention is that they relay the information, through their media, for consumption by their audiences. Obviously, the original message may be changed and subject to information deviance as it is processed, but audiences perceive much of this information as highly credible simply because opinion formers (Chapter 2) have bestowed their judgement on the item. Of the various forms of media relations, press releases, interviews, press kits and press conferences are most used.

Press releases

The press release is a common form of media relations activity. A one-page written report concerning an event or a change in the organisation is sent to various media houses for inclusion in the media vehicle as an item of news. The media house may cover a national area, but very often a local house will suffice. These written statements concern developments in the organisation, such as promotions, new products, awards, prizes, new contracts and customers. The statement is deliberately short and written in such a style that it attracts the attention of the editor. Further information can be obtained if it is to be included within the next publication or news broadcast. See the Toshiba press release (Exhibit 10.2). One of the characteristics of a good press release is that it is planned restricted in terms of when it can be used by media organisations. An 'embargo time' requires that the item cannot be used until a certain date. This means that instead of a single media house using the material ahead of others, the news opportunity is maximised as several organisations seek to utilise the material at the due time.

Press conferences

Press conferences are used when a major event has occurred and where a press release cannot convey the appropriate tone or detail required by the organisation. Press conferences are mainly used by politicians, but organisations in crisis (e.g. accidents and mergers) and individuals appealing for help (e.g. police requesting assistance from the public with respect to a particular incident) can use this form of communication. Press kits containing a full reproduction of any statements, photographs and relevant background information should always be available.

Interviews

Interviews with representatives of an organisation enable news and the organisation's view of an issue or event to be conveyed. Other forms of media relations concern by-lined articles (articles written by a member of an organisation about an issue related to the company and offered for publication), speeches, letters to the editor, and photographs and captions.

Viewpoint 10.3 Entertainment PR for TV Wars

There are two big UK Saturday night television shows, *The X Factor* (XF) and *Strictly Come Dancing* (SCD). These shows command audiences of approximately 11–12 and 7–8 million respectively, and they run head-to-head in the three months leading to Christmas. Public relations is used to support both of them, but in slightly different ways.

SCD is produced by the BBC and all the PR relating to the show is managed in-house. PR agencies are used to create attention but many of the celebrity contestants, one of the judges, and the two presenters have their own

TOSHIBA
Leading Innovation >>>

Toshiba premieres new 'Space Chair' ad campaign
Campaign to support Toshiba's SV REGZA LCD TV and Satellite T series laptops

London, UK, 16th November 2009 – Toshiba UK continues to lead innovation as it premieres its latest advertising campaign, 'Space Chair'; a piece of film which takes viewers on an awe-inspiring journey to the edge of space.

Created for Toshiba by Grey London, 'Space Chair' builds on the phenomenal success of 2008's record-breaking 'Timesculpture' ad campaign and has once again been filmed using Toshiba cameras. Shot in the wilderness of the Nevada Black Rock desert, the advertisement follows the journey of an ordinary living room chair to the extraordinary heights of the edge of space, lifted to an altitude of 98,268 feet by a simple helium balloon.

The advert is split into two executions, the first playing in 2009 for the **Toshiba REGZA SV LCD TV Series** and 2010 for the new range of **Satellite T Series** of ultra low voltage laptops. The REGZA SV is Toshiba's first ever model to include an LED backlight with local dimming, and is set to redefine the armchair viewing experience by delivering sharper, smoother images that clearly define every cloud and every star. The ultra portable, lightweight Satellite T Series enables users to go further by offering up to eleven hours of battery life – enough to take you to space and back.

The ad was shot by Haris Zambarloukos, the acclaimed cinematographer behind films including 'Enduring Love' and 'Mamma Mia' and was directed by Andy Amadeo, Creative Director at Grey London. The shoot was made possible via the construction of a unique custom-built camera rig engineered by John Powell of JP Aerospace – experts in this field who have successfully sent over 100 balloons into the upper atmosphere. A specially created full-sized model chair made of biodegradable balsa wood; light enough to make the 83 minute journey up towards space was tied to the rig and launched by the team.

Four independent GPS systems were placed on the rig to accurately record its height at any second to within 4 meters in altitude, and within 30cm in longitude and latitude position. This information was transmitted every 15 seconds back to ground control where it was monitored via a computer satellite system to enable the team to locate the rig once it had fallen back to earth.

The film is cinematic, opening with a shot of the solitary chair silhouetted against the Nevada sunrise and taking the viewer on its journey above the desert, into the clouds and beyond.

Matt McDowell, Marketing Director at Toshiba UK comments: 'Our aim was to create a new advertising campaign that would bring to life Toshiba's brand philosophy of leading innovation. We chose to send a chair on the journey as it is central to the user's experience of Toshiba's products; whether they are watching TV or using a laptop.'

'The ad features two exciting new products. The REGZA SV Series is the first-ever Toshiba LCD TV to combine Toshiba's Resolution+ technology and an LED backlight – delivering stunning high quality images that enhances the viewers' armchair experience. Offering the performance and functionality of full-sized laptops with portability and a battery life of up to eleven hours, the Satellite T Series frees users from the shackles of their desks, empowering them to explore new environments.'

Andy Amadeo, Creative Director at Grey London comments: 'Keeping with our tact of being as innovative as the brand, we once again created a mould-breaking commercial with Toshiba. Last year we set a new world record with "Timesculpture" and proved that their domestic camcorders could produce a breathtaking, never before seen piece of film. This time we have used Toshiba HD cameras to produce some of the most stunning footage shot at the edge of space.'

Facts about the shoot:

- The shots were taken at a staggering 98,268 feet above the earth using Toshiba's own cameras
- To reach the altitude required and to conform with Federal Aviation Administration regulations, the weight of the rig had to be carefully managed to a weight of no more than four pounds

Exhibit 10.2 Press release for the launch of the Toshiba Space Chair ad
Press release courtesy of Toshiba

Press Release

- Tied to the rig was a specially created full-sized model chair made of biodegradable balsa wood – the chair was made by a company called Artem and cost about £2,500
- Launch coordinates of the rig were – 119 degrees, 14 minutes by 40 degrees, 48 minute (12 miles North-East of the town of Gerlach, Nevada)
- The quality of the footage from the Toshiba IK-HR1S cameras was: 1920 × 1080 pixel count; 1080i @ 50hz; 100 Mbps
- The temperature dropped to minus 90 degrees when the chair reached 52,037 feet
- The chair took 83 minutes to reach an altitude of 98,268 feet where it broke and took just 24 minutes to fall back down to earth with the rig.

Notes to Editors

The full 60 second advert premieres on 16 November on ITV1 and runs for three weeks. The ad will then run again in February 2010.

Creative Credits

Creative Agency:	Grey London
Production Company:	Hungry Man LTD
Director:	Andy Amadeo
Editor and editing company:	The Whitehouse / Russell Ike
Post-production company:	The Mill

– Ends –

For more information, interview requests or photography, please contact:
Katy Ball @ Nelson Bostock Communications
E: katy.ball@nelsonbostock.com
T: 020 7792 7489

About Toshiba

Toshiba is a world leader and innovator in pioneering high technology, a diversified manufacturer and marketer of advanced electronic and electrical products spanning information & communications systems; digital consumer products; electronic devices and components; power systems, including nuclear energy; industrial and social infrastructure systems; and home appliances. Toshiba was founded in 1875, and today operates a global network of more than 740 companies, with 199,000 employees worldwide and annual sales surpassing 6.6 trillion yen (US$73 billion). Visit Toshiba's web site at www.toshiba.co.jp/index.html

About Grey London

We are 200 people, drawn from different marketing and media backgrounds, working together in a wonderfully open environment in Holborn, London. We do the lot: multi-channel, integrated, online, offline, above, through and below the line for a wide range of clients including Ryvita, P&G, GlaxoSmithKline, IPC Media, the British Heart Foundation, Dairy Crest and Toshiba.

We don't believe in agency positionings. We do believe in making our clients both successful and happy. We believe we're better than most agencies at listening to what clients really want. Which means we're better at understanding the problem and getting to the most exciting and effective answer.

Exhibit 10.2 *Continued*

personal PR support, all of which is coordinated by the BBC. The show has incurred many issues, varying from affairs between professional dancers and celebrities, the sacking of one of the judges and replacing her with a younger, former winner of the show, and issues concerning the positioning of the show, as a form of entertainment or dance competition. The latter issue is often exposed through the way the public votes to keep certain celebrities in.

XF is produced by ITV but all the judges have their own PR support. ITV's PR is involved but does not coordinate activities in the same way as the BBC. It appears that the central figure driving the show, and various offshoots, is Simon Cowell. When the show launched, his PR team (Max Clifford) drew attention by shaping Cowell's nasty image. Now, with the show well established, PR is used to manage the controversy and issues that emerge as the show moves forward and to cover relevant media stories concerning contestants and their backgrounds.

Interest in SCD is partly driven by providing exclusive information to websites and portals. This is achieved through the use of targeted niche blogs, forums and social networking groups. To increase the audience's experience of the show a new application was used in September 2009 which let online viewers interact with the live show by commenting on the performances and engaging emotionally with electronic 'boos', 'gasps' and 'wows'.

Source: Based on Magee (2009), O'Reilly (2009)

Question
What is the main role of entertainment PR?

Task
Storytelling can be powerful. Find stories that were used about SCD and X Factor.

Media relations can be planned and controlled, to the extent of what is sent to the media and when it is released. However, there is no control over what material is actually used or the perspective adopted through editing.

The quality of the relationship between an organisation and the media will dramatically affect the impact and dissemination of news and stories released by an organisation. The relationships referred to are those between an organisation's public relations manager and the editor and journalists associated with both the press and the broadcast media.

Publicity and events

Control over public relations events is not as strong as that for media relations. Indeed, negative publicity can be generated by other parties, which can impact badly on an organisation by raising doubts about its financial status or perhaps the quality of its products. Three main event activity areas can be distinguished: product, corporate and community events.

Product events

Product-oriented events are normally focused on increasing sales. Cookery demonstrations, celebrities autographing their books and the opening of a new store by the CEO or local MP are events aimed at generating attention, interest and sales of a particular product.

Alternatively events are designed to attract the attention of the media and, through stories and articles presented in the news, are able to reach a wide audience. For example, the public's attention was drawn to the launch of *The Simpsons Movie* in July 2007, by a stunt involving the painting of a giant Homer Simpson next to the 180-foot chalk cut Cerne Abbas giant in Dorset. News coverage of the new work of art, Homer holding a doughnut, was in most national newspapers, on ITV, Sky and BBC television, plus radio coverage (see Exhibit 10.3).

Corporate events

Events designed to develop the corporate profile are often designed to provide some entertainment. These can generate considerable local media coverage, which in turn facilitates awareness,

Exhibit 10.3 Chalky Homer
A paint line drawing of Homer Simpson next to the chalk cut Cerne Abbas Giant, used to attract media attention prior to the launch of *The Simpsons Movie* in July 2007
Image courtesy of Press Association Images/PA Wire

goodwill and interest. For example, events such as open days, factory visits and donations of products to local events can be very beneficial.

Community events

These are activities that contribute to the life of the local community. Sponsoring local fun runs and children's play areas, making contributions to local community centres and the disabled are typical activities. The organisation attempts to become more involved with the local community as a good employer and good member of the community. This helps to develop goodwill and awareness in the community.

The choice of events an organisation becomes involved with is critical. The events should have a theme and be chosen to satisfy objectives established earlier in the communications plan

In addition to these key activities the following are important forms of public relations:

- lobbying (out of personal selling and publicity);
- sponsorship (out of event management and advertising);
- corporate advertising (out of advertising);
- crisis management (out of issues management).

Lobbying

The representation of certain organisations or industries within government is an important form of public relations work. While legislation is being prepared, lobbyists provide a flow of information to their organisations to keep them informed about events (as a means of scanning the environment), but they also ensure that the views of the organisation are heard in order that legislation can be shaped appropriately, limiting any potential damage that new legislation might bring.

Moloney (1997) suggests that lobbying is inside public relations as it focuses on the members of an organisation who seek to persuade and negotiate with its stakeholders in government on matters of opportunity and or threat. He refers to in-house lobbyists (those members of the organisation who try to influence non-members) and hired lobbyists contracted to complete specific tasks.

His view of lobbying is that it is one of monitoring public policy-making for a group interest; building a case in favour of that interest; and putting it privately with varying degrees of pressure to public decision-makers for their acceptance and support through favourable political intervention (1997: 173).

Where local authorities interpret legislation and frame the activities of their citizens and constituent organisations, the government determines legislation and controls the activities of people and organisations across markets. The tobacco industry is well known for its lobbying activities, as are chemical, transport and many other industries.

Corporate advertising

In an attempt to harness the advantages of both advertising and public relations, corporate advertising has been seen by some as a means of communicating more effectively with a range of stakeholders. The credibility of messages transmitted through public relations is high, but the control that management has over the message is limited. Advertising, however, allows management virtually total control over message dispersion, but the credibility of these messages is usually low. Corporate advertising is the combination of the best of advertising and the best of public relations.

Corporate advertising that is, advertising on behalf of an organisation rather than its products or services, has long been associated with public relations rather than the advertising department.

The main purpose of corporate advertising appears to be the provision of cues by which stakeholders can identify and understand an organisation. This is achieved by presenting the personality of the organisation to a wide range of stakeholders, rather than presenting particular functions or products that the organisation markets. Schumann *et al.* (1991) conclude that a number of US studies indicate that the first goal of corporate advertising is to enhance the company's reputation and the second is to provide support for the promotion of products and services. However, research indicates that today the majority of organisations use corporate advertising to promote products and services.

Crisis communications

A growing and important part of the work associated with public relations is crisis communications. Crises can occur because of a simple or minor managerial mistake, an incorrect decision or because of a seemingly distant environmental event. All organisations face the prospect of managing a crisis, indeed, some commentators ominously suggest that all organisations have a crisis just around the corner (Fink, 2000). Jacques (2009) considers the lack of agreement in defining crises management and the various sections or stages through which a crisis proceeds. He suggests the need to identify the phases of the continuum. He offers the view of Mitroff (2004) who suggests that *crisis management* consists of a reactive phase, after a crisis has happened, whereas the preparation phase, before the crisis, should be characterised as *crisis leadership*.

Table 10.1	Common causes of disasters
Origin of crisis	Explanation
Economic	As the Western world currently experiences growth and high levels of employment and countries in the developing world follow a fluctuating path of revitalisation and competition, this has brought some organisations and industries in the West to collapse (e.g. UK shipbuilding).
Managerial	Human error and the pursuit of financial goals by some organisations give rise to the majority of disasters. For example, cutting costs at the expense of safety and repair of systems or deliberate sabotage as in Enron.
Political	Issues concerning war and terrorism have encouraged kidnapping, as well as organisations having to change the locations of their business.
Climate	The climate is changing substantially in certain parts of the world, and this has brought disaster to those who lie in the wake of natural disturbances. For example, the earthquakes in Haiti and Chile in 2010 and unusual rainfall patterns causing flooding in Australia.
Technology	The rate at which technology is advancing has brought about crises such as those associated with transportation systems and aircraft disasters. Human error is also a significant factor, which can be associated with the rate of technological change.
New media	The age of electronic media and instant communication means that information can be disseminated throughout the world within 30 minutes of an event occurring. Corporate blogging and use the use of Twitter can give immediate insight into events.
Consumer groups	The rise of consumer groups (e.g. Amnesty International and Greenpeace) and their ability to investigate and publicise the operations and policies of organisations.

Crises are emerging with greater frequency as a result of a number of factors. Table 10.1 sets out some of the main factors that give rise to crises for organisations.

Figure 10.2 describes organisational crises in the context of two key variables. On the horizontal axis is the degree to which management has control over the origin of the crisis. Is the origin of the crisis outside management's control, such as an earthquake, or is it within its control, such as those crises associated with poor trading results? The vertical axis reflects the potential impact that a crisis might have on an organisation. All crises, by definition, have a potential to inflict damage on an organisation. However, some can be contained, perhaps on a geographic basis, whereas others have the potential to cause tremendous damage to an organisation, such as those experienced through product tampering and environmental pollution.

The increasing occurrence of crises throughout the world has prompted many organisations to review the manner in which they anticipate managing such events, should they be implicated. It is generally assumed that those organisations that take the care to plan in anticipation of disaster will experience more favourable outcomes than those that fail to plan. When British Airways was faced with the prospect of strike action, the airline planned a response that included social media. This included a series of videos posted on YouTube and BA.com. These featured the CEO apologising for the inconvenience to their customers and providing updates on the current strike and operational situation (Kimberley, 2010).

However, when there is poor planning, poor results can be expected. Indeed, organisations that do not plan, experience crises that last over twice as long as those that do plan (Fink, 2000). For example, Eurostar have experienced a series of issues in recent years. In September 2008 a train caught fire, resulting in a 16 hour blaze. Brownsell (2009) reports that a full service was not resumed until February 2009. Later in December that year, trains ground to a halt in freezing weather, for no apparent reason. Passengers were stranded for hours, often in the dark, with no facilities and no support. Eurostar was thrown into crisis, experienced high levels of negative media visibility and was subsequently found not have a suitable crisis plan in position.

Figure 10.2 An organisational crisis matrix

Crisis planning is about putting into position those elements that can effect speedy outcomes to the disaster sequence. When a crisis strikes, it is the application of contingency based tactics by all those concerned with the event that will determine the strength of the outcome. Crises tend to move through a series of distinct phases. Coombs (2007) proposed three sequential phases:

- pre-crisis (signal detection, prevention, preparation);
- crisis event (recognition, containment);
- post-crisis (evaluation, learning, follow up communication).

Jaques (2007) developed clusters of action, as set out in Table 10.2.

For a long time the key issue associated with crisis communication has been speed. The speed of response has been crucial. However, as Borremans (2010) points out, speed is no longer the issue, as social media has enabled all organisations to respond quickly. The issue now is the impact of what is being communicated.

Social media not only disseminates bad news quickly it can also be used to gather information and to disperse positive news. For example, RSS feeds can be used to replace clipping

Table 10.2 Clusters of crisis management activities (Jacques, 2007)

Crisis stage	Management activities
Crisis preparedness	Planning processes, systems and manuals, documentation, training/simulations
Crisis prevention	Early warning, risk and issue management, social forecasting, environmental scanning, emergency response
Crisis incident management	Recognition, activation, damage mitigation, implementation
Post-crisis management	Recovery/resumption, post-crisis issue impacts, judicial inquiries, evaluation, modification

services and provide near real-time access to what is being said about the organisation at the centre of the crisis and it can do this 24/7. RSS feeds aggregate news items which can be read in one of three main ways. These are through email, an online 'feedreader', or through a 'feedreader application' which is downloaded to a PC.

Wikis can be used at all stages of the crisis, and even organised into the different phases of crisis planning process, from the 'preparedness' to 'post crisis management' stage. At the outset a 'wiki' can be used as a dynamic document, where all parties to the communication plan can input information and ideas to the same page. Draft statements, forms and other documents can be created, reviewed and managed throughout the crisis period, even from remote access.

Sponsorship

Sponsorship has become an increasingly popular element of the mix because of the quality of the communication it generates. It is a mix of advertising, with its capacity for message control, and public relations with its potential for high levels of credibility and message diffusion, directed through or with a third party. In this sense sponsorship lacks the harshness of advertising and the total lack of control that characterises much of the work of public relations. Sponsorship can be defined as a commercial activity, whereby one party permits another an opportunity to exploit an association with a target audience in return for funds, services or resources. In particular sponsorship;

- gives exposure to particular audiences that each event attracts, in order to convey simple awareness-based brand messages;
- suggests to target audiences that there is an association between the sponsored and the sponsor and that by implication this association may be of interest and/or value;
- allows members of the target audiences to perceive the sponsor indirectly through a third party and so diffuse any negative effects associated with traditional mass media and direct persuasion;
- provides sponsors with the opportunity to blend a variety of tools in the communication mix and use resources more efficiently and arguably more effectively.

Normally sponsorship involves two parties, the sponsor and the sponsee, although many sponsors may be assigned to a single sponsee. The degree of fit or congruence between these two parties partly determines the relative effectiveness of the relationship (Cornwell, *et al.*, 2006; Poon and Prendergast, 2006). The degree of fit, or product relevance as proposed by McDonald (1991) cited by Poon and Prendergast, can be considered in terms of two main dimensions. Function-based similarity occurs when the product is used in the event being sponsored. For example, the piano manufacturer *Bösendorfer* sponsoring a Viennese piano recital. The second dimension concerns image-based similarities, which reflects the image of the sponsor in the event. Here *Airbus*'s sponsorship of a major technical or even artistic exhibition serves to bestow prestige on all parties. Poon and Prendergast suggest that rather than treat these as mutually exclusive elements, there can be four interconnected dimensions. Figure 10.3 serves to illustrate their intentions.

Sponsorship, a part of public relations, should be used as part of an integrated approach to an organisation's communications. In other words, sponsorship provides a further tool that, to be used effectively, needs to be harnessed strategically. As Tripodi (2001) comments, the implementation of integrated marketing communications is further encouraged and supported when sponsorship is an integral part of the mix in order to maximise the full impact of this communication tool. For example, many companies and brands originating in south-east Asia and the Pacific regions have used sponsorship as a means of overseas market entry in order to develop name or brand awareness (e.g. Panasonic, JVC and Daihatsu).

Figure 10.3 Four interconnected dimensions of sponsorship
Source: After Poon and Prendergast (2006). Used with kind permission from WARC.

Coppetti *et al.* (2009) emphasise the value of congruence but also demonstrate that even when there is a lack of fit, the effectiveness of the sponsorship can be enhanced by involving the audience in what they refer to as 'attractive sponsor activities'. This suggests that by building in experiences for the audience and encouraging their participation, and by using advertising before and after the sponsorship event, such integration can serve to increase the value of the communication programme.

Sponsorship objectives

There are both primary and secondary objectives associated with using sponsorship. The primary reasons are to build awareness, developing customer loyalty and improving the perception (image) held about the brand or organisation. Secondary reasons are more contentious, but generally they can be seen to be to attract new users, to support dealers and other intermediaries and to act as a form of staff motivation and morale building (Reed, 1994).

Sponsorship is normally regarded as a communications tool used to reach external stakeholders. However, if chosen appropriately sponsorship can also be used effectively to reach internal audiences. Care is required because different audiences transfer diverse values (Grimes and Meenaghan, 1998). According to Harverson (1998), one of the main reasons IT companies sponsor sports events is that this form of involvement provides opportunities to 'showcase' their products and technologies, in context. Through application in an appropriate working environment, the efficacy of a sponsor's products can be demonstrated. The relationship between sports organisers and IT companies becomes reciprocal as the organisers of sports events need technology in order for the events to run. Corporate hospitality opportunities are often taken in addition to the brand exposure that the media coverage provides. EDS claims that it uses sponsorship to reach two main audiences, customers (and potential customers) and potential future employees. The message it uses is that the EDS involvement in sport is sexy and exciting.

A further important characteristic concerns the impact of repeat attendance on brand image. Work by Lacey *et al.* (2007) found that a car manufacturer's image improved modestly by sponsoring a sporting event. However, through repeat attendance positive opinion scores towards the sponsor improved. The obvious implication for marketing is that it is important to attract attendees back to sporting events.

Viewpoint 10.4 Sponsoring the geegees

The Cheltenham Festival is a major event in the horse racing calendar and with attendances and interest in all forms of the sport increasing, despite the recession, sponsorship remains an attractive from of marketing communications for many organisations. It was estimated that sponsorship was worth £1.68 million in 2010. Thomas Pink (the quality fashion retailer), Spinal Research (a charity) and Ryanair (the low cost airline) all sponsored events at the festival for the first time in 2010.

Thomas Pink sponsored the prestigious Leading Rider and Trainer Awards and so associated themselves with a sport and some of its most talented individuals, with their own heritage.

Cenkos Securities plc funded the Spinal Research Supreme Novices' Hurdle and so gave visibility to an important and racing related charity, as many involved in horse racing suffer spinal injury.

Sponsors can provide financial support for individual races and in return generate brand awareness and local visibility. In addition, the event provides a focus for the sponsor to provide corporate hospitality for selected customers and other stakeholders. The race also attracts media coverage and a certain level of word of mouth communication generated by spectators.

Source: Based on Turner (2010); www.cheltenhamfestival.net/New-sponsorship-of-Festival-awards.php
www.southwestbusiness.co.uk/news/Cheltenham-Festival-win/article-1918458-detail/article.html

Exhibit 10.4 Thomas Pink
Image courtesy of Alamy Images/John Warburton-Lee Photography

> **Question**
> How might a brand message integrated into a racing programme through a sponsor, be an effective form of marketing communication?
>
> **Task**
> Go to www.Utalkmarketing and find out why Ryanair chose to sponsor a race at the festival.

Following on from this is the issue about whether sponsorship is being used to support a product or the organisation. Corporate sponsorships, according to Thwaites (1994), are intended to focus on developing community involvement, public awareness, image, goodwill and staff relations. Product- or brand-based sponsorship activity is aimed at developing media coverage, sales leads, sales/market share, target market awareness and guest hospitality.

Types of sponsorship

It is possible to identify particular areas within which sponsorship has been used. These areas are sports, programme/broadcast, the arts and others that encompass activities such as wildlife/ conservation and education. Of all of these, sport has attracted most attention and sponsorship money.

Sports sponsorship

Sports activities have been very attractive to sponsors, partly because of the high media coverage they attract. Sport is the leading type of sponsorship, mainly for the following reasons:

- Sport has the propensity to attract large audiences, not only at each event but more importantly through the media that attach themselves to these activities.
- Sport provides a simplistic measure of segmentation, so that as audiences fragment generally, sport provides an opportunity to identify and reach often large numbers of people who share particular characteristics.
- Visibility opportunities for the sponsor are high in a number of sporting events because of the duration of each event (e.g. the Olympics or the FIFA World Cup).

Barclaycard's sponsorship of the football Premier League and Coca-Cola's sponsorship of the football championship have been motivated partly by the attraction of large and specific target audiences with whom a degree of fit is considered to exist. The constant media attention enables the sponsors' names to be disseminated to distant audiences, many of them overseas. Marshall and Cook (1992) found that event sponsorship (e.g. the Olympics or the Ideal Home Exhibition) is the most popular form of sponsorship activity undertaken by organisations. This was followed by team, league and individual support.

Vodafone sponsored Manchester United in order to boost global awareness. Then the company bought Mannesmann and found it then sponsored Benfica, Porto, Olympiakos and teams in La Liga in Spain and the Bundesliga in Germany. Rationalisation was necessary and wanting to maintain an association with football, it then became a Champions League sponsor (Murphy, 2007). AIG became United's next shirt sponsor in an attempt to fuel AIG's expansion out of North America and reach new markets, principally Asia, where a high percentage of the target market are football, and Manchester United fans. AIG have pulled out due to the financial crisis.

Golf has attracted a great deal of sponsorship money, mainly because it has a global upmarket appeal and generates good television and press coverage. Golf clubs are also well suited for corporate entertainment and offer the chance of playing as well as watching. Volvo sponsored the European Golf Championship for the period 1996–2000 for £20 million. Johnnie Walker continues to sponsor major golfing championships. Toyota used to support the World Matchplay Championship at Wentworth each year because the tournament fitted into a much wider promotion programme. Toyota dealers sponsored competitions at their local courses, with qualifiers going through to a final at Wentworth. The winner of that played in the pro-am before the World Matchplay. Toyota incorporated the tournament into a range of incentive and promotional programmes and flew in top distributors and fleet customers from around the world. In addition, the environment was used to build customer relationships. This championship is now supported by HSBC.

Programme sponsorship

Television programme sponsorship began to receive serious attention in Britain in the late 1990s. The market has grown, as reflected in TV sponsorship revenues, from £81.2 million in 2000 to nearly £200 million in 2009. This growth has occurred partly because of a relaxation in the regulations. For example, the visibility that each sponsor is allowed was strictly controlled to certain times, and before, during the break and after each programme with the credits. This was changed so that while sponsors are not allowed to influence the content or scheduling of a programme so as to affect the editorial independence and responsibility of the broadcaster, it is now permissible to allow the sponsor's product to be seen along with the sponsor's name in bumper credits and to allow greater flexibility in terms of the use of straplines. There is a requirement on the broadcaster to ensure that the sponsored credit is depicted in such a way that it cannot be mistaken as a spot advertisement. So, Hedburg (2000) gives the example of Nescafé sponsoring *Friends* showing a group of people sitting on a sofa and drinking coffee and of *Coronation Street* and former sponsor Cadbury's, which presented a whole chocolate street and set of chocolate characters.

Masthead programming, where the publisher of a magazine such as *Amateur Photographer* sponsors a programme in a related area, such as *Photography for Beginners*, is generally not permitted, although the regulations surrounding this type of activity are being relaxed. There are a number of reasons why programme sponsorship is appealing. First, it allows clients to avoid the clutter associated with spot advertising. In that sense it creates a space, or mini-world, in which the sponsor can create awareness and provide brand identity cues unhindered by other brands. Second, it represents a cost-effective medium when compared with spot advertising. Although the cost of programme sponsorship has increased as the value of this type of communication has appreciated, it does not command the high rates required for spot advertising. Third, the use of credits around a programme offers opportunities for the target audience to make associations between the sponsor and the programme.

Research by the Bloxam Group suggests that for a sponsorship to work there needs to be a linkage between the product and the programme. Links that are spurious, illogical or inappropriate are very often rejected by viewers. For example, a branded soft drink might work well with a youth-oriented programme, but a financial services brand supporting a sports programme or film series would not have a strong or logical linkage.

The line between product placement, brand entertainment and programme sponsorship becomes increasingly blurred. However, programme sponsorship should not be seen as a replacement for advertising. The argument that sponsorship is not a part of advertising is clearly demonstrated by the point that many sponsors continue with their spot advertising when running major sponsorships.

Arts sponsorship

Arts sponsorship, according to Thorncroft (1996), began as a philanthropic exercise, with business giving something back to the community. It was a means of developing corporate image and was used extensively by tobacco companies as they attempted to reach their customer base. It then began to be appreciated for its corporate hospitality opportunities: a cheaper, more civilised alternative to sports sponsorship, and one that appealed more to women.

Many organisations sponsor the arts as a means of enhancing their corporate status and as a means of clarifying their name. Another important reason organisations use sponsorship is to establish and maintain favourable contact with key business people, often at board level, together with other significant public figures. Through related corporate hospitality, companies can reach substantial numbers of their targeted key people.

Most recently, sponsorship has been used to reach specific groups of consumers. Orange sponsors a range of music-related events, one of them being the Glastonbury Festival. One of the key facilities is the 'chill 'n charge' tent. This is a bright orange-coloured tent in which people can use the phone-charging equipment or the Internet facilities to pick up their email and over 50,000 people used the tent at the 2007 festival. Orange see their sponsorship of the festival as a way to develop their brand and purchase consideration, but not as a means of directly acquiring customers (Bartlett, 2007).

The sponsorship of the arts has moved from being a means of supporting the community to a sophisticated means of targeting and positioning brands. Sponsorship, once part of corporate public relations, is now a significant aspect of marketing public relations.

Viewpoint 10.5 Robinsons supports juicy pantos

Robinsons has been involved with many sponsorship events over the years and is probably most associated with the Wimbledon tennis tournament. In 2009 Robinsons sponsored festive pantomimes in conjunction with First Family Entertainment. This is a large theatrical production company who had recruited several celebrities to star in pantomimes around the country. Robinsons wanted to raise awareness of the events and their association without using television, a costly route, one that they use for their Wimbledon work.

The result was a website to help children and parents develop and run their own pantomimes at home. The intention was to provide a way in which families could work together. The website contained information about writing scripts, costumes and promotional posters were all made available online. In order to enrich the experience an iPhone app was developed providing sound effects.

The launch was delivered through an on-pack promotion involving over 41 million bottles of Robinsons soft drinks. PR and promotional activity at pantomime events was also used to publicise the sponsorship. Ads were placed in First Family panto magazines, editorial content was seeded across 100 blog sites associated with motherhood and parenting, and a Flash game was placed on 25 children oriented game sites.

Source: Based on Anon (2009)

Question
To what extent might Robinson's be overly dependent on their relationship with Wimbledon?

Task
Make a list of the other activities Robinsons could sponsor successfully.

To support their global brand HSBC has a cultural sponsorship programme. In 2008 the bank supported cultural events in China, in 2009 they backed various Indian cultural initiatives and in 2010 they supported 'Festival Brazil'. This event was focused on exhibitions and various artistic performances by Brazilian artists in London at the festival. HSBC also supported events in South America, the Middle East, South-East Asia and the USA. The bank has co-partnered with the *Financial Times* and the Economist Intelligence Unit to advise companies thinking of exporting and setting up in Brazil (Brownsell, 2010).

Other forms of sponsorship

It has been argued that there is little opportunity to control messages delivered through sponsorship, and far less opportunity to encourage the target audiences to enter into a dialogue with sponsors. However, the awareness and image opportunities can be used by supporting either the local community or small-scale schemes. In March 2011 a Climate Week was held, with Aviva, RBS, EDF Energy and Kellogg as some of the first sponsors to sign up. These companies will be able to demonstrate what actions they are taking with regard to climate change as well as assist other organisations to become involved (Thomas, 2010).

Samsung Electronics use sponsorship to link up with a variety of activities. One of these is football and is a partner with Chelsea FC, Inter Milan FC, Palmeiras, Suwon Bluwings, Olympiacos and Feyenoord. The company is also an official sponsor for the Olympic Games, and the Asian Games. However, they feel that the greater the number of sponsors tied to an event the less opportunity there is to leverage the linkage. The one exception to this rule is the Olympics. This event involves all nations and Samsung signed an agreement in 2010 to be a main sponsor of the Olympics until 2016.

The majority of sponsorships, regardless of type, are not the sole promotional activity undertaken by the sponsors. They may be secondary and used to support above-the-line work or they may be used as the primary form of communication but supported by a range of off-screen activities, such as sales promotions and (in particular) competitions. For example, Sony Pictures developed a programme to encourage school pupils to be innovative and to develop their interest in science. Using an animated film, *Cloudy with a Chance of Meatballs*, the unbranded film provides a context for activities, quizzes and competitions (Thomas, 2009). More of a partnership than a straight sponsorship, the relationship furthers Sony's positioning as an innovator.

This section would not be complete without mention of the phenomenon called 'ambush marketing'. This occurs when an organisation deliberately seeks an association with a particular event but does so without paying sponsorship fees. Such hijacking is undertaken with the purpose of influencing the audience to the extent that they believe the ambusher is legitimate. According to Meenaghan (1998), this can be achieved by overstating the organisation's involvement in the event, perhaps through major communication activity using theme-based advertising or by sponsoring the media coverage of the event.

The role of sponsorship in the communications mix

Whether sponsorship is a part of advertising, sales promotion or public relations, has long been a source of debate. It is perhaps more natural and comfortable to align sponsorship with advertising. Since awareness is regarded as the principal objective of using sponsorship, advertising is a more complementary and accommodating part of the mix. Sales promotion from the sponsor's position is harder to justify, although from the perspective of the sponsored the value-added characteristic is interesting. The more traditional home for sponsorship is public relations (Witcher *et al.*, 1991). The sponsored, such as a football team, a racing car manufacturer or a theatre group, may be adjudged to perform the role of opinion former. Indirectly, therefore, messages are conveyed to the target audience with the support of significant participants who endorse and support the sponsor. This is akin to public relations activities.

Hastings (1984) contests that advertising messages can be manipulated and adapted to changing circumstances much more easily than those associated with sponsorship. He suggests that the audience characteristics of both advertising and sponsorship are very different. For advertising there are viewers and non-viewers. For sponsorship there are three groups of people that can be identified. First, there are those who are directly involved with the sponsor or the event, the active participants. The second is a much larger group, consisting of those who attend sponsored events, and these are referred to as personal spectators. The third group is normally the largest, comprising all those who are involved with the event through various media channels; these are regarded as media followers.

As if to demonstrate the potential sizes of these groups, estimates suggest that in excess of 4 million people attend the Formula 1 Grand Prix championship races (active participants) and over half a billion people (media followers) watch the races on television.

Exploratory research undertaken by Hoek *et al.* (1997) suggests that sponsorship is better able to generate awareness and a wider set of product-related attributes than advertising when dealing with non-users of a product, rather than users. There appears to be no discernible difference between the impact that these two promotional tools have with users.

The authors claim that sponsorship and advertising can be considered to work in approximately the same way if the ATR (attention, trial, reinforcement) model developed by Ehrenberg (1974) is adopted (Chapter 9). Through the ATR model, purchase behaviour and beliefs are considered to be reinforced by advertising rather than new behaviour patterns being established. Advertising fulfils a means by which buyers can meaningfully defend their purchase patterns. Hoek *et al.* regard this approach as reasonably analogous to sponsorship. Sponsorship can create awareness and is more likely to confirm past behaviour than prompt new purchase behaviour. The implication, they conclude, is that, while awareness levels can be improved with sponsorship, other communication tools are required to impact upon product experimentation or purchase intentions. Indeed, Smoliannov and Aiyeku (2009) make the point that integrated tv and major event sponsorship appear to work by influencing markets through TV audiences.

It was suggested earlier in this chapter that one of the opportunities that sponsorship offers is the ability to suggest that there is an association between the sponsored and the sponsor which may be of value to the message recipient. This implies that there is an indirect form of influence through sponsorship. This is supported by Crimmins and Horn (1996), who argue that the persuasive impact of sponsorship is determined in terms of the strength of links that are generated between the brand and the event that is sponsored.

These authors claim that sponsorship can have a persuasive impact and that the degree of impact that a sponsorship might bring is as follows:

$$\genfrac{}{}{}{}{\text{persuasive}}{\text{impact}} = \genfrac{}{}{}{}{\text{strength}}{\text{of link}} \times \genfrac{}{}{}{}{\text{duration}}{\text{of the link}} \times \left\{ \genfrac{}{}{}{}{\text{gratitude felt}}{\text{due to the link}} + \genfrac{}{}{}{}{\text{perceptual change}}{\text{due to the link}} \right\}$$

The strength of the link between the brand and the event is an outcome of the degree to which advertising is used to communicate the sponsorship itself. Sponsors that failed to invest in advertising during the Olympic Games have been shown to be far less successful in building a link with the event than those who chose to invest.

The *duration* of the link is also important. Research based on the Olympic Games shows that those sponsors who undertook integrated marketing communications long before the event itself were far more successful than those who had not. The use of mass media advertising to communicate the involvement of the sponsor, the use of event graphics and logos on packaging, and the creative use of pro-motional tie-ins and in-store, event-related merchandising facilitated the long-term linkage with the sponsorship and added value to the campaign.

Gratitude exists if consumers realise that there is a link between a brand and an event. For example, 60 per cent of US adults said that they 'try to buy a company's product if they support the Olympics'. They also stated that 'I feel I am contributing to the Olympics by buying the brands of Olympic sponsors'.

Perceptual change occurs as a result of consumers being able to understand the relationship (meaning) between a brand and an event. The sponsor needs to make this clear, as passive consumers may need the links laid out before them. The link between a swimwear brand and the Olympics may be obvious, but it is not always the case. Crimmins and Horn (1996) describe how Visa's 15 per cent perceived superiority advantage over MasterCard was stretched to 30 per cent during the 1992 Olympics and then settled at 20 per cent ahead one month after the Games had finished. The perceptual change was achieved through the messages that informed audiences that Visa was the one card that was accepted for the Olympic Games; American Express and MasterCard were not accepted.

This research, while based only upon a single event, indicates that sponsorship may bring advantages if care is taken to invest in communications long before and during the event to communicate the meaning between the brand and the event, which will leverage gratitude from a grateful audience. Finally, as if to confirm the point, Olson and Thjomoe (2009) find that combining television advertising increases the effectiveness of a sponsorship activity.

Summary

In order to help consolidate your understanding of public relations and sponsorship, here are the key points summarised against each of the learning objectives:

1 Explain the nature, characteristics and audiences for public relations

Public relations is a management activity used to convey messages about the organisation or its products and services, in order to build and maintain relationships with significant stakeholders. These relationships are noteworthy and they should be mutually beneficial.

The main characteristics of public relations are that it represents a very cost-effective means of carrying messages with a high degree of credibility. However, the degree of control that management is able to exert over the transmission of these types of messages can be limited.

Public relations can be used to communicate with a range of publics (or stakeholders). These vary from employees (internal public relations), financial groups (financial or investor relations), customers (media relations) and organisations and communities (corporate public relations).

2 Consider the issues relating to corporate responsibility and cause-related marketing

Organisations are under increasing pressure to act and be perceived as credible, transparent, responsible and ethically sound. Being able to present corporate brands as contributors to the wider social framework, a role beyond that of simple profit generators, has enabled many organisations to achieve stronger, more positive market positions. One of the avenues available to organisations to express their values and attitudes towards their need to be responsible is cause-related marketing.

3 Provide an overview of some of the main tools used by public relations, including media relations, lobbying, corporate advertising and crisis management

Public relations consists of a range of communication activities, of which media relations, publicity and event management appear to be the main ones used by practitioners. However, in addition, lobbying, corporate advertising and crisis communications form an important aspect of public relations activities.

4 Consider reasons for the use of sponsorship and the types of objectives that might be set

Sponsorship permits one party an opportunity to exploit an association with a target audience of another organisation, in return for funds, services or resources. Sponsorship can create awareness for an organisation (or brand), provide associations delivered indirectly and so avoid the issues associated with direct persuasion as well as use of resources effectively and efficiently.

The primary reasons are to build awareness, develop customer loyalty and improve the perception (image) held of the brand or organisation. Secondary reasons include attracting new users, supporting intermediaries and providing a form of staff motivation and morale building.

5 Appreciate the variety and different forms of sponsorship activities

Sponsorship is used in three key areas. These are sports, programme/broadcast, and the arts. There is also growing interest in other activities such as wildlife/conservation and education. Of all of these, sport has attracted most attention and sponsorship money.

6 Understand the role of sponsorship in the communication mix

Sponsorship has become an important part of the mix as it allows brands to be communicated without the clutter and noise associated with advertising. At the same time sponsorship enables associations and linkages to be made that add value for all the participants to the communication process.

There seems little doubt that the introduction of new products and brands can be assisted by the use of appropriate sponsorships. Indeed, it appears that sponsorship, in certain contexts, can be used to prepare markets for the arrival and penetration of new brands. It is perhaps more natural and comfortable to align sponsorship with advertising but it has also been associated with sales promotion and public relations. Since awareness is regarded as the principal objective of using sponsorship, advertising is a more complementary and accommodating part of the mix.

Review questions

1. Define public relations and set out its principal characteristics.
2. Using an organisation of your choice, identify the main stakeholders and comment on why it is important to communicate with each of them.
3. Highlight the main objectives of using public relations.
4. Select an industry of your choice, and consider the possible topics that might cause organisations in the industry to actively lobby the regulators.
5. Identify the main phases associated with crisis management.
6. Why do you think an increasing number of organisations are using sponsorship as a part of their marketing communications mix?
7. Name four types of sponsorship.
8. If the objective of using sponsorship is to build awareness (among other things), then there is little point in using advertising. Discuss this view.
9. Consider three television programmes that are sponsored and evaluate how viewers might perceive the relationship between the programme content and the sponsor.
10. Explain the role of sponsorship within the communications mix.

References

Anon (2007) KittenAid hits hard to save unwanted cats. Retrieved 16 January 2008 from http://www.prweek/uk/thisweek/campaigns/article/766679/CAMPAIGN-KittenAid

Anon (2009) The Work: Robinsons, *Revolution*, December, 56–57.
Bartlett, M. (2007) Glowing at Glastonbury, *theMarketer* (September), 20–23.
Bokaie, J. (2007) Coke commits to global water conservation drive, *Marketing*, 6 June, 1.
Borremans, P. (2010) Ready for anything: Support and enhance your crisis communication plan with social media, *Communication World*, (July–August), 31–33.
Brownsell, A. (2009) Getting back on track, *Marketing*, 8 July, 26–27.
Brownsell, A. (2010) HSBC launches Brazilian cultural sponsorship programme, *Marketing*, 13 June. Retrieved 13 July from www.brandrepublic.co/news
Bruning, S.D. and Ledingham, J.A. (2000) Perceptions of relationships and evaluations of satisfaction: an exploration of interaction, *Public Relations Review*, 26(1), 85–95.
Coombs, W.T. (2007) Protecting organization reputations during a crisis: The development and application of situational crisis communication theory, *Corporate Reputation Review* 10(3), 163–176.
Coppetti, C., Wentzel, D., Tomczak, T. and Henkel, S. (2009) Improving incongruent sponsorships and audience participation, *Journal of Marketing Communications*, 15(1) (February), 17–34.
Cornwell, B.T., Humphreys, M.S., Maguire, A.M., Weeks, C.S. and Tellegen, C.L. (2006) Sponsorship-Linked Marketing: The Role of Articulation in Memory, *Journal of Consumer Research*, 33(3), 312–321.
Crimmins, J. and Horn, M. (1996) Sponsorship: from management ego trip to marketing success, *Journal of Advertising Research* (July/August), 11–21.
Cropp, F. and Pincus, J.D. (2001) The mystery of public relations: Unravelling its past, unmasking its future, in R.L. Heath (ed.), *Handbook of public relations*. Thousand Oaks, CA: Sage, 189–203.
Ehrenberg, A.S.C. (1974) Repetitive advertising and the consumer, *Journal of Advertising Research*, 14 (April), 25–34.
Fink, S. (2000) *Crisis Management Planning for the Inevitable*. New York: AMACON.
Gregory, A. (2004) Scope and structure of public relations: a technology driven view, *Public Relations Review*, 30(3) (September), 245–254.
Grimes, E. and Meenaghan, T. (1998) Focusing commercial sponsorship on the internal corporate audience, *International Journal of Advertising*, 17(1), 51–74.
Grunig, J.E. (1992) Models of public relations and communication, in *Excellence in Public Relations and Communications Management* (eds J.E. Grunig, D.M. Dozier, P. Ehling, L.A. Grunig, F.C. Repper and J. Whits). Hillsdale, NJ: Lawrence Erlbaum, 285–325.
Grunig, J.E. (1997) A situational theory of publics: Conceptual history, recent challenges and new research, in *Public Relations Research: An International Perspective* (eds D. Moss, T. MacManus and D. Vercic). London: International Thomson Business, 3–48.
Grunig, J. and Hunt, T. (1984) *Managing Public Relations*. New York: Holt, Rineholt & Winston.
Harverson, P. (1998) Why IT companies take the risk, *Financial Times*, 2 June, 12.
Hastings, G. (1984) Sponsorship works differently from advertising, *International Journal of Advertising*, 3, 171–176.
Hedburg, A. (2000) Bumper crop, *Marketing Week*, 19 October, 28–32.
Hoek, J., Gendall, P., Jeffcoat, M. and Orsman, D. (1997) Sponsorship and advertising: a comparison of their effects, *Journal of Marketing Communications*, 3, 21–32.
Jaques, T. (2007) Issue management and crisis management: An integrated, non-linear, relational construct, *Public Relations Review* 33(2), 147–157.
Jaques, T. (2009) Issue and crisis management: Quicksand in the definitional landscape *Public Relations Review*, 35(3) (September), 280–286.
Kimberley, S. (2010) Pre-emptive strike, *Marketing*, 31 March, 15.
Kleinman, M. (2007) Coca-Cola commits $20m for water aid. *Daily Telegraph*, 5 June. Retrieved 5 December 2007 from http://www.telegraph.co.uk/money/main.jhtml?xml=/money/2007/06/05/cncola05.xml

Lacey, R., Sneath, J.Z., Finney, R.Z. and Close, A.G. (2007) The impact of repeat attendance on event sponsorship effects, *Journal of Marketing Communications*, 13(4) (December), 243–255.

Magee, K. (2009) Prime-time TV wars: Entertainment PR, *PR Week*, 27 November, 20–25.

Marshall, D.W. and Cook, G. (1992) The corporate (sports) sponsor, *International Journal of Advertising*, 11, 307–324.

McDonald, C. (1991) Sponsorship and the image of the sponsor, *European Journal of Marketing*, 25, 11, 31–38.

Meenaghan, T. (1998) Current developments and future directions in sponsorship, *International Journal of Advertising*, 17(1), 3–28.

Miller, G. (1989) Persuasion and public relations: two 'Ps' in a pod, in *Public Relations Theory* (eds C. Botan and V. Hazelton). Hillsdale, NJ: Lawrence Erlbaum.

Mitroff, I. (2004) *Crisis leadership: Planning for the unthinkable*, Hoboken, NJ: Wiley.

Moloney, K. (1997) Government and lobbying activities, in *Public Relations: Principles and Practice* (ed. P.J. Kitchen). London: International Thomson Press.

Murphy, D. (2007) Lost in the crowd, *Marketing*, 29, August, 36–37.

Olson, E.L. and Thjomoe, H.M (2009) Sponsorship effect metric: assessing the financial value of sponsoring by comparisons to television advertising, *Journal of the Academy of Marketing Science*, 37, 504–515.

O'Reilly. G. (2009) BBC hires Headstream to promote latest series of Strictly Come Dancing online, prweek.com. Retrieved 05 January 2009 from www.prweek.com/uk/news/929883/BBC-hires-Headstream-promote-latest-series-Strictly-Dancing-online/

Poon, D.T.Y and Prendergast, G. (2006) A new framework for evaluating sponsorship opportunities, *International Journal of Advertising*, 25(4), 471–487.

Reed, D. (1994) Sponsorship, *Campaign*, 20 May, 37–38.

Schumann, D.W., Hathcote, J.M. and West, S. (1991) Corporate advertising in America: a review of published studies on use, measurement and effectiveness, *Journal of Advertising*, 20(3), 35–56.

Smolianov, P. and Aiyeku, J.F. (2009) Corporate Marketing Objectives and Evaluation Measures of Integrated Television Advertising and Sports Event Sponsorships, *Journal of Promotion Management*, 15(1&2), (January), 74–89.

Thomas, J. (2009) Sony Pictures in school science tie, *Marketing*, 23 September, 10.

Thomas, J. (2010) Climate Week signs up key sponsors for event, *Marketing*, 20 June, 9.

Thorncroft, A. (1996) Business arts sponsorship: arts face a harsh set of realities, *Financial Times*, 4 July, 1.

Thwaites, D. (1994) Corporate sponsorship by the financial services industry, *Journal of Marketing Management*, 10, 743–763.

Tripodi, J.A. (2001) Sponsorship: a confirmed weapon in the promotional armoury. *International Journal of Sports Marketing and Sponsorship*, 3(1) (March/April), 1–20.

Utalk (2010) Nestle KitKat comes under attack with new Greenpeace viral. Retrieved 23 March 2010, from www.utalkmarketing.com

Witcher, B., Craigen, G., Culligan, D. and Harvey, A. (1991) The links between objectives and functions in organisational sponsorship, *International Journal of Advertising*, 10, 13–33.

Yun, S.-H. (2006) Toward public relations theory-based study of public diplomacy: testing the applicability of the excellence study, *Journal of Public Relations Research*, 18(4), 287–312.

Chapter 11
Direct marketing and personal selling

Direct marketing is a strategy used to create a personal and intermediary-free dialogue with customers. This should be a measurable activity and it is very often media-based, with a view to creating and sustaining a mutually rewarding relationship. Personal selling involves a face-to-face dialogue between two persons or by one person and a group. Message flexibility is an important attribute, as is the immediate feedback that often flows from use of this promotional tool.

Aims and learning objectives

The aims of this chapter are to first consider the characteristics of direct marketing and second to explore some of the principal issues and concepts associated with personal selling.

The learning objectives are to enable readers to:

1. define direct marketing and set out its key characteristics;
2. describe the different methods used to implement direct marketing;
3. explain the significance of the database in direct marketing and consider different direct response media;
4. discuss the different types, roles and tasks of personal selling;
5. consider the strengths and weaknesses of personal selling as a form of marketing communication;
6. explain the concept of multiple sales channels;
7. consider how direct marketing and personal selling might best be integrated with the other tools of the marketing communications mix.

Introduction

This chapter explores both direct marketing and personal selling. In many ways these topics complement each other in that they are both characterised by their personal and relatively transparent direct nature. Direct marketing is a term used to refer to all media activities that generate a series of communications and responses with an existing or potential customer. Direct marketing is mainly concerned with the management of customer behaviour and is used to complement the strengths and weaknesses of the other communication disciplines. To put this another way, advertising and public relations provide information and develop brand values but sales promotion, direct marketing and personal selling drive response, most notably behaviour. Both direct marketing and personal selling have the potential to engage customers directly, explicitly and can provide both an intellectual as well as emotional basis upon which interaction and dialogue can be developed.

The role of direct marketing

Direct marketing is concerned with the management of customer behaviour and is used to complement the strengths and weaknesses of the other communication disciplines. To put it another way, advertising and public relations provide information and develop brand values but sales promotion and direct marketing drive response, most notably behaviour.

Direct marketing is a tool of marketing communications used to create and sustain a personal and intermediary free communication with customers, potential customers and other significant stakeholders. In most cases this is a media based activity and offers great scope for the collection and utilisation of pertinent and measurable data. There are a number of important issues associated with this definition. The first is that the activity should be measurable. That is, any response(s) must be associated with a particular individual, a particular media activity and a particular outcome, such as a sale or enquiry for further information. The second issue concerns the rewards that each party perceives through participation in the relationship. The customer receives a variety of tangible and intangible satisfactions. These include shopping convenience, time utility and the satisfaction and trust that can develop between customers and a provider of quality products and services when the customers realise and appreciate the personal attention they appear to be receiving.

The direct marketer derives benefits associated with precision target marketing and minimised waste, increased profits and the opportunities to provide established customers with other related products, without the huge costs of continually having to find new customers. In addition, direct marketing represents a strategic approach to the market. It actively seeks to remove channel intermediaries, at least from the initial communication, reduce costs, and improve the quality and speed of service for customers, and through this bundle of attributes presents a new offering for the market, which in itself may provide competitive advantage. First Direct, Churchill and the pioneer, Direct Line, all provide these advantages, which have enabled them to secure strong positions in the market.

> **Viewpoint 11.1** Everyone likes the direct approach
>
> Direct marketing, in all of its different formats, is used by a great many organisations, some to a greater extent than others. In the Autumn of 2010 the prestige car brand Lexus launched its hybrid range and used direct marketing as the principal tool to deliver the communication strategy. Using the concept of evolution and natural selection, the direct and digital campaign was built around email and a direct mail pack. The goals were to generate awareness and interest among current Lexus customers and 'warm' prospects, with a view of stimulating brochure requests and test drives.
>
> In contrast The National Trust launched a direct marketing campaign to help secure funding for the acquisition of a stretch of coast on the Llŷn Peninsula in North West Wales. Using direct mail, the campaign directed people to a bespoke microsite which contained information about the ecological importance, the threats facing the peninsula and an opportunity to make donations.
>
> President Obama's election campaign was rooted in the use of direct and digital marketing, as he targeted swing voters, non-voters and others. Using database and email communications Obama generated so much in donations online that he was able to outspend the Republicans by 4:1 in TV advertising, and spend millions on a 30 minute ad that was then dissected by the media for 24 hours, dominating the media in the last days of the campaign.
>
> Financial services companies such as Santander, Axa, Aviva, Barclays, Direct Line all use direct marketing as a core element of their communications programmes. LoveFilm, the video rental company, charities such as Barnardos and Oxfam, and numerous B2B companies all invest heavily in direct marketing.
>
> *Source*: Based on Fernandez (2010a); Fernandez (2010b); Cooke (2008)
>
> **Question**
> If an organisation does not want to compete using advertising or direct marketing, what other methods could they use?
>
> **Task**
> Find two examples of companies using direct marketing and list the tools and media used.

Underpinning the direct marketing approach are the principles of trust and commitment, just as they support the validity of the other communication mix tools. If a meaningful relationship is to be developed over the long term and direct marketing is an instrumental part of the interaction, then the promises that the parties make to develop commitment and stability are of immense importance (Ganesan, 1994).

Types of direct brand

Direct marketing is assumed to refer to direct communication mix activity, but this is only part of the marketing picture. Using direct response media in this way is an increasingly common activity used to augment the communication activities surrounding a brand and to provide a new dimension to the context in which brands are perceived. However, direct marketing can be used by organisations in a number of different ways, very often reflecting the business strategy of the organisation. Four types can be identified and they should not be regarded as hierarchical, in the sense that there has to be progression from one type to another. They are reflections of the way different organisations use direct marketing and the degree to which the tool is used strategically.

Type 1: complementary tool

At this level, direct response media are used to complement the other communication mix activities used to support a brand. Their main use is to generate leads and to some extent awareness, information and reinforcement. For example, financial services companies, tour operators and travel agents use DRTV to stimulate enquiries, loans and bookings, respectively.

Type 2: primary differentiator

Rather than be one of a number of communication mix tools, at this level direct response media are the primary form of communication. They are used to provide a distinct point of differentiation from competitor offerings. They are the principal form of communication. In addition to the Type 1 advantages they are used to cut costs, avoid the use of intermediaries and reach finely targeted audiences (for example, book, music and wine clubs).

Type 3: sales channel

A third use for direct marketing and telemarketing in particular, concerns its use as a means of developing greater efficiency and as a means of augmenting current services. By utilising direct marketing as a sales tool, multiple sales channels can be used to meet the needs of different customer segments and so release resources to be deployed elsewhere and more effectively.

Type 4: brand vehicle

At this final level, brands are developed to exploit market space opportunities. The strategic element is most clearly evident at this level. Indeed, the entire organisation and its culture are normally oriented to the development of customer relationships through direct marketing activities. Prime examples are Lastminute.com and Amazon.

The growth of direct marketing

There can be little doubt that, of all the tools in the marketing communications mix, direct marketing has experienced the most growth in the past 15 years. The reasons for this growth are many and varied, but there have been three essential drivers behind the surge in direct marketing: technological advances; changing buyer lifestyles and expectations; and organisational expectations (see Figure 11.1). These forces for change demonstrate quite dramatically how a change in the context can impact on marketing communications.

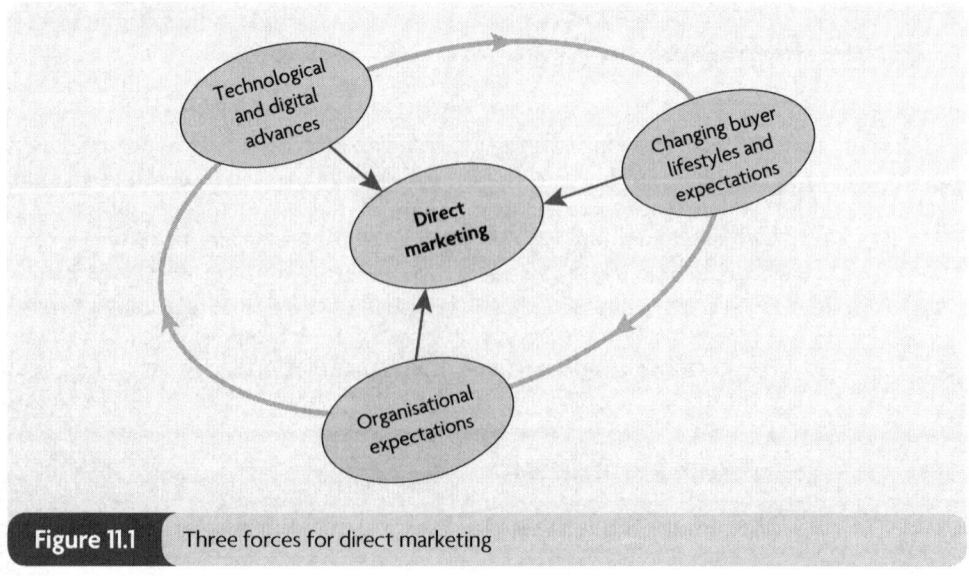

Figure 11.1 Three forces for direct marketing

Growth driver 1: technology

Rapid advances in technology have heralded the arrival of new sources and forms of information. Technology has enabled the collection, storage and analysis of customer data to become relatively simple, cost effective and straightforward. Furthermore, the management of this information is increasingly available to small businesses as well as the major blue chip multinational organisations. Computing costs have plummeted, while there has been a correspondingly enormous increase in the power that technology can deliver.

The technological surge has in turn stimulated three major developments. The first concerns the ability to capture information, the second to process and analyse it and the third to represent part or all of the information as a form of communication to stimulate interaction and perhaps dialogue to collect further information.

Growth driver 2: changing market context

The lifestyles of people in industrialised economies in particular, have evolved and will continue to do so. Generally, the brash phase of *selfishness* in the 1980s gave way to a more caring, society-oriented *selflessness* in the 1990s. The first decade of the twenty-first century suggests that a *self-oriented* lifestyle was prominent, reflected in short-term brand purchase behaviour and self-centred brand values and society behaviour. Perhaps the second decade will see further change as the global economy and forces for environmental adaptation bring about change to the way societies interact and individuals perceive their role within any one society. However, it seems as if there will be continued fragmentation of the media and finely tuned segmentation and communication devices will be necessary to communicate with discrete audiences.

Direct marketing offers a solution to this splintering and micro market scenario and addresses some of the changing needs of customers such as personalised, permission-based and informed communications. Management also benefits as direct marketing enables improved speed of response, lower waste and justification for the use and allocation of resources.

Growth driver 3: changing organisational expectations

Organisations can expect to continue experiencing performance pressures. These vary from the expectations of shareholders as they demand short-term returns on their investments to the impact this can have on managers. They are having to cope with an increasing cost base caused by demands on fuel and other resources by developing economies and a downward pressure on prices due to intense competition. This pressure on margins requires new routes to markets to reduce costs. Direct marketing addresses some of these changing management needs as there are no intermediary costs, there is fast access to markets (and withdrawal) plus opportunities to respond quickly to market developments and also justify their use and allocation of resources.

The impact of these drivers can be seen within the emergence of ideas about integrated marketing communications and an overall emphasis on relationship marketing principles. The enhanced ability of organisations to collect, store and manage customer lifestyle and transactional data, to generate personalised communications and their general enthusiasm for retention and loyalty schemes have combined to provide a huge movement towards an increased use of direct and interactive marketing initiatives.

The role of the database

At the hub of successful direct marketing and CRM activities is the database. A database is a collection of files held on a computer that contain data that can be related to one another and which can reproduce information in a variety of formats. Normally the data consist of information collected about prospects and customers that are used to determine appropriate segments and target markets and to record responses to communications conveyed by the organisation. A database therefore plays a role as a storage, sorting and administrative device to assist direct and personalised communications.

Age and lifestyle data are important signals of product usage. However, there will be attitudinal variances between people in similar groups demanding further analysis. This can, according to Reed (2000), uncover clues concerning what a direct mail piece should look like. So, older customers do not like soft colours and small type and sentences should not begin with 'and' or 'but'.

Increasingly, the information stored is gathered from transactions undertaken with customers, but on its own this information is not enough and further layering of data is required. The recency/frequency/monetary (RFM) model provides a base upon which lifestyle data, often bought in from a list agency, can be used to further refine the information held. Response analysis requires the identification of an organisation's best customers, and then another layer of data can be introduced which points to those that are particularly responsive to direct-response marketing activity (Fletcher, 1997). It is the increasing sophistication of the information held in databases that is enabling more effective targeting and communications.

Viewpoint 11.2 Tesco watches your trolleys

Tesco announced in the Spring of 2008 that they were going to monitor and record the shopping habits of over 60 million people in nine of the countries in which it operates.

Tesco Clubcard has 13.5 million current users in the UK, and versions of the card are available in South Korea, China and Malaysia. Each day an analysis is undertaken of their purchases. This data are then used to target discount coupons and promotions based on an individual's purchase patterns. The Clubcard is to be made available in Thailand, Hungary, Turkey, Slovakia, the Czech Republic and Poland.

Dunnhumby, who operate the database, have identified different types of shoppers:

- price sensitive shoppers – uses reward vouchers, few fresh foods, value lager;
- traditional shoppers – oldest group, buys small number of items from a list;
- mainstream shoppers – prefers easy-to-prepare family meals, saves Clubcard points for deals;
- healthy shoppers – any age but buys wholesome food, counts calories and fat;
- convenience shoppers – buys quick meals, often ready meals, prepared salads;
- finer foods shopper – affluent, older adults who prefer to cook with organic foods, exotic fruits and ovenware.

Source: Based on Hawkes (2008)

Question
To what extent does database information of this type provide Tesco with a competitive advantage?

Task
Visit dunnhumby.com and find out what they call relevance marketing.

Databases provide the means by which organisations, large and small, can monitor changes in customer lifestyles and attitudes or, in the business-to-business sector, the changing form of the interorganisational relationships and their impact on other members in the network as well as the market structure and level of competitive activity (Gundach and Murphy, 1993). It is through the use of the database that relationships with participants can be tracked, analysed and developed. Very importantly, database systems can be used not only to identify strategically important customers and segments but also to ascertain opportunities to cross-sell products (Kamakura *et al.*, 2003).

However, the merging of data generated through transactions with attitudinal and lifestyle data poses a further problem. In essence, this paints a picture of what has been achieved, it describes behaviour. What it does not do is explain why the behaviour occurred. It may be possible to track back through a campaign to examine the inputs, isolate variables and make a judgement, but the problem remains that the data itself, what has been collected, does not provide insight into what underpins the behaviour. Pearson (2003) suggests that direct marketing and market research data sets should be brought together into what has been referred to as 'consilience' (Wilson, 1998) or a unity of knowledge. This data-rich information should then be capable of providing organisations with data intelligence and an opportunity to predict behaviour and offer a new form of data value.

Permissions marketing

There are a number of tensions associated with the use of databases. These tensions can be related to concerns about privacy and the need to communicate sensitively with audiences who experience varying needs for privacy (Dolnicar and Jordaan, 2007). For example, customers have varying tolerances regarding the level of privacy that a database can exploit. These tolerances or thresholds (Goodwin, 1991) vary according to the nature of the information itself, how it was collected and even who collected it.

The information on a database very often exists simply because a customer entered into a transaction. The business entity that received the information as part of a transaction has a duty to acknowledge the confidential nature of the information and the context in which it was collected before selling the details to a third party or exploiting the information to the detriment of the individual who provided it in the first place. Breaking privacy codes and making unauthorised disclosures of personal details lays open the tenuous relationship an organisation thinks it has with its 'loyal' customers. These tensions have given rise to regulations requiring customers to provide organisations with their formal, express permission to use their personal data in particular ways.

It is commonly agreed that Godin (1999) is the pioneer of permission marketing (PM) (Krishnamurthy, 2001; Gomez and Hlavinka, 2007) and that the aim of PM is to 'initiate, sustain and develop a dialogue with customers, building trust and over time lifting the levels of permission, making it a more valuable asset' (Kent and Brandal, 2003: 491). To put it another way, PM is about 'getting the okay from individuals to market to them' (Smith, 2004: 52).

PM occurs when consumers give their explicit permission for marketers to send them various types of promotional messages (Krishnamurthy, 2001). Essentially customers authorise a marketer to transmit promotional messages in certain 'interest' categories. This is usually obtained when a customer registers to enter a website or completes a survey indicating their interests when registering for a service. Marketers are then able to target advertising messages more closely with the interests and needs of their registered customers. Definitions of PM vary according to the focus of the researchers, but they range from education, trust and share of wallet, to enticement and clutter.

Customers benefit from using PM through:

- a reduction in search costs and clutter;
- better organisation of the information search processes;
- improved message relevance through personalisation, customisation and recognition.

For organisations the benefits of using PM are related to:

- improved segmentation and targeting precision the acquisition of new customers, an increase of sales and the development of long-term, loyal customers;
- flexibility, resulting in improved interactivity, lower sales costs, enhanced direct communication with customers and increased profitability.

Direct response media

The choice of media for direct marketing can be very different from those selected for general advertising purposes. The main reason for using direct response media is that direct contact is made with prospects and customers in order that a direct response is solicited and a dialogue stimulated or maintained. In reality, a wide variety of media can be used, simply by attaching a telephone number, website address or response card.

Previously, broadcast media such as television and radio were the champions of the general advertiser. Now their adoption by direct marketers in the UK has changed the way these media operate. In terms of engagement, explored in Chapter 1, the broad cast format generated engagement through thinking and feeling. The use as a direct response implement changes the engagement to a behavioural orientation.

Direct mail, telemarketing and door-to-door activities are the main offline forms of direct response media, as they allow more personal, direct and evaluative means of reaching precisely targeted customers. Internet based direct work encompasses email, mobile and affiliate marketing as forms of direct linking.

Direct mail

Direct mail refers to personally addressed advertising that is delivered through the postal system. It can be personalised and targeted with great accuracy, and its results are capable of precise measurement.

The generation of enquiries and leads together with the intention of building a personal relationship with customers are the most important factors contributing to the growth of direct mail. Management should decide whether to target direct mail at current customers with the intention of building loyalty and retention rates, or whether they should chase new customers. The decision, acquisition or retention, should be part of the marketing plan but often this aspect of direct marketing lacks clarity, resulting in wastage and inefficiency. Direct mail can be expensive, at anything between £250 and £500 per 1,000 items dispatched. It should, therefore, be used selectively and for purposes other than creating awareness.

Organisations in the financial services sectors are the main users of this medium and the financial health of the sector is dependent to a large extent on some of the major financial services companies maintaining their spend on direct mail. However, an increasing number of other organisations are experimenting with this approach, as they try to improve the effectiveness of their investment in the communication mix and seek to reduce television advertising costs. The growth in consumer-based direct mail activities has outstripped that of the business-to-business sector. The number of direct mail items sent to consumers has increased considerably in comparison with the b2b sector.

Telemarketing

The prime qualities of the telephone are that it provides for interaction, is flexible and permits immediate feedback and the opportunity to overcome objections, all within the same communication event. Other dimensions of telemarketing include the development and maintenance of customer goodwill, allied to which is the increasing need to provide high levels of customer service. Telemarketing also allows organisations to undertake marketing research which is both highly measurable and accountable in that the effectiveness can be verified continuously and call rates, contacts reached and the number and quality of positive and negative responses are easily recorded and monitored.

Growth in telemarketing activity in the business-to-business sector has been largely at the expense of personal selling. The objectives have been to reduce costs and to utilise the expensive sales force and their skills to build on the openings and leads created by telemarketing and other lead generation activities. Some of the advantages of using the telephone as part of the media mix are that it allows for interaction between participants, it enables immediate feedback and sets up opportunities to overcome objections, all within the same communication event when both the sender and the receiver are geographically distant.

All of these activities can be executed by personal selling, but the speed, cost, accuracy and consistency of the information solicited through personal visits can often be improved upon by telemarketing. The complexity of the product will influence the degree to which this medium can be used successfully. However, if properly trained professional telemarketers are used, the sales results, if measured on a call basis, can outperform those produced by personal selling.

Contact centres use a variety of digital applications with the prime goals of reducing costs, improving efficiency and improving the client's reputation through quality of customer interaction. Automatic call distribution systems, call recording systems, computer–telephone integration, customer interaction management, predictive diallers and interactive voice response systems are just some of the ways in which technology is used in these environments.

Operator contact with customers can be also be supported by technology. Computer-assisted telephone interviewing (CATI) can provide varying degrees of technical support. The degree to which this is used depends on the task, the product and the nature of the target audience. The behaviour of call centre employees, however much they are regulated or controlled by various software applications, is a function of service quality, as perceived by callers. Referred to as customer orientation behaviours (COBs), Rafaeli *et al.* (2008) identify five COBs that are related to service quality. These are:

- anticipating customer requests;
- offering explanations and justifications;
- educating customers;
- providing emotional support;
- offering personalised information.

When these five COBs are used by call centre employees, customers perceive a high level of service quality. The implication of this, as pointed out by the researchers, is that as call centre managers invariably seek to minimise call length in order to reduce costs and increase the number of transactions, their actions appear to endanger service quality.

The costs of telemarketing are high. It is estimated for example, that is costs £15–£20 to reach a decision-maker in an organisation. When this is compared with £5 for a piece of direct mail or £150+ for a personal sales call to the same individual, it is the effectiveness of the call and the return on the investment that determines whether the costs are really high.

Carelines

Another reason to use telemarketing concerns the role which carelines can play within consumer/brand relationships. Manufacturers use contact centres to enable customers to:

- complain about a product performance and related experiences;
- seek product related advice;
- make suggestions regarding product or packaging development;
- comment about an action or development concerning the brand as a whole.

What binds these together is the potential all of these people have for repurchasing the brand, even those who complain bitterly about product performance and experience. If these people have their complaints dealt with properly then there is a reasonable probability that they will repurchase.

The majority of careline calls are not about complaints but seek advice or help about products. Food manufacturers can provide cooking and recipe advice, cosmetic and toiletries companies can provide healthcare advice and application guidelines while white goods and service-based organisations can provide technical and operational support.

Carelines are essentially a post-purchase support mechanism that facilities market feedback and intelligence gathering. They can warn of imminent problems (product defects), provide ideas for new products or variants and of course provide a valuable method to reassure customers and improve customer retention levels. Call operators, or agents as many of them are now being called, have to handle calls from a variety of new sources – web, email, interactive TV and mobile devices – and it is appreciated that many are more effective if they have direct product experience. Instant messaging channels enable online shoppers to ask questions that are routed to a call centre for response. Sales conversion ratios can be up by 40–50 per cent and costs are about £1 to answer an inbound question, compared with £3.50 by phone (Murphy, 2000). Kellogg's reports that its careline makes a 13:1 return on investment (Bashford, 2004).

While the Internet has provided further growth opportunities, it will also take on a number of the tasks currently the preserve of telemarketing bureaux. Websites enable product information and certain support advice to be accessed without the call centre costs and focus attention on other matters that are of concern to the customer. Chat room discussions, collaborative browsing and real-time text conversations are options to help care for customers in the future. However, it is probably the one-to-one telephone dialogue between customer and agent that will continue to provide satisfaction and benefits for both parties.

Inserts

Inserts are media materials that are placed in magazines or direct mail letters. These not only provide factual information about the product or service but also enable the recipient to respond to the request of the direct marketer. This request might be to place an order or post back a card for more information, such as a brochure.

Inserts have become more popular, but their cost is substantially higher than a four-colour advertisement in the magazine in which the insert is carried. Their popularity is based on their effectiveness as a lead generator, and new methods of delivering inserts to the home will become important to direct mailing houses in the future. Other vehicles, such as packages rather than letter mail, will become important.

Print

There are two main forms of direct response advertising through the printed media: first, catalogues and, secondly, magazines and newspapers.

Catalogues mailed direct to consumers have been an established method of selling products for a long time. Mail order organisations such as Freeman's, GUS and Littlewoods have successfully exploited this form of direct marketing. Organisations such as Tchibo and Kaleidoscope have successfully used mini-catalogues, but instead of providing account facilities and the appointment of specific freelance agents, their business transactions are on a cash-with-order basis.

Business-to-business marketers have begun to exploit this medium, and organisations such as Dell and IBM now use online and offline catalogues, partly to save costs and partly to free valuable sales personnel so that they can concentrate their time selling into larger accounts. Direct response advertising through the press is similar to general press advertising except that the advertiser provides a mechanism for the reader to take further action. The mechanism may be a telephone number (call free) or a coupon or cut-out reply slip requesting further information. Dell has transformed its marketing strategy to one that is based around building customised products for both consumers and business customers. Consumer direct print ads which offer an incentive, are designed explicitly to drive customers to the Dell website, where transactions are completed without reference to retailers, dealers or other intermediaries.

Exhibit 11.1 Direct response print ad from Dell
Image courtesy of Dell

Door-to-door

This delivery method can be much cheaper than direct mail as there are no postage charges to be accounted for. However, if the costs are much lower, so are the response rates. Responses are lower because door-to-door drops cannot be personally addressed, as can direct mail, even though the content and quality can be controlled in the same way.

> **Viewpoint 11.3** Onwards and upwards, direct to the sky
>
> In the grip of the recession Sky television made great use of direct marketing. In the year to June 2009 Sky invested £31.8 million on direct mail, a substantial 80 per cent increase on the previous year. However, this represents a mere 10 per cent of Sky's investment in direct marketing. Press advertising, media inserts and door-drop work accounts for the majority of its direct work. The result of this activity was that direct marketing accounted for 40 per cent of Sky's new customers in the period.
>
> Plans to continue this level of direct marketing are limited as the marketing strategy refocuses on the capabilities and facilities and in particular, subscriptions to Sky+ boxes and High Definition (HD) pictures. These benefits are not easily communicated through direct response and standard media. The need for face-to-face communication in order to demonstrate the benefits becomes more acute. As a result resources were reallocated to experiential marketing, such as shopping centre stands, consumer exhibitions and events, the field sales force and relationships with major high street retailers such as Dixons, Tesco and Comet.
>
> Source: Based on Murphy (2009)
>
> **Question**
> Why might you recommend Sky use direct marketing to launch an extension into radio?
>
> **Task**
> Buy a daily tabloid newspaper, cut out the direct response ads and consider what is similar about them.

Avon (Cosmetics) and Betterware are traditionally recognised as professional practitioners of door-to-door direct marketing. Other organisations, such as the utility companies (gas, electricity and water), and domestic cleaning company, Molly Maid, are using door-to-door to create higher levels of market penetration.

Radio and television

Of the two main forms discussed earlier, radio and television, the former is used as a support medium for other advertising, often by providing enquiry numbers. Television has greater potential because it can provide the important visual dimension, but its use in the UK for direct marketing purposes has been limited. One of the main reasons for this has been the television contractors' attitude to pricing. However, the industry has experienced a period of great change and has introduced greater pricing flexibility, and a small but increasing number of direct marketers have used the small screen successfully, mainly by providing freephone numbers for customers. Direct Line, originally a motor insurance organisation, has been outstanding in its use of television not only to launch but also to help propel the phenomenal growth of a range of related products.

The Internet and digital media

The explosion of activity around digital media, the Internet and email communications has been quite astonishing in recent years and now represents a major new form of interactive marketing communications. The establishment of digital television services and the imminent withdrawal of analogue services, has driven new forms of interactivity. Initially home shopping and banking facilities were attractive to those whose lifestyles complement the benefits offered by the new technology but fully interactive services now bring increased leisure and entertainment opportunities. For more information on interactive marketing communications see Chapter 14.

Personal selling

In an era where relationship marketing has become increasingly understood and accepted as the contemporary approach to marketing theory and practice, so personal selling characterises the importance of strong relationships between vendor and buyer. The traditional image of personal selling is one that embraces the hard sell, with a brash and persistent salesperson delivering a volley of unrelenting, persuasive messages at a confused and reluctant consumer. Fortunately this image has receded as the professionalism and breadth of personal selling become more widely recognised and as the role of personal selling becomes even more important in the communications mix.

Personal selling activities can be observed at various stages in the buying process of both the consumer and business-to-business markets. This is because the potency of personal communications is very high, and messages can be adapted on the spot to meet the requirements of both parties. This flexibility, as we shall see later, enables objections to be overcome, information to be provided in the context of the buyer's environment and the conviction and power of demonstration to be brought to the buyer when the buyer requests it.

Personal selling is different from other forms of communication in that the transmitted messages represent, mainly, dyadic communications. This means that there are two persons involved in the communication process. Feedback and evaluation of transmitted messages are possible, more or less instantaneously, so that these personal selling messages can be tailored and be made much more personal than any of the other methods of communication.

Using the spectrum of activities identified by the hierarchy of effects, we can see that personal selling is close enough to the prospective buyer to induce a change in behaviour. That is, it is close enough to overcome objections, to provide information quickly and to respond to the prospects' overall needs, all in the context of the transaction, and to encourage them directly to place orders.

The tasks of personal selling

The generic tasks to be undertaken by the sales force have been changing because the environment in which organisations operate is shifting dramatically. These changes, in particular those associated with the development and implementation of new technologies, have had repercussions on the activities of the sales force and are discussed later in this chapter.

The tasks of those who undertake personal selling vary from organisation to organisation and in accord with the type of selling activities on which they focus. It is normally assumed that they collect and bring into the organisation orders from customers wishing to purchase products and services. In this sense the order aspect of the personal selling tool can be seen as one of four order-related tasks:

1. *Order takers* are salespersons to whom customers are drawn at the place of supply. Reception clerks at hotels and ticket desk personnel at theatres and cinemas typify this role.
2. *Order getters* are sales personnel who operate away from the organisation and who attempt to gain orders, largely through the provision of information, the use of demonstration techniques and services and the art of persuasion.
3. *Order collectors* are those who attempt to gather orders without physically meeting their customers. This is completed electronically or over the telephone. The growth of telemarketing operations was discussed in the previous chapter, but the time saved by both the buyer and the seller using the telephone to gather repeat and low-value orders frees valuable sales personnel to seek new customers and build relationships with current customers.
4. *Order supporters* are all those people who are secondary salespersons in that they are involved with the order once it has been secured, or are involved with the act of ordering,

Table 11.1 Tasks of personal selling

Prospecting	Finding new customers
Communicating	Informing various stakeholders and feeding back information about the market
Selling	The art of leading a prospect to a successful close
Information gathering	Reporting information about the market and reporting on individual activities
Servicing	Consulting, arranging, counselling, fixing and solving a multitude of customer 'problems'
Allocating	Placing scarce products and resources at times of shortage
Shaping	Building and sustaining relationships with customers and other stakeholders

usually by supplying information. Order processing or financial advice services typify this role. In truly customer-oriented organisations all customer-facing employees will be an order supporter.

However, this perspective of personal selling is narrow because it fails to set out the broader range of activities that a sales force can be required to undertake. Salespeople do more than get or take orders. The tasks listed in Table 11.1 provide direction and purpose, and also help to establish the criteria by which the performance of members of the personal selling unit can be evaluated. The organisation should decide which tasks it expects its representatives to undertake.

Personal selling is the most expensive element of the communications mix. The average cost per contact can easily exceed £250 when all markets and types of businesses are considered. It is generally agreed that personal selling is most effective at the later stages of the hierarchy of effects or buying process, rather than at the earlier stage of awareness building. Therefore, each organisation should determine the precise role the sales force is to play within the communications mix.

The role of personal selling

Personal selling is often referred to as interpersonal communication and from this perspective Reid *et al.* (2002) determined three major sales behaviours, namely getting, giving and using information:

- Getting information refers to sales behaviours aimed at information acquisition, for example gathering information about customers, markets and competitors.
- Giving information refers to the dissemination of information to customers and other stakeholders, for example sales presentations and seminar meetings designed to provide information about products and an organisation's capabilities and reputation.
- Using information refers to the salesperson's use of information to help solve a customer's problem. Associated with this is the process of gaining buyer commitment through the generation of information (Thayer, 1968, cited by Reid *et al.*, 2002).

These last authors suggest that using the information dynamic appears to be constant across all types of purchase situations. However, as the complexity of a purchase situation increases so the amount of giving information behaviours decline and getting information behaviours increase. This finding supports the need for a salesperson to be able to recognise particular situations in the buying process and then to adapt their behaviour to meet the buyer's contextual needs.

However, salespeople undertake numerous tasks in association with communication activities. Guenzi (2002) determined that some sales activities are generic simply because they are performed by most salespeople across a large number of industries. These generic activities are selling, customer relationship management and communicating to customers. Other activities such as market analysis, pre-sales services and the transfer of information about competitors to the organisation are industry specific. Interestingly he found that information-gathering activities are more likely to be undertaken by organisations operating in consumer markets than in b2b, possibly a reflection of the strength of the market orientation in both arenas.

The role of personal selling is largely one of representation. In b2b markets sales personnel operate at the boundary of the organisation. They provide the link between the needs of their own organisation and the needs of their customers. This linkage, or boundary spanning role, is absolutely vital, for a number of reasons that will be discussed shortly, but without personal selling, communication with other organisations would occur through electronic or print media and would foster discrete closed systems. Representation in this sense therefore refers to face-to-face encounters between people from different organisations.

Many authors consider the development, organisation and completion of a sale in a market exchange-based transaction to be the key part of the role of personal selling. Sales personnel provide a source of information for buyers so that they can make the right purchase decisions. In that sense they provide a good level of credibility, but they are also perceived, understandably, as biased. The degree of expertise held by the salesperson may be high, but the degree of perceived trustworthiness will vary, especially during the formative period of the relationship, unless other transactions with the selling organisation have been satisfactory. Once a number of transactions have been completed and product quality established, trustworthiness may improve. As the costs associated with personal selling are high, it is vital that sales personnel are used effectively. To that end, some organisations are employing other methods to decrease the time that the sales force spends on administration, travel and office work and to maximise the time spent in front of customers, where they can use their specific selling skills.

The amount of control that can be exercised over the delivery of the messages through the sales force depends upon a number of factors. Essentially, the level of control must be regarded as low, because each salesperson has the freedom to adapt messages to meet changing circumstances as negotiations proceed. In practice, however, the professionalism and training that many members of the sales force receive and the increasing accent on measuring levels of customer satisfaction mean that the degree of control over the message can be regarded, in most circumstances, as very good, although it can never, for example, be as high as that of advertising.

This flexibility is framed within the context of the product strategy. Decisions that impact upon strategy are not allowed. There is freedom to adapt the manner in which products are presented, but there is no freedom for the sales representatives to decide the priority of the products to be detailed.

Viewpoint 11.4 Flexible sales teams

Personal selling can take many forms but the face-to-face form of communication can be a strong force for engagement and behaviour change. Emerging brands benefit when brand owners and entrepreneurs visit retailers in person, and start to establish a relationship. For example, when Sam Galsworthy launched Sipsmith, an alcohol based brand, he used his motorbike to visit high-end style bars in and around London to ensure that bottles of his brand were given a prominent position at the bar, and to persuade bar managers to promote and recommend the brand to customers. As a result the barmen get to know the face behind the brand, something that wholesalers are not able to do.

Many large organisations, especially those in the b2b sector, employ their own sales teams to visit customers to provide advice, technical support for the product line and to resolve any problems and difficulties. Grocery and

FMCG producers use their sales force teams to develop sales with the multiple supermarkets and independent grocers. Providing adequate coverage can be difficult and expensive so temporary sales force teams are often used for product launches and periods of high demand. Field marketing agencies can provide these facilities. When Kellogg's launched Rice Crispies Totally Chocolatey a field sales team was used to visit hundreds of outlets in the London area, to get the brand established.

Source: Based on Benady (2009)

Question

Why should organisations maintain an employed, and expensive sales force when they can rent a sales force at any time?

Task

Choose a brand that you would like to make, then consider the role a sales team might play in your communication strategy.

Strengths and weaknesses of personal selling

There are a number of strengths and weaknesses associated with personal selling. It is interesting to note that some of the strengths can in turn be seen as weaknesses, particularly when management control over the communication process is not as attentive or as rigorous as it might be.

Strengths

Dyadic communications allow for interaction that, unlike the other communication mix tools, provides for fast, direct feedback. In comparison with the mass media, personal selling allows for the receiver to focus attention on the salesperson, with a reduced likelihood of distraction or noise.

There is a greater level of participation in the decision process by the vendor than in the other tools. When this is combined with the power to tailor messages in response to the feedback provided by the buyer, the sales process has a huge potential to solve customer problems.

Weaknesses

One of the major disadvantages of personal selling is the cost. Costs per contact are extremely high, and this means that management must find alternative means of communicating particular messages and improve the amount of time that sales personnel spend with prospects and customers. Reach and frequency through personal selling are always going to be low, regardless of the amount of funds available. Control over message delivery is very often low and, while the flexibility is an advantage, there is also the disadvantage of message inconsistency. This in turn can lead to confusion (a misunderstanding perhaps with regard to a product specification), the ramifications of which can be enormous in terms of cost and time spent by a variety of individuals from both parties to the contract.

The quality of the relationship can, therefore, be jeopardised through poor and inconsistent communications.

When personal selling should be a major part of the communications mix

In view of the role and the advantages and disadvantages of personal selling, when should it be a major part of the communications mix? Table 11.2 indicates some key factors using advertising as a comparison.

Table 11.2 When personal selling is a major element of the communications mix

	Advertising relatively important	Personal selling relatively important
Number of customers	Large	Small
Buyers' information needs	Low	High
Size and importance of purchase	Small	Large
Post-purchase service required	Little	A lot
Product complexity	Low	High
Distribution strategy	Pull	Push
Pricing policy	Set	Negotiate
Web-enabled communications and exchanges	High	Low
Resources available for promotion	Many	Few

Source: Adapted from Cravens (1987)

The following is not an exhaustive list, but is presented as a means of considering some of the important issues: complexity, network factors, buyer significance and communication effectiveness.

Complexity

Personal selling is very important when there is a medium to high level of relationship complexity. Such complexity may be associated either with the physical characteristics of the product, such as computer software design, or with the environment in which the negotiations are taking place. For example, decisions related to the installation of products designed to automate an assembly line may well be a sensitive issue. This may be due to management's attitude towards the operators currently undertaking the work that the automation is expected to replace.

When the complexity of the offering is high, advertising and public relations cannot always convey benefits in the same way as personal selling. Personal selling allows the product to be demonstrated so that buyers can see and, if necessary, touch and taste it for themselves. Personal selling also allows explanations to be made about particular points that are of concern to the buyer or about the environment in which the buyer wishes to use the product.

Buyer significance

The significance of the product to the buyers in the target market is a very important factor in the decision on whether to use personal selling. Significance can be measured as a form of risk, and risk is associated with benefits and costs.

The absolute cost to the buyer will vary from organisation to organisation and from consumer to consumer. The significance of the purchase of an extra photocopier for a major multinational organisation may be low, but for a new start-up organisation or for an established organisation experiencing a dramatic turnaround, an extra photocopying machine may be highly significant and subject to high levels of resistance by a number of different internal stakeholders.

Communication effectiveness

There may be a number of ways to satisfy the communication objectives of a campaign, other than by using personal selling. Each of the other communication tools has strengths and weaknesses; consequently differing mixes provide different benefits. Have they all been considered?

One of the main reasons for using personal selling occurs when advertising alone, or any other medium, provides insufficient communications. The main reason for this inadequacy surfaces when advertising media cannot provide buyers with the information they require to make their decision. For example, someone buying a new car may well observe and read various magazine and newspaper advertisements. The decision to buy, however, requires information and data upon which a rational decision can be made. This rationality and experience of the car, through a test drive perhaps, balances the former, more emotional, elements that contributed to the earlier decision.

The decision to buy a car normally evokes high involvement, therefore car manufacturers try to provide a rich balance of emotional and factual information in their literature. From this perspective buyers seek further information at the website and seek experience and reassurance at a dealership. Car buyers sign orders with the presence and encouragement of salespersons. Very few cars are bought on a mail order basis, although some are bought over the Internet.

Personal selling provides a number of characteristics that make it more effective than the other elements of the mix. As discussed, in business-to-business marketing the complexity of many products requires salespeople to be able to discuss with clients their specific needs; in other words, to be able to talk in the customer's own language, to build source credibility through expertise and hopefully trustworthiness, and build a relationship that corresponds with the psychographic profile of each member of the DMU. In this case, mass communications would be inappropriate.

Channel network factors

When the number of members in a network is limited, the use of a sales force is advisable, as advertising is inefficient. Furthermore, the opportunity to build a close collaborative relationship with members may enable the development of a sustainable competitive advantage.

There are two further factors that influence the decision to use personal selling as part of the communications mix. When the customer base is small and dispersed across a wide geographic area it makes economic sense to use salespersons, as advertising in this situation is inadequate and ineffective.

Personal selling is the most expensive element of the communications mix. It may be that other elements of the mix may provide a more cost-effective way of delivering the message.

Integration and supporting the sales force

In an effort to increase the productivity of the sales force and to use their expensive skills more effectively, direct marketing has provided organisations with an opportunity to improve levels of performance and customer satisfaction. In particular, the use of an inside telemarketing department is seen as a compatible sales channel to the field sales force. The telemarketing team can accomplish the following tasks: they can search for and qualify new customers, so saving the field force from cold calling; they can service existing customer accounts and prepare the field force should they be required to attend to the client personally; they can seek repeat orders from marginal or geographically remote customers, particularly if they are low-unit-value consumable items; finally, they can provide a link between network members that serves to maintain the relationship, especially through periods of difficulty and instability. Many organisations prefer to place orders online or through telesales teams, as it does not involve the time costs associated with personal sales calls. The routine of such orders gives greater efficiency for all concerned with the relational exchange and reduces costs.

Direct mail activities are also becoming more important in areas where personal contact is seen as unnecessary or where limited field sales resources are deployed to key accounts. As with telesales, direct mail is often used to supplement the activities of the field force. Catalogue and electronic communications such as fax can be used for accounts, which may be regarded as relatively unattractive.

In addition to this, use of the Internet and mobile-based communications have provided new opportunities to reach customers. The website itself symbolises the changing orientation of marketing communications. Whereas once the brochure, mass media advertising and perhaps a communication mix incentive represented the central channel of communication, now the website and the database serve to integrate directed, sometimes interactive, one-to-one communications. These are supported in many cases by more call-to-action messages channelled through a variety of coordinated offline and digital media.

All of these activities free the field sales force to increase their productivity and to spend more time with established customers, key accounts or those with high profit potential.

Multichannel selling

A number of different sales channels have been identified so far and many organisations, in their search to reduce costs, have restructured their operations in an attempt to better meet the 'touchpoints' of their different customers.

Restructuring has often taken the form of introducing multiple sales channels with the simple objective of using less expensive channels to complete selling tasks that do not require personal, face-to-face contact. Technology-enhanced channels, mainly in the form of web-based and email communications, have grown considerably, often at the expense of telephone and mail facilities. Payne and Frow (2004) have developed a categorisation of sales channels and these are depicted in the vertical column of Table 11.3.

In order to better meet the needs of customers, organisations need to evolve their mix of channels. Customers will then be able to interact with their supplying organisations using the mix of channels that they prefer to use. Therefore, marketing communications needs to be used in order to best complement the different audiences, channel facilities and characteristics. Through mixing channels and communications in a complementary way, higher levels of

Table 11.3 Comparison of channel characteristics

Channel	Breadth	Dominant form of communication	Cost/contact
Field sales	Key account, service and personal representation	Dialogue	High
Outlets	Retail branches, stores, depots and kiosks	Interactive	Medium
Telephony	Traditional telephone, facsimile, telex and contact centres	One-way and two-way	Low to medium
Direct marketing	Direct mail, radio and traditional television	One-way and two-way	Low
ecommerce	Email, Internet, interactive television	Interactive	Very low
mcommerce	Mobile telephony, SMS, WAP and 3G	Interactive	Very low

customer service can be achieved. The proliferation of channels may, however, lead organisations to believe that the greater the number of channels the greater the chances of commercial success. In addition to the view that multichannel customers are known to spend up to 30 per cent more than single channel customers, the Internet and overseas call centres also offer substantial (short-term) cost savings (Myers *et al.*, 2004).

Categorising customers

One simple approach to managing channels is to categorise accounts (customers) according to their potential attractiveness and the current strength of the relationship between supplier and buyer (see Figure 11.2). A strong relationship, for example, is indicative of two organisations engaged in mutually satisfying relational exchanges. A weak relationship suggests that the two parties have no experience of each other or, if they have, that it is not particularly satisfying. If there have been transactions, it may be that these can be classified as market exchange experiences. Attractiveness refers to the opportunities a buying organisation represents to the vendor: how large or small the potential business is in an organisation.

For reasons of clarity, these scales are presented as either high or low, strong or weak. However, they should be considered as a continuum, and with the use of some relatively simple evaluative criteria accounts can be positioned on the matrix and strategies formulated to move accounts to different positions, which in turn necessitate the use of different sales channel mixes.

Based on the original approach developed by Cravens *et al.* (1991) appropriate sales channels are superimposed on the grid so that optimum efficiency in selling effort and costs can be managed (Figure 11.3). Accounts in Section 1 vary in attractiveness, as some will be

	Strength of relationship	
	High	Low
Account potential High	Section 1 Strategic investment	Section 2 Select and build
Account potential Low	Section 3 Adjust and maintain	Section 4 Reduce all support

Figure 11.2 Account investment grid

	Strength of relationship	
	High	Low
Account potential High	Key account management Field force selling	Field force selling Telemarketing/call centre Website Email
Account potential Low	Directed field force selling Telemarketing/call centre Website Email	Direct mail Telemarketing Email

Figure 11.3 Multichannel mix allocation
Source: After Cravens *et al.* (1991). Used with permission

assigned key account status. The others will be very important and will require a high level of selling effort (investment), which has to be delivered by the field sales force. Accounts in Section 2 are essentially prospects because of their weak relationship but high attractiveness. Selling effort should be proportional to the value of the prospects: high effort for good prospects and low for the others. Care should be given to allocating a time by which accounts in this section are moved to other parts of the grid, and in doing so save resources and maximise opportunities for growth. All the main sales channels should be used, commencing with direct and email to identify prospects, telesales for qualification purposes, field sales force selling directed at the strong prospects and telesales and website for the others. Website details provide support and information for those accounts that wish to remain distant. As the relationship becomes stronger, so field selling takes over from telemarketing and the coordinating activities of the contact or call centre. If the relationship weakens, then the account may be discontinued and selling redirected to other prospects.

Accounts in Section 3 do not offer strong potential and, although the relationship is strong, there are opportunities to switch the sales channel mix by reducing, but not eliminating, the level of field force activity and to give consideration to the introduction of telemarketing for particular accounts. Significant cost reductions can be achieved with these types of accounts by simply reviewing the means and reasoning behind the personal selling effort. Accounts in Section 4 should receive no field force calls, the prime sales channels being telesales, email, the website and perhaps catalogue selling depending upon the nature of the website.

Establishing a multiple sales channel strategy based on the grid suggested above may not be appropriate to all organisations. For example, the current level of performance may be considered as exceeding expectations, in which case there is no point in introducing change. It may be that the costs and revenues associated with redeployment are unfavourable and that the implications for the rest of the organisation of implementing the new sales channel approach are such that the transition should be either postponed or rejected. Payne and Frow (2004) suggest a range of channel options or strategies can be identified that relate to the channel needs of target segments. These range from a single dominant channel such as those used by Amazon and Egg, a customer segment approach designed for use with different channel types such as intermediaries, b2b end-user customers and consumers, one based on the different activity channels that customers prefer to use, such as a mix of online and offline resources to identify, see, demonstrate, select and pay for a computer and finally a truly integrated multi-channel strategy utilising CRM systems to integrate all customer information at whichever contact point the customer chooses to use. These strategies reflect some of the approaches that can be used and indeed various combinations can be used to meet customers' channel needs. However, experience has shown that costs can be reduced through the introduction of a multiple sales channel approach and that levels of customer satisfaction and the strength of the relationship between members of the network can be improved considerably. In addition, it is vital to remember that customers will move into and use new channel mixes over the customer lifecycle and that channel decisions should be regarded as fluid and developmental.

Summary

In order to help consolidate your understanding of direct marketing and personal selling, here are the key points summarised against each of the learning objectives:

1 Define direct marketing and set out its key characteristics

Direct marketing is a tool of marketing communications used to create and sustain a personal and intermediary free communication with customers, potential customers and other significant stakeholders. The key characteristic of direct marketing is that it has the capacity to provoke a behaviour response from the audience.

2 Describe the different methods used to implement direct marketing

Direct marketing can be used by organisations in a number of different ways, very often reflecting the business strategy of the organisation. Four types can be identified and they should not be regarded as hierarchical, in the sense that there has to be progression from one type to another. They are reflections of the way different organisations use direct marketing and the degree to which the tool is used strategically.

3 Explain the significance of the database in direct marketing and consider different direct response media

A database is a collection of files held on a computer that contain data that can be related to one another and which can reproduce information in a variety of formats. Normally the data consist of information collected about prospects and customers that are used to determine appropriate segments and target markets and to record responses to communications conveyed by the organisation. A database therefore plays a role as a storage, sorting and administrative device to assist direct and personalised communications.

Most media have a capacity of direct marketing applications, but television and radio, direct mail, telemarketing and the digital media are the most used.

4 Discuss the different types, roles and tasks of personal selling

There are four main ways of categorising personal selling. These are *order takers* who are salespersons to whom customers are drawn at the place of supply. *Order getters* are sales personnel who operate away from the organisation and who attempt to gain orders; *order collectors* attempt to gather orders over the telephone. Finally there are *order supporters* who are secondary salespersons in that they are involved with the order once it has been secured, or are involved with the act of ordering, usually by supplying information.

5 Consider the strengths and weaknesses of personal selling as a form of communication

Personal selling allows for interaction and dialogue, which entails both parties focusing on each other, with a reduced likelihood of distraction or noise. Both are able to tailor messages in response to the feedback provided by the other and solve customer problems. As a result there is a greater level of participation in the decision process by the vendor than in the other tools.

On the other hand the cost of personal selling is extremely high, and reach and frequency low. Control over message delivery can be low and message consistency variable.

6 Explain the concept of multiple sales channels

The introduction of multiple sales channels enables organisations the opportunity to complete some selling tasks without the expense or relative slowness of personal, face-to-face contact. Technology-enhanced channels, mainly in the form of web and email communications, have grown considerably, often at the expense of telephone and mail facilities.

In order to better meet the needs of customers, organisations need to evolve their mix of channels. Customers are better to interact with their supplying organisations using the mix of channels that they prefer to use.

7 Consider how direct marketing and personal selling might best be integrated with the other tools of the marketing communications mix

Advertising and public relations can play important roles creating awareness and shaping the attitudes and disposition of audiences. These help to drive web traffic where the complementary nature of direct marketing and personal selling enables organisations to improve levels of performance and customer satisfaction, through integration. By assigning each of them with roles within the overall decision-making process, efficiencies can be realised and costs slashed. Direct mail, telemarketing and web services have all served to improve the performance of organisations.

Review questions

1. Explain the different levels of direct marketing highlighting the key differences.
2. Write brief notes explaining the reasons why usage of direct marketing has grown in recent years.
3. Discuss the role of the database as the hub of marketing communications.
4. Why does direct mail continue to have a strong role to play in the direct marketing activities for many organisations?
5. Why might permission marketing be seen as an unnecessary cost and an infringement of civil liberties?
6. Which industries might use personal selling as a primary element of its marketing communications mix?
7. What are the different types of personal selling and what are the tasks that salespeople are normally expected to accomplish?
8. Describe the role of personal selling and highlight its main strengths and weaknesses.
9. Which factors need to be considered when determining the significance of personal selling in the communications mix?
10. Write brief notes outlining the way in which direct marketing might be used to assist personal selling activities.

References

Bashford, S. (2004) Telemarketing: customers calling, *Marketing*, 8 September. Retrieved 16 October 2004 from www.brandrepublic.com/news/

Benady, D. (2009) Field marketing comes into its own in the recession, *Marketing*. Retrieved 10 July 2010 from www.brandrepublic.com/features/

Cooke, C. (2008) Obama's Digital Campaign, *WPP*. Retrieved 12 August 2010 from www.wpp.com/wpp/marketing/digital/obamas-digital-campaign.htm

Cravens, D.W. (1987) *Strategic Marketing*. Homewood, IL: Irwin.

Cravens, D.W., Ingram, T.N. and LaForge, R.W. (1991) Evaluating multiple channel strategies, *Journal of Business and Industrial Marketing*, 6(3/4), 37–48.

Dolnicar, S. and Jordaan, Y. (2007) A market-orientated approach to responsibly managing information privacy concerns in direct marketing, *Journal of Advertising*, 36(2) (Summer) 123–149.

Fernandez, J. (2010a) Lexus unveils DM push for its hybrid range, *Marketing Week*, 10 August. Retrieved 12 August 2010 from www.marketingweek.co.uk/disciplines/direct-marketing/lexus-unveils-dm-push-for-its-hybrid-range/3016840.article

Fernandez, J. (2010b) National Trust uses DM for Welsh coastline appeal, *Marketing Week*, 10 August. Retrieved 12 August 2010 from www.marketingweek.co.uk/sectors/not-for-profit/national-trust-uses-dm-for-welsh-coastline-appeal/3016859.article

Fletcher, K. (1997) External drive, *Marketing*, 30 October, 39–42.

Ganesan, S. (1994) Determinants of long-term orientation in buyer–seller relationships. *Journal of Marketing*, 58 (April), 1–19.

Godin, S. (1999) *Permission Marketing: Turning Strangers into Friends, and Friends into Customers*. New York: Simon & Schuster.

Gomez, L. and Hlavinka, K. (2007) The total package: loyalty marketing in the world of consumer packaged goods (CPG), *Journal of Consumer Marketing*, 24(1), 48–56.

Goodwin, C. (1991) Privacy: recognition of a consumer right, *Journal of Public Policy and Marketing*, 10(1), 149–166.

Guenzi, P. (2002) Sales force activities and customer trust, *Journal of Marketing Management*, 18, 749–778.

Gundlach, G.T. and Murphy, P.E. (1993) Ethical and legal foundations of relational marketing exchanges, *Journal of Marketing*, 57 (October), 35–46.

Hawkes, S. (2008) Tesco rolls out trolley watch around the world, *The Times*, 12 April, 51.

Kent, R. and Brandal, H. (2003) Improving email response in a permission marketing context, *International Journal of Market Research*, 45(4), 489–503.

Krishnamurthy, S. (2001) A comprehensive analysis of permission marketing. *Journal of Computer-Mediated Communication*, 6(2) (January). Retrieved 8 March 2008 from www.jcmc.indiana.edu/vol6/issue2/krishnamurthy.html

Murphy, D. (2000) Call centres ponder price of technology, *Marketing*, 14 September, 43–44.

Murphy, D. (2009) Direct mail: finding its place in the mix, *Marketing: Top 100 Mailers*, 4 October, 4–9.

Myers, J.B., Pickersgill, A.D. and Metre van, E.S. (2004) Steering customers to the right channels, *McKinsey Quarterly*, 4, 16 November.

Payne, A. and Frow, P. (2004) The role of multichannel integration in customer relationship management, *Industrial Marketing Management*, 33(6) (August) 527–538.

Pearson, S. (2003) Data takes centre stage. Data 2003, *Marketing Direct*, sponsored supplement.

Rafaeli, A., Ziklik, L. and Doucet, L. (2008) The impact of call center employees' customer orientation behaviors on service quality, *Journal of Service Research*, 10(3) (February), 239–255.

Reid, A., Pullins, E.B. and Plank, R.E. (2002) The impact of purchase situation on sales-person communication behaviors in business markets, *Industrial Marketing Management*, 31(3), 205–213.

Reed, D. (2000) Too much, too often, *Marketing Week*, 12 October, 59–62.

Smith, J.W. (2004) Permission is not enough: empowerment and reciprocity must be included, too, *Marketing Management*, 13(3), 52.

Thayer, L. (1968) *Communication and Communication Systems*. Homewood, IL: Irwin.

Wilson, E.O. (1998) *Consilience: The Unity of Knowledge*. New York: Random House.

Chapter 12
Sales promotion, exhibitions and product placement

The additional value offered through sales promotions can form an important part of the communication mix and are often of strategic importance. By adding value to the offer and hoping to bring forward future sales, these techniques can be a source of competitive advantage, one that is invariably short-rather than long-run. Exhibitions and trade shows can be an integral and important component in the communications mix, especially in the b2b sector. Exhibitions are good at developing relationships with suppliers and customers. Product placement enables brands to be seen in the appropriate context and can help form brand associations for consumers. Product placement activities are growing as the regulations in many countries are becoming more relaxed.

Aims and learning objectives

The aims of this chapter are to consider the nature, role and characteristics associated with three important tools of marketing communications: namely sales promotion, exhibitions and product placement.

The learning objectives are to enable readers to:

1. discuss the nature, types and role of sales promotions;
2. explain how sales promotions can be used strategically in the communications mix;
3. describe the various sales promotion methods and techniques;
4. explain the characteristics and significance of exhibitions and trade shows;
5. consider the role of exhibitions in the marketing communications mix;
6. understand the concepts and issues associated with product placement.

Introduction

Three topics are explored in this chapter. The first part considers sales promotion and the tools and techniques used to incentivise customers. The middle part considers the characteristics of exhibitions, an important business-to-business tool. The final part of this chapter examines an interesting and developing tool, product placement.

If advertising is used to create brand values then the primary role of sales promotion is to engage audiences by delivering a call-to-action. These two tools complement each other as advertising seeks to work over the long term to create awareness and positive feelings, whereas sales promotion works in the shorter-term to encourage people to behave in particular ways and to create sales. Sales promotion offers buyers additional value, an inducement to generate an immediate sale. These inducements can be targeted at consumers, distributors, agents and members of the sales force. A whole range of network members can benefit from the use of sales promotion.

This promotional tool is traditionally referred to as a form of below-the-line communication because, unlike advertising, these agencies are not paid a commission by the media owners. The promotional costs are borne directly by the organisation initiating the activity, which in most cases is a manufacturer, producer or service provider.

Understanding the value of sales promotions

There are many sales promotion techniques, but they all offer a direct inducement or an incentive to encourage receivers of these messages to buy a product/service sooner rather than later. The inducement (for example, price deals, coupons, premiums) is presented as an added value to the basic product and is intended to encourage buyers to act 'now' rather than later. Sales promotion is used, therefore, principally as a means to accelerate sales. The acceleration represents the shortened period of time in which the transaction is completed relative to the time that would have elapsed had there not been a promotion. This action does not mean that an extra sale has been achieved, just that a potential future exchange is confirmed and transacted now.

Sales promotions consist of a wide range of tools and methods. These instruments are considered in more detail later but consideration of what constitutes sales promotion methods is important. In many cases price is the determinant variable and can be used to distinguish between instruments. Sales promotions are often perceived purely as a price discounting mechanism through price deals and the use of coupons. This, however, is not the whole picture, as there are many other ways in which incentives can be offered to buyers.

Reference has already been made to the idea that sales promotions are a way of providing value and it is this value orientation that should be used when considering the nature and essential characteristics of sales promotion. Peattie and Peattie (1994) established a useful way of discriminating between price and non-price sales promotion instruments. They refer to sales promotions that are value increasing and sales promotions that are value adding (see Table 12.1).

This demarcation is important because a large amount of research into sales promotion has been based on value-increasing approaches, most notably price deals and coupons (Gupta, 1988; Blattberg and Neslin, 1990; Krishna and Zhang, 1999). This tends to distort the way sales promotions are perceived and has led to some generalisations about the overall impact of this promotional discipline. There is a large range of other sales promotion instruments which add value and enhance the offering and which provide opportunities to derive longer-term benefits (see Table 12.2). However, research into these is limited (Gilbert and Jackaria, 2002).

As a result of this diversity of sales promotion instruments it should be of no surprise to learn that they are used for a wide range of reasons. Sales promotions can be targeted, with

Table 12.1	A value orientation of sales promotions
Value element	Explanation
Value-increasing	Value is increased by offering changes to the product quantity/quality or by lowering the price. Generally used and perceived as effective over the short term.
Value-adding	Value is added by offering something to augment the fundamental product/price offering. Premiums (gifts), information or opportunities can be offered as extras and the benefits realised over different periods of time: delayed (postal premiums), accumulated (loyalty programmes) or instant (scratch and win competitions). These have the potential to add value over the longer term.

Source: Based on Peattie and Peattie (1994)

Table 12.2	A typology of sales promotion
Value-increasing (alters price/quantity or price/quality equation)	Value-adding (offers 'something extra' while leaving core product and price unchanged)
Discount pricing	Samples
Money-off coupons	Special features (limited editions)
Payment terms (e.g. interest-free credit)	Valued packaging
Refunds	Product trial
Guarantees	In-pack gifts – premiums
Multipack or multi-buys	In-mail gifts – premiums
Quantity increases	Piggy back gifts – premiums
Buybacks	Gift coupons Information (e.g. brochure, catalogue) Clubs or loyalty programmes Competitions/prize draws

considerable precision, at particular audiences and there are three broad audiences to whom sales promotions can be targeted: consumers, members of the distribution network, and the sales forces of both manufacturers and resellers. It should be remembered that the accuracy of these promotional tools means that many subgroups within these broad groups can be reached quickly and accurately. However, sales promotions campaign can backfire. When KFC offered a downloadable coupon that was endorsed by Oprah Winfrey, franchises could not keep pace with demand, especially as KFC had not placed any control or limit on the number of coupons that could be downloaded.

The reasons why organisations use sales promotions are set out at Table 12.3.

Table 12.3 Reasons for the use of sales promotions

Reach new customers	They are useful in securing trials for new products and in defending shelf space against anticipated and existing competition.
Reduce distributor risk	The funds that manufacturers dedicate to them lower the distributor's risk in stocking new brands.
Reward behaviour	They can provide rewards for previous purchase behaviour.
Retention	They can provide interest and attract potential customers and in doing so encourage them to provide personal details for further communications activity.
Add value	They can encourage sampling and repeat purchase behaviour by providing extra value (superior to competitors' brands) and a reason to purchase.
Induce action	They can instil a sense of urgency among consumers to buy while a deal is available. They add excitement and interest at the point of purchase to the merchandising of mature and mundane products.
Preserve cash flow	Since sales promotion costs are incurred on a pay-as-you-go basis, they can spell survival for smaller, regional brands that cannot afford big advertising programmes.
Improve efficiency	Sales promotions allow manufacturers to use idle capacity and to adjust to demand and supply imbalances or softness in raw material prices and other input costs, while maintaining the same list prices.
Integration	They can provide a means of linking together other tools of the promotional mix.
Assist segmentation	They allow manufacturers to price discriminate among consumer segments that vary in price sensitivity. Most manufacturers believe that a high-list, high-deal policy is more profitable than offering a single price to all consumers. A portion of sales promotion expenditures, therefore, consists of reductions in list prices that are set for the least price-sensitive segment of the market.

As if in an attempt to categorise and manage this list, Lee (2002) suggests that the main reasons for the use of sales promotions can be reduced to four:

- as a reaction to competitor activities
- as a form of inertia – this is what we have always done
- as a way of meeting short-term sales objectives
- as a way of meeting long-term objectives.

The first three are used widely and Lee comments that many brand owners use sales promotion as a panic measure when competitors threaten to lure customers away. Cutting prices is undoubtedly a way of prompting a short-term sales response but it can also undermine a longer-term brand strategy.

> **Viewpoint 12.1** Participation in promotional programmes
>
> For the price of a tube of chewing gum, Trident offered music fans an opportunity to see Beyonce at the O$_2$ Arena. In order to promote awareness of the sales promotion event various stunts were staged. The first was in Piccadilly Circus, London, where 100 lookalike Beyonces performed a flash dance, and in doing so attracted extensive media coverage and over a million views of YouTube. Tickets were given to people donating to buskers who were hired to cover various Beyonce tracks, to people who sang Beyonce numbers in the Lucky Voice karaoke bar and to the winners in a an enormous game of musical chairs held in a shopping centre. As a result of this activity over 67,000 visited the Trident Unwrapped website.
>
> Downloading discount vouchers is now commonplace for many people. To captialise on this the convenience store Spar ran an online game called Shelf Sniper. This involved shooting products on a moving conveyor using the mouse to control a barcode scanner. By reaching level two of the game, individuals won a £1 voucher redeemable against £10 worth of shopping.
>
> *Source*: Based on Wallace (2010); Benady (2009)
>
> **Question**
> Why have these brands used games and events to run the promotion?
>
> **Task**
> What game might you use to support a sales promotion for a travel company?

Not too many years ago sales promotions were regarded as a key way of developing sales. However, the use of sales promotions, in particular the use of on-pack promotions, bonus packs, competitions and price deals have failed to maintain the growth of previous years. Reasons for the decline include changing consumer behaviour, the rise of digital media and a distinct lack of innovation in the industry. Another important factor has been the expectations and drive of resellers, and the main supermarket chains in particular. Most have followed low cost strategies (Porter, 1980) with an emphasis on reducing suppliers' costs to a minimum. Supermarkets also desire sales promotion programmes that are exclusive to them as this is seen as a major way of developing their retail brands. Supermarkets have become media owners and realise the value of their store space as a means of exposing others brands. Therefore, any form of sales promotion activity within their environments should be exclusive and tied into their brand. Providing on-pack promotions for individual stores is normally too expensive and uneconomic so this form of promotion has suffered a great deal.

New solutions have had to be found, and as Barrand (2004) suggests the use of digital media and the integration of sales promotion within other campaigns has been, and continues to be successful. The use of SMS, email, viral campaigns and the Internet are used increasingly to drive sales by providing the call-to-action, which for a long time was the province of sales promotion activities.

The use of sales promotion has soared during the recession as consumers trade down in search of economies. 'Bogofs' and twofers' were popular forms of promotion, as they represent quantity at low prices. Benady (2009) reports that today straight price discounts are valued most, exemplified by Tesco's 'buy one now, get one free later' campaign.

The role of sales promotion

The role of sales promotion has changed significantly over recent years. At one time, the largest proportion of communications budgets was normally allocated to advertising. In many cases advertising no longer dominates the communications budget and sales promotion has assumed the focus of the communications investment, for reasons that are described below. This is particularly evident in consumer markets that are mature, have reached a level of stagnation, and where price and promotion work are the few ways of inducing brand switching behaviour.

Short termism

The short-term financial focus of many industrialised economies has developed a managerial climate geared to short-term performance and evaluation, over periods as short as 12 weeks. To accomplish this, communications are required that work quickly and directly impact upon sales. Many see this as leading to an erosion of the brand franchise.

Managerial accountability

Following on from the previous reason is the increased pressure upon marketing managers to be accountable for their communications expenditure. The results of sales promotion activities are more easily justified and understood than those associated with advertising. The number of coupons returned for redemption and the number of bonus packs purchased can be calculated quickly and easily, with little room for error or misjudgement. Advertising, however, cannot be measured so easily, in either the short or the long term. The impact of this is that managers can relate this type of investment in communications to the bottom line much more comfortably than with advertising.

Brand performance

Technological advances have enabled retailers to track brand performance more effectively. This in turn means that manufacturers can be drawn into agreements that promulgate in-store promotional activity at the expense of other more traditional forms of mass media promotion. Barcode scanners, hand-held electronic shelf-checking equipment and computerised stock systems facilitate the tracking of merchandise. This means that brand managers can be held responsible much more quickly for below-par performance.

Brand expansion

As brand quality continues to improve and as brands proliferate on the shelves of increasingly larger supermarkets, so the number of decisions that a consumer has to make also increases. Faced with multiple-brand decisions and a reduced amount of time to complete the shopping expedition, the tension associated with the shopping experience has increased considerably over the last decade.

Promotions can make decision-making easier for consumers: they simplify a potentially difficult process. So, as brand choice increases, the level of shopping convenience falls. The conflict this causes can be resolved by the astute use of sales promotions. Some feel that the cognitive shopper selects brands that offer increased value, which makes decision-making easier and improves the level of convenience associated with the shopping experience. However, should there be promotions on two offerings from an individual's repertoire then the decision-making is not necessarily made easier.

Competition for shelf space

The continuing growth in the number of brands that are launched and the fragmentation of consumer markets mean that retailers have to be encouraged to make shelf space available. Sales promotions help manufacturers win valuable shelf space and assist retailers to attract increased levels of store traffic and higher utilisation of limited resources.

The credibility of this communication tool is low, as it is obvious to the receiver what the intention is of using sales promotion messages. However, because of the prominent and pervasive nature of the tool, consumers and members of the trade understand and largely accept the direct sales approach. Sales promotion is not a tool that hides its intentions, nor does it attempt to be devious (which is not allowed, by regulation).

The absolute costs of sales promotion are low, but the real costs need to be evaluated once a campaign has finished and all redemptions received and satisfied. The relative costs can be high, as not only do the costs of the premium or price discount need to be determined, but also the associated costs of additional transportation, lost profit, storage and additional time spent organising and administering a sales promotion campaign need to be accounted for.

In its favour, sales promotion allows for a high degree of control. Management is able to decide just when and where a sales promotion will occur and also estimate the sales effect. Sales promotions can be turned on and off quickly and adjusted to changed market conditions. The intended message is invariably the one that is received, as there is relatively little scope for it to be corrupted or damaged in transmission.

Sales promotion plans: the objectives

The objectives of using this tool are sales oriented and are geared to stimulating buyers either to use a product for the first time or to encourage use on a routine basis. One objective of sales promotion activity is to prompt buyers into action, to initiate a series of behaviours that result in long-run purchase activity. These actions can be seen to reflect high or low involvement and they occur in the conative stage of the attitudinal set. If the marketing objectives include the introduction of a new product or intention to enter a new market, then the key objective associated with low-involvement decisions is to stimulate trial use as soon as possible. When high-involvement decisions are present, then sales promotions need to be withheld until a suitable level of attitudinal development has been undertaken by public relations and advertising activities.

If a product is established in a market, then a key objective should be to use sales promotions to stimulate an increase in the number of purchases made by current customers and to attract users from competing products (see Figure 12.1). The objectives, therefore, are either

	Involvement	
	High	Low
New product or market	Withhold sales promotion	Use sales promotion to stimulate trial
Established product or market	Non-loyals – use for switching Loyals – use carefully	Non-loyals – use sales promotions to attract for trial Loyals – use sales promotion to reward for increased usage

Figure 12.1 A sales promotion objectives grid

to increase consumption for established products or to stimulate trial by encouraging new buyers to use a product. Once this has been agreed then the desired trial and usage levels need to be determined for each of the target audiences.

The strategic use of sales promotions

For a long time sales promotions have been regarded as a short-term tactical tool whose prime purpose is to encourage customers to try a brand or to switch brands (within their repertoire), attracted by the added value of the sales promotion. Indeed, Papatia and Krishnamurthi (1996) claim that coupons can actively promote switching behaviour and so reduce levels of loyalty. As discussed earlier what happens after a sales promotion activity finishes is debatable. Some claim that once a promotion is withdrawn satisfied customers will return to the brand unsupported by a sales promotion, but supported by other elements of the marketing communications mix: in particular advertising, to maintain awareness of the brand and its values; direct marketing, to provide personal attention and the opportunity to take immediate action; and public relations to sustain credibility and relevance.

By way of contrast it can be argued that sales promotion serves to discount a brand, either directly through price-based reductions or indirectly through coupons and premiums. Customer alignment is to the deal rather than to the brand itself. This serves to lower expectations of what a brand stands for and what it is capable of delivering. So, once a sales promotion is removed, the normal price is perceived as representing inferior value and so repeat purchase behaviour is deterred.

However, despite these less than positive views, some writers (Davis, 1992; O'Malley, 1998) argue that sales promotions have a strategic role to play in the communications mix. Traditionally they have been viewed as short-term tactical tools that can be used offensively to induce the trial of new products, or defensively for established products to retain shelf space and consumers. Sales promotions that do not work as intended may have been used to support inappropriate products or may have been devised without adequate planning. An example of the latter issue may be the Hoover free flights misjudgement and the associated over-subscription which followed the launch of that particular sales promotion activity. There can be no doubt that sales promotions oriented to consumer deals and Temporary Price Reductions (TPRs), in particular, do little to contribute to the overall strategy adopted for an organisation or even a product.

One of the consequences of competitive sales promotions, especially in consumer markets, is the spiral effect that retaliatory actions can have on each organisation. A sales promotion 'trap' develops when competitors start to imitate each other's activities, often based upon price reductions. This leads eventually to participants losing profitability and consumers losing value and possibly choice as some products are forced to drop out of the market.

With the development of relationship marketing and the move towards integrated marketing communications has been the realisation that employees are an important target audience. There is a strong need to motivate the workforce and sales promotion activities have an important role to play. However, employee incentives need to be made accessible to everyone and not just a few (such as the sales force). This means that rewards need to be more broadly spread and there needs to be choice. Vouchers, for example, enable the prizewinner to make a choice based on their circumstances and they are easier to administer than many of the other types of reward. Incentive schemes should be designed in such a way that they do not fall into the trap of creating winners and losers which can be the case when, for example, the top 20 in a scheme win a prize, which effectively creates 80 losers out of every 100 employees.

Many schemes are based around product prizes, typically electrical goods. However, for many people these are no longer attractive (or sufficiently motivating) as rewards. Virgin vouchers provide activity-based rewards where there is an experience that gives the recipient a memory. Activities such as hot-air ballooning, sky diving, visits to the theatre or to health farms appeal to a wide cross-section of people.

> ### Viewpoint 12.2 Blitzing the independent stores
>
> When Britvic Soft Drinks launched a key new product named Drench Juicy they needed quick penetration in the convenience and independent channels. This was because a planned summer tv ad would drive consumer demand so there had to be product availability.
>
> To do this they used Reach, a field marketing team, in order to establish the 'water with a fruity taste' brand in the key retail outlets. A dedicated team of 100 people was appointed, with a goal of working across the top 17,000 outlets, selling three variants of Drench Juicy, merchandising them in chillers. They also sold price marked packs to ensure maximum rate of sale in stocking stores. In store sampling also took place, particularly at high footfall stores at peak times (e.g. lunch hours). The benefit of this was that not only did the brand get increased visibility but it also increased trial rates.
>
> A direct mail campaign was used in the next best 6,000 independent stores. The blitz approach was repeated over three days, four weeks later. This drove increased volume and encouraged repeat purchase where the brand had sold through.
>
> Using livewire technology the team was able to not only report results quickly but also react quickly to any issues that arose. The result of this activity was that the brand was sampled in over 600 stores, direct sales of over 40,000 cases was achieved and every new distribution point was supported with POS. Some 90 per cent distribution was achieved, with current listings in Boots, Morrisons, McColls, Sommerfield and WHSmith Travel, and over 15,000 independent stores.
>
> *Source*: Based on Anon (2009)
>
> #### Question
> What other sales promotion techniques could have been used to support the launch?
>
> #### Task
> Go to www.promotion.com and read the advice about promotional activities.

The true strategic effect of sales promotion activities can only be achieved if they are coordinated with the other activities of the communications mix, and this requires planning. In particular, the complementary nature of sales promotion and advertising should be exploited through the use of common themes and messages, timing, targeting and allocation of resources (in particular budgets). Sales promotions that are planned as a sequence of predetermined activities, reflecting the promotional requirements of a product over the longer term, are more likely to be successful than those sales promotions that are simply reactions to competitors' moves and market developments.

The strategic impact of sales promotions is best observed when they are designed or built into a three- to four-year plan of promotional activities, coordinated with other elements of the communications mix, and integrated with the business strategy.

The manner in which many of the loyalty programmes are managed signals a move from pure sales promotion to direct marketing. The integration of these two approaches has become necessary in order that the advantages of both are realised. This does raise an interesting conflict, in that sales promotion is essentially a short-term tool, and direct marketing needs to work over the long term. The former is product oriented (albeit giving added value to consumers) and often oriented to mass audiences, whereas the latter is based upon developing a personal dialogue (Curtis, 1996).

Finally, the huge sums of money involved in some of the mainstream loyalty or reward-based programmes suggest that these should be seen as longer-term promotional investments. As the return will spread over many years, a medium-term perspective may be more appropriate rather than a short-term view based on a sales 'blip'.

Sales promotion methods

There are a variety of sales promotion methods or techniques. These vary in their characteristics but they are essentially incentives, which are rewards for buyers behaving in particular ways. There are some sales promotion activities run by brand owners that are targeted at the sales forces of the manufacturers and resellers. However, the two principal audiences for sales promotions are those targeted at distributors and those at consumers.

Manufacturers to distributors

Manufacturers and distributors, including retailers, see sales promotions as important devices to encourage trial among non-users and to stimulate repeat purchase among users. Retailers prefer in-store promotions (push) instead of promotions aimed at consumers (pull) strategies. This has implications for the communication mixes deployed by manufacturers. Essentially distributor-oriented promotions represent a business orientation and Table 12.4 sets out the main methods and techniques that can be used in this context.

Marketing communications between manufacturers and resellers are vitally important. Sales promotions play an increasingly important role in the coordination between the two parties. Resellers look for sales promotions to support their own marketing initiatives. Wheeler and Fermer (2009) estimate that the value of funding paid by consumer packaged goods manufacturers to grocery multiple retailers, to support promotional activities is approximately £8 billion per year, in the UK.

Supplier selection decisions depend in part upon the volume and value of the communications support. In other words, will supplier X or Y provide the necessary level of

Table 12.4 Distributor-oriented sales promotion techniques

Method	Explanation
Advertising allowance	A percentage allowance is given against a reseller's purchases during a specified campaign period. Instead of providing an allowance against product purchases, an allowance can be provided against the cost of an advertisement or campaign.
Buying allowance	In return for specific orders between certain dates, a reseller will be entitled to a refund or allowance of x per cent off the regular case or carton price.
Count and recount	Manufacturers may require resellers to clear old stock before a new or modified product is introduced. One way this can be achieved is to encourage resellers to move stock out of storage and into the store. The count and recount method provides an allowance for each case shifted into the store during a specified period of time.
Buy-back	Purchases made after the count and recount scheme (up to a maximum of the count and recount) are entitled to an allowance to encourage stores to replenish their stocks (with the manufacturer's product and not that of a competitor).
Dealer contests	Used to hold a reseller's attention by focusing them on a manufacturer's products not a competitor's.
Dealer conventions and meetings	These enable informal interaction between a manufacturer and its resellers and can aid the development and continuance of good relations between the two parties.
Training and support	This is an important communications function, especially when products are complex or subject to rapid change, as in IT markets. This can build stronger relationships and manufacturers have greater control over the messages that the resellers transmit.

communication support, either within the channel or direct to the consumer? Indeed, Wheeler and Fermer see trade based promotional support increasing and because of the balance of power in the marketing channels, this looks unlikely to change in the medium term. They see a move away from multibuy to price led activity, which all lead to a reduced ROI. In essence, suppliers are funding a disproportionate amount of the discounts demanded by consumers.

Manufacturers to consumers

Manufacturers use sales promotions to communicate with consumers mainly because they can be a cost-effective means of achieving short-term increases in sales. The objectives are twofold: first, to stimulate trial use by new users or second, to increase the amount of product used by current customers. Methods relating to these two main tasks are set out in Table 12.5.

These methods represent a pull-positioning strategy, as they are targeted at consumers. They can stimulate a shift in sales and they can be instigated and withdrawn at any time, subject to any contractual arrangements. Most brands outsource the design and implementation of sales promotion activities to specialist agencies. They in turn often employ fulfilment houses, organisations that manage the logistics associated with particular promotions. For example, premiums require the receipt and accountability of coupons or finance and then the dispatch of the designated product. Cadbury's ran a premium based promotion with their chocolate digestives brand of biscuit. Research shows that 90 per cent of biscuit consumption involves a drink, so a mug/biscuit combination is highly complementary. The promotion was based on people uploading a picture and personalising a mug, for just £7.99 (Wilde, 2009).

Finally, bonus packs and 2-4-1 offers in particular have been used by manufacturers to provide increased value to customers, move stock, reduce working capital and take customers out of the next purchase cycle by loading them with product and so disadvantage competitors. Whilst this works perfectly well for some, the offer does not work for all customers. Single person households are not always able to consume the extra product within the use by dates and therefore are unable to realise the value offered. In recognition of this situation, Tesco now

Table 12.5 Consumer-oriented sales promotion techniques

Method	Explanation
Sampling	Although very expensive, sampling is an effective way of getting people to try a product. Trial-size versions of the actual product are given away free. Sampling can also take the form of demonstrations, trial-size packs that have to be purchased or free use for a certain period of time.
Coupons	These are vouchers or certificates that entitle consumers to a price reduction on a particular product. The value of the reduction or discount is set and the coupon must be presented at purchase.
Price-offs	These are a direct reduction in the purchase price with the offer clearly labelled on the package or point of purchase display.
Bonus packs	These offer more product for the regular pack price, typically a 2 for 1 offer. They provide direct impact at the point of purchase and represent extra value.
Refunds and rebates	Used to invite consumers to send in a proof of purchase and in return receive a cash refund.
Premiums	Items of merchandise that are offered free or at a low cost in return for product purchase.
Contests and sweepstakes	A contest is a customer competition based on skill or ability. Entry requires a proof of purchase and winners are judged against a set of predetermined criteria. A sweepstake determines winners by chance and proof of purchase is not required. There is no judging and winners are drawn at random.

offer a deal based on 'buy one, get one free – later'. Customers can now reclaim their second item at a date that is convenient to them.

Trade shows and exhibitions

Trade shows and exhibitions fulfil a role for customers by enabling them to become familiar with new developments, new products and leading-edge brands. Very often these customers will be opinion leaders and use word-of-mouth communications to convey their feelings and both product and exhibition experiences to others. The role of trade fairs is to enable manufacturers, suppliers, and distributors to meet at a designated location. Drawn from a particular industry or related industries, the purpose is to exchange information about products and services and to build relationships. These events normally exclude consumers. Exhibitions are attended by consumers.

In the b2b market, trade shows are very often an integral and important component in the communications mix. Meeting friends, customers, suppliers, competitors and prospective customers is an important sociological and ritualistic event in the communication calendar for many companies. In the consumer sector, exhibitions provide a point of difference and offer continuity for those people who make the brand choice decisions at the point of purchase.

The idea of many suppliers joining together at a particular location in order to set out their products and services so that customers may meet, make comparisons and place orders is far from new. Indeed, not only does this form of promotional activity stretch back many centuries, it has also been used to explain the way the Internet works (Bertheron *et al.*, 1996).

At a basic level, trade shows can be oriented for industrial users and exhibitions for consumers and the content or purpose might be to consider general or specialised products/markets. According to Boukersi (2000), consumer-oriented general exhibitions tend to be larger and last longer than the more specialised industrial shows and it is clear that this more highly segmented and focused approach is proving more successful, based on the increasing number of these types of exhibitions.

Reasons to use exhibitions

There are many reasons to use exhibitions, but the primary reasons appear not to be 'to make sales' or 'because the competition is there' but because these events provide opportunities to meet potential and established customers and to create and sustain a series of relational exchanges. Li (2007) cited by Geigenmüller (2010) stresses that the impact of trade shows on the development of valuable long-term buyer-seller relationships is important.

The main aims therefore, are to develop long-term partnerships with customers, to build upon or develop the corporate identity and to gather up-to-date market intelligence (Shipley and Wong, 1993) and to exchange information about products, services and corporate developments. This implies that exhibitions should not be used as isolated events, but that they should be integrated into a series of activities, which serve to develop and sustain buyer relationships.

After a tentative start to the 1990s, the exhibition industry in this century has grown considerably. With managers increasingly accountable for their promotional spend, a greater number of budgets are now channelled into exhibitions and related events. In 1995, visitors attended 773 exhibitions in the UK, where venues exceeded 2,000 square feet. By 2005, the number had risen to 944 exhibitions (Advertising Association, 2008).

Costs can be reduced by using private exhibitions. The increased flexibility allows organisations to produce mini or private exhibitions for their clients at local venues (e.g. hotels). This can mean lower costs for the exhibitor and reduced time away from their businesses for those attending. The communication 'noise' and distraction associated with the larger public events can also be avoided by these private showings.

Viewpoint 12.3 Making an exhibit of cars in Beijing

The Beijing car show is a major event in a country where car sales increased 45 per cent in 2009. This rate growth should be considered against a background where only 50 out of a 1,000 people own a car. In Germany this figure is 500 in every 1,000. So, the potential for car manufacturers is huge and this is why the Beijing car show is well attended.

Some 80 per cent of the 1,000 cars on show are made locally and compete with American, European and Japanese brands. Car shows in Europe are largely about dealers and dealerships, the media and specialist journalists, and suppliers and parts equipment manufacturers. The emphasis is on relationships, news, and profiling each form of development. Very few orders are agreed at the shows, although many pre-show agreements are ceremoniously signed for photographers and the crowds.

The Chinese show is a sales extravaganza. The country's car network is relatively young and there are an insufficient number of dealerships. As a result, consumers having completed their Internet-based searches, arrive at the show armed with bags of cash, ready to secure their chosen vehicle.

Source: Based on Madden (2010); Bristow (2010)

Question
How would you use marketing communications to attract visitors to a car show?

Task
Make a list of the 10 critical activities associated with organising a trade show.

Exhibit 12.1 Scene from the Beijing Car Show... it's official
A security guard takes pictures of a Lamborghini Murciélago LP 670-4 Super Veloce China Limited Edition
Image courtesy of Getty Images/Feng Li

Characteristics of exhibitions and trade fairs

The main reasons for attending exhibitions and trade fairs are that they enable organisations to meet customers (and potential customers) in an agreeable environment, one where both have independently volunteered their time to attend; to place/take orders; to generate leads; and to gather market information. The reasons for attending exhibitions are set out in Table 12.6.

From this it is possible to distinguish the following strengths and weaknesses of using exhibitions as part of the marketing communications programme.

Strengths

The costs associated with exhibitions, if controlled properly, can mean that this is an effective and efficient means of communicating with customers. The costs per inquiry need to be calculated, but care needs to be taken over who is classified as an inquirer, as the quality of the audience varies considerably. Costs per order taken are usually the prime means of evaluating the success of an exhibition. This can paint a false picture, as the true success can never really be determined in terms of orders because of the variety of other factors that impinge upon the placement and timing of orders.

Viewpoint 12.4 Making an exhibition of Ireland

The development of Ireland's tourism market involves attracting both individuals for vacations and also the business market in terms of conferences, events and meetings. One thing that is common to both groups is the opportunity to visit and enjoy the breathtaking scenery and the warmth and friendliness of the people.

Some of Ireland's recent economic changes included an advantageous set of tax breaks designed to encourage investment in the construction industry. One of the results of this initiative has been the development of a huge number of recently completed high-quality hotels, many with conference centres. Thus, with a wealth of excellent suppliers, the challenge for Tourism Ireland at the International Confex 2007 exhibition was to stand out among the other 1,075 exhibitors and attract conference organisers to their exhibition platform.

To encourage visitors it was decided to send out mailers to key conference organisers prior to the exhibition and give them a reason to visit the Tourism Ireland stand. These mailers were designed to be personal invitations and included an invitation to experience some genuine Irish hospitality in the form of a Hot Irishman (coffee liqueur) or a Guinness. This was to be symbolic of the opportunities to relax away from a conference. Normally a return of 3 per cent might be expected for a mailer of this type. However, 2.9 per cent responded asking for more information because they were unable to attend the exhibition, while a further 7.1 per cent attended the stand. An overall response rate of 10 per cent was achieved.

Source: Based on UTalk (2007).

Question
Why was direct mail used to reach conference organisers?

Task
How would you attract business people to attend an exhibition on office equipment?

Products can be launched at exhibitions, and when integrated with a good PR campaign a powerful impact can be made. This can also be used to reinforce corporate identity. Exhibitions are an important means of gaining information about competitors, buyers and technical and political developments in the market, and they often serve to facilitate the recruitment process. Above all else, exhibitions provide an opportunity to meet customers on relatively neutral ground and, through personal interaction, develop relationships. Products can be demonstrated, prices agreed, technical problems discussed and trust and credibility enhanced.

Table 12.6   Reasons exhibitors choose to attend exhibitions

To meet existing customers
To take orders/make sales
To get leads and meet prospective new customers
To meet lapsed customers
To meet prospective members of the existing or new marketing channels
To provide market research opportunities and to collect marketing data

Weaknesses

One of the main drawbacks associated with exhibition work is the vast and disproportionate amount of management time that can be tied up with the planning and implementation of exhibitions. However, good planning is essential if the full potential benefits of exhibition work are to be realised.

Taking members of the sales force 'off the road' can also incur large costs. Depending on the nature of the business these opportunity costs can soar. Some pharmaceutical organisations estimate that it can cost approximately £5,000 per person per week to divert salespeople in this way.

The expected visitor profile must be analysed in order that the number of quality buyers visiting an exhibition can be determined. The variety of visitors attending an exhibition can be misleading, as the vast majority may not be serious buyers or, indeed, may not be directly related to the industry or the market in question. Research by Gopalakrishna *et al.* (2010) has found that approximately 40 per cent of first-time exhibitors, spanning a range of industries, do not return to the same show the following year. As Galea (2007) cited by Gopalakrishna *et al.* (2010) pointed out, a growing concern for managers is the ability to reach relevant decision-makers. The researchers response was to attempt an understanding of attendee behaviour, as this would help trade show organisers segment their audiences. From their research data they determined a typology of business show visitors. These are depicted at Table 12.7.

Exhibitions as a form of marketing communications

As a form of marketing communications, exhibitions enable products to be promoted, they can build brands and they can be an effective means of demonstrating products and building industry-wide credibility in a relatively short period of time. Attendance at exhibitions may also be regarded from a political standpoint, in that non-attendance by competitors may be taken as an opportunity by attendees to suggest weaknesses.

In the b2b sector new products and services are often introduced at exhibitions, especially if there are to be public relations activities and events that can be spun off the launch. In other words, exhibitions are not activities independent of the other communication tools. Exhibitions, if used effectively, can be part of an integrated communications campaign.

Advertising prior to, during and after a trade show can be dovetailed with public relations, sponsorship and personal selling. Sales promotions can also be incorporated through competitions among customers prior to the show to raise awareness, generate interest and to suggest customer involvement. Competitions during a show can be focused on the sales force to motivate and stimulate commercial activity and among visitors to generate interest in the stand, raise brand name awareness and encourage focus on particular products (new, revised or revolutionary) and generate sales leads and enquiries.

Table 12.7 A typology of trade show visitors

Segment name	Key characteristics
The basic shopper (40%)	Basic shoppers make about seven 'serious' visits to booths, 75 per cent are planned, and 70 per cent of visits are made to stand-alone booths which are accessible on all four sides.
The enthusiast (17%)	Enthusiasts make an average of 24 visits while at the trade show, more than three times that of the basic shopper. 80 per cent of their visits are planned and they prefer to be 'where the action is'.
The niche shopper (17%)	The niche shopper makes an average of 9.2 visits, which is greater than the basic shopper but lower than the enthusiast. The key characteristic of this type of shopper is that 40 per cent of their serious visits are made to small sized booths. The niche shopper prefers to work with specialty exhibitors who do not have a big presence at the show.
The brand shopper (17%)	Brand shoppers make about 10 serious visits and show the highest high preference for large booths. Their plan for the booths attended is also the highest, reflecting their need to plan and make their visit to the show as efficient as possible.
The apathetic shopper (11%)	Only 33 per cent of the apathetic shopper's booth visits are planned. They also prefer booths that are open on three sides, and which have a wide selection of products. The suggestion is that apathetic shoppers might represent 'newcomers' or attendees who are unfamiliar with the trade show.

Source: Gopalakrishna *et al.*, (2010). Used with permission

Perhaps above all else, trades shows and exhibitions play a major role in the development of relationships.

Digital media and trade shows

In many ways the use of a website as brochureware represented a first attempt at an online exhibition. In these situations, commercial organisations provided opportunities for people who physically could not get to see a product to gain some appreciation of its size, configuration and capability (through text).

Online trade shows are web-based platforms enabling manufacturers, suppliers and distributors an opportunity to exchange information, virtually. This facilitates speed, convenience and cost factors that influence small and medium sized organisations. As noted by Geigenmüller (2010), online show visitors can call on virtual halls and booths to obtain information about a firm's products and its services. Interaction between buyers and sellers occurs through chat rooms or video conferences, and forums. Online diaries or blogs are also used to discuss issues or leave messages for other participants.

However, the development of multimedia technologies has given not only commercial but also not-for-profit organisations the opportunity to showcase their wares on a global basis. One type of organisation to explore the use of this technology has been museums and art collections (static exhibits). Khoon *et al.* (2003) refer to the American History Documents (at www.indiana.edu/liblilly/histy/), Exploring Africa (at www.sc.edu/library/spcoll/sccoll/africa) and SCRAN (at www.scran.ac.uk) (which is a multimedia resource for Scottish history and culture) as examples of previous work and facilities in this area.

The use of multimedia technologies enables audiences across the world to access these collections and with the use of audio, video clips and streaming video, in addition to pictures and extensive text, these exhibitions can be brought to life, visited repeatedly, focus given to particular exhibits, materials updated quickly and unobtrusively, and links made to other similar facilities. The key difference between this development and previous brochureware-type facilities is the feeling of virtual reality, the sense that a digital visitor is actually in the exhibition, even though seated several thousand miles away.

The use of ecommerce and digital media in the management and presentation of exhibitions is increasing. It is unlikely that online exhibitions will ever replace the offline, real-world version, if only because of the need to form relationships and to network with industry members, to touch and feel products and to sense the atmosphere and vitality that exhibitions generate. However, there is huge scope to develop specialised exhibitions, online showcases that incorporate exhibits (products and services) from a variety of geographically dispersed locations.

Marketing management of exhibitions

Good management of exhibitions represents some key aspects of marketing communications in general. Successful events are driven by planning that takes place prior to the exhibition, with communications inviting a range of stakeholders, not just customers, in advance of the exhibition event. Stands should be designed to deliver key messages and press releases and press information packs should be prepared and distributed appropriately.

During the event itself staff should be well briefed, trained and knowledgeable about their role in terms of the brand and in the exhibition process. After the exhibition it is vital to follow up on contacts made and discussions or negotiations that have been held. In other words, the exhibition itself is a planned marketing communications activity, one where activities need to be planned prior to, during and after the event. What is key is that these activities are coordinated, themed and supported by brand-oriented staff.

Above all else, exhibitions are an important way of building relationships and signalling corporate identity. Trade shows are an important means of providing corporate hospitality and showing gratitude to all an organisation's customers, but in particular to its key account customers and others of strategic interest. Positive relationships with customers, competitors and suppliers are often reinforced through face-to-face dialogue that happens both formally in the exhibition hall and informally through the variety of social activities that surround and support these events.

Product placement

One way of overcoming the irritation factor associated with advertisements screened in cinemas prior to a film showing is to incorporate the product in the film that is shown. This practice is referred to as product placement, which is the inclusion of products and services in films (or media) for deliberate promotional exposure, often, but not always, in return for an agreed financial sum. It is regarded by some as a form of sales promotion, by others as sponsorship, but for the purposes of this text it is treated as an advertising medium because the 'advertiser' pays a third party for the opportunity to present the product in their channel.

A wide variety of products can be placed in this way, including drinks (both soft and alcoholic), cameras, laptops, confectionery, newspapers, cars, airlines, perfume and even holiday destinations and sports equipment. However, the development of product placement has inevitably led to new formats and fresh approaches, some of which only serve to muddy the waters.

Hudson and Hudson (2006) set out the development of product placement. Early forms of product placement concerned brand owners making deals with film producers and film stars to openly endorse the brand. The brand owner would fund props and facilities for the film in return for spoken and visual endorsement. Some of the first television programmes were named after the brands that sponsored them, for example, *The Colgate Comedy Hour* and the *Kraft Television Theatre* (Hudson and Hudson, 2006).

The establishment of product placement agencies in the 1980s helped formalise the process and removed much of the barter and haggling that had typified arrangements. The turning point occurred when the film *ET* depicted an alien being lured by Reese's Pieces. Hershey, the manufacturer, saw sales rise 65 per cent following the release of the film and since then product placement has grown year on year.

Two distinct forms of product placement-related activity have emerged, partly as a result of the proliferation of the media, the consequential surge in the production of entertainment programmes, and the media industry's need to generate income streams. Rather than place a product within a film, television or radio programme where it assumes a passive role, hoping to get noticed, a new approach sees entire entertainment programmes built around a single product. In contrast to the passivity of product placement, here a brand is actively woven into the theme or the plot of the programme. This latter approach has been labelled 'branded entertainment'. Hudson and Hudson (2006) depict this as a continuum, represented in Figure 12.2.

Hackley and Tiwsakul (2006) suggest the term 'entertainment marketing'. They believe the term reflects the diversity of ways in which brands are inserted into entertainment vehicles. This perspective subsumes product placement and incorporates celebrity endorsement and sponsorship, elements discussed elsewhere in this book.

Characteristics of product placement

Strengths

By presenting the product as part of the film, not only is it possible to build awareness, but source credibility can be improved significantly and brand images reinforced. The audience is assisted to identify and associate itself with the environment depicted in the film or with the celebrity who is using the product.

Levels of impact can be very high, as cinema audiences are very attentive to large-screen presentations. Rates of exposure can be high, particularly now that cinema films are being released through video outlets, satellite and various new regional cable and television organisations.

Perhaps the major advantage is that the majority of audiences appear to approve of this form of marketing communications, if only because it is unobtrusive and integral to the film (Nebenzahl and Secunda, 1993).

Weaknesses

Having achieved a placement in a film (video, television or radio programme) there is still a risk that the product will run unnoticed, especially if the placements coincide with distracting or action-oriented parts of the film. Associated with this is the lack of control the advertiser has over when, where and how the product will be presented. If the product is noticed, a small minority of audiences claim that this form of communication is unethical; it is even suggested that it is subliminal advertising, which is, of course, illegal. The absolute costs of product placement in films can be extremely high, counteracting the low relative costs or cost per contact. The final major drawback concerning this form of communication concerns its inability to provide explanation, detail, or indeed any substantive information about the product. The product is seen in use and is hopefully associated with an event, person(s) or objects that provide a source of pleasure, inspiration or aspiration for the individual viewer.

Viewpoint 12.5   Entertaining placement

Product placement originated in television shows, progressed into films and has now been utilised in other media and entertainment vehicles. The music industry for example has been looking for new income streams as illegal downloading fails to abate. Product placement in promotional videos is a partial solution. For example, Lady Gaga and Beyonce made a nine-minute long promotional video to support their collaborative single, 'Telephone'. Placements include state of the art LG handsets, the Virgin Mobile network, Diet Coke cans, an HP Envy laptop, and the website for dating agency 'PlentyofFish' is featured.

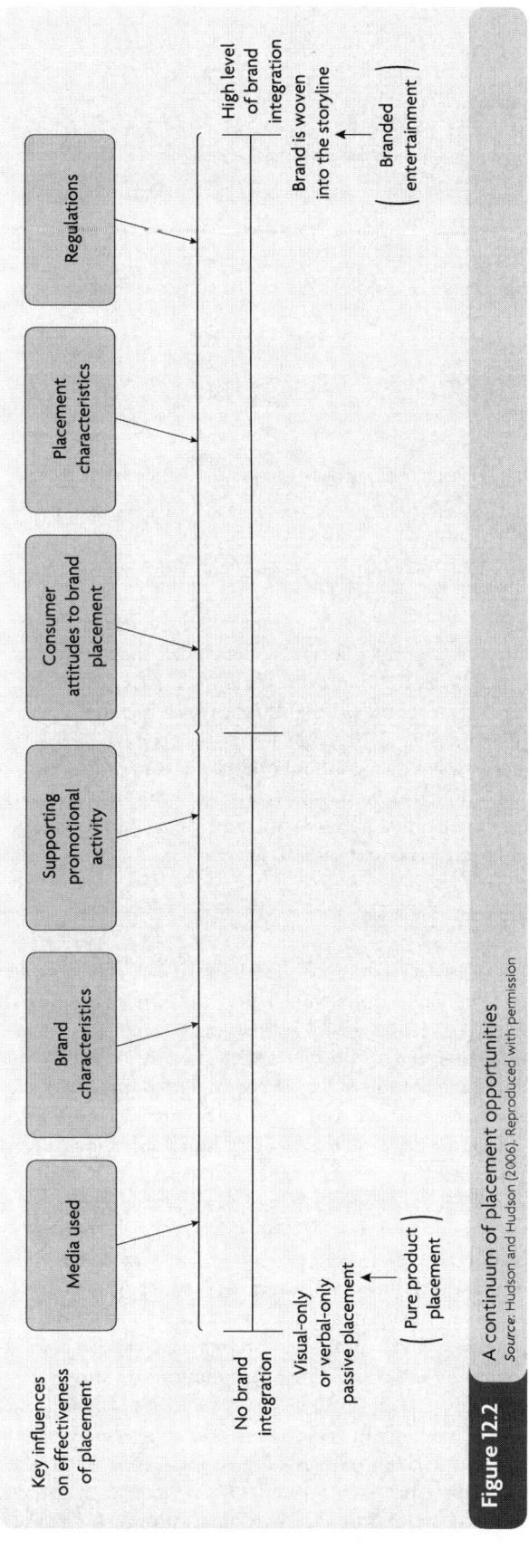

Figure 12.2 A continuum of placement opportunities
Source: Hudson and Hudson (2006). Reproduced with permission

> The hit tv show, *American Idol* works closely with three particular sponsors, Coca Cola, Ford and AT&T. In 2009 Apple became the fourth sponsor. As a result these brands feature in or make maximum use of their association with the show. Nielsen report that Coke achieved 2,000 views in the last season. This was through the placement of Coke cups in front of the judges, plus Coke's decoration of the 'Red Room'. The show can only be accessed through iTunes, whilst Ford make promotional videos with the contestants.
>
> Source: Based on various including Utalk (2010); Pemberton (2010); Dawn and Block (2009); Jones (2010)
>
> ### Question
> Should there be a limit on the number of products placed in a film, if so, how many and why?
>
> ### Task
> Watch a film or television programme of your choice and note how many placements have been made.

As indicated earlier, product placement is not confined to cinema films. Music videos, television plays, dramas and soap operas can also use this method to present advertisers' products. The novel *The Sweetest Taboo*, written by novelist Carole Matthews, includes frequent references to various Ford cars, which is not surprising as Ford paid her to mention their cars in her work (Plaut, 2004).

Pervan and Martin (2002) found that product placement in television soaps was an effective communications activity. They also concluded that the way a product is used in the soap, i.e. positive and negative outcomes, may well have important implications for the attitudes held towards these brands. In addition, they suggested that organisations should study the consumption imagery associated with placed products as this might yield significant information about the way in which these products are actually consumed. Product placement is not confined to offline communications. For example, the toothpaste brand Pearl Drops has been written into the plotline and was integrated into the social network Bebo's interactive drama called *Sofia's Diary*, a teen-targeted programme.

Placement Issues

The nature of a placement and the impact it has on the audience appear to be affected by a number of variables. Important issues concern: the nature of the placement (Sung *et al.*, 2009) and its association with the storyline; whether the actors use the product or it remains a background object; if the product fits the plot; the degree to which the product is prominently displayed; the medium used (de Gregorio and Sung, 2009) and the amount of time that the product is actually exposed. Karrh *et al.* (2003) refer to the relative lack of control that marketers have over product placement activities, but confirm that in comparison to advertising equivalents, product placement can have a far greater impact on audiences and in most cases at a fraction of the cost of a 30-second advertisement.

Cultural background and ethical disposition can influence an audience's perception of product placements (Nelson and Devanathan, 2006) whilst Russell and Belch (2005) refer to difficulties relating to the way the value of product placement is perceived. There is a view, held by creative and media agencies, that the 'number of seconds on screen' is a valid measurement of effectiveness. Many do not agree and prefer to consider the context of the placement and the level of continuity within a defined communications strategy as more meaningful measures.

Research indicates that product placement has little impact on changing brand attitudes. Homer (2009) found that two key variables concern the type of placement (subtle versus prominent) and the degree to which the placement is repeated. She finds that brand attitudes fall when product placements are prominent, especially so when they are repeated. When the placement is subtle consumer attitudes are relatively positive but repeated exposures have little impact.

Summary

In order to help consolidate your understanding of sales promotions, exhibitions and product placement, here are the key points summarised against each of the learning objectives:

1 Discuss the nature, types and role of sales promotions

Sales promotion offers buyers additional value, as an inducement to generate an immediate sale. These inducements can be targeted at consumers, distributors, agents and members of the sales force. Sales promotions used by resellers (largely retailers) to influence consumers are normally driven by manufacturers, although some price deals and other techniques are used to generate store traffic.

2 Explain how sales promotions can be used strategically in the communications mix

Sales promotions have a strategic role to play, particularly when they are used to complement the other activities in the promotional mix. By attempting to develop a consistent theme to a promotional plan, sales promotions can follow advertising's awareness-building activities with a series of messages that continue the theme already established.

3 Describe the various sales promotion methods and techniques

Sales promotions used by manufacturers to communicate with resellers are aimed at encouraging resellers to either try new products or purchase more of the ones they currently stock. To do this, trade allowances, in various guises, are the principal means. The majority of sales promotions are those used by manufacturers to influence consumers. Again, the main tasks are to encourage trial or increase product purchase. A range of techniques, from sampling and coupons to premiums, contests and sweepstakes, are all used with varying levels of success, but there has been a distinct shift away from traditional promotional instruments to the use of digital media in order to reflect consumer's preferences and media behaviour.

4 Explain the characteristics and significance of exhibitions and trade shows

The main reasons for attending exhibitions and trade fairs are that: it enables organisations to meet customers (and potential customers) in an agreeable environment, one where both have independently volunteered their time to attend; to place/take orders; to generate leads; and to gather market information.

5 Consider the role of exhibitions in the marketing communications mix

As a form of marketing communications, exhibitions enable products to be promoted, they can build brands and they can be an effective means of demonstrating products and building industry-wide credibility in a relatively short period of time. Positive relationships with customers, competitors and suppliers are often reinforced through face-to-face dialogue that happens both formally in the exhibition hall and informally through the variety of social activities that surround and support these events.

6 Understand the concepts and issues associated with product placement

Product placement is the inclusion of products and services in films (or media) for deliberate promotional exposure, often, but not always, in return for an agreed financial sum. It is regarded by some as a form of sales promotion, by others as sponsorship, but the most common linkage is with advertising, because the 'advertiser' pays a third party for the opportunity to present the product in their channel.

There are distinct forms of product placement. One involves the passive placement of a product within the media; the other sees whole entertainment programmes built around a single product, one where it is actively woven into the theme or the plot of the programme. This is known as 'branded entertainment'.

Review questions

1. Why do organisations use sales promotion and why has sales promotion assumed such a large share of promotional expenditure?
2. How might use of technology assist the development of loyalty and retention programmes?
3. List the main sales promotion methods used by manufacturers and targeted at consumers. How can coupons be used to reduce levels of buyer perceived risk?
4. Explain the objectives that manufacturers might have when encouraging resellers to take stock of more product.
5. How would you advise a newly appointed assistant brand manager on the expected outcomes of a sales promotion programme? (Choose any sector/industry of your choice.) Suggest four ways in which sales promotions can be evaluated.
6. Evaluate the differences between exhibitions and trade shows.
7. As sales manager for a company making plastic mouldings for use in the manufacture of consumer durables, set out the reasons for and against attendance at trade shows and exhibitions, as an exhibitor and as a visitor.
8. Write brief notes explaining the role exhibitions might play in a company's integrated marketing communications strategy.
9. Name two strengths and two weaknesses of product placement.
10. Identify four examples of product placement. Evaluate their effectiveness.

References

Advertising Association (2008) *Advertising Statistics YearBook 2008*. Henley on Thames: Advertising Association.
Anon (2009) Drench Juicy field marketing launch campaign, Utalk, 14 September. Retrieved 8 July 2010 from www.utalkmarketing.com/Pages/Article.aspx?
Barrand, D. (2004) Promoting change, *Marketing*, 6 October, 43–45.
Benady, D. (2009) Brands struggle to kick the sales promotion habit, *Marketing*, 11 December. Retrieved 13 July 2010 from www.brandrepublic.com/news
Bertheron, P., Pitt, L.F. and Watson, R.T. (1996) The World Wide Web as an advertising medium, *Journal of Advertising Research*, 6(1) (January/February), 43–54.
Blattberg, R.C. and Neslin, S.A. (1990) *Sales Promotion: Concepts, Methods and Strategies*. Englewood Cliffs, NJ: Prentice-Hall.
Boukersi, L. (2000) The role of trade fairs and exhibitions in international marketing communications, in *The Handbook of International Marketing Communications* (ed. S. Moyne). London: Blackwell, 117–135.
Bristow, M. (2010) Grand ambitions at Beijing car show, BBC News, 27 April 2010. Retrieved 14 July 2010 from www.news.bbc.co.uk/1/hi/8644730.stm
Curtis, J. (1996) Opposites attract, *Marketing*, 25 April, 28–29.
Davis, M. (1992) Sales promotions as a competitive strategy, *Management Decision*, 30(7), 5–10.

Dawn, R. and Block, A.B. (2009) Brands Take the 'American Idol' Stage, Billboard.com. Retrieved 31 March 2010 from www.adweek.com/aw/content_display/news/strategy/

de Gregorio, F. and Sung, Y. (2009) Giving a shout to Seagram's gin: extent of and attitudes towards brands in popular songs, *Journal of Brand Management*, 17(3), 218–235.

Galea, C. (2007) Show me the money: maximizing your trade show investment, available at: managesmarter.com. Accessed 20 September 2007.

Geigenmüller, A. (2010) The role of virtual trade fairs in relationship value creation, *Journal of Business and Industrial Marketing*, 25(4), 284–292.

Gopalakrishna, S., Roster, C.A. and Sridhar, S. (2010) An exploratory study of attendee activities at a business trade show, *Journal of Business & Industrial Marketing*, 25(4), 241–248.

Gilbert, D.C. and Jackaria, N. (2002) The efficacy of sales promotions in UK supermarkets: a consumer view, *International Journal of Retail & Distribution Management*, 30(6), 325–332.

Gupta, S. (1998) Impact of sales promotions on when, what and how much we buy, *Journal of Marketing Research*, 25(4), 342–355.

Hackley, C. and Tiwsakul, R. (2006) Entertainment marketing and experiential consumption 1, *Journal of Marketing Communications*, 12(1) (March), 63–75.

Homer, P.M. (2009) The Impact of Placement Type and Repetition on Attitude, *Journal of Advertising*, 38(3) (Fall), 21–31.

Hudson, S. and Hudson, D. (2006) Branded entertainment: a new advertising technique or product placement in disguise? *Journal of Marketing Management*, 22(5/6), 489–504.

Jones, L. (2010) Lady Gaga and Beyoncé's sexy music video 'Telephone' is trending on Twitter. What a surprise, *The Daily Telegraph*, 12 March. Retrieved 5 April 2010 from http://blogs.telegraph.co.uk/culture/lucyjones/100007056/lady-gaga-and-beyonce%E2%80%99s-sexy-music-video-telephone-is-trending-on-twitter-what-a-surprise/

Karrh, J.A., McKee, K.B., Britain, K. and Pardun, C.J. (2003) Practitioners' evolving views of product placement effectiveness, *Journal of Advertising Research*, 43(2) (June), 138–150.

Krishna, A. and Zhang, Z.J. (1999) Short or long duration coupons: the effect of the expiration date on the probability of coupon promotions. *Management Science*, 45(8), 1041–1057.

Lee, C.H. (2002) Sales promotions as strategic communication: the case of Singapore, *The Journal of Product and Brand Management*, 11(2), 103–114.

Li, L.Y. (2007) 'Marketing resources and performance of exhibitor firms in trade shows: a contingent resource perspective', *Industrial Marketing Management*, 36, 360–370.

Madden, N. (2010) Taking a spin around the China auto show, *Advertising Age*, 81(18), 17.

Nebenzahl, I.D. and Secunda, E. (1993) Consumer attitudes toward product placement in movies, *International Journal of Advertising*, 12, 1–11.

Nelson, M.R. and Devavathan, N. (2006) Brand placements, Bollywood style, *Journal of Consumer Behaviour*, 5(3), 211–221.

O'Malley, L. (1998) Can loyalty schemes really build loyalty? *Marketing Intelligence and Planning*, 16(1), 47–55.

Papatia, P. and Krishnamurthi, L. (1996) Measuring the dynamic effects of promotions on brand choice, *Journal of Marketing Research*, 33(1) (February), 20–35.

Peattie, S. and Peattie, K.J. (1994) Sales promotion, in *The Marketing Book* (ed. M.J. Baker), 3rd edn. London: Butterworth-Heinemann.

Pemberton, A. (2010) Is Lady Gaga's Video For 'Telephone' Just One Big Ad?, 23 March. Retrieved 30 March 2010 from www.new.music.yahoo.com/blogs/musictoob/

Pervan, S.J. and Martin, B.A.S. (2002) Product placement in US and New Zealand television soap operas: an exploratory study, *Journal of Marketing Communications*, 8, 101–113.

Plaut, M. (2004) Ford advertises the literary way, *BBC News/Business*. Retrieved 20 March 2008 from http://news.bbc.co.uk/1/hi/business/3522635.stm.

Porter, M.E. (1980) *Competitive Strategy: Techniques for Analyzing Industries and Companies*. New York: Free Press.

Russell, C.A. and Belch, M. (2005) A managerial investigation into the product placement industry, *Journal of Advertising Research*, 45(1) (March), 73–92.

Shipley, D. and Wong, K.S. (1993) Exhibiting strategy and implementation, *International Journal of Advertising*, 12(2), 117–130.

Sung, Y., de Gregorio, F. and Jung, J. (2009) Non-students consumer attitudes towards product placement: Implications for public policy and advertisers, *International Journal of Advertising*, 28(2), 257–285.

Utalk (2007) How direct mail boosted Tourism Ireland's conference market. Retrieved 4 January 2008 from www.utalkmarketing.com/pages/article.aspx?

Utalk (2010) Lady Gaga abnd Beyonce 'Telephone' video is a brand showcase. Retrieved 30 March 2010 from www.utalkmarketing.com

Wallace, C. (2010) Trident has Beyonce fans chewing up, *PR Week*, 15 April. Retrieved 13 July 2010 from www.brandrepublic.com/news

Wheeler, M. and Fermer, I. (2009) Who would be a sales director? *Warc Exclusive* (May). Retrieved 9 July 2010 from www.warc.com

Wilde, C. (2009) Cadbury Digestive's free personalised mug promotion, Promotions and Incentives, 2 October. Retrieved 13 July 2010 from www.brandrepublic.com/news/